The SAGE Handbook of
International Higher Education

The SAGE Handbook of
International Higher Education

Edited by

Darla K. Deardorff
Duke University, Durham, North Carolina, USA

Hans de Wit
Amsterdam University of Applied Sciences, The Netherlands

John D. Heyl
CEA Global Education, Tempe, Arizona, USA

Tony Adams
Tony Adams+
Tony Adams & Associates, Melbourne, Australia

A Publication of the Association of International Education Administrators
Published in cooperation with the *Journal of Studies in International Education*

Los Angeles | London | New Delhi
Singapore | Washington DC

Los Angeles | London | New Delhi
Singapore | Washington DC

FOR INFORMATION:

SAGE Publications, Inc.
2455 Teller Road
Thousand Oaks, California 91320
E-mail: order@sagepub.com

SAGE Publications Ltd.
1 Oliver's Yard
55 City Road
London EC1Y 1SP
United Kingdom

SAGE Publications India Pvt. Ltd.
B 1/I 1 Mohan Cooperative Industrial Area
Mathura Road, New Delhi 110 044
India

SAGE Publications Asia-Pacific Pte. Ltd.
3 Church Street
#10-04 Samsung Hub
Singapore 049483

Printed in the United States of America

Library of Congress Cataloging-in-Publication Data

The SAGE handbook of international higher education / edited by Darla K. Deardorff, Hans de Wit, John Heyl.

p. cm.
Includes bibliographical references and index.

ISBN 978-1-4129-9921-2 (cloth)

1. International education—Cross-cultural studies. 2. Education, Higher—Cross-cultural studies. I. Deardorff, Darla K. II. Wit, Hans de, 1950- III. Heyl, John.

LC1090.S26 2012
378—dc23   2012010922

This book is printed on acid-free paper.

Acquisitions Editor: Brian Normoyle
Editorial Assistant: Megan Koraly
Production Editor: Laura Stewart
Copy Editor: Jacqueline Tasch
Typesetter: C&M Digitals, Ltd.
Proofreader: Eleni Georgiou
Indexer: Sylvia Coates
Cover Designer: Janet Kiesel
Marketing Manager: Katie Winter
Permissions Editor: Adele Hutchinson

Certified Sourcing
www.sfiprogram.org
SFI-00453

12 13 14 15 16 10 9 8 7 6 5 4 3 2 1

CONTENTS

FOREWORD

When I meet new people who learn I am associated with higher education, they invariably ask what my "specialization" is. Everybody is apparently expected to have one, so I often answer "international education." Yet, I always feel that such an answer is totally inadequate to explain that my field is untraditional; that it is not a disciplinary "specialty"; that it does not reside in its own "box" but that it is found in many boxes; that it is a composite of borrowings from virtually every academic discipline and every culture; and that international education is therefore multidimensional, multidisciplinary, and cross-cultural. This Handbook goes a long way to explain and interpret this growing field not only to outsiders, but perhaps—unexpectedly—also to insiders, international education professionals themselves.

The editors are to be congratulated for putting together such an impressive collection of chapters that help define the field and do what such handbooks are designed to do. A Handbook of this kind tends to upgrade the field; to increase, codify, and solidify its knowledge base; and by implication to raise the standard of the profession that is associated with this academic venture. If there were a "Who's Who in International Education," the editors and contributors would be prominently featured in it because they are serious scholars with distinguished professional records.

The complexity and structure of the field are reflected well by the way the Handbook is organized. Thus, the table of contents tells a great deal about the intellectual and cognitive frameworks of the writers and their mental maps, which determine their categories and units of analysis. Furthermore, the way a book is put together reveals the extent to which the authors raise the levels of their analyses each time a new variable, such as *culture* is introduced, thus also raising the complexity of the field, as in the case in this Handbook.

It is especially good to see the Handbook reflecting a variety of cultural and national perspectives by including prominent educators and scholars from a variety of countries where international education has made extraordinary strides, especially in Europe, Africa, and Asia. We should strive to internationalize international education just as we internationalize domestic education.

The Handbook is broken down into several sections that represent the trajectory of the field, from its history, context, and conceptual foundations, to a look at future trends.

I was especially delighted to see a chapter on the context of international education within the larger field of higher education. Context is extremely important in this field and is often also neglected. Here we have a paradox, in that international education in practice is a small segment of higher education, while its subject is much larger than any part of the system of education, indeed of any country—because it deals with the entire world. International education literature touches on three important aspects: First, it is leadership driven; second, it is for the future; and third, its primary foundation is knowledge and its production, dissemination, transfer, and utilization. All these three aspects are taken into account in this Handbook.

As I reflect on the past 60 years of my own career in this field, I can hardly recognize how far the international education field has evolved—from the time when we were essentially pioneers with no prior training, without road maps and tools of the trade, handbooks or research that might guide our practice. So it is especially fitting that this Handbook also addresses the leadership of the profession as the reason why the field prospers and advances. In my own writings, I claim that there are no other functions in higher education that are as comprehensive, knowledge driven, multidimensional, intellectually demanding, and creative as the posts occupied by these international education professionals. Moreover, international educators possibly function at a higher level of organizational complexity than most educational administrators, including college presidents, vice presidents, and deans, who may understand the level of domestic and internal intricacies but who seldom demonstrate that level of complexity internationally.

The idea that international education is for the future is found and replayed throughout the Handbook. Trends are difficult to identify because they do not begin and end at any particular time and often change dramatically and rapidly. I am fond of a quote that is attributed to a futurist, Kenneth Boulding, who was skeptical of the obsession with causation of some in the social sciences, when he stated famously that "things are the way they are because they got that way."

Internationalization means change, in this case, planned change that brings a large number of issues out into the open, and international education professionals can provide the necessary leadership and vision to move institutions forward. Such leadership is desperately needed, given that universities' mission statements do not often appear to address adequately what it is that we are doing differently by educating students for the future. Institutional strategic plans tend to reflect more the limits of their capacities and the present problems than anticipated future global needs. Similarly, these strategic plans do not explain what happens to the *domestic* knowledge after the infusion of *international*

knowledge occurs. Thus, leadership and future orientation are major themes of this Handbook.

I broke into the field when some literature and research was beginning to be made available through publications and support of major foundations and the U.S. government. In fact, I was fortunate to be invited to a 2-week international education seminar back in 1961 where we examined some 180 pieces of research and publications dealing with international education and more specifically with international students. This is all that we could find then, but we concluded that this exercise was very useful. Now when I see the extent of published works that deal with various aspects of the field, I am amazed not only at the size and scope of the literature but also at the relative lack of interconnectedness. As I suggested earlier in this foreword, I always look at bibliographies because they tell you what theories and concepts are being taken into account by the authors. It amazes me to find that many seminal pieces of research are dominated by narrow conceptual and theoretical frames of a single discipline and are neglecting relevant knowledge from others. This Handbook, however, addresses the need not only to do research internationally but also to research this interdisciplinary and intercultural field itself.

I am honored to be asked to provide these thoughts as part of an extraordinary venture that will raise the bar of competencies and knowledge of the field and highlight the roles of international educators who have come a long ways—often alone—to develop the field to the point at which it is now, and that is a very high point indeed.

Josef Mestenhauser
St. Paul, Minnesota, United States

PREFACE

The 21st century, characterized by expanding globalization, has impacted higher education in multiple ways. In the course of the millennial transition, the internationalization of higher education has moved from a marginal to a core dimension of higher education worldwide. This increased mainstreaming of internationalization is a fascinating phenomenon: new concepts, programs, providers, and methods of delivery are emerging; impressive national and regional scholarship programs and networks have been established; radical reforms have been undertaken to make higher education globally competitive; and mobility of students and scholars has increased around the world. This publication presents a broad and interpretive overview of these developments in a combination of issues and regional accounts.

In 1992, the Association of International Education Administrators, a professional organization for leaders in the international education field, published *Bridges to the Future: Strategies for Internationalizing Higher Education,* edited by Charles Klasek with contributions by U.S.-based association members. One of the first landmark publications to document and conceptualize a relatively new field at that time, *Bridges'* purpose was to present the major issues in international education in a period of important changes in world history: the collapse of the Iron Curtain and the fall of the Berlin Wall, the first Gulf War, the acceleration of globalization, and the initial spread of the Internet, all at the end of the 20th century. As editor Charles Klasek (1992) stated then, international education was moving "from a peripheral activity in higher education to one which was integral to the teaching, research, and service mission of the colleges and universities in the United States" (p. i). At the time of the publication of the 1992 edition of *Bridges,* the Cold War was over,

a period of dramatic growth in cross-national immigration was beginning, U.S. higher education had emerged as a global model, and the liberalization of global trade was about to occupy the attention of world leaders. For these reasons, Klasek noted that *Bridges* was seen as a way "to assist higher education in the creation, development, and enhancement of international programs in colleges and universities in an effusive growth period" (p. ii).

Twenty years later, the world and the field of international higher education have changed dramatically, which necessitates not just a revision of the seminal *Bridges to the Future,* but a new publication that documents the issues, trends, and conceptualizations of the current field within a broader global context. *The SAGE Handbook of International Higher Education* is written in a period of even bigger challenges and change. On the one hand, the attacks of 9/11 catapulted the United States into long and costly wars in Afghanistan and Iraq, as well as an aggressive approach to a "global war on terrorism." The subsequent neglect of diplomacy and "soft power" left the United States increasingly isolated in the world. At the same time, the rising prominence of other nations and regional associations such as the European Union impacted the flow of educational mobility and immigration. Meanwhile the global economy appeared to be booming throughout most of this period, particularly spurred by a worldwide housing speculation in the early 21st century and the greed of large multinational financial institutions. When this boom came to an abrupt halt in 2008, the most severe economic downturn since the Great Depression of the 1930s threatened the entire global economy. The economic crisis, however, coincided with the election in the United States of the first African American president, who had a decidedly multiethnic and international background and who faced leadership in a time of increased ethnic tensions around the world. Furthermore, pressing global problems such as poverty, health care, ethnic and gender diversity, and sustainable development created a context in which global cooperation was no longer a choice but rather an imperative. Higher education and research play a more important and international role than ever in a global economy that is driven by knowledge and innovation.

Given these global changes and challenges, the questions posed by the current volume—in terms of what this all means for international higher education—are not so different from those in 1992, but the context and the relevance have changed substantially. Will the next decades lead to increasing nationalism and protectionist politics? Will divisions grow between the Western Judeo-Christian world and the Islamic world? Or will the world move into an era of economic recovery, increasing mutual understanding among nations and cultures, narrowed inequality between global North and South, and a healthy environment? How will international higher education ensure that students are well prepared to live and work in this century and to engage globally in addressing world problems? As in 1992, the internationalization of higher education can and must play an important role in a world that is more global and at the same time more local than ever before.

This Handbook serves as an ambitious guide to international education in this millennium and offers global perspectives and new strategies for the further creation, development, and enhancement of the internationalization of higher education in the years to come. The time is right to bring new voices into the current and future role of internationalization in postsecondary education. While the pioneering generation of senior international education administrators and scholars involved in this field and its professional associations, such as the Association of International Education Administrators, developed the initial strategies of institutional internationalization, the succeeding generations are engaged in moving the field forward around the globe. Increasingly more international, more intentional, more strategic, and more self-consciously global in their thinking, these leaders in international education are not only internationalizing their institutions but also engaging globally within the broader contexts of the pressing issues of the 21st century.

In a conscious attempt to bridge two generations of scholars and practitioners, this Handbook includes contributions by experienced authors as well as by emerging scholars, in most cases writing together. Often, coauthors have been intentionally paired together in a way that brings different perspectives to the issues discussed in the chapters. Furthermore, each chapter's focus is sharpened through boxes that highlight concrete institutional, national, or regional experiences in an effort to bring theory and practice together, as well as to infuse the book with multiple perspectives. The global tenor of this Handbook, set by the editorial team spanning three continents, provides a unique contribution to the field of international education as it comes of age in the 21st century.

Inspired by *Bridges to the Future* and building on the legacy of that publication, this Handbook comprises five sections. The first section includes chapters placing internationalization of higher education in a conceptual and historic context. This section includes a chapter focusing on recent developments in internationalization in the United States, as well as a chapter on the Bologna Process in Europe and its global implications. The second section presents seven chapters with different strategic dimensions of internationalization. These include leadership, institutional strategies (including partnerships), outcomes assessment, risk management, international student security, and employee perspectives. The third section offers four chapters on "internationalization at home"—that is, what international educators can do on their own campuses to infuse more global dimensions into their institutions. This includes helping to internationalize the curriculum, exploring the teaching and learning processes, developing intercultural and global competences, and examining the intersections between the local and the global. Some chapters in this section also discuss ways in which study abroad experiences can be better integrated into the institution. The fourth section turns outward and addresses the mobility of students, scholars, institutions, programs, and projects around the globe in various ways, including through international development. The fifth and concluding section contains two chapters that provide insights, future directions, and global trends in international education, as well as a discussion of remaining issues that must be considered.

The coeditors intentionally decided not to organize this Handbook by various components of international education such as education abroad, international student advising, foreign language learning, and so on since international education in the 21st century requires a more wide-ranging discussion of salient issues, given that these components by themselves (or even together) cannot adequately measure or achieve the comprehensive internationalization that is needed at higher education institutions today. Rather, this volume reaches for a more strategic approach to internationalization that goes beyond its (presumed) component parts and aims at changing the quality of higher education itself. Most chapters include text boxes with a regional, national, thematic or institutional focus. These boxes are intended as case studies to underline the trends as described in the chapter. They are in general written by external authors, who are mentioned by their name and current position. In some cases, the boxes are written by one or all the chapter authors, in which cases no names are mentioned.

This comprehensive publication will be of interest to everyone involved in higher education as a leader, senior administrator, scholar, researcher, trainer, or commentator. In addition, we hope that those newer to the profession will also feel that this volume provides a baseline of knowledge and informed perspectives that will shape the future of the field and, quite possibly, their careers; we also hope to inform emerging leaders in higher education as they educate the next generation.

Darla K. Deardorff,
Hans de Wit, John D. Heyl

ACKNOWLEDGMENTS AND DEDICATION

We express deep appreciation to all of the chapter authors for the contributions that are the substance of this volume, as well as to the authors of the focused boxes found throughout the chapters. We owe special thanks both to the Association of International Education Administrators (AIEA), which conceived and supported this multiyear effort, and to the *Journal of Studies in International Education,* whose authors have provided the data and research insights that have shaped so much scholarship in the field of international education. SAGE and its editors have been very generous with both their support and guidance, for which we are most grateful. And thanks goes to Harvey Charles, chair of AIEA's Editorial Board, for his support throughout this process, as well as to Gulnaar Kaur and Rosemary Holland for their staffing support of this project.

We dedicate this volume to Dr. Tony Adams, a most valued Australian colleague and giant in the field of international education. Tony was a member of the editorial team from the beginning of this project, and his imprint can be found throughout its pages. He offered insightful and collegial advice on every chapter until his death on May 12, 2011. We miss him and hope that this volume adds to his very substantial legacy to our profession.

SECTION A

Contextual, Conceptual, and Historical Frameworks

1

Internationalization Within the Higher Education Context

Laura E. Rumbley, Philip G. Altbach, and Liz Reisberg

Internationalization has been one of the most powerful and pervasive forces at work within higher education around the world during the last two decades. With remarkably few exceptions, no corner of the globe or institutional type has proven itself immune to the call to "internationalize" in some fashion. In this process, practical applications and conceptual understandings of internationalization have evolved significantly, while the overall stakes in the internationalization game have become noticeably higher. Whereas at the beginning of the 21st century, international orientations, characteristics, and programmatic offerings of a college or university may have been perceived as merely an interesting and appealing component of an institution's profile, today internationalization is a core issue of concern to the higher education enterprise, touching directly on questions of social and curricular relevance, institutional quality and prestige, national competitiveness, and innovation potential. More recently, for better or worse, institutions also view internationalization as a source of potential revenue.

The authors of this chapter have previously asserted that it is "not possible for higher education to opt out of the global environment, since its effects are unavoidable" (Altbach, Reisberg, & Rumbley, 2009, p. 7). Yet, in spite of the powerful influence of the global context, "local realities of wealth, language, academic development, and other factors all affect the extent to which institutions are motivated and able to internationalize" (Altbach et al., 2009, p. 7). This means that leaders in higher education must be prepared to track and understand the broadest global trends in higher education, as well as the internationalization of higher education more specifically, while at the same time attending effectively to the unique needs and aspirations of their particular institutions, local communities, and regional or national contexts. Thus it can be quite challenging in today's complex and fast-moving environments, which are often characterized by scarce resources and competing priorities, to mention just two common yet critical challenges.

The good news is that senior international officers and administrators who are faced with the daunting task of making sense of this complex and shifting landscape have an increasing array of information and resources from which to draw insight and ideas. Internationalization and globalization have been the subject of much analysis over the last two decades. This work has resulted in a substantial body of literature exploring many facets of these phenomena within the context of higher education. There has also been a great deal of focus on translating theory to practice, with the aim of providing meaningful pathways from the realm of ideas about internationalization to practical implementation, particularly at the institutional level. Indeed, 20 years ago, the AIEA's first *Bridges to the Future* publication (Klasek, 1992) broke important new ground in this area.

Many have since contributed to an evolving set of definitions for globalization and internationalization. For the purposes of this analysis, *globalization* is characterized by "the broad economic, technological, and scientific trends that directly affect higher education and are largely inevitable in the contemporary world" (Altbach, 2006, p. 123). *Internationalization*, meanwhile, is defined as a "process of integrating an international, intercultural, or global dimension in the purpose, functions, or delivery of postsecondary education" (Knight, 2003, p. 2). Understood as both a reaction and a companion trend to globalization, internationalization has long been considered the toolkit of responses available (primarily at institutional and national levels) to address the many and diverse opportunities and imperatives presented by the overwhelming forces of globalization. This chapter addresses the significance of the current shift as internationalization moves beyond the concept of the toolkit. Today, internationalization is considered central to the academic enterprise, particularly in terms of planning for the future by policymakers and institutional leaders (International Association of Universities [IAU], 2010), and the phenomenon stands out clearly as a strategic objective essential to the relevance, dynamism, and sustainability of the world's 21st-century institutions and systems of higher education. What is more, internationalization has emerged as a compelling agent of change in its own right, serving as a potent catalyst for new models for the organization, delivery, and even the stated mission of the higher education enterprise in many different contexts across the globe.

A central goal of this chapter is to put various key aspects of internationalization into a broader context for deeper understanding and more nuanced reflection. In addition to more general considerations, brief overviews of internationalization developments in four major regions of the world—Africa, Asia, Europe, and Latin America—are also presented in this chapter. These supplements provide insight into how many of the issues touched on in this analysis are playing out in specific regional contexts.

INTERNATIONALIZATION AS A GLOBAL PHENOMENON

Eva Egron-Polak, secretary-general of the International Association of Universities (IAU), has said that "even though there is still no such thing as global higher education," internationalization is "creating a sense of 'global' in higher education" (Soilemetzidis, 2011, p. 1). Indeed, one of the most important aspects of internationalization today is that the frame of reference for this phenomenon extends well beyond the local and even the national. This is evident in two very visible ways. First, news about internationalization moves rapidly across borders. Indeed, where there is Internet access, information about developments in the internationalization of higher education in one location seems to be widely and nearly instantly available almost everywhere else. Second, approaches to internationalization in one part of the world are often emulated (or, at the very least, examined and considered for application) in other parts of the world. Specific trends and practices are being duplicated in different regions. For example, the growth in the number of countries working to position themselves as regional higher education/innovation "hubs" (Knight, 2011) may be seen as an embodiment of isomorphic trends in internationalization, as is the spreading interest in stronger regional cooperation and integration. One of the most compelling examples of regionalization in the contemporary era emerged in Europe in the context of the Bologna Process, but regionalization has also been taken up as a serious topic of discussion in Asia (Maslen, 2008) and Latin America (Travers, 2011). The expanding use of English as the primary international language of research, scholarly publication, and (increasingly) teaching (Altbach, 2007; Wächter & Maiworm, 2002, 2008) provides another example of an internationalization trend being tested out broadly across the globe. The IAU has been particularly interested in tracking how internationalization is understood and operationalized around the world, and it has produced three reports that endeavor to capture the perspectives of higher education leaders around the world with regard to the phenomenon (IAU, 2003, 2006, 2010).

The proliferation of information can be attributed to advancements in information technologies, but the dramatic upswing in recent years in coverage about international higher education issues is perhaps more important. In 1995, the Boston College Center for International Higher Education (CIHE) launched *International Higher Education*. This quarterly newsletter—published in English, Chinese, Spanish, and Russian and distributed internationally both by CIHE and in conjunction with partner organizations in China, Colombia, Germany, and Russia—was an early trendsetter. The CIHE newsletter is now complemented by the center's blog, "The World View," in collaboration with InsideHigherEd.com. Momentum in this area has been promoted by the introduction of other media outlets focused specifically on higher education regionally or worldwide—such as *University World News* and the Academic Cooperation Association's *ACA Newsletter–Education Europe*—as well as the considerable growth in coverage of international issues by longstanding higher education media sources such as the *Chronicle of Higher Education* and *Times Higher Education*. In addition, more mainstream, high-profile, and internationally circulated news sources, such as *The Economist* and *New York Times*, now devote significant space to stories and analysis about international issues in higher education, particularly in regard to the social and economic impact of new trends and models. Book series on international higher education topics—sponsored, for example, by CIHE and the Academic Cooperation Association—also have an important bearing on this trend, along with the significant body of studies and reports produced by such organizations as the International Centre for Higher Education Research Kassel (INCHER-Kassel), based at the University of Kassel in Germany, and the Center for Higher Education Policy Studies (based at the University of Twente in the Netherlands), to name just a very few examples.

Chapter 6 in this volume provides a more extensive treatment of the issue of internationalization resources. Still, it is impossible to overstate the influence of the international orientation of many information resources, as well as the easy access to much greater quantities of information about higher education around the world, on the way institutional leaders and policymakers understand issues and strategic options in local contexts. Internationalization is truly a global phenomenon.

ETHICAL CHALLENGES

The global resonance of internationalization is simultaneously exciting and worrisome. While international engagement—for individuals, institutions, and systems of higher education—has the potential to bring with it enormous opportunities and benefits, the global playing field is inherently uneven (Altbach et al., 2009). In this context, well-resourced actors will have more options and opportunities when it comes to how (and to what degree) to internationalize. Fundamental differences in the quality and quantity of internationalization activities and outcomes will result. In short, an increasingly competitive international environment has the potential to generate real winners and losers.

All of this has significant, real-world implications for the educational opportunities of individual students, the orientation and operation of higher education institutions, and even the performance of national economies. For example, smaller, developing economies are particularly vulnerable as they may find it difficult to integrate (and regulate) opportunities offered by foreign providers with greater capital. For-profit providers, in particular, may expand (and sometimes exploit) local opportunities, but not always in line with national priorities or objectives. Indeed, fundamental conflicts may arise in the introduction and development of for-profit higher education activities, which by definition are designed to advance owners' or (in many cases) shareholders' interests above and beyond the interests of other key stakeholders (such as students, professors, or society more broadly speaking). The activities of international student recruiters, agents, and other commercially oriented actors, who may play close to ethical boundaries, are also coming under closer scrutiny in the United States and elsewhere (National Association for College Admission Counseling, 2011).

The commercialization of higher education on a global scale raises many additional ethical questions, which are addressed later in this chapter, but, fundamentally, if higher education is to contribute to the advancement of the public good—even where many "private good" objectives exist—global activities should be guided by core principles of ethical engagement. At a minimum, ethical internationalization requires a commitment to such fundamental values as transparency, quality in academic programming and support services, academic freedom, fair treatment of partners and stakeholders, respect for local cultures, and thoughtful allocation of resources. These may sound like mere lofty words, but cultural conflicts are difficult to avoid when issues such as academic integrity, institutional accountability, gender roles, and sexual orientation are viewed from different cultural perspectives. International initiatives often confront dilemmas where the values of cultures are incompatible and the line between what is wrong or right and what is the prerogative of culture is not always clear.

Active engagement with internationalization can put decision makers at all levels into challenging situations where critical decisions must be made in complex and changing environments. Thus, a guiding principle should exist to attend appropriately to the opportunities and imperatives to internationalize, with a long-term perspective firmly rooted in considerations of ethics and quality.

A COMPLEX AND SHIFTING LANDSCAPE

Internationalization is expressed in many and varied ways. However, an examination of several key aspects of the phenomenon provides a useful framework for understanding its scope and complexity. The central elements in this analysis include:

- The increasing number of internationally mobile students and scholars, moving to and from ever more diverse locations

- The rapid growth in cross-border educational provision

- The push to achieve world-class status

- The interest in producing globally competent graduates capable of understanding and

functioning in a complex and interconnected world

- The increasing prevalence of the English language for teaching and research

- The significant emphasis on cooperative networking among higher education institutions and national higher education systems

- The overt efforts by individual institutions and national higher education systems to compete internationally

- The dramatic increase in the commercialization of international education, particularly in terms of the growing opportunities available to for-profit enterprises.

This is by no means an exhaustive list of manifestations of internationalization. However, these selected topics should serve to highlight the multifaceted nature of the phenomenon and its effects at multiple levels (including individuals, institutions, and national and regional systems of higher education) and across many aspects of the higher education enterprise, from mission and management, to teaching and learning, enrollment and staffing, and more.

International Student and Scholar Mobility

The movement of students, faculty, researchers, and even nonacademic staff is one of the most obvious and important aspects of internationalization today (see Chapters 21 to 23, this volume, for detailed discussion.). Although the international migration of students is not without precedent, the scale of mobility around the world today is greater than ever before. Mobility represents a basic component of internationalization—ostensibly easily documented and understood. However, on closer inspection, international mobility is a remarkably complex phenomenon, particularly when considered at a global level.

International mobility is increasing. The Organization for Economic Cooperation and Development (OECD, 2010) estimates that, as of 2008, there were some 3.3 million internationally mobile students around the world. This figure is up from the estimated figure of 3 million in 2007 and represents an increase of some 85% over the 1.8 million students thought to have been mobile in 2000 (OECD, 2010). There is speculation that this number will grow to at least 5.8 million by the year 2020 (Böhm et al., 2004) and 7.2 million by 2025 (Böhm, Davis, Meares, & Peace, 2002). However, it is extremely difficult to compile accurate data. Around the world, mobile students are defined by different criteria and, as a result, counted inconsistently. In some cases, citizenship is used to assess the international or domestic status of students, while in other instances a student is considered to be international if he or she completed the previous level of schooling in a country other than where the current degree (or credential) is being pursued. In still other cases, students may be counted only if they remain to complete a degree, while elsewhere they may factor into the mobility statistics if they are participating in an exchange program of some duration.

Figures generated by different data collection methods are not only difficult to compare across countries but also potentially misleading. For example, Turkish nationals are estimated to make up about a quarter of the foreign population in Germany. For a variety of reasons, many children born into this 1.7 million-strong group have assumed their parents' nationality, rather than German citizenship (*Deutsche Welle*, 2009). In this unusual situation, if citizenship is the measure of international student status, it is conceivable that many thousands of individuals would be counted as international students, despite being lifelong residents and having been educated since childhood in Germany. This is a rather unusual example, but it is illustrative of the many inconsistencies that can complicate data comparisons (de Wit, Agarwal, Said, Sehoole, & Sirozi, 2008; Kelo, Teichler, & Wächter, 2006; Teichler, Ferencz, & Wächter, 2011).

The process of gathering credible numbers on outbound students is also difficult. This is more easily achieved for short-term sojourns abroad used toward completion of a degree at the home institution. However, it is largely impossible to track the phenomenon of outgoing degree mobility, whereby students move internationally to complete a full degree, unless the host country carefully documents these individuals as inbound students. Furthermore, in many places the procedures for capturing and recording international mobility are simply not rigorous enough to allow for time series analyses (Teichler et al., 2011).

BOX 1.1 A View From Africa

Chika Sehoole

Associate Professor, University of Pretoria (South Africa)

Higher education systems in Africa—as elsewhere—have been directly affected by the rapidly globalizing environment and the resulting growth in internationalization. While internationalization is often considered a recent phenomenon, it is nothing new to parts of the world, such as Africa, that were once colonized. Indeed, the internationalization of African education in general (and higher education in particular) is directly related to the colonial experience on this continent. For example, the first degree-awarding institution in Nigeria was the University of Ibadan, established in 1948 as a University College of London. In the same year, the University of the Gold Coast in Ghana was also founded as a University of College of London, as was the University of Dar es Salaam in Tanzania, opened after independence in 1961. The three countries share a common legacy of British colonization.

Contemporary patterns of international student and staff mobility also reflect Africa's colonial past. Students and staff who go abroad tend to go to institutions and countries with links to the

(Continued)

(Continued)

former colonialists. For this reason, students from Anglophone African countries will often go to study in the United Kingdom, students and staff from Francophone Africa will flow to France, and those from Lusophone countries will gravitate toward Portugal.

Dependence continues to be an endemic feature of African higher education's engagement with the rest of the world, most notably in terms of the continent's widespread reliance on external or foreign assistance. The Partnership for Higher Education in Africa, a consortium of U.S.-based foundations, was a major player in the period 2000 to 2010 supporting internationalization efforts in higher education in countries such as Egypt, Ghana, Tanzania, Kenya, Mozambique, and Nigeria. Foreign embassies and diplomatic missions also serve as agents of internationalization by offering scholarships and study opportunities for Africans abroad. Meanwhile, transnational organizations such as the World Bank and the United Nations have played a major role in higher education in some sub-Saharan countries. Ethiopia, for example, is benefiting from the bank's Development Innovation Fund, which supports international institutional linkages, visiting faculty, new and innovative undergraduate and graduate programs, and short-term staff training overseas.

National governments also play a crucial role in the international activities of African higher education. Ministries of various types—such as foreign affairs and home affairs—have oversight in different countries for a range of responsibilities such as determining national human resource needs; negotiating bilateral agreements that facilitate student, staff, research, and knowledge exchange; and issuing visas and study permits. For example, the Mauritian Ministry of Foreign Affairs negotiates all bilateral cooperation agreements between Mauritius and other countries, including those covering scholarships for Mauritius nationals and branch campuses on its soil. The governments of Egypt, Kenya, South Africa, and Botswana play similar roles for the higher education sector in their countries.

Despite enormous challenges, African institutions of higher education are adopting many of the same internationalization activities employed at institutions across the world, including institutional partnerships; joint research projects; inbound and outbound student, faculty, and staff mobility; the introduction of international dimensions into the curriculum; the establishment of branch campuses; and transnational virtual delivery of higher education. Yet, Africa's place in the global higher education network remains disadvantaged. For example, apart from Egypt and South Africa, the flow of international students is more outbound than inbound for the countries of Africa, and relatively few internationally mobile students and staff return to the continent after completing their studies elsewhere, leading to significant brain drain. The dominance of English as the lingua franca of international communication, research, and business adds another layer of difficulty for many of Africa's non-English speaking countries eager to engage with the global knowledge economy and cutting-edge academic networks. The rapid growth of private higher education in Africa—while clearly meeting some needs for access—presents real challenges for quality, a critical issue for international engagement and competitiveness.

In short, providing an accurate global picture of international student mobility is extremely difficult. This is a particular challenge for national and regional policymakers who may wish—as is the case in Europe in the context of the Bologna Process—to articulate clear quantitative goals for mobility as part of larger social, political, or economic strategies (Leuven/Louvain-la-Neuve Ministers' Communiqué, 2009).

It is notable that while growth in international student numbers has been robust, it has not quite kept pace with overall increases in higher education enrollment around the world. Over the last

35 years, global higher education enrollment is estimated to have risen by more than 400%, whereas the worldwide growth rate in international student mobility has risen somewhat less dramatically by 350% (Bruneforth, 2010). Although the increases in both areas are impressive, they indicate that a smaller percentage of the total enrollment in higher education may be internationally mobile today than was the case 35 years ago. In the absence of reliable data, it is difficult to say conclusively why these trends are not more perfectly aligned. Among the plausible explanations, however, are the efforts in the last couple of decades to expand access to higher education, particularly in developing and middle-income countries. By improving both the quantity and quality of higher education provision at home, some countries are diminishing the influence of one of the fundamental push factors that sends large numbers of students abroad—namely, the inability to find either access to higher education or educational opportunities of sufficiently high quality (de Wit et al., 2008). The dramatic growth in student demand is, among other things, a function of demographics as well as notable increases in secondary school completion rates around the world. These trends show few signs of slowing soon, especially in much of the developing world (Altbach et al., 2009), but it is unclear exactly how these developments will affect international student mobility rates in the future.

Although smaller in scale, measuring and summarizing the movement of scholars, researchers, and staff present even greater challenges (Teichler et al., 2011), since much of this mobility occurs on an ad hoc, short-term basis and is often organized at an individual if not department level. Yet, this kind of activity is understood to be increasingly vital to successful internationalization. Research has indicated that (at least in the U.S. context) faculty members with international experience have a direct and positive effect on student participation in study abroad. In addition, the presence of foreign faculty enhances efforts to infuse curricula and campus life with an international dimension, and domestic faculty with international experience are more likely to "buy in" to initiatives designed to advance campus internationalization (O'Hara, 2009).

The mobility of top international talent is also a major concern of both sending and receiving countries at the highest policy levels (Gibson & McKenzie, 2011; World Economic Forum, 2011). Skilled migration plays out in educational and governmental circles alike. Visa regulations in different countries—including Australia, the Netherlands, the United Kingdom, United States, Saudi Arabia, and others—actively confer privilege on highly educated applicants or those with expertise in key fields connected to innovation and economic growth. There are also formal initiatives in place to attract such talent. The Banting Fellowship program in Canada is one of many examples of national-level efforts to encourage the pursuit and exchange of international talent, as is a Russian "mega-grant" scheme. The Canadian initiative will invest CAD$45 million over five years to support 70 two-year fellowships—available to Canadians and non-Canadian citizens—whose work should serve to support the country's science and technology strategy. Interestingly, the effort is also specifically designed to foster international connections by allowing up to one quarter of fellowship recipients to take placements at research institutions outside of Canada (Office of the Prime Minister of Canada, 2010). Meanwhile, the Russian Ministry of Education and Science announced in late 2010 the names of 40 winners of awards up to 150 million rubles (or USD$5.3 million) "to conduct research at a Russian university working with a team comprised of researchers from the host institution." Notably, half of the grant winners were Russian citizens, but just 5 of the 40 award recipients reside in Russia (*ACA Newsletter: Education Europe*, 2010). Talent attraction efforts—or re-attraction, in the case of expatriate scientists and academics—are becoming increasingly common (and high profile) in different parts of the world. China offers another notable example. Of the 1.62 million students who went overseas since 1978, only 497,000 returned, including only 8% of the Chinese who earned PhDs abroad in science and engineering. Having lost so much of its native talent, China is creating new initiatives to cultivate, attract, and repatriate human capital (Wang, 2010). For a more detailed discussion of skilled migration and top talents, see Chapter 23.

Although many of the specifics about international academic mobility dynamics remain to be clarified, it appears certain that the population of internationally mobile students and scholars will continue to grow. That said, this population is likely to exhibit some new characteristics and behaviors. Whereas for decades students and scholars have moved from the less-developed countries of the global South (particularly in Africa, Asia, and Latin America) to the wealthier and more economically powerful countries and regions of the North (including Australia, Canada, the United States, and Western Europe), new destinations are emerging as viable options for internationally mobile academic talent, with a strong attraction to one's own region for such opportunities. For example, South Africa has become a destination for many sub-Saharan African students on the move. China, too, is beginning to position itself as a key player in Asia, and South Korea is also devoting resources to building up its international attractiveness. The newly established regional hubs for higher education in Singapore and the Middle East (including Education City in Qatar and the Dubai Knowledge Village) also aim to create a profile for themselves within their respective regions, while Egypt stands out as a destination of choice where religion is a key factor in mobility decision-making (de Wit, et al., 2008). Indeed, de Wit et al. (2008) note that "religious factors are becoming increasingly important, not only in higher education student mobility but also in elementary and secondary education" (p. 248).

Of course, the pull of the world's academic powerhouses will no doubt continue to be significant. Indeed, in 2007, North America and Western Europe captured nearly 65% of the world's mobile students. However, this is down from the 2000 figure of about 70%, while Asia's share of the pie, for example, grew from 13% to 18.5% in the 2000 to 2007 period (Altbach et al., 2009). The so-called regionalization of international student mobility (and other manifestations of internationalization)—whereby individuals and institutions look more readily within their own geographic region rather than to traditional destinations or better-known partner countries outside of the immediate region—is an important trend to watch (IAU, 2006, 2010).

International mobility of academic talent is unquestionably an important issue. There is a widely shared belief that international study is, on balance, a good thing, with positive ramifications for individuals and societies aiming to leverage the contributions of a better educated and more globally competent workforce. But real risks and challenges must be considered. For example, students who move internationally, for

both short-term credit mobility and full degree programs, are largely self-funded and therefore tend to come from more privileged socioeconomic backgrounds. As a result, the experience is often limited to elite groups and to the retention of privilege (IAU, 2010). If internationalization—and student mobility as a key component of the phenomenon—is to adequately reflect other fundamental values of higher education, such as equitable access, then international mobility opportunities need to be made available more broadly to more diverse groups of students. Student organizations in Europe, where student mobility has been a high-profile policy matter for more than two decades, have been particularly vocal in recent years about concerns in this area (European Students' Union, 2008).

Just as international opportunities are unevenly distributed, so too are effects. Although increasingly viewed through the more neutral lens of "brain circulation," the international movement of academic talent can represent a net loss (so-called "brain drain") for some countries (especially the poorest countries across Africa) while escalating the advantages of developed countries. More and better data on student mobility, including analyses of the quality and impact of these experience and their long-term effects for individuals, institutions, and societies are sorely needed. (For a longer discussion on this issue, see Chapter 21, this volume.)

Cross-Border Education

The movement of people has long characterized the international dimension of higher education but, increasingly, programs and entire institutions are on the move, as are institutional models and approaches to teaching and learning (see Chapters 18 to 20, this volume, for detailed discussion). Cross-border education—also commonly referred to as *transnational* or *borderless* education—takes many different forms, including

> fully fledged "sister" institutions of existing universities (such as New York University in Abu Dhabi), branch or satellite campuses of parent institutions . . . , and collaborative arrangements (such as the one between the University of Nottingham and Zhejiang Wanli Education Group-University, which allows for the operation of the University of Nottingham Ningbo, China). Also prevalent are single programs or narrow

fields of study being offered overseas by one institution or jointly by two or more (Altbach et al., p. 25).

Joint and double degree programs, "twinning," and franchise arrangements also figure into this landscape. The international reach of distance learning may also be considered relevant in this context.

Efforts to catalogue a comprehensive list of cross-border programs (including that of Verbik & Merkley, 2006) are hampered by the fact that there are so many different configurations of this phenomenon. There are, however, strong indications that both supply and demand are growing. As mentioned previously, in much of the developing world, demand for higher education is outpacing the ability of domestic suppliers (public or private) to respond. This unmet need represents a real opportunity for foreign providers, many of whom are for-profit entities eager to expand their markets. Even traditional universities see the potential for a return from investing in operations overseas. Benefits sought by these actors include the extension of an international profile and brand, as well as the establishment of a convenient base of operations for study abroad, international research activities for faculty, and cooperation with foreign partner institutions (Verbik & Merkley, 2006).

The potential for problems when crossing national borders is often underestimated, however. On the provider side, foreign institutions may not have an adequate understanding of the cultural and regulatory framework into which they are moving. This can result in unrealistic expectations of partnership dynamics, what can be achieved in the host country, and on what timetable. Decisions to launch a branch campus are frequently based on short-term financial aspirations, often encouraged by subsidies provided by host countries or institutions rather than mission-driven rationales. Objectives should reflect a meaningful and sustainable combination of local needs and foreign provider goals (Knight, 2005; Rumbley & Altbach, 2007). Indeed, major missteps have resulted in significant losses for institutions trying to establish outposts overseas. Examples include Michigan State University, which decided to end its undergraduate programs in Dubai (at a loss of over $4 million) (Mills, 2010; Swan, 2010), and George Mason University (2009), which pulled out of its

Ras Al Khaimah campus in 2009, just four years after opening its doors there. More dramatically, in 2007, the University of New South Wales (UNSW) reportedly agreed to pay back all of the grants and loans—totaling $22.4 million—that the Australian university had received from Singapore to launch a branch campus there. UNSW had opened the campus just a few months before the closure was announced (Overland, 2007).

Time and money are clearly key considerations in this discussion, but so are issues of academic quality, academic freedom, and the basic rights of individuals. How does an institution ensure that the quality of its international offerings will be comparable to the home campus, particularly when home campus faculty may be unwilling to relocate overseas? For a research university, can the branch campus offer the same opportunities for research? Are the same principles of academic freedom upheld on both the home and branch campus? Are individuals—for example, women, ethnic and religious minorities, homosexuals, students with special needs—afforded the same rights, protections, and opportunities? These questions shed light on the range of issues that providers and hosts must consider in the cross-border education discussion.

The stakes for host countries in all of this are arguably higher, however. Poorer countries, in particular, and those with nascent or otherwise ineffective regulatory frameworks, can find it exceedingly difficult (if not impossible) to protect the public from low-quality or deceptive educational programming offered by some foreign providers, not to mention outright fraud perpetrated by rogue providers. Meanwhile, imported curricula and teaching methods may not be appropriate or effective in a specific national or cultural context (Teferra, 2008b). Developing economies are keen to train ever-larger cohorts of young people to help drive economic development and innovation. But these efforts are undermined if attention is not paid to both the quality and content of the education (Knight, 2005, 2008; Teferra, 2008b).

Cross-border initiatives often disregard local priorities. A foreign provider will typically avoid fields that require large investment in infrastructure such as laboratories or high-tech equipment. The end result is that, while cross-border providers may help to increase higher education enrollment, they may not deliver the training most urgently needed in the host country. Yet, some of the world's most prestigious institutions are participating in cross-border activity. For example, the Weill Cornell Medical College, Cornell University's medical school, operates a campus in Qatar, where it trains physicians and conducts medical research, notably in the areas of "genetic and molecular medicine, women's and children's health, gene therapy, and vaccine development" (Weill Cornell Medical College in Qatar, 2009, p. 1) Other examples include the University of Chicago's Booth School of Business in London, Boston University's longstanding campus in Brussels, and Stanford University's collaboration with the National University of Singapore to deliver an Executive Program in International Management. Cross-border education is generally delivered by much less prestigious institutions.

In addition to programs and institutions, approaches to higher education appear to be moving across borders, as well. For example, from Hong Kong (Rumbley, 2008) to Amsterdam (Rumbley, 2010), there is an emerging interest—or, some are careful to specify, "renewed" interest (Rumbley, 2010)—in liberal education for undergraduate students around the world (Peterson, 2011). Many point to the United States as the cradle of this kind of higher education and therefore see this model as an export to other parts of the world. Yale University's initiative to open a liberal arts program in Singapore (in conjunction with the National University of Singapore) and Bard College's initiatives in Russia, Central Asia, and Palestine (Peterson, 2011) may be seen as examples of such developments. Advocates for the current "global migration" of liberal arts (Peterson, 2011, p. 11) argue that they are not opportunistically riding a wave of simple fascination with liberal learning. Rather, they assert that the kind of education provided by liberal arts programs—with attention to multidisciplinarity, the development of students' critical thinking skills, and the overt emphasis on enabling students to "learn how to learn"—is critically important for local and national stakeholders everywhere, where the focus is on building stronger multicultural societies as well as dynamic workforces capable of innovating and adapting to change (Peterson, 2011; Rumbley, 2008, 2010).

BOX 1.2 A View From Asia

Yuto Kitamura

Associate Professor, Sophia University (Japan)

Today, the international profile of Asian universities is rising steadily, and the higher education market within Asia is undergoing rapid expansion. Competition among universities is intensifying beyond national borders, and universities from outside Asia are eagerly launching themselves in Asian countries. It must be noted, however, that the region is far too diverse to be described under the one umbrella term, *Asian*. On the one hand, in countries like Japan and South Korea, more than half of the respective age cohort goes on to higher education. On the other hand, in some countries in South and Southeast Asia, higher education enrollments remain low and in single figures. Yet, an overview of the state of higher education in Asian countries alerts us to the fact that a considerable number of issues are common to all countries. The most prominent of these is the strong interest in the internationalization of universities.

Until now, Asian countries tended to send their human resources to North America, Europe, and Australia. Moreover, prestigious universities from those areas have moved to open branch campuses in Asian countries such as Singapore and Malaysia, particularly since the 1990s. Thus, universities in Asia are rapidly undergoing internationalization in an effort not to lose their own students, and students of neighboring countries, to Western universities. Also, the international recruitment of teaching staff and researchers has become easier today, thanks to a flexible employment system being created by such trends as incorporating universities (notably in Japan and Malaysia) and by making universities self-governing (as seen in Thailand and Indonesia).

Asian countries have endorsed these internationalization initiatives. In Japan, for instance, the government in 2010 inaugurated the Global 30 project, aimed at vastly increasing the number of foreign students in the country. To enhance international competitiveness in a knowledge-based economy, governments are also targeting focused support on core research facilities to promote the growth of world-class research centers; Project 211 in China, BrainKorea 21 in South Korea, and the Center of Excellence Program in Japan are relevant examples. In this way, governments are endeavoring to attract excellent researchers regardless of nationality. Furthermore, internationalization of the higher education market in Asia is stimulating regional political networks—for example, the Association of Southeast Asian Nations (ASEAN) and the South Asian Association for Regional Cooperation—to get involved in university issues, thereby speeding up the drive toward regional coordination. The ASEAN University Network is evidence of this trend.

Many Asian countries are working to boost the international competitiveness of their own universities by focusing on quality assurance efforts. But there is huge variation in quality assurance capacity within the region. In Southeast Asia, for example, the countries of Indonesia, Thailand, the Philippines, and Malaysia have already developed or established their own mechanisms for monitoring quality. By contrast, in countries such as Cambodia, Myanmar, and Laos, no adequate progress has been made in the design and implementation of effective quality assurance systems. This intraregional gap is a large obstacle in developing a common framework for quality assurance in Southeast Asia. Therefore, organizations such as the Asia-Pacific Quality Network are assisting those member countries with limited capacity to develop further efforts to enhance quality assurance.

For Asian universities to survive and to develop successfully in the international higher education market of the 21st century, each needs to build its own distinctive university profile while meeting global standards. At the same time, to differentiate themselves from Western universities, they must also delineate distinctive features of universities that clearly reflect the unique and multifaceted character of "Asia."

In spite of very real challenges, and in the face of spirited debate surrounding the appropriateness and viability of specific initiatives, cross-border activities are increasing in number and scope. One of the most interesting developments involves—much like the student mobility trends—a visible increase in South-South movement, although the trend for educational programming to flow North-South still dominates. And while such initiatives are still relatively small in number, the announcement by the Open University of Malaysia that it will soon offer master's programs in Ghana and Vietnam (Observatory on Borderless Higher Education, 2010) is just one example of how emerging actors in this area may change the dimensions of the playing field in coming years. There is, without question, a "sense of opportunity and also of urgency . . . felt by many institutions keen to engage internationally" (Altbach et al., 2009, p. 26). But experience suggests caution in this highly complex and fluid area of international engagement.

World-class Aspirations

Internationalization is increasingly understood as a transformative phenomenon, moving institutions—and even national and supranational actors—to adjust everything from administrative policies to entire frames of reference. A very tangible example of this development can be seen in the way that universities around the world are embracing (at least in principle) the notion that their missions and strategic development must incorporate a perspective beyond the local and even the national horizon. The widespread aspiration to world-class status provides especially clear evidence of such developments.

Excellence at a world-class level has become an objective for higher education institutions and systems across the globe (Altbach, 2004; Hazelkorn, 2011; Salmi, 2009). Organized efforts to achieve international recognition for quality higher education can be seen on all continents. The proliferation of international university rankings—from the *Academic Ranking of World Universities* (originally compiled by Shanghai Jiao Tong University in 2003 and now produced by the Shanghai Ranking Consultancy) to the *Ranking Iberoamericano*, released for the first time in 2010 by SCImago Institutions Rankings of Spain—has increased pressure on institutions to measure excellence against subjective, externally defined criteria (Hazelkorn, 2011). Excellence in higher education at the highest levels has arguably always had an international dimension, but today a vast number of institutions choose to benchmark against international standards, whether by competing for spots on a league table (Hazelkorn, 2011) or seeking accreditation by organizations (often in the United States and Europe) perceived to confer prestige (Eaton, 2004; OECD, 2004)

There are many positive aspects to these developments. Indeed, who can argue with the pursuit of excellence? But at a global level, the quest exacerbates the dominance of specific influences and the gaps among the "haves" and "have nots." Responses to the various global ranking efforts are particularly notable for bringing these disparities into stark relief. Hazelkorn (2011) notes that

> because rankings use quantification as the basis for determining quality and performance, they privilege older, well-resourced universities, which are highly selective in their recruitment of students and faculty and whose comparative advantages have been accumulated over time (p. 23).

Developing countries, many struggling simply to provide space for all of the university-eligible students in the population, cannot compete equally. Yet—from Nigeria to Sri Lanka to Vietnam—the developing world is also drawn inexorably into the contest for global visibility and prestige (Hazelkorn, 2011). The economically privileged countries of the world, meanwhile, continue to strengthen and expand their knowledge system infrastructures, often at the expense of the developing world, through the recruitment of top talent. In developing and industrialized countries alike, the effort to perform well on the international rankings has, in some cases, concentrated already limited funds on just a small number of privileged institutions or functions—often favoring research over teaching or "fields and units which are likely to be more productive, have faculty who are more prolific especially at the international level, and more likely to trigger (upward) changes in the appropriate indicators" (Hazelkorn, 2011, p. 107). U-Multirank, a project supported by the European Commission, is one example of an effort to move attention away from what are perceived as simplistic and overly subjective approaches to defining excellence. The U-Multirank aims to deliver a "multi-dimensional global university ranking" focused on five key dimensions: teaching and learning, research, knowledge transfer, international orientation, and regional engagement. The goal is to make more transparent and accessible to key stakeholders the "institutional and programmatic diversity" of European higher education, with aspirations to apply this model more globally (U-Multirank, n.d.). It is uncertain if this effort will yield the intended results.

U-Multirank notwithstanding, the quest for excellence at the institutional level, as defined by international rankings and excellence initiatives, is clearly skewed toward research productivity (Altbach, 2011). No one disputes the enormous importance of research or its links to innovation, which in turn can have a powerful effect on economic performance. What is worrisome is that the emphasis on research can eclipse the importance of teaching and other functions in higher education, causing national governments to direct limited resources toward strengthening the research capacity at a small number of institutions. A more broadly conceived notion of excellence that takes into account activities beyond research might yield more meaningful long-term results for more institutions, as well as strengthen *systems* of higher education as a whole. Indeed, aspiring to the development of a world-class system, rather than a select few world-class institutions (Altbach, 2010), is a strategic objective that deserves more emphasis in policy and planning circles.

Educating for Global Engagement

Working to achieve enhanced visibility on the global stage is not the only way in which internationalization is affecting the priorities and orientations of institutions, which are also looking inward and redefining educational objectives for their students. Striving to produce global competence, or a sense of civic responsibility that extends beyond the local or even national level, is now explicit in the mission and strategic planning documents of countless higher education institutions. In many cases—for example, Duke University's 2006 strategic plan—this effort is guided by a framework of understanding with the following orientation:

> We operate in an interdependent world where what were once hard and fast borders are now permeable, where individuals are part of an increasingly global community and where problems transcend traditional boundaries. To be citizens of this world, we must be knowledgeable about issues that impact that world, such as global warming, poverty and pandemics, and conflicting cultures and proactive in using that knowledge to make a difference. (Duke University, 2006, as quoted in Childress, 2010, p. 48)

Acting on these laudable aspirations can be challenging, however. First, it can be quite difficult to articulate what terms like global competence and global citizenship actually mean or how these objectives dovetail effectively with more traditional educational objectives (Deardorff, 2009; see Chapters 14 to 17, this volume). In addition, it can be a slow and difficult process to move stakeholders to agree on exactly how the curriculum and co-curriculum should support this work, especially when higher education is under ever-greater public pressure to address so many diverse social responsibilities.

Still, internationalization as it relates to educating human resources for optimal performance in a more global knowledge economy resonates across the spectrum of higher education provision. In some ways, this has been most visible among elite liberal arts institutions and high-powered research universities, but the interest in educating for global engagement is also visible at the level of vocational and technical education. Although typically considered a resource for highly localized education and workforce development needs, the U.S. community college sector and its counterparts in Europe and elsewhere are looking more than ever to incorporate elements of internationalization into their strategic activities. For example, the Bruges Communiqué on Enhanced European Cooperation in Vocational Education and Training (2010) speaks specifically about the need to internationalize the sector in its vision for the period 2011 to 2020, notably through mobility channels. Likewise, the American Association of Community Colleges (AACC) has, since 2006, included references to global engagement in its mission statement, specifically "supporting community colleges to prepare learners to be effective in a global society" and "empowering community colleges to grow as a global force for learning by disseminating information and promoting international partnerships between American community colleges and countries seeking collaborative opportunities" (AACC, 2006).

Ultimately, moving institutions, faculty, staff, and students to see themselves and the work that they do in a larger global context is increasingly necessary in light of 21st-century realities such as economic interdependency, terrorism, and global warming, which cross national boundaries. The real work, however, lies in actually moving institutions beyond rhetoric and the mere recognition of these issues toward meaningful action that balances global and local interests in ways that make sense for individual institutions and their constituents.

English and More English

Language is a central issue in any discussion of internationalization of the world's higher education institutions and systems. In many parts of the world, the move to conduct research and deliver all or significant parts of educational programming in English is a strategic decision to increase international openness, attractiveness, and competitiveness. There are no definitive data about the extent to which English dominates the academy worldwide, but there is a consensus that the movement is far-reaching. Two studies in Europe (Wächter & Maiworm, 2002, 2008) have attempted to analyze the trend of English-taught programs in that context. This work revealed that between 2002 and 2007 the number of English-taught programs more than tripled (from slightly over 700 to almost 2,400). At the same time, such programming is unevenly spread across Europe and "still not a mass phenomenon" (Wächter & Maiworm, 2008, p. 10), and English is unlikely to "take over" (Wächter & Maiworm, 2008, p. 91) as the language of instruction in Europe, at least in the near future. In the European context, implementation of English-taught programs appears to be a strategic choice to strengthen internationalization efforts by enhancing attractiveness to international students, improving domestic graduates' readiness for employment in a more global or international context, and serving to "sharpen the profile of the institution" (Wächter & Maiworm, 2008, p. 13).

BOX 1.3 A View From Europe

Irina Ferencz

Policy Officer, Academic Cooperation Association (Belgium)

Home to many of the world's oldest universities, Europe is closely acquainted with internationalization. In fact, one of the core activities of this phenomenon, the international mobility of scholars, has a centuries-long history here. Nevertheless, only during the past two decades has internationalization moved center stage in Europe, gradually appearing at the core of institutional missions, policies, and strategies.

It remains fairly difficult, if not impossible, to talk about internationalization in Europe in generic terms. "Unity in diversity," which has famously described much of the political and economic integration in the framework of the European Union, is equally valid in the sphere of higher education. Indeed "internationalization(s) at different speeds" may be one of the best ways to describe the European context. First, internationalization itself has been defined differently across the European higher education community—in some cases as the institutional response to the pervasive forces of globalization, in others as the very counterpart to globalization. Furthermore, European countries and the nearly 4,000 institutions of higher education there find themselves at various stages of internationalization, having initiated these efforts at different moments in time and with different resources at hand. Countries like the United Kingdom, Germany, France, and the Nordic countries are among the trendsetters in internationalization in Europe and beyond, while many other European countries are only beginning to get their feet wet in this area.

What unites most European higher education institutions is their strong interest in acquiring or enhancing their (unique) international profile and reputation, but there has been some uniformity and joint action. The Bologna Process and the initiatives of the European Union, with its mobility programs (like Erasmus and Erasmus Mundus), have fostered enormous interest in international student (and staff) mobility. The guiding principle here has been that more mobility is both a positive and necessary development. European states have been encouraged to cooperate with other European counterparts in a range of international activities, particularly in terms of mobility and creating joint and double degrees. The trend has also been to foster a friendly yet competitive approach with the rest of the world.

Support for internationalization activities has also penetrated the nation-level policy discourse. The governments of several European countries have had strategies for internationalization in place for years now. In ideal cases, such policies are also in tune with institutional strategies in the country. National agencies for internationalization like the DAAD (Germany), the British Council (the United Kingdom), CampusFrance, or Nuffic (the Netherlands) play a crucial role in these efforts, and there is a growing tendency to develop such national-level actors across Europe. Mutual learning is in full swing in this area. For example, websites of the type "Study in . . ." have already become widespread, and so has the presence of European actors at promotional fairs and similar events around the world.

Europe currently enjoys a positive global profile. It hosts about half of the world's mobile student population and has managed to preserve this market share over the past decade, despite growing competition and the multiplication of study destinations worldwide. Yet, there are clear national differences here, as well; about two thirds of all foreign students in Europe study in just three countries – the United Kingdom, Germany, and France. European students who study abroad tend to choose other European countries and only occasionally opt to study outside of Europe.

Many European countries are now shifting from *more* internationalization to *better* internationalization, for example, seeking to attract the best and brightest students from abroad, to forge strategic partnerships and alliances, and to measure and assure the quality of international activities. Concerns about the unintended consequences of internationalization are also on the rise, in relation to such issues as brain drain, monolingualism (English as the *lingua franca*), and the impact of internationalization indicators on public funding of institutions. Continuing to internationalize with the same level of enthusiasm will require European higher education institutions to deal effectively and creatively with these challenges.

In other parts of the world, however, English has arguably taken over, and more by necessity than by choice. In Ethiopia, for example, English is the official language of instruction in universities (although not of primary or secondary education). This policy has been considered critically important to Ethiopia's highly ambitious plan to expand the enrollment capacity and quality of its postsecondary system. A great deal of foreign aid and expertise has been invested to this end, with English serving as the lingua franca of this engagement. Given that so much of the world's global knowledge economy turns on communication in English, there is some merit to this development in Ethiopia, but there are also serious drawbacks. Many Ethiopian students and faculty are simply not operating effectively in English, putting them at a disadvantage for both teaching and learning. Furthermore, if the aim of the country's massive push to upgrade its national higher education system is to address key Ethiopian challenges—of poverty, food insecurity, unemployment, environmental degradation, public health problems, and the like—does the widespread use of a non-native language (often supported by curricula and materials from abroad) contribute effectively to the understanding of local problems or the cultivation of local solutions?

From a more general standpoint, de Wit (2011) has singled out teaching in English as the first of nine fundamental misconceptions about internationalization, all of which in some way reflect a situation where the means to achieve internationalization have evolved into goals in and of themselves and in the process have lost much, if not all, of their meaning. In the case of English usage, it can also lead to a series of unintended consequences and "absurd situations" that devalue internationalization and reduce educational quality (de Wit, 2011, p. 6).

How and to what extent to incorporate English—or other dominant languages, for that matter—into the higher education enterprise is under discussion in countless countries and institutions across the globe. It provides an especially vivid example of the complex considerations involved for many institutions when it comes to formulating rational approaches to "glocal" action; that is, how best to take into account broad international perspectives and concerns as well as more immediate local needs and issues?

Cooperative Networking

Another notable aspect of internationalization today is the pervasiveness of regional and cross-border networking in higher education at institutional and national levels. Perhaps the most obvious manifestation of this kind of engagement has been the Bologna Process, an intergovernmental agreement now involving nearly 50 countries that has facilitated the effort to build a European Higher Education Area (EHEA).

The EHEA aspires to "a common, Europe-wide framework of understanding around tertiary education and lifelong learning, with significant cross-border intelligibility of degrees and qualifications, and a high level of quality, attractiveness, and competitiveness on a global scale" (Altbach et al., 2009, p. 28; Bologna Declaration, 1999). The Bologna Process has attracted the interest of higher education leaders and policymakers in many corners of the world, and has served as a key point of reference for other regions (see Chapter 5, this volume). Indeed, cooperative networking and the focus on regionalization appear to be strongly correlated, as seen in initiatives such as ENLACES in Latin America and the Caribbean (UNESCO-IESALC, 2008); the establishment of the African Network for Internationalization of Education (Teferra & Knight, 2008); the African Union Harmonization Strategy, now under development; discussions among Association of South East Asian Nations (ASEAN) members to work more collaboratively in Asia (English.news.cn, 2010); and the Catania Declaration (2006), which aims to bring more than a dozen countries that border the Mediterranean Sea into closer contact through greater "comparability and readability of higher education systems" (Catania Declaration, 2006, p. 2).

International cooperation in higher education is also seen through the countless institutional and professional organizations that have proliferated in recent years and purposefully incorporate an international focus into their membership and activities. Student networks, university and rectors' conferences, administrators' and practitioners' associations, scholarly

networks, and quality assurance and accreditation bodies all figure into this discussion (Schneller, Lungu, & Wächter, 2009). It is not surprising that NAFSA, originally established in the United States in 1948 as the National Association of Foreign Student Advisors, kept the acronym by which it is best known but changed the name of the organization in 1990 to the Association of International Educators to better reflect the scope of its international membership, which has swelled to more than 10,000.

International organizations with a wide range of profiles are also understood to be playing ever more important roles in higher education policy, planning, and development (Bassett & Maldonado-Maldonado, 2009). Key actors in this area include OECD, UNESCO, the World Bank, and the World Trade Organization. In addition, private philanthropic organizations—such as the Carnegie Corporation and the Ford, MacArthur, and Rockefeller foundations—as well as government aid agencies (notably, although certainly not exclusively, from northern Europe) have contributed heavily to initiatives focused on higher education, particularly in Africa. The involvement of these organizations in the higher education enterprise, particularly in the developing world, has been the subject of much critique. However, they must also be recognized for an array of positive contributions when it comes to pooling significant resources in support of higher education and drawing attention to the needs of less-developed countries when it comes to tertiary education development and sustainability.

Meanwhile, international cooperation in research also has become increasingly common and important, involving national agreements, institutional arrangements, and the activity of countless individual researchers. Central to this trend has been the rising sense that the most cutting-edge research (particularly in the high-stakes STEM fields of science, technology, engineering, and mathematics) can be most effectively achieved when leveraging the expertise of strong international teams. This is a function of both the complexity of this kind of research—which may demand top minds in several different disciplines, all of whom are unlikely to be at the same institution or even in the same country—and the cost of highly technical, often long-term research projects, which cannot realistically be borne by one institution or country. Reductions in international travel costs and innovations in digital communications arguably have also served to smooth the way for more international research activity. In a 2007 report commissioned by the United Kingdom's Office of Science and Innovation, the authors noted dramatic growth in the volume of collaborative papers during the 10 years from 1995 to 2005. In absolute volume of collaborative papers, increases varied from 30% for France to 50% for the United Kingdom and more than 100% for China (Adams, Gurney, & Marshall, 2007). Many of the most compelling research issues of the day are understood to be borderless, international, or even global, in their origins and effects, adding another powerful incentive for international academic collaboration.

Networking, although practical and beneficial, also presents risks and challenges. Networks can be highly elite, keen to draw in members with the best resources to share. This can make it highly difficult for stakeholders from the world's fledgling higher education systems or more poorly resourced institutions to participate or to benefit from their output. If "different" (and, notably, less affluent and influential) partners are not involved—at any level—in such cooperative activities, the agendas and discourse of these networks and partnerships may not effectively incorporate the perspectives of importance to these already marginalized stakeholders (see Chapter 9, this volume, for further discussion on partnerships). For example, some observers have raised frequent questions about who is driving the agenda for higher education development in Africa—international donors or local stakeholders (Teferra, 2008a). The prominent use of English as the language of international cooperation in higher education (research-oriented or otherwise) is another example of how the process of international engagement skews perspective, priorities, and activities toward the more powerful partners.

International Competition

While cooperation has become a hallmark of internationalization today, so has competition. The international rankings are an obvious manifestation of this trend, as are the aforementioned efforts to attract top academic talent from around the world in the race to generate the highest levels of marketable new knowledge.

Competitive advantage brings with it prestige, influence, and greater access to funding; this plays out not only at the institutional level, but also within national higher education systems, and even at the supranational level.

Many higher education institutions today aggressively leverage their international profile as a way to stand out in an increasingly crowded marketplace of postsecondary possibilities. Most often, this involves highlighting the international dimension on institutional websites and in other promotional materials, making sure that potential students and other stakeholders are aware of the institution's work in this area. Although hardly considered groundbreaking today, the emphasis on internationalization as a unique element of the institution is a significant departure from the way that colleges and universities presented themselves 15 or even 10 years ago. Meanwhile, a very small but increasingly visible set of institutions is taking this idea further by aiming to position themselves as fundamentally global, ostensibly for innovative academic purposes but also with the aim of increasing competitive advantage. Not surprisingly the list of institutions that now include *international* in their name is growing. More substantive initiatives to strengthen international profiles and enhance cachet are also on the rise. There are a considerable number of examples, but New York University Abu Dhabi stands out as an especially vivid case in point, touted as an extraordinary experiment in international education, but also openly acknowledged by NYU president, John Sexton, as an effort to outmaneuver other highly prestigious universities in the high-stakes race for international excellence and recognition (Krieger, 2008).

National education systems are also in competition with one another, even while they may be cooperating. National governments actively pursue internationalization goals for competitive purposes that relate to excellence in research, technological innovation, economic strength, and relevance. *World-class* is a term that pervades much of this discourse. In a clear maneuver to establish world-class institutions, a wide range of countries have launched excellence initiatives in recent years. These efforts are overwhelmingly government-sponsored and focus heavily on strengthening the work of existing or emerging institutions through competitive funding schemes. They also support the recruitment and retention of top academic talent. Examples of these initiatives include China's 211 and 985 programs, Denmark's Investment Capital for University Research effort, Brain Korea 21, and Spain's Network for International Campuses of Excellence (Behrenbeck, 2010). In all cases, the benchmarks for excellence are clearly international, in the sense that success is to some degree measured on a global scale.

Finally, competition as a consequence of internationalization can also be seen at the supranational level. Europe offers perhaps the best example of this kind of region-wide thinking, which was succinctly captured in the language of the European Union's so-called Lisbon Strategy of 2000. This called for Europe "to become the most competitive and dynamic knowledge-based economy in the world" (European Council, 2000), in no small part through a process of strengthening various aspects of the European higher education and research landscape. By all accounts, the Lisbon Strategy fell short of many of its stated goals, but the new European Union (EU) policy that replaced it, known as ET 2020, continues to advocate for support of knowledge, training,

and innovation activities within higher education (and through lifelong learning) that serve to strengthen Europe from within and maintain its dynamic position of leadership in the fast-moving global knowledge economy. Meanwhile, the Bologna Process is also concerned with the question of Europe's ability to compete globally in higher education. An evolving Bologna external working group has for several years been exploring a number of questions related to the promotion and marketing of European higher education to the world beyond Europe. And indeed some tangible efforts have been made to achieve a European brand and facilitate a central portal for access to information on and contacts within European higher education. Still, none of these coordinated activities has gained much traction. A lack of strong European-level leadership in this area may be one reason for this limited success. The size and diversity of European higher education also defies easy generalizations; first and foremost, Bologna signatory countries must attend to their own national issues and objectives, over and above the questions of joint European promotion and marketing of the higher education sector.

BOX 1.4 A View From Latin America

Alma Maldonado-Maldonado

Researcher, Centro de Investigaciones Avanzadas (Mexico)

Latin America is more a cultural category than a geographical one. Most definitions include only Spanish- and Portuguese-speaking countries. Although there are French-speaking countries in the region, it is less common for them to be included under the Latin American umbrella. Besides language, other characteristics that define this group of countries are common historical experiences (colonialism and independence), cultural elements, and economic and political developments. Nevertheless, Latin America has many differences of geography, race, and size. We should therefore be cautious in considering Latin America as a single monolithic region.

One of the most striking characteristics of Latin American higher education institutions is their sense of identity. This derives from a number of sociohistorical events, such as the reform movement that took place in Córdoba, Argentina, in 1918 and subsequent student and intellectual movements. By then, building a regional identity was a key aspect of the agenda. Currently, the central issues for Latin American higher education relate to competition, the relevance of the private sector, and accreditation and quality assurance, all with significant international dimensions. Internationalization itself is evident in three key areas: student mobility, cross-border education activities, and network building and collaboration. These speak to great potential in the region but are also very real challenges.

In terms of student mobility, the region faces an asymmetric situation with respect to developed countries. A great many Latin American students go abroad, compared to the far lower number of international students who study in Latin America (with the exception of Cuba, the largest recipient of international students in the region). Unfortunately, this issue is connected to brain drain. There is also an imbalance regarding degree seeking and non-degree seeking students: The region receives more of the latter than of the former.

Meanwhile, international providers of higher education services are more and more aware of the potential Latin American market. The national public and private sectors seem insufficient to satisfy demand, encouraging new providers to focus on the region. For instance, Laureate International Universities have bought at least 23 universities in Latin America (it also owns 18 in Europe, 4 in Asia, 2 in Australia and 4 in the United States), and the Apollo group is present in Chile and Mexico. On the other hand, very few Latin American programs are competitive at the global level. Although some question the reliability of global rankings, they provide an indication of the international standing of higher education systems and institutions. It is not a surprise that very few Latin American universities are included in the three most important global rankings. Only six universities from Brazil and one each from Argentina, Chile, and Mexico appear among the top 400 in the Shanghai Jiao Tong university ranking. Only one (from Mexico) appears in the top 200 of the Times Higher Education ranking, and just nine Latin American universities (three from Brazil and two each from Argentina, Chile, and Mexico) appear among the top 400 in the *U.S. News & World Report* standings, the most recent global ranking.

Finally, in the area of establishing collaborative arrangements and building networks, most Latin American higher education institutions are signing interinstitutional agreements with as many universities as they can, but the effectiveness of this practice has been questioned. There are also attempts to collaborate regionally: for example, the Network of Macro-universities of Latin America and the Caribbean, whose purpose is to connect the largest universities of the region; the *Universia* network whose goal is to create a Hispanic-American space of socially responsible knowledge; and the Tuning project, which is looking to apply the Tuning methodology used to harmonize European higher education to the Latin American region.

Overall, the main challenge for Latin American higher education institutions seems to be that of moving toward deeper engagement with the knowledge-based economy, instead of remaining at the more traditional level of just "becoming more international" (via such mechanisms as the promotion of academic mobility, participation of cross-border providers, and inter-university collaborations and networks). It is fair to say that, even in these areas, the region lags far behind the world leaders. Catching up will require Latin American institutions to begin by enhancing regional links with a medium- to long-term vision that considers the ways these institutions will transcend traditional internationalization to participate more actively in the knowledge based-economy.

Internationalization reflects new kinds of competition within higher education today, particularly at the higher levels of the prestige hierarchy. Competition often encourages innovation and excellence, yet all nations and institutions risk getting caught up in the powerful forces of international competition without carefully considering what outcomes are truly desirable and achievable.

Commercialization

An element of internationalization that is not much researched but is beginning to receive greater attention is the growing commercialization of international higher education initiatives. For quite some time, many universities (and some countries) have seen internationalization as an important source of revenue. Major receiving countries of international students—such as Australia, the United Kingdom, and the United States— have quantified the earnings gained when higher education is assessed as an export activity, and some strategies acknowledge international initiatives as a means of earning income to compensate for funding deficits. Recruiting students from abroad, establishing branch campuses, and implementing other initiatives are strategies often intended to earn revenue for the sponsoring institutions, even when these institutions are considered to be nonprofit.

There is also a rapidly growing for-profit higher education industry involved in a range of services including establishing new universities, recruiting students, providing language training (mainly in English), and preparing students for testing. Many of these for-profit enterprises are multinational, with activities in numerous countries. Some of the highest-profile actors in this sphere are Laureate Education (formerly Sylvan Learning Systems), Kaplan, Inc., and the Apollo Group (the parent company of the University of Phoenix) (Altbach & Knight, 2010). In addition, an illicit international market offers fake degrees and other questionable higher education services.

While the profit motive has always been an unmistakable part of the internationalization landscape, it seems to be growing in size and scope. At a global level, there remains the unresolved issue of the General Agreement on Trade in Services (GATS) of the World Trade Organization (WTO). While the specifics of GATS are not explored here, it is important to recognize that higher education is now discussed in a free trade context "as a commodity to be freely traded internationally." Another topic of debate is the idea that higher education is a private good rather than a public responsibility. Altogether, these "powerful economic references place higher education in the domain of an international market and promote the view that commercial forces have a legitimate place in higher education" (Altbach & Knight, 2010, p. 120).

The diverse rationales for internationalization may draw heavily from such issues as educational quality, intellectual relevance, and institutional

strengthening, but they are not likely to be divorced from commercial potential, which is increasingly salient. The global monetary value of international higher education is difficult to assess, but it is arguably substantial, given that foreign students are estimated to have contributed $18.8 billion to the U.S. economy alone during the 2009–2010 academic year (NAFSA, 2010). The standard warning of *caveat emptor* applies in this discussion, however. Indeed, business and education are not always easy partners. The 2010 U.S. congressional investigations into improprieties among for-profit postsecondary education providers called into question motives and practices among this group that can easily be extrapolated to an international higher education context. In the same year, all distance education providers in Ethiopia were shut down in an effort to restrain what the government believed to be poor educational provision by private institutions. This is another dramatic indication of the tensions between commercial and noncommercial interests in different higher education contexts.

"So What?" A Few Practical Implications for Senior Administrators

Twentieth-century American inventor and businessman Charles Kettering is credited with having said, "You can be sincere and still be stupid." This pithy insight, if a little blunt, does capture an important aspect of the challenges facing senior higher education administrators today with regard to internationalization: Believing in it is not enough. Indeed, institutional leaders and managers may be deeply convinced of the relevance of internationalization, but for such beliefs to achieve meaningful and sustainable results, an informed vision and tangible resources are necessary as well. Internationalization may be effectively implemented, cultivated, refined, and sustained in many ways, and each institution needs to think carefully about the extent and the direction that this development will take. Some institutions will opt for a highly centralized approach, while others will work to embed internationalization more broadly across the institution. However, in terms of crafting the unifying vision and marshalling the resources necessary to move substantively toward the realization of their vision, most higher education institutions will benefit from having at least one internationalization advocate situated at or near the top of the decision-making hierarchy. This increases the likelihood that the international agenda will be visible internally and externally, and puts internationalization on a par with the other core activities and initiatives of the institution. (See Chapters 7 and 8, this volume, for further discussion.)

In conjunction with the appropriate designation of leadership for internationalization, the international agenda requires "care and feeding" in the form of resources—financial, human, and intellectual. The most effectively internationalized institutions—no matter how that label may be defined—steer funding, staffing, creative energy, and expertise explicitly toward the achievement of results, whether the goals include attracting international students and scholars, developing innovative new program offerings, providing students with opportunities to learn abroad, or supporting inter-institutional partnerships.

This kind of commitment does not and cannot take place devoid of context. There is a daily (if not hourly) barrage of new information circulating about internationalization in higher education. In addition, a host of new issues emerge regularly in social, political, and economic spheres that may have a direct effect on the ways that institutions can and must think about their international profiles and agendas. To address this, senior administrators in this field today must have a coherent strategy for information management. Ideally, this should involve a balance between access to the most vital and relevant news of the day and exposure to additional sources of information that provide deeper analysis and varied perspectives that take into account long-term implications.

The fast-moving world of internationalization also requires clear thinking. The pace of new developments is dizzying, and the pressure to act or be left behind seems more intense than ever before. The international agendas that seem to survive the test of time and achieve long-lasting impacts are those that are squarely rooted in the missions of the actors involved. Quality, (mission) coherence, and sustainability are three fundamentally important elements that should be at the core of institutional planning and decision-making with regard to internationalization.

CONCLUSION

Internationalization represents a phenomenon of interest to an extraordinarily broad cross-section of higher education institutions in all parts of the world. This is a notable development (particularly) of the last two decades. From a relatively marginal position on the agendas of institutions, nations, and international organizations, internationalization has acquired a significant profile at the highest levels of policymaking and institutional leadership in many corners of the world. This has been driven by a very real sense of the opportunities and imperatives inherent in the phenomenon. The perception is that much can be gained by attending to the international dimension, while real opportunities may be forfeited by failing to advance or engage with this agenda.

To be sure, the potential to bring about positive change through internationalization in such areas as relevance, quality, and even prestige is quite exciting. All signs point to the fact that it makes little (if any) sense for institutions to opt out of international engagement altogether. Indeed, internationalization is affecting what, how, where, and from whom students learn; how higher education institutions and systems conceive of their missions and roles; how research is carried out and disseminated; and how fundamental paradigms of cooperation and competition in higher education are understood and elaborated.

But there are real risks and challenges associated with these developments. Central among these are the fundamental mismatch (costly in both the short and long-term) that can occur between international aspirations, local needs, and institutional resources; the very real potential for poor planning and execution of misguided internationalization strategies; the risk of further cleavages between wealthier and poorer individuals, institutions, and countries, all approaching internationalization on an inherently uneven playing field; and (sadly) new opportunities for corruption and exploitation.

The complex and shifting landscape of internationalization, along with the speed with which new developments present themselves in the current context, makes managing internationalization strategies (and their practical components) extremely challenging. Perhaps even more difficult is the process of articulating a clear hierarchy of interests to guide efforts in this area in a coherent fashion. Presented with a world of opportunities but only limited resources, this is a most daunting task. Making informed and creative choices about internationalization—with a clear sense of the interplay between risks and benefits, opportunities and imperatives, obstacles and resources—requires unique skills and talents, real vision, and sustained commitment.

REFERENCES

ACA Newsletter: Education Europe. (2010, November). Russian "megagrants" generate excitement, criticism. Retrieved from http://www.aca-secretariat.be/index.php?id=29&tx_smfacanewsletter_pi1[nl_uid]=70&tx_smfacanewsletter_pi1[uid]=2292&tx_smfacanewsletter_pi1[backPid]=50&cHash=9500ff3595892deb062eb9195481dfa4

Adams, J., Gurney, K., & Marshall, S. (2007). *Patterns of international collaboration for the UK and leading partners.* Leeds, England: Evidence, Ltd. Retrieved from http://image.guardian.co.uk/sys-files/Education/documents/2007/07/13/OSICollaborationSummaryRepo.pdf

Altbach, P. G. (2004). The cost and benefits of world-class universities. *Academe, 90* (January-February). Retrieved from http://www.aaup.org/aaup/pubsres/academe/2004/jf/feat/altb.htm

Altbach, P. G. (2006). Globalization and the university: Realities in an unequal world. In J. J. F. Forest & P. G. Altbach (Eds.), *International handbook of higher education* (Vol I, pp. 121–140). Dordrecht, The Netherlands: Springer.

Altbach, P. G. (2007). The imperial tongue: English as the dominating academic language. *International Higher Education, 49*(Fall), 2–4.

Altbach, P. G. (2010, October 15). World-class universities and their undergrowth: The systemic link. Paper delivered at *World-class: The brave new world of global higher education and research.* The Academic Cooperation Association European Policy Seminar No. 26, Brussels, Belgium.

Altbach, P. G. (2011). Rankings season is here. *International Higher Education, 62*(Winter), 2–5.

Altbach, P. G., & Knight, J. (2010). Higher education's landscape of internationalization: Motivations and realities. In P. G. Altbach (Ed.),

Leadership for world-class universities: Challenges for developing countries (pp. 117–137). Chestnut Hill, MA: Center for International Higher Education.

Altbach, P. G., Reisberg, L., & Rumbley, L. E. (2009). *Trends in global higher education: Tracking an academic revolution.* Paris: UNESCO.

American Association of Community Colleges. (2006). Mission statement. Retrieved from http://www.aacc.nche.edu/About/Pages/mission.aspx

Bassett, R. M., & Maldonado-Maldonado, A. (Eds.). (2009). *International organizations and higher education policy: Thinking globally, acting locally?* New York: Routledge.

Behrenbeck, S. (2010, May 16–18). Attracting researchers: Initiatives for excellence. Presentation at *Brains on the move: Gains and losses from student mobility and academic migration.* The Annual Conference of the Academic Cooperation Association, Córdoba, Spain, 2010.

Böhm, A., Davis, D., Meares, D, & Peace, D. (2002). *Global student mobility 2025: Forecasts of the global demand for international higher education.* Sidney: IDP Education Australia.

Böhm, A., Follari, M., Hewett, A., Jones, S., Kemp, N., Meares, D., Pearce, D., & Van Cauter, K. (2004). *Vision 2020. Forecasting international student mobility: A UK perspective.* London: British Council.

Bologna Declaration of 19 June 1999. (1999). Retrieved from http://www.bologna-bergen2005.no/Docs/00-Main_doc/990719BOLOGNA_DECLARATION.PDF

Bruges Communiqué on Enhanced European Cooperation in Vocational Education and Training. (2010). Retrieved from http://ec.europa.eu/education/lifelong-learning-policy/doc/vocational/bruges_en.pdf

Bruneforth, M. (2010 May 16–18). The mobility of students: Where they come from and where they go. Presentation at *Brains on the move. Gains and losses from student mobility and academic migration.* The Annual Conference of the Academic Cooperation Association, Córdoba, Spain.

Catania Declaration: Euro-Mediterranean Area of Higher Education and Research. (2006). Retrieved from http://www.miur.it/UserFiles/2209.pdf

Childress, L. (2010). *The twenty-first century university: Developing faculty engagement in internationalization.* New York: Peter Lang.

Deardorff, D. K. (Ed.). (2009). *The Sage handbook of intercultural competence.* Thousand Oaks, CA: Sage.

Deutsche Welle. (2009, March 23). More ethnic Turks becoming German citizens, study shows.

Retrieved from http://www.dw-world.de/dw/article/0,,4121209,0.0.html

de Wit, H. (2011). Internationalization of higher education: Nine misconceptions. *International Higher Education, 34*(Summer), 6–7.

de Wit, H,. Agarwal, P., Said, M. E., Sehoole, M. T., & Sirozi, M. (Eds.). (2008). *The dynamics of international student circulation in a global context.* Rotterdam, The Netherlands: Sense Publishers.

Eaton, J. S. (2004). Accreditation and recognition of qualifications in higher education: The United States. In *Quality and recognition in higher education: The cross-border challenge* (pp. 63–74). Paris: OECD.

English.news.cn. (2010, August 3). *Chinese state councilor proposes integrated education with ASEAN countries.* Retrieved from http://news .xinhuanet.com/english2010/ china/2010-08/03/c_13428618.htm

European Council. (2000, March 23–24). Presidency conclusions. Lisbon European Council. Retrieved from http://www.europarl.eu.int/ summits/lis1_en.htm

European Students' Union. (2008, May). *Policy paper "mobility."* Retrieved from http://www.esib.org/ index.php/documents/policy-papers/ 336-policy-paper-qmobilityq

George Mason University. (2009, July 15). *Ras Al Khaimah campus in the United Arab Emirates.* Retrieved from http://rak.gmu.edu/

Gibson, J., & McKenzie, D. (2011). *Eight questions about brain drain* (World Bank Policy Research Working Paper 5668). Retrieved from http://www-wds. worldbank.org/external/default/WDSContent Server/WDSP/IB/2011/05/24/000158349_2011052 4155759/Rendered/PDF/WPS5668.pdf

Hazelkorn, E. (2011). *Rankings and the reshaping of higher education: The battle for world-class excellence.* London: Palgrave MacMillan.

International Association of Universities (IAU). (2003). *Internationalization of higher education: Practices and priorities.* Paris: Author.

International Association of Universities (IAU). (2006). *Internationalization of higher education: New directions, new challenges.* Paris: Author.

International Association of Universities (IAU). (2010). Internationalization of higher *education: Global trends, regional perspectives.* Paris: Author.

Kelo, M., Teichler, U., & Wächter, B. (2006). *EURODATA: Student mobility in European higher education.* Bonn: Lemmens.

Klasek, C. B., (Ed.). (1992), *Bridges to the future: Strategies for internationalizing higher education.* Carbondale, IL: Association of International Education Administrators.

Knight, J. (2003). Updating the definition of internationalization. *International Higher Education, 33*(Fall), 2–3.

Knight, J. (2005). Cross-border education: Not just students on the move. *International Higher Education, 41*(Fall), 2–3.

Knight, J. (2008). The internationalization of higher education: Complexities and realities. In D. Teferra & J. Knight, J. (Eds.), *Higher education in Africa: The international dimension* (pp. 1–43). Chestnut Hill, MA, and Accra, Ghana: Boston College Center for International Higher Education & Association of African Universities.

Knight, J. (2011). Education hubs: A fad, a brand, an innovation? *Journal of Studies in International Education, 15,* 221–240.

Krieger, Z. (2008, April 13). The emir of NYU. *New York.* Retrieved from http://nymag.com/news/ features/46000/

Leuven/Louvain-la-Neuve Ministerial Communiqué. (28-29 April 2009). *The Bologna Process 2020: The European Higher Education Area in the new decade.* Communiqué of the Conference of European Ministers Responsible for Higher Education. Retrieved from http://www .europeunit.ac.uk/sites/europe_unit2/bologna _process/decision_making/leuven_louvain_la _neuve_2009.cfm

Maslen, G. (2008, November 23). Southeast Asia: Bold plan to duplicate Bologna. *University World News,* 0054. Retrieved from http://www .universityworldnews.com/article. php?story=20081120154941889

Mills, A. (2010, July 6). Low enrollment led Michigan State U. to cancel most programs in Dubai. *Chronicle of Higher Education.* Retrieved from http://chronicle.com/article/Low-Enrollment- Led-Michigan/66151/

NAFSA. (2009). *The economic benefits of international education to the United States for the 2008–2009 academic year: A statistical analysis.* Retrieved from http://nafsa.org/_/ File/_/eis2010/usa.pdf

National Association for College Admission Counseling. (2011, July). *Statement on Incentive-Based Compensation for International Student Recruitment Approved by NACAC Board of Directors.* Retrieved from http://www .nacacnet.org/AboutNACAC/Policies/ Documents/BoardApprovedStatement.pdf

Observatory on Borderless Higher Education. (2010, February 1). *Spreading its wings: The Open University Malaysia is venturing out into Ghana and Vietnam.* Retrieved from http://www.obhe .ac.uk/documents/view_details?id=805

Office of the Prime Minister of Canada. (2010, July 6). Backgrounder: Banting postdoctoral fellowships. Retrieved from http://pm.gc.ca/ eng/media.asp?id=3531

O'Hara, S. (2009, May). Vital and overlooked: The role of faculty in internationalizing U.S. campuses.

In *Expanding study abroad capacity at U.S. colleges and universities* (IIE Study Abroad White Paper Series, Issue No. 6, pp. 38–45). New York: Institute of International Education.

Organization for Economic Cooperation and Development (OECD). (2004). *Quality and recognition in higher education: The cross-border challenge*. Paris: Author.

Organization for Economic Cooperation and Development (OECD). (2010). *Education at a glance 2010*. Paris: Author.

Overland, M. A. (2007, December 12). Australian university to pay back $22.4-million for Singapore campus failure. *Chronicle of Higher Education*. Retrieved from http://chronicle.com/article/Australian-University-to-Pay/40121.

Peterson, P. M. (2011). Liberal education in the global perspective. *International Higher Education, 62*(Winter), 10–11.

Rumbley, L. E. (2008, May 8). *Humanities and social science education in Hong Kong and East Asia* (podcast recorded with Kai-ming Chen). Retrieved from http://www.bc.edu/research/cihe/podcasts/archives03.html

Rumbley, L. E. (2010, April 16). *Liberal arts education: A Dutch perspective* (podcast recorded with Marijk van der Wende). Retrieved from http://www.bc.edu/research/cihe/podcasts.html

Rumbley, L. E., & Altbach, P. G. (2007, July 26). International branch campus issues. Memorandum submitted to the U.S. House of Representatives, Committee on Science and Technology hearing, *The globalization of R&D and innovation, Part II: The university response*. Retrieved from http://frwebgate.access.gpo.gov/cgi-bin/getdoc.cgi?dbname=110_house _hearings&docid=f:35857.wais.pdf

Salmi, J. (2009). *The challenge of establishing world-class universities*. Washington, DC: The International Bank for Reconstruction and Development / The World Bank.

Schneller, C., Lungu, I, & Wächter, B. (2009). *Handbook of international associations in higher education*. Brussels: Academic Cooperation Association.

Soilemetzidis, I. (2011, April 21). International Association of Universities (IAU), 3rd global survey report: Anglohigher®. Retrieved from http://www.anglohigher.com/casestudies/casestudy_detail/45/39

Swan, M. (2010, July 1). Michigan State University shuts most of its Dubai campus. *The National*. Retrieved from http://www.thenational.ae/news/uae-news/education/michigan-state-university-shuts-most-of-its-dubai-campus

Teferra, D. (2008a). The international dimension of higher education in Africa: Status, challenges, and prospects. In D. Teferra & J. Knight, J.

(Eds.), *Higher education in Africa: The international dimension* (pp. 44–79). Chestnut Hill, MA, and Accra, Ghana: Center for International Higher Education and Association of African Universities.

Teferra, D. (2008b). Internationalization of higher education: Legacy and journey in the African landscape. In D. Teferra & J. Knight, (Eds.), *Higher education in Africa: The international dimension* (pp. 553–558). Chestnut Hill, MA, and Accra, Ghana: Center for International Higher Education and Association of African Universities.

Teferra, D., & Knight, J. (Eds.). (2008). *Higher education in Africa: The international dimension*. Chestnut Hill, MA, and Accra, Ghana: Center for International Higher Education and African Association of Universities.

Teichler, U., Ferencz, I., & Wächter, B. (Eds.). (2011). *Mapping mobility in European higher education* (Vols. I & II). Brussels: Directorate General for Education and Culture, European Commission.

Travers, E. (2011, June 12). Latin America: Partnerships to boost higher education. *University World News*, 175. Retrieved from http://www.universityworldnews.com/article.php?story=20110610213548370

U-Multirank (n.d.). Multi-dimensional gloal ranking of universities; a feasibility project. Retrieved from http://www.u-multirank.eu/

UNESCO-IESALC. (2008). *Espacio de encuentro latinoamericano y caribeño de educación superior*. Retrieved from http://www.iesalc.unesco.org.ve/index.php/option=com_contents&view=article&id=186&catid=3&Itemid=14&lang=es

Verbik, L., & Merkley, C. (2006). *The international branch campus: Models and trends*. London: Observatory on Borderless Higher Education.

Wächter, B., & Maiworm, F. (2002). *English-taught programmes in European higher education: Trends and success factors* (ACA Papers on International Cooperation in Education). Bonn: Lemmens.

Wächter, B., & Maiworm, F. (2008). *English-taught programmes in European higher education: The picture in 2007* (ACA Papers on International Cooperation in Education). Bonn: Lemmens.

Wang, H. (2010, September). *China's talent plan: Where will it lead China to?* Retrieved from http://www.brookings.edu/~/media/Files/events/2010/0920_china_talent/0920_china _powerpoint.pdf

Weill Cornell Medical College in Qatar. (2009). *Fact sheet 2009–2010*. Retrieved from http://qatar -weill.cornell.edu/media/mediacenter/othermedia/pdf/09-10%20Fact%20Sheet _English.pdf

World Economic Forum. (2011). *Global talent risk: Seven responses*. Retrieved from http://www3.weforum.org/docs/PS_WEF_GlobalTalentRisk _Report_2011.pdf

2

CONCEPTS, RATIONALES, AND INTERPRETIVE FRAMEWORKS IN THE INTERNATIONALIZATION OF HIGHER EDUCATION

JANE KNIGHT

Internationalization has been one of the most critical factors shaping higher education in the last three decades. Beyond transforming higher education, internationalization has substantially changed itself. The bifurcation of internationalization into two interdependent pillars—"at home" and "abroad"—is evidence of this change. The international dimension of the curriculum has progressed from an area studies and foreign language approach to the integration of international, global, intercultural, and comparative perspectives into the teaching/learning process and program content. Academic mobility has moved from student to provider and program mobility. Cross-border education has gradually shifted from a development cooperation framework to a partnership model and now to commercial competition orientation.

The term *internationalization* began to be used widely by the higher education sector in the 1980s to promote international studies, educational exchange, and technical assistance (Klasek, 1992). Since then there has been an explosion in the number and types of international initiatives undertaken by higher education institutions, organizations, and governments. Internationalization strategies, programs, and policies developed by these actors have evolved over the years in response to and as agents of the pervasive force of globalization. As the 21st century progresses, the international dimension of postsecondary education is becoming increasingly important and, at the same time, more and more complex.

Recent developments—increased privatization and commercialization of higher education, the knowledge economy, GATS, for-profit providers, new quality assurance and accreditation regulations, global higher education ranking systems, international research networks, and increased emphasis on learning outcomes—have all influenced how the tertiary sector has interpreted and promoted the international dimension of higher education. There have been many benefits of internationalization, some risks, and as internationalization matures, some unintended consequences as well.

The purpose of this chapter is to present an analytical framework to understand the key concepts and elements of internationalization and to gain a more comprehensive understanding of this complex and multilayered process. Although a diversity of institutional, national, regional, and international stakeholders are involved with the international dimension of higher education, the focus of this chapter is primarily at the higher education institution level. The analysis will include a discussion of the meaning of internationalization, new actors, changing rationales and expectations, strategies related to internationalization on campus and abroad, and a look at benefits, risk, and unintended consequences. Any examination of internationalization needs to take into account the differences among countries and regions of the world recognizing that priorities, rationales, approaches, risks, and benefits differ between east and west, north and south, sending and receiving, and developed and developing countries.

DEFINING INTERNATIONALIZATION

Internationalization is a term that is being used more and more to discuss the international dimension of higher education and, more widely, tertiary education. Because it means different things to different people, it is used in a myriad of ways. While it is encouraging to see increased attention to and use of internationalization, there is often a great deal of confusion about what it means.

For some people, it means a series of international activities such as academic mobility for students and teachers; international linkages, partnerships, and projects; and new international academic programs and research initiatives. For others, it means delivering education to other countries using a variety of face-to-face and distance techniques and such new types of arrangements as branch campuses or franchises. To many, it means including an international, intercultural, or global dimension in the curriculum and teaching/learning process. Still others see international development projects or, alternatively, the increasing emphasis on commercial cross-border education as internationalization. Finally, the term is being used to describe

regional education hubs, zones, hotspots, education cities, and knowledge villages.

Clearly, internationalization is used to describe a vast array of issues, strategies, and new developments around the world. Yet, there is concern that internationalization is becoming a catch-all concept for anything that is related to the international dimension of higher education. The concept may have been stretched too far when internationalization is described as or interpreted as international league tables. The current obsession among higher education institutions with their global standing and brand is a sign of the times. Definitely, there is an appetite for international and regional rankings of institutions, but one needs to question whether this is part of an internationalization process or part of an international marketing and public relations campaign.

It is interesting to see how the terminology used to describe the international dimension of higher education has evolved over the past 50 or more years. Table 2.1 illustrates how vocabulary reflects the priorities and phases over the years. Who would have guessed in the 1960s, when the emphasis was on scholarships for foreign students, international development projects, and area studies, that today we would be discussing branding, cross-border education, global citizenship, franchising, and education visa factories? International education has been a much-used term throughout the years and still is a preferred term in many countries, but the processes of internationalization, globalization, regionalization, and now planetization, are actively debated concepts and central to promoting and sustaining the international dimension of higher education.

Internationalization: A Working Definition

The purpose of trying to develop a clear and somewhat comprehensive definition for internationalization is to help clarify the current confusion and misunderstanding. It is appropriate that there will never be one universal definition. Yet, it is important to have a common understanding of the term so that when we discuss and analyze the phenomenon, we understand each other and there is solidarity when advocating for increased attention and support from policymakers and academic leaders.

Generic Terms			
Last 10 years	Last 20 years	Last 30 years	Last 50 years
Regionalization Planetization Glocalization Global citizenship Knowledge enterprise Green internationalization Global rankings	Globalization Borderless education Cross-border education Transnational education Virtual education Internationalization 'abroad' Internationalization 'at home'	Internationalization Multicultural education Intercultural education Global education Distance education Offshore or overseas education	International education International development cooperation Comparative education Correspondence education
Specific Elements			
Last 10 years	Last 20 years	Last 30 years	Last 50 years
Regional education hubs International competencies Degree mills Visa factories Joint, double, combined degrees Branding, status-building	Education providers Corporate universities Liberalization of educational services Networks Virtual universities Branch campus Twinning and franchise programs	International students Study abroad Institution agreements Partnership projects Area studies Bi-national cooperation	Foreign students Student exchange Development projects Cultural agreements Language study

Table 2.1   Evolution of Main International Education Terminology

Source: Knight updated 2010

The challenging part of developing a definition is the need for it to be generic enough to apply to many different countries, cultures, and education systems. In the past several years, various definitions of internationalization have been proposed (Arum & van de Water, 1992; de Wit, 2002; Van der Wende, 1997), but their universal application has been severely curtailed by the inclusion of specific rationales, actors, strategies, and outcomes embedded in the description. It is contrary to the spirit of internationalism to have a definition biased toward a particular country or cultural perspective. Recent debates about whether internationalization is a western or eastern or northern construct reflect the ongoing concern that internationalization is interpreted as westernization, Americanization, Europeanization, or modernization (Dzulkifli,

2010; Odin & Mancias, 2004). These debates often focus on the driving rationales and implementation strategies that reflect national/cultural norms. That is precisely why a definition of internationalization of higher education needs to be neutral and void of motivations, benefits, activities, and results, as these vary enormously across nations and from individual to individual, institution to institution, region to region.

The working definition proposed for this chapter is the following: Internationalization at the national/sector/ institutional levels is defined as: "the process of integrating an international, intercultural, or global dimension into the purpose, functions or delivery of post-secondary education" (Knight, 2004, p. 11).

This is intentionally a neutral definition of internationalization. Many would argue that the process of internationalization should be described in terms of promoting cooperation and solidarity among nations, improving quality and relevance of higher education, or contributing to the advancement of research. While these are noble intentions and internationalization can contribute to these goals, a definition needs to be objective enough to describe a phenomenon that is universal but has different purposes and outcomes depending on the actor or stakeholder. Central to understanding internationalization is to see it as an *ization* or a process and not an *ism* or an *ideology*. Internationalism is different than internationalization even though both stress the concept of "between and among nations." Globalization is also a process, albeit different from internationalization as it addresses the idea of worldwide or global, not the notion of relations among countries.

Specific terms and concepts have been carefully chosen for this working definition of internationalization: The term *process* is deliberately used to convey that internationalization is an ongoing effort and to note the evolutionary quality of the concept. Process is often thought of in terms of a tri-part model of education: input, process, and output. The concepts of input and output were carefully not used, even though today there is increased emphasis on accountability and outcomes. If internationalization is defined in terms of inputs, outputs, or benefits, it becomes less generic as it must reflect the particular priorities of a country, an institution, or a specific group of stakeholders.

The notion of *integration* is specifically used to denote the process of embedding the international and intercultural dimension in policies and programs to ensure sustainability and centrality to the mission and values of the institution or system.

International, intercultural, and *global* are three terms intentionally used as a triad, as together they reflect the breadth of internationalization. *International* is used in the sense of relationships between and among nations, cultures, or countries. However, internationalization is also about relating to the diversity of cultures that exist within countries, communities, institutions, and classrooms so *intercultural* is used to address aspects of cultural diversity. Finally, *global* is included to provide the sense of worldwide scope. These three terms complement each other and together give richness

both in breadth and depth to the process of internationalization.

The concepts of *purpose, function,* and *delivery* have been carefully chosen. *Purpose* refers to the overall role that higher education has for a country or region or, more specifically, to the mission of an institution. *Function* refers to the primary elements or tasks that characterize a national higher education system and an individual institution. Usually these include teaching/learning, research, and service to the community and society at large.

Delivery is a narrower concept and refers to the offering of education courses and programs, either domestically or abroad. This includes delivery not only by traditional higher education institutions but also by new providers, such as companies that are more interested in the global delivery of their programs than in the international or intercultural dimension of the curriculum, research, and service.

This definition purposely addresses the institutional and national or system levels of higher education, but not the individual level or the regional level. This does not ignore that individuals like students, faculty, or researchers are deeply involved in and impacted by internationalization. Quite the contrary, individuals are the promoters, implementers, participants, targets, beneficiaries, and some may say innocent victims of the internationalization process. But the underlying principle of the definition is not to include individual actors, stakeholders, and beneficiaries as doing so narrows its scope and loses its universal application and objectivity.

Thinking about the regional level and internationalization is still a work in progress. In a geographic sense, *international* includes supranational groupings such as regions, but regionalization is being thought of in a variety of new ways, such as regional political alliances, economic groupings, and sector networks.

The emerging importance of regionalization of higher education, in part stimulated by the European Bologna Process, is launching a new discourse on the purposes, strategies, and definition of regionalization. A new definition of regionalization of higher education is likely to emerge along the lines of "a process of promoting, recognizing, and formalizing opportunities for regional collaboration among national governments, nongovernmental education bodies, and individual higher education institutions."

Collaboration is the key concept even though regional higher education collaboration can be motivated by and lead to the region's increased competitiveness. This is clearly the case in Europe, where one of the goals of the Bologna process has been to increase the attractiveness and competitiveness of Europe.

Regionalization in Africa, described as a harmonization process, is seen as key to Africa's development and its emergence into the knowledge society and economy (Hoosen, Butcher, & Khamati, 2009). Higher education regionalization initiatives in the Middle East are currently focusing on regional quality assurance networks and of course university associations, but pan-regional discussions on higher education collaboration at the national systems level are not well developed. The situation in Asia is more active and complex (Kuroda & Passarelli, 2009). Region-wide initiatives in quality assurance, such as the Asia Pacific Quality Network, and student mobility schemes (University Mobility of Asia Pacific) have been established for several years. However, as in all other regions, subregional groupings in Asia are taking major steps toward closer alignment and collaboration. For instance, the South East Asia Ministers of Education currently have projects promoting student mobility, common credit systems, and quality assurance (Supachai, 2009). In Latin America and the Caribbean, a major new initiative for the regionalization of higher education has been established by IESCALC-UNESCO: ENLACES, which in English means the Latin America and the Caribbean Area for Higher Education. ENLACES is a regional platform formally created for the mobilization of projects and studies that support academic cooperation and knowledge sharing in the region. A major activity is the development of a Map of Higher Education in Latin America and the Caribbean. This project brings together data on national higher education systems in order to facilitate academic mobility and the development and alignment of national and institutional policies. For example, there is a strong commitment to facilitate the convergence of national and subregional assessment and accreditation systems. Two other priorities are the mutual recognition of studies, titles, and diplomas based on quality assurance, as well as the establishment of common academic credit systems accepted throughout the region.

Fostering the intraregional mobility of students, researchers, faculty, and administrative staff through the implementation of funded programs is another area of activity. Finally, strengthening the learning of the region's languages to foster the kind of regional integration that incorporates cultural diversity and multilingualism is a primary concern and modality for building the common higher education area.

These few examples serve to acknowledge that regionalization, in terms of greater collaboration and alignment of national or subregional systems, is an important element of internationalization. Accompanying the discussion of system-level changes and alignment is a debate on the essence of regional identity, such as Africanization, Asianization, or Europeanization. Both discourses merit further research and reflection and indicate a key stage in the evolution of internationalization.

GROWTH IN NUMBER AND DIVERSITY OF ACTORS

For several reasons, it is important to examine the different levels and types of actors involved in promoting, providing, and regulating the international dimension of higher education. First, internationalization now encompasses a vast array of initiatives that have brought new actors into play. Second, these activities and issues have implications for policies and regulations at the international, regional, and domestic levels. Third, the lines or boundaries separating these different levels are becoming increasingly blurred and porous.

Table 2.2 illustrates that actors represent a diversity of groups: not only the educational institutions and providers themselves, but also government departments and agencies; nongovernmental and semi-governmental organizations; private and public foundations; and conventions and treaties. The categories of actors can be further analyzed by considering the nature of their mission: policy-making, regulating, funding, programming, advocacy, and networking. It is important to note that actors often occupy more than one role and that these categories are therefore not mutually exclusive (Jaramillo & Knight, 2005).

The activities of these actors are diverse and include, for example, student mobility, research,

Levels of Actors	Types of Actors	Roles of Actors
National Bilateral Subregional Regional Interregional International	Government departments or agencies Non (or semi-) governmental organizations Professional associations or special interest groups Foundations Public/private educational institutions and providers	Policymaking Regulating Advocacy Funding Programming Networking Research Information Exchange

Table 2.2   Actors and Their Roles in the Internationalization of Higher Education

This plethora of actors means that a diversity of rationales is driving the process of internationalization at all levels and especially at the institutional and national levels. The multiplicity of motives and the fact that they are changing is what contributes to the intricacy of internationalization and the growing confusion and fascination about what it means and involves.

Source: Knight Updated 2010

information exchange, training, curriculum, scholarships, and quality assurance. The analysis becomes more complex when actors at the national, bilateral, subregional, regional, interregional, and international level are considered. It is also important to note that, in many circumstances, all levels of actors can be involved or influence the development and implementation of policy, programs, and regulations of international higher education.

Rationales Driving Internationalization

The need for clear, articulated rationales for internationalization cannot be overstated. Rationales are the driving force for why an institution (or any other actor) wants to address and invest in internationalization. Rationales are reflected in the policies and programs that are developed and eventually implemented. Rationales dictate the kind of benefits or expected outcomes. Without a clear set of rationales, accompanied by a set of objectives or policy statements, a plan, and a monitoring/ evaluation system, the process of internationalization is often an ad hoc, reactive, and fragmented response to the overwhelming number of new international opportunities available.

The motivations and realities driving internationalization are undergoing fundamental changes (Altbach & Knight, 2006). Traditionally,

rationales have been presented in four groups: social/cultural, political, academic, and economic (Knight & de Wit, 1999). This provides a useful macro view, but as internationalization becomes more widespread and complex, a more nuanced set of motives is necessary. Furthermore, it is important to distinguish between rationales at different levels of actors, especially the institutional level and national level. Table 2.3 summarizes the four categories of rationales as defined in the mid 1990s and the rationales at the institutional and national levels as differentiated 10 years later (Knight, 2008).

The International Association of Universities (IAU) conducted worldwide surveys on internationalization in 2003, 2005 and 2009 (IAU, 2010; Knight, 2006). Given the importance of understanding why higher education institutions invest in internationalization, respondents (primarily heads of institutions in more than 100 countries) were asked in all three surveys to identify the top rationales driving their efforts to internationalize.

Of particular importance is the fact that the top rationale for 2005 and 2009 surveys was preparing students to be interculturally competent and more knowledgeable about international issues in a more globalized world. This clearly puts the emphasis on human resource development and academic-oriented rationales. Strengthening research and knowledge capacity

Four Categories of Rationales (1999)	Two Levels of Rationales (2008)
Academic	Institutional
International dimension to research and teaching	International branding and profile
Extension of academic horizon	Income generation
Institution building	Student and staff development
Profile and status	Strategic alliances
Enhancement of quality	Knowledge production
International academic standards	National
Economic	Human resources development
Revenue generation	Strategic alliances
Ecompetitiveness	Commercial trade
Labor market	Nation building
Financial incentives	Social cultural development
Political	
Foreign policy	
National security	
Technical assistance	
Peace and mutual understanding	
National identity	
Regional identity	
Social	
National cultural identity	
Intercultural understanding	
Citizenship development	
Social and community development	

Table 2.3   Change in Rationales Driving Internationalization

Source: Knight, 2008.

dropped from second place in 2005 to fourth place in 2009, which is surprising given the emergence of the knowledge society and economy. For both years, creating and enhancing the institution's profile and reputation ranked in third place. This finding is perhaps the most revealing as it indicates the weight placed on developing an international brand, which relies more on a smart and successful marketing campaign than on integrating an international, global, and intercultural dimension into the teaching learning process, research, and service to community/society. The quest for an international reputation and hence the obsession with worldwide ranking tables is a trend that no one predicted 10 years ago.

Of interest is that diversifying sources of income remains the least important rationale across both surveys. This finding raises eyebrows and speculation, given the reliance of some universities in several countries on revenue from international student recruitment and cross-border education. But this dependence on international student fees applies only to higher education institutions in 8 or 10 countries (i.e., Australia, United Kingdom, New Zealand) and not to the majority of institutions in the 95 countries that responded to the survey in 2005 and 115 countries in 2009. It is a potent reminder that economic rationales are the top driver in only a handful of countries around the world, although the impact of these countries is significant as they are the most active and aggressive in terms of international education.

INTERNATIONALIZATION: "AT-HOME" AND "CROSS-BORDER"

An interesting development in the conceptualization of internationalization has been the division of internationalization into "internationalization at home" and "cross-border education." Figure 2.1 illustrates that these two pillars are separate but closely linked and interdependent. Cross-border education has significant implications for campus-based internationalization and vice versa.

Campus-Based Internationalization

The "at home" concept has been developed to give greater prominence to campus-based strategies given the recent heightened emphasis on international academic mobility. These strategies can include the intercultural and international dimension in the teaching/learning process, research, extracurricular activities, relationships with local cultural and ethnic community groups, and integration of foreign students and scholars into campus life and activities. Most institutions—and in fact most countries—have realized that the number of domestic students who have some kind of study abroad or international research or field experience is frustratingly low. This requires that more attention be paid to campus- and curriculum-based efforts to help students live in a more interconnected and culturally diverse world. Students

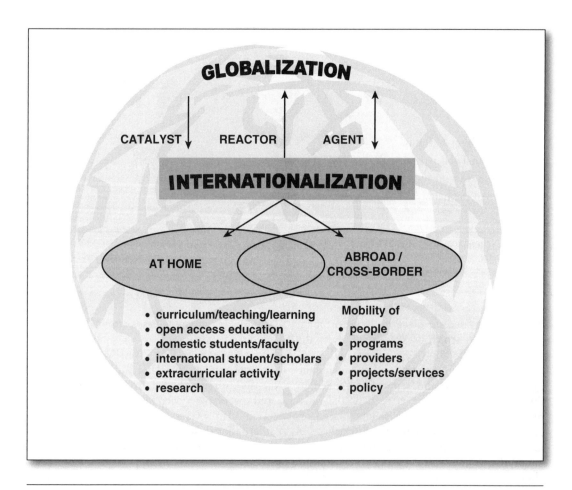

Figure 2.1   Two Pillars of Internationalization: At Home and Cross-Border

Source: Knight, 2010.

and faculty need increased understanding of inter-national and global issues and greater intercultural understanding and skills, even if they never leave their community or country (Deardorff, 2006). Such is the world we live in now, and it will be even more so in the future. Universities thus have the responsibility and challenge to integrate international, intercultural, and comparative perspectives into the student experience through campus-based and virtual activities in addition to international academic mobility experiences.

The strategies included in campus-based or "at home" internationalization are listed in Table 2.4. This elaboration is perhaps broader

Curriculum and programs	New programs with international theme infused international, cultural, global, or comparative dimension into existing courses
	Foreign language study
	Area or regional studies
	Joint or double degrees
Teaching/ learning process	Active involvement of international students, returned study abroad students and cultural diversity of classroom in teaching/learning process
	Virtual student mobility for joint courses and research projects
	Use of international scholars and teachers and local international/intercultural experts
	Integration of international, intercultural case studies, role plays, problem solving scenarios, project-based learning, teams, learning communities, resource materials
	Service-learning
	Integration of global learning outcomes and assessment
Research and scholarly activity	Area and theme centers
	Joint research projects
	International conferences and seminars
	Published articles and papers
	International research agreements
	Research exchange programs
	International research partners in academic and other sectors
	Integration of visiting researchers and scholars into academic activities on campus
Co-curricular activities	International/global leadership development programs
	Interdisciplinary seminars and think tanks
	Distinguished speaker seminar
Extracurricular activities	Student clubs and associations
	International and intercultural campus events
	Language partners, friendship programs, student speaker programs
	Liaison with community based cultural and ethnic groups
	Peer support groups and programs
Liaison with local community based cultural/ ethnic groups	Involvement of students in local cultural and ethnic organizations through internships, volunteering, placements and applied research
	Involvement of representatives from local cultural and ethnic groups in teaching/ learning activities, research initiatives and extra-curricular events and projects

Table 2.4 Framework for Internationalization "At Home"

Source: Knight, Updated 2010

than the original concept of internationalization "at home" (Nilsson, 2003), which put more focus on the intercultural aspects of the teaching/learning process and the curriculum. For a more detailed discussion of internationalization at home, see Section C.

Cross-Border Education

Cross-border education refers to the movement of people, programs, providers, policies, knowledge, ideas, projects, and services across national boundaries. Delivery modes range from face-to-face to virtual. Cross-border education can be part of development cooperation projects, academic partnerships, or commercial trade. It includes a wide variety of arrangements ranging from study abroad to twinning to franchising to branch campuses. It is a term that is often used interchangeably with *transnational, offshore,* and *borderless education,* which causes some confusion and misunderstandings (Knight, 2007).

The demand for international education is forecasted to increase from 1.8 million international students in 2000 to 7.2 million international students in 2025 (Böhm, Davis, Meares, & Pearce, 2002). These are staggering figures and present enormous challenges and opportunities. It is not known what proportion of the demand will be met by student mobility, but exponential growth in the movement of programs and institutions/providers across national borders clearly lies ahead.

Table 2.5 provides a schema to understand the nature of cross-border education and illustrates two significant trends. The first trend is the vertical shift downward from student mobility to program and provider mobility. It is important to note that the number of students seeking education in foreign countries is still increasing; however, there is growing interest in delivering foreign academic courses and programs to students in their home country. The second shift is from left to right, signifying substantial change in orientation from development cooperation to competitive commerce, or in other words, from aid to trade. The focus of this discussion is on the movement of programs and providers.

Cross-border mobility of programs can be described as the movement of individual education/training courses and programs across national borders through face-to-face and distance learning or a combination of these modes. The sending foreign country-provider or an affiliated domestic partner can award credits toward a qualification, or they can do so jointly. Franchising, twinning, double/joint degrees, and various articulation models are the more popular methods of cross-border program mobility (Knight, 2007).

Given that several modes for program mobility involve partnerships, there are questions about who owns the intellectual property rights to course design and materials. What are the legal roles and responsibilities of the participating partners in terms of academic, staffing, recruitment, evaluation, financial, and administrative matters? While the movement of programs across borders has been taking place for many years, it is clear that the new types of providers, partnerships, awards, and delivery modes are challenging national and international policies and regulatory frameworks.

Cross-border mobility of providers can be described as the physical or virtual movement of an education provider (institution, organization, company) across a national border to establish a presence in order to offer education/training programs or services to students and other clients. The difference between program and provider mobility is one of scope and scale in terms of programs and services offered and the local presence (and investment) by the foreign provider. A distinguishing feature between program and provider mobility is that with provider mobility, the learner is not necessarily located in a different country than the awarding institution, which is usually the case in program mobility (Knight, 2010).

Credits and qualifications are awarded by the foreign provider (through foreign, local, or self-accreditation methods) or by an affiliated domestic partner. Different forms of cross-border provider mobility include branch campus, bi-national universities, acquisition/mergers, teaching sites, and research offices. Whether one is a sending or a receiving country, there are a variety of important policy issues and implications to consider. This raises questions as to whether receiving countries have the requisite policies in place for registration and accreditation of foreign education programs and providers and also for the regulation of the financial aspects (i.e., taxes, degree of foreign/local

Category	Forms and Conditions of Mobility		
	Development Cooperation	Educational Linkages	Commercial Trade
People Students Professors/scholars Researchers/ Experts/consultants	Semester/year abroad Full degrees Field/research work Internships Sabbaticals Consulting		
Programs Course, Program Sub-degree, Degree, Post Graduate	Twinning Franchised Articulated/ Validated Joint/Double Award Online/Distance		
Providers Institutions Organizations Companies	Branch Campus Virtual University Merger/Acquisition Independent Institutions		
Projects Academic projects Services	Research Curriculum Capacity Building Educational services		
Policies Academic Management Institutional and National	Quality Assurance Degree Levels Credit Accumulation and Transfer Academic Mobility		

Table 2.5   Framework for Cross-Border Education

ownership, profit sharing and repatriation etc.) For a more detailed discussion of internationalization abroad, see Section D.

BENEFITS AND RISKS

While the process of internationalization affords many benefits to higher education, serious risks are clearly associated with this complex and growing phenomenon. Tables 2.6 and 2.7 present the IAU 2005 and 2009 survey results on perceived benefits and risks. In terms of benefits, it is reassuring to note that the most highly ranked benefits, across both years, correspond to the rationales driving internationalization (see Table 2.3). These include internationally aware and prepared students and staff, improved quality, and strengthened research capacity. This correlation between rationale and benefits demonstrates that internationalization, to a certain extent, is fulfilling expectations at the institutional level.

Benefits	Percentage	
	2005	2009
More internationally oriented students and staff	22	
Increased international awareness of students		25
Improved academic quality	21	
Strengthened research and knowledge production	15	16
Innovation in curriculum, teaching and research	14	
Enhanced internationalization of the curriculum		11
Enhanced international cooperation and solidarity	12	12
Enhanced prestige/profile for the institution		10

Table 2.6   Top Five Benefits of Internationalization 2005 and 2009: Results of the IAU Global Surveys on Internationalization

Source: Knight, 2010.

The survey results on perceived risks merit close attention. The top risks: (1) commodification and commercialization, (2) increase in foreign degree mills and low quality providers, and (3) brain drain are consistent for 2005 and 2009. While the rankings are the same across the years, the percentages differ because more options were offered in the 2009 survey, resulting in lower number of responses for each option. One of the new options in 2009 was "overemphasis on internationalization at the expense of other priorities of importance for staff and students." Interestingly, it ranked fourth in importance and signals the potential for backlash about the priority currently being given to internationalization at the institutional level. This risk warrants close monitoring as there is bound to be a tipping point where support for internationalization weakens, especially in light of the emerging unintended consequences.

Risks	Percentage	
	2005	2009
Commodification and commercialization of education programs	23	11
Increase in number of foreign degree mills and low quality providers	17	10
Brain drain	15	9
Growing elitism in access to international education opportunities	12	
Over-emphasis on internationalization at the expense of other priorities of importance for staff and students		8
Overuse of English as a medium of instruction	9	
Greater competition among higher education institutions		8

Table 2.7   Top Five Risks of Internationalization 2005 and 2009: Results of the IAU Global Surveys on Internationalization

Source: Knight, 2010.

UNINTENDED CONSEQUENCES

As internationalization changes to meet new challenges it is important to examine some of the unexpected developments and results. While the benefits of internationalization are many and varied, there are clearly risks and also unintended consequences attached to the process, which need to be addressed and monitored (Knight, 2009).

The Brain Drain-Gain-Train

Little did we know 25 years ago that the highly valued and promoted international academic mobility for students, scholars, and professors would have the potential to grow into a highly competitive international recruitment business. Several countries are investing in major marketing campaigns to attract the best and brightest talent to study and work in their institutions in order to supply the brain power for innovation and research agendas. The difficulties and challenges related to academic and profession mobility should not be underestimated. Nor should the potential benefits. But it is impossible to ignore the latest race to attract international students and academics as means to acquire brain power and generate income. The original goal of helping students from developing countries study in another country to complete a degree and return home is fading fast as nations compete to retain needed human resources.

While brain drain and brain gain are well-known concepts, research is showing that international students and researchers are increasingly interested in taking a degree in Country A, followed by a second degree or perhaps internship in Country B, leading to employment in Country C and probably D, finally returning to their home country after 8 to 12 years of international study and work experience. Hence, the emergence of the term *brain train*. In the final analysis, whether one is dealing with brain gain, brain drain, or brain train, this phenomenon is presenting benefits, risks, and new challenges for both sending and receiving countries. From a policy perspective, higher education is becoming a more important actor and is now working in closer collaboration with immigration, industry, and the science and technology sectors to build an integrated strategy for attracting and retaining knowledge workers. The convergence of an aging society, lower birth rates, the knowledge economy, and professional labor mobility is introducing new issues and opportunities for the higher education sector and producing some unanticipated results and challenges in terms of international mobility.

Quality, Accreditation, and Credential Recognition

The increase in student, program, and provider mobility is intended to increase access to higher education and meet the appetite for foreign credentials, but there are serious issues related to the quality of the academic offerings, the integrity of the new providers, and the recognition of credentials. The increase in the number of foreign degree mills (selling parchment-only degrees), accreditation mills (selling bogus accreditations for programs or institutions), and rogue for-profit providers (not recognized by national authorities) are realities that students, parents, employers, and the academic community now need to be aware of. Who would have guessed two decades ago that international education would be struggling increasingly to deal with issues such as (a) fake degrees and accreditations, (b) academic credentials that are earned but not recognized, and (c) nonregulated "fly by night" institutions. Of course, it is equally important to acknowledge innovative developments by bona fide new providers and traditional universities who are delivering high-quality programs and legitimate degrees through new types of arrangements and partnerships (franchise, twinning, branch campus). The perpetual challenge of balancing cost, quality, and access significantly impacts the benefits and risks of cross-border education.

Double and Joint Degrees: Twice the Benefit or Double Counting?

Improvement in the quality of research, the teaching/learning process, and curriculum has long been heralded as a positive outcome of international collaboration. Through exchange of good practice, shared curricular reform, close research cooperation, and mobility of professors/students, internationalization can offer many benefits. A recent trend has been the establishment of joint programs between institutions in different countries that lead to double (or multiple) degrees and in some cases joint degrees, although the latter face steep legal constraints.

Joint programs are intended to provide a rich international and comparative academic experience for students and to improve their opportunities for employment. With all new ideas, however, come questionable adaptations and unintended consequences. For instance, in some cases, double degrees can be nothing more than double counting one set of course credits. Situations exist where two or three credentials (one from each participating institution) are conferred for little more than the workload required for one degree. While it may be very attractive for students (and potential employees) to have two degrees from institutions in two different countries, the situation can be described as academic fraud if course requirements for two full degrees are not completed or differentiated learning outcomes not achieved. It is important to point out that there are many excellent and innovative joint and double degree programs being offered, but one of the unanticipated consequences is the potential misuse or abuse of degree-granting and recognition protocols.

Commodification and Commercialization: For-profit Internationalization

For many educators, the heart of the debate about increased commercial cross-border education and the view that education is an industry is the impact on the purpose, role, and values of higher education. The growth in new commercial and private providers, the commodification and market orientation of education, and the prospect of new trade policy frameworks are catalysts for stimulating serious reflection on the role, social commitment, and funding of public higher education institutions. The trinity of teaching/learning, research, and service has traditionally guided the evolution of universities and their contribution to the social, cultural, human, scientific, and economic development of a nation and its people. Is the combination of these roles still valid, or can they be disaggregated and rendered by different providers?

Cultural Diversity or Homogenization?

The impact of new forms of international academic mobility on the recognition and promotion of indigenous and diverse cultures is a subject that evokes strong positions and sentiments. Many believe that modern information and communication technologies and the movement of people, ideas, and cultures across national boundaries present new opportunities to promote one's culture to other countries and to enhance the fusion and hybridization of cultures. Supporting this position is the assumption that the flow of culture across borders is not new at all; only the speed has been accelerated and the modes broadened.

Others see both the movement and the speed as alarming. They contend that these same forces are eroding national cultural identities and that, instead of creating new hybrid cultures, indigenous cultures are being homogenized, which in most cases means Westernized. Because education has traditionally been seen as a vehicle of acculturation, these arguments focus on the specifics of curriculum content, language of instruction (particularly the increase in English), and the teaching/learning process in international education. See also Chapter 19.

Competition and Profile: World Rankings

International and regional rankings of universities have become more popular and problematic in the last five years. The heated debate about their validity, reliability, and value continues. But at the same time university presidents declare in their strategic plans that a measurable outcome of internationalization will be the achievement of a specific position in one or more of the global ranking instruments. Some institutions see internationalization as a means to gain a worldwide profile and prestige. Is this really internationalization, or is it international marketing and branding? The intense competition for world rankings would have been impossible to imagine a mere 20 years ago, when international collaboration among universities through academic exchanges and development cooperation projects were the norm. Of course, these types of activities still occur, but the factors driving internationalization are becoming increasingly varied, multifaceted and competitive. Is international cooperation becoming overshadowed and trumped by competition for status, bright students, talented faculty, research grants, and membership in global networks?

Conclusion

This discussion has shown without a shadow of a doubt that internationalization has come of age. No longer is it an ad hoc or marginalized part of the higher education landscape. University strategic plans, national policy statements, international declarations, and academic articles all indicate the centrality of internationalization in the world of higher education.

As it has transformed higher education, internationalization has itself experienced dramatic change, especially in the area of education and research crossing national borders. The section on cross-border education illustrates the staggering growth in the scope and scale of cross-border initiatives including branch campuses, international double-degree programs, regionalization initiatives, faculty and student mobility schemes, franchised programs, and research networks. Education hubs, virtual mobility opportunities, and bi-national universities are recent developments.

It is prudent to take a close look at the policies, plans, and priorities of the key actors, such as universities, government ministries, national/regional/international academic associations, and international government agencies. These documents reveal that internationalization of education and research is closely linked with economic and innovation competitiveness, the great brain race, the quest for world status, and soft power. Economic and political rationales are increasingly the key drivers for national policies related to international higher education, while academic and social/cultural motivations appear to be decreasing in importance. But perhaps what is most striking is that the term *internationalization* is becoming a catch-phrase to describe anything and everything remotely linked to the worldwide, intercultural, global, or international dimensions of higher education; thus, it is at risk of losing its meaning and direction.

Recent national and worldwide surveys of university internationalization priorities and rationales show that establishing an international profile or global standing is seen to be more important than reaching international standards of excellence or improving quality. Capacity building through international cooperation is being replaced by status-building projects to gain world-class recognition. International student mobility is now big business and becoming more closely aligned to recruitment of brains for national science and technology agendas. Some private and public education institutions are changing academic standards and transforming into visa factories in response to immigration priorities and revenue generation imperatives. More international academic projects and partnerships are becoming commercialized and profit-driven, as are international accreditation services. Diploma mills and rogue providers are selling bogus qualifications and causing havoc for international qualification recognition. Awarding two degrees from institutions located in different countries based on the workload for one degree is being promoted through some rather dubious double degree programs. And all of this is in the name of internationalization.

Who could have forecasted that internationalization would evolve from the traditional process based on values of cooperation, partnership, exchange, mutual benefits, and capacity building to one that is increasingly characterized by competition, commercialization, self-interest, and status building? Is internationalization having an identity crisis, given this apparent shift in values? Critics question whether internationalization is now an instrument of the less attractive side of globalization instead of an antidote.

At the same time, there are countless examples of positive internationalization initiatives, which illustrate how internationalization at home, cross-border education, and collaborative scholarship contribute to the development of individuals, institutions, nations and the world at large.

As we enter the second decade of this century it may behoove us to look back at the last 20 or 30 years of internationalization and ask ourselves some questions. Has international higher education lived up to our expectations and its potential? What values have guided it through the information and communication revolution, the unprecedented mobility of people, ideas, and technology; the clash of cultures; and the periods of economic boom and bust? What have we learned from the past that will guide us into the future? What are the core principles and values underpinning internationalization of higher education that in 10 or 20 years from now will make us look back and be proud of the track record and contribution that international higher education has made to the more interdependent world we live in, the next generation of citizens, and the bottom billion people living in poverty?

REFERENCES

Altbach, P. G., & Knight, J. (2006). The internationalization of higher education: Motivations and realities. *NEA Almanac of Higher Education* (pp. 27–36). Washington, DC: National Education Association.

Arum, S., & Van de Water, J. (1992). The need for a definition of international education in U.S. universities. In C. Klasek (Ed.), *Bridges to the future: Strategies for internationalizing higher education* (pp. 198–206). Carbondale, IL: Association of International Education Administrators.

Böhm A., Davis, D., Meares, D., & Pearce, D. (2002). The global student mobility 2025 report: Forecasts of the global demand for international education. Canberra, Australia: IDP.

Deardorff, D. K. (2006). Identification and assessment of intercultural competence as a student outcome of internationalization. *Journal of Studies in International Education, 10*(3), 241–266.

de Wit, H. (2002). Internationalization of higher education in the United States of America and Europe: A historical, comparative, and conceptual analysis. Westport, CT: Greenwood Press.

Dzulkifli, A. R. (2010). *Is internationalization a Western construct?* Presentation at British Council Going Global 4 Conference, London. Retrieved from http://www.britishcouncil.org/goingglobal-gg4-speakers-dzulkifli-abdul-razak.htm

Hoosen, S., Butcher, N., & Khamati, B. (2009). Harmonization of higher education programmes: A strategy for the African Union. *African Integration Review, 3*(1), 1–36.

International Association of Universities. (2010). *Internationalization of higher education: Global trends, regional perspectives* (3rd Global IAU Survey, International Association of Universities). Paris: Author. Retrieved from http://www.iau-aiu.net/internationalization/pdf/Key_results_2009.pdf

Jaramillo, I., & Knight, J. (2005). Key actors and programs: Increasing connectivity in the region. In H. de Wit, I. Jaramillo, J. Gacel-Avila, & J. Knight (Eds.), *Higher education in Latin America: The international dimension.* Washington, DC: World Bank.

Klasek, C. B. (Ed.). (1992). *Bridges to the future: Strategies for internationalizing higher education* (pp. 198–206). Carbondale, IL: Association of International Education Administrators.

Knight, J. (2004). Internationalization remodeled: Definitions, rationales, and approaches. *Journal for Studies in International Education, 8*(1), 5–31.

Knight, J. (2006). *Internationalization of higher education: New directions, new challenges.* (2005 International Association of Universities Global Survey Report). Paris: International Association of Universities.

Knight, J. (2007). Cross-border tertiary education: An introduction. In *Cross-border tertiary education: A way towards capacity development* (pp. 21–46). Paris: OECD, World Bank, and NUFFIC.

Knight, J. (2008). *Higher education in turmoil: The changing world of internationalization.* Rotterdam, the Netherlands: Sense Publishers.

Knight, J. (2009). New developments and unintended consequences: Whither thou goest, internationalization? In R. Bhandari & S. Laughlin (Eds.), *Higher education on the move: New developments in global mobility* (Global Education Research Reports, pp. 113–125). New York: Institute for International Education.

Knight, J. (2010). Higher education crossing borders: Programs and providers on the move. In D. B Johnstone, M. B. D'Ambrosio, & P. J. Yakoboski (Eds.), *Higher education in a global society* (pp. 42–69). Northampton, MA: Edward Elgar.

Knight, J., & de Wit, H. (Eds.). (1999). *Quality and internationalization in higher education.* Paris: Organization for Economic Cooperation and Development (OECD), Programme on Institutional Management in Higher Education (IMHE).

Kuroda, K., & Passarelli, D. (Eds.). (2009). *Higher education and Asian regional integration symposium report.* Tokyo: Waseda University, Global Institute for Asian Regional Integration.

Nilsson, B. (2003). Internationalization at home: Theory and praxis. *European Association for International Education Forum, 12.*

Odin, J., & Mancias, P. (Eds.). (2004). *Globalization and higher education.* Honolulu: University of Hawaii Press.

Supachai, Y. (2009). Experiences of Asian higher education frameworks and their implications for the future. In K. Kuroda & D. Passarelli (Eds.), *Higher education and Asian regional integration symposium report.* Tokyo: Waseda University, Global Institute for Asian Regional Integration.

Van der Wende, M. (1997). Missing links: The relationship between national policies for internationalization and those for higher education in general. In T. Kalvermark & M. Van der Wende (Eds.), *National policies for the internationalization of higher education in Europe* (pp. 10–31). Stockholm, Sweden: National Agency for Higher Education Hogskoleverket Studies.

3

The History of Internationalization of Higher Education

Hans de Wit and Gilbert Merkx

This chapter focuses on the historical development of international education in Europe and the United States. It is important to relate the internationalization of higher education in today's world to the original roots of the university and to place the present developments in historical perspective. Only in this way is it possible to identify the specific character of the internationalization of higher education as currently encountered.

The Middle Ages and Renaissance

Altbach (1998) calls the university the one institution that has always been global: "With its roots in medieval Europe, the modern university is at the center of an inter-national knowledge system that encompasses technology, communications, and culture" (p. 347). Kerr (1994) states that "universities are, by nature of their commitment to advancing universal knowledge, essentially international institutions, but they have been living, increasingly, in a world of nation-states that have designs on them" (p. 6). These references to history ignore the fact that universities mostly originated in the 18th and 19th centuries and had a clearly national orientation and function (de Wit, 2002, pp. 3-18). Neave (1997) speaks of an "inaccurate myth." Scott (1998) also criticizes the "myth of the international university" dating from the medieval period. Very few universities founded in that period were ultimately transformed by the modern world, he says, classifying this myth as "internationalist rhetoric." The university of the Middle Ages could not be "international," given that nation-states did not yet exist.

Most publications on the internationalization of higher education still refer back to the Middle Ages up to the end of the eighteenth century in Europe, making a side reference to the only known non-European university, the Al Azhar University in Egypt. Before the nineteenth century, in addition to religious pilgrims, "pilgrims or travellers (peregrini) of another kind were also a familiar sight on the roads of Europe. These were the university students and professors. Their pilgrimage (peregrinatio) was not to Christ's or a saint's tomb, but to a university city where they hoped to find learning, friends, and leisure" (de Ridder-Symoens 1992, p. 280). Although the academic pilgrimage started long before the twelfth century, it became a common phenomenon at that time. De Ridder-Symoens describes the impact of the mobility of students and scholars on higher education and society in that period in a way that reminds us of many of the arguments used to promote mobility today:

> The use of Latin as a common language, and of a uniform programme of study and system of examinations, enabled itinerant students to continue their studies in one 'studium' after another, and ensured recognition of their degrees throughout Christendom. Besides their academic knowledge they took home with them a host of new experiences, ideas, opinions, and political principles and views. (pp. 302–303)

Owing to the creation of more universities in the fifteenth century, recruitment of students became more regionalized, and migration of students came nearly to a halt. By the end of the Middle Ages, three quarters of all students went to a university in their region. The exceptions were those who wanted "to continue their studies in an internationally renowned university and in disciplines not taught in their own schools" (p. 287).

Because nations as political units did not yet exist, one can speak of a medieval "European space," defined by this common religious identity and uniform academic language, program of study, and system of examinations (Neave, 1997, p. 6). This medieval European space, although limited in comparison to present-day mass higher education, bears a resemblance to the recent development of a new European higher education space, particularly given the gradual emergence of English language as the common academic language of the present, resembling the medieval role of Latin.

THE EIGHTEENTH AND NINETEENTH CENTURIES

With the emergence of the nation-state, universities became de-Europeanized and nationalized. This transition did not take place in a radical way.

As Kolasa (1962) notes, toward the end of the seventeenth century and in the eighteenth century,

> European culture continued, to a considerable degree, its universalistic spirit. . . . National cultures became more differentiated but the most prominent savants and artists still belonged to the whole of Europe, and the French language was commonly spoken by cosmopolitan aristocracy, which managed all political and a good deal of non-political affairs. (p. 12)

According to Kolasa, the Middle Ages, the Reformation, and the Enlightenment were periods of "natural, not organized or regimented, flow of culture, and of free wandering of the creators of that culture across political frontiers" (p. 12). This domain of international cultural relations was challenged in the second half of the nineteenth century, with the emergence of political and cultural nationalism.

Hammerstein (1996, p. 624) illustrates this with the following examples: prohibition of study abroad in many countries; displacement of Latin as the universal language by vernacular languages; and the disappearance of the *peregrinationes academicae* and its gradual replacement by the *grand tour,* which differed in its emphasis on cultural experience compared to the academic objectives of the former. Universities became institutions that served the professional needs and ideological demands of the new nations in Europe. "Paradoxically perhaps," observes Scott (1998), "before it became an international institution the university had first to become a national institution—just as internationalization presupposes the existence of nation states" (p. 123).

Between the 18th and 19th century, three international aspects of higher education can be identified: dissemination of research, individual mobility of students and scholars, and export of higher education systems (see Box 3.1).

Research and publications were one international element of higher education in the eighteenth and nineteenth centuries. Although much of the research in that period had a national focus and interest, the international exchange of ideas and information through seminars, conferences, and publications has remained a constant feature of international scholarly

BOX 3.1 Export of Higher Education Systems

The most important international element of higher education in this era was probably the export of systems of higher education. This took the form of export from the colonial powers to their colonies and later to the newly independent states. Higher education in Latin America has been, and still is to a large extent, modeled on higher education in the Iberian Peninsula. Higher education in India and other Asian, African, Caribbean, and North American countries belonging to the British Empire was modeled on British higher education. In the same way, the Asian, African, Caribbean, and North American universities in the former French colonies have been built according to the structure of French higher education. After independence, these influences prevailed and only more recently have other national and international influences had their impact on higher education in these countries. As Roberts, Rodrígues Cruz, and Herbst (1996) describe, by the end of the eighteenth century, universities and other institutions of higher education could be found in North, Central, and South America, as implants from Europe. Altbach and Selvaratnam (1989) describe this phenomenon for Asia.

Countries with a noncolonial heritage, such as Japan, China, and Thailand developed also largely Western university systems. Higher education in Japan, for instance, was seen as an important part of the modernization process, which took place in the nineteenth century under pressure of Western economic, political, and military power. To this day, contemporary higher education in Japan includes elements of German origin and of current American higher education (Altbach & Selvaratnam 1989, p. 10).

Even higher education in the United States, often regarded today as the dominant model in international developments of higher education, was based on European influences and continued to reflect these for a long time. Oxford and Cambridge were the models for the first colleges established in the American colony (colonial colleges such as the New College, later Harvard, which delivered its first degree in 1642; the College of William & Mary in Dartmouth; the Collegiate School, later Yale University; the Academy of Philadelphia, later University of Pennsylvania; the College of New Jersey, later University of Princeton; and King's College, later Columbia University). Later, with the creation of Johns Hopkins University, the German model of the research university was also imported. As a side effect, many students sojourned to the universities in Europe, on which these institutions were modeled, to pursue further studies. The American system of higher education, which emerged in its modern form between the 1860s and the early 1900s, can be considered, according to Ben-David (1992), as "one of `secondary reform' and belongs to the same category of externally inspired change as the establishment of modern systems of higher education in Russia, Japan and elsewhere in Asia, and Africa" (p. 25).

Scott (1998, p. 124) calls this export of higher education models the first of two main forms of internationalization of higher education that continued well into the twentieth century. This can hardly be seen, however, as a process of integrating an international and intercultural dimension. It would be tempting to call it a primitive form of globalization of higher education or globalization of higher education avant-la-lettre, but that would ignore the role of the nation-state in the process. The best description of this stage of internationalization is "academic colonialism" or "academic imperialism."

contact. Kolasa (1962, pp. 15, 163) notes that the international academic associations and societies of the nineteenth century were private in character and dedicated to individual and professional relationships. This element comes closest to the notion of universalism that has always been present in higher education.

Although there is very little statistical information on the mobility of students and scholars in the eighteenth and nineteenth centuries, mobility never completely came to an end but changed character. De Ridder-Symoens (1996) describes this change as follows: "Renaissance teachers looked upon study abroad as the culmination of the humanist education of young members of the elite. In Renaissance times wandering students were strongly attracted by the renown of teachers" (p. 417), while most of the traveling students in early modern Europe were mainly concerned with the cultural and intellectual advantages of educational travel.

If the first decades of the sixteenth century were, according to de Ridder-Symoens (1996), "the golden age of wandering scholars" (p. 418), by the mid-sixteenth century the Reformation and counter-Reformation had a strong negative impact on mobility. Study abroad was prohibited in many countries, based on the argument that foreign universities were "sources of religious and political contamination" (p. 419). As in today's flow of foreign students, economic and financial arguments were important. Emigration of students was seen as a loss for the sending cities and a threat to the development of their own universities. At the same time, the reduction in the number of foreign students affected the cities that most of them had visited. In the seventeenth and eighteenth centuries, the grand tour revived student mobility, at first in order to get a degree and later, in the period of Enlightenment, mainly for pleasure. All in all, de Ridder-Symoens (p. 442) concludes that until about 1700, student mobility was an important element of university life, and even afterward, it continued to influence intellectual and political life in Europe.

Until the 20th century, in sharp contrast to the present situation, the mobility of students was greater from the United States to Europe than from Europe to the United States. For many Americans, the pursuit of study in Europe was considered the final step in their cultural integration into American society: the grand tour (see Box 3.2). The same can be said of Canadian and Australian higher education.

BOX 3.2 The Grand Tour

Higher education in the United States was based on European influences and continued to reflect these for a long time. During colonial times, the children of rich planters often went to Europe, in particular the United Kingdom, for studies such as medicine and law. But as Halpern (1969) notes, opposition developed after the American Revolution: "Jefferson and Webster opposed sending young Americans to study abroad because they shared a common distrust of European ways and because they feared that American students would become denationalized" (p. 17).

Although many American scholars and educators still went to Europe in the nineteenth century for further study and insight, these same people in their later careers became hostile to study abroad, in particular by undergraduate students. Halpern (1969) provides several examples of political and educational leaders in the United States speaking out against foreign study. An example is Harvard President Charles W. Eliot, who wrote in 1873:

Prolonged residence abroad in youth, before the mental fibre is solidified and the mind has taken its tone, has a tendency to enfeeble the love of country, and to impair the foundations of public spirit in the individual citizen. This pernicious influence is indefinable, but none the less real. In a strong nation, the education of the young is indigenous and national. It is a sign of immaturity or decrepitude when a nation has to import its teachers, or send abroad its scholars. (p. 24)

According to Halpern (1969), this attitude can be explained by a strong desire to break with the educational and cultural dependence on Europe (p. 25). Nonetheless, American faculty and students continued to flow to Europe throughout the nineteenth century, as David McCullough (2011) describes in *The Greater Journey: Americans in Paris,* which features Americans studying in Paris in the 19th century.

Around the turn of the century one can see a shift. On the one hand, the emergence of American graduate schools presented American students the opportunity to study at home rather than abroad. On the other hand, for the first time foreign students began to come to the United States.

Note: This text was written by chapter author Hans de Wit.

International education in the United States was enhanced by that nation's engagement in the global arena. The United States has been involved in wars and national security crises since it emerged as a great power in the 1890s with the Spanish-American War. This new role stimulated both international studies and political science. During the late nineteenth century, academic mobility from and to the United States became a regular phenomenon, but without a formal and institutional structure. This began to change toward the turn of the twentieth century.

In 1890, the American Association of University Women created the first fellowship to enable a college professor to pursue research abroad. In 1902, the Rhodes Scholarships were founded to promote understanding between English-speaking people. In 1905, the American Academy in Rome established research fellowships for study in Italy, and in 1911, the Kahn Foundation started to offer fellowships for secondary school teachers to travel abroad. Another organization that dates from this period is the American-Scandinavian Foundation (1910). In 1911, the Committee on Friendly Relations Among Foreign Students was established with the objective of counseling foreign students and gathering statistics on foreign students in the United States. Between 1905 and 1912, Harvard and Columbia, along with the Universities of Chicago and Wisconsin, established exchange agreements with German and French universities (Halpern 1969, pp. 27–28; see also Hoffa, 2007).

In summary, one can describe the period from the end of the Renaissance to the beginning of the twentieth century as being oriented toward predominantly national higher education.

The main areas of international academic attention in that period were the individual mobility of a small group of well-to-do and academically qualified students to the top centers of learning in the world, the export of academic systems from the European colonial powers to the rest of the world, and cooperation and exchange in academic research, gradually involving American higher education. This confirms the suggestion of Kerr (1994), Altbach (1998), and Scott (1998) that the focus of higher education in that period became more directed to developing a national identity and serving national needs and less to amassing universal knowledge.

BEFORE WORLD WAR II

The creation of the Institute of International Education (IIE) in 1919 in the United States, the Deutscher Akademischer Austauschdienst (DAAD) in 1925, and the British Council in 1934 indicates the growing attention to international cooperation and exchange before World War II. Academic cooperation at that time was more focused on scholars than on students. And in the aftermath of World War I, it was driven by political rationales of peace and mutual understanding. The International Committee on Intellectual Co-operation, created in 1921 under the auspices of the League of Nations and the predecessor of UNESCO, was a manifestation of that new emphasis. As Kolasa (1962) observes, "The co-operation of intellectuals with politicians within the framework of the League of Nations is one of the most essential differences between the unofficial organizations of the nineteenth century and the League organization for intellectual co-operation" (p. 41).

In Europe, the colonial presence continued to play an important role in foreign area and language studies. World War I produced an initial burst of enthusiasm for international and foreign area studies in the United States. Thus, in 1917, the American Association of Teachers of Spanish was founded, and in 1918, the first issue of the *Hispanic American Historical Review* appeared with a preface by President Woodrow Wilson. However, following World War I, the new interest in foreign affairs and foreign places abated rather quickly. By 1921, the *Hispanic American Historical Review* had to cease publication.

Institutions were less active than foundations. The first junior-year-abroad program was established in France in 1923 by the University of Delaware. Women's colleges were most frequently involved in setting up such programs in Europe: Marymount College in 1924 (Paris), Smith College in 1925 (Paris) and 1931 (Florence), and Rosary College in 1925 (Fribourg). Taylor (1978, p. 1518) argues that this arose because women needed more chaperoning when studying abroad, and while female students went abroad for cultural enrichment, the men remained in the United States to work on their careers.

As Goodwin and Nacht (1991) make clear, what happened with exchange and cooperation also applied to the curriculum:

> The demonstrated unpreparedness of the United States to comprehend the process of which it was part, both during World War I and at the Peace Conference afterward, suggested to many young Americans the need both to understand other countries better and to reflect on different ways to arrange relations among states. The study of international relations increased in the United States between the wars, with practitioners lodged both in universities and in nongovernmental research institutions like the Council on Foreign Relations, the Carnegie Endowment for International Peace, and the Brookings Institution. (p. 3)

The first two decades of the twentieth century show a growth in mobility, in particular movement toward the United States; more attention from private organizations and foundations for study abroad; and the start of institutional exchange and study abroad programs. What is striking in all this is the nearly exclusive focus on Europe.

Bilateral links and exchanges existed also between European countries such as between France and Germany. Also, student travel companies emerged in that period; the development of the Student Identity Card and the International Student Travel Conference occurred during that time. The International Committee on Intellectual Cooperation of the League of Nations and the *Confédération Internationale des Étudiants* were created in 1919, the latter in Strasbourg, with the objective to strengthen ties of respect and to cultivate solidarity. Both organizations were international but European dominated, showing the increased importance of study abroad and exchange in Europe and the rest of the world. More concrete information on European mobility is lacking for this period.

With the advent of World War II, the United States began looking to its southern neighbors. President Franklin D. Roosevelt named Nelson Rockefeller Coordinator of Inter-American Affairs. Rockefeller vigorously promoted educational exchanges as a means of combating Axis propaganda and encouraging rejection of fellowships for study in Germany and Italy. The government asked the Institute for International Education to administer an exchange program offering scholarships to more than 1,000 Latin American students between 1941 and 1943 (IIE, 1994, pp. 7–9).

AFTER WORLD WAR II

After World War II, international educational exchange expanded, first and foremost in the United States. Europe was still too heavily focused on recovering from the severe wounds of two world wars and on reconstruction to be able to invest in international educational exchange and cooperation. In the field of area studies, it was barely able to maintain its historical strength in the knowledge of other cultures and languages. Many of its academics had either become victims of the wars or migrated to other parts of the world, mainly the United States, Canada, and Australia. The world of academia was turned upside down, as Goodwin and Nacht (1991) describe: "Views of the world in U.S.

higher education were transformed almost overnight by World War II. From a cultural colony the nation was changed, at least in its own eyes, into the metropolis; from the periphery it moved triumphantly to the center" (pp. 4-5).

Cunningham (1991) describes the same phenomenon for Canada:

> Until the Canadian higher education system was well established, Canadians often had to study in the United States and Europe to obtain their qualifications, particularly in the professions. Then, as our own infrastructure matured, students from other countries began to arrive here for advanced studies. But this phenomenon

is quite recent. Students from overseas began arriving in Canada in significant numbers only after World War II. (p. 1)

While the early development of international education between the two wars was focused on Europe and strongly driven by private initiative and the rationale of peace and understanding, World War II caused a radical change. Although peace and mutual understanding continued to be a driving rationale in theory, national security and foreign policy were the real forces behind its expansion, and with it came government funding and regulations (see Box 3.3).

BOX 3.3 National Security as a Driving Rationale in the United States

World War I, in which U.S. preparedness was conceived in strictly military terms, had relatively few lasting effects on U.S. international competence. In contrast, World War II led to institutions that initiated the rise of international education in the United States. The Japanese attack on Pearl Harbor in 1941 galvanized the American public and swept away opposition to joining the Allies. The War Department realized that it would have to fight a two-front war and that it lacked the foreign area competence to do so.

The Office of Strategic Services (OSS) began to recruit university faculty for their language and area expertise and put them to work as intelligence analysts. Studies of national character were commissioned for every country on both fronts. Some were later declassified and published after the war. The most famous of these was the anthropologist Ruth Benedict's 1946 study of Japanese national character, *The Chrysanthemum and the Sword,* which became both an anthropology classic and a best seller in Japan.

Also, the U.S. Army established the Army Specialized Training Program, or ASTP, which sent officers to institutions of higher education for crash courses in needed skills, including foreign languages and foreign area studies. The total number of officers trained is not known, but at its high point, the ASTP had 150,000 officers enrolled in 55 colleges and universities. In 1943, the Navy set up a similar program, the V-12 Navy College Training Program, which enrolled more than 125,000 officers before it was terminated in 1946. The success of these ventures led the U.S. Army in 1945 to establish an American-style university in Biarritz, France, complete with faculty, college credit courses, and several thousand GI students (Lambert, Barber, Jordan, Merrill, & Twarog, 1984). Unfortunately, this experiment was soon the victim of budget cuts. The ASTP and V-12 programs were highly effective, and they established a model of university-government collaboration that was to be the inspiration for Title VI of the National Defense Education Act (NDEA) of 1958. Other spin-offs of World War II include the Fulbright Act of 1946, Marshall Plan of 1947, the Point Four Program of 1949, the Foreign Assistance Act of 1961, and the Title XII overseas agriculture assistance program of BIFAD, passed in 1975.

(Continued)

(Continued)

World War II veterans, who become internationalists because of their overseas service, were the promoters of these federal programs. The late Frederick Wakeman, a China specialist who served as president of the Social Science Research Council, called attention to this generational effect in a talk to National Research Council directors in 1996. Wakeman argued that an elite network of World War II veterans emerged, committed to enabling the United States as a world power. Members of this elite moved back and forth among the major foundations, universities, and government agencies, using their contacts to promote America's international competence. McGeorge Bundy, for example, worked in Army intelligence during World War II, served as an assistant to Secretary of War Henry Stimson, went to the Council on Foreign Relations, became a professor at Harvard and then dean of Harvard College, returned to government as chairman of John F. Kennedy's National Security Council, and finally became president of the Ford Foundation. Wakeman also observed that the retirement of the World War II generation meant the loss of elite support for international competence.

The Fulbright Act of 1946 (replaced by the Fulbright-Hays Act of 1961) was conceived as a way of spending down lend-lease loans owed to the United States by World War II allies, whose weak currencies could not be converted into dollars. By sending faculty and graduate students to foreign countries and receiving faculty and students from those same countries, the Fulbright program established personal networks and stimulated interest in overseas research. It also familiarized Americans with foreign universities and foreigners with American universities.

Soon foreign faculty began to use their U.S. connections to place their students in American universities. Foreign student enrollments in the United States had been virtually nonexistent before World War II. After the passage of the Fulbright Act of 1946, enrollments of foreign students began to grow, at first slowly and then exponentially. In 1959, there were 48,000 foreign students in American colleges and universities. By 2009, there were 690,000 such students.

A second spin-off of the Fulbright program was that American faculty began to use their foreign connections to establish study abroad programs for their own students. Before 1950, only six U.S. academic year study abroad programs existed, a number that grew to 103 in 1962 and 208 in 1965. Summer study abroad programs grew from 63 in 1962 to 97 in 1965

(Freeman, 1966). The Institute for International Education reported 18,000 Americans studying abroad in 1965, 49,000 in 1985, and 224,000 in 2005.

At the same time, the Soviet Union expanded its political, economic, social, and academic control over Central and Eastern Europe in a quite different and clearly repressive way, bringing academic freedom and autonomous cooperation and exchange almost to an end. Kallen (1991) describes the situation of higher education in Central and Eastern Europe during the Communist period:

> Higher education, as well as the educational system in general, had been made subservient to the political and economic interests of the State and in fact the Party. The universities were among the chosen and most prestigious instruments for transforming human minds and for providing the State economy with the right numbers and the right kind of highly qualified manpower. (p. 17)

For academic cooperation, the Western world was not a priority:

> Much higher importance was attached to co-operation with other socialist countries, whether in Central/Eastern Europe itself or elsewhere in the world. Large numbers of

students with scholarships attended higher education in the USSR and in other socialist countries, and considerable numbers of staff were invited to teach or learn, particularly in the USSR. The Third World at large represented the second priority. Apart from receiving large numbers of students on state scholarships and inviting considerable numbers of staff, the Central/Eastern European countries carried out a vast programme of development assistance in Third World countries." (pp. 27–28)

In Europe, higher education in the first decade after the Second World War was not very international. Countries were focused on reconstruction after the great Depression and the Second World War, with their impact on society and the economy. What little international dimension existed was primarily the movement of elite degree-seeking students in developing countries to the colonial and imperialist powers with which they were linked: the United Kingdom, France, Germany, and, to a lesser extent, countries like Belgium and the Netherlands. In addition, governments signed cultural and scientific agreements to exchange small numbers of students and staff. In general, the period 1950 to 1970 was characterized by a foreign policy among receiving countries of "benevolent laissez–faire" (Baron 1993, p. 50): open doors to foreign students.

That policy, "humanitarianism and internationalism" (Chandler 1989, p. viii), and its one–way dimension were the main characteristics of the process of internationalization of higher education at a global level and in Europe in particular. The universities themselves played a mainly passive role as receivers of foreign students. The effects on higher education cooperation within Europe were marginal. International activity was mainly oriented toward the cooperation of European higher education with the United States (outward mobility) and with the Third World (inward mobility). A European policy for internationalization did not exist, and the same applies to the institutional level. At the national level, international cooperation and exchange were included in bilateral agreements between nations and in development cooperation programs, driven by political rationales. Institutions were passive partners in these programs.

Neave (1992) characterizes academic mobility in Europe in the period 1950 to 1970 as follows: "overwhelmingly voluntarist, unorganized and individual" (p. 15).

> The relatively small numbers of students involved and though organized under the aegis of national agencies, whether public or private, continued in the main along a North-North axis, between North America and the United States in particular and Western Europe, or, from the standpoint of the Eastern bloc, between the Soviet Union and its satellites. (p. 18)

Another feature of this period was the rise of competition between the Soviet Union and the United States with respect to North-South academic exchanges. "More than a few development projects in the Third World became something of a chess game between the superpowers," as Holzner and Greenwood (1995, p. 39) observe. The USSR saw developing countries as an important region in which to expand their political and economic power, and they invested in development aid programs for universities. Likewise, the United States and soon after Western Europe, Canada, and Australia provided development funds for higher education in Asia, Latin America, and Africa. Academic personnel were sent to these regions for teaching, training, and curriculum development; junior faculty received grants for postgraduate training in the donor countries; and equipment and books were sent to improve the infrastructure of the universities in the developing world. A massive movement of students from South to North, in particular to the five most important receiving nations—the Soviet Union, Germany, France, the United Kingdom, and the United States—characterized the second half of the twentieth century, the only changes being that Australia moved in as a serious competitor in the Asian market and the Soviet Union lost its position.

Technical assistance was another dominant factor in North-South relations in higher education. Cooperation for the development of agriculture, based on the agricultural extension programs of the Roosevelt Administration, was one of the components of the Point Four Program of 1949, expanded by later legislation, most notably the Foreign Assistance Act of 1961. Administered since 1961 by the U.S. Agency for International Development (USAID), technical assistance programs, as Holzner and Greenwood

(1995) remark, also came to be seen "almost exclusively in the light of Cold War conceptions of the national interest" (p. 39). In 1975, these agricultural assistance programs were consolidated in U.S. Title XII of the legislation authorizing the establishment of the Board for International Food and Agricultural Development (BIFAD). Long-term contracts were established with major land-grant universities in the United States to enable them to participate in overseas AID agricultural projects. Such universities often had dozens, or even hundreds, of faculty, staff, and students working overseas.

The Cold War also played a central role in the development of foreign language and area studies programs in the United States (see Box 3.4).

Overall, in the post-World War II period, the Cold War drove the U.S. government, for reasons of defense, public diplomacy, and security, to stimulate international exchange and cooperation. Even after the end of the Cold War,

continued international instability gave new relevance to these rationales for federal support. In Europe, however, the development of international education took a different shift, as Box 3.5 makes clear.

In the 1980s, the global context changed. The strengthening of the European Community and the rise of Japan as an economic world power challenged U.S. dominance, not only in the political and economic arenas but also in research and teaching. Both Japan and the European Community invested in research and development (R&D) programs to compete with the United States. The European Community invested in programs of cooperation for R&D between the member states, with specific reference to the technological race with Japan and the United States. Following the example of countries such as Germany and Sweden, the European Commission decided to expand its role to the promotion of international cooperation in curriculum development, mobility

BOX 3.4 The Cold War and International Education in the United States

The Soviet Union's 1957 success in launching the first orbiting satellite, Sputnik, led to a wave of public hysteria in the United States, comparable to the reactions to Pearl Harbor and the destruction of the World Trade Towers on 9/11/2001. The Eisenhower administration was suddenly on the political defensive, accused of letting the Soviets get ahead of the United States. In response, the Eisenhower Administration proposed a new federal program to support science, engineering, language, and area studies in higher education, called the National Defense Education Act (NDEA) of 1958. The NDEA, according to Vestal (1994), was a direct reaction to the launch the year before of Sputnik I by the Soviet Union and an effort by the United States to regain international leadership. The point man for this legislation was World War II veteran Eliot Richardson, the assistant secretary for education in the Department of Health, Education, and Welfare.

The NDEA included Title VI, which was a new version of the Army Specialized Training Program. Title VI authorized partnerships between government and higher education to train foreign language and area experts. NDEA was passed in 1958 and signed by President Eisenhower. Over the next decades, new Title VI missions were added, such as outreach, citizen education, internationalization of the undergraduate curriculum, international business education, minority recruitment, language research, and support for overseas research centers (Scarfo, 1998).

All these initiatives indicate that higher education was considered an instrument in the Cold War. At the same time, they stimulated the internationalization of higher education in the United States.

Note: This text was written by chapter author Gil Merkx.

BOX 3.5 International Education in Europe in the 1980s

The 1980s produced some radical changes in Europe. With respect to the individual mobility of students, European nations and universities began changing their benevolent laissez–faire policy to a more controlled acceptance and in some cases the active recruitment of fee-paying foreign students. At first, this applied nearly exclusively to the United Kingdom, where the British decided in 1979 to introduce full-cost fees for foreign students. Higher education as an export commodity quickly became dominant in the United Kingdom, as it also did in Australia. For most people on the European continent, considering the education of foreign students as an export commodity was still anathema at that time.

On the European continent, the hosting of foreign students was and in most cases still is based more on foreign policy arguments than on considerations of export policy. At the end of the twentieth century, the international movement of students as an export commodity had spread over the European continent and became a more important element of higher education policy than it had been in the past, both at the national and institutional level.

In the late 1970s and early 1980s, the notion of studying abroad, in the sense of sending students to foreign institutions of higher education as part of their home degree program, became an issue on the continent that overshadowed the developments in individual mobility of students. Since the 1980s, student mobility as a one-way, individual process stimulated by political or economic considerations has (with the exception of the United Kingdom) lost prominence as a policy issue. It has been marginalized by the greater attention given to student mobility in the framework of exchange programs, which have been among the top priorities in higher education policies of the 1980s and 1990s. Before this period, organized programs for the exchange of students and staff existed, but these programs were limited in both funding and scope, stimulating mainly unrelated exchanges at the graduate level.

The 1976 Joint Study Programmes scheme of the European Community (EC) was aimed at the promotion of joint programs of study and research between institutions in several member states. The focus of this experimental program was primarily the stimulation of academic mobility within the EC. This scheme was replaced in 1987 by the European Action Scheme for the Mobility of University Students (Erasmus). The action program of 1976 was the basis for future activities in academic cooperation and exchange within the European Community. Since the implementation of the Erasmus program in 1987, significant results have been achieved in cooperation and exchange within higher education in the European Union. Thanks to Erasmus, in the period 1987–2011, more than 2 million students have been exchanged, and the program expanded to other European countries outside the European Union.

Note: This text was written by chapter author Hans de Wit.

of students, and faculty and university-industry networks. In terms of internationalization during this period, the international dimension of higher education moved from the incidental and individual into organized activities, projects, and programs, based mainly on political rationales and driven more by national governments than by higher education itself. Kerr (1994) notes that "it has been to the advantage of nation-states to support the expansion of higher education and its internationalization within and beyond their borders" (p. 20).

After the Cold War: A Shift From Political to Economic Rationales

The collapse of communism at the end of the 1980s and the beginning of the 1990s changed the map even further. The countervailing political and military superpower, the USSR, fell apart at a time when the United States was being increasingly threatened as the economic superpower by the European Union.

The end of the Cold War, according to Shaw (1994), created an atmosphere of global anarchy: on the one hand, a contradictory context of growing nationalism was based on the exclusivity of ethnic groups, in itself the result of "disintegration of nation-states and national societies," and the other a global culture and society, a "global complex of social relations," was developing at the level of both systems and values. This global society can be best understood as a diverse social universe in which the unifying forces of modern production, markets, communications, and cultural and political modernization interact with many global, regional, national, and local segmentations and differentiations. Global society should be understood not as a social system but as a field of social relations in which many specific systems have formed, some of them genuinely global, others incipiently so, and others still restricted to national and local contexts. (p. 19)

No longer dominated by the superpowers, the global environment is characterized by Friedman (1994) as "ethnicization and cultural pluralization of a dehegemonizing, dehomogenizing world incapable of a formerly enforced politics of assimilation or cultural hierarchy" (p. 100). This is a development that is expressed in the stronger emphasis on globalization of economics, social and political relations, and knowledge but at the same time by tendencies toward ethnic conflicts and nationalism and isolation, tendencies that increasingly manifested themselves in the next decade.

In the post-Cold War period, economic arguments were emphasized in promoting international cooperation and exchange in higher education. Lyman (1995) describes this for the United States: "For too long, international education, especially exchange and study abroad programs, were justified by a vague sense that such studies were the path to mutual understanding and world peace, [but] today, internationalizing education in the US is proposed as a way to help restore our economic competitiveness in the world" (p. 4). Harari (1992, p. 57) also stresses the growing importance of the argument of economic competitiveness. Callan and de Wit (1995) have stated that the same applies for the arguments used by the European Commission for their programs to promote cooperation and exchange within the European Union and with the rest of the world. Neave (1992, p. 21) uses terms such as the *market ethic* and the *cash nexus* for this period. Van der Wende (2001) speaks of a change in paradigms from cooperation to competition, although she also states correctly: "Not surprisingly most continental European countries pursue a cooperative approach to internationalization, which in terms of international learning and experience is more compatible with the traditional value of academia" (p. 255).

Competitiveness as a popular rationale for international education was added to the older rationales of foreign policy and national security. In the United States, the creation of Centers for International Business Education and Research at universities under Part B of Title VI of the U.S. Higher Education Act is an illustration that "national interest came to be supplemented (but certainly not replaced) by the competitiveness paradigm" (Holzner & Greenwood 1995, p. 40). Mestenhauser (2000, p. 34) also refers to the change of rationale from international understanding and avoiding wars and conflicts to global competitiveness in U.S. international education.

President Bill Clinton circulated a memorandum on "international education policy" for the heads of executive departments and agencies, dated April 19, 2000 (White House, 2000), which underlines the competitiveness rationale:

> To continue to compete successfully in the global economy and to maintain our role as a world leader, the United States needs to ensure that its citizens develop a broad understanding of the world, proficiency in other languages, and knowledge of other cultures. America's leadership also depends on building ties with those who will guide the political, cultural, and economic development of their countries in the future. A coherent and coordinated international education strategy will help us meet the twin challenges of

preparing our citizens for a global environment while continuing to attract and educate future leaders from abroad.

In Europe in the 1990s, the creative and informal period of educational policy of the European Community came to an end. The Maastricht Treaty, signed in 1992 and ratified on November 1, 1993, included education for the first time. The importance of strengthening the European dimension in education was placed high on the agenda. The role of the European Commission in higher education has not been limited to educational mobility and exchange within the European Union. It has impacted, in the first place, the opening up of Central and Eastern Europe. Through its so-called PHARE program, the commission in 1989 initiated several forms of cooperation, both in R&D and in education. Thanks to the program for support to higher education in these countries, TEMPUS, and other programs supported by national governments and other international private and public organizations, a rapid improvement in the educational infrastructure and the quality of education in Central and Eastern Europe has been achieved. Now most of these countries have become members of the European Union (EU) or at least are accepted as participants in the EU programs. Also, all the countries, including Russia since 2003, have signed the Bologna Declaration (see Chapter 5, this volume) and take part in its development process.

The cooperation programs of the EU go beyond Europe. The early fear on the part of some governments and academics outside Europe of the emergence of a "Fortress Europe" in international education has proved to be unfounded by a booming number of exchange agreements and programs of cooperation linking institutions of higher education in Europe with counterpart institutions all over the world. This is reflected in the creation of the new Erasmus Mundus program, started in 2004 and intended to create high-level joint degree programs between EU institutions and those elsewhere in the world.

At the Start of the Twenty-First Century

The end of the Cold War, the deepening of European integration, and the globalization of our societies started a process of strategic development of the international dimension of higher education. Although one could disagree with Callan's (2000) emphasis on the role of analysts in this process, her description of the change between the 1980s and 1990s is correct:

> A dominant concern through the 1990s has been with internationalization as a process of strategic transformation of institutions. This concern makes a clear departure from earlier, piecemeal and limited, concerns with the management of student mobility. . . . "Striving for strategy" has become a recurrent motif in the construction of internationalization, both descriptively and prescriptively. (p. 17)

Teichler (1999) argues that this period is one of substantial qualitative changes, referred to as the three quantum leaps in the internationalization of higher education. The first one is the leap from "a predominantly 'vertical' pattern of cooperation and mobility, towards the dominance of international relationships on equal terms." That leap coincides with the "piecemeal and limited" focus on internationalization Callan (2000) describes. The second leap is "from casuistic action towards systematic policies of internationalisation." That leap refers to the emergence of a strategic perspective on internationalization, as Callan mentions. The third one is "from a disconnection of specific international activities on the one hand, and (on the other) internationalisation of the core activities, towards an integrated internationalisation of higher education" (pp. 9–10). This analysis is the more appropriate view of the developments in this period, where the third leap can be seen as the millennium leap, the leap at the beginning of the 21st century: the leap in which internationalization as a strategic issue becomes an integrated part of the overall strategy of institutions of higher education.

The landscape of international higher education has been changing over the past decade (de Wit, 2002, 2008; Knight, 2008). The international dimension and the position of higher education in the global arena are more prominent than ever in international, national, and institutional documents and mission statements. Increasingly influenced by globalization, higher education is also becoming a more dynamic actor in the global knowledge economy. Teichler

(2004), Scott (1998, 2005), Altbach (2006), Knight (2008), de Wit (2008, 2011), Foskett and Maringe (2010), and others address the complex relationship between globalization and internationalization of higher education.

The most striking trend over the past 40 years is the increase in the number of globally circulating students, from about 250,000 in 1965 to 2.5 million in 2005 and 3.7 million in 2011. The cross-border delivery of higher education, with programs, projects, and providers moving across borders instead of students, is an important growth market for Australia, the United States, and the United Kingdom, while continental Europe lags behind (see Chapter 18, this volume). For the United Kingdom and Australia, the number of students in offshore activities is increasing more rapidly than those onshore. Global competition for highly skilled manpower is becoming a strong pull factor in international student circulation. The graying societies of Europe, North America, Australia, and Japan are competing for top talent around the world, all of which need to fill the gaps in their knowledge economies. At the same time, they have to compete with the emerging economies in Asia, Latin America, the Middle East, and Africa, where such talents may be needed even more (see Chapters 23 and 25, this volume).

CONCLUDING REMARKS

From this description of the historical development of the international dimension of higher education, it becomes obvious that changes in the external and internal environments of higher education over the centuries have been extremely influential in this process. Macrohistorical changes affecting the international dimension of Europe's higher education over the past decades were: the emergence of nation-states in the nineteenth century and earlier; Europe's historical role in the world, in particular its role in colonization and in the process of decolonization; the impact of higher education in countries such as France, Germany, and the United Kingdom on higher education in the rest of the world; recent trends in European integration; the collapse of the former Soviet Union and associated East-West rapprochement; recession and financial constraint; "massification" of higher education; the dissolution

of some structures and blocs and the emergence of others.

One can say that until the twentieth century this dimension was rather incidental and individual: the wandering scholar and student, the grand tour, the student flows from South to North. The export of higher education models in the eighteenth and nineteenth centuries, seen by some as an important manifestation of the internationalization of higher education, is difficult to understand as such and is better seen as academic colonialism.

After World War II, international educational efforts became structured into activities, projects, and programs, mainly in the United States and to a lesser extent in the Soviet Union, Germany, France, the United Kingdom. National scholarship programs for students and staff (Fulbright); institutional study abroad programs (the American junior-year abroad); the development of area studies, international studies, and foreign language training in the United States (NDEA, the Higher Education Act, Title VI); scientific and cultural agreements between countries; and the creation of national agencies (IIE, DAAD, and British Council) were manifestations of more organized activity-based approaches to internationalization. Referred to in the literature collectively as "international education," they were driven in particular by the Cold War.

A second manifestation appearing in the 1960s was technical assistance and development cooperation, an area that in some countries, such as Australia, Canada, and The Netherlands, was the most dominant international program until the 1980s and is also strongly present elsewhere (see also Chapter 20, this volume). In addition, although less organized, the international flow of students, mainly from South to North, continued and even expanded.

Major changes in internationalization took place in the 1980s. The move from aid to trade in Australia and the United Kingdom; the development of the European programs for research and development (the Framework programs and their predecessors) and for education (SOCRATES, LEONARDO, and their predecessors); the development of transnational education; the presence of internationalization in mission statements, policy documents, and strategic plans of institutions of higher education, in particular in Europe, Northern America, and

Australia; and the emergence of senior policy advisers for internationalization and their membership organizations (Association of International Education Administrators, IEA, NAFSA, European Association for International Education, International Education Association of Australia) were clear manifestations of these changes.

Globalization and the related knowledge society based on technological developments, as well as the end of the Cold War and the creation of regional structures (in particular the EU), influenced these changes. The need for higher education to make an organized response to these external developments resulted in internationalization strategies that were based on more explicit choices (rationales) and a more integrated strategy (process approach). It was only in the 1980s that the internationalization of higher education became a strategic process, resulting, for instance, in the establishment in 1982 of the Association of International Education Administrators (AIEA) in the United States. Competitiveness in the international market became a key rationale. Incidents, isolated activities, projects, and programs were still present, both at the national and institutional level, but internationalization as a strategic process became more central in higher education institutions.

However, the period 1990-present is one of transition, the beginning of a great transformation, according to Kerr (1994, p. 9). The globalization of our societies and markets and its impact on higher education, along with the new knowledge society based on information technology, will change higher education profoundly and will also change the nature of internationalization of higher education, as discussed in Chapter 24, this volume. Will that change be, as Kerr argues, "in the direction of the supremacy of the pure model of academic life consistent with reasonable guidance by the nation-state [and] a universal reconvergence where universities best serve their nations by serving the world of learning"? That would be too simplistic and naive a conclusion. Internationalization will take place in the context of globalization processes, processes that, as Scott (1998) states, "cannot simply be seen as reiteration of the old internationalism, still dysfunctionally dominated by the West (or, at any rate, the developed world) but are now intensified by the new

information (and knowledge) technologies" (p. 124).

The changing global environment, the changes in global higher education itself and the way its international dimension is evolving, call for a debate on the future of internationalization. The historical roots and changes of the internationalization of higher education should not be ignored in that debate. Although so far Europe and North America, in particular the United States, as well as to a certain extent Australia, have played a key role in the development of internationalization, there is an increasing concern, correct or not, that internationalization is a synonym to Westernization or neocolonialism. At the same time, the other continents, in particular Asia but also Latin America, Africa, and the Middle East, will undoubtedly influence the debate on internationalization by their practice and by their position in the global knowledge society and economy in the coming decades.

Author's Note: This chapter owes to previous work by the authors, in particular Chapters 1 and 2 in de Wit, 2002, and Merkx, 2000.

REFERENCES

Altbach, P. G. (1998). Comparative perspectives in higher education for the twenty-first century. *Higher Education Policy, 11,* 347–356.

Altbach, P. G. (2006). Globalization and the university: Realities in an unequal world. In P. G. Altbach & J. J. F. Forest (Eds.), *International handbook of higher education.* Dordrecht: Springer.

Altbach, P. G., & Selvaratnam, V. (1989). *From dependence to autonomy: The development of Asian universities.* Dordrecht: Kluwer Academic.

Baron, B., (1993). The politics of academic mobility in Western Europe. *Higher Education Policy, 6*(3), 50–54.

Ben-David, J. (1992). *Centers of learning: Britain, France, Germany, United States.* New Brunswick, NJ: Transaction.

Callan, H. (2000). The international vision in practice: A decade of evolution. *Higher Education in Europe, 25*(1), 15–23.

Callan, H., & de Wit, H. (1995). Internationalization of higher education in Europe. In H. de Wit (Ed.), *Strategies for internationalisation of higher education: A comparative study of Australia,*

Canada, Europe and the United States of America. Amsterdam: European Association for International Education.

Chandler, A. (1989). *Obligation or opportunity: Foreign student policy in six major receiving countries* (IIE Research Report No. 18). New York: Institute for International Education.

Cunningham, C. G. (1991). *The integration of international students on Canadian post-secondary campuses.* Ottawa: Canadian Bureau for International Education.

De Ridder Symoens, H. (1992). Mobility. In H. de Ridder-Symoens (Ed.) *A history of the university in Europe: Vol. I. Universities in the Middle Age.* Cambridge, UK: Cambridge University Press.

De Ridder-Symoens, H. (1996). Mobility. In W. Rüegg (Ed.), *A history of the university in Europe: Vol. 2. Universities in early modern Europe.* Cambridge, UK: Cambridge University Press.

de Wit, H. (2002). *Internationalization of higher education in the United States of America and Europe: A historical, comparative, and conceptual analysis.* Westport, CT: Greenwood Press.

de Wit, H. (2008). The internationalization of higher education in a global context. In P. Agarwal, M. E. Said, M. Sehoole, M. Sirozi, & H. de Wit (Eds.), *The dynamics of international student circulation in a global context.* Rotterdam: Sense Publishers.

de Wit, H. (2011). *Trends, issues, and challenges in internationalisation of higher education.* Amsterdam: Center for Applied Research on Economics and Management, School of Economics and Management HvA.

Foskett, N., & Maringe, F. (2010). *Globalization and internationalization in higher education: Theoretical, strategic and management perspectives.* London: Continuum International Publishing Group.

Freeman, S. A. (1966). Undergraduate study abroad. In *International education: Past, present, problems, and prospects: Selected reading to Supplement H.R. 14643* (pp. 387-392). Washington, DC: Government Printing Office.

Friedman, J. (1994). *Cultural identity & global process.* London: Sage.

Goodwin, C. D., & Nacht, M. (1991). *Missing the boat: The failure to internationalize American higher education.* Cambridge, UK: Cambridge University Press.

Halpern, S. (1969). *The Institute of International Education: A history.* Doctoral dissertation, Columbia University, New York.

Hammerstein, N. (1996). The Enlightenment. In W. Rüegg (Ed.), *A history of the university in Europe: Vol. II. Universities in early modern*

Europe. Cambridge, UK: Cambridge University Press.

Harari, M. (1992). Internationalization of higher education. In A. S. Knowles (Ed.), *The international encyclopedia of higher education.* San Francisco: Jossey-Bass.

Hoffa, W. A. (2007). *A History of US study abroad: Beginnings to 1965.* Carlisle, PA: Forum on Education Abroad.

Holzner, B., & Greenwood, D. (1995). The institutional policy contexts for international higher education in the United States of America. In H. de Wit (Ed.), *Strategies for internationalisation of higher education, A comparative study of Australia, Canada, Europe, and the United States of America.* Amsterdam: European Association for International Education.

Institute of International Education (IIE). (1994). Investing in People Linking Nations. 1919–1995: The First 74 Years of the Institute of International Education. New York: IIE.

Kallen, D. (1991). Academic exchange in Europe: Towards a new era of cooperation. In *The open door: Pan-European academic co-operation, an analysis and a proposal.* Bucharest: CEPES/ UNESCO.

Kerr, C. (1994). Higher education cannot escape history: Issues for the twenty-first century. Albany: State University of New York Press.

Knight, J. (2008). Higher education in turmoil. The changing world of internationalization. Rotterdam, the Netherlands: Sense Publishers.

Kolasa, J. (1962). *International intellectual co-operation (the League experience and the beginnings of UNESCO)* (Series A. no. 81). Wroclaw, Poland: Prace Wroclawskiego Towarzystwa Naukowego.

Lambert, R. D., Barber, E. G., Jordan, E., Merrill, M. B., & Twarog, L. I. (1984). *Beyond growth: The next stage in language and area studies.* Washington, DC: Association of American Universities.

Lyman, R. (1995). Overview. In K. H. Hanson & J. W. Meyerson (Eds.). *International challenges to American colleges and universities: Looking ahead.* Phoenix, AZ: Orix Press.

McCullough, D. (2011). *The greater journey: Americans in Paris.* New York: Simon & Schuster.

Mestenhauser, J. A. (2000). Missing in action: Leadership for international and global education for the 21st century. In *Internationalization of higher education: An institutional perspective* (Papers on Higher Education). Bucharest: UNESCO/CEPES.

Neave, G. (1992). *Institutional management of higher education: Trends, needs and strategies for* co-operation. Unpublished document, International Association of Universities. Paris: UNESCO.

Neave, G. (1997). The European dimension in higher education. An historical analysis. Background document for the conference on *The Relationship between Higher Education and the Nation-State,* Enschede, the Netherlands.

Roberts, J., Rodrígues Cruz, A. M., & Herbst, J. (1996). Exporting models. In W. Rüegg. (Ed.), *A history of the university in Europe: Vol. 2. Universities in early modern Europe.* Cambridge, UK: Cambridge University Press.

Scarfo, R. D. (1998). The history of Title VI and Fulbright Hays. In J. N. Hawkins, C. M. Haro, M. A. Kazanjian, G. W. Merkx, & D. Wiley (Eds.), *International education in the new global era.* Los Angeles: University of California at Los Angeles.

Scott, P. (1998). Globalisation and the university. In P. Scott (Ed.), *The globalization of higher education.* Buckingham, UK: SRHE and Open University Press.

Scott, P. (2005). The global dimension: Internationalising higher education. In B. Khem & H. de Wit (Eds.), *Internationalization in higher education: European responses to the global perspective.* Amsterdam: European Association for International Education.

Shaw, M. (1994). *Global society and international relations.* Cambridge, UK: Polity Press.

Taylor, M. L. (1978). Study abroad. In A. S. Knowles (Ed.), *The international encyclopedia of higher education.* San Francisco: Jossey-Bass.

Teichler, U. (1999). Internationalisation as a challenge of higher education in Europe. *Tertiary Education and Management, 5,* 5–23.

Teichler, U. (2004). The changing debate on internationalization of higher education. *Higher Education, 48,* 5–26.

Van der Wende, M. 2001. Internationalisation policies: About new trends and contrasting paradigms. *Higher Education Policy, 14,* 249–259.

Vestal, T. M. (1994). The international student experience: A U.S. industry perspective. *Journal of Studies in International Education 3*(2), 57–72.

White House. (2000). International education policy: Memorandum for the heads of executive departments and agencies by President Clinton. Oklahoma City: Office of the Press Secretary.

4

COMPREHENSIVE AND STRATEGIC INTERNATIONALIZATION OF U.S. HIGHER EDUCATION

JOHN K. HUDZIK AND MICHAEL STOHL

Globalization and companion forces propel internationalization of higher education worldwide. The global expansion of higher education instructional and research capacities is likely to flatten the historic advantages enjoyed by North American and European systems and constitutes one of the most potent challenges and opportunities to face U.S. higher education in the coming decades. This challenge occurs in the context of an ongoing but already substantial rebalancing of public U.S. higher education away from heavy reliance on government funding toward greater private investment, which shapes additional changes in the basic financial structure and assumptions underlying higher education. Successful internationalization of U.S. higher education will have to be responsive to these changing dynamics as well as to heightened demands for higher education accountability and outcome assessment to justify investment.

What follows is an analysis of the key indicators underlying changes in the global and domestic environments affecting higher education. This provides the backdrop for presenting the model for a more *comprehensive internationalization*

(CI), which has emerged over the last decade (e.g., Childress, 2009; Dewey, 2009; Engberg & Green, 2002; Hudzik, 2011; Knight, 1999, 2002; NAFSA: Task Force on Internationalization, 2008) and is gaining momentum as an organizing paradigm for thinking about the likely direction that a globally engaged U.S. higher education system will take.[1] This is followed by a framing of issues that provide the starting point for change as well rationales for it. Prerequisites for, and key features of, a comprehensive approach to internationalization are then introduced. The chapter concludes by examining a set of broader changes likely in U.S. higher education within which the impacts of internationalization will be embedded and play out.

As discussed in following sections, research on developments in global higher education leads to a number of fairly consistent conclusions about paths and directions of change. First, global higher education capacity and participation are spreading dramatically, both in instructional and research terms. Second, higher education providers are increasing in number regionally and in type, particularly in the private sector. Third, both cross-border competition and collaboration among providers of higher education are expanding. Fourth, the mechanisms of funding across the globe for higher education continue to be transformed, most notably a continuing transition that blends public good and private investment, ever more heavily weighting toward the latter. Fifth, the global student-customer pool will diversify to include more lifelong and part-time learners and a more socioeconomically diverse clientele. Sixth, cross-border trade in ideas, students, scholars, and collaboration will continue to increase as a matter of institutional prestige and competitive necessity, and higher education trade will expand in both physical and virtual terms. The next section of this chapter examines a subset of these issues, ones that are likely to be most salient in shaping directions of both global and U.S. higher education, including funding, global growth in instructional and research capacity, and widening rationales for internationalization.

SALIENT ENVIRONMENTAL DRIVERS OF CHANGE

Funding

Given problematic fiscal conditions and budget policy uncertainty at both the state and federal levels within the United States, U.S. higher education internationalization will play out in an environment of financial stress. The current financial crises follow a three-decade period of public disinvestment in higher education and a cost shift to students and families through increasing tuition. Illustrative of this disinvestment are the descriptors employed to characterize the states' declining financial role in their public universities from *state universities,* to *state-supported universities,* to *state-assisted universities,* and most recently to *state-regulated universities* (Gibbons, 2007, pp. 11–12; McDowell, 2001, p. 13).

Tuition now accounts for more than 50% of the revenue of public research universities, up from 39% in 2002; tuition has increased more than 500% since 1983 (National Governors Association, 2010). The great recession beginning in 2008 was so severe that some predict it will be many years if not a full decade before the

economy and public budgets recover to even 2008 levels (Pew Center on the State, 2010; State Higher Education Executive Officers, 2011) and that, regardless, the longer term fiscal situation is such that the existing public higher education-funding model is unsustainable (National Association of Budget Officers, 2010). As more of the cost burden falls to consumers, voices rise for greater cost control, more value for money, and more robust outcomes (Hurley, 2009; National Governors Association, 2010; White & Eckel, 2008).

Funding trends play out as important variables in other countries and regions as well (Kearney & Yelland, 2010). Growth in private for-profit and not-for-profit higher education is demand-absorbing and a critical component of enrollments in many countries (e.g., 26% in the United States, 77% in Japan, 80% in Korea, 75% in Brazil, and a third in Mexico and Poland; Program for Research, 2010). Tuition has been introduced into European nations that did not have it in the past, and tuition costs continue to rise throughout many countries and world regions (Organization for Economic Cooperation and Development [OECD], 2010, Chapter B), and private-like forces (Teixeira, 2009) are reshaping public higher education globally as well (e.g., revenue diversification and surplus-producing activity; full-cost and market-demand accountability; growth of a government-dependent private sector.) As one observer has noted:

> Higher education is being asked to cater to a growing and increasingly diverse population and to do so in a more economic and efficient way ... and [is being] asked to strengthen responsiveness to the demands of the economic and social environment ... One response to these challenges has been to promote the adoption of market elements, ... particularly through increased privatization. (Teixeira, 2009, p. 232)

Global Instructional Capacity and Mobility

A number of international bodies project significant changes in the composition of global higher education capacity in the coming decades: Global participation in higher education will increase 150% to 250 million participants annually by 2025 (Ruby, 2010). Altbach, Reisberg, and Rumbley (2009) reported a 53% increase from 2000 to 2007. Global student mobility will nearly double to 7 million students annually by 2020 to 2025 (Banks, Olsen, & Pearce, 2007; Haddad, 2006) from 2010 levels of about 3.6 million. The OECD's (2010a) report notes an 11% increase from 2007 to 2008 alone. It may become the case that 7 million mobile students will be achieved much earlier, and the number by 2025 will be much larger.

For the United States, the Institute of International Education (IIE, 2010) reports a nearly 3% increase for 2009–2010 (and nearly a 15% increase cumulative for the 2 previous years) in incoming international students and a very slight decline in outbound students (the decline no doubt prompted by the great recession). Given global growth in mobility and barring unforeseen circumstances and events, the number of students inbound to the United States is likely to continue to grow, although almost assuredly the U.S. global market share will decline. The same pattern will likely be the case for outbound study abroad.

IIE (2011) data indicate a 4.7% increase in international students into the U.S. from FY (fiscal year) 2009–2010 to FY 2010–2011 and a 3.9% increase in U.S. study abroad comparing FY 2008–2009 to FY 2009–2010. Both sets of figures indicate resilience of mobility in and out of the United States despite the severe recession.

Demographic data indicates that most of the growth overall in student enrollments will occur outside Western Europe, North America, and Australia/New Zealand, as will a larger share of mobility. The other world regions, for reasons relating to growth in size and quality of their educational institutions, will significantly reshape the *global* higher education profile and the scale and quality of global instructional capacity will expand and flatten.

Global Research Capacity

Research capacity is spreading and flattening globally. For example, the U.S. National Science Foundation (National Science Board, 2010) reports that (a) researchers in the labor force increased annually from about 7% to 11% in Asian countries, but only 3% in North America and Europe; (b) cross-border joint publications tripled as a share of total publications (mainly intraregionally) from 1988 to 2007; (c) while between 1996 and 2007, annual R&D expenditures grew at about 6% in North America and

Europe, they grew at about 10% in India, Korea, and Taiwan, and at about 15% to 20% in Thailand, Singapore, Malaysia, and China; and (d) output of scholarly publications (e.g., in the sciences and engineering) increased from 1988 to 2008 by about 17% in the United States and about 60% in Europe, while in the same period, some countries in Asia had triple-digit percentage increases. The result is that foundations are being laid for new centers of excellence in research and teaching throughout most world regions, and consequently, competition for the best students and faculty to produce the best graduates and most new knowledge will intensify globally (Wildavsky, 2010).

Widening Institutional Rationales for Internationalization

The business of universities is ideas—their creation and their dissemination. Increasingly the business of universities throughout the world occurs across borders, as evidenced by increased cross-border flows of students, scholars, and scholarly collaborations. Mobility, often defined as students crossing borders for education and learning, is now also very much about the mobility of scholars and institutional administrators (Wildavsky, 2010). Also, the mobility is multidirectional (China, for example, now has as many inbound as outbound students).

The advent of global ranking schemes (e.g., QS Top Universities, 2010; Shanghai Jiao Tung, 2010; *Times* Higher Education, 2010) represents a paradigm shift in reference points for higher education institutions throughout the world. U.S. public and private institutions fare well in the rankings. Currently, U. S. private institutions account for 14, and U.S. public institutions 15, of the top 50 in the Times rankings, 18 and 17, respectively of the top 50 in the Shanghai Jiao Tung rankings, and 16 and 4, respectively, of the top 50 in the QS rankings. One can expect significant alterations in the future. A number of institutions and nations in Asia and elsewhere have indicated aspirations to raising their ranks to the top 25, 50, or 100 institutions in the world.

There is an interesting difference between the response and public reactions of many U.S. public versus private universities in the current fiscal and political climate. Private universities consistently trumpet their rankings to all audiences.

Public universities trumpet the rankings to incoming graduate students and other scholars but often downplay the rankings when discussing their teaching and undergraduate student profiles with state legislative bodies, which frequently worry that their faculties spend too much time building their research profiles and not enough time "being a teacher."

In the United States and elsewhere, the institution's customers are global. As the world moves toward a more integrated global labor market, a "work force-ready" graduate has a global meaning in terms of graduates finding jobs across borders or, at minimum, increasingly working closely with colleagues in other countries. As diverse immigrant populations join local communities, knowledge of their cultures is important. As businesses large and small engage global markets, they need access to country and regional knowledge and expertise. Customers at home increasingly are global customers, too. Issues of peace, justice, cross-cultural communication, and understanding (Deardorff, 2009) are of greater complexity and importance than any time in history.

CONSEQUENCES OF HIGHER EDUCATION GLOBAL GROWTH

The globalization of higher education has both competitive and collaborative cross-border dimensions. Strong aggregate demand and short supply will likely characterize global higher education for some time. Growth in the private sector in all regions is likely and will continue to absorb unmet demand. The U.S. system of higher education of the future, long envied worldwide, will function within a much more robust and competitive environment, with the rapid growth of capacity and quality in Asia and modernizing systems in an expanding and rationalizing European Union (EU). Development of capacity in Latin America is under way, albeit at a less robust pace than in Asia, and at least for the time being, the emphasis seems more focused on building instructional rather than research capacity per se.

The need to meet and sustain increased capacity coincides with a philosophical switch to neoliberal notions of higher education as a private investment (Teixeira, 2009). Questions in the United States about the value-added of current higher education models and outcomes

further impact the debate on financing. Funding model discussions are accompanied by increasing pressure for outcome assessments, better alignment with societal needs, and greater efficiency and effectiveness (see, e.g., Hurley, 2009; McPherson & Shulenburger, 2006; Spellings, 2006).

Strong global demand and short supply, coupled with a flattening of global capacity and quality, increase the opportunities for trade and competition, "brain circulation," and competition for the short supply of the best in faculty, students, staff, and leaders. Brain drain in the direction of highly developed systems such as those of the United States is likely to continue. The United States is unlikely suddenly to become an unattractive place to research scholars, but it is no longer on its own: Attractive pockets of excellence, cutting edge research, and personal and research financial rewards have expanded in Europe and developed in Asia and the Antipodes.

Although, global ranking schemes and quality competition fuel a wider competitive net, countervailing pressures for cross-border partnerships and collaborations arise from a flattening of capacity and increased inability for institutions to "go it alone," particularly in cutting-edge research. Thus, the tension between competition and collaboration is likely to be ongoing, with strong manifestations of both tendencies for the foreseeable future.

The National Science Foundation study (NSB, 2010) points to a rise in cross-border joint authorship, and there is little reason to think this won't increase. Yet, government policymakers, as Simon Marginson of the University of Melbourne points out, often see an us versus them view about funding cross-border research collaborations. "As the national policy maker sees it, 'These public-knowledge goods are all very well, but what's in it for us? Why should we pay for everyone's free benefit?'" (Marginson, 2010). Legal prohibitions against the sharing or transport of sensitive technology or research findings across borders (especially to unfriendly or suspect states or their citizens) and country-specific sanctions complicate partnerships (Knezo, 2006).

Stephen Toope (2010), president of the University of British Columbia, notes that the reality of what we can do on our own from the point of view of cost, infrastructure, and access to cutting edge thinking (all of which exist in a growing number of locations around the world) is increasingly constrained. Toope suggests that the best cross-border collaborations are likely to grow organically out of the interests of research scholars rather than being pushed "top down" by either governments or institutional leadership (the latter perhaps having facilitator rather than creator roles). A nationally decentralized higher education system, but one with huge and diverse capacity, such as in the United States, is likely to fare quite well in Toope's organic cross-border environment, although an increasing proportion of the talent driving it will itself come from cross-border sources.

A Global Higher Education System?

A fully integrated global higher education system is unlikely to emerge solely as a result of the growth in global capacity and expansion of mobility, competition, and collaboration. However, in classic systems-science terms, a *system* has already emerged if we define the system as institutions interacting with one another (e.g., cross-borders collaborations and exchanges), impacting one another (e.g., competing for research funding and the best in students and staff), and establishing mutual ground rules (e.g., quality mechanisms, cross-border credential certifications). The ebb and flow of forces produces ongoing disequilibrium as well as equilibrium.

These aspects of global and cross-border systems confound nationally based systems, institutions, markets, and purposes, but it seems most unlikely in the near future that a global higher education system in political and highly bureaucratized top-down terms will emerge to supersede nationally based funding and regulatory systems and national higher education priorities. Rather, it is more likely that global and nationally based systems will coexist within the global system for decades, and bilateral and multilateral trans-border relationships will occur within the context of the larger set of global forces.

Top-Tier Globally Engaged and Lower-Tier Locally Engaged?

Some speculate that higher education will divide into a two-tier system (Wildavsky, 2010) with the highest-ranked institutions globally engaged and those not so ranked locally engaged. Part of the idea is that global partnerships will form more easily among similarly high-ranked institutions, which are also more likely to have resources to support global engagement. However, as it seems highly likely that higher education will more generally internationalize, a continuum of global-local engagement seems the more likely outcome rather than two polar extremes. Just as the forces of globalization play out in but are also mediated by the local context, higher education also faces the challenge of being *both* globally engaged and locally useful. It seems only a matter of common sense that some institutions, partly because of mission, will be more comprehensively engaged globally, but it seems equally plausible that others will participate in differing ways as well. While true that some top-tier global institutional networks or clubs are forming consortia (e.g., Universitas 21, Association of Pacific Rim Universities, The Worldwide Universities Network [WUN]) to span continents, the realities of globalization seem likely to dissuade all or most institutions from a purely local orientation.

COMPREHENSIVE INTERNATIONALIZATION: AN ORGANIZING PARADIGM FOR U.S. HIGHER EDUCATION

The challenge facing U.S. higher education concerns the scale and scope of how internationalization is defined in concept and practice as it grapples with the realities of globalization. During the 1960s, if not significantly before, the United States and higher education began to sense with alarm the uneven playing field created by its traditional inward-looking national focus (Wiley, 2001). Such unease was responsible, at least in part, for the growth of area study centers and language programs, which were supported significantly by Title VI of the National Defense Education Act. Since then, there has been a half-century of interest in and commitment to international programming, including growth in study abroad, the further internationalization of some key professional programs (e.g., business and engineering), and a widening of institutions involved in development activity abroad (for example, through USAID funding and programs such as Higher Education for Development involving a broad range of teaching, research, and outreach activities).

What distinguishes these earlier efforts from emerging models of internationalization such as CI is the scale and scope of the conception of what higher education internationalization encompasses. There is a growing sense that internationalization is an institutional imperative, not just a desirable option. In short, the discussion over internationalization increasingly focuses on institutional ethos and mission, a broadly shared commitment to a widening scope of international programs and activities. A working definition of CI is the following:

> Comprehensive internationalization is commitment and action to infuse international, global and comparative content and perspective throughout the teaching, research and service missions of higher education. It shapes institutional ethos and values, and touches the entire higher education enterprise . . . .
> Comprehensive internationalization not only impacts all of campus life, but the institution's external frames of reference, partnerships and relationships. (Hudzik, 2011, p. 10)

CI is not a synonym for student mobility, exchange, or international education; rather, these are parts of the larger CI concept. This conceptualization of CI is consistent with the perspective of Mestenhauser (1998), who foresaw over a decade ago "an advanced level of internationalization . . . involv[ing] not only internationalizing key courses but also identifying the international dimensions of every single discipline."

CI is an organizing paradigm to think and act systemically and holistically about higher education internationalization in all institutional missions. It influences all academic units and content and pedagogy throughout curricula and involves all students, all institutional clientele, and all faculty. In addition, CI includes the often ignored but critical factors for internationalization that are within institutional services units and established institutional rules and regulations. Rules, regulations, and policies developed for a domestic setting often do not translate well across borders and across cultures. A broad-scale institutional commitment to internationalization challenges (to name a few) established institutional housing and food policies, institutional travel regulations and procedures, definitions and assessment of risk, insurance coverage, intellectual property regulations, and supports

for increasing numbers of international students not familiar with U.S. pedagogies and expectations.

CI's challenge is in the intended mainstreaming of international content and perspective, moving it from the campus periphery to a core element of the entire higher education enterprise and "working to change the internal dynamics of an institution to respond and adapt appropriately to an increasingly diverse, globally focused, ever-changing external environment" (Ellingboe, 1998, p. 199). As recognized by the 2008 NAFSA Taskforce report, "Internationalization is the conscious effort to integrate and infuse international, intercultural, and global dimensions into the ethos and outcomes of postsecondary education." Seen this way, CI is infused throughout the institution to be a reality and a credible response to globalization. However, as Hudzik and Stohl (2009) have noted previously, this is still a controversial view in some quarters.

> Many see internationalisation as one of the shops in the university mall from which some elect to purchase the product, rather than as something to which all shops in the mall contribute in unique ways. Yet, this limited view of internationalisation seems anathema to the fundamental conceptualization of a "university" or a "forum" . . . [because] learning and thinking across cultures, borders and systems is at the heart of both classical and contemporary discovery and learning in education. (p. 9)

Marginson (2010) identifies three contemporary factors that strengthen the interconnections between higher education internationalization and the processes of globalization: (1) global electronic networking for high-speed communication and collaboration; (2) the heightened role that research universities have in generating competitive positions for knowledge societies and the ability to promote and sustain economic growth and entrepreneurship; and (3) expanded access globally to higher education. The first speeds inexpensive cross-border spread of ideas and collaborative scholarship. The second pressures institutions to remain abreast of cutting-edge discoveries and applications emerging throughout the world. The third creates a global market for higher education and for cross-border trade and competition to obtain the best faculty and students from global sources. An implication of Marginson's view is that strategically planned internationalization can turn higher education into a contributor shaping globalization and enhances its influence locally and regionally.

A Countervailing Argument: The "End of Internationalization?"

A recent short treatise by Brandenburg and de Wit (2011) carried the provocative title, "The End of Internationalization." Brandenburg and de Wit begin by describing how higher education internationalization changed from the 1970s onward and through the rise of globalization as a "rivaling term" in the late 1990s. They describe a "post-internationalization age" with components including: (a) moving away from dogmatic and idealistic concepts of internationalization and globalization; (b) understanding internationalization and globalization not as goals but rather as means to other ends; (c) viewing mobility and other activities as instruments and not goals in themselves; and (d) investing more time into questions of rationales and outcomes.

Their main points are pertinent and largely consistent with their more detailed consideration in NAFSA's publication on comprehensive internationalization (Hudzik, 2011). Given the body of their arguments and analysis, the title should probably not be the *end* of internationalization, but rather the *migration* of the concept of internationalization into a far more sophisticated and comprehensive approach to internationalization of higher education. Even with widening rationales for internationalization and the realities of globalization, institutions will for the most part not jettison their national connections and identities. Rather, identities will be revised to take into account an environment shaped by forces that transcend national boundaries (globalization). CI creates the bridge from old to new concepts of internationalization that are responsive to globalization.

U.S. Higher Education Internationalization: Framing Issues

Goal or Means

Globalization generally, and the globalization of higher education particularly, will press U.S. higher education to transition toward more comprehensive forms of internationalization. Some may see CI as the goal itself. However, just as national security was the driving force behind passage of both Title VI and Fulbright Hays and provided the enormous post-Sputnik investments in science and engineering education and research capacity in the American university system, the more commanding motivations for CI are more likely to be a means to advance other objectives. These include enhancing preparation of all graduates for work and life in a global environment, improving the competitive connection of local economies to global markets, strengthening research capacity through collaborations abroad, and contributing to a more globally aware citizenry. This is consistent with Knight's (2002, p. 1) assertion that internationalization is "the process of integrating an international dimension into the teaching, research and public service function of the institution." Internationalization's instrumental values are already being driven by institutional clientele, U.S. accreditation bodies, and higher education leadership groups such as the American Council on Education, as well as the increasing portion of the global business community that demands better globally prepared employees.

System Decentralization and Prospects for a Federal Government Role

U.S. higher education, with its decentralized system of 4,300 institutions of various kinds and its over 18 million students, is a very large and complex system and one with substantial variety in types of institutions. There is no national system of higher education. The diversity of U.S. higher education and the constitutional reservation to the states of the functions of education are powerful forces that auger against emergence of a strong national system of higher education.

> The organisation and administration of colleges and universities in the United States can be understood only if it is recognised at the outset that there is no system of higher education which can be described definitively. There is no sharp line of distinction even in types of control and every generalisation could be refuted by the policy of some individual institutions. American higher education is characterised more by its variability than its uniformity, more by the local autonomy of each institution than by its organization into a system. (Brown, 2007, p. 453)

The existing diversity of the American higher education system is a touted core value (Ruby, 2010) and is likely to prevent any attempts to nationalize the public higher education system.

The impacts of the federal government on internationalization can be positive but sometimes are strongly negative as a result of regulatory decisions tightening visa regulations and restrictions of cross-border research collaborations. The federal government can be encouraging and supportive through conducive visa and immigration policies and by facilitating conditions for research collaboration across borders and funding for programs such as Title VI, scholarships, and portability of scholarship funding. But there is little to suggest in the present and foreseeable budget climate much growth in federal financial support and quite possibly little in the way of proactive positive regulatory policies. Indeed, the more likely impetus for change will come from within higher education and its clientele in response to the challenges discussed above. Some states may take a more active role in supporting internationalization of their states' higher education systems by reducing or eliminating premium tuition rates, fees, or regulations for international students as some public universities have already done.

Prospects for Change

There are strong catalysts for change in U.S. higher education (also see Hudzik, 2010). However, there are also powerful inhibitors to change, particularly for the scale and scope of the changes being discussed. Principal among these inhibitors are self-satisfaction and the status quo. In an address in Vienna in 2009, James Duderstadt (2009), former president of the University of Michigan, described U.S. higher education as "risk averse, self-satisfied, unduly expensive." Duderstadt flags two important concepts that are in tension: the drag of mature enterprise and change forced by globalization. A self-satisfied U.S. higher education system is a powerful narcotic for inhibiting change. On the other hand, the critique of U.S. higher education from the inside and the challenges posed by heightened competition from the outside may combine to weaken the barrier imposed by the status quo.

One small example of such change in a traditional area of international engagement by U.S.

higher education relates to recruiting international students. Much of the U.S. strategy in the past was based on a philosophy, "we have built it, and they are coming." The current active discussion pro and con about the use of agents, which is in part a reflection of their greater use by U.S. institutions, is an indicator of a likely switch from passive international recruitment to more proactive marketing and recruitment coalition building.

Some of the barriers to structural change generally in U.S. higher education are systemic: for example, state appropriations based on headcount instead of measureable outcomes (Brewer & Tierney, 2010); inadequate market information to drive responsiveness to changing market conditions (Tucker, 2010); and the fear of being first. In the midst of the spiraling economic downturn and at the front edge of serious consequences for higher education budgets, the October 25, 2009, edition of *The Chronicle of Higher Education* reported that college leaders may be thinking strategic change but few are engaging in it (Blumenstyk, 2009). Yet, these structural or systemic impediments are under challenge.

There are no guarantees of change, and certainly the kind of far-reaching change implied by this discussion does not occur in the short run. Nonetheless, the prospects for serious structural change in direction suggested by a CI approach and as identified at the end of this chapter are stronger now than in the past few decades. In Everett Rogers's (2003) terms, the strategy for innovation and change has three important components: First, to create the conditions for "early innovators," who are subsequently rewarded for their success; second, to create the conditions and rewards for "early adopters," who spread the innovation; and third, to build toward a majority. There are already enough examples of successful forms of international engagement by U.S. higher education to have satisfied Rogers's first stage. The rhetoric of college and university presidents and provosts makes it sound as if Rogers's second and third stages have commenced, but the reality in terms of follow-through, particularly when set against a CI frame of reference, suggests that there still is very much to do to actualize Roger's second and third stages.

Institutional Diversity in Responding to Comprehensive Internationalization

Although more comprehensive approaches to internationalization are likely to emerge as a matter of necessity, their operational meaning, form, and scale will vary substantially across the highly decentralized and diverse U.S. higher education landscape. Institutions will vary their responses to fit their extant or evolving missions and their institutional frames of reference with respect to clientele, alumni, their publics, their communities, and their histories and perceived ethos. They will also respond to an evolving set of rationales and motivations for internationalization.

U.S. institutions vary in their starting points from little or no international engagement; to limited focus on student mobility (incoming and outgoing); to wider efforts to internationalize the on-campus curriculum; to the addition of cross-border research collaborations, development work abroad, and various forms of institutional presence abroad (e.g., branch campuses, offices). From varying starting bases, however, a CI impetus will expand to touch more and more students and enrich modes of international engagement consistent with institutional missions. In other words, not all institutions will do everything, but all institutions will do more and impact more of their stakeholders/constituencies/clienteles.

Exemplars of diversity in approach and success can be seen in the composite of annual NAFSA Simon Award winners (NAFSA, 2010). A review of these provides varied models for success and differing programmatic foci; all, however, are good examples involving widely differing institutional types and circumstances of progress toward a more comprehensive engagement of internationalization.

CI needs linkage to core institutional missions or its sustainability will be doubtful and opportunity for marginalization increased. Although arguably all higher education institutions engage in instructional, research, and service missions, they vary greatly in the emphasis given to each. Four-year liberal arts institutions will engage comprehensive internationalization differently and with different priorities and foci than will graduate and graduate research institutions, and all of them will operate differently than community colleges.

BOX 4.1 Comprehensive Internationalization in Context: The Community College

Borough of Manhattan Community College

The Borough of Manhattan Community College enrolls 21,000 students, of whom about 85% are minority students; most are part-time students and also work. The college pursued internationalization in the classroom curriculum, study abroad, and increased enrollment of international students.

A key component of CI is internationalizing the curriculum so that it infuses every student's course of study, both general education and major courses. The college created a Global Pedagogy Handbook in 2007 outlining pedagogical best practices for bringing global insights into the classroom. Distributed to the entire faculty, it includes course descriptions, assignments, and other materials for 31 courses in 11 academic departments as well as the Center for Ethnic Studies. Courses with a global perspective can be found in career programs like nursing and business, science and teacher education, and in the traditional programs of the liberal arts.

Second, the college adopted a model (approved in a referendum by the students) to allocate a portion of student fees directly to study abroad scholarships to enable a greater range of students to participate in programs, which include both faculty-led programs in Ghana, Italy, Spain, France, Costa Rica, and China and the Salzburg Seminar.

Third, the Borough of Manhattan Community College's commitment to internationalization may be seen in its growing population of international students. The college now enrolls more than 1,600 students, hailing from more than 100 countries, on nonimmigrant visas.

The rationales and motivations for U.S. higher education internationalization are diversifying as well. With the end of the Cold War, the dominant security-related rational for internationalization (as well as the dominant driver of the original Title VI legislation) ended. Biddle (2002) characterized the replacement rationale in the late 20th century as, "In the context of an increasingly interdependent world . . . the goal was to promote in students an awareness of their role in an interdependent world and how as citizens and professionals they could contribute to and shape it" (p. 5).

In a global context, Knight and de Wit (de Wit, 1995, 1998; Knight & de Wit, 1999) categorized the motivations for higher education internationalization as (a) academic, searching for global or universal truth and knowledge; (b) socio-cultural, acquiring cross-cultural knowledge and understanding; (c) political, maintaining or expanding global power and marketplace. The rationales expressed over the last several years in conferences by U.S. administrators and institutional clientele suggest a list of motivations similar to those of Knight and de Wit but perhaps more institution-centric (suggesting that CI will be driven in part from the inside of higher education by clientele and in response to changing global and funding dynamics). The drivers of continuing U.S. internationalization will include a more diverse set of perceived needs including:

- national and global security
- cross-cultural knowledge and understanding to improve relations
- labor force and local economic competitiveness
- knowledge, skills, attributes, and careers for graduates
- institutional stature in a global system of higher education
- institutional revenue and markets
- research and scholarship reputation and capacity building

Commonalities and Differing Operational Meanings of *Comprehensive*

The absence of common operational meanings for terms such as *internationalization* has been a feature of the higher education landscape for some time (Knight, 1999). The operational meaning of *comprehensive* will also vary across institutions in large part because of the very different missions of institutions. For four-year liberal arts institutions, the meaning of *comprehensive* will focus on undergraduate curriculum and learning; for research-intensive institutions, the institution's research missions and graduate education will be included. For institutions with heavy community and outreach engagement, internationalizing the service/outreach mission will be an added focus.

Mission-induced differences aside, there are intended commonalities underlying use of the term *comprehensive* in the CI context. One is breadth of clientele coverage: that is, no matter who the focal audience (e.g., undergraduates, graduate students, or research faculty fit in with institutional mission), the idea is to mainstream internationalization for that audience. Second are the modes of engaging them internationally: For example, internationalizing the undergraduate curriculum to be comprehensive would engage general education, curricula in the majors, and link on-campus curriculum with education abroad. In research, institutions would look broadly to link domestic capacities and interests with those in the wider global system. The third commonality concerns who is involved in supporting or delivering CI. CI in any of its operational forms requires broad-gauge involvement—not a few faculty and staff being engaged but many, and also not just the faculty but service and support units. The fourth is institutional ethos. For CI to have a chance, it needs to be part of institutional guiding values and operating principles—a core part of the corporate culture.

Institutional Organization for Comprehensive Internationalization

As Biddle (2002) notes, "Ultimately, the plan put in place [for internationalization] must reflect the university's particular history and culture; failure to respect the institutional context puts the initiative at risk" (p. 10).

Top-down command and control models do not usually fit well within U.S. higher education institutions. Academic governance, key features of crucial curricular and academic personnel decision-making originating in departments and colleges, and the influence and powers of academic deans confound top-down command

BOX 4.2 Comprehensive Internationalization in Context: The Liberal Arts College

Hobart and William Smith College

Hobart and William Smith College is a liberal arts college of 2,000 students located in the small town of Geneva, New York. It is a 2010 Simon Award winner on the strength of its integrated global approach to the curriculum, campus programs, and outreach. Particularly highlighted was study abroad: 60% of its students participate in study abroad programs, and study abroad and global education are woven into every facet of the institution. Planning was guided by a new mission statement that clearly infused the global. This led to the creation of the Center for Global Education and numerous international initiatives and fund raising to support them. The president's passion and reward structures were connected and faculty drivers for the plans that were created were identified and encouraged. The result has been dramatic growth in international content across the curriculum and growth in locations for study abroad on both institutional and faculty-led programs, primarily directed to non-European destinations. These programs have significant pre-departure and reentry programs, which link students learning in the disciplines across the campus and connect what goes on "out there" with the core of student learning. The campus has also reached out to the local community, emphasizing global citizenship and events that link town and gown, such as the campus and town being encouraged to read and discuss *Three Cups of Tea*.

models. Discussions about organization and structure on campuses often center on a false dichotomy: to centralize or to decentralize. The former is touted as delivering coordination, efficiencies, and focus on strategic objectives while the latter sees centralization as synonymous with red tape and stifling creativity and diversity. A "middle" way may reside in matrix organizational structures with elements of hierarchy, decentralization, and crosswalks for collaboration among those engaged in various aspects of internationalization. Already a number of the largest and most complex U.S. institutions are organized this way to support CI. It can be hypothesized that as international engagement expands in breadth and scope, organizational structures will tend to evolve toward matrix models.

BOX 4.3 Comprehensive Internationalization in Context: The Comprehensive Research University

Comprehensive research universities have the basis to engage all three missions of undergraduate and graduate education, research, and engagement service. The University of Minnesota and Michigan State University, both land grant institutions and both Simon Award Winners, benefit from long traditions of international engagement, reinvigorated by successive campus leadership and ongoing faculty and student commitments.

The University of Minnesota, Twin Cities

The University of Minnesota Twin Cities is a public land grant university with more than 50,000 students. CI has been a strategic priority under the leadership of the past two presidents of the

(Continued)

(Continued)

university. Following recommendations of a 2004 university taskforce, the institution significantly strengthened its institution-wide office to lead and coordinate expansion of international engagement throughout the institution. The Office of International Programs became a central hub of international activity on campus with responsibility for coordinating campus-wide efforts.

Since 2007, the university has required that the annual planning compacts of all institutional units include a section on international engagement. This has elevated the priority and expectations of international dimensions in campus planning and budgeting. An assistant vice president position was created to promote and coordinate faculty international engagement and provided grants and awards. In 2008, the Board of Regents policy was updated to strengthen support of international education and engagement.

A post-9/11 institutional goal was set to increase international enrollment to 5% of the undergraduate student body, compared to about 1% at the time, incorporating some funds for nonresident tuition waivers and a reduction of nonresident tuition rates. The curriculum integration and learning-abroad project has had a major impact on undergraduate study abroad enrollment, bringing the university closer to its goal that 50% of graduates will have a study abroad experience (currently about 30%). The university also identified means to fund students at the master's and professional degree level and, in 2001, initiated a fellowship program to assist these students in gaining a study or research experience abroad. The Multicultural Study Abroad Group works to increase the numbers of students of color who study abroad by helping overcome barriers and provide resources. The CI project and increased understanding of study abroad and student advising have been effective in bringing less-informed faculty and staff on board. To encourage greater faculty participation in international research, the university created an internal grants program to promote research and global engagement in interdisciplinary and transnational partnerships.

Michigan State University

Michigan State University is a public land grant university of nearly 47,000 students in East Lansing. The university can trace its internationalization from the post-World War II era, through its participation in European and Asian reconstruction, and later expansion to development projects throughout every major world region. In the mid-1950s, it created the first dean of international programs, a university position charged with providing campus-wide leadership and coordination in this area. Throughout the 1960s and onward, the institution added five area study centers, language centers, a CIBER (Center For International Business, Education And Research), and a number of other internationally focused research and outreach institutes, many of which won Title VI funding and national resource center status. A leader in study abroad participation among large universities since the 1970s, MSU began a major initiative in 1995 to increase study abroad participation to 30% of graduates, with new goals to increase that percentage further in the longer run. Over the last decades, MSU has attracted tens of thousands of international students and scholars, particularly to its graduate and research programs. New initiatives seek to expand undergraduate numbers. Currently, the university has about 7,000 international students and scholars in residence.

It has a presence in one form or another in more than 70 countries at any particular point in time. In 1995, requirements were added to the annual institutional budget planning process for all colleges and significant academic units to address their goals for international engagement; earlier, the university promotion and tenure forms were revised to include international activities as a category in all major areas of faculty efforts.

A significant new symbolic and programmatic initiative at the institution recognizes globalization and globalization of higher education. Titled "from land grant to world grant" by its president, Lou Anna K. Simon, the planned transformation of MSU into a "world grant" institution reflects an institutional commitment to retain traditional land grant values of access/inclusion, quality, and community engagement but to expand their connection to the world scene. It is a commitment to serve the needs of and to be engaged with not only the state and nation but the world and to recognize the increasingly borderless world reality. World grant is symbolically and programmatically the connection of the local and the global in learning, discovery, and engagement and seeks to further weave international and global engagement seamlessly into campus core values, ethos, and actions.

Offices of international programs and senior international officers (SIOs) are essential for CI success (see Heyl, 2007). SIOs have come from a variety of backgrounds, depending in large measure on campus culture and the scope of campus internationalization efforts. Some SIOs come from the faculty ranks, others rise through international programming or support units (e.g., director of an area center, director of mobility), and others from outside careers (e.g., former ambassadors). A more recent phenomenon is the creation of vice presidential positions, with some of these more strategically focused on the course of long-range institutional directions in international engagement, including entrepreneurial objectives.

In an organizational sense the great challenge in the coming decades will be to develop leadership that is credible throughout campus and that not only can provide strategic and intellectual direction but also is administratively savvy enough to orchestrate and coordinate a wider, deeper, and systemic internationalization effort.

What Are the Objectives and Outcomes for Comprehensive Internationalization?

Learning and discovery are the intellectual capital of higher education, but they can be easily confused or subverted by the revenue motivations that drive some aspects of internationalization (e.g., revenue from student mobility, contracts abroad on a cost plus or high overhead return basis). A key future challenge will be the balancing of market forces with core intellectual

values. The challenge of pecuniary motivations and commoditization, set against those of high-quality learning and discovery, will test core institutional values and ethics in revenue diversification and marketing. The role of accreditation bodies in U.S. higher education, as well as periodic federal investigations of practices and the role of an open press, can combine to ward against the worst excesses.

If the core mission of higher education is ideas, then a fundamental issue is how U.S. higher education's response to global forces will be driven by and respond to intellectual objectives and applications—for example, learning outcomes, research and scholarship of students and faculty, institutional curricula or research thrusts, community service and problem solving, and sustained institutional capacity building.

A related issue is how the success of CI will be defined: Will it include, for example: the numbers of its "customers" (e.g., students, public or private organizations) or degree of market penetration; maintenance or enhancement of standards and quality; customer satisfaction evaluations; faculty assessments of intellectual value added; financial viability (e.g., breakeven, surplus, profit); and outcome measures (e.g., completion rates, student academic performance, employer assessments of graduates, income from discoveries, grants, contracts).

Clear Goals and Accountability

As goals and motivations for internationalization widen, so will concepts and measures of CI success. While Einstein made the significant observation that, "Everything that can be counted does not necessarily count; everything that counts cannot necessarily be counted" (http://www. einstein-quotes.com/Life.html), in an organizational sense, it is what gets counted and measured that becomes most important in setting institutional and financial agendas. If internationalization is defined and measured mainly as student mobility of resident students or the number of international students studying on the campus (which appears to be the case at many institutions), then counting these numbers becomes the measure of internationalization and its success.

But a fundamental change takes place in what is measured and how internationalization is operationally defined for accountability when institutional standards incorporate learning outcomes, problem-solving outcomes, and research outcomes as the focus of measurement and accountability. A succession of views on this point has unfolded (Deardorff, 2005; Hudzik, 2011; Hudzik & Stohl, 2009; Olson, Evans, & Shoenberg, 2007; Olson et al., 2005). In almost any endeavor, when institutional investments in time, energy, and redirected priorities enlarge, attention focuses questions on value added, outcomes, and impacts. It seems inescapable that given the general rise in calls for increased outcome accountability in higher education, institutional efforts to more fully engage globally will require attention to CI outcome assessment on indicators such as the following, undertaken in a systematic fashion connected to institutional missions and values (Hudzik & Stohl, 2009):

Learning Outcomes

- Identifiable knowledge competencies or learning objectives
- Standardized levels of language competency
- Positive impacts on attitudes, beliefs, skills, careers
- Increased capacity to learn from and with others from different cultures
- Meeting requirements of internationally defined credentials

Discovery (research, scholarship, engagement) Outcomes

- Refereed publications in international journals
- Invited speakers at international conferences and similar events

- Institutional position in global rankings
- International awards, prizes, and recognition
- Strategic cross-border collaborations that contribute to institutional mission objectives
- Global strategic alliances that strengthen institutional capacities
- Commercial applications income
- Impact on peoples' and communities' condition: economic, health, education, nutrition
- Safety/security and access

WHICH ACADEMIC DISCIPLINES AND PROFESSIONS?

The humanities and the social and behavioral sciences have been the principal disciplines undergirding higher education internationalization. The knowledge base they provide in languages, history, and culture and in comparative political, social, and economic systems remains core subject matter in international engagement. Over the past two decades, however, there has been an expansion of academic and professional programs incorporating international dimensions into their teaching and research. This reflects the changing global context. Thus, it is inadequate to understand business without understanding its global connections, to study food production and safety without reference to global trade in food, to examine communicable disease without understanding its cross-border origins and solutions, or to study the environment without understanding connections to the global environment. These changes indicate that all disciplines and programs of U.S. higher education will require international engagement to remain relevant.

Faculty

The most important factor in comprehensive internationalization is the faculty. Faculty control the curriculum and decisions to award academic credit, they do the research (along with graduate students), and they determine whether standards and criteria have been met for promotion and tenure. They are among the most powerful elements in the governance of an institution. An institution cannot internationalize without the active and agreeable participation of a majority of its faculty. A faculty barrier is potentially the most constraining (see Stohl, 2007).

Faculty need incentives, and funding is a significant inducement to internationalization, but it is not a sufficiently powerful inducement on its own. It is one thing to signal that international engagement is a permissible activity to include in a tenure package (e.g., internationalizing a course, being an invited speaker at an international conference, being engaged in collaborative research and publication with colleagues abroad), and quite another to suggest that it carries added or special weight, or further to suggest that it is expected or required. Brewer (2010) discusses a variety of strategies to encourage greater faculty commitment to internationalization, including recognizing the importance of "faculty ownership, choice and support" (Green & Olson, 2003, p. 78). Emmanuel (2010) identifies five dominant extrinsic motivational factors that have significant positive or negative effects on the internationalization of the curriculum by U.S. faculty:

> More funds to support student participation in internationalized programs; recognition, support and encouragement from dean or chair; more funds to support curriculum development and internationalization for off-campus courses (e.g., study abroad, exchange programs); more funds to support curriculum development and internationalization for on-campus courses (e.g., infusion, international subject matter courses); [and] inclusion of participation in internationalization efforts in your evaluation processes (salary increases, tenure, and promotion). (p. 177)

Cooper's and Mitsunaga's (2010, p. 79) research on faculty collaborations further support Stohl's (2007) argument that colleges and universities must emphasize the intrinsic benefits of international work in order to engage faculty understanding of the learning and discovery benefits that come with cross-cultural collaborative efforts.

The critical issue turns on what criteria are applied de facto by department-level promotion and tenure committees and administrators. As Fairweather (2002) argues, tenure and promotion are "the ultimate faculty evaluation." What actually happens is usually a matter of department culture, priorities, and interpretations of national disciplinary standards (see Amey & Brown, 2004). In general, the level of departmental recognition for international activity is likely to be uneven, running from hostile to heavily and actively supportive and rewarding, but balanced more toward the former than the latter (Amey & Brown, 2004). While administrators at the campus level more frequently recognize these difficulties, they also note that it will require a complete reorientation of the campus culture for changes in the key issue of faculty evaluation to occur.

Overarching Pressures on U.S. Higher Education With Implications for Comprehensive Internationalization

There are substantial pressures in U.S. higher education for change, from both internal and external sources (e.g., Hurley, 2009; National Governor's Association, 2010). Some pressures originate in budget shortfalls and the changing U.S. public- and private-sector financial landscapes, some come from a vocal customer pool that is now paying more for higher education, and some from calls for reform originating with basic concerns about quality (e.g., among other issues, whether graduates are workforce-ready and whether higher education is meeting social needs). We have selected eight topics of general reform to which we think CI also will have to be responsive.

1. Funding, accountability, and stature based on outcomes (e.g., what students actually learn, what they can do, what jobs they get, or the reputation and applications of faculty research) (Deardorff, 2009; Hudzik & Stohl, 2009; McPherson & Shulenburger, 2006; U.S. Department of Education, 2006). The growing pressure to measure value-added outcomes is spreading to internationalization.

2. Time and cost to degree (American Association of State Colleges and Universities, 2010; National Governors Association, 2010). Internationalizing the curriculum will require integrating new elements within existing requirements so as not to delay time to degree by adding requirements.

3. Growing use of strategic financial and cost/benefit analysis. The benefits of internationalization must survive its full cost assessment and not add significant new costs. Integration of CI into the academic core is essential (e.g., integrating international content into existing degree requirements, general education as well as majors) if it is to survive budget crises.

4. Pressure to spread cost by establishing interinstitutional partnerships/collaborations. Strategic and transformative partnerships (Sutton, 2010) across institutions and borders can help spread and control costs and build mutual capacity (Toope, 2010).

5. Pressure for innovation in practices. Campus internationalization leaders will need to be innovative in expanding access and delivery. Merely scaling up existing methods is not a practical solution. Of necessity, this will include jettisoning some traditional modes of delivery (e.g., traditional forms of language learning) and content. Further advances in CI will be inextricably tied to systematic creativity and innovation in its definition and delivery beyond merely scaling up (American Council on Education, 2008).

6. The pressure to build cross -mission synergies. Budget constraints prioritize investments that produce synergies across institutional missions. The internationalization of learning, research, and outreach will require their interconnection. As CI becomes intertwined with all relevant institutional missions (teaching, research, and outreach), it will require structures throughout campus to connect and coordinate interests and centers of capacity.

7. Responding to nontraditional students who are becoming the "usual." Internationalization must facilitate access and mobility for a more diverse client pool and for the many (part-time students, adult learners, those from more diverse socioeconomic groups), not just the few.

8. Global competition for the best faculty and students. As research capacity is critical in a knowledge society and as faculty and graduate students are the research engines of higher education, global recruitment for faculty and students will expand. This will require U.S. higher

education to recruit more systematically globally and will require government policies to facilitate it.

Summary

U.S. higher education generally and its international engagement will undergo substantial change in current and future decades in response to a combination of domestic factors and global forces. At home, the transition from public support to private investment for higher education, rising higher education costs overall, and calls for increased accountability will force their own sets of changes relating to improving system efficiency and effectiveness, which will provide a new context for further internationalization.

The rise of instructional and research capacity in global higher education will increase the level of competition as well as the need for collaboration between U.S. higher education and other national and emerging global systems. Signs are already emerging to suggest other additional changes that will emerge to further impact U.S. higher education, including mechanisms of quality control stretching across borders; more demand for value added from customers, both individuals and the public; a global higher education market and system expanding to confound nationally defined higher education policy; and challenges to balancing global market forces with key intellectual learning and discovery values as the drivers of change.

CI requires a paradigm shift in how U.S. higher education is likely to engage the altered global landscape. Although not all institutions will engage CI in the same ways, and although CI saliency will depend on its connection to institutional missions and values, it seems highly likely that the proportion of students, faculty, staff, and other clientele who become connected in learning, scholarship, and actions to a global higher education environment will expand. For this to be effective, internationalization efforts must move from campus periphery to campus core and be integrated more fully into institutional ethos. These changes are necessary if U.S. higher education is not to be marginalized in the rapidly changing domestic and global environments that now provide the wider arena of higher education. While the further internationalization of U.S. higher education institutions seems almost certain to continue, achieving successful outcomes will require an institutional approach to internationalization that is both strategic and comprehensive.

REFERENCES

Altbach, P. G., Reisberg, L., & Rumbley, L. (2009). *Trends in global higher education: Tracking an academic revolution.* Paris: UNESCO. Retrieved June 15, 2011, from http://unesdoc.unesco.org/images/0018/001832/183219e.pdf

American Association of State Colleges and Universities (AASC&U). (2010). *The top 10 higher education state policy issues for 2010* (Higher Education Policy Brief). Washington, DC: AASC&U.

American Council on Education (ACE). (2008). *Comprehensive internationalization.* Retrieved June 8, 2010, from http://www.acenet.edu/AM/Template.cfm?Section=Home%20&%20Template

Amey, M. J. (2010). Administrative perspectives on international partnerships. *New Directions for Higher Education, 57–67.*

Amey, M. J., & Brown, D. F. (2004). Breaking out of the box: Interdisciplinary collaboration and faculty work. Boston: Information Age Publishing.

Banks, M., Olsen, A., & Pearce, D. (2007). *Global student mobility: An Australian perspective five years on.* Canberra, Australia: IDP Education.

Biddle, S. (2002). *Internationalization: Rhetoric or reality* (ACLS Occasional Paper, No. 56). New York: American Council of Learned Societies.

Blumenstyk, H. (2009, October 25). In a time of uncertainty, colleges hold fast to the status quo. *The Chronicle of Higher Education.* Retrieved October 25, 2009, from http://chronicle.com/article/In-a-Time-of-Uncertainty/48911/

Brandenburg, U., & de Wit, H. (2011). The end of internationalization. *International Higher Education, 62,* 15–17.

Brewer, D. J., & Tierney, W. G. (2010, June). Barriers to innovation in U.S. higher education. Paper presented at the American Enterprise Institute Conference, *Reinventing the American University: The Promise of Innovation in Higher Education.* Retrieved June 15, 2011, from http://www.aei.org/event/100218.

Brewer, E. (2010). Leveraging partnerships to internationalize the liberal arts college: Campus internationalization and the faculty. *New Directions for Higher Education, 83–96.*

Brown, F. (2007). The organisation and administration of colleges and universities. *Higher Education Quarterly, 3,* 453–461.

Childress, L. K. (2009). Internationalization plans for higher education institutions. *Journal of Studies in International Education, 13,* 289–303.

Childress, L. K. (2010). Twenty-first century university: Developing faculty engagement in internationalization. New York: Peter Lang.

Cooper, J., & Mitsunaga, R. (2010). Faculty perspectives on international education: The nested realities of faculty collaborations. *New Directions for Higher Education, 69–81.*

Deardorff, D. K. (2005, May/June). A matter of logic. *International Educator, 26–31.*

Deardorff, D. K. (Ed.) (2009). *The SAGE handbook of intercultural competence.* Thousand Oaks, CA: Sage.

Dewey, P. (2009). Reason before passion: Faculty views on internationalization in higher education. *Higher Education, 58,* 491–504.

de Wit, H. (1995). *Strategies of internationalization of higher education. A comparative study of Australia, Canada, Europe, and the United States.* Amsterdam: European Association for International Education.

de Wit, H. (1998). *Rationales for internationalisation of higher education.* Viseu, Portugal: Polytechnic Institute of Viseu. Retrieved May 11, 2010, from http://www.ipv.pt/millenium/witll.htm

Duderstadt, J. J. (2009, March). *Current global trends in higher education and research: Their impact on Europe.* Dies Academicus 2009 address presented at Universitat Wien, Vienna, Austria.

Ellingboe, B. J. (1998). Divisional strategies to internationalize a campus portrait: Results, resistance, and recommendations from a case study at a U.S. university. In J. A. Mestenhauser & B. J. Ellingboe (Eds.), *Reforming the higher education curriculum: Internationalizing the campus* (pp. 198–228). Phoenix, AZ: Oryx.

Emmanuel, J. F. (2010). Motivational factors and worldview dimensions associated with perceptions of global education initiatives by U.S. college professors (Paper 1668). Theses and Dissertations, University of South Florida.

Engberg, D., & Green, M. F. (Eds). (2002). *Promising practices: Spotlighting excellence in comprehensive internationalization.* Washington, DC: American Council on Education.

Fairweather, J. S. (2002). The ultimate faculty evaluation: Promotion and tenure decisions. In C. L. Colbeck (Ed.), *Evaluating faculty performance.* San Francisco: Jossey-Bass.

Gibbons, J. H. (2007). The university of the twenty-first century: Artifact, sea anchor, or pathfinder. In W. T. Greenough,

P. J. McConnaughay, & J. P. Kesan (Eds.), *Defining values for research and technology: The university's changing role.* Plymouth, UK: Rowman & Littlefield.

Green, M. F. (2005). Internationalization of U.S. higher education: A student perspective. Washington, DC: American Council on Education.

Green, M., & Olson, C. (2003). *Internationalizing the campus: A user's guide.* Washington, DC: American Council on Education, Center for Institutional and International Initiatives.

Green, M. F., Luu, D., & Burris, B. (2008). *Mapping internationalization on U.S. campuses.* Washington, DC: American Council on Education.

Haddad, G. (2006). *The importance of internationalization of higher education.* Paper presented at the International Association of Universities Conference on the Internationalization of Higher Education: New Directions, New Challenges. Beijing, China.

Heyl, J. D. (2007). *The senior internationalization officer (SIO) as change agent.* Durham, NC: Association of International Education Administrators.

Hudzik, J. K. (2010, May/June). The economy, higher education and campus internationalization. *International Educator, 96–102.*

Hudzik, J. K. (2011). *Comprehensive internationalization: From concept to action.* Washington, DC: NAFSA Association of International Educators.

Hudzik, J. K., & Stohl, M. (2009). Modeling assessment of outcomes and impacts from internationalization. In H. de Wit (Ed.), *Measuring success in the internationalisation of higher education* (EAIE Occasional Paper 22). Amsterdam: European Association for International Education.

Hurley, D. J. (2009). *Considerations for state colleges and universities in a post-recession America.* Washington, DC: American Association of State Colleges and Universities. Retrieved from http://www.congressweb.com/aascu/docfiles/Considerations-AASCU11-09.pdf

Institute of International Education (IIE). (2010). *Open doors 2010 fast facts.* Retrieved June 15, 2011, from http://www.iie.org/en/Research-and-Publications/Open-Doors

Institute of International Education (IIE). (2011). *Open Doors 2011 fast facts.* Retrieved November 17, 2011, from http://www.iie.org/en/Research-and-Publications/~/media/Files/Corporate/Open-Doors/Fast-Facts/Fast-Facts-2011.ashx

Kearney, M. L., & Yelland, R. (2010). *Higher education in a world changed utterly: Doing more with less* (Discussion Paper). Paris: OECD/IMHE General Conference Institutional Management in Higher Education.

Knapp, L. G., Kelly-Reid, J. E., & Grinder, S. A. (2008). Postsecondary institutions in the United States: Fall 2007. First look. Washington, DC: U.S. Department of Education, IES National Center for Education Statistics. Retrieved June 15, 2010, from http://nces.ed.gov/pubs2008/2008159rev.pdf

Knezo, G. J. (2006). "Sensitive but unclassified" information and other controls: Policy and options for scientific and technical information (CRS Report for Congress). Washington, DC: The Library of Congress.

Knight, J. (1999). Internationalisation of higher education. In *Quality and internationalisation in higher education.* Paris: Organization for Economic Cooperation and Development.

Knight, J. (2001). Monitoring the quality and progress of internationalization. *Journal of Studies in International Education, 5,* 228–243.

Knight, J. (2002). *Developing an institutional self-portrait using the internationalization quality review process guidelines.* Retrieved June 10, 2010, from http://www.aucc.ca/events/2010/e-group/iqrp.pdf

Knight, J. (2007). Internationalization brings important benefits as well as risks. *International Higher Education, 46.*

Knight, J., & de Wit, H., (Eds.). (1999). Internationalisation of higher education. In *Quality and internationalisation in higher education.* Paris: OECD.

Marginson, S. (2010, May 30). The rise of the global university: 5 new tensions. *The Chronicle of Higher Education,* Commentary. Retrieved July 19, 2010, from http//chronicle.com/article/The-Rise-of-the-Global/65694/

McDowell, G. R. (2001). *Land-grant universities and extension into the 21st century: Renegotiating or abandoning a social contract.* Ames: Iowa State University Press.

McPherson, P., & Shulenburger, D. (2006). *Toward a voluntary system of accountability (VSA) for public universities and colleges.* Washington, DC: National Association of State Universities and Land-Grant Colleges (now Association of Public and Land-grant Universities (APLU)). Retrieved June 10, 2010, from http://www.aplu.org/NetCommunity/Document.Doc?id=2556

Mestenhauser, J. A. (1998). International education on the verge: In search of new paradigm. *International Educator, 7*(2–3): 68–76.

NAFSA: Association of International Educators. (2010). *Senator Paul Simon Award for campus internationalization.* Retrieved June 15, 2011,

from www.nafsa.org/about/default
.aspx?id=16296

NAFSA Task Force on Internationalization. (2008).
*NAFSA's contribution to internationalization
of higher education.* Washington, DC: NAFSA
Association of International Educators.
Retrieved June 1, 2010, from www.nafsa.org/
uploadedFiles/nafsas contribution.
pdf?n=8167

National Association of State Budget Officers and
the National Association of State Legislators.
(2010, November 15). *A new funding paradigm
for higher education* (Miller Center Paper on
Higher Education Funding. Retrieved May 8,
2011, from http://www.nasbo.org/Link
Click.aspx?fileticket=MEqFX1WtTPY%3
D&tabid=38

National Governors Association. (2010, February
23). *The big reset: State government after the
great recession.* Paper prepared by J. Thomasian
of the National Governors Association Center
for Best Practices. Washington, DC: Author.

National Science Board (NSB). (2010). *Science and
engineering indicators (2010).* Arlington, VA:
National Science Foundation Board.

Olson, C. L., Evans, R., & Shoenberg, R. F. (2007). *At
home in the world: Bridging the gap between
internationalization and multicultural education.*
Washington, DC: American Council on
Education.

Olson, C. L., Green, M. F., & Hill, B. A. (2005).
*Building a strategic framework for
comprehensive internationalization.*
Washington, DC: American Council on
Education.

Organization for Economic Cooperation and
Development (OECD). (2008). *Education at a
glance 2008.* Paris: Author.

Organization for Economic Cooperation and
Development (OECD). (2010a). *Education at a
glance 2010.* Paris: Author.

Organization for Economic Cooperation and
Development (OECD). (2010b). *Highlights from
education at a glance 2010.* Paris: Author.

Paige, M. R. (2005). Internationalization of higher
education: Performance assessment and
indicators. *Nagoya Journal of Higher Education,
5,* 99–122.

Pew Center on the State. (2010). *The state of the
states 2010: How the recession might change
states.* Washington, DC: The Pew Charitable
Trusts.

Program for Research on Private Higher Education.
(2010). *Private and public higher education
shares for 117 countries* (updated November
2010). Retrieved June 15, 2011, from http://
www.albany.edu/dept/eaps/prophe/data/
international.html

QS Top Universities. (2010). *QS world university
rankings 2010.* Retrieved June 1, 2011, from
http://www.topuniversities.com/university
-rankings/world-university-rankings/2010.

Rogers, E. M. (2003). *Diffusion of innovations.* New
York: Free Press.

Ruby, A. (2010). *The uncertain future for
international higher education in the Asia-
Pacific region.* Washington, DC: NAFSA:
Association of International Educators.
Retrieved June 1, 2011, from www.nafsa.org/
uploadedFiles/NAFSA Home/Resource Library
Assets/Networks/SIO/UncertainFuture.pdf

Shanghai Jiao Tung. (2010). *Academic ranking of
world universities.* Retrieved from http://www
.shanghairanking.com/

Spellings, M. (2006). *A test of leadership: Charting the
future of U.S. higher education.* Washington, DC:
U.S. Department of Education.

State Higher Education Executive Officers. (2011).
State higher education finance: FY 2010.
Retrieved from http://www.sheeo.org

Stohl, M. (2007). We have met the enemy and
he is US: The role of the faculty in
internationalization of higher education in the
coming decade. *Journal of Studies in
International Education, 11*(3–4), 359–372.

Sutton, S. B. (2010). Transforming internationalization through partnerships. *International
Educator, 19*(1), 60–63.

Teixeira, P. (2009). Mass higher education and
private institutions. In *Higher education to 2030:
Vol. 2. Globalization* (pp. 231–258). Paris:
Organization for Economic Cooperation and
Development.

Times Higher Education. (2010). *The world
university rankings.* Retrieved June 1, 2011, from
http://www.timeshighereducation.co.uk/
worlduniversity-rankings/

Toope, S. J. (2010). Global challenges and the
organizational-ethical dilemmas of universities.
Inside Higher Education. Retrieved June 1, 2011,
from http://www.insidehighered.com/blogs/
globalhighered/stephen_toope_ubc_on_global
_challenges_and_the_organizational_ethical
_dilemmas_of_universities

Tucker, R. (2010). Four barriers to innovation.
Inside Higher Education. Retrieved June 1, 2011,
from http://insidehighered.com/
news/2010/06/04/aei

U.S. Department of Education. (2006).
*A test of leadership: Charting the future of
U.S. higher education* (A report of the
Secretary of Education's Commission on the
Future of Higher Education). Washington, DC:
Author.

U.S. Department of Education. (2009). *Fast facts:
Total enrollment in degree granting*

institutions 2007. Washington, DC: U.S. Department of Education, IES National Center for Education Statistics. Retrieved June 1, 2010, from http://nces.ed.gov/ fastfacts/display.asp?id=98

White, B. P., & Eckel, P. D. (2008). *Leadership challenges for higher education's future.* Washington, DC: American Council on Education.

Wildavsky, B. (2010). *The great brain race: How global universities are reshaping the world.* Princeton, NJ: Princeton University Press.

Wiley, D. (2001). Forty years of the Title VI and Fulbright. In P. O'Meara, H. D. Mehlinger, & R. Ma Newman (Eds.), *Changing perspectives on international education* (pp.11–29). Bloomington: Indiana University Press.

NOTES

1   The American Council on Education (ACE) initially popularized use of the term *comprehensive internationalization* in works such as *A Handbook for Advancing Comprehensive Internationalization* (2006) and *Building a Strategic Framework for Comprehensive Internationalization* (2005). NAFSA's Senator Paul Simon Award for Comprehensive Internationalization has served to highlight campuses whose policies and practices are among the best in advancing aspects of comprehensive internationalization. The term, however, has not had a universal operational meaning. For example, much of ACE's use of the term focuses on the instructional missions of institutions rather than research and outreach per se.

5

Europe's Bologna Process and Its Impact on Global Higher Education

Jeroen Huisman, Clifford Adelman, Chuo-Chun Hsieh, Farshid Shams, and Stephen Wilkins

This chapter describes the developments in the Bologna Process, which started in 1999. The attempt to realize the European Higher Education Area (EHEA) is arguably one of the largest reform projects in higher education, and such reform initiatives warrant a critical assessment of their achievements. The reform has impacted or will impact the specific context in which many internationalization practitioners, not only in Europe but also beyond, will have to carry out their professional activities. The intended consequences include easier international cooperation and related activities, but—as with many reforms—there are unintended side effects that complicate matters of international cooperation and exchange. The chapter will focus on achievements in terms of policies and progress in the member states of the EHEA and will also look in some depth at the spin-off of the Bologna Process: Has the process triggered similar reform processes in other regions? And if so, how and what are the impacts? And what does this all imply for practitioners in the area of international higher education? These questions are addressed in part with boxes that review Bologna-responsive events in other parts of the world.

Introduction

The year 1999 will very likely appear in the history books as a key moment in European higher education. Representatives of 29 European countries signed the Bologna Declaration on June 19. The document's four pages (excluding the pages with signatures) stressed the need to collectively work toward an internationally competitive EHEA, which would promote mobility and employability of its citizens and would aim at greater compatibility and comparability of the higher education systems.

In many respects, the Bologna Declaration and the ensuing process are special. For instance, various analysts have pointed at its ambiguous and vague objectives (Neave, 2002), the high ambitions, the long-term perspective of the process (Witte, Huisman, & Purser, 2009), the changing policy agenda over time (Kehm, Huisman, & Stensaker, 2009), and the changing composition of the stakeholders involved in the process (e.g., Keeling, 2006; Neave & Maassen, 2007).

Despite—or possibly thanks to—these unique characteristics, much has been achieved in the first decade of the process. This chapter, first, sets out the background of the process and how it unfolded. Second, the key achievements across the signatories will be summarized, answering the question of what has been accomplished with respect to the various action lines of the process. Third, responses of other world regions will be addressed. As soon as the Bologna Process gained momentum, those involved were curious to learn to what extent the Bologna Process should or could be extended to other parts of the world (Zgaga, 2006, p. iv). This was called the "external dimension" of the Bologna Process. Zgaga's report yields insight about what happened in the first 5 years, and it is worthwhile to reassess the situation after the first decade. This chapter is, however, broadly interested in the external responses to the process and the extent to which other regions have developed collective policies to tackle the challenges put forward by the Bologna Declaration and subsequent communiqués. Fourth, the chapter looks ahead and focuses on what could happen toward 2020. The final section reflects on the consequences for policy and practice.

In the description and analysis, we rely on publicly available information in the academic, policy, and practice domains. The findings of earlier evaluations of the Bologna Process, particularly the 2007 report (Huisman, Witte, & File, 2007), and included, with heavy reliance on the independent evaluation project of the Bologna Process (Westerheijden et al., 2010), in which the lead author of this chapter was involved.

THE PROCESS

Historical Roots

Seeds for many elements of the Bologna Process were sown decades earlier. From the 1970s onward, student mobility had been on the rise. Students, either on their own or participating in structural arrangements, increasingly looked for opportunities to have an educational experience abroad. Initially, structural arrangements were national or bilateral, allowing students to stay abroad for a certain period of study with the support of a national grant system. Organizations like the Netherlands Organization for International Cooperation in Higher Education, the German Academic Exchange Service, and the British Council supported their national students and staff in going abroad, mostly through grants for short visits.

European initiatives such as the Joint Study Program Scheme (launched in 1976) and the European Action Scheme for the Mobility of University Students (Erasmus, launched in 1987) brought a supranational dimension to mobility and exchange and paved the way for a broader set of study abroad options for European students. The programs provided financial support for students and staff staying abroad. Initially, these supranational programs were only for students from countries part of the then-European Economic Community, the predecessor of the current European Union (EU). Later, non-EU members were also allowed to participate in the program.

Both the national and European mobility policy initiatives were largely driven by academic and cultural rationales. For the British Council, the primary focus was to promote the cultural understanding of Britain through partnership (Fisher, 2009), and the European objective in the 1970s was to cooperate for improvement and development. This European objective was arguably driven by political constraints. The then-member states were somewhat reluctant to go beyond cooperation and toward supragovernmental steering, coordination, and integration. At that time, education as a social-cultural phenomenon was seen as falling under the principle of national sovereignty, hence the strong preference of most member states for an intergovernmental approach (de Wit & Verhoeven, 2001; Teichler, 1998).

Obviously, the national and European objectives of the time regarding mobility and student and staff exchange did not persist, and various factors contributed to gradual changes in the objectives. Internal and external dynamics of the mobility programs contributed largely to the changes. First, because of the increasing success of the mobility programs, broader internationalization questions started to emerge on the agendas of higher education institutions, national governments, and their internationalization agencies. From the perspective of the higher education institution, the question of which institutions were comparable and thus suitable for an Erasmus exchange became important. From the government's perspective, the issue of transparency (and recognition) of foreign programs and degrees became much more pertinent. From the students' perspective, questions were raised regarding how the experience abroad would fit in with the home experience. This question was followed by the more specific question of whether and how credits earned abroad would count toward the home degree. In many European countries, the attention to issues beyond mobility led to broader internationalization policies at the national level and broader internationalization strategies at institutions (Huisman & Van der Wende, 2004, 2005; Kälvemark & Van der Wende, 1996).

Second, an external dynamic played a significant role. Mobility and internationalization in the broader sense, previously driven largely by social and cultural objectives, became increasingly connected to broader economic imperatives. For example, the British initiative to recruit international fee-paying students was a higher education policy based on an explicit economic export and trade perspective (Elliot, 1998). Also, at the European level, (higher) education was put forward as a key driver for further economic development and growth. The European idea of free movement of capital, goods, services, and people gradually spilled over to the domain of higher education (de Wit & Verhoeven, 2001, p. 204). Consequently, the sharp edges of previous debates on sovereign and subsidiary—in the past strongly fueled by particular national sentiments—disappeared, and there was generally more acceptance of the fact that steps *could*—and in some actors' minds *should*—be taken to explore how the traditional cooperation efforts could be tilted to another plane: that of harmonization and integration.

Sorbonne Declaration

Taking the internal and external dynamics together, considerable scope emerged for initiatives beyond mobility and student and staff exchange. The theme of harmonization is taken up by the signatories of the immediate predecessor of the Bologna Declaration, the 1998 Sorbonne Declaration. As part of the celebration of the 800th anniversary of the Sorbonne University in Paris, four ministers responsible for higher education in France, Italy, Germany, and the United Kingdom signed a declaration about harmonizing the architecture of the European higher education system. The declaration aimed at creating a European area of higher education, and concrete measures were mentioned: a common two-cycle degree structure, mutual recognition of degrees, and an increase of mobility. The declaration added that the aim of harmonization should not be taken too literally, however, and the objective should not be achieved at all costs. It stressed that the creation of the European area was subject to those situations "where national identities and common interests can interact and strengthen each other" (Sorbonne Declaration, 1998; see Witte, 2006, pp. 124–129 for details).

Even with this understanding of the objectives—that harmonization would be voluntary, as long as collective interests were served and national identities preserved—one would wonder why four national ministers would put so much effort into an intergovernmental process. The key for understanding this lies in the political fact that three of the four ministers saw the initiative as a strategy to address domestic higher education problems (Witte, 2006, pp. 125–126). This is also visible in the motives and actions of some countries that later joined the Bologna Process (see, e.g., Gornitzka, 2006; Välimaa, Hoffman, & Huusko, 2006). Neave (2002, p. 186) also alludes to this by noting that existing developments are included or presented under the Bologna banner, suggesting progress and considerable consensus. The Sorbonne Declaration closes with an invitation to other European countries to join the initiative.

Bologna Declaration and Process

A year later, representatives of 29 European countries met in Bologna to discuss a follow-up to the Sorbonne Declaration. They agreed to work towards the realization of the EHEA. Various interrelated objectives are mentioned throughout the document, including increasing the attractiveness of European higher education, promoting European citizens' mobility and employability, and enhancing comparability and compatibility of the higher education systems.

Six action lines were proposed:

- the adoption of a system of easily readable and comparable degrees (including the implementation of the diploma supplement)
- adoption of a system essentially based on two main cycles: undergraduate and graduate
- establishment of a system of credits as a proper means of promoting mobility
- promotion of student and staff mobility
- promotion of European cooperation in quality assurance
- promotion of the necessary European dimensions in higher education (Bologna Declaration, 1999)

The key objectives were to be achieved by 2010, and bi-annual meetings were suggested to take stock of progress and consider changes to the policy agenda. In the successive meetings of the ministers responsible for higher education (in Prague, 2001; Berlin, 2003; Bergen, 2005; London, 2007; Leuven/Louvain-la-Neuve, 2009; Budapest/Vienna, 2010), the communiqués addressed additional action lines and changed some of the directions. For instance, lifelong learning was added to the agenda in Prague (2001), and the third cycle—doctoral training— was added in Berlin (2003). Also in Berlin, the quality action line was further operationalized. The European Network for Quality Assurance in Higher Education (ENQA) was asked to cooperate with the higher education institutions' umbrella organizations and with the European Student Union to develop a set of standards, procedures, and guidelines on quality assurance.

The Significant Others

Readers may now have a sense of the background of the Bologna Process and understand that it was to some extent a logical follow-up to policy developments in the preceding decades. In terms of the declaration's wording, the text should not be taken too literally; it is an attempt to set a policy train in motion. In addition, the policy train is a "moving target," as Kehm et al. (2009) have said. The agenda changed during the first decade of the reform process, and new targets have been set for the next decade.

This leaves one issue that is generally misunderstood by relative outsiders, and that is the ownership of the process. From the outset, the Bologna Process is presented as an intergovernmental process. However, supranational agencies played an important role in the preparations for the meeting in Bologna. Shortly after the Bologna Declaration, the European Council (2000) launched the Lisbon process, which aimed at making the EU the most competitive and dynamic knowledge-based economy in the world by 2010. The focus of this process—rather similar to the Bologna Process (see also Van der Wende & Huisman, 2004)—is more on research, development, and innovation, but it definitely touches on elements of the teaching and learning fabric, if only because many higher education institutions in Europe deal with both teaching and research. More explicitly, the involvement of the European Commission is visible in two ways. First, it was a supporter of the Bologna Process in helping to prepare the text of the declaration and a sponsor of the background report, *Trends in Learning Structures in Higher Education* (Haug, Kirstein, & Knudsen, 1999) (see Witte, 2006, pp. 129–130). After the Bologna Declaration appeared, the European Commission continued to fund research, professionalization, and network projects under the Lifelong Learning Program, which would help to disseminate Bologna (and Bologna-related) best practices. The Tuning project is a good example of a project initially endorsed with EU-funding that had a considerable impact on the further development of the Bologna Process, especially further thinking, conceptually and practically, about learning outcomes and their comparability across countries. Second, the European Commission has developed its own higher education strategy, building upon the Lisbon process but skilfully bringing on board elements of the Bologna Process. The European Commission's communications (e.g., European Commission, 2005, 2006) focus on funding, governance, and curriculum and—not surprisingly—many of the suggestions made regarding curriculum resonate with the Bologna Process. Keeling (2006) details the gradual interweavements of the supranational and intergovernmental processes (see also Gornitzka, 2010).

To complicate things further, various interest groups involved in the Bologna Process must be mentioned. Obviously, the Bologna

Process is ultimately about change processes to take place in reality (Neave & Maassen, 2007, p. 138). After the Bologna meeting, a steering and consultative group were set up to coordinate the process. A few years later, the Bologna Follow Up Group would be institutionalized, consisting of representatives of all signatory countries, the European Commission, and consultative members: the European Association of Universities, the European Association of Institutions in Higher Education, the National Unions of Students in Europe (later European Student Union), ENQA, Council of Europe, UNESCO (through its *Centre Européen pour l'Enseignement Supérieur*), Education International (representing the European academics), and Business Europe. Although being observers, obviously they have been able to influence the process to some extent and to communicate their views externally (see also Lažetić, 2010, for an analysis of dynamics in the follow-up group). The students have, for example, been trying to influence and steer the Bologna Process through the bi-annual "Bologna with student eyes" reports (European Student Union, 2009) and the European Association of Universities has been involved in the bi-annual stock-taking exercises (e.g., Reichert & Tauch, 2003).

In sum, the Bologna Process quickly developed from an intergovernmental policy process into a multilevel, multi-actor governance process, which revolves largely around the concept of mutual adjustment as the mode of coordination (Witte, 2006).

The Outcomes So Far

Although changes in the action lines over the years make it difficult to determine exactly what they are today, there is considerable agreement (see Rauhvargers, 2011; Westerheijden et al., 2010) that the following issues are key to the Bologna Process:

- three-cycle degree structure
- national qualifications frameworks
- quality assurance
- recognition of qualifications and credits, and prior learning
- student and staff mobility
- social dimension of the EHEA

What follows is a stock-taking exercise, without an attempt to attribute the state of the art to the Bologna Process as such, or—indeed—an attempt to qualify the Bologna Process as a success (or not) (see Westerheijden et al., 2010, for a thoughtful reflection, see also Neave, 2002).

The overall assessment of the Westerheijden et al. (2010, pp. 5–7) report is helpful to understand the general achievements. The report states that most of the architectural elements have been implemented in most of the Bologna countries: That is, elements of legislation and regulation are in place at the national levels. Also, governments have often allocated funds to higher education institutions to realize the national and intergovernmental objectives. There are, however, important differences between the signatory countries. Some have moved much faster than others, and—not that surprisingly—newcomer countries (about 17 of the current 47 Bologna countries joined in 2001–2005)—were often slower compared to the early adopters. Because of the different starting points, different domestic issues and problems, and different governance arrangements, Bologna countries followed different policy trajectories to reach the objectives. In addition, because of the different contexts, the reforms and achievements sometimes differed from the Bologna intentions. The different contexts also explain to some extent why some countries have been able to achieve some objectives earlier or better than others, while they at the same time may be lagging in realizing other objectives.

Three-Cycle Degree Structures

Before the Bologna Declaration, degree structures differed considerably, both in terms of the overall length of programs and in terms of cycles constituting the structure. Although about 30 countries already had clear or sometimes informal distinctions between two cycles, the length of the cycles differed significantly. In some countries, undergraduate programs took 3 years, in others—particularly in central and eastern Europe (see, e.g., File & Goedegebuure, 2003)—they could be much longer, up to 5, 6, or even 7 years. The same goes for the graduate level, with various lengths for master's-type degrees (1 to 3 years) and the doctoral cycle. The latter cycle might take 2 to 4 years, but in many countries, this was not specified at all, based on the idea that it would take as long as it takes the student to deliver the thesis. But many countries also had intermediary qualifications, either at the undergraduate level (associate degrees) or at the graduate level (diploma, certificates) (see, e.g., Schrier & Kaiser, 1998). Also, there were considerable differences between the disciplines, with professional qualifications in medicine, dentistry, and veterinary sciences—and sometimes also engineering—taking more time than programs in arts, humanities, and social sciences.

At the end of the first Bologna decade, the signatory countries all have adopted a two- or three-cycle degree system. The length of the first cycle ranges from 3 to 4 years (180 to 240 credits), the length of the second cycle is between 1 and 2 years (60 to 120 credits). The combination "180 + 120" is now the most prominent model (19 countries) in the EHEA. Many countries have structured their doctoral programs and integrated these in the cycle structure. Short-cycle programs and intermediary qualifications continue to exist or were introduced during the Bologna Process. Also, all countries make use of the European Credit Transfer and Accumulation System (ECTS), are working toward this, or are using a domestic system that is compatible with ECTS.

It is important to point out potential differences between politics and reality (Neave & Maassen, 2007). Whereas the architecture for the EHEA may be in place, it does not mean that everything is in place at the institutional level. Westerheijden et al. (2010, p. 7) report, for example, that in seven signatory countries—including Germany and Russia—the percentage of students in the two-cycle structures is still below 50%. Also, in the majority of countries, one or more disciplines are exempted from having to comply with the Bologna cycle structure (see Huisman et al., 2007). Although ECTS has been implemented, many programs and higher education institutions have not yet made the necessary connections between credits and student workload and learning outcomes.

National Qualification Frameworks

Qualification frameworks, defining graduates' competences (knowledge, skills, and attitudes) and learning outcomes (what the learner will know, understand, and be able to demonstrate

on graduation) at the various qualification levels were marginal in pre-Bologna higher education. After it became a topic on the Bologna agenda in 2003, various countries started developing qualification frameworks. The so-called Dublin descriptors (defining in general terms what knowledge and skills students should acquire for the different cycles) were accepted at the 2005 meeting in Bergen as the building blocks for the European-level qualification framework. That framework would then guide countries to work toward national qualification frameworks. Some countries, for example, Ireland and Scotland, could relatively easily adjust their existing frameworks to the European framework.

After the first decade, only eight EHEA countries have national qualification frameworks in place. The deadline for meeting this objective was extended to 2012. It should be emphasized that the development is only a first step toward the next important phase: that of adjusting curricula and (re)defining learning outcomes for programs at the higher education institutions to the frameworks.

Bearing in mind that a top-down approach may be seen as a highly abstract and complicated issue, it is important to mention a highly relevant bottom-up initiative. From 2000, the Tuning Educational Structures in Europe project (in short: Tuning) has worked on defining workload, level, learning outcomes, competences, and profiles for different areas of knowledge. Apparently, it was easier to discuss issues of competences at the level of the (sub)discipline, and the involvement of experts in the disciplines across Europe has certainly contributed to the success of the Tuning project (Tuning, 2011b).

Quality Assurance

Some European countries had external quality assurance systems in place before Bologna. Pioneers in Western Europe started developing and implementing these systems in the 1980s (United Kingdom, France, the Netherlands). The pattern for many central and eastern European countries was different. After the fall of the communist regimes, many countries adopted a state-controlled accreditation system at the program or institutional levels (Van der Wende & Westerheijden, 2003). Gradually, other countries started to adopt quality assurance systems as well. A 1994 EU pilot project and the launch of ENQA in 2000 gave impetus to the spread of the quality movement (Van der Wende & Westerheijden, 2003, pp. 178–179). By that time, almost all Western European countries had a governmental policy regarding quality assurance in place (Scheele, Maassen, & Westerheijden, 1998). Although models differed considerably across countries, common elements were a managing agent, self-evaluation, peer review, public reporting, and funding consequences, mostly indirect (Van Vught & Westerheijden, 1994).

After a decade of Bologna reform, almost all countries now have internal and external quality assurance systems in place on a system-wide scale. ENQA—in cooperation with the European Student Union, the European Association of Institutions of Higher Education, and the European University Association—has developed European Standards and Guidelines (ESG) for quality assurance, and these were adopted in 2005. The ESG consist of three parts: internal quality assurance, external quality assurance of higher education institutions, and external quality assurance of quality assurance agencies. As such, the ESG provide a model for countries and national agencies setting up or adjusting their quality assurance systems.

As such, the objective to promote European cooperation in quality assurance and to develop comparable criteria and methodologies—however vague this may have sounded in 1999—has largely been achieved. The ESG contribute to achieving consensus on good practice, and some transparency has emerged, for it is relatively clear which quality assurance agencies are trustworthy. To broaden the transparency beyond European agencies, an independent register of quality assessment agencies (EQAR) has also been set up.

Also here, reservations must be noted regarding progress. Arguably, much more attention is paid to quality assurance than a decade ago, but that does not imply that internal quality assurance mechanisms are in place at all higher education institutions. The ESG are particularly important for national level organizations, so they can show compliance (and hence be accepted as legitimate actors). In their analysis of reviews of national quality assurance agencies, however, Stensaker, Harvey, Huisman, Langfeldt, and Westerheijden (2010) note a lack of transparency in how assessments are actually made. A similar comment relates to the relationship between ENQA and EQAR: all EQAR-listed agencies are full members of ENQA, and some agencies are—on the basis of the same criteria—accepted by ENQA but not by EQAR. Most important, the impact on shop-floor level quality assurance and improvement and enhanced student experience is questionable (Huisman & Westerheijden, 2010).

Recognition of Qualifications, Credits, and Prior Learning

The issues under the heading of recognition all point in the direction of creating greater transparency about what students have learned. The assumption is that students could be much more mobile if they could easily carry their credentials—formulated in a language easily accessible to all higher education institutions in signatory countries—with them on their intellectual journeys across the EHEA.

The overwhelming majority of Bologna countries have signed the 1997 Lisbon Recognition Convention. This convention, developed before the Sorbonne and Bologna Declaration by the Council of Europe and UNESCO, entails multilateral legal agreements between signatories. The agreement specifies that countries recognize foreign academic qualifications as similar to the corresponding qualification in the domestic system, unless evidence can be provided that there are substantial differences between domestic and foreign qualification. Here it is important to formally distinguish between recognition of academic qualification and recognition of professional qualifications, the latter being regulated by directives of the EU (and therefore applying only to EU members). Other parts of the Lisbon Recognition Convention detail that countries should provide the necessary information on the higher education system and institutions in their country and to maintain national information centers in charge of supplying information and advice regarding recognition. During the Bologna Process, it became clear that signing and ratifying the Lisbon convention was an important step but did not ensure harmonization. Consequently, signatory countries had quite different procedures and instruments in place (see Rauhvargers & Rusakova, 2008). In fact, the differences were substantial, and Westerheijden et al. (2010) found no coherent approach to recognition yet. In June 2010, a revised recommendation on criteria and procedures for the assessment of foreign qualifications appeared (UNESCO & Council of Europe, 2010).

Specific tools to increase transparency, mentioned in the Lisbon convention and taken up in the Bologna Declaration, are ECTS and the Diploma Supplement. Qualification frameworks are another tool for recognition. The implementation of Diploma Supplements, giving evidence of courses taken and credits earned in a language widely spoken in Europe, has been achieved in most countries. Most of the institutions in two thirds of the Bologna countries automatically issue a Diploma Supplement free of charge.

More transparency on the recognition of prior learning is the least developed topic in the context of recognition. This is an (intermediate) objective, both to support increasing recognition and to support widening access and increasing participation. Fourteen of the Bologna signatories have domestic recognition policies to assess nonformal prior learning to pass a judgment on access to specific forms or levels of higher education. That said, there are also countries where national policies are not in place, but where many of the higher education institutions recognize prior learning. Also, limited use of recognition policies was found in many countries. Overall, the pattern is very varied, which calls for further actions.

Student and Staff Mobility

Acknowledging the importance of staff mobility, this section focuses on student mobility. Ultimately, many elements of the Bologna Process should be judged in light of the overall aim to increase citizens' mobility and employability across Europe but also, with respect to inward mobility, to increase the attractiveness of European higher education. The aim of improving mobility goes back to earlier initiatives to increase student and staff mobility, for example, through the Erasmus program. Although institutionalized supranational and national mobility programs have played and continue to play an important role, it should be emphasized that most student mobility takes place at the students' own initiative, outside the mobility programs. This has implications for the visibility of student mobility. Although data have improved, there is still a lack of insight in individual mobility and limited data on credit mobility. A conceptual

issue is how to define international mobility. Many sources use citizenship as a criterion, but residency would be a better one (see also Kelo, Teichler, & Wächter, 2006).

With respect to actual change in student degree mobility across EHEA countries, Westerheijden et al. (2010) compared 1999 and 2007 data on foreign students in the EHEA, looking separately at foreign students from other EHEA countries and students from outside the EHEA. The percentage of foreign non-EHEA students in the total student population has increased from 1.6% to 2.6%. That growth is very uneven, with countries showing significant increases (more than double the number of foreign students in 2007) and countries showing decreases. This makes it hard to maintain that a significant "Bologna effect": an increase in the overall attractiveness of the EHEA. More likely, the increase is due to increased attractiveness of particular countries (United Kingdom, France, Germany, the Netherlands, Sweden, Denmark, and Norway), partly related to the fact that many degree programs are offered in English. The percentage of foreign students from other EHEA countries has increased from 3.5% to 4.6%. The patterns for individual countries are varied here, too, with great differences particularly in the balance between receiving and sending students abroad. Overall, there seems to be a division between eastern and western EHEA countries, the latter being the main recipients of foreign EHEA students and the former being minor destinations.

Evaluations of the Erasmus program, the largest mobility program, reveal that financial barriers and problems with recognition of study abroad are the most important barriers to mobility (see, e.g., Vossensteyn et al., 2010). The implementation of portable study grants and loans would contribute to solving some of these problems. A majority (80%) of countries now have some kind of portable support for mobile students (Rauhvargers, 2011), but there is still scope for further improvement.

Social Dimension of the
European Higher Education Area

Arguably the least developed action line of the Bologna Process is the social dimension, perhaps because it is the newest action line, appearing in the 2001 Prague communiqué and becoming more operational in 2003. Another explanation is that the social dimension is a "wicked problem" (Rittel & Webber, 1973) in higher education, involving issues such as widening participation and battling inequalities. These problems are termed "wicked" for solutions are not obvious; many stakeholders are involved in the problem, and they disagree. Finally, the social dimension is a rather abstract action line, and throughout the Bologna Process, different aspects have been emphasized. Connected to this is the problem of clearly delineating means to achieve the objectives. In this section, we focus on the promotion of wider access to higher education and increasing participation. The general means to achieve these objectives are flexibility in the admission to higher education, flexibility in its provision, student services, and student finance.

With respect to flexible access, a fair number of countries have nationally accepted procedures in place for recognizing prior learning and show widespread use of such practices. Flexible study paths are implemented—sometime were in place before the Bologna Process—in about one third of the countries, mostly by offering distance education or part-time studies. Short-cycle higher education degrees are also provided, and flexibility of programs (modularization, elective courses) is also in place, but overall flexibility in study paths is not a widespread practice. Regarding student services (guidance and counselling), the research carried out by Katzensteiner, Ferrer-Sama, and Rott (2008), updated by the independent evaluation report on the Bologna Process (Westerheijden et al., 2010, p. 55), points out that in one third of the signatories, these services are widespread; in another third, they are less readily available or lacking quality; and in the remaining countries, services were not available (or data were lacking). With respect to financial support, the pattern across countries differs significantly. In one group of countries, mostly in the northwest of Europe, direct financial aid to students is high, and the personal contributions of students to the costs of their education are low. Another group of countries, many of these in the eastern part of Europe, have low levels of governmental aid, with the students making high contributions to their education.

Because of the nature of the "wicked problem" and the recent implementation of policies to change the situation, progress in the social dimension is limited. Studies (e.g. Orr, Schnitzer, & Frackmann, 2008) continue to report some societal groups being underrepresented in higher education (students from a lower socio-economic background, students with an immigration/ethnic background or with disabilities, and those who enrol in higher education through alternative routes).

Summary

The picture that emerges is one of many changes—past and still taking place in the EHEA. Some convergence emerges in terms of the infrastructure of higher education systems, regarding the cycle structure, ECTS, diploma supplements, and quality assurance procedures. That said, underlying this broad pattern are many national idiosyncrasies and even outright deviations from the general pattern. The key explanations for the differences are (a) different points of departure and different speeds of implementing change; (b) different nationally driven political agendas, emphasising different priorities and interpreting elements of the Bologna Process to fit in with the national context; (c) different perceptions at the shop-floor level (institutions, managers, professionals) of how important and relevant all the proposed changes are, from their perspectives.

RESPONSES FROM OTHER REGIONS

In a globalized context, major developments in one region will be noticed by actors in other regions, particularly when policy change has considerable support from a significant number of national governments and when much change is apparently taking place in all those higher education systems. Moreover, such large-scale developments in one part of the world will have real consequences for other regions. At one time, Europe was at a disadvantage because of the relative length of its undergraduate and graduate programs, compared to the United States. The new structure resulting from the Bologna Process has changed the competition. Also, the introduction of quality assurance systems across various regions may have a positive impact on quality and the recognition of quality, with an impact on the competitive landscape and potential choice patterns of (international) students. Before describing developments outside of Europe, text boxes will describe "Bologna-type" developments in the Asia-Pacific region, Latin America, the United States, and Africa.

Box 5.1 Asia-Pacific Region

Developments in Asian-Pacific higher education systems are intimately connected with Western models, notably provided by France, Germany, the United Kingdom, and the United States (Huang, 2007), although it can also be argued that there are indigenous models such as the Confucian model (see Marginson, 2011, for a contemporary version of that model). In contrast to the national policies and structures transplanted from the West before the 1990s, recent influences on the region heavily feature cross-border initiatives at the institutional level. The development encompasses initiatives of Western providers in, for example, Malaysia, Singapore and China, and those exported from Asian countries, for example, Singapore and Hong Kong). The cross-border initiatives stem from expanding demand for higher education in conjunction with global and economic competition. As a result, higher education in the region has gradually been seen as an important service industry, serving the economy (Mok, 2007). As in other regions, cross-border higher education in the Asia-Pacific region brings along important issues high on the policy agenda, for example, relating to comparability, recognition of degrees, mobility (and brain drain), and compatibility.

Therefore, it is no surprise that several regional organizations started to focus on specific higher education issues, such as the enhancement of mobility, the assurance of the quality of provision across the region, and mutual recognition arrangements. For example, the Association of Southeast Asian Nations (ASEAN) has mounted a series of higher education projects in collaboration with the European Union (EU). Also, through the Brisbane Communiqué (2006), initiatives were launched in accordance with the conclusions of the meeting of Asia-Pacific Education Ministers in 2006, aimed at encouraging and facilitating regional student and academic mobility and exchange.

Mobility

Programs for exchanging students and academics are the most common types of schemes that have been initiated in Asia. The University Mobility in Asia and the Pacific project, based on a voluntary association of universities, was already established in 1993. Moreover, ASEAN set up a University Network in 1995 to facilitate cooperation between institutions with respect to teaching and research in the 10 member countries of Southeast Asia. In 2001, the network was extended into the ASEAN-EU University Network Program (AUNP), funded by the EU. Another project of the European Commission, Asia-Link, had similar aims. Funds were made available for partnership projects initiated to promote sustainable relationships and for network initiatives designed to share experiences, particularly those that European institutions had acquired through the Bologna Process, for example, in relation to quality assurance, credit transfer systems, and the initiatives for student and lecture mobility, promoting joint research and convergence of curricula (European Commission, 2002).

Quality Assurance

Unlike their counterparts in Europe, which incorporated quality assurance into their systems, Asian countries were inclined to adopt international benchmarking as the means for assessing university performance (see Mok, 2007). The ASEAN aims at developing quality assurance systems at program and institutional levels to promote mutual recognition and networking (ASEAN University Network [AUN], 2010b). More specifically, a network of quality assurance commenced in 2000 and consists of chief quality officers of ASEAN member universities. Guidelines for quality assurance were generated and endorsed in 2004, and a manual for the implementation of the guidelines was distributed in 2006. In the meantime, AUNP launched technical assistance in 2005 to help ASEAN members not only in applying external and internal quality assurance at national and institutional levels, respectively, but also in promoting the regional quality assurance approach (see also AUN, 2010a). Other important developments were the start of the Asia-Pacific Quality Network in 2004 and—as a follow-up to the Brisbane communiqué—the development of the so-called Chiba principles for quality assurance in the Asia-Pacific region (2008), the latter clearly mirroring the European Standards and Guidelines.

Structures

The ASEAN is preparing a credit transfer system to be realized by 2015, thereby enhancing student mobility among member universities and facilitating student exchange programs (AUN, 2010b). In light of the European experience in the Bologna Process, a report of the Australian government (Department of Education, 2008), drawing on a follow-up survey of the Brisbane Communiqué, recommended that member countries should focus on the establishment of national information centers and the development of diploma supplements and credit systems, which would further enhance the transparency of higher education systems. Accordingly, a draft model of diploma supplement was provided in 2010, and in Australia, the higher education graduation statement is now commonplace.

Box 5.2 Latin America

Historical Background

Higher education in Ibero-American countries has witnessed considerable change in the past few decades. Two major trends are worth mentioning: massification and diversification. Massification started in the 1950s, but particularly after 1985, there was a significant increase in the number of institutions (Ferrer, 2010). At the same time, institutional diversification started and has continued in most South American countries. It encompasses the emergence and the rise of private providers and a growing diversity in institutional types (Brunner, 2009). However, the investments in research and development (R&D) remain significantly limited, with Brazil as an exception. The lack of funding caused a growing trend of brain drain.

Echoes of the Bologna Process

Inspired by the Bologna Process, Latin American governments embraced the idea of creating an Ibero-American knowledge area, with the objective of strengthening the traditional ties with Spanish and Portuguese universities to enrich the knowledge capital in the region. Early seeds for strengthening these ties had been sown in 1992, when the North American Free Trade Agreement (NAFTA) was signed. The United States was not very successful in taking advantage of the Latin American higher education market (see Aboites, 2010, for review and discussion) and thus created

(Continued)

(Continued)

space for developing links between Latin America and Europe. The postcolonial links, including language similarities, accommodated the adoption of Bologna in Latin America. The Declaration of Guadalajara, signed in 1991, followed by the declaration of Salamanca in 2001 and 2005, stressed the need for regional developments toward creating a common knowledge area, hence the need for greater academic cooperation toward the common area of higher education (Brunner, 2009).

In addition, a number of projects were launched to accomplish a similar goal. The EU-LA-Caribbean HE [European Union-Latin America-Caribbean higher Education] area (EULAC), the Tuning Latin America project (Tuning, 2011a), and a Latin American version of the European Reflex Project, which is called Proflex, are some of these endeavors (Zgaga, 2006). Despite all the signs of moving toward regional integration and cooperation, it has been argued that Latin America and the Caribbean are still at the early stages of this movement (Gacel-Ávila, forthcoming; Gacel-Ávila, Jaramillo, Knight, & de Wit, 2005).

Quality Assurance and Quality Framework

Ferrer (2010) reports on the emergence of university evaluation and accreditation bodies in Latin American countries during the last couple of decades (e.g., CONAEVA in Mexico and CONEAU in Argentina). He argues that this is due to the increasing awareness of the potential quality-undermining hazards that could be introduced by the growing higher education private sector.

In May 2003, the Ibero-American Network for Higher Education Accreditation (RIACES) was established as a nonprofit and independent organization (for more on networks in Latin America, see Jaramillo & Knight, 2005). It promotes cooperation in quality assurance, information exchange, and the development of accreditation systems (Red Iberoamericana Acreditación de la Calidad de la Educación Superior, 2011). RIACES has managed to develop common regional quality criteria for higher education in certain disciplines, and work continues in other disciplines. Accreditation and mutual recognition of degrees is also seen as an important requirement to boost student and staff mobility (see, e.g., Osorio, 2010).

Mobility

Student and professional migrations have become a challenging issue for many countries around the world, those in Latin America. The concept of brain drain often sounds quite appalling to the less developed countries, which are not capable of keeping their professionals, let alone enticing new highly skilled workers from other countries (Holm-Nielsen, Thorn, Brunner, & Balán, 2005). The Academic and Scientific Mobility Observatory is a recently launched project that aims to provide a centralized virtual portal to observe and report on the changes in the migration of professionals and students in the South American region (Academic and Scientific Mobility Observatory, 2011).

The lack of transparency of quality assurance systems and quality frameworks, as well as the absence of an integrated credit transfer system, has negative impacts on the growth of student mobility between Ibero-American countries. The Pablo Neruda program (for postgraduate student mobility) and the RIACES project are serious attempts to enable greater academic mobility particularly for master's and PhD students.

Structure

The Tuning Latin America project report (Beneitone et al., 2007) reveals no dominant model for academic credits in Latin American universities. In some countries, there is no credit system in place. The Republic of El Salvador has implemented a mandatory unit scoring system. Many initiatives are emerging, but it is difficult to move toward a common transferable credit system because many very different agencies are involved.

BOX 5.3 United States

The large and complex system of higher education in the United States has moved through three stages and themes of response to the Bologna Process, responses that affect some segments of the enterprise more than others.

Information Distribution

The channels of communication about Bologna and its action lines have been limited but growing. The online *World Education News and Reports* (WENR) carried explications of Bologna developments early, but they went to a limited audience with limited concerns: deans and admissions officers of graduate (second- and third-cycle degrees) programs concerned with the nature and impact of the shift to three-year bachelor's degrees among European applicants to their programs. Presentations and panels on other Bologna topics at national conferences started only in 2006. In between, knowledge of Bologna among U.S. faculty and administrators was carried principally by isolated personal contacts with European colleagues and among U.S. institutions with either branch campuses or cooperative agreements with universities in Europe (see also Brookes & Huisman, 2009). Neither the broad-distribution trade press (*Chronicle of Higher Education* and the online *Inside HigherEd*) nor the general press gave prominence to Bologna Process stories until research and analyses of Bologna began to appear in 2008 (Adelman, 2008a, 2008b, 2009; Gaston, 2010). These were all featured in articles in the trade press, with considerable commentary and response. The audience for Bologna information grew exponentially. Research centers in flagship institutions such as the University of Wisconsin-Madison, the University of California at Berkeley, and the University of Michigan all devoted papers, online analyses, and conferences to Bologna, and in the United States, such flagships have considerable leverage on knowledge distribution.

Qualification Frameworks

The Lumina Foundation for Education sponsored much of the research and analysis on Bologna. Following the recommendations in that research, the foundation selected two related projects that responded to the general concern that U.S. degrees lacked transparency, meaning, and understanding. The first of these was an adaptation of the European Tuning model. Three state higher education systems (Indiana, Minnesota, and Utah) were recruited in the spring of 2009 to

(Continued)

(Continued)

select two disciplines each (Indiana picked three) and try out the Tuning sequence to produce both templates of reference points for student learning in those fields and statements of student learning outcomes. The undertaking differed from its European original in that ISCED 5B degree programs (theoretically oriented tertiary education) were included with 5A (professionally oriented tertiary education); hence, community colleges were part of each disciplinary team (as was at least one student representative). The Texas system joined Tuning USA in 2010 with four subdisciplines of engineering, and the Kentucky system entered in 2011 with five fields. The Midwestern Higher Education Compact is putting together a multistate Tuning effort, and, in another departure from the original model, the American Historical Association (a leading learned society), building on the fact that both Indiana and Utah had picked history as one of their disciplines, is designing a Tuning-type project as well. All of these are being funded by the Lumina Foundation.

The second undertaking, now running parallel to Tuning USA, was the development of a Beta Degree Qualifications Profile (DQP) under Lumina Foundation sponsorship (Adelman, Ewell, Gaston, & Schneider, 2011). Released in January 2011, the DQP is intended to be more of an iterative process than a final statement. It follows the qualifications framework of the EHEA in setting forth degree-qualifying competencies at short cycle, first cycle, and second cycle levels, but it does so in five learning outcome territories: specialized knowledge, broad integrative knowledge, intellectual skills (analytic inquiry, use of information resources, diverse perspectives, quantitative fluency, and communication fluency), applied learning, and civic learning. Lumina has funded two regional accrediting bodies to explore the potential of the DQP in quality assurance, one consortium of private institutions to explore the potential of the DQP in their graduation requirements, and two national higher education organizations that put together teams of community colleges and four-year institutions to work through variations in the initial DQP presentation. One state higher education system, too, should be funded for a vertical (short, first, and second cycles) DQP exploration beginning in 2012. U.S. participants know that Europeans have spent a decade or more on qualification framework construction and anticipate doing the same.

BOX 5.4 Africa

Historical Background

Africa is the least developed region globally in terms of higher education institutions and enrollments (Teferra, 2008). The majority of African countries were previously colonies of European countries. Higher education in Africa has been shaped by colonialism and organized according to European models. Since the 1980s, African higher education has been starved of adequate funding, a policy recommended by the World Bank, which argued that investment would be better spent on primary and secondary education and on vocational training (Teferra, 2005). However, during the last few years, higher education has become more widely recognized as a key sector in regional development.

Cooperation and Actions Toward Reform

In 2003, the signatory countries agreed to cooperate with countries in other parts of the world as a part of the external dimension of the Bologna Process. The report of a special working group identified the southern Mediterranean countries (in North Africa) as a region of priority interest. The main aims of cooperation included promoting the idea and practice of regional cooperation, strengthening cultural contacts and mutual understanding, enhancing quality in higher education, and creating a coherent regional labor market with transparency in qualifications (Zgaga, 2006, p. 13). From 2004, representatives from countries outside the Bologna Process were invited to attend Bologna conferences and seminars. In addition, a series of conferences have been held in Africa to discuss the adaptation of African universities to the Bologna Process. The African Union, an EU-style cooperation body, has suggested that Bologna be studied as a model for higher education harmonization across Africa. The rationale and benefits put forward by the AU for harmonization include greater intraregional mobility of students and academics and increased sharing of information, intellectual resources, and research (African Union, 2007, p. 3).

France has been the most active European country promoting Bologna-style reforms in its former colonies and the French-speaking countries of the Maghreb: Algeria, Morocco, and Tunisia. The Catania Declaration (2006), with objectives similar to the Bologna Declaration, created a Euro-Mediterranean higher education and research area, which promotes collaboration between Europe and North African countries including Egypt and those in the Maghreb. Some countries clearly build on the French Bologna-type structure of *licence-master-doctorat*, with support from the French government, EU, and World Bank.

Similar developments are taking place in West Africa among the countries of the Western African Monetary and Economic Union. The *Reseau pour l'Excellence de l'Enseignement Supérieur en Afrique de l'Ouest* network of higher education institutions in seven countries has also adopted the French structure, and it hopes to fully implement this system, including modularization and a credit transfer system.

Quality Assurance

Quality assurance features prominently in the African Union's harmonization strategy. In some countries, quality assurance development is occurring at both institutional and national levels, and the African Association of Universities (AAU) has been instrumental in driving forward the reforms. While institutions are developing formal quality assurance policies and mechanisms, national structures for quality assurance and accreditation are also being established (Singh, 2010). In 2006, only 15 African countries had functioning quality assurance agencies (Shabani, 2008). In 2008, UNESCO and the World Bank supported an AAU project to develop quality assurance systems in its member universities, encourage collaboration on quality assurance, and strengthen the capacity of national bodies. An African Quality Assurance Network was launched in 2009 as part of this project.

Student and Staff Mobility

The African Union has suggested the achievement of intra-African mobility of students and academics as a potential benefit of introducing Bologna-style harmonization across Africa. Other organizations, like the Reseau network in West Africa and those involved in the Lusophone Higher Education Area, echo this. South Africa and Egypt in particular attract large numbers of incoming students from other African countries (Mulumba, Obaje, Kobedi, & Kishun, 2008). By aligning their higher education systems with those in Europe, African nations may be able to encourage further student mobility toward Europe as well as increased flows between African nations. Jowi (2009, p. 274) has warned that the largest threat of internationalization in Africa may be brain drain. The increased mobility of academics envisaged by the harmonization reforms now in progress in Africa is not intended to create winning and losing countries or institutions, but this may be an unavoidable result of increased academic mobility.

Developments Outside Europe

Higher education in the four regions has obviously been influenced by the Bologna Process. It is evident that the external incentives (mostly from Europe) have had impacts on the propensity to move toward an integrated system of higher education. That said, specific regional issues (and problems) have put a particular stamp on the regional initiatives, which explains why regions stress different Bologna elements. Also, governments in these regions used references to the EHEA to boost domestic change they feel should be realized. Despite the regional differences, however, all regions pay considerable attention to improving quality assurance arrangements and mobility.

It is difficult to assess the impact of the regional change processes, given they are only recent, and policies have not yet been fully developed and implemented. Positive views, for example, are expressed by Khelfaoui (2009), qualifying the French-patterned reforms in Africa as a "turnkey" product (for good or for bad), addressing universities' internal and recurring problems, especially concerning the large increases in enrollments and inadequate facilities (Charlier & Croché, 2009). Some scholars are pessimistic about the developments. One important reason is the disparity of structures and systems and, therefore, a lack of common ground (see Brunner, 2009; Figueroa, 2008; on Latin America). Another impediment is the lack of capacity to bring about the change or skepticism regarding the reforms (see, e.g., Khelfaoui, 2009, on Africa). Critical analysts point out that the regions may have overlooked carefully translating the EHEA policies into the specific regional context (see, e.g., Aboites, 2010). Some analysts even qualify the policies as neocolonial (Figueroa, 2008). Regions, therefore, run the risk of that implementation failing. Jowi (2009), however, argues that if collaborations are structured reciprocally, optimal benefits can be achieved.

THE IMPLICATIONS

From the above analysis it is clear that the Bologna Process has brought about considerable change since 1999 in the countries that signed the declaration. Obviously, change has been much more abundant in some countries than others, and sometimes, change has been more ceremonial than real. All governments and higher education institutions, nevertheless, have dealt with the challenges of restructuring their curricula, introducing or changing their quality assurance regimes, introducing credit transfer systems, developing mobility programs, and implementing policies to improve participation. While acknowledging patterns of similarity, various studies point out that the Bologna action lines have been translated in very different ways.

Similar observations pertain to the responses to and adaptations of the Bologna Process in other world regions. Apparently, the issue of curriculum structure is less pertinent in other regions (if only for the fact that in many regions, the undergraduate-graduate structure was already part and parcel of the institutional fabric), but issues around qualification frameworks, mobility, and quality assurance have certainly been picked up in other regions as a consequence of attention to these issues in the EHEA. Here again, or arguably even more profoundly, contextual differences come to the fore. Each region picked up issues that were deemed most relevant/urgent, for example, transparency of qualifications in the United States, quality assurance in Asia, and mobility in Africa.

The manifold regional and national interpretations of the Bologna-type challenges make it difficult to assess the implications for those working in internationalization. The two lessons that can be gleaned are, first, that the Bologna reform process will inevitably continue to impact internationalization activities across the globe and, second, that however disappointing, there is no reason to assume straightforward answers to the challenges. The Bologna Process cannot be disregarded as a temporary policy fashion: It has already had many important effects (stressing again that some change has been real and some rhetorical). It would be unwise to ignore the strategic consequences. At the same time, practitioners must assess Bologna's relevance against their own national and institutional contexts. This means carefully reflecting on the question of which Bologna elements are most important and translating these elements into context-bound policy and strategic solutions that address the local challenges.

References

Aboites, H. (2010). Latin American universities and the Bologna Process: From commercialisation to the Tuning competencies project. *Globalisation, Societies and Education, 8,* 443–455.

Academic and Scientific Mobility Observatory. (2011). About OBSMAC. Retrieved March 1, 2012, from http://www.iesalc.unesco.org.ve/index.php?option=com_content&view=article&id=1813:sobre-obsmac&catid=194&Itemid=746&lang=en

Adelman, C. (2008a). *The Bologna Club: What U.S. higher education can learn from a decade of European reconstruction.* Washington, DC: Institute for Higher Education Policy.

Adelman, C. (2008b). *Learning accountability from Bologna: A higher education policy primer.* Washington, DC: Institute for Higher Education Policy.

Adelman, C. (2009). *The Bologna Process for U.S. eyes: Re-learning higher education in the age of convergence.* Washington, DC: Institute for Higher Education Policy.

Adelman, C., Ewell, P., Gaston, P. L., & Schneider, C. G. (2011). *The degree qualifications profile.* Indianapolis, IN: Lumina Foundation for Education.

African Union. (2007). *Harmonisation of higher education programs in Africa: a strategy for the African Union* (Summary report). Addis Ababa, Ethiopia: African Union.

ASEAN University Network. (2010a). *About the AUN-QA.* Retrieved March 1, 2012, from http://www.aunsec.org/site/main/web/index.php?option=com_content&view=article&id=210%3Aabout-the-aun-qa&catid=150%3Ageneral-info&Itemid=188&lang=en

ASEAN University Network. (2010b). *History and background.* Retrieved March 1, 2012, from http://www.aunsec.org/site/main/web/index.php?option=com_content&view=article&id=50&Itemid=35&lang=en

Beneitone, P., Esquetini, C., González, J., Maletá, M. M., Siufi, G., & Wagenaar, R. (2007). *Reflections on and outlook for higher education in Latin America: Final report Tuning Latin America project.* Bilbao, Spain: Universidad de Deusto.

Bologna Declaration. (1999). *The European higher education area: Joint declaration of the European ministers of education convened in Bologna at the 19th of June 1999.* Bologna.

Brisbane Communique. (2006). *Communique issued by the ministers attending the Asia-Pacific Education Ministers' Meeting.* Brisbane: International Education Forum.

Brookes, M., & Huisman, J. (2009). The eagle and the gold stars: Does the Bologna Process affect US higher education? *Higher Education in Europe, 34*(1), 3–23.

Brunner, J. J. (2009). The Bologna Process from a Latin American perspective. *Journal of Studies in International Education, 13,* 417–438.

Catania Declaration. (2006). *Euro-Mediterranean Area of Higher Education and Research.* Catania, Italy.

Charlier, J. E., & Croché, S. (2009). Can the Bologna Process make the move faster towards the development of an international space for higher education where Africa would find its place? *Journal of Higher Education in Africa, 7*(1/2), 39–59.

Department of Education. (2008). *Recognition of higher education qualifications across the Brisbane Communique region.* Canberra, Australia: Author.

de Wit, K., & Verhoeven, J. (2001). The higher education policy of the European Union: With or against the member states? In J. Huisman, P. Maassen, & G. Neave (Eds.), *Higher education and the nation state. The international dimension of higher education* (pp. 175–231). Amsterdam: Pergamon.

Elliot, D. (1998). Internationalizing British higher education: Policy perspectives. In P. Scott (Ed.), *The globalization of higher education* (pp. 32–43). Buckingham, UK: Society for Research into Higher Education and Open University Press.

European Commission. (2002). *ASEAN-EU university network program.* Luxembourg: Office for Official Publications of the ECs.

European Commission. (2005). *Mobilising the brainpower of Europe: Enabling universities to make their full contribution to the Lisbon Strategy.* Brussels: Author.

European Commission. (2006). *Delivering on the modernisation agenda for universities: education, research and innovation.* Brussels: Author.

European Student Union. (2009). *Bologna with student eyes 2009.* Leuven, Belgium: Author.

Ferrer, A. T. (2010). The impact of the Bologna Process in Ibero-America: Prospects and challenges. *European Journal of Education, 45*(4), 601–611.

Figueroa, F. E. (2008). European influences in Chilean and Mexican higher education: The Bologna Process and the Tuning project. *European Education, 40*(1), 63–77.

File, J., & Goedegebuure, L. (Eds.). (2003). *Real-time systems. Reflections on higher education in the Czech Republic, Hungary, Poland and Slovenia.* Brno, Czech Republic: Vutium Press.

Fisher, A. (2009). *A story of engagement: The British Council 1934–2009.* London: British Council.

Gacel-Ávila, J. (forthcoming). Comprehensive internationalisation in Latin America. *Higher Education Policy.*

Gacel-Ávila, J., Jaramillo, I. C., Knight, J., & de Wit, H. (2005). The Latin American way: Trends, issues, and directions. In H. de Wit, I. C. Jaramillo, J. Gacel-Ávila, & J. Knight (Eds.), *Higher education in Latin America: The international dimension* (pp. 311–368). Washington DC: The International Bank for Reconstruction and Development/The World Bank.

Gaston, P. L. (2010). *The challenge of Bologna: What U.S. higher education has to learn from Europe and why it matters that we learn it.* Sterling, VA: Stylus.

Gornitzka, Å. (2006). What is the use of Bologna in national reform? The case of Norwegian quality reform in higher education. In V. Tomusk (Ed.), *Creating the European Area of Higher Education: Voices from the periphery* (pp. 19–41). Dordrecht, the Netherlands: Kluwer.

Gornitzka, Å. (2010). Bologna in context: A horizontal perspective on the dynamics of governance sites for a Europe of Knowledge. *European Journal of Education, 45*(4), 535–548.

Haug, G., Kirstein, J., & Knudsen, I. (1999). *Trends in learning structures in higher education I.* Copenhagen, Denmark: Danish Rectors' Conference.

Holm-Nielsen, L. B., Thorn, K., Brunner, J. J., & Balán, J. (2005). Regional and international challenges to higher education in Latin America. In H. de Wit, I. C. Jaramillo, J. Gacel-Ávila & J. Knight (Eds.), *Higher education in Latin America: The international dimension* (pp. 39–69). Washington DC: The International Bank for Reconstruction and Development/The World Bank.

Huang, F. (2007). Internationalization of higher education in the developing and emerging countries: A focus on transnational higher education in Asia. *Journal of Studies in International Education, 11*(3/4), 421–432.

Huisman, J., & Van der Wende, M. (Eds.). (2004). *On cooperation and competition. National and European policies for the internationalisation of higher education.* Bonn, Germany: Lemmens.

Huisman, J., & Van der Wende, M. (Eds.). (2005). *On cooperation and competition II. Institutional responses to internationalisation, Europeanisation and globalisation.* Bonn, Germany: Lemmens.

Huisman, J., & Westerheijden, D. F. (2010). Bologna and quality assurance: Progress made or pulling the wrong chart? *Quality in Higher Education, 16*(1), 63–66.

Huisman, J., Witte, J., & File, J. M. (2007). *The extent and impact of higher education curricular reform across Europe.* Enschede, the Netherlands: Center for Higher Education Policy Studies.

Jaramillo, I. C., & Knight, J. (2005). Key actors and programs: Increasing connectivity in the region. In H. de Wit, I. C. Jaramillo, J. Gacel-Ávila, & J. Knight (Eds.), *Higher education in Latin America: The international dimension* (pp. 301–339). Washington DC: The International Bank for Reconstruction and Development/The World Bank.

Jowi, J. O. (2009). Internationalization of higher education in Africa: developments, emerging trends, issues and policy implications. *Higher Education Policy, 22*(3), 263–281.

Kälvemark, T., & Van der Wende, M. (Eds.). (1996). *National policies for the internationalisation of higher education in Europe.* Stockholm: National Agency for Higher Education.

Katzensteiner, M., Ferrer-Sama, P., & Rott, G. (2008). *Guidance and counselling in higher education in European Union member states.* Aarhus, Denmark: University of Aarhus.

Keeling, R. (2006). The Bologna Process and the Lisbon research agenda: The European Commission's expanding role in higher education discourse. *European Journal of Education, 41*(2), 203–223.

Kehm, B., Huisman, J., & Stensaker, B. (Eds.). (2009). *The European Higher Education Area: Perspectives on a moving target.* Rotterdam: Sense.

Kelo, M., Teichler, U., & Wächter, B. (2006). Towards improved data on student mobility in Europe: Findings and concepts of the Eurodata study. *Journal of Studies in International Education, 10*(3), 194–223.

Khelfaoui, H. (2009). The Bologna Process in Africa: Globalization or return to "colonial situation"? *Journal of Higher Education in Africa, 7*(1/2), 21–38.

Lažetić, P. (2010). Managing the Bologna Process at the European level: institution and actor dynamics. *European Journal of Education, 45*(4), 549–562.

Marginson, S. (2011). Higher education in East Asia and Singapore: Rise of the Confucian model. *Higher Education, 61*(5), 587–611.

Mok, K. H. (2007). Questing for internationalization of universities in Asia: Critical reflections. *Journal of Studies in International Education, 11*(3/4), 433–454.

Mulumba, M. B., Obaje, A., Kobedi, K., & Kishun, R. (2008). International student mobility in and out of Africa: challenges and opportunities. In D. Teferra & J. Knight (Eds.), *Higher education in Africa: The international dimension* (pp. 490–514). Chestnut Hill, MA: Boston College, Center for International Higher Education, and Association of African Universities.

Neave, G. (2002). Anything goes: Or, how the accommodation of Europe's universities to European integration integrates an inspiring number of contradictions. *Tertiary Education and Management, 8*(3), 181–197.

Neave, G., & Maassen, P. (2007). The Bologna Process: An intergovernmental policy perspective. In P. Maassen & J. P. Olsen (Eds.), *University dynamics and European integration* (pp. 135–153). Dordrecht, the Netherlands: Springer.

Orr, D., Schnitzer, K., & Frackmann, E. (2008). *Social and economic conditions of student life in Europe.* Bielefeld, Germany: Bertelsmann.

Osorio, F. C. (2010). Accreditation, recognition of titles, and mobility as instruments for integration. *Bulletin IESALC Reports, 203.*

Rauhvargers, A. (2011). Achieving Bologna goals: Where does Europe stand ahead of 2010. *Journal of Studies in International Education, 15*(4), 4–24.

Rauhvargers, A., & Rusakova, A. (2008). *Improving recognition in the European Higher Education Area: An analysis of national action plans.* Strasbourg, France: Council of Europe.

Red Iberoamericana Acreditación de la Calidad de la Educación Superior (RIACES). (2011). *Welcome to RIACES.* Retrieved March 1, 2012, from http://www.riaces.net/index.php/en/riaces-cols2-what-is-riaces/what-is-riacesgroup1.html

Reichert, S., & Tauch, C. (2003). *Trends 2003: Progress towards the European Higher Education Area.* Geneva/Brussels: European University Association.

Rittel, H. W. J., & Webber, M. M. (1973). Dilemmas in a general theory of planning. *Policy Sciences, 4,* 155–169.

Scheele, J. P., Maassen, P., & Westerheijden, D. F. (Eds.). (1998). *To be continued . . . follow up of quality assurance in higher education.* The Hague: Elsevier/De Tijdstroom.

Schrier, E., & Kaiser, F. (1998). *Intermediate qualifications. Thematic report V. CHEPS Higher Education Monitor.* Enschede, the Netherlands: Center for Higher Education Policy Studies.

Shabani, J. (2008). The role of key regional actors and programs. In D. Teferra & J. Knight (Eds.), *Higher education in Africa: The international dimension* (pp. 464–489). Chestnut Hill, MA: Boston College, Center for International Higher Education, and Association of African Universities.

Singh, M. (2010). Re-orienting internationalisation in African higher education. *Globalisation, Societies and Education, 8*(2), 269–282.

Sorbonne Declaration. (1998). *Joint declaration on harmonisation of the architecture of the European higher education system by the four Ministers in charge for France, Germany, Italy and the United Kingdom.* Paris: the Sorbonne.

Stensaker, B., Harvey, L., Huisman, J., Langfeldt, L., & Westerheijden, D. F. (2010). The impact of the European Standards and Guidelines in agency evaluations. *European Journal of Education, 45*(4), 577–587.

Teferra, D. (2005, May 18–20). *The Bologna Process: The experience and challenges for Africa.* Paper presented at the Third Conference on Knowledge and Politics, Bergen, Norway.

Teferra, D. (2008). The institutional dimension of higher education in Africa: status, challenges and prospect. In D. Teferra & J. Knight (Eds.), *Higher education in Africa: the international dimension* (pp. 44–79). Accra/Boston: AAU/CIHE.

Teichler, U. (1998). The role of the European Union in the internationalization of higher education. In P. Scott (Ed.), *The globalization of higher education* (pp. 88–99). Buckingham, UK: Society for Research into Higher Education & Open University Press.

Tuning. (2011a). *Proyecto Tuning América Latina.* Retrieved March 1, 2012, from http://tuning.unideusto.org/tuningal/

Tuning. (2011b). *Tuning educational structures in Europe.* Retrieved March 1, 2012, from http://www.unideusto.org/tuningeu/

UNESCO & Council of Europe. (2010). *Revised recommendation on criteria and procedures for the assessment of foreign qualifications.* Strasbourg/Paris: UNESCO & Council of Europe.

Välimaa, J., Hoffman, D., & Huusko, M. (2006). The Bologna Process in Finland. Perspectives from the basic units. In V. Tomusk (Ed.), *Creating the European Area of Higher Education: Voices from the periphery* (pp. 43–67). Dordrecht, the Netherlands: Springer.

Van der Wende, M., & Huisman, J. (2004). Europe. In J. Huisman & M. Van der Wende (Eds.), *On cooperation and competition National and European policies for the internationalisation of higher education* (pp. 17–49). Bonn, Germany: Lemmens.

Van der Wende, M., & Westerheijden, D. F. (2003). Degrees of trust or trust of degrees? Quality assurance and recognition. In J. M. File & L. Goedegebuure (Eds.), *Real-time systems. Reflections on higher education in the Czech Republic, Hungary, Poland and Slovenia.* Brno, Czech Republic: Vitium.

Van Vught, F. A., & Westerheijden, D. F. (1994). Towards a general model of quality assessment in higher education. *Higher Education, 28*(3), 355–371.

Vossensteyn, H., Beerkens, M., Cremonini, L., Huisman, J., Souto-Otero, M., Botas, P., et al. 2010. *Improving participation in the Erasmus program.* Strasbourg, France: European Parliament.

Westerheijden, D. F., Beerkens, E., Cremonini, L., Huisman, J., Kehm, B., Kovač, A., et al. (2010). *The first decade of working on the European Higher Education Area: Bologna Process independent assessment: Vol. 1. Main report.* Enschede, the Netherlands: Center for Higher Education Policy Studies.

Witte, J. (2006). *Change of degrees and degrees of change: Comparing adaptations of European higher education systems in the context of the Bologna Process.* Enschede, the Netherlands: Center for Higher Education Policy Studies.

Witte, J., Huisman, J., & Purser, L. (2009). European higher education reforms in the context of the Bologna Process: How did we get here, where are we, and where are we going? In Organization for Economic Cooperation and Development (OECD)(Ed.), *Higher education to 2030: Vol. 3. Globalisation.* Paris: OECD.

Zgaga, P. (2006). *Looking out: The Bologna Process in a global setting.* Oslo: Norwegian Ministry of Education and Research.

6

AN OVERVIEW AND ANALYSIS OF INTERNATIONAL EDUCATION RESEARCH, TRAINING, AND RESOURCES

HANS DE WIT AND DAVID URIAS

The study of the internationalization of higher education has developed rapidly over the past two decades. A great percentage of materials continue to be strongly dominated by North American and Western European conceptions, although there has been a recent increase of information being disseminated from Asia, Latin America, and Africa. The purpose of this chapter is to present an overview of key resources and act as a primary foundational collection of pertinent, contemporary resources in international education. The focus is to provide a primer concerning which journals, centers, books, databases, and Web sites are of relevance for those involved in the study and practice of international education, while placing such resources in perspective of trends/developments in the field. Also some information on educational and training programs is provided.

In the beginning of the 1990s, as Teichler (1996) observed, there was a lack of comprehensive documentation on the internationalization of higher education. He expressed the hope that "a network of key institutions cooperating in joint provision of the global state of the art" (p. 338) would emerge. He also called for a broader thematic range and improvement in theoretical basis and research methods. Research on international education, according to Teichler, was focused mainly on psychological research about student attitudes and behavior, experiences of students from developing countries studying abroad, and descriptions and evaluations of international programs and projects. He also stated that most of the research was "occasional, coincidental, sporadic, or episodic" (1996, p. 341), with most of the research conducted in the United States.

In 1997, in the inaugural issue of the *Journal of Studies in International Education,* de Wit also noted a lack of a strong research tradition on the internationalization of higher education and, as such, a lack of academic recognition of the field. Ten years later, de Wit (2007) observed in the same journal:

An increasing number of manuscripts in the field of international education are published in more generic (higher) education journals, and the quality of the discourse in journals, at conferences, and at seminars or workshops . . . has improved as well. Internationalization of (higher) education has become more important on the policy agenda but also on the research agenda. (pp. 258–259)

In the same issue, Kehm and Teichler (2007) note a substantive growth in the number of such studies and assert that internationalization has become a more visible component of general publications on higher education. They also observe that studies on this topic are not easily accessible, are targeting more practitioners and policymakers than higher education researchers, are more closely linked to other topics than the theme of internationalization itself, and are more complex and highly normative. Over the past 5 years, this trend has continued, with more and more higher education media paying attention to the internationalization of higher education—increasingly online. Many new books and articles have been published on the theme. Furthermore, one can see an increasing interest among graduate students to focus their master's and doctoral research on the internationalization of higher education.

The point by Kehm and Teichler (2007) concerning a lack of sufficient access and familiarity with resources on internationalization of higher education is still valid. They state that there are "only a few researchers who continuously engage with the issue and have made it their field of specialization. There are even fewer centers or institutes that have internationalisation of higher education as a core theme of their research activities" (pp. 263–264).

Although it is detailed in identifying the key sources on the internationalization of higher education in terms of books, articles, centers, Web sites, and training programs, this chapter does not intend to be comprehensive in the depth of its coverage.

Research Centers

Centers for research on higher education that focus some attention on internationalization are still limited in their consideration of this topic, and there is a concern that the continuity of their focus on internationalization is in danger. Over the years, the Center for International

Higher Education at Boston College, United States, the International Center for Higher Education Research at the University of Kassel, Germany, and the Center for Higher Education Policy Studies at the University of Twente, the Netherlands, have given ample attention to research on international education. The Ontario Institute of Education, Toronto; the Center for Studies in Higher Education at the University of California, Berkeley; the Centre for the Study of Higher Education at the University of Melbourne; and the International Centre for Higher Education Management of the University of Bath in the United Kingdom—to mention just a few—are increasingly adding an international dimension to their research. In the United Kingdom, the Centre for Academic Practice and Research in Internationalisation of Leeds Metropolitan University should be mentioned. The start of the Centre for Higher Education Internationalisation at the Università Cattolica del Sacro Cuore in Milan in 2012 is an example of a recent research center specifically focused on internationalization of higher education.

There is also an increase in graduate education and research as well as other types of professional research on the internationalization of higher education among young scholars and practitioners around the world. Four examples illustrate this: NAFSA's Teaching, Learning, Scholarship Knowledge Community; the European Association for International Education's (EAIE) Special Interest Group, "Researchers in International Higher Education"; and the International Education Research Network, an initiative of the International Education Association Australia in cooperation with Australian Education International (www.ieaa .org.au/researchnetwork). The African Network for Internationalization of Education is another example of this development: an independent, nonprofit, nongovernmental network committed to the advancement of high-quality research, capacity-building, and advocacy on internationalization of higher education with prime focus on Africa (www. anienetwork.org). Members of these research networks see exchange of information and sources as a key need.

Journals

The main journal in the field of internationalization of higher education is the *Journal of*

BOX 6.1 *Journal of Studies in International Education*

The first issue of the *Journal of Studies in International Education* was published in Spring 1997 by the Council on International Educational Exchange on the occasion of its 50th anniversary and in a cooperative agreement with the European Association for International Education. With the publication of Volume 4 in 2000, the Association for Studies in International Education (ASIE) took over as publisher. For Volume 5 in 2001, ASIE signed a contract with Sage Publications, by which Sage would publish the journal on behalf of ASIE. The number of issues expanded from two to four issues a year and, in 2010, to five issues a year.

The *Journal of Studies in International Education* is a unique journal in the sense that it is created and owned by an international group of professional associations, all active in the field of international education: membership-based and intermediate and service-oriented organizations, representing all different continents of the world. At present, 13 organizations and associations belong to ASIE, including large membership associations such as the Association of International Educators (NAFSA) and the Association of International Education Administrators in the United States; the Canadian Bureau for International Education; the European Association for International Education (EAIE); the Asia-Pacific Association for International Education and the Japan Network for International Education in Asia; the International Education Association of Australia; the International Education Association of South Africa; and the Mexican Association for International Education (AMPEI) in Latin America. Also participating are organizations like the British Council in the United Kingdom, Nuffic in the Netherlands, and World Education Services (WES) in the United States. These groups have joined efforts in stimulating the study of international education by creating this research-based journal, which is peer reviewed and covers the broad field of internationalization of higher education. For more information, see www.nuffic.net/asie or http://jsi.sagepub.com.

Studies in International Education. For an overview, see Box 6.1. Over the 15 years of its existence, this academic journal has become broadly respected by both researchers and practitioners in international higher education. Kehm and Teichler (2007) conclude in their analysis of the journal that "altogether, the *Journal of Studies in International Education* has been a mirror of the diversity of themes, concepts, and findings relevant to understanding international aspects in higher education. It also mirrors changes of emphasis over time" (p. 269). At the same time, they observe that "its publications deserve more careful comparative analyses about the differences in emphasis in various countries and the underlying conditions and rationales" (p. 269).

The *Journal of Studies in International Education* is not the only journal in the field.

The journal *Frontiers* appeared in the United States a bit earlier. Since its founding at Boston University in 1994, *Frontiers* has established itself as a relevant journal for international educators, with a specific focus on study abroad. *Frontiers* is sponsored by a consortium of American institutions. This journal is a strategic partner of the Forum on Education Abroad (www.forumea.org), sharing and supporting the work and goals of that organization. (See Box 6.2.)

Educación Global is another journal that since 1997 has published an annual issue by the *Mexican Association for International Education* (AMPEI). Its aim is to disseminate articles on the internationalization of education and international cooperation. For more information about AMPEI and its journal, see Box 6.3 (www.ampei.org.mx).

BOX 6.2 Frontiers: The Interdisciplinary Journal of Study Abroad

The purpose of *Frontiers* is to publish thought-provoking research articles, insightful essays, and concise book reviews that may provide the profession of study abroad an intellectual charge, document some of the best thinking and innovative programming in the field, create an additional forum for dialogue among colleagues in international education, and ultimately enrich our perspectives and bring greater meaning to our work.

Frontiers aspires to publish excellent writing that reflects deeply on the critical issues and concerns of study abroad. In particular, this journal is interested in the intellectual development of students in an international and intercultural context. Study abroad offers great promise both to individual students and to institutions committed to international education.

Frontiers is an interdisciplinary journal. It publishes manuscripts from a wide range of disciplines and encourages approaches to topics that use multiple and mutually supporting forms of analysis. Research on the issue of student learning abroad, for example, might make use of research in anthropology, linguistics, psychology, philosophy, and education. *Frontiers* encourages researchers in particular fields of study to submit manuscripts that relate well to study abroad. Examples of such articles might include: an analysis of the meaning of study abroad for a particular historical figure; an examination of study abroad themes as they appear in a literary work; a business case study analysis of a study abroad program; or a research article on the psychological processes that shape study abroad experiences.

Since its founding at Boston University in 1994, *Frontiers* has established itself as an important and serious journal for international educators. Currently, more than 1,300 institutions and individuals in over 25 countries subscribe. *Frontiers* is sponsored by a consortium of institutions that includes Arcadia University, Beloit College, Binghamton University, Central College, Dickinson College, James Madison University, Kalamazoo College, Macalester College, Middlebury College, New York University, Partnership for Global Education of Hobart and William Smith Colleges and Union College, Pomona College, The School for International Training, Tufts University, University of Richmond, University of Texas, Austin, University of Tulsa, Villanova University, and Yale University. *Frontiers* is a strategic partner of the Forum on Education Abroad, sharing and supporting the work and goals of that organization. The journal's editorial offices are housed at Dickinson College.

Frontiers generally publishes two volumes per year, alternating between a general, eclectic volume and a thematic volume that covers a specific topic in-depth. Each volume typically contains research articles, an essay, book reviews, and an update of a particular theme or topic in study abroad. *Frontiers* has also published special issues, in particular *A History of US Study Abroad: Beginnings to 1965*, and *1965-present*. For more information, visit www.frontiersjournal .com.

An important journal for those interested in international higher education trends and issues from a thematic and regional perspective is *International Higher Education*, published quarterly by the Center for International Higher Education at Boston College. Since 2008, it is also published in Chinese, since 2010 in Russian, and since 2011 in Spanish. The center also regularly publishes important books on developments in international higher education. Although the articles and books are not primarily focused on internationalization of higher education, several of them deal with this theme, and the other publications are relevant for insight into the general

BOX 6.3 Mexican Association for International Education (Asociación Mexicana para la Educación Internacional; AMPEI)

The Mexican Association for International Education (Asociación Mexicana para la Educación Internacional; AMPEI) was founded in July 1992. With more than 150 members belonging to over 50 higher education institutions, AMPEI is a nonprofit association whose mission is to assist in the strengthening of the academic quality of Mexican educational institutions through international cooperation.

Sponsored by funds from different organizations that support higher education institutions at the international level, as well as by annual membership fees, AMPEI carries out different activities related to:

- Training of academic exchange professionals through specialized workshops
- Promotion of academic exchange and collaboration among local and foreign higher education institutions
- Investigation and analysis of negotiations for academic exchange activities
- Permanent dissemination of information regarding the activities of the association
- Promotion of the professional improvement of its members
- Recommendation of policies and practices that promote the development of educational programs and research projects in which faculty members, students, and university staff members from Mexico and other countries participate
- Training, systematization, and dissemination of information concerning the mission of the association
- Representation of the interests of the membership before national and international organizations
- Promotion of meetings and academic and professional events regarding international education and international cooperation
- Training tools and new practices of international education activities that increase the efficiency of AMPEI's work

Educación Global is the AMPEI journal, with one issue per year since 1997. Its aim is to disseminate articles on the internationalization of education and international cooperation. Its articles cover developments in Mexico and Latin America, but also include other parts of the world and thematic and conceptual developments as well. The articles are published in either Spanish or English. For more information, visit www.ampei.org.mx/publicaciones.

trends in international higher education. (For more information: www.bc.edu/cihe). In addition to these journals, other (higher) education research journals increasingly publish articles on the theme of the internationalization of higher education, for example, the *Comparative Education Review*, published by the University of Chicago for the Comparative and International Education Society (www.cies.us), and other journals in comparative education.

Finally, journals of the different associations such as NAFSA's *International Educator* (www .nafsa.org), the EAIE's *Forum* (www.eaie.nl), and the Institute of International Education's *IIE Networker Magazine* (www.iie.org) write about internationalization of higher education, although primarily with a focus on policy and practice. Also, the newsletter of the International Association of Universities publishes regularly on internationalization of higher education. Its *Global Surveys* on this topic, published in 2003, 2005, and 2010, provide insight into global and regional trends with respect to internationalization of higher education (see www.Iau-aiu.net).

WEBSITES

Websites are increasingly important sources of information, particularly as more and more printed sources move to the electronic realm. Some websites have already been mentioned above. Other valuable websites include the Manitoba International Education News Service (www.studyinmanitoba.ca/news-service-home), the Higher Education International Unit site and newsletter (www.international.ac.uk), and the service by the Dutch Organization for International Cooperation in Higher Education (Nuffic) (www.nuffic.nl/international-organizations/international-education-monitor). World Education Services (WES) has an online newsletter with relevant information on international higher education: *World Education News and Reviews* (www.wes.org/ewenr).

Important sources of information also include web-based news sites on higher education that write regularly on international education, for example, *University World News* (www.universityworldnews.com), *Inside Higher Education* (www.insidehighered.com), *The Chronicle of Higher Education* (www.chronicle.com, includes a global edition), the *Guardian* (www.guardian.co.uk/higher-education-network), and the *Times Higher Education* (www.timeshighereducation.co.uk).

There are also some interesting blogs on international education, such as the one by David Comp, University of Chicago, *International Higher Education Consulting Blog* (http://ihec-djc.blogspot.com/), and the one by Erik Beerkens, Leiden University, *Higher Education, Science & Innovation from a Global Perspective* (http://blog.beerkens.info/).

DATABASES

The most substantive database of studies in internationalization of higher education is the IDP Database of Research on International Education. This searchable database contains details of more than 7,500 books, articles, conference papers, and reports on various aspects of international education from publishers in Australia and abroad. The database houses material published from 1990 to the present. It contains references and publications by publishers and several organizations, not only from Australia but also from elsewhere, providing an informative overview of organizations, publishers, countries, and links. (See www.idp.com/research/database_of_research).

Another source of studies is The Observatory. This resource was originally a collaborative initiative with the Association of Commonwealth Universities and Universities UK. Since 2010, it is linked to I-Graduate. The Observatory tracks a wide range of media and news sources to keep subscribers up-to-date with the latest developments in borderless higher education around the world. The Observatory's full archive of news headlines, articles, and reports is available on an unlimited basis only to subscribers. However, a range of resources and services can be accessed by nonsubscribers (www.obhe.ac.uk).

It is important to note that several organizations and centers provide regular updates on key publications about internationalization and international higher education. Two that immediately come to mind are the Academic Cooperation Association and their newsletter *Education Europe* (www.aca-secretariat.be), and the Center for International Higher Education (www.bc.edu/cihe).

GENERAL BOOKS ON INTERNATIONALIZATION

It is not the intention here to provide a bibliography of publications on the theme. In 1996, Albert Over (1996) published such a bibliography as part of the book *Academic Mobility in a Changing World*. He identified 1,500 references since 1980 in English, French, and German. The strong presence of English was already clear, as only 8% of the publications were not in English; those were primarily in German, funded by the Deutscher Akademischer Austausch Dienst [German Academic Exchange Service], and even those were mainly official documents. At the time of the bibliography's publication, the focus with respect to internationalization was on mobility, which was also the central theme of the book in which it appeared. Since then, topics under *internationalization* have become much more diverse, and the number of publications has drastically increased. An attempt to update Over's (1996) bibliography would be an enormous exercise, even if limited to publications in English and the period 1990 to 2010. Kehm and

Teichler wrote in 2007: "In looking at authors addressing the international dimension of higher education, we often find references to persons such as—in alphabetical order—Philip G. Altbach, Jane Knight, Peter Scott, Ulrich Teichler, Marijk van der Wende and Hans de Wit" (p. 263). The list of authors of the *Sage Handbook on International Higher Education* reflects the broader pool of researchers in international education in recent years.

At the same time, the range of topics under the umbrella theme of internationalization of higher education has increased and the terms *globalization* and *regionalization* have become closely linked to and regularly overlap with *internationalization*.

The first publication to mention in this overview is:

Klasek, Charles B. (Ed.). (1992). *Bridges to the future: Strategies for internationalizing higher ducation.* Carbondale, IL: Association of International Education Administrators.

This seminal book was one of the first to examine the creation, development, and enhancement of international programs in U.S. colleges and universities. Its contribution rests in creating a debate, both in northern America and Europe, on the concept of internationalization, and it resulted in an initiative by the Institutional Management of Higher Education (IMHE) program of the Organization for Economic Cooperation and Development (OECD).

In 1995, a study appeared that attempted to provide a regional comparative overview of internationalization of higher education. It was based on the aforementioned initiative by the IMHE program of the OECD to map developments with respect to the international dimensions of higher education. The first study focused on Europe, northern America, and Australia. Later studies spotlighted the Asia-Pacific region, Latin America, and Africa. These studies still play an important role in the comparative analysis of internationalization of higher education and were funded by the OECD (the first two), the World Bank (the third), and the Carnegie and Ford Foundations (the fourth).

de Wit, H. (Ed.). (1995). *Strategies for internationalisation of higher education: A comparative study of Australia, Canada, Europe and the United States of America.*

Amsterdam: EAIE (in cooperation with IMHE/ OECD and AIEA).

de Wit, H., Jaramillo, I. C., Gacel A. J., & Knight, J. (Eds.). (2005). *Higher education in Latin America: The international dimension.* Washington, DC: World Bank, Directions in Development. Spanish edition: *Educacion Superior en America Latina, la Dimension Internacional.* Bogota, Colombia: Banco Mundial en Cooperacion con Mayol Ediciones.

Knight, J., & de Wit, H. (Eds.). (1997). *Strategies for internationalisation of higher education in Asia Pacific countries.* Amsterdam: EAIE in cooperation with IMHE/OECD and IDP-Education Australia.

Teferra, D., & Knight, J. (Eds.). (2008). *Higher education in Africa: The international dimension.* Boston and Accra, Ghana: Boston College, Center for International Higher Education, and Association of African Universities.

In addition, the study for IMHE/OECD on quality and internationalization of higher education may be included in that series:

Knight, J., & de Wit, H. (Eds.). (1999). *Quality and internationalisation of higher education.* Paris: OECD. French Edition: *Qualité et Internationalisation de l'Enseignement Supérieur,* Paris: OCDE. Spanish Edition (2001): *Calidad y Internacionalización de la Educación Superior,* Mexico: Asociación Nacional de Universidades e Instituciones de Educación.

Although these studies are outdated in their concrete data, still relevant today is their conceptual framework for understanding the internationalization of higher education.

Other general overviews and analyses of internationalization of higher education have been published as well, including:

de Wit, H. (2002). *Internationalisation of higher education in the United States of America and Europe: A historical, comparative and conceptual analysis.* Greenwood, CT: Greenwood Studies in Higher Education.

Knight, J. (2008). *Higher education in turmoil: The changing world of internationalization.* Rotterdam, the Netherlands: Sense Publishers.

Ninnes, P., & Hellsten, M. (Eds.). (2005). *Internationalizing higher education: Critical explorations of pedagogy and policy* (CERC Studies in Comparative Education: Vol. 16). New York: Springer.

Scott, P. (1998). Globalisation and the university. In Peter Scott (Ed.), *The Globalization of Higher Education*. Buckingham, UK: Society for Research into Higher Education and Open University Press.

In addition, general higher education works have been giving increasing attention to the internationalization of higher education, such as:

Altbach, P., Reisberg, L., & Rumbley, L. (2009). *Trends in global higher education: Tracking an academic revolution*. Boston: Boston College, Center for International Higher Education.
Enders, J., & Fulton, O. (Eds.). (2002). *Higher education in a globalising world: International trends and mutual observations*. The Netherlands: Kluwer.
Forest, J., & Altbach, P. (Eds.). (2006). *International handbook of higher education*, Vols 1 and 2. The Netherlands: Kluwer.
Larsen, K., & Vincent-Lancrin, S. (2004). *Internationalisation and trade in higher education: Opportunities and challenges*. Paris: OECD.

In the area of internationalization of the curriculum and international/intercultural competencies, some key publications that are referenced frequently include:

Beelen, J. (Ed.). (2007). *Implementing internationalisation at home*. Amsterdam: EAIE.
Deardorff, D. K. (Ed.). (2009). *The SAGE handbook of intercultural competence*. Thousand Oaks, CA: Sage.
Jones, E. (Ed.). (2010). *Internationalization and the student voice*. New York: Routledge.
Nilsson, B., & Otten, M. (Eds.). (2003). Internationalisation at home [Special issue]. *Journal of Studies in International Education, 7*(No. 1), 5–119.
Olson, C., Evans, R., & Shoenberg, R. F. (2007). *At home in the world: Bridging the gap between internationalization and multicultural education*. Washington, DC: American Council on Education.
Savicki, V. (2008). *Developing intercultural competence and transformation: Theory, research, and application in international education*. Sterling. VA: Stylus.

The above books owe a lot to two studies from the 1990s:

Mestenhauser, J., & Ellingboe, B. J. (1998). *Reforming the higher education curriculum: Internationalizing the campus*. Phoenix, AZ: American Council on Education/Oryx Press Series on Higher Education.

Van der Wende, M. C. (1996). Internationalising the curriculum in Dutch higher education: An international comparative perspective. *Journal of Studies in International Education, 1*, 53–72.

At the regional and national level, numerous books, too many to mention here, have been published over the past years, including those from several organizations that publish book series on internationalization. Previously mentioned was *The Observatory*. In addition, the Academic Cooperation Association (ACA), in cooperation with Lemmens Publishers in Bonn, Germany, publishes regular books on this theme, as do the EAIE and NAFSA: Association for International Educators. In the United States, the Institute of International Education (IIE) has a valuable series of publications. In addition to its annual report *Open Doors*, IIE also publishes, with support from the American Institute of Foreign Study, a series of books on global higher education research. The American Council on Education has published several series on mapping internationalization, as well as a series on campus leadership focused on internationalization. The European University Association (EUA), in cooperation with ACA and Raabe publishers, published the *EUA/ACA Handbook Internationalisation of European Higher Education*, which, as of 2011, is published as the *EAIE Handbook* and the *EUA Bologna Handbook, Making Bologna Work*, both with regular supplements (www.raabe.de). Other publishers like Sage Publications, Routledge, Stylus, and Sense Publishers regularly publish books on internationalization.

Recently, some interesting readers and books have been published that illustrate the increase of publications in the field:

Childress, L. K. (2010). *The twenty-first century university: Developing faculty engagement in internationalization*. New York: Peter Lang.
Lewin, R. (Ed.). (2009). *The handbook of practice and research in study abroad: Higher education and the quest for global citizenship*. New York: EECA/ Routledge, New York.
Maringe, F., & Foskett, N. (Eds.). (2010). *Globalization and internationalization in higher education: Theoretical, strategic and management perspectives*. London: Continuum.
Stearns, P. N. (2009). *Educating global citizens in colleges and universities: Challenges and opportunities*. New York: Routledge.

Wildavsky, B. (2010). *The great brain race: How global universities are reshaping the world.* Princeton: Princeton University Press

EDUCATION AND TRAINING IN INTERNATIONAL EDUCATION

One can see an increase in students and practitioners who consider international education a specialized career and look for master's and doctoral programs, as well as professional training modules. Professional associations such as NAFSA, EAIE, Association of International Education Administrators, and International Education Association of Australia offer training programs and resources to their members on a broad range of subjects.

In the United Kingdom, programs are also offered on international(ization of) higher education at the master's and professional doctorate level. Examples are the online master's in management of international higher education of Edge Hill University and the doctor of business administration in higher education management, a part-time professional doctoral program at the University of Bath, which has several students focusing on internationalization of higher education. The Centre for Higher Education Internationalisation in Milan is developing a doctoral and master's program in internationalization of higher education. Also, institutions in Australia, Canada, and the United States offer graduate programs that allow students to focus on internationalization of higher education, as is the case at centers such as the International Center for Higher Education Research in Kassel, Germany, and the Center for Higher Education Policy Studies in Twente, The Netherlands, earlier mentioned.

CONCLUDING OBSERVATIONS

The field is too broad to present a comprehensive overview of sources, publications, and training programs on the internationalization of higher education, and it has evolved over the years so drastically that this is an impossible task. However, the chapter attempted to provide an overview of key sources and trends in publications in this field.

An increase in researchers and publications from Asia, Latin America, and Africa should be noted. As a case in point, if one looks at the submitted and accepted manuscripts to the *Journal of Studies in International Education*, there is an ever increasing diversity, not only in themes and topics, but also in authors and the regions they come from and write about. At the same time, the field is still dominated primarily by English-speaking researchers, publications, and resources from Europe and northern America. It will be interesting to see if this will change in the years to come due to the increasing importance of Asia and emerging economies in the Middle East, Africa, and Latin America.

SECTION B

STRATEGIC DIMENSIONS IN INTERNATIONAL HIGHER EDUCATION

7

LEADERSHIP IN INTERNATIONAL HIGHER EDUCATION

JOHN D. HEYL AND JOSEPH TULLBANE

For international educators, leadership remains an elusive concept. Leadership is crucial to success in the role of senior international officer (SIO), a term used primarily in the United States (but with analogs in other countries) to refer to an institution's lead international administrator. Still, styles of successful leadership clearly vary greatly from individual to individual, from institution to institution, and at different stages of the internationalization process. Moreover, as professionals interacting with colleagues around the world, international educators intuitively understand that leadership is itself a culturally determined construct, and its practice is shaped significantly by culture. This chapter will focus on the role of the SIO in the U.S. context but will also highlight exemplars of leadership in other world regions and in different higher education settings. These highlights are not intended to be all-inclusive, in terms of covering every possible situation or region worldwide, but serve as examples of cultural and situational differences that permeate leadership challenges within the field of international education. The chapter concludes with speculations on critical global leadership skills required of international educators in the 21st century.

LEADERSHIP THEORIES: A BRIEF OVERVIEW

Theories or models of leadership have gained large audiences in the past 20 years. More recently, theories drawn mainly from the business world have penetrated higher education. That noted, the field of formalized leadership study is quite young, and many of these approaches, therefore, present different emphases. Collins (2005) speaks of 5th Level Leadership, which moves organizations from "good" to "great." Senge (2006) emphasizes the importance of becoming a "learning organization." Bolman and Deal (2003) urge "reframing" organizations to find the levers for leadership. Lipman-Blumen (2000) identifies nine "achieving styles" that can lead to "connective leadership."

Many commentators speak about *transformational* leadership, but most professionals have only a vague idea of what this term really means. Most day-to-day leadership theory focuses on what the field calls transactional leadership, that is, as the name implies a transaction between leader and follower, often entailing a focus on incentives such as promotions or other recognition for good work. Transformational leadership, originally espoused by James MacGregor Burns in *Leadership* (1978), suggests that a transformational leader engages his or her followers in a concept or idea that is so compelling that it creates a connection that motivates and increases the potential that the followers will reach their highest potential. Transformational leadership creates something more than just transactional exchanges. In this concept of leadership, the followers expand on the leader's original idea or vision and feed it back to the leader, ultimately causing a reciprocal positive spiral that lifts the leader, the followers, and the vision itself to new heights, creating something bigger than originally imagined. In the process, both leader and follower are morally uplifted and more concerned with the collective good than with their personal needs and demands. In international higher education, the American Council on Education has focused many of its publications on university leadership on *transformational* change (Eckel, Green, & Hill, 2001; Heyl, 2007, pp. 5–19). In more general treatments, other writers, such as Bass (1985), Howell and Ovolio (1993) and Kouzes and Posner (2002), have expanded on Burns's original ideas and are worth noting.

Theories of leadership are useful to higher education leaders because they help individuals identify their own strengths, weaknesses, and opportunities within a broader context than their immediate situation. Similarly, these theories can aid a leader in identifying the strengths and weaknesses of subordinates and colleagues alike, thereby, adapting their leadership style to the situation at hand. Finally, they can provide guides to lead from strengths, remedy weaknesses, and exploit opportunities for transformational change.

Speaking of transformational leadership presupposes a basic knowledge of the theories behind successful leading. At this level, leadership is a fairly simple concept: It is a process of interaction between two individuals (usually a leader and a follower or multiple followers) in pursuit of some goal to better the entity or organization within which they operate. In practical terms, however, this relationship or interaction can be quite complex, especially as the process expands to include multiple actors on multiple levels of interaction. For most college or university administrators, this process includes three tiers of relationships: (a) supervisor-subordinate;

(b) colleague-colleague, within the constraints of the institution; and (c) colleague-colleague, at the regional or national level. For SIOs, an additional tier must be included, that of colleague-colleague at the international level. This last tier is particularly important because it entails the added concepts of diplomacy and cross-cultural understanding between one's own society and that of other nations and cultures.

One striking example, taken from headlines, may be sufficient to show that however powerful (and popular) a model or theory of leadership may be, all such models have limitations.

In his widely read book *The Toyota Way,* Jeffrey Liker (2004) explained the phenomenal success of the Japanese automaker as a consequence of leadership and company culture. Then came the 2009 recalls over gas pedal engineering and the global media focus on the failures of leadership during a period of rapid expansion. Akio Toyoda, Toyota CEO and the founder's grandson, apologized to a global audience for failures of leadership. In an unprecedented appearance before a U.S. House committee investigating the sudden acceleration of Toyota vehicles, Toyoda admitted that the company had perhaps grown too fast and lost its focus on quality (Vartabedian & Bensinger, 2010). The Toyota Way had apparently gone astray, perhaps because it was so culturally insular.

And yet the Toyota Way offers positive lessons, as well, with regard to the importance of working toward staff development and empowerment, planning long term, and growing leaders who know the work in detail but also think strategically. The main lessons for the international educator: Do not be too tied to a single leadership model because, in the long run, all leadership theories are imperfect. Indeed, in universities one is typically dealing with multiple stakeholders: upper administration, faculty, students, staff colleagues, unions, parents, alumni, benefactors, perhaps state government—all of whom can claim a measure of legitimacy. In this context, international educators should identify their strengths and weaknesses in a clear-eyed process of self-reflection, know the "invisible tapestry" (Kuh & Whitt, 1988) of their own institution, and continually grow in skill, sensitivity, and judgment in leading others (Van de Water, 2006).

The Toyota Way also suggests that there may be distinctive Asian versions of leadership.

Although some elements of Japanese manufacturing clearly draw on non-Japanese insights into high-quality/high-morale production management techniques—mainly W. Edwards Deming's focus on quality control—recent discussions of leadership have emphasized distinctive Eastern and Western approaches. Chen and An (2009), for example, have argued that there is a distinctive Chinese model of leadership that is based on "self-cultivation, context profundity, and action dexterity" (pp. 200–203). More recently, leadership has been placed in a global context and led to conjectures about characteristics of truly *global* leadership (Pusch, 2009).

Another cultural dimension that is of increasing interest to students of leadership focuses on features that distinguish between male and female leadership styles. Leadership models or theories noted thus far—with the exception of that formulated by Lipman-Blumen (2000)—have been developed by (and for) mainly male investigators or practitioners. This evident bias may well be more the result of the ratio of male to female leaders at the time the theories were developed, rather than an intentional slight. That noted, with the increasing number of highly qualified women moving into SIO ranks, international educators have been asking if there are leadership differences between men and women in positions of international education leadership (Williamson, 2010). The political successes of Julia Gillard in Australia, Angela Merkel in Germany, and Dilma Vana Linhares Rousseff in Brazil (to mention only a few leading examples) and the financial/business successes of Christine Lagarde (IMF), Meg Whitman (Hewlett-Packard), and Virginia Rometty (IBM) suggest that female perspectives on leadership deserve more attention than they have received in the past (Barsh, Cranston, & Lewis, 2009; Tarr-Whelan, 2009).

International education at women's colleges and universities provides a particularly focused effort to combine leadership and internationalization. Carol Christ (2011), president of Smith College (in Massachusetts), recalling Smith students traveling to Paris in the 1920s, says, "At Smith College, our mission is to educate women of promise who will change the world." A recent summit in the United States brought together female campus presidents to review "lessons learned" from building executive careers on university campuses (Stripling, 2011). Teresa Sullivan, the first female president of the University of Virginia, offered some advice on speaking up at meetings: "Have the sound bite at the end of the conversation." Good advice for anyone trying to shape an institution's agenda.

These lessons are also relevant to the growing number of female leaders in international education, both in the United States and around the world. Of the first 10 presidents of the Association of International Education Administrators (AIEA, 1982–1992), none were female; of the last 10 presidents of AIEA (2003–2012), five have been female. Moreover, AIEA's 2011 and 2012 annual conferences were the first to host conference sessions on female SIOs ("The Rise and Shine of the Female SIO"; "The Evolving Role of Female SIOs").

LEADERSHIP IN PRACTICE

SIOs are inevitably middle managers in what has been termed a "loosely coupled" organization, the contemporary university (Heyl, 2007, pp. 10, 35). They must be familiar with planning strategically, building coalitions, pooling resources, and approaching new issues with "out of the box" solutions. In short, they must be masters of the institutional culture and change agents. But any institutional change requires vision, resources, and time. Sometimes, those resources—those that actually expand annually budgeted resources—lie surprisingly close at hand, perhaps right in one's own back yard, but external to the academic institution. A term has been coined to reflect this promising interaction between the global and the local: *grounded globalism* (see Chapter 17, this volume). Grounded globalism assumes that every successful global initiative, just as it must meet a real need in the global partner, must link back to the local history and culture of the initiating institution. Since *global* and *local* are often housed in distinct disciplines and assert competing claims on campus budgets, seeing and mobilizing links between them often requires a special kind of vision.

No doubt such local resources for internationalization—corporate headquarters, ethnic alliances, consulates (or honorary consuls)—are more abundant in urban centers. But such resources/partners exist sometimes in unexpected places, as well. One university and one SIO who has achieved more with this resource than most is Joel Glassman at the University of Missouri-St. Louis (See Box 7.1).

BOX 7.1 Leadership and the Local Community

Joel Glassman

Director, Center for International Studies, University of Missouri-St. Louis, USA

The University of Missouri-St. Louis takes its land grant mission seriously. Outreach, or community service, is an integral part of the mission of every academic unit on campus, including for the Center for International Studies. Early in the development of the center, we initiated outreach, or community education programs, designed to make the international education resources of the campus available to the community. For example, soon after the center was established, we conducted seminars and conferences about NATO, the United Nations, and U.S.-Asian relations to share our faculty expertise with those in the community interested in keeping informed about international affairs.

As our ties to St. Louis's international communities, including many ethnic communities, began to mature, we came to see them as a source of educational resources and not just the beneficiary of our educational programs. Rather than seeing these as one-way relationships, with the University providing information to them, we started to see these external audiences/communities as simultaneously providing resources to the university. Once we conceptualized the flow of information and resources moving in both directions, we were able to form genuine partnerships with many communities. An early partnership was with the St. Louis Stuttgart, Germany, Sister City Committee, which wanted to develop additional formal ties with Stuttgart. Working together, we established a student exchange program with the University of Stuttgart, and the committee helped raise funds for scholarships for the exchange students.

Many ethnic communities have enormous pride in their heritage culture. They are eager to see that heritage made accessible, both to their own community and to the community-at-large. They increasingly look to the university to create a "space" for teaching about their heritage, and we look to them for the resources to enable us to further our mission of cross-cultural education.

And through these partnerships, what has been accomplished? We have funded endowed professorships in African, Chinese, Greek, Irish, and Japanese studies. We have established German and Greek culture centers. We have funded lecture series about Greece, Israel, and Mexico and endowed annual study abroad scholarships to several destinations. We also enjoy robust and growing partnerships with the Bosnian, French, Indian, Indonesian, and Polish communities. In each of these still developing relationships, we are exploring the possibility of formally establishing an academic base.

In some instances, funds have been raised locally, while in others the local community, in partnership with the university, has raised funds internationally. Of course, every encounter has not been successful. In several cases, we found communities that are unwilling, or unable, to develop ties to a majority community institution. In the case of the two most notable failures, imagined commitments to another local university made it difficult to develop a partnership.

As the university's SIO, it has been a great opportunity to work to build and nurture these relationships. Enjoying the support of the senior campus administrator, president or chancellor, of your university is essential. We have been privileged to enjoy that support.

Beyond that, it has been important to recognize the real diversity beneath the surface of our community. Our ethnic communities enjoy a strong sense of identity and have very real aspirations to see their heritage recognized and given a place in the educational efforts of this community. In short, they want to be stakeholders. Building these alliances and partnerships has enhanced the profile and visibility of the University of Missouri-St. Louis in this community. It also has enabled us to raise millions of dollars to support international education, both on campus and in the community.

Mobilizing resources for internationalization—whether local, private, corporate, institutional, or governmental—is a key challenge for international educators. This is particularly true in the U.S. higher education context in this period of shrinking public support and declining endowment accounts. Colleges and universities have consolidated divisions, frozen hiring, and reduced international and even some domestic travel. As institutions seek to protect their most fundamental elements, areas that are perceived as tangential are particularly targeted for personnel and funding cuts and sometimes elimination. To bolster revenues, campuses have raised tuition and fees and urged all units to explore ways to raise funds to support their programs.

Although the dire fiscal context at the time of this writing is not likely to be a permanent feature of campus financing, SIOs will continue to be asked to justify their investments in new ventures in ways that are, at worst, revenue neutral. This puts international educators in a challenging situation. While part of their role is highly valued for the additional tuition revenue it might bring (i.e., international student recruitment and enrollment) other aspects of their role—for example, study abroad and foreign visiting scholars—are seen as cost centers to be carefully audited and cautiously managed. Widely held perceptions of international education operations as peripheral to the core mission of the institution adds to the leadership challenge facing the international educator. Part of the leadership challenge for SIOs is to convince senior leadership at their institutions that internationalization is both mainstream and institution enhancing.

Inevitably, an important aspect of the SIO's case for a seat at the leadership table within the institution has to do with resources: how to expand institutional resources in a sustainable way that also benefits the broader internationalization process. Many practices at the office level demonstrate efforts at efficiency and an entrepreneurial spirit (McCarthy, 2010). These include creating more efficient workflows; using technology wisely; and, in selected areas such as study abroad data management, overseas recruitment, and English language instruction, outsourcing services. On the resource development side, there are opportunities to seek support through grants and gifts, joint ventures with private sector organizations, alumni development, and the kind of local partnerships illustrated in Box 7.1.

Mitch Leventhal, Vice Chancellor for Global Affairs at the SUNY system's Global Center in New York, has presented a bold new approach to building resources for internationalization. Leventhal (2011) calls his strategy *performance-based reinvestment.* (See Chapter 22, this volume, for further discussion of this strategy.) Basically, he sees an unusual opportunity not only to become more efficient with current resources but also to expand dedicated resources for internationalization because of twin demand forces working on U.S. higher education. With first-year college cohorts likely to decline in coming years—and foreign demand for U.S. study (especially at the undergraduate level) expanding again after declines following the September 11, 2011, attacks and subsequent visa restrictions—SIOs have the opportunity to make a case for a marginal sweep of international student tuition to support broader internationalization. He summarizes his strategy as follows:

> The United States remains the most desired destination for international students, and demand for international education continues to grow at a high rate. Yet despite the large numbers of international students on our shores, these students comprise less than 4% of our total enrollment in higher education.
>
> Furthermore, although overall enrollment is currently at a national high water mark, all projections show looming declines in domestic enrollment, as the current demographic bulge moves through the system and the economy improves—both of which are inevitable over the next two to four years. In other words, we must anticipate increasing absorptive capacity at many U.S. institutions.
>
> We must strategically tap into this market to both internationalize our campuses and provide the financial resources to achieve our objectives. It is critical to create a "virtuous circle," connecting new income associated with international student tuition with the other imperatives of internationalization, i.e., study abroad scholarships, faculty internationalization grants, scholars-at-risk funding, international services infrastructure, etc.

Leventhal (2011) addresses the special situation in the United States, which is a net importer of globally mobile students and thus a net exporter of higher education. SIOs in the

United States have been aware for many years of the extraordinary revenue streams associated with special services for international students, especially through English language programs (ESL). But other countries could also learn lessons from Leventhal's model, both net importers of transnational students (e.g., Australia, Canada, Italy, Spain, United Kingdom), as well as net exporters of these students (e.g., China and India). Clearly, the SIO must be alert to the opportunities—and risks—of pooling both internal and external resources to further institutional internationalization.

LEADERSHIP IN A GLOBAL CONTEXT

As noted earlier in this chapter, there can be significant differences in how international education operations are viewed and implemented in different parts of the world. The societal context and educational traditions of a country or region influence the form and function taken by all levels of education, including international education. To communicate and negotiate successfully in that fourth dimension of SIO leadership, the leader must have a sense of where international colleagues are coming from and where their needs and demands are driving them. An understanding of the trends in degree structures, regional alignments, assessment, and funding patterns elsewhere in the world is more than a matter of cross-cultural communication (de Wit, 2009). It is a major factor for the success or failure of SIOs in the global knowledge society of the 21st century. What follow are examples of some regional differences that play into the global role of SIOs today and in the future.

Europeans, as founders of the world's first Western universities, have been active in various forms of international activities from earliest times. As pointed out in earlier chapters, the forms and rationales for transnational travel by students and scholars have changed radically over the centuries. In recent times, the evolution and enlargement of the European Union, the Bologna Process launched in 1999 to create a European Higher Education Area, and the global competition for student and scholar talent have profoundly changed the environment in which SIOs work. If anything, the challenges to leadership in this very active context may well be greater than ever – as Box 7.2 by Hans de Wit demonstrates.

BOX 7.2 International Education Leadership in Europe

Hans de Wit

Professor of Internationalization of Higher Education, (Netherlands) and Centre for High Education Internationalisation (Italy)

Talking in general terms about leadership in international education in Europe is not easy, as the higher education systems, structures, and cultures are quite diverse. Higher education in Europe is based on different traditions in the United Kingdom, northern continental Europe and southern Europe and, due to many years of communism, has evolved differently in central and eastern Europe as well. The result is many varied paths to internationalization. Over the last decade, one can observe a stronger convergence in these systems and in the organization of international education, influenced by global (the global knowledge economy) and regional (the Bologna Process) developments. Still, higher education and therefore its international dimension are strongly embedded in national systems, legislation, and cultures.

International offices have been a common feature of northern European higher education for more than 25 years. In the United Kingdom, they are focused more on recruitment of international students, whereas in continental Europe, they are more directed to cooperation and exchange of students and faculty, stimulated by European programs such as Erasmus. The offices and their leaders originally held a marginal position in the university hierarchy, positioned under either student or academic affairs. In southern Europe, they were and in several cases still are primarily administrative units with little role in policy and strategic development.

In the 1990s, in northern Europe—and to a certain extent also in central and eastern Europe—the role and influence of international offices increased, as internationalization became a more central part of higher education policy. International offices expanded, and their SIOs became more involved in strategic development of their institutions; in several cases, one can observe the development of new senior positions (vice presidents or deputy vice presidents international). Such a development also can be observed in other parts of Europe, reflecting the increased role of international education in European higher education. This broader role includes bilateral and multilateral agreements, European programs, exchanges, foreign student advising and service (including housing, visa and credential evaluation), technical assistance projects, and study abroad. Although requiring a broad background, the typical European SIO does not have academic credentials and is little involved in academic issues, with the internationalization of the curriculum falling outside his or her role.

Also in the 1990s, with the growth of activities and the complexity of their administration, the administration of international education in many institutions became more decentralized, with faculties, schools, and departments opening their own offices and appointing their own international education officers. This radical expansion of international education is reflected in the growth of the European Association for International Education (EAIE), whose annual conferences grew from an attendance of 600 in its founding year (1989) to more than 3,500 in 2011.

Currently, a new trend in leadership of international education is emerging, as one can see, for example, in the Netherlands. With the increased importance of international education, it has also become more mainstreamed. International offices and separate policies for internationalization—islands within institutions—are viewed as ineffective and not in accordance with the central role international education should play in the mission and plans of the institution. As a result, the positions of vice presidents international are gradually disappearing, as internationalization is seen more as an integrated part of education and research policy of all units instead of as a separate position. At the departmental and school level, the increased focus on internationalization of the curriculum is seen more as an integral part of curriculum development than as a function of the international office.

If this trend continues, it will have important implications for leadership in international education in Europe. The professional development and support for the administration of international education will continue to be important, and a professional organization like EAIE will continue to play a crucial role. Regarding policy and strategy and the increased priority for internationalizing the curriculum, however, the role of the SIO in these areas will continue to decline. This will require a different approach to issues such as advocacy, strategic development, and policy debates.

In the African context, international educators work amid the transition to a more open society, dealing with the twin realities of an underfunded educational system and sharp disparities of wealth and opportunity (Marmolejo, 2011). As Nico Jooste suggests in Box 7.3, international education leaders are thus required to maximize limited resources, while addressing key societal needs.

BOX 7.3 African Challenges for International Education Leadership

Nico Jooste

Director, Office for International Education, Nelson Mandela Metropolitan University (South Africa)

The internationalization of higher education institutions in Africa is as important for institutional leaders elsewhere in the world as it is on the continent. The fact that local experts on higher education in Africa are mostly absent from global debates on the internationalization of their institutions of higher learning promotes a global debate lacking the true intricacies of higher education within Africa. Only those who are directly committed to the success of African higher education institutions can provide a true understanding of this unique subject. From the outset, it needs to be recognized that, contrary to popular belief, African higher education is a national competency and, as such, functions within national systems and not as part of an African system of higher education. This in itself is one of the major challenges facing international education leaders on the continent. In many cases, these leaders operate as one of a few institutional leaders in the country, and in some cases, the sole international education leader within their country.

Being a leader of a higher education institution in Africa requires a unique, multiskilled individual who is invested in internationalization and one who can employ international partnerships as more than just a useful tool in internationalization. Due to a leader's lack of experience, exposure, and resources, these partnerships become the only links with other higher education institutions globally, with the result that internationalization, as practiced in the developed world, becomes an unobtainable dream.

Leaders in African higher education institutions seldom have the luxury of SIOs to provide dedicated capacity to lead internationalization at the institution. The lack of capacity, both from a skills and from a resource point of view, results in limiting the scope of internationalization and reduces internationalization to a process that focuses solely on institutional linkages. This limitation results in international offices becoming linkage offices, and those practitioners of internationalization being reduced to linkage officials. This places a restriction on the practice of internationalization and makes the mainstreaming of internationalization very difficult to achieve. Although this reality is indicative of a much greater problem for African higher education institutions, the limits on internationalization are driven by higher education leaders who are required to function under extremely challenging circumstances. This includes resource scarcities as well as a relative lack of institutional autonomy. Institutional leadership is constantly challenged by the demands of an ever globalizing knowledge society on the one hand, and the narrow agendas of the ever changing—and in many cases unstable—political condition of their country on the other.

To overcome these obstacles to internationalization leaders in most higher education institutions on the continent need to recognize that strength and opportunity lies in the practice of the African value of *ubuntu: the recognition of mutual interdependence and the promotion of compassionate and responsible leadership.*

The reasonable success of South African higher education institutions in internationalization lies in the accomplishments of the International Education Association of South Africa, which provides, in the spirit of *ubuntu*, collective leadership and guidance to South African universities in their internationalization efforts. In a resource-scarce environment, the association collectively provides leadership and creates capacity that would be impossible to achieve on an institutional basis alone.

Those leaders who many years ago invested in this mindset are succeeding in their international efforts and are reaping the fruits of their success.

On a broader African scale, the same concept is being introduced by the African Network for Internationalization of Education. The promotion of a common understanding of internationalization among African higher education institutions will take place only if this forum is given the space and resources to grow into a continent-wide leadership resource that would be able to guide and empower internationalization and higher education leaders throughout Africa.

To conclude, the successful international education leader in the African higher education context needs to be an innovative individual with compassion for the success of the institution, the broader society, and the environment. The person should also understand the great benefits of collective leadership as well as the challenges it brings.

As the most populous and, in many ways, most dynamic region of the world, educational leaders in Asia-Pacific face unique higher education challenges in coming decades. On the one hand, they must deal either with a rapidly expanding demand for university education (India, China, Vietnam, Thailand) or with shrinking cohorts of university age students (Japan, South Korea, Taiwan). As net exporters of globally mobile students, these countries must try to turn brain drain to brain circulation that can benefit their economies in an increasingly competitive global environment. As Sonny Lim discusses below in Box 7.4, Asian SIOs must be highly attuned to new directions from their institutions, national economies, and globalization.

BOX 7.4 Asian-Pacific Issues in International Education Leadership

Sonny Lim
Director of the Office of Public Affairs, Yale-NUS College (Singapore)

In contrast to many universities in Western Europe and America, higher education institutions in the Asia-Pacific region have long embraced a "flat world." Decades before Pulitzer Prize-winner Thomas Friedman wrote *The World is Flat* (2005), discussing the impact of the "new players" and new technologies in evolving globalization, many societies in Asia-Pacific were forced to reinvent and retool their economies in the aftermath of World War II and decolonization. Most had little choice but to build export-led economies to meet the demands of consumers in wealthier nations. On campuses, in response to centralized growth plans, university administrators were tasked to expand teaching and training capacity, while at the same time managing change and crises with every ebb and flow of globalization.

Singapore, South Korea, Taiwan, and Hong Kong (the Tiger nations) are prime examples of globalized economies. In the 1950s, when confronted with great odds to even survive amid Cold War realignments, the Tigers exhorted their people to embrace change by working hard and putting off personal consumption. Their future would be to produce quality goods and to export the best to the West. This future also depended on all students studying feverishly, while also accepting that not all who desired a university education would get the opportunity.

In government and on campuses, higher education leaders also accepted the overriding need to train and produce a workforce for multinational corporations and foreign investors. With

(Continued)

(Continued)

international projects high on the agenda, the Senior International Officer (SIO) on campus was required to possess not only global knowledge but also crisis-mode instincts and savvy: She or he needed to take action ahead of the next wave of change and to constantly refresh teaching, research, and institutional strategy. In addition, the SIO was expected to have the vision and vigor of a chief executive to engage foreign partners and programs. For this reason, the de facto SIO on campus was and typically is the president, rector, or vice chancellor.

On other administrative levels, there are directors and managers similar to the SIOs described in this chapter, but most operate with a significant advantage: SIOs in Asia-Pacific do not have to worry as much as their Western counterparts about gaining their share of funding for programs and projects. Internalization is a high priority almost by definition, and most international departments are funded well and report directly to the president or provost.

Meanwhile, millions of Chinese, Indian, and Asia-Pacific students continue to travel to study in North America, Australia, New Zealand, and Western Europe. Within the data, however, there is a looming fork in the road: More and more of these students are drawn to studying management and business versus, for instance, applied sciences and engineering. Some may even seek a liberal arts education (Institute of International Education, 2011). No longer just focused on the sciences or engineering, and supported by burgeoning middle classes from Bangalore to Busan to Beijing, future cohorts will eventually acquire a wider educational base and return to a modernized Asia-Pacific to create and lead more private- and public-sector institutions. In time, one could well expect higher professional standards and practices to take root among leadership circles from boardrooms to classrooms in an "Asia Anew."

Campus leadership models and practices in Asia-Pacific will thus likely evolve and improve, with internationalization remaining a core mission and catalyst for change. Initially confronting and then embracing a "flat world," Tiger nation universities might well offer a distinctive model of campus leadership, one that defines change-management skills and crisis-mode instincts as indispensable to tackling a more connected and more complicated global environment.

LEADERSHIP SKILLS
FOR THE 21ST CENTURY

Understanding that the key skills the SIO will need may change in coming decades, this section tries to identify current requirements for effective leadership. Clearly, the SIO must be a multitalented and multitasking professional, adapting to and shaping multiple environments. But with changes in institutional missions, shifting funding patterns, and new arenas of cooperation and competition in higher education globally, it appears that a few key skills deserve special attention.

Entrepreneurship

The precipitous decline in public funding for higher education—what is sometimes called the *privatization* of public higher education—and the dramatic advance of private and for-profit higher education globally are forcing all university administrators to think as entrepreneurs. Deans are encouraged to develop fee-based professional training programs; continuing education units (now often called outreach) are mandated to expand adult and nontraditional enrollment (in particular through online teaching); U.S. athletic departments seek ever more lucrative television contracts for their major sports; student services build cash-cow residence halls (built with state-issued bonds)—and international education administrators are charged with expanding international student enrollments and English as a Second Language (ESL) centers, charging large fees to support study abroad, and working with central administration to support the launching of branch campuses abroad. If college presidents in an earlier era might have thought a fine arts building, a new library, or new science lab facilities were their largest ambitions, they now unveil plans for ambitious online offerings and a physical presence in Buenos Aires, Shanghai, or Abu Dhabi (Wildavsky, 2010, pp. 42–69). International education leaders need to be familiar with all of these initiatives and to help shape those that have the potential to truly internationalize the entire institution. It should be noted that private institutions, more tuition-driven than their public counterparts, have applied these lessons for many years. Whereas relatively high "home school tuition" and more flexible "discounting" have often supported internationalization efforts at these institutions, shrinking or slow-growth endowments and high recruitment costs for a diminishing pool of first-year domestic students will continue to make it challenging for SIOs at private institutions to achieve their internationalization goals.

The role of international educators in the context of the continuing globalization of higher education is complex and sometimes treacherous. On the one hand, they must provide accurate, unbiased information relevant to the university's decision to embark on a global project. On the other hand, SIOs should bring professional values of cross-cultural sensitivity, transparency, academic integrity, and ethical behavior, as well as respect for all stakeholders to the project—even if these clash with the purely business perspective of the venture. Heightening the complexities of the position and the leadership role of the international educator is the inherent conflict between the need to use the leader's expertise in a field that few others in the institutional leadership fully understand, to advise and support the president, rector, or dean and the need, for the very same reason, to serve as a standard bearer for the internationalization of the institution (often seen as a partisan stance)

The values of global business tend to focus on competitiveness, branding, margins, and opportunity costs. The values of international educators tend to focus on integration, acknowledgment of difference, and the continuous expansion of global consciousness (Herrera, 2008). The latter values are closer to those of the faculty than those of the CEO. Of course, these need not be in conflict. The successful global project combines both sets of values in integrative ways. What is new for SIOs is that the professional values of the international education community must be integrated with both the cultural values of the broader society and the competitive/collaborative values of their institution (de Wit, 2009, pp. 2–3). For these reasons, the SIO must become a globally minded academic entrepreneur.

Cross-cultural Collaboration

International educators know that they must support programs that encourage the development of intercultural competence in students and in faculty and staff colleagues. But pivotal to their ultimate success may well be knowledge of their own intercultural competence or, as the case may be, incompetence. Although some SIOs bring to their role extensive experience in other cultures, most SIOs do not come from academic disciplines such as area studies or foreign languages that build skills of cultural adaptation. Moreover, they have typically learned the role of SIO through on the job training. This includes developing skills of cross-cultural collaboration.

Several commentators have emphasized the importance of knowing oneself as a prerequisite for successful leadership. For example, Paige and Goode (2009, p. 341) note that international educators must develop "cultural self awareness" to be effective trainers and study abroad administrators. "Cultural self awareness is the foundation for intercultural competence because understanding one's own culture makes it easier to recognize other cultural practices, anticipate where cultural differences are greater, and thus be better prepared for those cultural challenges" (p. 336). Pusch (2009, p. 71) takes the argument a step further by suggesting that knowledge of their own culture is not sufficient: Global leaders must also understand the impact of their own culture on themselves.

SIOs operate in a unique set of cultural contexts that require diverse leadership skills. On the one hand, they must understand the culture of their institution, whether it be a university campus, a professional association, a government or profit/nonprofit agency, or a corporate entity. SIOs must understand the levers for change at a college or university, the institutional readiness for change, and the identities of both allies and obstructers. The role of trainer is important because international education leaders are often called on to train both colleagues and the boss—the president, rector, provost, or dean— the person who has the authority to make critical budget and prioritizing decisions.

But, perhaps unique to the role, SIOs must also operate collaboratively across cultures worldwide. This requires knowledge of the nuances of other cultures, other languages, and certainly an awareness of the constraints under which foreign colleagues operate.

None of this is easy to acquire, but globalization is making this repertoire of skills increasingly essential. As Western SIOs interact more consistently and increasingly face-to-face with non-Western colleagues and the global mobility of students and faculty accelerates, the burden will fall on them to lead effective cross-cultural collaboration to expand opportunities (Hofstede, 2009, pp. 94–98).

Collaboration is the other element in cross-cultural collaboration. Virtually nothing happens in international education, almost by definition, as the work of a single individual. The SIO's work is the opposite of the solitary scholar's dogged labor in dusty archives. International education is essentially an interpersonal, collaborative field. The power of collaboration is the central theme of Disney executive Michael Eisner's (2010) *Working Together: Why Great Partnerships Succeed.* In the field of international education, Ralph Smuckler (2003), long-time SIO at Michigan State University, has written a memoir *A University Turns to the World: A Personal History of the Michigan State University International Story.* University presidents also value the power of "leveraging human resources," especially in the context of diminishing financial resources, as Victor Boschini, Jr. (2011), chancellor at Texas Christian University (Houston), has noted: "The creation of a common working community has been another key element in transforming international education [at TCU]" Taken together, these diverse perspectives from both business and higher education highlight what can be accomplished when leadership and collaborative chemistry work together.

Finally, collaboration is becoming increasingly urgent as globalization narrows prospects for individual institutions operating alone. As Stockley and de Wit (2011) point out, whether an association, a consortium, or a network, and whether faculty-driven (bottom-up) or leadership-driven (top-down), all such collaborations require leaders who can articulate shared goals, identify institutional complementarities, balance institutional self-interest and group benefit, mobilize human and financial resources, and support strong communication among partners. SIOs will be increasingly called on to provide this kind of leadership. Stockley and de Wit (2011) conclude:

> Strategic partnerships in research, teaching and transfer of knowledge, between universities and of universities with business and beyond national borders, will be the future for higher education, in order to manage the challenges that globalisation will place on it. Cooperation for competition and competition for cooperation: this will be driving higher education globally in the years to come." p. 58)

Assessment and the Learning Organization

Traditionally colleges and universities have thought of themselves as "producing" knowledge and knowledge seekers—or at least students exposed to certain key traditions in the arts, cultures, science, and technology. In some higher education systems, especially in Europe and Latin America, university study often results in a license (literally, a *licenciatura* or *diplom*) or national examination that is a gateway to a profession, more like legal and medical education in the United States. Globally today, stakeholders both inside and outside higher education, and whatever the field of study, increasingly expect evidence that a certain level of learning has in fact taken place. This requires assessment. (See Chapter 10, this volume, for a discussion of Outcomes Assessment in International Education.)

Assessment has come to mean many things in a university environment. The most familiar to faculty, at least in the United States, is the attempt to measure the effectiveness of professors, initially through student evaluations and tenure reviews and, most recently, through public posting of professors' teaching load and salary (June, 2011). In international education, assessment has focused thus far on two related topics: campus internationalization and student learning on global knowledge or competence.

SIOs must be familiar with both of these streams of assessment since they impinge directly on their work and the ultimate justification for their role as educators.

Assessing campus internationalization has become a central feature of the SIO role in recent years. Indeed, this theme is treated in different ways throughout this volume (in particular, see Chapters 10 and 24). In the United States, the American Council on Education made the first systematic effort to tackle this topic by launching a series of studies on leadership and "comprehensive internationalization" in 2001 (Heyl, 2007, pp. 8–10). This has more recently been expanded in a transatlantic study that focuses more on issues related specifically to assessment (de Wit, 2009). Of special interest is the assessment tool developed by a group of Dutch institutions, the so-called MINT questionnaire, which offers an institutional self-evaluation that tracks internationalization policies and goals to resources and through to activities and implementation (van Gaalen, 2009). Even broader in the range of institutions involved, the IMPI (Indicators for Measuring and Profiling Internationalization) project is an effort to develop both quantitative and qualitative measures launched by institutions in six European countries in 2010 (IMPI, 2012). By introducing this kind of assessment to the broader university community, the SIO can raise the profile of internationalization by linking assessment to diverse units on campus, from academics to student affairs and institutional research.

The assessment of student global learning has taken many forms, initially with the development of area studies, foreign language, and other interdisciplinary (global studies) programs and, more recently, with certificates to document a specific set of coursework and other activities with a coherent international theme (see Heyl, 2007, pp. 32–34 and Chapter 14, this volume). But these programmatic innovations fall largely within the traditional framework of courses completed, not necessarily knowledge acquired. The current movement toward global learning assessment rests on prospects for statistically measuring changes in student knowledge, skills, and attitudes. A plethora of assessment instruments have emerged that claim to measure this kind of learning (see Fantini, 2009; Chapters 10 and 16, this volume). Much of the

application of these assessment tools relates to study abroad, but there are important opportunities to apply them to the home campus as a measure of comprehensive institutional internationalization (Deardorff, Pysarchik, & Yun, 2009).

Being proactive in the assessment arena places the SIO within a major trend in higher education today and helps make the university a true *learning organization* in Senge's (2006) sense of the term. Seen in this context, SIOs can contribute to the continuous assessment and renewal of the university's human capital, a key to the future of institutional vitality in the 21st century. As Llopis (2011) contends for the private sector:

> Leaders today must approach their business like a think-tank, where every member of the supply chain is an asset to the business they serve and thus accountable to contribute in ways that support continuous innovation. Leaders must be accountable for thinking strategically not just about their own business, but also about their marketplaces and industries.

For the SIO, this means valuing all resources at the institutional level while also understanding and applying the trends in international education at large.

ETHICS IN INTERNATIONAL EDUCATION LEADERSHIP

The area of professional ethics in education has expanded significantly in recent decades. Some of the impetus for promoting an explicit set of ethical guidelines stems from the increasing legal exposure of colleges and universities. The prospect of litigation over criminal acts—or even over casual remarks recorded on a smart phone or sent via e-mail—now forces universities to regularly train their faculty and staff, including international educators, on a wide variety of ethical and legal issues. Another impetus has been the effort at self-regulation within various specialty areas in higher education. Thus, professional associations in international education have developed robust codes of ethics for their members, member institutions, and partners. These codes may apply specifically to education abroad (Forum, 2011); international student recruitment, enrollment and support (American International Recruitment Council, 2010; Australian Government, 2009; Australian Vice-Chancellors' Committee, 2005; Nuffic, 2009; UK Council for International Student Affairs, 2011); or more broadly to the field in general (NAFSA, 2003).

These ethical guides focus mainly on four themes: truthfulness in public statements, focus on service to students, conflicts of interest, and transparency in contractual arrangements with various university clienteles. This development is of special relevance to leaders in international education because they typically have responsibility for multiple areas of institutional services (such as international partnerships/agreements, international student recruitment, study abroad, faculty development, even instruction, and research), all of which can pose ethical issues. Moreover, SIOs typically supervise staff who deliver these services, thus introducing ethical issues in employer-employee relations.

Ethics and values are, of course, closely related. (Bass & Steidlmeier, 2004) Although ruthless, amoral, and long-tenured leaders can be cited throughout history and, indeed, in our own time, effective long-term, transformational leadership in business, politics, or higher education requires a moral compass. Some have called this a sense of True North (Garten, 2001, pp. 112–131); others have focused more on constructing an international education philosophy to provide guideposts for action (Van de Water, 2006, pp. 58–59).

In comparing various codes of ethics currently in use in international education, a few salient values emerge. These are: (a) ensuring transparency and accuracy in communicating the international education programs and services that an institution offers, including various fees for service that are increasingly common in international education; (b) placing the goals of student learning foremost in any program recommendations, whether regarding the curriculum, a study abroad vendor, a foreign partner, a development contract, or insurance options; (c) avoiding conflicts of interest that may involve the financial interests of international educators themselves. This last value is increasingly relevant to SIOs as they take part in professional consulting, join governing boards, and otherwise engage in pay-for-service activities outside their institution. The final value (d) is advancing

the internationalization of the entire institution, not merely to enlarge the office or administrative unit SIOs direct. SIOs bear the unique responsibility to drive the kind of internationalization that enhances the overall education provided by their institution. As Rumbley, Altbach, and Reisberg noted earlier in this volume (Chapter 1), "At a minimum, 'ethical internationalization' requires a commitment to such fundamental values as transparency, quality in academic programming and support services, academic freedom, fair treatment of partners and stakeholders, respect for local cultures, and thoughtful allocation of resources."

Ethical issues in practice are often made even more complex because international education leaders routinely deal with global partners, sometimes from cultures and legal systems that are dissimilar from their own. Recent reports on transparency and corruption worldwide indicate that risks of unethical behavior among colleagues abroad can vary substantially from country to country (Corporate Executive Board, 2011, p. 11; Transparency International, 2010). Although the education sector tends to rank lower in corruption than the police or business globally, this is not always the case. Thus, SIOs frequently have to confront an additional layer of trust and ethics in their international dealings.

Internationalization is itself a process of change. Therefore, ethical issues can emerge in novel circumstances for which there are no precedents or institutional history. It is part of the leader's responsibility to identify the risks— legal, ethical, and logistical—for a new partnership or endeavor. Ideally, experience with an apparent "one-off" case will lead to consensus among institutional colleagues and other professionals that helps shape guidelines for future cases and future decision-making.

Conclusion

At its heart, the concept of leadership in general is one of successfully influencing an organization to accomplish its mission. In its highest form, that of transformational leadership, it pulls subordinates and colleagues into a unifying vision of something greater. Leaders at this level are change agents not just in the arena of international education or the broader arena of internationalization, but for a higher quality of education for the entire academic institution. Synergistic relationships may develop and grow in this process, making the vision everyone's and literally changing the organization forever.

Within a university or college, the position of SIO is quite unusual among administrators. Organizationally, within the higher education context, it typically resides at a level at least two below the president, rector, or chancellor and works under the auspices of either academics, *rectorat*, student affairs, or outreach. The SIO is the quintessential *middle manager*. The very nature of internationalizing an institution, however, demands that its projects exist in some form across every facet of the institution: curricular, co-curricular, and interaction with the community at large. In effect, SIOs are expected to exert influence on elements completely outside of their organizational niche. To achieve such goals entails crossing organizational boundaries and entering fiefdoms of other power brokers (deans and other senior administrators) around the campus community. Unless those barriers are breached on a fairly regular basis, the task of internationalizing the institution will most probably fail. To suggest that this is a difficult and challenging situation is to understate both the political realities of any institution and the complexity of the overall process.

With little real power, how does the SIO accomplish the daunting and lofty goal of successfully spreading an internationalization ethos throughout the fabric of the campus tapestry? More important, how does the SIO achieve not just buy-in of the various competing constituencies on a campus, but also ownership of internationalization by those constituent groups? To answer these relatively complex problems of leadership, one might ask: What does the SIO bring to the table that will influence acceptance and campus-wide change in what is a notoriously conservative institution? The last thing SIOs should wish for is that the rest of the institution simply points toward their office or building and says, "Oh, international! They handle those things over there." This sort of marginalization and isolation are a constant threat to genuine and broad-based internationalization of an institution, which demands inclusion and participation in the process. But even if SIOs achieve complete ownership by the wider campus community, they must still exert

that gentle hand at the tiller of the institutional ship, or it can easily drift off course (Harari, 1992).

It is in the complexity of the four dimensions of the job mentioned earlier in this chapter that one can discover what SIOs bring to their institution. Leadership challenges, but huge opportunities as well, are wrapped into those dimensions. Working in the regional, national, and especially the international dimensions, as a natural course of the requirements of the job, SIOs can bring new resources, ideas, and practical solutions that readily adapt to the needs of the organization overall. Senior administrators value such input and will reciprocate with support when needed. Once they begin looking to the SIO as that independent voice of value, they see the SIO's vision in a different light as well. Thus, never forget your mission and your employer: Many brilliant SIOs have gotten caught up in a single facet or dimension only to find themselves shut out or left behind in another. The key is balance, focusing on the long-term and the institution-wide effort (de Wit, 2011a, 2011b; McCarthy, 2007).

Leadership in international education is a challenge that goes beyond SIOs at colleges and universities. To use a metaphor from international economics: The "supply chain" for expanding globally oriented higher education has many links. International education leaders who are not SIOs—and do not work for universities—make important and lasting contributions through their work in professional associations, consortia, and government agencies, and as bloggers and scholars. This chapter has focused on the institutional setting because that is the setting in which a leader can directly impact the student experience and help shape an institution's future. But many others in international higher education are also critical to the growth and maturity of the profession.

How does this leadership discussion apply to SIOs outside the United States? The principles and leadership skills treated here are general and adaptable and will be effective in most situations and in other cultural environments. The specifics of each SIO's situation, however, will require flexibility and agility. While the regions of the world share certain similarities in issues confronting the SIO, each institution really does form an entity unto itself, with its own problems.

Here are a few questions for further reflection on SIO leadership. Is your vision powerful enough to draw others into it and create a direction for the entire institution? Does it fit within the overall direction of the institutional mission and goals? Are you genuinely and positively committed to that vision? Indeed, are you willing to put your career "on the line" to make positive change happen? As Mestenhauser and Ellingboe (2005) have concluded, "To accomplish the task of internationalization . . . requires knowledge about change, for internationalization is about change and the future" (p. 37). The SIO has a crucial role to play as change agent within the institution and beyond.

References

American International Recruitment Council. (2010). *Certification standards.* Retrieved from http://airc-education.org/

Australian Government. (2009). *National code – Part D: Standards for registered providers.* Retrieved from Australian Education International: http://www.aei.gov.au/AEI/ESOS/ NationalCodeExplanatoryGuide/PartD/default .htm

Australian Vice-Chancellors' Committee. (2005). *Provision of education to international students: Code of practice and guidelines for Australian universities.* Retrieved from http://www .universitiesaustralia.edu.au/resources/337/324

Barsh, J., Cranston, S., & Lewis, G. (2009). *How remarkable women lead: The breakthrough model for work and life.* New York: Crown.

Bass, B. M. (1985). *Leadership and performance beyond expectation.* New York: Free Press.

Bass, B. M., & Steidlmeier, P. (2004). Ethics, character, and authentic transformational behavior. In J. Ciulla (Ed.), *Ethics, the heart of leadership* (2nd ed. pp. 175–196). Westport, CT: Praeger.

Bolman, L. G., & Deal, T. E. (2003). *Reframing organizations: Artistry, choice, and leadership* (3rd ed.). San Francisco: Jossey-Bass.

Boschini, V. J. (2011). Learning to change the world: Making international education core to the institutional mission. *AIEA: Presidential perspectives.* Retrieved from http://www .aieaworld.org/publications/ PresidentialPerspectives

Burns, J. M. (1978). *Leadership.* New York: Harper & Row.

Corporate Executive Board (CEB). (2011). *Turning ethics into outcomes: Three steps to build "integrity capital" to manage risk and drive performance.* Retrieved from http://www .executiveboard.com/executive-guidance/2011/ Q2/index.html?cid=70180000000ZFhS&sourc eid=1

Chen, G., & An, R. (2009). A Chinese model of intercultural leadership competence. In D. Deardorff (Ed.), *The Sage handbook of intercultural competence* (pp. 196–208). Thousand Oaks, CA: Sage.

Christ, C. T. (2011). A world college for the world's women. *AIEA: Presidential perspectives.* Retrieved from http://www.aieaworld.org/ publications/PresidentialPerspectives

Ciulla, J. (2004). *Ethics, the heart of leadership* (2nd ed). Westport, CT: Praeger.

Collins, J. (2005). *Good to great and the social sectors.* New York: Collins.

Deardorff, D. K. (2009). *The SAGE handbook of intercultural competence.* Thousand Oaks, CA: Sage.

Deardorff, D. K., Pysarchik, D., & Yun, Z. (2009). Towards effective international learning assessment: Principles, design and implementation. In H. deWit (Ed.), *Measuring success in the internationalization of higher education* (EAIE Occasional Paper 22, pp. 23–37). Amsterdam: European Association for International Education.

de Wit, H. (2009). *Measuring success in the internationalisation of higher education* (EAIE Occasional Paper 22). Amsterdam: European Association for International Education.

de Wit, H. (2011a). Internationalization of higher education: Nine misconceptions. *International Higher Education, 64*(summer), 6–7.

de Wit, H. (2011b). *Trends, issues, and challenges in internationalisation of higher education.* Amsterdam: Centre for Applied Research on Economics and Management.

Eckel, P., Green, M., & Hill, B. (2001). *On change V: Riding the waves of change: Insights from transforming institutions.* Washington, DC: American Council on Education.

Eisner, M. (2010). *Working together: Why great partnerships succeed.* New York: HarperCollins.

Fantini, A. (2009). Assessing intercultural competence: Issues and tools. In D. K. Deardorff (Ed.), *The SAGE handbook of intercultural competence* (pp. 456–476). Thousand Oaks, CA: Sage.

Forum on Education Abroad. (2011). *Code of ethics for education abroad* (2nd ed.). Carlisle, PA: Author. Retrieved from http://www.forumea .org/documents/ForumEA-CodeofEthics 2011-2ndEdition.pdf

Friedman, T. (2005). *The world is flat: A brief history of the twenty-first century.* New York: Farrar, Straus & Giroux.

Garten, J. (2001). *The mind of the C.E.O.* New York: Basic Books.

Harrari, M. (1992). The internationalization of the curriculum. In C. Klasek (Ed.), *Bridges to the future: Strategies for internationalizing higher education* (pp. 52–79). Carbondale, IL: Association of International Education Administrators.

Herrera, S. (2008). *Effectiveness of study abroad in developing global competence and global consciousness: Essential outcomes for internationalizing the curriculum.* Unpublished doctoral dissertation, University of Florida. Retrieved from http://purl.fcla.edu/fcla/etd/UFE0022495

Heyl, J. (2007). *The senior international officer (SIO) as change agent.* Durham, NC: AIEA.

Hofstede, G. (2009). The moral circle in intercultural competence. In D. Deardorff (Ed.), *The Sage handbook of intercultural competence* (pp. 85–99). Thousand Oaks, CA: Sage.

Howell, J. M., & Ovolio, B. J. (1993). The ethics of charismatic leadership: Submission or liberation? *Academy of Management Executive, 6*(2), 43–54.

IMPI. (2012). *General Information about IMPI.* Retrieved from http://www.impiproject.eu/index.php?option=com_content&view=article&id=12&Itemid=17

Institute of International Education (IIE). (2011). *Open doors 2011.* Retrieved from http://www.iie.org/Research-and-Publications/Open-Doors/Data/International-Students/Fields-of-Study-Place-of-Origin/2010-11

June, A. (2011, May 6). Release of faculty-productivity data roils U. of Texas. *Chronicle of Higher Education.* Retrieved from http://chronicle.com/article/Release-of/127439/

Kouzes, J. M., & Posner, B. Z. (2002). *The leadership challenge: How to get extraordinary things done in organizations* (3rd ed.). San Francisco: Jossey-Bass.

Kuh, G., & Whitt, E. (1988). *The invisible tapestry: Culture in American colleges and universities* (ASHE-ERIC Higher Education Report, *17*(1)). Washington, DC: Association for the Study of Higher Education.

Leventhal, M. (2011, February 13). U.S.: New funding models for international education. *University World News.* Retrieved from May 21, 2011, at http://www.universityworldnews.com/article.php?story=20110211204106430

Liker, J. (2004). *The Toyota way: 14 management principles from the world's greatest manufacturer.* New York: McGraw-Hill.

Lipman-Blumen, J. (2000). *Connective leadership: Managing in a changing world.* New York: Oxford University Press.

Llopis, G. (2011, September 20). Is leadership irrelevant? *Forbes.* Retrieved from http://www.forbes.com/sites/glennllopis/2011/09/20/is-leadership-irrelevant/

Marmolejo, F. (2011, March 31). African higher education in the world: Are they (and we) ready? *Chronicle of Higher Education.* Retrieved from http://chronicle.com/blogs/worldwise/african-higher-education-in-the-world-are-they-and-we-ready/28025?sid=at&utm_source=at&utm_medium=en

McCarthy, J. (2007, June 29). A roadmap for creating the global campus. *The Chronicle of Higher Education, 53*(43), p. B12.

McCarthy, J. (2010, February 15). *Resource development.* Workshop presentation at AIEA Annual Conference, Washington, DC.

Mestenhauser, J., & Ellingboe, B. (2005, November-December). Leadership knowledge and international education. *International Educator,* pp. 36–43.

NAFSA. (2003). *NAFSA's code of ethics.* Washington, DC: NAFSA, Association of International Educators. Retrieved from http://www.nafsa.org/about.sec/governance_leadership/ethics_standards/nafsa_s_code_of_ethics

Nuffic. (2009). *Code of conduct international student higher education.* Retrieved from http://www.internationalstudy.nl/images/Herziene_Gedragscode_Engels_tcm32-22629.pdf

Paige, M., & Goode, M. (2009). Intercultural competence in international education administration. In D. K. Deardorff (ed.), *The SAGE Handbook of Intercultural Competence,* pp. 333-349. Thousand Oaks, CA: Sage.

Pusch, M. (2009). The interculturally competent global leader. In D. K. Deardorff (Ed.), *The SAGE handbook of intercultural competence* (pp. 66–84). Thousand Oaks, CA: Sage.

Senge, P. (2006). *The fifth discipline: The art and practice of the learning organization* (Rev. ed.). New York: Currency Doubleday.

Smuckler, R. (2003). *A university turns to the world: A personal history of the Michigan State University international story.* East Lansing: Michigan State University Press.

Stockley, D., & de Wit, H. (2011). The increasing relevance of institutional networks. In H. de Wit (Ed.), *Trends, issues, and challenges in internationalisation of higher education.* Amsterdam: Centre for Applied Research on Economics and Management.

Stripling, J. (2011, March 24). For women seeking to advance in academe, advice from 4 who made it to the top. *Chronicle of Higher Education.* Retrieved from http://forums.chronicle.com/article/For-Women-Seeking-to-Advance/126889/

Tarr-Whelan, L. (2009). *Women lead the way: Your guide to stepping up to leadership and changing the world.* San Francisco, CA: Berrett-Koehler.

Transparency International. (2010). *Corruption perceptions index 2010.* Berlin: Transparency International. Retrieved from http://transparency.org/policy_research/surveys_indices/cpi/2010/results

UK Council for International Student Affairs. (2011). *Code of practice for members and subscribers.* Retrieved from http://www.ukcisa.org.uk/join/code_of_practice.php

Van de Water, J. (2006). Lessons learned: musings on a 30-year career in international education. *International Educator, 15*(1), 57–61.

Van Gaalen, A. (2009). Developing a tool for mapping internationalisation: A case study. In H. de Wit (Ed.), *Measuring success in the internationalization of higher education* (EAIE Occasional Paper 22, pp. 77–91). Amsterdam: European Association for International Education.

Vartabedian, R., & Bensinger, K. (2010, February 24). Toyota president Akio Toyoda apologizes for safety lapses. *Los Angeles Times.* Retrieved from http://articles.latimes.com/2010/Feb/24/business/la-fi-toyota25-2010Feb25).

Wildavsky, B. (2010). *The great brain race: How global universities are reshaping the world.* Princeton, NJ: Princeton University Press.

Williamson, W. (2010). *Male vs. female leadership in international education/international education leadership men vs. women II.* Retrieved from http://webcache.googleusercontent.com/search?q=cache:http://www.facultyled.com/international-education-men-vs-women/

8

INSTITUTIONAL STRATEGIES AND INTERNATIONAL PROGRAMS: LEARNING FROM EXPERIENCES OF CHANGE

RIALL NOLAN AND FIONA HUNTER

Internationalization is a key challenge for higher education today, one that is shifting in its role and scope. One of these shifts involves a move away from an activity-based approach toward one that is more strategic (Knight & de Wit, 1997). This leads to greater integration, as internationalization becomes part of vision and values and is increasingly embedded across functional areas and into policies, structures, and processes (Lewis, 2007). A second shift is toward a stronger emphasis on economic rationales and competitive dynamics (van der Wende, 2001), as strengths in international cooperation are often exploited and transformed through alliances, partnerships, and networks that enable universities to enter new markets or position themselves strategically (Enders, 2004; Scott, 1998; Sporn, 2003; van der Wende, 2001).

Although colleges and universities are coming to recognize the importance and value of internationalization, the fact remains that few of them, to date, have managed to successfully transform themselves accordingly. Moreover, not enough is known about how internationalization as a change strategy actually takes place at the institutional level (Marginson & Rhodes, 2002). It is important, therefore, to look closely at such efforts across the world, to learn what works and, most important, why. Thus, this chapter, departing from the format of other chapters in this volume, explores institutional strategies for internationalization by discussing four detailed concrete case studies within the context of the chapter (as opposed to using text boxes as many of the other chapters do).

With that in mind, specific strategies for internationalization at four institutions in Europe and the United States were examined. While it is recognized that there will always be both similarities and differences across universities and colleges in the various world regions as national traditions and structures impact institutional responses (Dale, 1999) and also internationalization strategies, it is also true that there are always lessons to be learned from each institutional story, however unique it might appear to be. In exploring the different strategies and programs, the focus has been placed on what has been accomplished in each institution according to its own specific set of objectives and—more important—how this had been achieved. In some cases, the strategy or program has been fully implemented, while in others, a significant process of change is under way, creating the foundations for a new approach to internationalization. Whether it was an institutional strategy or program that was being examined, a number of key concepts shaped the approach to examining institutional change.

The first thing to recognize is that there is no single model for internationalization: Each institution will identify an internationalization effort in accordance with its own ability and ambition. However, it is equally important to recognize that without certain key elements in place, efforts to internationalize—whatever their substance or intent might be—are probably doomed to failure in the long run.

One is reminded of the opening lines of Tolstoy's *Anna Karenina:* "All happy families are alike; each unhappy family is unhappy in its own way." For internationalization, this might be rephrased as: "Every successfully internationalized university will succeed in its own particular way; universities that fail to internationalize will fail in remarkably similar ways."

So the first framing concept is that of *organizational culture*: the basic identity of an institution. According to Schein (1992), organizational culture develops through interaction among organizational members in response to their environment and can be thought of as shared learning. While it is recognized that institutional response will depend on factors beyond shared experience—age, academic configuration, location, reputation, and availability of resources, for example—efforts to change must be consonant with the organization's character and sense of self. However, it is also acknowledged that institutions can change through agency and the power of imagination (Marginson, 2007) and that these, too, are key to the process of change and performance.

The second notion that framed the inquiry was Donald Schön's (1983) concept of the *reflective conversation* that occurs among certain professionals and leads to shared understandings and, in some cases, original and synergistic ideas.

This notion is connected to the concept of narrative (Roe, 1995), which is interpreting the stories told within and about an institution. These stories shape and define its public character and culture and constitute both frames and constraints for innovation and change.

It is useful here to take a moment to elaborate on the idea of reflective conversations and narratives. As investigative techniques, these are similar to how anthropologists look at the life histories of individuals. By looking at individual lives, one also learns about the overall culture. Life histories, for individuals, allow understanding about:

- what events were significant in someone's life
- what choices those events offered to someone
- why specific choices were made
- how the results or outcomes of choices were assessed
- what the individual learned going forward from the experience

In a similar way, by building case studies situated in the current context of globalization (Deem, 2001; Marginson, 2007), it is possible to learn from institutions about how and why they chose the path they did. These institutional accounts, in turn, will greatly illuminate the way for other institutions, as they, too, seek to internationalize according to their own set of objectives.

The third notion that framed the inquiry concerns the *essential enablers* of successful change. Experience has shown that without a set of enablers in place, innovation in international higher education will rarely turn into long-term and sustainable institutionalization. Among the essentials that seem to matter are these:

- Leadership: It is the task of leadership to create a vision for internationalization and to convince the community of the need for change. Leadership links the vision for internationalization to the institutional mission, communicates it effectively, and creates the right conditions for its realization. Insightful leadership has an acute sense of institutional development and dynamics and is able to identify the most appropriate line of action (Davies, 1991; Eckel, Green, & Hill, 2001; Lockwood & Davies, 1987; Shattock, 2003).

- Faculty engagement: It is well known that without commitment from those who will implement the change, strategies and programs run the risk of failure. Institutional leaders should be prepared to invest time and energy to gain broad consensus and identify key change agents with the necessary skills to drive the new vision forward. Open leadership draws on expertise in the community and builds the right teams to facilitate and embed the change (Olson & Eoyang, 2001; Olson, Green, & Hill, 2005). People are key to the process.

• Policy support: Once the new direction has been established, a set of mechanisms will be needed to sustain the process and realize the goals. The vision must be supported by a clearly articulated strategy that sets out key objectives, targets, and timelines. New procedures, policies, and processes will most likely be required not only to implement, but also to communicate and evaluate the change. New or modified governance arrangements may be required to support the strategy and enable those entrusted with its implementation to execute the necessary tasks at hand and drive the process forward (Davies, 2001; Shattock, 2003).

• Financial support: People and policies will not be able to achieve much without the necessary financial resources to carry out the change and sustain it over time. This may require innovative thinking, entrepreneurial effort in identifying new income streams, and a willingness to undertake a degree of risk. Investments should involve not only the strategy or program itself but also incentives to reward achievement and innovation (Davies, 2001; Shattock, 2003; Sporn, 1999, 2003).

To understand how these essential enablers were put in place, four educational institutions were identified—two in Europe and two in the United States—that had successfully instituted innovation in the area of internationalization. Interviews with key players in each institution were carried out with the aim of understanding not simply what had been accomplished, but how the change had been made and what lessons could be learned from each story. The cases do not seek to be representative of internationalization in Europe or in the United States but rather to highlight range of response and degree of change. They are stories of vision and ambition that testify to change in the field, and such stories can be narrated in almost any country in the world today.

EUROPE

The transformation of European higher education is forcing universities into a much more competitive international environment. This section will examine how two universities—the University of Lausanne in Switzerland and LUISS Guido Carli in Rome, Italy—are responding strategically to the challenges they face.

University of Lausanne

The University of Lausanne (UNIL) has 12,000 students from bachelor's to doctoral level across seven faculties: theology and religious studies, law and criminal justice, arts, social and political sciences, business and economics, biology and medicine, and geosciences and environment.

The last decade has been a turbulent one, setting the university on a path of transformational change. The first shock came with a reshuffling of academic disciplines in 2003. The university shares its breathtakingly beautiful campus on the shores of Lake Leman with the prestigious Swiss Federal Institute of Technology at Lausanne (EPFL), and the difficult decision was taken to transfer science faculties to EPFL, provoking significant internal disruption and resistance. The second shock came with the Bologna Process, which generated reform upheaval across all degree programs as the university aligned with the requirements of the emerging European Higher Education Area. The third shock was a new law in 2006 in the Swiss Canton of Vaud, where UNIL is located, which transformed historical governance arrangements into new requirements for greater autonomy and accountability.

UNIL defines itself as a modern university with ancient foundations (1537) and has skillfully transformed these challenges into unique opportunities that have placed it on a path of institutional improvement and internationalization. While it lost its scientific core to EPFL, it did retain biology and geology and strategically merged them with other groupings to create new and unique interdisciplinary competences. Biology joined medicine and created a new institute for genomics. Geology and geography came together to create geosciences and environment opening up new opportunities for development. Strong academic resistance was

partially overcome by a generous budget allocation to the new units with money that had been
freed up from the original science faculties.

The timing was right. The areas involved
were poised to enter the international arena and
the new groupings created innovative niches
that sparked international interest. While the
loss of science created vulnerability in global
university rankings (UNIL was placed 136 in the
Times Ranking and 152 in the QS World
University Ranking in 2010), the unique composition of the new groupings enabled them to
gain advantage in a different way. In any case,
UNIL sees participation in the rankings as a tool
for learning and self-improvement rather than
as a means to compete for students or enhance
earnings, since it has the enviable good fortune
to be adequately funded by the canton.

While this internal transformation was under
way, the Bologna Process was bringing
Switzerland closer to Europe. (Although not a
European Union member, Switzerland enjoys
special arrangements for participation in
European Higher Education programs.) The
university was engaged in a 10-year project that
would transform the substance and structure of
its academic offerings and bring it in line with
the requirements of the European Higher
Education Area. The model proposed by the
Bologna Process is one of curricular reform and
institutional autonomy, calling for new relations
with the state. Under Canton Vaud's new autonomy law, the rector is now appointed for 5 years,
rather than being elected by peers, and is given
extensive managerial and financial power. The
new arrangements also require the rector to produce a detailed strategic plan and hold the university directly accountable to the canton.

UNIL did not have a tradition of strategic
planning but had relied on various commissions
that identified directions for the institution. The
main goals of the first plan 2006–2011 was to
create a solid base for development by resolving
a number of outstanding financial and management issues and to put UNIL on the global map
by enhancing its prestige and influence.

Key to building the new identity and profile
of UNIL is the innovative leadership of the rector, Dominique Arlettaz. He is ideally placed to
lead the change, having had the experience of
being the vice rector for the Bologna Process and
the Dean of the Science Faculty involved in the
management of the academic reorganization.

He chose his team of five members carefully and
broke with tradition by bringing two nonaca-
demics on board. One is the previous administrative director, who has brought management
and financial expertise to the table, and the
other is a quality expert, appointed as the vice
rector for enhancement and quality. The rector
had identified the creation of a quality culture as
one of the main engines for change. Carried out
with a focus on collaboration for continuous
improvement and recognition for achievement,
the work has revolutionized the way of thinking
and working in both the academic and administrative communities.

Another key innovation has been the appointment of a vice rector for research. Research had
previously been managed exclusively in the
departments, but now there is a small central
structure with the mission to support promising
research projects with funds and services. As
successes are communicated and celebrated
across campus, the concept of research excellence has begun to emerge, and the institutional
culture is changing.

The strategic plan identifies seven priority
areas, and internationalization is integrated
into each one. UNIL already had a strong international tradition, with one fifth of its student
population and one third of the teaching staff
from abroad, and so it was deemed unnecessary to identify internationalization as a separate priority area. International Director
Antoinette Charon Wauters disagreed. She
spoke up at an internal meeting, requesting—
and obtaining—the right to a specific internationalization plan to support the strategy. The
international plan, approved in 2009, makes
international activities more explicit and
coherent and thus more able to make a contribution to the institutional strategy. It identifies
five areas for improvement in internationalization: increased competencies in teaching and
research through greater international collaboration; stronger international positioning for
the attraction of talent; enhanced internationalization of students and international recognition of qualifications; greater international
competences in the student body; and active
participation in international developments
for teaching and research. Like the strategy
itself, the first plan is one of consolidation.

The creation of a specific plan for internationalization has also had a significant impact

on the International Office itself. Its role and profile have gained in visibility and prestige within the university, which has led to the positive outcome of an increase in both staff and budget as well as greater involvement in institutional matters. The international director has a direct link to the rector, a relationship that has worked well since Wauters had already collaborated with Arlettaz when he was vice rector for the Bologna Process. She has had a significant impact on the strategy, which in turn has impacted her role and that of her office. Her function is becoming increasingly strategic, and she is now present in all the internal committees, ready and willing to share her international knowledge and experience. "Now they listen to me," she says.

The institutional strategy has produced tangible results. The financial house has been put in order, and the foundations of a quality culture have been laid. More efficient resource management has effectively increased the available funding, and strategic allocation of funds has provided clear direction and established institutional priorities. While central management controls funding, it encourages and rewards innovation. International projects may also receive co-funding from the International Office, creating a key link between the office and the academic departments.

A focus on quality has changed the way the university thinks about itself. People are learning to ask questions about the way they work and seek solutions for improvement. Rather than comparing with others, they benchmark against themselves, seeking to enhance performance on a year-by-year basis. The new culture is to do well and better, and these values are increasingly linked to internationalization. New staff have a stronger international profile, and innovative projects involve more international partners.

The international plan has led to more exchanges for students and teaching staff, but it is not just a question of increasing numbers. It has also led to thinking more strategically about the alliances and partnerships that can create real added value and learning opportunities. This includes developing closer relations with EPFL on the shared campus to enhance both local and international profiles.

The rector has gained the confidence of the university and of the canton, which has confirmed him for a further five years. The next phase of the strategy will make internationalization a priority, and the portfolio of the vice rector for research has been extended to include internationalization. Wauters looks forward to the opportunity to move from a period of consolidation to one of innovation. "We have not always been proud of ourselves," she says, "but that is changing. This is now a good place to be and the transformation is a happy one."

A series of internal and external events generated the levers for change, but the right leader with the right combination of talent and tools has set the university on a pathway for institutional transformation that creates an explicit link between quality and internationalization. The carefully planned actions of a patient but determined rector, with enhanced authority and power to act as well as the insight and ability to identify talent in different parts of the university and let it flourish, have led to a change in the values and practices of its members. There is greater trust toward senior management, and stronger collaboration between the different parts of the university in a more dynamic and positive atmosphere. The intuition of the international director that the time was ripe to move center stage has given internationalization and the International Office a major role to play in the future creation of a new global identity for the University of Lausanne.

LUISS Guido Carli in Rome

LUISS Guido Carli in Rome, Italy is a young, specialized university that developed out of a pre-existing educational institution in the 1970s. It is a private university, which means that it is regulated by the Ministry for Higher Education but is essentially privately funded through tuition fees. Currently, it has 7,100 students from bachelor's to doctoral level in business, law, and political science. In its short history, it has demonstrated the capacity to pre-empt the need for change and adapt accordingly. It has always had a mission for "useful learning" and service to its stakeholder community and has built a reputation for excellence, focusing on its ability to attract talented students and provide top employment opportunities for its graduates, thus positioning itself in an international market. Its focus had been a national one, but the arrival of the Luca Cordero di Montezemolo, formerly president of the Italian racing car company Ferrari, as the new university president in 2005 sparked off a process of rapid and profound transformation. Aware of the far-reaching effects of globalization in the business world, Montezemolo saw the university falling out of step if it did not undertake the strategic choice to internationalize.

The vision was to make LUISS an innovative university that provides an international education in response to changing professional profiles and internationally competitive research. It aimed to position itself among the top 25 European universities in economics, political science, and law, with the ability to attract students and scholars from all over the world. Once the board had established the vision, it appointed a new managing director, Pierluigi Celli, who has extensive experience in the business world, and a new rector, Massimo Egidi, who has a proven track record for strategic change in higher education. They were vested with the authority to develop and execute the university's first long-term strategy and to appoint administrative and academic teams with the appropriate competences to realize the vision.

A five-year plan for internationalization with five key areas was launched in 2006. It started with a series of internal improvements since quality of service is key to its reputation. Investments were made in new purpose-built facilities and in the range, relevance, and efficiency of student services to raise satisfaction and provide a tangible sign of change to both current and prospective students. This was linked to an intensive national media campaign to raise institutional visibility.

The next step was to align all educational offerings, including executive education, with market needs and with a strong international focus, either in terms of content or delivery, that would open up part of the portfolio to an international student market. New curricula were designed to meet the needs of emerging professions, and undergraduate and graduate programs taught in English were introduced. The long-term objective is to provide one third of its academic offerings in English. The English-taught master's programs with an international profile are proving to be attractive to international students, who account for between 70% and 90% of the enrollment. The new curricula are linked to an enhanced scholarship program

and the creation of pathways of excellence for talented students. New international exchange partners were identified to ensure adequate opportunity for mobility, and the first double-degree programs were set up with partners in Europe and around the world. The International Office was restructured and enhanced with more qualified personnel to meet the new demands.

Initiatives to upgrade teaching and learning methods, introduce a new internal quality system, and encourage closer interaction with key stakeholders have also been undertaken. The overall aim has been to identify niches where the university could excel and build an international reputation without expanding the academic portfolio significantly.

These changes have been further enhanced by taking advantage of a recent Italian law for governance reform. LUISS has done away with traditional faculties; instead, departments are responsible for academic programs and research, and schools are responsible for professional education. LUISS has also appointed its first vice rector for teaching and learning.

The third step was to build up its research capacity to internationally competitive levels. Its previous focus had been as a teaching institution, and it recognized the need to reorganize its research efforts and renew its academic community. LUISS has identified strategic research areas and set up research communities that are funded according to output. It has hired 10 senior researchers with an international profile and redesigned research careers according to international standards. It is also exploiting its partnership network (and the attractiveness of Rome as a destination) to invite renowned researchers on short-term contracts to make a contribution to its new strategy. Research effort is now coordinated by a vice rector for research. Investment in research not only builds an international reputation but also serves as a source of transferable knowledge for the local business community.

Developing international visibility is the fourth step of the plan. LUISS is developing strategic partnerships, building an international advisory board, and creating a multidisciplinary research institute. International visibility is not only entering the international community but opening itself up to international evaluation standards. LUISS has a number of benchmarking initiatives under way that will enable it to apply for international accreditation, such as EQUIS, which will not only enhance its reputation but also enable it to revise current tuition levels.

Income generation is the fifth step in the plan and key to its success, since the strategic goals exceed LUISS's current financial capacity. Tuition has always been its main source of income, and it is seeking to diversify its income streams through fund-raising, alumni development, sponsorship from the stakeholder community, and greater outreach into the business community through executive education and technology transfer. More effective use of resources alongside enhanced tuition revenues and new income streams are opening up new investment possibilities.

The internationalization strategy has led to years of extreme and demanding activity in every area and at every level of the university, and the process is still under way as the university evaluates how best to move forward with its next phase of internationalization. Change has been tangible from the very early stages as the actions are rolled out and results accumulate. Each success gives new confidence and provides new energy to move forward. This sense of achievement is leading to a stronger sense of institutional cohesion and shared direction, making it easier to build the teams and realize the change. Success also brings financial returns, which can be reinvested, and the University has been able to increase its tenured academic staff from 80 to 120 in the space of only two years. All new staff come in according to the new international profile and contribute directly to the change.

While the initial trigger came from the president, the university leadership is making the change happen. The managing director and the rector were chosen on the basis of specific competences; they share their commitment to the strategy, work together as a team, and have enhanced powers to take action. Their ability to achieve results has boosted the confidence of the board, and consequently, it has further released the purse strings, thus making broader and bolder action possible.

The rector identified a brand new team of forward-thinking academics who could contribute knowledge from their own international experience and inject fresh thinking. He calculated carefully how much change could be implemented at each stage, aware of the delicate balance between sending out a clear signal of new direction while still maintaining trust within the academic community. He sees it as his leadership responsibility to communicate the vision, give clear direction, and broaden consensus while at the same time maintaining a tight control over process through clear assignment of responsibilities and close monitoring of the tasks at hand.

The rector and his team have spoken with one voice to persuade, convince, motivate, and bring colleagues on board, often painstakingly and one by one, investing endless amounts of individual energy and never losing sight of the main objective. Academic leadership is unrelenting in its determination to push through change but able to combine drive with patience, working within institutional or individual constraints. Mixed with a heavy dose of determination is a strong sense of realism.

The administrative leadership was able to take a more incisive approach and has been radical in eradicating practices that prevented it from developing a quality culture and an ability to respond opportunistically to changing conditions. Significant reorganization and a series of new appointments in the early stages of the plan laid the groundwork for stronger cohesion and focus in the management team.

Both leaders have given new meaning and energy to the mission and convinced their members to make an uncommon effort for the internationalization strategy. This is not without its daily challenges, but it is being achieved progressively by building on internal desire for excellence and by reinterpreting the original values in line with external shifts, not only in the graduate labor market but also in the national and European higher education systems, transformed by the Bologna Process into a more international and competitive environment. "It will take 10 to 15 years to carry out the change so we need to create the spirit, culture, desire to compete as a European university," says Rector Egidi. In the current higher education context, Europe has become the new market, and LUISS has chosen internationalization as its new identity.

This discussion has highlighted the strategic initiatives and steps undertaken by two European universities to internationalize their institutions. See Box 8.1 for an example from another Italian university.

BOX 8.1 An Italian University Internationalizes

Edilio Mazzoleni

Head of Operations, International Office, Università Cattolica del Sacro Cuore (Italy)

In the late nineties, some European universities, in reaction to globalization, took a new approach to internationalizing their institutions. The traditional form of internationalization based mainly on student mobility and reciprocal exchanges had become obsolete. It no longer satisfied the students' needs to acquire the necessary skills to function and prosper in a globalized context. Employers, multinationals, and small and medium enterprises started seeking multilingual candidates able to function in an intercultural environment.

In addition to the new global context, the institutional rationales for international mobility have changed in the last 20 years. In the United States, and in other English-speaking countries, higher education has become a market that attracts degree-seeking students from other countries. In Europe, the interest in higher education has only recently begun to move from a focus on mobility and cooperation programs to other forms of internationalization, motivated by a need to increase the number of international fee-paying students. This change has been assisted by the actions of the Bologna process (The Council of Europe, 2010) and the Lisbon Convention (The Council of Europe/UNESCO, 2002), both aimed at building a competitive knowledge society.

There are three main reasons why Italy has fallen behind northern Europe in the process of internationalization of higher education. The first is the absence of an English-language instruction base, which exists principally in the southern half of continental Europe. The second is the strong national culture and state tradition that characterize these countries. The third, and most important, is the inadequacy of policymakers to push and implement significant educational reforms to meet the demands of globalization.

Università Cattolica del Sacro Cuore (UCSC), with more than 40,000 students and five campuses throughout the Italy, is the largest private university in Europe and is ranked in the 400 to 500 group globally (Shanghai Jiao Tong University, 2010). It is a comprehensive university with disciplines that include law, political science, sociology, arts and philosophy, education, economics, banking and insurance, psychology, languages, agriculture, mathematics and the natural sciences, and medicine and surgery.

The University has also established itself as a European and global leader in student mobility, with 23% of its graduating undergraduate cohort having an international experience.

UCSC has implemented fully the prescribed changes dictated by the European Union, which have generated since 1999 a strong increase in national and international competition, further emphasized by the emergence of new universities. UCSC was the only Italian university honored in 2006 and 2008 for the quality of its implementation of the Bologna reform.

To remain a leader in higher education in Italy and in Europe, UCSC has adopted a new strategic plan, with the International Relations Office becoming responsible for the promotion, recruitment, induction, administration, and support of all international and outbound students to ensure their success in the globalized society of the 21st century.

By 2013, more than 800 international degree-seeking students will be recruited annually as well as some 1,600 non degree-seeking exchange, semester, year, and short-term study abroad students (12% of the university's student body). UCSC currently has 2,453 international students, about 1,000 of which are mobility students whereas about 1400 students enroll yearly in degree programs.

UCSC is the first comprehensive research university in Italy that has introduced both undergraduate and graduate curricula and degree programs taught in English to generate and sustain this massive increase in international students. Within the same time frame, UCSC expects to increase its outbound student mobility from 23% to 35% of its annual graduating cohort, that is, from 1,200 today to 2,500 by 2013.

Initiatives being developed include: a free-standing international website, Web and Facebook marketing, specific international branding, prospect management using a conventional CRM system, the engagement of agents, specific country and regional recruiting strategies, and dedicated international student advisers. In this work, UCSC is beginning to resemble a U.S., English, or Australian university.

UCSC's international activities are designed to financially benefit the university, impact the multicultural teaching and research environment and the local and Italian economies, and contribute to the development of emerging countries through cooperation projects. The success of these activities will be measurable by benchmarking with counterpart universities at the national and international level.

UNITED STATES OF AMERICA

In the United States, the focus is on two innovative programs for internationalization—one at the University of Denver, the other at the University of Michigan's School of Art and Design—and how they have been developed strategically.

The University of Denver

The University of Denver, founded in 1864, is the oldest private institution in the Rocky Mountain region, with a total enrollment of nearly 12,000 students, about 5,500 of them undergraduates. DU, as it is called, has become well known in international education circles for its Cherrington Scholars Program. This program, initiated under Chancellor Dan Ritchie, essentially pays the additional costs for undergraduate students to participate in a wide variety of study-abroad programs. The cost of overseas traveling and living is generally acknowledged as one of the most formidable obstacles to student participation in study abroad. Cherrington in effect picks up these costs; DU students pay tuition, room, and board costs at home, and Cherrington pays the rest, which includes airfare and other associated travel costs.

The program was initially conceived after September 11, 2001, when DU's chancellor became concerned about the event's impact on international learning and on the visibility of young American students in the rest of the world. In many ways, overseas opportunities seemed to be closing for US students in the wake of 9/11, and Cherrington was intended to counter this trend.

A small set of key players at DU—the chancellor, the vice chancellor, and Ved Nanda, then vice provost for internationalization and now professor of international law—conceived of the program. At the time, 80% of the students at Denver who studied abroad did so on programs organized by other universities and third-party providers.

Chancellor Ritchie contributed an initial sum of $100,000 from his own budget as seed money, with a request to set up a program whereby Denver students could go, with virtually full support, directly to overseas universities.

With the approval of the board of trustees, the program went forward. A faculty committee (the Cherrington Global Scholars faculty) was formed to ensure support and to work out details, a process that took 18 months. The work also involved administrators across the campus, including the offices of housing, registrar, financial aid, and study abroad. Sites and partners overseas had to be identified and developed. In 2004, the first group of Denver's Cherrington scholars went abroad.

The program budget amounts to some $10 million (a sum that includes redirected tuition, room, and board), run through the provost's office, with contributions coming from all participating academic units. Eric Gould, the current vice provost for internationalization, chaired the original faculty committee. "Once the idea had been laid out," he said, "it was not a hard sell."

Today, the committee that oversees the Cherrington Scholars Program (the Internationalization Advisory Board) is composed of faculty members, chosen by the deans and the Faculty Senate, plus people in International Programs and Study Abroad. It meets monthly.

The program has come to be seen as an educational plus for DU, helping attract applicants, and contributing to DU's identity. To an increasing extent, thanks to Cherrington, study abroad is coming to be seen as part of a liberal education at DU.

How has the Cherrington Scholars Program evolved, and how has it changed the University of Denver? To begin with, people at DU emphasize that Cherrington is only one part of the international portfolio at DU. It is, however, a major part, and serves in a sense as a flagship program for much of the university. Since 2004, the program has encouraged people at DU to seek better integration of study abroad with the established curriculum and to learn about how to manage student mobility on a relatively major scale. By the time they graduate, 74% of DU undergraduate students now participate in the program giving the university an exceptionally high participation rate for an institution of its size and character.

It is also important to note that significant financial resources were put into the program. Of necessity, the initial concept required faculty and administration to work together closely to design sustainable programs, assure academic quality, and build in sustainability. Administrative offices responsible for parts of Cherrington got new staff and resources. Academic departments sending 10 or more students abroad each year were given an adviser's position.

Over time, more and more faculty have become interested in participating in the program. Destinations and courses have been added. More than 50% of Cherrington's programs are offered by third-party providers or in partnership with other universities. As the budget requirements have grown, there have been resource questions, but DU made an early and consistent decision not to cut Cherrington's budget, but rather, to be prudent and seek cost savings where appropriate.

What has the university learned from its experience? For one thing, it has learned a great deal about the planning and management of study-abroad programs, including logistical details. There are now a wide variety of international experiences available to DU's Cherrington scholars, and their professors increasingly value the time students spend away from the home campus. Attention on campus has turned to issues of assessment, quality assurance, and curricular integration. There is some movement toward a required portfolio (including foreign language and cultural training) for students. There is also interest today in diversifying the programs to include summer and inter-session programs, as well as service learning.

Cherrington continues to evolve. The costs for overseas study continue to climb, and there is increasing concern today about the long-term sustainability of the present arrangements. Some programs are much more expensive than others and may have to be cut back or curtailed.

But there is no doubt that the program has had a tremendous impact on the university, and its image of itself. Nearly 75% of Denver's students now participate in study abroad, 61% of these for a full academic year. Students now say that they come to DU in part because of the study-abroad programs.

School of Art and Design of the University of Michigan

The University of Michigan, a public institution, enrolls nearly 42,000 students, of which 26,000 are undergraduates. Michigan is one of the largest and most prestigious research universities in the United States. It is also highly decentralized, and while it prides itself on its many international connections and activities, there is very little enthusiasm for centralized planning and strategy with respect to international education. Innovation and change in this institutional environment must come from within constituent units, not from the top.

The College of Art and Design is relatively small: 500 students, of whom 30 are graduate students. They have 40 full-time faculty. The current dean of the School of Art and Design, Bryan Rogers, came to Michigan in 2000.

Previously, he had been at Carnegie-Mellon University as head of their school of art. Although he had always been interested in international education, it was only after an international sojourn of his own at the age of 30 that he began to see the importance of such experiences, not just in his own life, but in his role as an educator of others.

Dean Rogers describes what happened in the School of Art and Design as "a fortuitous conflation of events and people." It became important for him to provide students with international experience sooner rather than later in their educational career, because, as he put it, "you find out where home is when you leave," and understanding oneself as being of, and shaped by, a particular place and culture is important for education. At Carnegie-Mellon, he had set up various exchange programs for students, with the result that over a 10-year period, the number of art students with international experience rose to about 50%. By the time he came to Michigan, internationalization was high on his list of priorities.

At that time, Michigan's School of Art and Design had one program, in Japan. Dean Rogers began to lay the groundwork for change by providing funding to send faculty overseas, provided that they used the trips to identify and set up exchange arrangements. At the same time, he began to work on internal organization for internationalization. He set up an International Council of faculty members and appointed a director of international engagement. Such initiatives were looked on very favorably by Michigan's top administration, for whom internationalization had been a priority for some time. In monthly meetings of the deans, international initiatives were a high priority.

In 2009, the decision was made to require overseas experience for the School of Art and Design's students. This decision was first discussed in the school's Executive Committee and then by the full faculty, resulting in a unanimous vote. The initiative has been helped by money from two major outside donors, which now makes it possible to offer need-based scholarships to some students. Staff and faculty also participate in some of the summer programs, as internships. The school requires each student to do something when he or she comes back to use the learning gained overseas.

What has the School learned so far? Internationalizing a program is a bigger job than people might think. It takes students time to make good decisions, and it takes work to publicize and explain the program. Faculty have had to learn to work together more closely than in the past, and there is a lot of record-keeping and administration involved. All of the people in the School have had to learn a lot. The success of the effort was due to a critical mass, combined with leadership within the School and support from the university's top administration. Today, the School has 20 overseas partners, and another 20 partnerships being developed. The pipeline of students with overseas experience is now well-established, and, the students who come back from their overseas studies are the program's best and most persuasive advocates.

Discussion

What emerges from these accounts, and what can be learned from them? While the cases reflect the unique nature and culture of each institution, there are lessons that can be relevant for a wider audience.

First, the stories both contradict and reaffirm aspects of institutional narrative. They contradict the widely held (and oft-repeated) notion that faculty must initiate and drive institutional change and that innovations can succeed only to the extent that they involve things the faculty is already comfortable with. In the cases examined, a visionary leader, who was not a rank-and-file faculty member, first proposed significant change. Following that, a team or group of advocates came together to push the change forward, defend it, and eventually implement it. As the results of the change began to appear and became woven into the institution's fabric, a new narrative about institutional identity and internationalization began to emerge, one in which innovation figured prominently.

Power of imagination enabled the vision, but in all cases, the changes that were introduced built on key aspects of institutional culture and quickly became part of the story that the institution told itself and others about what it was becoming. It shows that a strong sense of identity can act as a powerful resource in finding the willingness to make decisive commitments and uncommon efforts for change.

Here, Schön's (1983) notion of reflective practice becomes evident. Schön points out that many professionals do not really prescribe but rather engage in a long-term reflective dialogue with their clients or colleagues, and that it is this dialogue, or reflective conversation, which shapes the product or outcome. Architects do this, psychotherapists do this, and community planners do this. It is likely that on many campuses, international initiatives develop in very much the same way: as the result of a continuing dialogue between different constituencies. Furthermore, as the dialogue develops, the parties' understanding of issues, opportunities, and options changes and expands. What results, in other words, is not only a joint product but a product that may look quite different from what the group initially set out to create.

Second, some interesting and possibly important differences between the European and American cases can be seen, as well as some strong similarities. Although internationalization, it could be argued, is being driven by fundamentally different forces in the United States and in Europe, the end results—higher rates of mobility, enhanced internationalized curricula, and faculty with more capacity for complex international activity—tend to be very much the same.

One of the objectives that Europe has set for itself is the removal of obstacles to intra-European mobility. This, in turn, has had a profound effect on Europe's ability to connect and interact with extra-European institutions. With the rise of English as the academic lingua franca within Europe, the region is acquiring the ability to attract more talent than before from elsewhere and to compete more directly with established Anglophone institutions.

In the United States, in contrast, there has been little interest in "harmonizing" higher education and much more effort at attempts to overcome the cultural, geographic, and linguistic isolation of the country through (in some cases) fairly aggressive internationalization campaigns.

While the local characteristics and conditions vary considerably and lead to different responses, all four universities are examples of how opportunity has been identified and exploited to institutional advantage, in response to both external and internal challenges. Internationalization becomes the new direction, and the shift undertaken is toward greater integration and institutionalization. Internationalization thus becomes central to mission and strategy, altering academic and administrative behaviors. It becomes both an institutional effort and a force for innovation.

Third, returning to the four strategic enablers, it can be seen more clearly how these operated in the cases under consideration.

• *Leadership*: In each case, the presence of strong, visionary advocates at the upper administrative levels was crucial in getting the innovations "on the table" and then in bringing the community on board. These leaders had a strong sense of the institution and of what could be achieved. They understood how to use institutional narrative and culture to strategic advantage and set the pace and degree of change accordingly. They displayed different leadership traits, but all gained the confidence of their funders and the respect of their community. Some used a more top-down and others a more bottom-up approach, but all displayed the crucial combination of passion and patience. They were all chosen according to a precise profile for a precise purpose. Without the right leadership, change cannot happen.

• *Faculty engagement*: Leadership alone is not enough. Although the faculty are not always—and perhaps not often—in the vanguard of change, they are crucial for the institutionalization of change, once change is proposed. They may not be the initiators but will necessarily become the embedders of the change. The number of faculty may be a small group of carefully chosen individuals in the beginning, but as their success develops—and is communicated and celebrated—it becomes best practice and influences further changes across the institution. Daily actions in the new environment slowly but steadily change beliefs and behaviors and increase levels of engagement. Without the right faculty engagement, the change cannot be sustained.

• *Policy support*: In all cases, the "new idea" led to the generation of new procedures, policies, and processes that would support it and drive it forward. In the European cases, the whole fabric of the universities changed to accommodate the new strategic direction, while in the U.S. cases, new programs called for changes of a more administrative nature to the established curriculum, schedule, or working pattern. But as the changes became embedded, they changed the behaviors of individuals and the way they thought about the organization. As new learning accumulates, new ideas and opportunities emerge, creating a dynamic process of regeneration. Without appropriate policy support, innovation will quickly wither and die.

- *Funding*: Finally, of course, there is the matter of money. Funding can come from many sources, including tuition, external grants, administrative set-asides from the central budget, donors, and the private sector. In each change that was examined, the institutions took pains at the outset to ensure that needed resources were there, and could continue to be there on a sustainable basis. "Sustainability" here means several things: that the needed resources will be available into the foreseeable future; that the transaction costs of obtaining these resources are not too great; and that resource acquisition does not engender too much competition with other institutional priorities. The universities were also prepared to engage in a certain amount of risk-taking in order to get the new projects off the ground. Although other resources are also important for the promotion of change, financial support is, in many respects, the *sine qua non* of any successful innovation.

The four enablers are closely interconnected, and all four institutions used them creatively and carefully to ensure the success of their strategy or program for internationalization. This demonstrates that leaders must identify not only *what* to change but also *how* to implement the change in the specific context of each institution. A combination of understanding the institutional environment and a sense of mission is what made it possible for the four institutions examined to think beyond their usual way of operation and create the institutional energy to undertake a process of change that made internationalization an essential component of their identity.

Finally, these cases demonstrate that while it is not possible to accurately forecast the course of change, once begun, the benefits and challenges of the experience offer opportunity to the institutions to engage in a process of continuous learning and improvement (Senge, 2006). This, the *reflective conversation* referenced earlier, arises from, is shaped by, and feeds back into core elements of institutional culture. Each institution, in other words, has a different story

to tell and a different way of creating and re-creating that story.

LESSONS FOR SENIOR INTERNATIONAL OFFICERS

What can senior international officers (SIOs) working in our colleges and universities learn from these four cases and the example in Box 8.1? Perhaps the first thing to note is that in each of our cases, the SIO was *not* the initiator or driver of change. Instead, top leadership provided the impetus for innovation.

Years ago, Schein's (1992) work showed us that organizational culture comes, by and large, from the top. Leadership behavior shapes, for example, what others in the organization pay attention to, what they are rewarded for doing, and, in the most fundamental sense, where they are going. Leadership and culture are the two faces of the same coin.

What, then, should the role of an SIO be? SIOs, despite their lack of authority, can play key intermediary roles here, as visionaries and as emissaries from the outside world. The paradox is that although it seems that high-level administrators are often the only ones capable of initiating change, these same individuals may be relatively unaware of both opportunity and danger in the wider international world. The SIO can play a crucial role here as provider of information about opportunities outside the university and what has worked and what has not worked elsewhere; perhaps most important, the SIO can be the narrator of stories of both success and failure from elsewhere that bring to light the real costs and benefits of a course of action.

Once changes have been proposed, of course, SIOs can play another role as advocates and go-betweens with academic units and upper administration to mobilize supporters, identify early gains and issues, and troubleshoot and resolve implementation problems. They can also become active players in the process of change, as the Lausanne case exemplifies.

This has several fairly straightforward implications for the institutional context within the international education profession. Although SIOs need to be extremely skilled—as always—at working with students, staff, and faculty, they also need to improve their skill at working with presidents, provosts, and rectors. Specifically, they need to be able to develop and promote effective and workable visions of internationalization to people in those high-level positions, who can initiate and drive change.

Training in more effective networking, in change-agency, and in the development of reflective dialogues with top decision makers would go a long way toward making SIOs more effective in supporting, if not leading, internationalization in higher education.

Most institutions present a fairly complex sociopolitical arena, one in which different interests collide, collude, and combine. To some extent, successful institutional change is luck: a combination of having the right factors in the right place at the right time. But as Louis Pasteur reminded us, "chance favors the prepared mind." An astute SIO is often able, with a word here and nudge there, to seize the moment, as the UNIL international director demonstrated.

Concluding Thoughts

While organizational change theories and an expanding literature on internationalization of higher education (Kehm & Teichler, 2007) can provide much insight and guidance, it nevertheless is important to have more institutional stories to compare and contrast. Until now, the emphasis has been on ideas and results in internationalization, but not so much at the process by which the ideas were turned into lasting results. These four cases point to the interplay in the roles of leadership, faculty engagement, policy support, and funding as key elements for success. The cases also show how internationalization is changing in response to a changing higher education environment. Internationalization is both the agent and the object of the change as each institution develops its own unique response based on its specific context, but similarities across institutions can be transformed into lessons for all. However, surely there is more to say, and learn, about the paths along which institutions find their way as they internationalize, for the institutions themselves and for those who work directly with internationalization. As pressure to internationalize grows, it becomes all the more important to learn as much as possible about how to turn vision and ideas into sustained, positive outcomes.

If it is true that each institution's story is unique, it must also be true that closer examination would reveal patterns in the stories, patterns that would indicate some of the fundamental factors, elements, and conditions that promote or discourage internationalization. A theory of internationalization cannot be constructed without more ground-level data on how specific initiatives succeeded or failed. Both success and failure can provide useful lessons. For this, more stories of organizational change need to be told—ethnographies of transformation, as it were—in order to help institutions meet their present challenges in internationalization.

References

Dale, R. (1999). Specifying globalisation effects on national policy: A focus on the mechanisms. *Journal of Educational Policy, 14*(1), 1–17.

Davies, J. L. (1991). New universities: Their origins and strategic development. In P. G. Altbach (Ed.), *International higher education: An encyclopaedia.* (Vol. 1, pp. 205–231). New York & London: Garland.

Davies, J. L. (2001). The emergence of entrepreneurial cultures in European universities. *Higher Education Management, 13*(2), 25–43.

Deem, R. (2001). Globalisation, new managerialism, academic capitalism, and entrepreneurialism in universities: Is the local dimension still important? *Comparative Education, 37*(1), 7–20.

Eckel, P., Green, M. F., & Hill, B. (2001). *On change V: Riding the waves of change: Insights from transforming institutions.* Washington, DC: American Council on Education.

Enders, J. (2004). Higher education, internationalization, and the nation-state: Recent developments and challenges to governance theory. *Higher Education, 47*(3), 361–382.

Kehm, B. M., & Teichler, U. (2007). Research on internationalisation in higher education. *Journal of Studies in International Education, 11*(3–4), 260–273.

Knight, J., & de Wit, H. (Eds.). (1997). *Internationalisation of higher education in Asia Pacific countries.* Amsterdam: European Association for International Education.

Lewis, V. (2007). *"Integrated internationalism" in UK higher education: Interpretations, manifestations, and recommendations.* DBA thesis, University of Bath.

Lockwood, G., & Davies J. (1985). *Universities: The management challenge* (Society for Research into Higher Education). Guildford, UK: NFER-NELSON.

Marginson, S., & Rhodes, G. (2002). Beyond national states, markets, and systems of higher education: A glonacal agency heuristic. *Higher Education, 43*(3), 281–309.

Marginson, S. (2007). Five somersaults in Enschede: Rethinking public/private in higher education for the global era. In J. Enders & B. Jongbloed (Eds.), *Public-private dynamics in higher education, expectations, developments and outcomes.* Bielefeld, Germany: Transcript Verlag.

Olson, E. E., & Eoyang G. H. (2001). *Facilitating organizational change: Lessons from complexity science.* San Francisco: Jossey-Bass/Pfeiffer.

Olson, C. L., Green, M. F., & Hill, B. A. (2005). *Building a strategic framework for comprehensive internationalization.* Washington, DC: American Council on Education.

Roe, E. (1995). *Narrative policy analysis: Theory and practice.* Durham, NC: Duke University Press.

Schein, E. H. (1992). *Organizational culture and leadership.* San Francisco: Jossey-Bass.

Schön, D. (1983). *The reflective practitioner.* New York: Basic Books.

Scott, P. (Ed.). (1998). *The globalization of higher education.* Buckingham, UK: Society for Research into Higher Education and Open University Press.

Senge, P. (2006). *The fifth discipline: The art and practice of the learning organization* (Rev. ed.). New York: Doubleday.

Shattock, M. (2003). *Managing successful universities.* Maidenhead, UK: Society for Research into Higher Education/Open University Press.

Sporn, B. (1999). *Adaptive university structures* (Higher Education Policy Series, No. 54). London: Jessica Kingsley.

Sporn, B. (2003). Trends relating to higher education in Europe: An overview. In H. Eggins (Ed.), *Globalization and reform in higher education* (pp. 117–130). Maidenhead, UK: Society for Research into Higher Education/Open University Press.

Van der Wende, M. (2001). Internationalization policies: About new trends and contrasting paradigms. *Higher Education Policy, 14*(2), 249–259.

9

Collaborating on the Future

Strategic Partnerships and Linkages

Susan Buck Sutton, Everett Egginton, and Raul Favela

The past two decades have witnessed a remarkable repositioning of institutional partnerships so that they are not simply one tactic among many, but rather a defining characteristic of academic internationalization. The 21st century is giving rise to a global reorganization of higher education that makes the boundaries of institutions and nations extremely porous and gives new importance to linkages that cross these boundaries. International partnerships have moved much closer to the center, not just of institutional efforts at internationalization, but of institutional definitions of core mission as well. This chapter explores the new shape and ever-widening functions of such affiliations and identifies the practices that lead to successful, mutually beneficial collaborations, as well as the forces that can undermine them. It also places international partnerships within the more general context of emerging transnational structures of higher education.

In so doing, this chapter builds on earlier discussions of inter-institutional agreements between U.S. universities and those overseas.

Klasek's (1992) short chapter in the precursor to this volume noted that such agreements were increasing in number and that it might be time to regularize the institutional procedures that governed these linkages. Reprints of guidelines from six U.S. universities, concerning what should go into a Memorandum of Understanding (MOU) and who should sign it, constituted three quarters of the chapter's pages. The partnerships most common at that time focused on student and faculty exchange, and these MOUs were sometimes referred to simply as "exchange agreements." Klasek noted, however, that collaborative research and what were called "technical cooperation" projects[1] were also sometimes at stake (pp. 108–110), which indicates that at least some colleges and universities were thinking about such matters more broadly. The subsequent expansion in the number of institutions looking to do more with partnerships is where the present chapter begins, examining the changing nature of internationalization that frames this expanded use of partnerships, the new forms partnerships now take, the practices that sustain them over time, and where they may be headed in the future.

Rethinking Academic Boundaries in the 21st Century

At the time Klasek (1992) wrote his chapter, academic internationalization was generally conceived as a process of infusing international perspectives into an institution. There was an emphasis on the internal workings of institutions, including the home-based accumulation of international resources (faculty, students, research centers, study abroad options) and restructuring of curricula.

Over the last 20 years, however, it has become increasingly apparent that conceiving internationalization this way misses the bidirectionality inherent in the very word *international,* as well as the benefits and even philosophical imperatives that argue for a more collaborative approach. Internationalization is as much a process of institutions reaching beyond their own boundaries as it is of accumulating resources within their walls (Hudzik, 2011, p. 10; Sutton, 2010). It is as much a process of moving out into the world as studying that world from a distance. Increasingly, internationalization is as much a process of joining broader alliances as it is one of promoting the interests of single institutions. This bidirectionality has, however, been historically muted by certain ways of conceiving (and talking) about academic institutions as self-contained units, as well as the ways in which existing structures, processes, and vested interests reflect this conception.

It is becoming increasingly clear that international knowledge is best constructed through international dialogue, that institutions have much to gain by sharing resources across national borders, and that higher education itself is now conducted on a global stage. This context has repositioned international affiliations as both key strategy and core philosophy for internationalization. The goals of internationalization are no longer simply what individual institutions can do for themselves, but also what multiple institutions can do together that they could not do alone.

The forces that produced this recognition of internationalization as bidirectional and boundary-bending are varied and even sometimes conflicting (Altbach, Reisberg, & Rumbley, 2009; Knight, 2008; Stockley & de Wit, 2011). Postcolonial perspectives have increasingly argued that student learning requires the authentic inclusion of multiple voices about the human condition. Advances in science, technology, scholarship, and most professional fields are no longer limited to a few nations but increasingly the result of collaboration across many. Internationalization now spreads across all academic disciplines, and many of the newcomers approach it as much through working with their international colleagues as studying about them. The marketing of degree programs, the search for students, and the quest for institutional ranking and accreditation are now worldwide ventures. At the same time, many of the most serious issues of the 21st century call for globally coordinated responses, the communities served by colleges and universities have themselves been globalized, and human mobility is at an all-time high. Finally, advances in information technology have made cross-border collaboration much easier than in the past, at the same time that they have introduced another player/partner/competitor into the mix: universities that teach solely through distance means.

These varied forces have piled new meanings onto the term *internationalization,* including some that contrast with the long-standing usages of diversifying an institution's student base and enhancing international understanding (Altbach et al., 2009; de Wit 1998; Egron-Polak & Hudson, 2010, p. 62; Hudzik, 2011, pp. 12–13; Knight 2008). The result is a volatile mix, a rapidly changing landscape, a state of turmoil in the words of Knight (2008), and a recognition that internationalization can carry negative as well as positive implications (Egron-Polak & Hudson, 2010; Ishikawa, 2009; Teferra, 2008; Wildavsky, 2010). Institutions are wrestling with their positioning in a global system of higher education, individuals can mean different things when invoking the term, and competitive and collaborative impulses are both at work.

As institutions navigate this situation, few any longer see internationalization simply in terms of infusing perspectives inwardly, even if they have not yet found the language to describe a bidirectional approach. Most are moving toward a conception of internationalization that revolves around international engagement or connection. In this regard, many institutions are weighing three overlapping possibilities for outward engagement: spreading institutional reach through branch campuses, research centers, and distance delivery; competing for global ranking and market share; and collaborating for joint projects, resource sharing, and mutual benefit (Altbach & Knight, 2010; Coclanis & Strauss, 2010; de Wit, 2004, Marginson & van der Wende, 2007).

This chapter focuses on the last of these. More specifically, this discussion examines the evolving use of institutional partnerships as agents of internationalization. The linkages discussed here are not one faculty member with another, but rather a number of institutions with each other. These affiliations fit the definition given by Kinser and Green (2009): "cooperative agreements between a higher education institution and another distinct organization" (p. 13). Such agreements may link academic institutions with each other in both one-on-one affiliations and multi-institutional consortia (Sternberger, 2005; Stockley & de Wit, 2011). They may also link academic institutions with private businesses, nonprofit organizations, community groups, international associations, or government agencies. What such partnerships have in common is that they are recognized at the highest levels of each institution, and they draw academic institutions out beyond themselves to achieve institutional goals. As will become clear, some partnerships even create international academic units with functions and lives of their own, well beyond their constituent institutions.

While all such alliances merit discussion, this chapter focuses on those that link academic institutions, either in pairs or larger networks. Many of the conclusions presented, however, apply with only slight modification to other kinds of linkages and consortia. The institutional affiliations on which we focus are rapidly expanding in number and importance (Altbach & Knight, 2010, p. 29; Bhandari & Motwani, 2010; Chan 2004; Hartle 2008; van de Water, Green, & Koch, 2008, pp. 1–5). A 2005 International Association of Universities survey showed that the internationalization strategy most valued by universities (across all world regions) was that of institutional agreements and networks, a strategy that registered as a close second in the 2009 edition of the survey (Egron-Polak & Hudson, 2010, p. 91). What is happening might, in fact, be labeled the *internationalization of internationalization,* signaling that the process of internationalization has itself become internationally collaborative.

BOX 9. 1 The Intersection of Internationalization and Civic Engagement

Gil Latz

Associate Vice Chancellor for International Affairs, Purdue University (USA)

Portland State University (PSU) began the process of formulating and implementing a university-wide internationalization strategy in 1999. A Strategy for Comprehensive Internationalization was developed with six priorities focused on achieving global excellence by providing opportunities for students and faculty and by pursuing partnerships that have an international dimension with our metropolitan community. A central idea shaping this strategy has been exploring the intersection of internationalization and civic engagement.

Since 2003, strategic partnerships with Vietnamese institutions have been a priority, putting PSU on the leading edge of efforts to collaborate with a nation undergoing profound economic,

(Continued)

(Continued)

social, and political change. From the outset, PSU focused on academic, government, and business network opportunities, building directly on the university motto, *"Let Knowledge Serve the City,"* and emphasizing two key elements of the internationalization strategy:

- To have students enter the 21st century as leaders in an emerging global community
- To embrace internationalization as a scholarly activity that connects educational programs with innovative research and community-based service

Programmatically, PSU sought to deepen its three spheres of recognized excellence in a synergistic manner:

- *Boundary-breaking research:* innovative sustainability projects (augmented by a recent $25 million Miller Foundation Grant).
- *Student-centered education:* faculty and student engagement in relevant service-learning projects, learning communities, first-year programs, and community-based capstone courses.
- *Community-based service:* building on four decades of experience partnering with governments, corporations, and nonprofit entities that share a commitment to the collective good.

Our vision for working with Vietnam was to focus our efforts by creating a network of institutions (academic and otherwise) that could leverage reciprocal benefits in these three areas of excellence. Initially, we explored a linkage between the Vietnam Fulbright Office and PSU's strategy for institutional, community, and business partnerships. Ultimately this dialogue has led to four distinct projects exploring how the United States and Vietnam might interact on commonly defined problems: a Community-University Engagement Program (in collaboration with Higher Education for Development/U.S. AID), an Advanced Program in Computer Science (supported by the Ministry of Education and Training), the Intel Vietnam Scholars Program (a 3 + 2 university engineering education reform project), and political leadership for sustainable development (with the Ho Chi Minh Political Academy). Table 9.1 summarizes these strategic partnerships and their significant outcomes for all involved.

Global Issue Areas	Vietnam-related Initiatives	Engaged Groups	Outcomes and Benefits
Mitigating urban environmental problems	University of Sciences, Vietnam National University PSU's Center for Academic Excellence and Community-University Engagement Program	PSU City of Portland/METRO Nike Community groups Vietnam universities Ho Chi Minh City Environmental Bureau	New urban Environmental Education Centers (3) Community-university service-learning projects (12) Short-term faculty led program (annual); faculty immersion (2010) on environmental problems and rapid urban development Contribution to PSU theme of Global Excellence

Global Issue Areas	Vietnam-related Initiatives	Engaged Groups	Outcomes and Benefits
Developing new academic programs and curricula	PSU-University of Sciences Computer Science Program w/MOET Intel Vietnam scholars program Leadership for sustainable development	PSU's Maseeh College of Engineering/Computer Science PSU's Hatfield School of Government Intel and businesses Vietnam universities Ho Chi Minh Political Academy	Resources for pursuing PSU's academic mission and PSU theme of global excellence Contributing to Vietnam's agenda for academic reform Relationship development Governance issues associated with rapid economic development

Table 9.1   Portland State University's (PSU's) Engagement With Vietnam, 2003–2011

The Evolving Scope, Goals, and Form of International Partnerships

In short, international academic partnerships are being asked to do more than they have in the past. Partnerships are, in fact, a major testing ground for institutional efforts at connecting with an increasingly global system of higher education. There are dozens of new partnership models in existence, as different institutions move forward in different ways (Stockley & de Wit 2011; Van de Water et al., 2008, pp. 16–23). This is a moment of great flux, creativity, and experimentation, and senior international officers (SIOs) can find themselves navigating different international partnership goals held by different constituencies even within their own institutions.

Still the most common and often default interpretation of the term *partnership* is an affiliation directed toward increasing student mobility, although the locations of such exchange partners are evolving, as institutions in the global North seek partners in the global South, and Asian institutions grow in importance. These exchanges are most often of students for a semester or two (sometimes matched with the occasional exchange of faculty). They can occur between a single pair of institutions, on a one-for-one basis, or be spread across a larger consortium. Their basic goals are twofold: increasing opportunities for students and faculty

from the home institution, while simultaneously diversifying its study body through the influx of visitors. To such core motivations may be added using exchange opportunities for student recruitment, curricular expansion, and development of regional educational systems (as in the Erasmus program). A more and more common variation on this theme are partnerships that set up largely one-way flows of students through dual degree and facilitated transfer arrangements (Chan, 2004).

As common as exchange partnerships are, international affiliations are increasingly taking on new functions and spreading across the traditional tripartite categories (also sometimes conceived as "deliverables") of higher education: teaching, research, and service or civic engagement, a point well-illustrated in Box 9.1. In terms of the first of these domains, affiliations are used to provide overseas study opportunities for students, solicit outside expertise in curriculum development, develop joint courses and degrees, infuse global perspectives into existing courses, and trade or combine faculty resources for teaching, both at a distance and in the classroom (e.g., Cogan, 1998). Under the heading of research, partnerships are now directed toward establishing joint research centers, conferences, publications, Web sites and databases, as well as connecting faculty for collaborative research projects. Partnerships focused on service often create collaborative teams pursuing community development, workforce preparation, conflict resolution, public health, environmental threats, legal and governmental reforms, increased access to education, and similar issues in the nations of one or all partners.

Closely related and even overlapping the goals just mentioned are linkages concerned with capacity-building on one side of the partnership. Such affiliations, under the heading of technical cooperation or educational cooperation for development, have been significant in the advancement of colleges and universities in Africa and other parts of the global South (European University Association, 2010; Kellogg, 2009; Some & Khaemba, 2002; Teferra 2008). The driving purpose of such linkages has been institutional development through visiting teams of faculty, students, and administrators from the global North (as well as the welcoming of students from the South at universities in the North). There has, however, been increasing recognition that these visiting teams learn as much as they teach and that such projects work best when fully collaborative (Canto & Hannah, 2001; Duval, 2009; Gillespie, 2003; Ishikawa, 2009).

Colleges and universities are not the only entities interested in international academic partnerships. Nations, foundations, religious organizations, and international associations sometimes fund such affiliations and introduce societal goals (Stockley & de Wit, 2011) that range across peace-building, public diplomacy, national security, workforce development, poverty alleviation, democratization, international business linkages, and global issues of health, environment, education, conflict, and poverty. These goals are sometimes consonant with what academic institutions already wish to do but sometimes channel institutions in ways that Neave (1992) labels reactive.

The partnership goals mentioned thus far were all present 20 years ago, albeit in a different mix, and with some less elaborated than they now are. New on the scene, however, are goals that stem from the increasing globalization of higher education itself. Colleges and universities now participate in a worldwide academic system, and partnerships have acquired goals connected to positioning institutions within this system and even—in some cases—directly shaping the system. In the first instance, partnerships are now often made with considerable concern for advancing an institution's international ranking through association with highly regarded collaborators (Chan, 2004; Knight, 2008). Some multiuniversity consortia are also constructed with an eye toward creating globally recognized tiers of high and low prestige. At the same time, a number of international academic associations have recently examined the emerging global system of higher education in a more analytical way and opened up space for discussing the negative implications of what is happening, as well as the positive (Stockley & de Wit, 2011).

In short, not all partnerships are the same, and different individuals can promote the same partnership for different reasons. What all partnerships have in common, however, is their emphasis on collaboration over isolation, even when the primary motivator is individual institutional gain. Kanter's (1994) concept of *collaborative advantage*, derived from her analysis of international business—provides a useful theoretical framework. As she says, "In the global economy, a well-developed ability to create and sustain fruitful collaborations gives companies a significant competitive leg up" (p. 96).

In this regard, it is useful to distinguish between two levels of collaboration. Exchange partnerships concerned with student mobility stand at one end of a continuum from what might be called *transactional* to what might be called *transformational* collaborations (Sutton, 2010). Exchange partnerships are at the transactional end because human resources are traded in a manner that resembles transactions in a marketplace. The individuals who travel from one institution to another are changed as a result of the exchange, but the institutions themselves remain largely separate and unaffected. Transformational partnerships, in contrast, are those that change or transform entire departments, offices, and institutions, through the generation of common goals, projects, and products.[2] Both sides emerge from the relationship somewhat altered. Transformational partnerships combine resources; they view linkages as a source of institutional growth and collaborative learning. They often produce new initiatives that go beyond what was originally planned. They are greater in scope than exchanges and constitute a direct effort at outward engagement. Bard College's development of what it defines as *authentic partnerships* provides an apt example (Gillespie, 2003; see Box 9.2).

BOX 9.2 How to Form an Authentic Partnership, or Working With Colleagues Overseas to Democratize Education and Change Ourselves

Susan Gillespie

Director of the Institute for International Liberal Education and
Vice President for Global Initiatives, Bard College (USA)

Many of us in international education are in this line of work because we—like good teachers and good citizens everywhere—hoped and still hope to make the world a better place. Often, our hopes were nurtured by the life-changing experience of studying and living in a foreign country. (Mine was Germany, where I studied for six and a half years.) The cognitive, social, and epistemic challenges we encountered helped us understand the point of view of people in other countries or deepened our yearning to understand them more fully. We found friends, equals, sympathetic interlocutors. Equally important, we learned to see ourselves, and our country, through the minds of others. We began to become globally aware. Why not make this experience available to young people from our communities and institutions? And how best to do this? These are some of the questions we came back asking.

These turned out to be the very same questions that young people from eastern Europe asked after coming to Bard College for a year as exchange students in the early 1990s. We had invited them, raised the funds to cover their costs, and eagerly welcomed them as they took their first drive through New York City's Central Park, encountered U.S. mall culture, and turned their sharp young minds to the questions raised in our liberal arts classrooms. Something we had not anticipated was how conscious they were of the benefits of liberal arts education, the difference between the academic atmosphere at, say, Bard, and their home universities. Many of them went home hoping to introduce this kind of education in their countries. Ten years later, when we organized a reunion of these students, the top two things they wanted to discuss were the impact of liberal education and educational reform.

Bard's far-flung and ambitious partnership programs in Russia, South Africa, Kyrgyzstan, and Palestine began with the outspoken concerns of these international students. We soon met faculty members who were equally passionate about bringing liberal education to their countries as a means of fostering democracy. We wanted to support and learn from their struggles. We also wanted to see what we ourselves could learn by becoming deeply engaged not just individually, but as an institution.

Bard's partnerships are all based on the awarding of a dual degree or dual credit. This means, on the one hand, that we have to work very closely with our partners to align our curricula, evaluation criteria, assessment, planning, and administration. It also means that faculty and administrators on both sides visit frequently, in both directions, work together on a day-to-day basis, and become intimately (sometimes excruciatingly) familiar with the institutional and sociopolitical culture of the partner institution. This makes life interesting. The dual degree is the lynchpin of our joint ventures and contributes, we believe, to equality and mutuality, the two watchwords of Bard's Institute for International Liberal Education, which administers these ventures.

The Bard College–Al-Quds University partnership illustrates this philosophy well. Established in 1984, Al-Quds is the only Arab university in Jerusalem. Al-Quds and Bard share a commitment to

(Continued)

(Continued)

educational reform and to the liberal arts as a force for both personal and societal growth. They have recently joined forces in a comprehensive partnership that seeks to provide a distinctive liberal arts education as a means of preparing young Palestinians to assume the responsibilities of leadership and self-governance in a democratic state and as an opportunity for Bard students to study with Palestinian students across a variety of academic disciplines, including classes analyzing a range of discourses surrounding the Israeli-Palestinian conflict. Bard and Al-Quds faculty share responsibility for this program, collaborating on curricular and faculty development, recruitment, and governance. The collaboration includes a dual-degree master's of arts in teaching program, as well as the Al Quds Bard Honors College, which offers a four-year program leading to a B.A. Honors from Al-Quds and a B.A from Bard. The curriculum combines traditional disciplines and innovative interdisciplinary programs, the language of instruction is English, and classes emphasize student-centered learning, the development of independent inquiry, and the free exchange of ideas.

THE TWISTS AND TURNS OF PARTNERSHIPS OVER TIME: A CASE STUDY

As partnerships gain in range and importance, it is also becoming clear that they are always— and inevitably—works in progress. It is not just that partnership goals and forms have changed over the last 20 years, it is also that partnerships are inherently dynamic. The give-and-take of partnership activity, the "lived experience" of partnerships (to borrow a term from anthropology) creates change. In some cases this change is toward less activity, in others, toward more. No two pathways are precisely the same. This is a point perhaps best made by recounting a sample partnership history in depth, in this case, an affiliation between a Mexican university and one in the United States. This case demonstrates both how partnerships can twist and turn over time, and it also reflects the trend toward more multifaceted partnerships that has marked the last 20 years.

The partnership between New Mexico State University (NMSU) and the Universidad Autónoma de Chihuahua (UACH) has clearly been transformational. It did not start this way, however. The partnership grew and matured as the result of an evolving and increasingly comprehensive set of activities linking NMSU, UACH, and other institutions and agencies in Chihuahua and New Mexico over three decades. These relationships and activities created an environment that nurtured the NMSU-UACH relationship. This was not anticipated, however, when activities began.

The story began in 1992 when NMSU became involved in the development and implementation of alternative energy technologies in the State of Chihuahua. NMSU's alternative energies group in the College of Engineering conducted solar and wind energy development for U.S. AID and the U.S. Department of Energy in Chihuahua from 1992 to 2005. During this period, NMSU collaborated with a variety of Mexican state and federal agencies in Chihuahua, as well as universities (including UACH), research centers, and the local solar energy industry. This was a grant-driven educational-cooperation-for-development project, which also provided exchange and work opportunities for NMSU students in Chihuahua and vice versa.

The unintended consequence of this initial work was the emergence of a network of U.S. and Chihuahuan agencies, industries, laboratories, and educational institutions concerned with renewable energy. This meant an engaged workforce was ready for collaborative activities, both educational and developmental. Moreover, the concrete successes of the initial work created greater openness to proposals for new activities. Through the new initiatives that resulted, NMSU eventually signed agreements and carried out collaborative activities with more than a dozen institutions and organizations in Chihuahua.[3]

Ultimately, NMSU's deep engagement in Chihuahua created the matrix that transformed the partnership between NMSU and UACH. Things began to build in 2002–2003 when the NMSU provost and UACH rector led delegations to each other's campuses.[4] The delegations discussed ongoing programs, proposed new initiatives, and brainstormed ideas. Enthusiasm and commitment were much in evidence. It was clear that the foundation on which to build had been laid. The NMSU president struck a chord when he emphasized the importance of continuing NMSU-UACH initiatives, assuring all present that much could be done despite resource limitations on both sides of the border. UACH colleagues wholeheartedly agreed, pointing out that they were indeed accustomed to accomplishing "*mucho con menos.*"

In 2003, NMSU created a new position reflecting this greater commitment to partnership activities with Chihuahua. Egginton (one of the authors of this chapter) took up this post: vice provost of international and U.S./Mexico border programs. At the same time, a Chihuahuan trade official, Armando Martinez, became head of the new Chihuahua Trade Office (CTO), established by Chihuahua, in which NMSU funded office space in Chihuahua in return for unspecified economic and educational trade opportunities for NMSU and the state of New Mexico. CTO members included heads of small companies, directors of schools and research centers, and leaders of nonprofit organizations throughout Chihuahua. Connections between NMSU and Chihuahua had grown so much they warranted offices to manage and advance them. These offices, in turn, increased activities between Chihuahuan and New Mexican institutions across the domains of government, research, education, and work with indigenous populations.[5]

Within a year of these developments, in late 2004, NMSU and UACH secured support from U.S. AID for work with the indigenous community of Sierra Tarahumara. By this time, Raul Favela (another author of this chapter) had taken up the post of leading international initiatives for UACH. In announcing this award, U.S. Ambassador to Mexico Tony Garza noted, "These new partnerships promote economic development in Mexico's rural areas by assisting this sector to become more competitive and to provide more economic opportunities." The project addressed the need for economic development through education and training opportunities, food production, small-farm development, natural resource management, income production, and marketing for nascent enterprises in the region.

This project brought talented students from Chihuahua to earn master's degrees at NMSU in various disciplines and offered workshops and seminars in the Sierra Tarahumara region organized by faculty from NMSU and UACH. It moved the NMSU-UACH relationship from one that was moderately collaborative to one that was transformational. From this one externally funded project, NMSU and UACH began to consider additional ways to collaborate—thinking automatically of each other whenever an opportunity presented itself. A subsequent and enduring collaboration was the design of a joint aeronautical engineering program that brings UACH students to NMSU to earn bachelor's degrees in this field of great interest and importance. The two institutions have also developed a joint doctoral degree program in civil engineering with a focus on transportation.

Support for this expanding partnership has come from the highest levels, with institutional presidents frequently taking part in cross-border activities, a key signal of the importance each institution holds for the other.[6] Students and faculty who had never before participated in international activities were given a platform on which to explore their interests, and their engagement has been facilitated by working closely with international counterparts. The expanding knowledge and competence of both institutions and their members have come through dialogue and mutual learning deeply contextualized in specific social, cultural, and economic settings. New binational approaches to science and scholarship have emerged, and cross-border issues have been addressed in a collaborative way.

NMSU's relationship with UACH has enjoyed periods of significant activity and periods when activities were more sporadic. The diversity of events and programs, however, has meant that as one arena waned, another waxed, and the partnership continued forward. At present, the activity level is shifting once again as both institutions face administrative changes, the global recession poses economic challenges, and violence escalates in Mexico's border states, particularly Chihuahua. Already, the violence has seriously hampered NMSU travel to Mexico. Many aspects of this situation are beyond the universities' control. Given the foundation now established, however, it is hoped that both institutions will sustain the partnership, adapt to adversity, and once again do "*mucho con menos.*"

BUILDING PARTNERSHIPS THAT WORK

The NMSU/UACH partnership is remarkable but not unique. Sutton has a similar tale to tell, in her case about partnership evolution between Indiana University Purdue University Indianapolis and Moi University in Kenya (Quigley, 2009; Sutton, 2010). So do those who wrote text boxes for this chapter. No matter their particular twists and turns, all of the programs reflect the trend toward multifaceted, strategic, transformative collaborations. Duval (2009) refers to such robust linkages as "high-performing partnerships," and the growing list of factors that lead to these is remarkably similar to that identified for the NMSU/UACH partnership (Anderson, 1999; Chan, 2004, pp. 38-39; de Wit, 2004; Kellogg, 2009; Kinser & Green, 2009, p. 16; Prichard, 1996, p. 5; Van Ginkel, 1996, p.100; Wiley 2006).[7]

• Making a good institutional match, based on mission, strengths, community connections, and partnership goals

• Devoting time to building and sustaining the relationship, communicating frequently, dealing with disagreement, and maintaining trust through fairness, integrity, and the honoring of commitments

• Operating on the basis of shared decision-making, reciprocity, mutual benefit, and collaborative determination of goals and projects

• Clarifying what is to be provided by each side in a transparent manner that also addresses possible inequalities of resources and imbalances in exchanges

• Spreading activities across multiple arenas, engaging multiple constituencies, and building a large network of supporters

• Flexibility, adaptability, and openness to change

• Engaging relevant decision-makers and supporting the partnership through an overall institutional partnership strategy, as discussed in the next section

DEVELOPING AN INSTITUTIONAL APPROACH TO INTERNATIONAL PARTNERSHIPS

Not all partnerships are as complex and multitiered as that between NMSU and UACH. Nor should they be. Such robust transformational partnerships are at one end of the continuum, and most institutions have a broad portfolio of partnerships, including some that reside more on the transactional side. Each serves its purpose, even if there is a general move toward fewer, more strategic partnerships (Stockley & de Wit, 2011). Whatever array of partnerships they pursue, many institutions are articulating partnership goals and policies in a more systematic way than in the past. The practice of partnership-making is becoming more deliberate, and MOUs are signed with greater care and less abandon, even as the activities they authorize encompass a wider set of possibilities.

The development of articulated partnership policies and programs rarely occurs in linear fashion (Edwards, 2007; Green & Olson, 2003; Kinser & Green, 2009; Van de Water et al., 2008). Pilot projects coexist side-by-side with policy-setting initiatives. In whatever order they occur, however, the following overlapping steps are often part of the process by which institutions organize their partnership efforts, The points that follow owe much to both Van de Water et al. (2008) and Kinser & Green (2009).

1. *Making an inventory of existing affiliations.* Creating a centralized registry of current partnerships and assessing levels of activity provides the basis for decisions concerning continuation or dissolution, as well as identifying gaps (or concentrations) in geographical distribution and types of partnerships.

2. *Establishing a partnership approval process.* Partnerships commit resources, both human and financial, and therefore require the approval and engagement of key decision-makers at various levels. The development of application templates and approval sheets with multiple signature lines, the routing of these documents through appropriate offices, and the

establishment of an affiliations committee that reviews proposed new partnerships are common methods for ensuring this happens.

3. *Articulating overall partnership goals and strategies.* Institutions are increasingly setting goals with respect to number and location of partnerships, activities to be pursued, balance between transactional and transformational outcomes, criteria by which partners will be selected, impact they are expected to have, and the ways in which the institution will support them (Kinser & Green, 2009, pp. 7–9; Van de Water et al., 2008, pp. 8–10). As with Portland State and Osaka Universities, these goals are often geared to institutional mission, as well as an overall internationalization plan.

4. *Spreading a culture of partnership.* Partnering beyond the institution comes no more easily than developing interdisciplinary centers within one. Both require ample discussion of what is gained by collaboration. Both require institutional support to initiate and sustain work outside one's own unit. International partnerships also require professional development activities to deepen the knowledge and intercultural competence of those who participate.

5. *Developing policies, procedures, and organizational structures for managing partnerships.* As partnerships move from occasional exchanges to more robust forms, they require more complex policies and organizational forms to guide them. Many institutions are establishing partnership offices or committees to coordinate the myriad activities and constituencies involved and to articulate principles for participating in these activities (Chan, 2004, pp. 40–41). Some are also tackling procedural roadblocks to partnership development, such as overly restrictive limits on spending institutional funds overseas (as in the University of Washington's Global Support Project).

6. *Providing financial and other support.* Many exchanges are revenue neutral (when balance in numbers is achieved), and transformational partnerships can result in significant external funding. The increasing importance of partnerships, nevertheless, asks institutions to provide some baseline funding and support, equivalent to what is provided for other key institutional functions: personnel; information technology, which enables effective communication at a distance; and seed grants for faculty, students, and administrators to become involved (Hartle, 2008). The case for such funding is not easy to make in difficult economic times, but it rests on the increasing need for institutions to become internationally engaged. Partnerships constitute one of the most philosophically defensible and cost-effective modes of internationalization. Special fees, a portion of international student tuition, or a percentage of the indirect costs of external international grants are possible revenue streams (Leventhal, 2011).

7. *Thoughtful practices for initiating partnerships.* In the past, it was not unusual for MOUs to be signed after a single meeting. The increasing importance of partnerships, however, calls for greater deliberation, beginning with a clear idea of institutional goals and the kinds of partners being sought. Moving toward partnership requires multiple conversations (some internal, some with the potential partner), the engagement of relevant decision makers, the candor to raise problems and potential trouble spots (Van de Water et al., 2008, pp. 38–41), and the patience to let relationships and understandings mature. It is a dialogical process (Kinser & Green, 2009; Sternberger, 2005; Van de Water et al., 2008, pp. 10–11) in which mutual understandings are developed, agendas modified, and human relationships built.

8. *Well-crafted MOUs and Implementation Plans.* Partnerships are increasingly governed by a general MOU that serves as an umbrella for a succession of separate, more specific implementation plans outlining each new activity (Thullen, Tillman, Horner, Carty, & Kennedy, 1997, pp. 34–65; Van de Water et al., 2008, pp. 20–22, 37–45). The MOU is a commitment to work toward the goals that arise during collaboration. It sets general parameters of the partnership, dates when it will be reviewed, the manner in which difficulties and disagreements will be handled, and conditions under which the MOU may be terminated. Implementation Plans contain some of these elements but also identify specific activities, the financial and other responsibilities of each institution, the outcomes that are expected, and when and how these will be assessed.

9. *Thoughtful practices for sustaining partnerships over time.* Once established, partnerships

should be guided by the factors leading to long-lasting, high-performing collaborations given in the previous section. This requires considerable organization and leadership, as well as practices that enable newcomers to become active participants and ensure that the partnership will endure, even when its original proposers have retired or pulled back.

10. *Procedures and benchmarks for reviewing, revising, and terminating partnerships.* Partnerships are dynamic entities, enhanced by periodic assessment concerning level of activity, quality of projects or products, number of students and faculty involved, effectiveness of the working relationship, cost, and impact on teaching, research, civic engagement, and institutional positioning (see also Anderson, 1999).

Pursuing such a comprehensive institutional approach to partnerships both amplifies and changes the work of international offices. It asks that those guiding international affiliations be conversant with more than the logistics of exchange and that they participate in institutional decision-making at various levels. Such partnership programs work best when integrated with overall institutional mission, as illustrated by Osaka University's approach (Box 9.3).

BOX 9.3 Osaka University's Global Commitment

In 2005, Osaka University's International Affairs Board initiated a new, comprehensive approach to internationalization, captured in a widely disseminated document entitled *Osaka University's Global Commitment and Strategies* (Osaka University, 2005). All three of the defining international goals established by this document committed the university to expanding its international partnerships:

1. To promote research collaboration with scholars and institutions overseas and share the research results for the benefit of global society

2. To promote education that fosters transcultural communicability and encourages constructive, creative action

3. To build regional academic communities in Asia and work for human security and sustainable development

The strategies put forth to achieve these goals focused on moving beyond individual or departmental collaborations toward institution-wide partnerships and networks by "introducing collective measures" and "organizational support" to facilitate joint research projects, student and staff exchanges, and significant efforts to address issues of health, environment, and development across Asia.

Two interlocking offices support these initiatives and have enabled Osaka University to move to a new level of international partnership. The first is the Office for International Plans and Programs (IPP), which directly develops and supports partnerships, exchanges, and affiliations. IPP formulates strategies to carry out the university's international goals, collects data on the current state of its internationalization including its partnerships, conducts research on international issues in higher education, and works to improve support for students and faculty visiting the university. Besides managing Osaka University's international partnerships, IPP has become a think tank for new approaches to international academic collaboration, and its staff are active contributors to worldwide discussions on these matters (see, e.g., Ishikawa, 2009). Whereas international outreach consisted almost entirely of individual research collaborations in 2005, the university has now focused its efforts around three overseas education and research centers: San Francisco (U.S.), Groningen (the Netherlands), and Bangkok (Thailand). These centers provide bases for Osaka University faculty and students to pursue research and educational interests with partners in these targeted areas.

The second office provides a broad theoretical framework for the university's collaborative activities. It is the Global Collaboration Center (GLOCOL), a unit that not only studies the many forms of global cooperation, but also is itself globally collaborative in its composition and activities. GLOCOL was established in 2007 when Osaka University merged with the Osaka University of Foreign Studies, an amalgamation that brought significant expertise in international studies to the institution. The result is a center that explores the factors that enhance or block global collaboration in the contemporary world, in ways that enrich and expand Osaka University's approach to its own partnerships. As the GLOCOL mission statement says:

> Ultimately, our goal at GLOCOL is to contribute to the betterment of society through the promotion of global collaboration. Just as it is impossible to envisage a future entirely free from diseases, disasters, and misfortunes, our efforts may not lead to a complete resolution of wars and conflicts, poverty, ecological degradation, and other problems in the contemporary world. Still, we firmly believe in the importance of making sustained and practical efforts to alleviate our shared problems, and recognize global cooperation as essential to these endeavors.

GLOCOL thus places international academic collaboration in its broadest context, while raising critical questions concerning the purposes such affiliations serve and the ways in which they are best pursued.

Note: This box was prepared by chapter author Susan Buck Sutton.

A brief discussion on the use of information technology (IT) in advancing partnerships is also in order. Gone are the days when successful partnerships depended on face-to-face meetings, extensive international travel with long and expensive stays, and numerous costly one-on-one telephone conversations. IT has reduced costs, expanded the level of participation in both real-time and asynchronous meetings, and expedited the collaboration of faculty, students, and administrators. IT in all its varied manifestations—from landline telephones and fax machines to smart phones and Skype; from traditional desktop computers to e-pads and "cloud-based" technology—is essential to effective partnerships. At the same time, IT presents challenges that must be addressed, from the North/South digital gap to the need to protect confidentiality and also obtain written consent and confirmation for partnership activities.[8]

THE FUTURE OF INTERNATIONAL PARTNERSHIPS

Whatever form they take or goal they pursue, international academic partnerships are currently on the rise. It is risky, nevertheless, to predict that this increase will continue indefinitely. The turmoil in which higher education now finds itself contains forces that could reverse the move toward partnership, from funding challenges to online delivery of degrees, branch campuses, the possible rise of a small set of dominant global universities (Wildavsky, 2010), and political unrest both within and among nations.

There is also a tension between institutional advancement and partnership advancement inherent in any collaborative venture and only partially overcome through Kanter's (1994) *collaborative advantage.* The extent to which particular institutions remain invested in significant partnership strategies will thus depend on what benefits partnerships produce (both intended and unintended) in comparison to what is achieved by going it alone; whether or not these benefits outweigh the costs and difficulties of maintaining the linkages; whether participating institutions can develop sustainable structures and procedures; and how strong other institutional priorities are. In making these assessments, the full transaction costs of partnerships (the balance or imbalance in exchange numbers, staffing to oversee the partnership, support for faculty and student participation, and funding for possible overseas centers) must be weighed against what it might cost to engage in international work without partnership platforms on which to build.

Continued institutional engagement with partnerships will also reflect the extent to which ethical standards emerge to grapple with issues of justice, equity, and integrity. Partners must be held to standards of accountability, delivery on commitments, accurate representation of themselves and the partnership, and confidentiality with respect to project records and communications.[9] Ethical assurances are particularly important for partnerships between institutions in wealthy, high-income countries and poor, low-income countries. Philpott (2010) argues that such alliances are often initiated with great fanfare and enthusiasm but scant attention to the ethical issues involved. She then poses several tests that can be applied to ensure that ethical principles are at work, partnerships are balanced, and neither side benefits more than the other (see also Bhutta, 2002; Canto & Hannah, 2001; Edejer, 1999; Gillespie, 2003; International Association of Universities, 2000; Shue, 1995; Teferra 2008).

• Informed consent: Full information concerning partnership activities is provided; there are assurances it is understood; participation is voluntary; allowance is made for language and cultural differences.

• Risks and benefits: Risks (cost and time factors, distractions from regular work and resultant realigned priorities, cultural misunderstandings) and benefits (enhanced individual and institutional capacity for both partners, reciprocal learning) are clear to all.

• Exploitation: Concrete steps are in place to assure the partnership is not being used simply to gain advantage and that benefits, workload, and commitments are distributed equitably.

• Standard of education: What is taught and the research that takes place are in the best interests of the host country and the host institution.

The general Statement on Internationalization adopted by the International Association of Universities in 2000 provides valuable additional framing for the ethical issues involved in partnerships, particularly in its call to use educational cooperation to address issues of inequity, brain drain, and the preparation of students as global citizens.

Should the present trend toward increasing numbers of partnerships as well as greater range and creativity in the activities they pursue continue, certain other developments are likely. One might be the rise of a new subfield of international educators who specialize in developing and guiding partnerships, as well as organizations that broker partnership arrangements (Altbach & Teichler, 2001, p. 23). Another might be the further elimination of procedural roadblocks to partnerships, making institutions more limber in their ability to engage internationally. It would also be reasonable to expect the development of common, internationally understood definitions of different types of partnerships, as well as quality standards, conflict resolution methods, and ethical principles.

Continued growth in partnerships would also likely alter existing structures of research and teaching in interesting ways. Joint degrees, the trading or joint teaching of courses, and the swirling of multinational cohorts of students and even faculty among partner institutions is likely to become more common. Bi- or multinational research centers would likely become more prominent, as would consortia among smaller institutions. Because partnerships operate beyond the institutional boundaries that have given higher education its shape for so long, an increase in such affiliations might rework this shape. Paired with the move toward greater civic engagement, international partnerships lend themselves to open-ended, interactive, porous models of higher education, in which knowledge comes from engagement beyond the institution as much as it does from work within it.

International partnerships also hold promise for addressing critical global issues, from environmental sustainability to ethnic conflict, in ways that bring different national perspectives and resources together. The interactive global conversation developed by Skelly at the University of Ulster (Box 9.4) heads in this direction and also raises the possibility of

BOX 9. 4 The Global Conversation: A Transformational Partnership that "Connects the Dots"

James Skelly

Visiting Professor of Peace Studies,
University of Ulster in Derry (Northern Ireland)

The Global Conversation is a course that helps students develop a better understanding of the environmental problems associated with economic globalization and thus prepares them for active participation in a conversation in a civil society that is increasingly global in scope. At a basic level, *The Global Conversation* is about how we live on the planet, both individually and collectively, and it poses two fundamental questions: Can we sustain the way we have been living on the earth? How ought we to live? The unsustainable manner in which humans are currently living on our planet requires that we try to connect the dots both in terms of issues and in terms of partnership with others throughout the world.

Central to *The Global Conversation* from its inception has been the idea that the classroom had to be global, and it also had to stimulate dialogue among students in different parts of the world about the compelling issues that humanity faces. It accomplishes this by connecting students at various institutions in online discussions of course issues and collaborative projects developed through organized exchanges in Learning Circles using the Internet, where all course materials are hosted using a Moodle platform.

The course was developed by Brethren Colleges Abroad (BCA) and James Skelly, BCA's coordinator for peace and justice programming, who oversees the course, which is also part of the international politics curriculum at the University of Ulster's Magee Campus in Derry, Northern Ireland. Partnership with colleagues and institutions in other countries was essential to the creation of a global classroom, and the networks of BCA, Ulster, and the peace studies community were used to accomplish this.

The course was initially an optional offering for students studying abroad through BCA's programs in China, France, and Mexico, and it is now offered at several of its other program sites. In addition, the course was also made a part of the curriculum at the Institute for Social & European Studies in Hungary, where there is a significant cohort of international students. As of the winter-spring term 2011, *The Global Conversation* had also become part of the curriculum at the Burren College of Art in Ballyvaughan, Ireland; Elizabethtown College and Juniata College in Pennsylvania; Regis University in Colorado; and the Universidad Veracruzana in Veracruz, Mexico. Still other students are able to take the course through University of California, San Diego, Extension and as an independent study at U.S. institutions such as the University of Minnesota and the University of San Diego. Since 2007, students from nearly 50 U.S. colleges and universities have participated in the course, and in the spring semester of 2010, there were 45 students studying in, or from, 20 different countries including: Argentina, Belarus, Cameroon, Canada, Cyprus, France, Germany, Hungary, Ireland, Kosovo, Lithuania, Mexico, Moldova, Russia, Serbia, Spain, Turkey, Ukraine, United Kingdom, and the United States.

institutions developing a sense of their own global citizenship in much the same way as we expect overseas study to engender ideas of personal global citizenship in our students.

Ultimately, partnerships have the potential to be transcendental, enabling students, faculty, and institutions to both understand but also go beyond their settings. Partnerships can have a similarly transcendental impact on the process of internationalization. In the words of Favela, the most philosophical author of this chapter,

> It is not enough simply to say we want to internationalize. We must consider the direction in which we want to internationalize. This is parallel to saying that economic success should not be a goal unto itself but rather a means to achieve peaceful equilibrium. For internationalization, the challenge is to enable students and institutions to think more broadly, more universally; to be simultaneously intellectual, imaginative, innovative, independent, interdependent, idealistic, interdisciplinary, intercultural, and interiorized; to understand themselves in the context of economic, political, and social forces that shape education and drive perceptions of wealth, power, and success. If we attempt to internationalize without thinking of such goals, we leave behind a space of moral emptiness.

In this lies the full power of international partnerships, providing—as they do—nothing less than the opportunity to create dialogical modes of higher education that are internationally constructed and ever-evolving and that transcend what any institutions could do alone.

References

Altbach, P. G., & Knight, J. (2010). The internationalization of higher education: Motivations and realities. *Journal of Studies in International Education, 11,* 290–305. doi: 10.1177/1028315307303542

Altbach, P. G., Reisberg, L., & Rumbley, L. E. (2009). *Trends in global higher education: Tracking a revolution.* A report prepared for the UNESCO 2009 World Conference on Higher Education. Paris: UNESCO. Retrieved from http://unesdoc .unesco.org/images/0018/001831/183168e.pdf

Altbach, P. G., & Teichler, U. (2001). Internationalization and exchanges in a globalized university. *Journal of Studies in International Education, 5,* 5–25. doi: 10.1177/102831530151002

Anderson, W. (1999). Cooperating internationally. *New directions in higher education* (106), 101–107. doi: 10.1002/he.10612

Bhandari, R., & Motwani, A. (2010, Spring). U.S.-India exchange: Ready for a "new era"? *IIE Networker,* pp. 18–20. Abstract and locator information retrieved from http://cinemalu4u .com/new/2010/05/07/iie-networker-u-s-india -exchange-ready-for-a-new-era/

Bhutta, A. Z. (2002). Ethics in international health research: A perspective from the developing world. *Bulletin of the World Health Organization, 80*(2), 114–120. Retrieved from http://www.ncbi.nlm.nih.gov/pmc/articles/ PMC2567726/

Canto, I., & Hannah, J. (2001). A partnership of equals? Academic collaboration between the United Kingdom and Brazil. *Journal of Studies in International Education, 5,* 26–41. doi: 10.1177/102831530151003

Chan, W. W. Y. (2004). International cooperation in higher education: Theory and practice. *Journal of Studies in International Education, 8,* 32–55. doi: 10.1177/1028315303254429

Coclanis, P. A., & Strauss, R. P. (2010, September 2). Partnerships: An alternative to branch campuses overseas. *The Chronicle of Higher Education* (commentary). Retrieved from http://chronicle.com/article/Partnerships-a -Different/124286/

Cogan, J. J. (1998). Internationalization through networking and curricular infusion. In J. A. Mestenhauser, & B. J. Ellingboe (Eds.), *Reforming the higher education curriculum: Internationalizing the campus* (pp. 106–117). Washington DC: American Council on Education/Oryx Press.

de Wit, H. (1998). *International workshop on academic consortia.* Hong Kong: Hong Kong Baptist University, David C. Lam East-West Center.

de Wit, H. (2004). Academic alliances and networks: A new internationalization strategy in response to the globalization of our societies. In D. Theather (Ed.), *Consortia: International networking alliances of universities* (pp. 28–48). Melbourne: University of Melbourne.

Duval, J. M. (2009, July). *Crafting strategic partnerships.* Paper presented at the Annual Meeting of the Commission of International Programs of the Association of Public and Land-grant Universities [APLU], Colorado Springs.

Edejer, T.T. (1999). North-South research partnerships: the ethics of carrying out research in developing countries. *British Medical Journal, 319*(7207), 438–441. Abstract retrieved from http://www.bmj.com/content/319/7207/438 .extract/reply

Edwards, J. (2007). Challenges and opportunities for the internationalization of higher education in the coming decade: Planned and opportunistic initiatives in American institutions. *Journal of Studies in International Education, 11,* 373–381. doi: 10.1177/1028315307303920

Egron-Polak, E., & Hudson, R. (2010). *Internationalization of higher education: Global trends, regional perspectives.* Paris: International Association of Universities.

Enos, S., & Morton, K. (2003). Developing a theory and practice of campus-community partnerships. In B. Jacoby (Ed.), *Building partnerships for service learning* (pp. 20–41). San Francisco: Jossey-Bass.

European University Association. (2010). *Africa-Europe higher education cooperation for development: Meeting regional and global challenges.* Brussels: European University Association White Paper. Retrieved from http:// www.eua.be/Libraries/Publications_homepage_ list/Africa-Europe_Higher_Education_ Cooperation_White_Paper_EN.sflb.ashx

Gillespie, S. (2003). Toward "genuine reciprocity": Reconceptualizing international liberal education in the era of globalization. *Liberal Education, 89,* 6–20. Retrieved from http://www .aacu.org/liberaleducation/le-wi03/ le-wi03feature.cfm

Green, M. F., & Olson, C. (2003). *Internationalizing the campus: A user's guide.* Washington DC: American Council on Education.

Hartle, T. (2008). *Expanding partnerships to strengthen Africa's higher education institutions.* Washington DC: U.S. AID and Higher Education for Development.

Hudzik, J. (2011). *Comprehensive internationalization: From concept to action.* Washington DC: NAFSA. Retrieved from http:// www.nafsa.org/resourcelibrary/Default. aspx?id=24045

International Association of Universities. (2000). *Toward a century of cooperation: Internationalization of higher education* (Policy statement). Paris: International Association of Universities. Retrieved from http://www.iau-aiu .net/content/other-statements

Ishikawa, M. (2009). University rankings, global models, and emerging hegemony. *Journal of Studies in International Education, 13,* 159–173. Abstract retrieved from http://jsi.sagepub.com/ content/13/2/159.abstract

Kanter, R. M. (1994, July-August). Collaborative advantage: The art of alliances. *Harvard Business Review, 72,* 96–108. Abstract retrieved from http://hbr.org/1994/07/collaborative -advantage-the-art-of-alliances/ar/1

Kellogg, E. D. (2009, May). *Partnerships for development.* Paper presented at Annual Meeting of NAFSA: Association of International Educators, Minneapolis.

Kinser, K., & Green, M. F. (2009). *The power of partnerships: A transatlantic dialogue.* Washington DC: American Council on Education.

Klasek, C. B. (1992). Inter-institutional cooperation: Guidelines and agreements. In C. B. Klasek (Ed.), *Bridges to the future: Strategies for internationalizing higher education.* (pp. 108–128). Carbondale, IL: Association of International Education Administrators.

Knight, J. (2008). *Higher education in turmoil: The changing world of internationalization.* Rotterdam: Sense Publishers.

Leventhal, M. (2011). US: New funding models for international education. *University World News,* p. 158. http://www.universityworldnews.com.

Marginson, S., & van der Wende, M. (2007). To rank or to be ranked: The impact of global rankings in higher education. *Journal of Studies in International Education, 11,* 306–329. doi: 10.1177/1028315307303544. Abstract retrieved from http://jsi.sagepub.com/content/11/3-4/306 .short

Neave, G. (1992). *Managing higher education international co-operation: Strategies and solutions* (Reference Document UNESCO). Paris: International Association of Universities (IAU). Retrieved from http://unesdoc.unesco. org/images/0009/000986/098679eb.pdf

Osaka University. (2005). *Osaka University's global commitments and strategies* (Policy statement). Osaka, Japan: Osaka University. Retrieved from www.osaka-u.ac.jp/jp/international/iab/e/osaka -u_e.pdf

Philpott, J. (2010). Applying themes from research ethics to international education partnerships. *Virtual Mentor, 12*(3), 171–178. Abstract retrieved from http://virtualmentor.ama-assn .org/2010/03/medu1-1003.html

Prichard, R. (1996). Networking for research and development: Necessity or new religion. *Inter-American Journal of University Management, 10,* 5–11.

Quigley, F. (2009). *Walking together, walking far: How a U.S. and African medical school partnership is winning the fight against HIV/AIDS.* Indianapolis: Indiana University Press.

Shue, H. (1995). Ethics, the environment and the changing international order. *International Affairs (Royal Institute of International Affairs), 71*(3), 453–461. Abstract retrieved from http://www.jstor.org/stable/2624835

Some, D. K., & Khaemba, B. M. (Eds.). (2002). *Internationalization of higher education: The African experience and perspective.* Eldoret, Kenya: Moi University Press.

Sternberger, L. (2005). Partnering for success. *International Educator, 14*(4), 12–21. Retrieved from http://am.nafsa.org/_/File/_/InternationalEducator/PartneringforSuccessJulAug05.pdf

Stockley, D., & de Wit, H. (2011). The increasing relevance of institutional networks. In H. de Wit (Ed.), *Trends, issues, and challenges in internationalization of higher education* (pp. 45-58). Amsterdam: Center for Applied Research on Economics & Management, Hogeschool van Amsterdam.

Sutton, S. B. (2010). Transforming internationalization through partnerships. *International Educator, 19*(1), 60–63.

Teferra, D. (2008). The international dimension of higher education in Africa: Status, challenges, and prospects. In D. Teferra, & J. Knight (Eds.), *Higher education in Africa: The international dimension* (pp. 44–79). Boston: Center for International Higher Education.

Thullen, M., Tillman, M. J., Horner, D. D., Carty, S., & Kennedy, S. (1997). *Cooperating with a university in the United States: NAFSA's guide to interuniversity linkages.* Washington DC: NAFSA.

Van de Water, J., Green, M. F., & Koch, K. (2008). *International partnerships: Guidelines for colleges and universities.* Washington DC: American Council on Education.

Van Ginkel, H. (1996). *Networking and strategic alliances: Dynamic patterns of organization and co-operation.* Geneva: CRE-Action 109.

Wildavsky, B. (2010). *The great brain race: How global universities are reshaping the world.* Princeton, NJ: Princeton University Press.

Wiley, D. (2006). *Best practices for international partnerships with higher education institutions in Africa.* Lansing: Michigan State University, African Studies Center.

NOTES

1   Such projects aimed at capacity-building for institutions outside the United States and/or educational, health, and economic development for their surrounding communities.

2   The term *transformational* is here borrowed from the ways in which service-learning programs collaborate with community organizations, whether at home or overseas (Enos & Morton 2003).

3   Among these partners are the Secretary of Education and Culture for the State of Chihuahua, Universidad Autónoma de Ciudad Juárez, Fundación del Empresariado Chihuahuense, Centro Investigación de Materiales Avanzadas, and Centro de Investigación en Alimentación y Desarrollo.

4   In February 2002, an NMSU delegation, led by Provost William Flores, was hosted by UACH Rector Ing. José Luis Franco Rodriguez. The return visit to NMSU, headed by Rector Franco Rodriguez and Chihuahua State Senator Ricardo Arturo Lopez Castro, took place in May 2003.

5   Egginton and Martinez worked to create greater communication and partnership between Chihuahuan and New Mexican institutions at the political level (meetings among the mayors), socioeconomic level (nonprofit organizations focused on providing services to the *colonias* in New Mexico and the indigenous population of the Sierra Tarahumara in Chihuahua), research laboratories, and educational institutions (Chihuahua's foremost agricultural and technical high school, UACH, and others).

6   For example, in 2005, several UACH administrators attended the installation of Michael Martin as president of NMSU, and he, in turn, invited the UACH engineering faculty and Folklorico dancers to the subsequent homecoming festivities. After the departure of President Martin, Interim President Waded Cruzado embraced the relationship with enthusiasm, traveling to Chihuahua on a number of occasions, meeting with the governor, José Reyes Baeza, the UACH president, Raul Chavez, and other administrators.

7   In recent years, NMSU and UACH have taken the story of their transformative partnership on the road, organizing presentations at international meetings to discuss the factors contributing to their long-lasting and active collaboration. At the 2009 annual meeting of NAFSA, for example, Egginton and Favela, along with NMSU Interim President Cruzado and Sutton acting as an outside observer, explored the factors that had made this partnership so transformational.

8   Some other rules of thumb regarding the use of IT to expedite international partnerships follow. (a) cell phones (do not hold confidential conversations; do not disclose identifying information); (b) fax machines (call ahead to avoid others seeing the fax or having the fax misplaced; make a reasonable attempt to remove faxes from the machine promptly; partners with confidentiality or privilege protections should make all attempts to have their own fax machines); (c) computers (only use your own computer or one that has been entirely and

exclusively assigned to you); (d) electronic records (should be properly secured; user access levels should be limited to the minimum access level necessary for job performance; clear written policies and procedures on record maintenance and destruction); (e) networks and databases (security measures should always be taken to ensure that networks are protected and sensitive information is available to only select individuals); (f) data retention (data should be backed up regularly and policies regarding data retention in place); (g) online tools (Wikis, Web-based databases, and others should be used only with care, and confidential personal information not put online).

9   In light of the earlier discussion of IT, partnerships should consider the importance of developing written guidelines and agreements that clearly describe the risks and benefits involved in using IT and assign ownership of all equipment (computers, fax machines, hard drives, etc.) as well as the files, records, and communications that derive from their use.

10

OUTCOMES ASSESSMENT IN THE INTERNATIONALIZATION OF HIGHER EDUCATION

DARLA K. DEARDORFF AND ADINDA VAN GAALEN

What is the purpose of higher education, and what role does the internationalization of education play in achieving this purpose? Indeed, what does successful internationalization of higher education mean? What is the evidence of such success? Within higher education, more and more attention is being given to discussing the results of internationalization. Often, though, the focus is on output indicators rather than on outcome and impact indicators (Beerkens et al., 2010), frequently developed for specific institutional or national contexts and thus reducing the possibility of broader international comparisons. This is partly caused by the development of an increasing number of institutional rankings, which are rather one-dimensional and rarely factor in internationalization efforts, educational quality, or student learning.

Even when measuring the actual success of internationalization efforts, the focus tends to be on counting the numbers of students in student exchange, number of institutional agreements or partnerships, the economic impact of international students, and so on. But what about measuring and assessing student learning outcomes, enhancement of the quality of education or employability, and the outcomes that address the central goals of higher education, as results of internationalization?

This chapter addresses these questions from the context of international education. What should administrators know about assessing the impact of internationalization on learning outcomes and the impact on the quality of education? While this provides a limited view on comprehensive internationalization evaluation and long-term impacts, it does offer the opportunity to relate specific policies to outcomes and to explore a core mission of postsecondary institutions, that of knowledge dissemination and learning. This also means that other outcomes—for instance, in the area of research, or outcomes related to other stakeholders beyond students (such as faculty, government, industry, society or partner institutions)—will only be noted within the context of the quality of education. (See Chapters 4, 5, 17, and 24, this volume, for further discussion on other outcomes.)

This chapter starts with definitions before providing an overview of key theoretical frameworks of assessment and the context of assessment in the internationalization of higher education around the globe through organizational and research efforts. Included in this chapter are specific examples of assessment efforts in Japan, South Africa, and the Netherlands and Flanders. The chapter explores practical suggestions for implementing outcomes assessment in international education and concludes with some practical recommendations for international education administrators, drawn from the various efforts and research around the globe on outcomes assessment in internationalization.

Definitions

Before continuing to explore assessment topics, it is important to highlight definitions used in this chapter.

Internationalization

Internationalization, although currently under discussion and revision, has been defined in a variety of ways and is therefore a rather flexible term. This chapter embraces the definition by Knight (2004): "Internationalization is the process of integrating international, intercultural, or global dimensions into the objective function and provision of higher education." (See Chapter 2 and Chapter 25, this volume, for further discussion on the concept of internationalization.)

Hudzik and Stohl (2009) state that internationalization needs to contribute to core missions and values of institutions, or it will never rise above secondary status. The internationalization of higher education is viewed similarly in this chapter as a means to reach the core goals of an institution rather than as an end in itself. These core goals can be defined as: (a) knowledge creation/discovery (research); (b) knowledge dissemination/learning (education); and (c) service (a U.S. term), engagement or third mission[1] (a term used in Europe meaning contribution to society). This implies that the outcomes and impact of internationalization should always be studied in terms of how they contribute to achieving the mission and core goals of an institution.

Outcomes

There are currently different ways of viewing outcomes and impact assessment. According to Beerkens et al. (2010), outcomes can be considered as the end results of internationalization activities and are typically formulated at a higher level of abstraction than outputs, which include, for instance, quality enhancement of education or reputation enhancement. Another way of viewing outcomes is through the student lens, where, for example, definitions of outcomes (American Council on Education, 2007; Deardorff, 2007) focus primarily on student learning. Whatever the level—individual or program—of the outcomes examined, these need to be viewed in the context of longer term impact. The Organization for Economic Cooperation and Development (OECD) (2002) formulates outcomes as "the likely or achieved short-term and medium-term effects of an intervention's outputs." *Outcome* is closely related to the term *impact,* which is described by the OECD (2002) as "positive and negative, primary and secondary long-term effects produced by an intervention, directly or indirectly, intended or unintended." Martin and Sauvageot (2011) distinguish between *result*—an immediate measure of education—and *impact*—the consequences for the situation of an individual, a group, or society. Often, the terms *outcome* and *impact* are defined similarly and are used interchangeably, leading to inevitable confusion over terminology.

What stands out in these definitions is that outcomes (or results) come after outputs and before impact. Interesting in the OECD definition of *impact* is the term *negative long-term effects,* which concurs with Huisman (2007), who notes that internationalization is often conceived as an inherent good, while negative consequences are also possible. This chapter focuses on outcomes of internationalization efforts on which institutions can have an immediate influence, such as those related to student learning, which in turn leads to quality enhancement of education.

Theoretical Frameworks

One model that provides a concise framework for addressing outcomes within a program context, regardless of the field, is the program logic model (Rogers, 2000), also known as the logic model. This model takes into account the inputs as well as the overall impact and includes the following dimensions: inputs, activities, outputs, outcomes, and impact. It is widely used in the private, public, and nonprofit sectors and by such entities as the U.S. Department of State, the Kellogg Foundation, and United Way, a charitable service association in the United States. This model is also used by NONIE, the Network of Networks on Impact Evaluation, which was set up to improve development effectiveness through the use of impact evaluations.[2] This logic model can address both student learning outcomes and program outcomes. This chapter focuses primarily on student learning outcomes as a means to improving the quality of education.

This framework can be used to provide not only a road map for clarifying intended outcomes but also an analytical tool that leads to lasting change within the program or organization. In the end, the program logic model addresses three essential questions that underlie internationalization efforts: Where are we going? How will we get there? How will we know when we've arrived?

Here are the specific components of the program logic framework, with more discussion on the last three components, given the focus on results:

Inputs

What is needed to achieve the stated goals? Inputs are the resources needed to develop and implement activities that will achieve the goals. Inputs can include staff, faculty, administrators, time, money, partners, facilities, or other resources available to the institution. These inputs can be mapped and assessed in terms of ways in which they may impact the following four components.

Activities

What are the specific activities undertaken to achieve the goals? In the case of internationalization efforts, activities can involve learning opportunities that occur through curriculum, education-abroad experiences, research, involvement of faculty abroad, and so on. (See Chapters 14 and 15, this volume, for further discussion on curriculum and teaching/learning processes within internationalization.

Outputs

What are the direct results of activities? Who is involved and being reached through the activities? Outputs often include participation numbers, such as the number of students in education-abroad programs or the number of students benefitting from a joint program (Teekens, 2011). A prime example are participation numbers published in the annual *Open Doors* report published by the Institute of International Education. Another output example is the European University Association (EUA) project on Mapping University Mobility of Staff and Students (MAUNIMO) in 2010. The project encourages universities to design individual approaches toward mobility, while at the same time managing and possibly influencing national and regional data collection requirements. Participating institutions are encouraged to explain the challenges and show proof of the benefits of mobility to complement the quantitative data required by national or regional administrations.[3] (See Chapter 21, this volume, for further discussion on mobility numbers as outputs.)

Outcomes

What are the results of the activity for individuals, programs, the institution, and society? These are the expected or resulting effects of the outputs of an intervention (activities). Outcomes are directly related to the set goals and therefore often identified on a deeper level than outputs. They may be explained, for example, in terms of knowledge and skills obtained by students. Measuring outcomes involves both short-term outcomes and more medium-term outcomes, such as the quality enhancement of education. Examples of outcomes include specific learning outcomes such as the ones developed through the American Council on Education's Global Learning for All project (see Chapter 17 for more on this), as well as outcomes of international students (see Ward, 2006; Williams, 2008).

Impact[4]

What is the long-term impact (consequences/results) of the internationalization strategy on the institution, educational program, and students/alumni—and on stakeholders such as students, staff, business and industry, the local community, and international partners? One example is economic impact (Vickers & Bekhradnia, 2007; Parey & Waldinger 2011). Longitudinal studies are often necessary to assess long-term impact. One example of such a study is the Dwyer and Peters (2004) survey among participants of the IES Abroad programs. This study is valuable for its use of data over a considerable time period (alumni from 1950 to 1999) on mid- and long-term (50 years) impact on the participants' career and personal development. Another impact example is The Study Abroad for Global Engagement (SAGE) project,[5] which ran from 2006 to 2009 and aimed at documenting the long-term personal, professional, and global engagement outcomes of study abroad experiences.

Figure 10.1 illustrates the program logic model adapted to the internationalization of higher education. Using a framework such as program logic is often one of the first steps in assessment. This model helps to move institutions and international programs beyond counting numbers to providing the meaning behind the numbers, such as the enhancement of educational quality through achievement of student learning outcomes that result from student participation in institutional learning experiences; these experiences can be courses, education abroad, or co-curricular experiences. Limitations of the program logic model include the challenge of making any causal attribution since many factors may influence outcomes, especially in education-abroad experiences, and the long-term impact may not be addressed in initial assessment efforts. (For a further discussion on this model, see Deardorff 2005.)

Like the logic model, an assessment framework for thinking about institutional strategies on internationalization, developed by Nuffic (Van Gaalen, 2009), constitutes five broad categories of goals of internationalization, including: (1) enhanced quality of education programs, including the competences of graduates; (2) enhanced quality of research; (3) financial benefits; (4) benefits to the wider community; and (5) enhanced reputation. To reach the selected goal(s), an institution will undertake activities and invest time and resources (input).

Inputs/Resources

(what is needed for implementation of components of internationalization—includes time, funding, faculty, staffing, facilities, etc.)

↓

Activities/Components of Internationalization

(curriculum, foreign language courses, service learning, education abroad, international student programs, international co-curricular units)

↓

Outputs of Internationalization

(number of international students, number of education abroad programs, number of students studying foreign languages, etc.)

↓

Outcomes of Internationalization

(student learning outcomes, course/program outcomes, faculty outcomes, institutional outcomes, community outcomes, etc.)

= Long-Term Impact of Internationalization

Figure 10.1   Logic Model: Internationalization at Higher Education Institutions (HEIs)

Source: Adapted from general program logic model applied to internationalization (Deardorff, 2005).

The chosen combination of activities and resources can be assessed to determine resulting outcomes and impact in these different categories. Using models such as these to frame assessment efforts can aid institutional leaders in developing a more comprehensive strategy for internationalization.

TYPE OF OUTCOMES AND IMPACT

This chapter focuses primarily on the outcomes dimension of the program logic model, specifically at the student level. However, it is important to place these outcomes within the larger context of overall impact of internationalization so as to gain a more holistic picture. Possible impacts that have been identified are, among others:

1. Increased international prestige of the institution (Westerheijden, 2010). Institutional rankings are fast becoming a desired institutional outcome within the global arena. (For further discussion on rankings, see Chapter 24, this volume.)

2. Income generation (Westerheijden, 2010)

3. Employment and career enhancement (Paige, Fry, Stallman, Josić, & Jon, 2009, Sindt, 2007; Westerheijden, 2010)

4. Global engagement and understanding of citizenship and identity (Paige et al., 2009; Sindt, 2007)

5. Achieved learning outcomes/academic impact (De Decker, 2003; Paige et al., 2009), including achievement of foreign language competencies (Westerheijden, 2010), cultural understanding and appreciation (Sindt, 2007), and personal development (Sindt, 2007).

In looking more closely at impact, macro-, meso- and microlevels of impact can be distinguished; some examples (nonexhaustive) are shown in Figure 10.2.

Outcomes are viewed as occurring on three levels: (supra) national, organizational, and individual. This chapter does not delve into (supra) national outcomes, nor into institutional outcomes; rather, it focuses primarily on the micro and, where applicable, on the meso level. In fact, one of the main themes in assessing outcomes in international education has been the outcomes of study abroad at the micro level. For example, the impact of mobility on careers is a widely studied topic, as is the impact of mobility on the development of intercultural skills. Many related studies have been published in the *Journal of Studies in International Education,* for example, involving outcomes and impact of study abroad experiences. While these are certainly important, it is crucial to note that outcomes assessment in internationalization must go beyond study abroad experiences.

One of the few examples of studies on internationalization outcomes at the meso level was conducted among 77 U.S. higher education institutions (Jang, 2009). This study showed a clear relationship between internationalization and the quality of higher education, with the presence of international students positively impacting faculty competitiveness, undergraduate competitiveness, advanced training competitiveness, financial stability, constituents' satisfaction and institutional reputation. Conversely, an Australian study (McGowan & Potter, 2008) showed that international students, especially in for-profit institutions, can influence the quality of education in a negative way, such as lowering entry standards, given that institutions recruiting students mainly for income generation tend to be less strict in setting quality criteria for admitting students, especially when it comes to English proficiency.

Results of outcomes assessment are numerous and varied. Sindt (2007) points out that knowledge on outcomes of internationalization allows enhancement or development of institutional policies as well as programs and facilities. Sutton and Rubin (2010) found enhanced overall academic performance for students who studied abroad, as well as greater intercultural development. Sakurai, McCall-Wolf, and Kashima (2010) found that participants in a multicultural intervention program in Australia made more (local) friends and were more interested in local culture than students with the same characteristics who did not join the program. Research on employability in the Netherlands among 7,000 alumni of higher education (Berkhout & Smid, 2011) showed that a stay abroad decreased the time research university graduates needed to find their first jobs. The Association of Universities and Colleges of Canada (AUCC, 2009) adds one more reason to

Macro	Input	Expected outcomes	Intended Impact
International	Mobility programs Competitive higher education systems in world market Harmonizing educational systems and their quality assurance	Social integration (European Integration) Attracting knowledge workers Easier exchange of knowledge and expertise Higher quality of education worldwide.	World peace Economic growth Solutions to global issues
National	International recruitment, economic competitiveness Development aid	Educating/attracting skilled workers Knowledge export Capacity building	Competitive advantage Income generation Strengthening countries to promote social integration and trade
Meso			
Institutional	International benchmarking International cooperation Branch campuses Faculty/staff	Reputation building Access to data, instruments, and peer reviews Student competences/effectiveness of education Capacity building	Improving the quality of education Improving the quality of research Financial benefits Benefits to the wider community (third mission) Enhanced reputation
Program	Internationalization at home Internationalized curriculum	Student and industry satisfaction Enhanced educational offer	Increase in reputation Increase in student applications
Micro			
Students	Study abroad International classroom Internationalized curriculum	Acquiring 21st-century knowledge and skills Developing intercultural competence	Personal enrichment, Better labor market opportunities Better job performance

Figure 10.2   Macro/Meso/Micro Levels of the Internationalization of Higher Education

Source: van Gaalen, 2010 adapted version.

the list: Serious assessment of learning outcomes from internationalization enhances the credibility and prestige of student transcripts and, by extension, of degrees and diplomas.

This section has introduced some frameworks and relevant studies that can be used to guide internationalization assessment efforts within institutions. It is important to remember, however, that assessment begins first with the institutional (or program) mission, goals, and objectives and that any assessment must align with those key aspects of internationalization.

ASSESSMENT RESEARCH

In concluding this brief discussion of a few studies in various parts of the world related to research on outcomes assessment in higher education, it is helpful to understand limitations and future directions, given that much research is still needed regarding assessment of internationalization. (See also Cutberth, Smith, & Boey, J. 2008). Some research limitations to consider include:

1. There are a wide variety of institutions, policies, approaches, and even rationales in terms of models of internationalization or assessment. Leeuw and Vaessen (2009) noted that no single method is best to address the complexity of the issues at hand. Depending on the focus of the assessment and the availability of sources, some methods may have comparative advantage over others.

2. There is no one-size-fits-all in regard to assessing outcomes, given that assessment measures must be aligned with mission, goals, and objectives, which vary by institution and program.

3. Studies on the impact of education abroad, especially related to intercultural competence development, are often based on self-perspective tools as well as limited by self-selection of participants. It should be noted that multiple assessment methods may complement each other and jointly offer a more complete picture than any single method could if used individually. Deardorff (2009, pp. 477–491), for instance, found that a multiperspective method provides a more complete assessment picture, following principles of good assessment practice.

4. Most studies can indicate only correlations but not causations. As Leeuw and Vaessen (2009) point out, directly relating interventions to effects requires knowledge about what the situation would have been without the intervention. However, studies on outcomes and impact of internationalization, with some exceptions such as Sutton and Rubin (2010) and Sakurai et al. (2010), rarely use control groups.

5. Studies on impact on students tend not to include the backgrounds and basic skills of these students. In contrast to other skills, intercultural skills are usually not assessed on graduation from secondary education and can thus be difficult to attribute to a specific intervention, given the complexity of intercultural skill development.

6. Not all factors influenced by internationalization are assessed. Most studies are based on readily available data on outputs rather than applying more complex and rigorous methods of outcomes assessment.

7. Studies on outcomes of internationalization show a tendency to focus on conditions for desired outcomes rather than the actual outcomes themselves. They focus on results of specific support structures (input), activities or policies, and outputs (numbers) rather than outcomes or impact. In addition, most studies measure near-term impact rather than mid-term or long-term impact. This near-term impact is especially useful for higher education institutions, while mid-term impact is interesting for students and long-term impact for society at large.

8. One of the factors influencing the research questions and thereby the methods used is the interest of the sponsor. When assessments are aligned with institutional goals and mission, assessment not only justifies funding but also can lead to more focused priority on these efforts.

9. Impacts tend to be a mixture of several outcomes, which cannot easily or usefully be distinguished separately (Earl, Carden, & Smutylo, 2001). As a consequence, it can be studied as a whole—for example, Parsons (2010), who studied the combined effects of study abroad, contact with international students, an internationalized curriculum, and attendance at international events—or the separate parts (e.g. intercultural competences) of impact can be studied, which seems to be the case in most assessment studies. Therefore, most impact studies focus on the individual level rather than the institutional or societal level.

10. Studies obviously vary by quality, and it is important to examine the research methodologies, data, and data analyses to determine the

strength and quality of each study, including use of control groups.

Obviously, many of these characteristics of current studies limit the degree to which the results can be generalized.

Numerous research gaps exist in outcomes assessment of internationalization. More studies are needed on the actual assessments of international and intercultural learning outcomes, since many tools are inherently biased. Also, little research has been done on causality and how— or if—internationalisation leads to quality improvement of education.

Areas for future outcomes research include:

- Explaining the relation between internationalization activities and goals by showing the impact these activities have on the quality or effectiveness of education, research, and staff. In addition, the following outcomes could be further researched: reputation enhancement, financial revenues enhancement, student competence in general, student satisfaction,[6] and industry satisfaction.

- Defining how the internationalization process should be shaped to lead to quality improvement of higher education.

- Examining the long-term effects of study abroad participation (through longitudinal study) as well as the long-term effects of global learning (often used to refer to the process and scope of acquired knowledge, skills, and attitudes applied within the global context), whether at the institution or abroad.

- Reviewing published outcome studies in the international education field to determine quality of the studies and corresponding results and conclusions.

- Exploring the effect of national and international policies on the outcomes of internationalization in higher education.

- Studying different outcomes of internationalization policies in different national and institutional or cultural settings.

- Building on theoretical frameworks from other disciplines, such as political science, public policy, psychology, or sociology.

- Conducting empirical studies rather than case studies.

CONTEXT OF INTERNATIONALIZATION ASSESSMENT

When institutions engage in assessment, they must understand the larger context of higher education assessment and the various projects and initiatives occurring around the globe, so as to inform specific institutional efforts. The higher education field in general shows an increased focus on outcomes assessment, especially on student learning outcomes (see Box 10.1 on South Africa). Specific to international education, what projects have been undertaken in regard to outcomes assessment nationally or regionally? In the United States, this focus on student learning outcomes is often driven by state legislatures, for public institutions; by accrediting bodies, both regional and discipline-specific; and by federal granting agencies. While accrediting agencies do not themselves engage in assessment, they mandate that assessment of student learning occur. In some cases in the United States, this has led to institutional focus on global learning through institutional-wide Quality Enhancement Plans, which are connected directly to student learning outcomes and assessment. (See Figure 10.3 for a list of some institutions with internationally oriented Quality Enhancement Plans; see also Chapter 24, this volume, for more on accreditation and quality frameworks.)

In Europe, the Bologna Process has certainly increased the emphasis on learning outcomes (Morgan & Lydon, 2009, see also Chapter 5, this volume). Bologna communiques, European Union (EU) policy, and several projects for instance on Competences in Education and Recognition (CoRe 1 and 2), sponsored by the European Commission, include attention to learning outcomes.

Other educational associations have also focused efforts on internationalization outcomes in recent years, including the American Council on Education, with its Global Learning For All project involving several U.S. universities; the American Association of Colleges and Universities, with its Global Learning project; the Association of International Education Administrators, with conference sessions addressing key aspects of assessment; and the European Association of International Educators, with its publication entitled *Measuring Success in the Internationalisation of Higher Education* (de Wit,

BOX 10.1 Outcomes-based Assessment in Postsecondary Education in South Africa

Chrissie Boughey

Professor and Dean of Teaching & Learning, Rhodes University (South Africa)

Like many other countries across the world, South Africa uses a National Qualifications Framework (NQF) to facilitate the articulation of qualifications and learning with other postsecondary systems. The NQF has ten levels, with postsecondary education occupying Levels 5 through 10.

The NQF uses the concept of the *learning outcome* as a means of registering qualifications. This means that qualifications are described in relation to what students will be able to do once the degree, diploma, or certificate is awarded. Assessment criteria, usually defined as what an assessor needs to see to ensure that candidates meet an outcome, are then developed for each outcome, and tasks are designed that will allow students to demonstrate that they meet the criteria. Assessment, therefore, involves a process of aligning outcomes, criteria, and tasks to ensure that it is valid, reliable, and fair.

An example of a learning outcome might be "Students will be able to design a piece of research." Assessment criteria for this outcome might then include "A clear, concise statement of a problem is provided" and "Research aims and objectives are clearly stated." Assessment tasks intended to allow students to demonstrate that they have met the criteria might then involve an oral presentation and a written research proposal.

In some cases, assessment grids are produced involving descriptions of performance at a number of levels, which are then aligned with numerical marks. For example, the range of marks between 50 and 74 might fall into the category *competent,* with a description of competence then written using learning outcomes and assessment criteria. Marks of 75 and above might then fall into a *highly competent* category, with assessment criteria adjusted to match the level of performance. Practice varies across the system and even within institutions, however.

All universities have assessment policies that lay out the principles of assessment adopted within the institution and the procedures followed. These can usually be accessed via institutional websites.

In recent years, many South African universities have begun to either require or encourage faculty members to demonstrate competence as an assessor in order to be awarded tenure. Formal courses intended to accredit faculty as professional educators in postsecondary education have been developed, and assessor competence is a focus of these.

At the undergraduate level, universities require assessment at the exit level to be moderated using a system of external examiners. Postgraduate qualifications are all externally moderated.

2009), which features contributions from international educators from around the world. The World Bank also includes learning outcomes in the READ project. In Japan, there is also increased interest in learning outcomes (see Box 10.2)

University/City/State	QEP Plan Title
Anderson University, Anderson, SC	Global Engagement: Anderson University Abroad
Appalachian State University, Boone, NC	Global Learning: A World of Opportunities for Appalachian Students
Austin College, Sherman, TX	The Globe Program
Bellarmine University, Louisville, KY	Liberal Education in an International Context: Preparing Students for a Globally Competitive World
Belhaven College, Jackson, MS	Worldview Curriculum
Centenary College, Shreveport, LA	Experience Centenary: Careers, Community, Culture
Covenant College, Lookout Mountain, GA	Quality Enhancement Plan for Intercultural Competencies
Duke University, Durham, NC	Global Duke: Enhancing Students' Capacity for World Citizenship
Florida International University, Miami, FL	Global Learning for Global Citizenship
George Mason University, Fairfax, VA	Fostering a Culture of Student Scholarship
Georgia Gwinnett College, Lawrenceville, GA	Internationalization of the Curriculum
Georgia Institute of Technology, Atlanta, GA	Strengthening the Global Competence and Research Experiences of Undergraduate Students
Kennesaw State University, Kennesaw, GA	Get Global
Mary Baldwin College, Staunton, VA	Learning for Civic Engagement in a Global Context
Motlow State Community College, Lynchburg, TN	No title (http://www.mscc.edu/qep/reports.aspx)
Randolph College, Lynchburg, VA	Bridges Not Walls
Regent University, Decatur, GA	Developing Globally Competent Christian Leaders
Rollins College, Winter Park, FL	Education for Citizenship and Leadership In Local and Global Communities
Saint Augustine's College, Raleigh, NC	Global Learning for Success
Spelman College, Atlanta, GA	Spelman Going Global!
University of Tampa, Tampa, FL	Building International Competence: An Integrated Approach to International Education
University of Tennessee, Knoxville, TN	The International and Intercultural Awareness Initiative
Wake Forest University, Winston-Salem, NC	Beyond Boundaries: Preparing Students to be Become Global Citizens
Winthrop University, Rock Hill, SC	The Global Learning Initiative

Figure 10.3   SACS Institutional Quality Enhancement Plants (QEP) With Focus on Internationalization, Cultural Diversity, Global Learning, Global Citizenship, or Multiculturalism (sample institutional listing)

BOX 10.2 Recent Trends in University Internationalization in Japan—Institutional Review and Learning Outcome Assessment

Shingo Ashizawa

Professor, Division of International Cooperation, Meiji University, (Japan)

In Japan, the Ministry of Education, Culture, Sports, Science and Technology (MEXT) has launched a series of incentive projects to promote an international strategic approach at universities around the country. For example, in 2005, MEXT initiated the Strategic Fund Project, which established international headquarters within a number of universities. The aim of the project was to promote the creation of an "internationally competitive research environment" within Japanese higher education institutions. Another important project springing from government initiative is Global 30 (known as G-30), which was launched in 2009. The G-30 plays an integral role in helping achieve the goal of attracting 300,000 international students by the year 2020. As of 2011, 13 universities have been selected to receive G-30 funding. Furthermore, in 2011, MEXT launched several new grants for educational exchange. The government also subsidizes institutional partnerships and has called on about 20 institutions to establish joint teaching or even joint-degree programs with universities overseas. Among them, 10 schools will work on the Campus Asia Program, a trilateral student mobility project joining China, South Korea, and Japan.

By way of these government policies, higher education institutions are expected to develop a more strategic approach toward internationalization of their campuses. Also, universities are required to be accountable for quality assurance. Thus, program-based evaluation is becoming a key topic for international educators. Government agencies and business community leaders are advocating for educational reform. They are calling on Japanese higher education institutions to produce more "*Global JINZAI* (Global Talent)", graduates who can participate in and contribute to the global workforce. Universities are expected to provide diverse study abroad programs to educate future global leaders. Although a number of joint research projects and academic seminars have focused on ways to evaluate international programs and good practice, quality assessment, including institutional review, has only recently become an important topic among Japanese universities, particularly for comprehensive research schools. A research project that focused on developing evaluation criteria was conducted in 2005–2006 at Osaka University. It was supported by a Japan Society for Promotion of Science research fund. The final report can be seen at the following URL. http://www.gcn-osaka.jp/project/project-finalreport.htm

Also, Ritsumeikan University in Kyoto developed a pre- and post-experience online assessment project for students who participated in internship programs in 2011. This is one example of an ongoing assessment program that focuses on off-campus learning outcomes.

In April 2011, a 3-year research project focusing on learning outcome assessment of study abroad was launched. This project is also supported by a JSPS fund, and project members consist of scholars and practitioners in international education throughout Japan. The first stage of this research project will be a comparative study of learning outcome assessment in the United States and Europe. Next, the research team will develop an e-portfolio based on the comparative studies

(Continued)

(Continued)

of existing assessment programs. This e-portfolio will be designed to meet the needs of students who participate in study abroad programs, international internships, and volunteer experiences abroad. The project team will also conduct a survey of employers to learn more about their preferences and needs for a workforce with education-abroad experience.

Finally, a number of practitioners' groups are actively promoting service learning and the gap year system. For example, since 2004, a group of international educators (*Daigaku Kyouiku ni okeru Kaigai Taiken Gakushuu Kenkyuukai*) has organized a series of study sessions to establish quality assurance schemes for the overseas learning experiences of college students. In the future, by using professional networks and the ideas generated from the kind of research and group activities outlined here, further discussions among scholars, practitioners, and business leaders about how to cultivate and assess future Global JINZAI will be promoted throughout Japan.

Several higher education projects have attempted to define and measure internationalization outcomes, including GLOSSARI, Tuning, AHELO and NVAO and ECA quality certificates. These initiatives will be discussed in more detail in the section below.

GLOSSARI Project

The Georgia Learning Outcomes of Students Studying Abroad Research Initiative (GLOSSARI) was started in 2000. Sutton and Rubin (2010), reviewing this project, compare results of study abroad students with students in a control group with similar characteristics, aiming to isolate the effect of study abroad. Objectives of the GLOSSARI (http://glossari.uga.edu/) project are:

• Identify cognitive learning outcomes attributable to (a) diverse study abroad experiences and (b) for students at a wide variety of public institutions

• Identify impact on academic performance indicators

• Identify impact of study abroad on core liberal arts goals (critical thinking, leadership, adaptability, etc.)

• Identify program characteristics that optimize learning outcomes to guide future program development

• Identify student characteristics that predict (a) likely participants and (b) successful participants

• Refine, replicate, and disseminate methods for assessing the impact of study abroad on student learning outcomes.

The GLOSSARI database will be made available to other researchers.

TUNING in Europe, Latin America, and United States

Tuning Educational Structures in Europe (Tuning) has attempted to develop specific outcomes for different disciplines. Tuning supports the idea that universities should look for points of reference, convergence, and common understanding rather than for uniformity. Tuning (http://tuning.unideusto.org) was developed in 2000 in the framework of the Life Long Learning Program, to support the Bologna Process. It offers, among several tools, *A Guide to Formulating Degree Program Profiles*. The guide includes the formulation of Program Competences and Learning Outcomes. These could be useful for measuring the impact of internationalization as well.

Tuning supports a bottom-up approach in which university faculty formulate learning outcomes for each discipline. A methodology has been designed to understand curricula and to make them comparable:

1. Generic (general academic) competences

2. Subject-specific competences

3. The role of the European Credit Transfer and Accumulation System (ECTS) as an accumulation system

4. Approaches to learning, teaching, and assessment

5. The role of quality enhancement in the educational process (emphasizing systems based on internal institutional quality culture)

Generic competences include three internationally oriented competences:

1. Ability to communicate in a second (foreign) language

2. Ability to interact constructively with others regardless of background and culture, while respecting diversity

3. Ability to work in an international environment

Latin America also started a Tuning project involving 186 universities and 19 tuning centers. Similarly, in the United States, a Tuning Pilot was started in three states (Utah, Minnesota, and Indiana) through the Lumina Foundation. Given the great decentralization of higher education in the United States, Tuning proved a challenge but nonetheless was found to be a useful process, especially since employers were also involved in discussions on what students should know, understand, and be able to do (Birtwistle & McKiernan, 2011). Most recently, African countries have agreed to set up an African version of Tuning. In 2007, the Canadian Ministers of Education came to an agreement on a Canadian Degree Qualifications Framework (http://www. cicic.ca/docs/cmec/QA-Statement-2007.en.pdf). See Chapter 5, this volume, for more on Tuning.

AHELO Project

The OECD is working toward a tool for the Assessment of Higher Education Learning Outcomes (AHELO) The AHELO project (www .oecd.org/edu/ahelo) is aimed at assessing learning outcomes and examining which criteria influence these outcomes (OECD, 2010). Higher education students in more than 10 different countries took part in a feasibility study.

Current assessment methods were considered to be inadequate to value the diversity of higher education institutions because they reduced quality to a handful of criteria that left out more than they included, much as rankings do.

The AHELO project aims to develop criteria to evaluate the quality and relevance of what students learn in institutions around the world, focusing on teaching and learning, the two items that rankings usually exclude. The project is ambitious in its attempt to assess learning outcomes on an international scale by creating measures that are valid for all cultures and languages. However, according to Rauhvargers (2011), OECD is still grappling with important questions, such as: Is it possible to develop instruments to capture learning outcomes perceived as valid in different national and institutional contexts? The results of AHELO could have potential impact on assessing internationalization learning outcomes if AHELO is successful in creating measures that are valid in all cultures and languages.

See Box 10.3 for more discussion on AHELO.

NVAO and ECA

Accreditation organizations paying specific attention to the internationalization of higher education are a rare phenomenon in Europe (van Gaalen, 2010). Yet, an interesting pilot (see Box 10.4) was undertaken in 2010 by the Accreditation Organization of the Netherlands and Flanders (NVAO). The European Consortium for Accreditation (ECA) is now considering pilot projects in different European countries to test the NVAO methodology, with an eye toward developing an ECA certificate regarding internationalization. The methodology includes monitoring the impact of internationalization on the achievement of learning outcomes.

This brief discussion of various national or regional projects targeted at refining learning outcomes assessment indicates that such assessment in international education is not unique but rather, is part of a larger trend within higher education institutions around the world to focus on the evidence of student learning in an effort to document and improve the quality of education. This increased focus across higher education on (learning) outcomes has led to the challenge of defining and actually measuring these outcomes.

BOX 10.3 A Global Test for Undergraduate Learning Outcomes: The Assessment of Higher Education Learning Outcomes (AHELO)

Madeleine Green

Senior fellow, International Association of Universities (IAU)
and NAFSA: the Association of International Educators

Francisco Marmolejo

Executive director, Consortium for North American Higher Education Cooperation

Eva Egron-Polak

Secretary general, International Association of Universities (France)

The most direct way to find out what students know is to test them. Although most testing takes place in the classroom, many nations administer national tests for admissions to different levels of education and for professional certification. Until recently, there was no methodology on the horizon to compare student learning outcomes in higher education across nations or institutions. But the emerging global test of college achievement, the Assessment of Higher Education Learning Outcomes (AHELO) sponsored by the Organization for Economic Cooperation and Development (OECD), is a potential game-changer. AHELO is still a feasibility study, seeking to determine whether it is possible to create a series of tests that would assess both general and discipline-specific learning by students nearing the end of their undergraduate degree. Sixteen countries are participating in the feasibility study. Each country has selected to participate in the generic skills or discipline strand, with nine, including the United States, participating in the generic skills study.

AHELO has its supporters and skeptics. The fact that 18 governments have provided financial support for the first phase and secured institutional participation indicates that policymakers see such a tool as useful. Their very interest, however, creates anxiety among some institutional leaders and representatives who fear government-led efforts. Not everyone is convinced that it is possible to devise a globally relevant test that is also reliable and valid. Some of the skepticism about AHELO is based on doubts about standardized testing in general (Banta, 2007; Thomson & Douglas, 2009).

Comparing institutions with different missions, cultures, and languages also is a source of doubt. The problem is compounded for a global test. As Terry Hartle, senior vice president of the American Council on Education, put it, "If we haven't been able to figure out how to do this in the United States, it's impossible for me to imagine a method or standard that would work equally well for Holyoke Community College, MIT, and the Sorbonne" (Wildavsky, 2010, p. 133).

Other objections to AHELO derive from criticisms of the Collegiate Learning Assessment (CLA), the U.S. instrument that is being adapted for the generic strand. Some are alarmed by the use of a *U.S.* test, even though AHELO will engage testing experts and faculty to adapt it to different countries and languages. Methodological criticisms of CLA abound, including a small sample size, testing for different groups of freshman and seniors, and the difficulty of assessing value-added. Finally, some concerns center on how the results will be used. Although OECD professes no intention of using the results as another form of ranking, some think that this will be inevitable, and the publicly available institutional scores will create a de facto ranking system. Others point to the potential for policymakers to use the results as a tool for decision making rather than for analysis and improvement. AHELO is still in its early stages, and many issues have yet to be resolved, but the underlying reservations about standardized testing and the potential politics of AHELO are not likely to go away. In addition, the high costs of developing AHELO make its future uncertain.

BOX 10.4 Impact of Internationalisation on Students' Learning Outcomes as the Basis for a Distinctive (Quality) Feature for Internationalization

Frederik de Decker

Senior education adviser, Ghent University Association (Belgium)

In Flanders (Belgium) and the Netherlands, programs can apply for a distinctive (quality) feature in internationalization. The Accreditation Organization of the Netherlands and Flanders (NVAO), in consultation with a small group of experts, decided to do this *at the program level* to allow for diversity in the application of internationalization. Furthermore, NVAO issues all accreditations at program level. Finally, this is also the level where a link with intended learning outcomes for internationalization is best assessed. A dimension lacking in other instruments but considered to be a crucial feature for internationalization.

A framework for the assessment of internationalization as a distinctive (quality) feature was established. *Distinctive* in this framework means that "the program's desired internationalisation must have a significant impact on the overall quality of the program" (NVAO, 2011). The vision/ policy on internationalization is defined by the program applying for a distinctive (quality) feature. It will then be determined if this vision/policy (including verifiable objectives and benchmarks) has been made explicit, whether it is shared by the staff, and whether stakeholders have been consulted during its formulation or revision. Equally it will be determined whether the elements of the vision/ policy on internationalization are evaluated periodically and form the basis for improvement measures.

NVAO takes an innovative approach: The program itself defines the content and level of the expected learning outcomes of students as a result of internationalization. This approach is in line with the importance given to linking internationalization to learning outcomes. A program applying for the certificate will thus have to demonstrate that—because of the program's explicit attention to internationalization (however defined)—students develop, in the course of their study, the specified learning outcomes in terms of international and intercultural competences.

To obtain the certificate, programs need to score *good* or *excellent* on these two key standards: (1) vision/policy and (2) learning outcomes. Furthermore, the program's curriculum, educational concept, and assessment must be in line with the vision/policy on internationalization and the intended international learning outcomes. Student cohort composition, international experience, and expertise are taken into account. Also assessed is whether the services provided to national and international students are sufficient, in view of the vision/policy on internationalization and the intended international learning outcomes. Finally, the composition of the student group and in- and outbound mobility of students are factors that count. But these four standards (program, staff, services, students) are considered to be merely facilitating: They need to be of a sufficient level to allow for graduates to have achieved the learning outcomes in line with the vision/policy on internationalization.

It should be clear from the above that this approach deliberately does not impose a specific vision on how internationalization should be interpreted. Internationalization remains a container that programs can fill as they like with qualitative ingredients. At the same time, NVAO wants to be explicit about what the outcomes and impact of internationalization should be: a clear and proven enhancement of specific competences.

(Continued)

(Continued)

This concept was tested in the summer/fall of 2010 for 21 volunteering programs, primarily in the Netherlands and some in Flanders. Eighteen programs were granted the certificate in December 2010 (http://www.nvao.net/pilot_bijzonder_kenmerk_internationalisering) The assessments in the pilot phase were based on (a) a self-assessment report by the program, where possible in combination with an application for accreditation, and (b) a site visit with an international team, including a domain-specific expert, a student, an international quality assurance expert, and an expert on internationalization.

IMPLEMENTING OUTCOMES ASSESSMENT IN INTERNATIONAL EDUCATION

What are practical implications for institutions attempting to assess outcomes in international education? How should these outcomes be measured, evaluated, or otherwise mapped? Where do institutions even start regarding outcomes assessment? This section explores some of these questions and, in addition, offers questions that can guide institutions in assessing internationalization outcomes.

Getting Started on Assessment

Many institutions struggle with knowing exactly which assessment tools to use, especially given the increasing variety of available assessment tools. It is important to note that there is no one single best way to assess outcomes or best tools for the job (Deardorff, 2006, 2009; Leeuw & Vaessen, 2009). However, certain methods are more applicable to certain situations and stated learning outcomes than to others, and the Network of Networks on Impact Evaluation (NONIE) gives some examples of these in their publication *NONIE Guidance On Impact Evaluation* (Leeuw & Vaessen, 2009).

Combining the NONIE suggestions with suggestions made by the American Council on Education (2008) leads to the following list of steps to take in implementing outcomes assessment in international education:

Methodological guidance:

1. Identify the context and scope of the desired assessment.
   a. What is being measured within the course, program, or institution based on

stated mission and goals? In other words, which specific dimensions of internationalization are being assessed?
   b. What are the levels of assessment? Is the assessment at the level of institutional outcomes, program outcomes, or individual student outcomes?

2. Agree on what is valued.
   a. What is the purpose of the assessment and how will the data be used? (Note: If the data will not be used, there is no need to collect the data.)
   b. Does the assessment tool(s) actually measure what institutions desire to have measured, and do assessments collect actual evidence specified by stated outcomes?

3. Develop an assessment plan early in the process, through dialogue with stakeholders and university personnel skilled in assessment.

4. Build on existing knowledge relevant to the impact of interventions.
   a. What specific methods and tools have been used in assessing outcomes at the institution? What has worked and what can be improved and adapted to collect needed data/evidence?
   b. What literature and expertise are available on outcomes assessment that can help inform institutional efforts?

5. Carefully articulate the theories linking interventions to outcomes, define terminology based on literature, and determine assessment methods based on stated outcomes. What is the evidence of success that the stated goals have been achieved?

6. Determine what degree of assessment is feasible and worth the cost.
   a. Is there infrastructure in place to support assessment? Are there staff with assessment expertise?

b. Is there technical support available for electronic assessment methods such as e-Portfolios?

c. Is there professional development support available for those who work on assessment?

7. Address the validation issues: What are the reliability and validity statistics on the assessment tools being used, and what are the methods of assessment validation?

8. Use a mixed-methods approach: More than one data point is needed to ascertain reliable results and to provide a more holistic picture of what has been achieved. When possible, use a control group given the challenges of determining cause/effect.

9. Who are the stakeholders, and how will the assessment results be communicated to them?

10. To assure quality, how will the assessment process be assessed? What were the strengths and weaknesses of the assessments used? What will be done differently next time?

In-depth: Assessing Intercultural Learning Outcomes

Given that intercultural learning outcomes, often centered on the development of students' intercultural competence, are the current focus of outcomes assessment within internationalization, it may be helpful to examine this area more closely in an effort to provide a concrete example.

Too often, institutions use terms such as *intercultural competence* or *global citizenship* without adequately defining these terms based on the literature. For example, the Association of Universities and Colleges of Canada (AUCC, 2009) explains that higher education institutions have difficulty in defining measurable learning outcomes of internationalization as it includes not only skills and knowledge development but also personal development. Deardorff (2009, Chapter 28) states that definitions and clarity must occur before outcomes can be measured adequately. Her research-based definition of intercultural competence, for example, has been used by institutions in bringing more focus to assessment efforts around intercultural competence (see Chapter 16, this volume, for further discussion on intercultural and global

competences). Clearly, defining outcomes is one of the first steps in implementing assessment.

Thus, the important first step in assessing intercultural competence is in defining the concept itself, using the existing literature and work as a basis for the definition/framework. Most definitions and models tend to be somewhat general in terminology, so once a definition has been determined, it is important to develop a process that generates measurable outcomes and indicators within the context to be assessed. To begin that process, it is best to prioritize specific aspects of intercultural competence, based on the overall mission, goals, and purpose of the course or program. The definition that is used for intercultural competence will determine both the aspects that will be assessed and the level of assessment (i.e., individual, program, organization). As in the case of learning outcomes, the level is usually that of the individual and the learning that occurs for each individual. For example, based on the overall mission, "understanding others' perspectives" may be an essential aspect of intercultural competence to assess and thus becomes a stated goal. From that point, one would engage other key persons in dialogue about the specific measurable outcomes related to this overall goal of "participants' ability to understand others' perspectives" as to the best ways to achieve this goal. These ways of achieving the stated goal become the specified objectives, which will be discussed in more detail shortly.

Stating Goals and Measurable Outcomes

It is important to spend sufficient time on defining internationalization goals in such a way that they can be measured whether they were reached or not. Thus, assessment literature (Driscoll & Wood, 2007; Palomba & Banta, 2001) calls for taking broader goals and developing more specific measurable outcomes statements that can in turn be assessed. In developing specific outcomes statements, the SMART objective guide can be followed:

- **Specific:** Is the objective well defined and clear to all stakeholders?
- **Measurable:** In what form will this objective be reached and under what (observable) conditions?
- **Agreed upon:** Do the stakeholders and staff accept this objective?

- **R**ealistic: Is assessment possible within the available resources, knowledge, and time?
- **T**ime-bound: When should the objective be reached?

The SMART objectives work well in regard to student learning outcomes. However, within other contexts such as broader institutional goals, there may be obvious limitations with stating objectives in this format.

Learning outcomes statements should be based on the goals and prioritized foci of intercultural competence aspects (instead of the concept as a whole). Once specific aspects of intercultural competence have been prioritized (such as greater cultural self-awareness or increased perspective-taking), it is time to write measurable objectives, or outcomes statements, related to each of the prioritized aspects. A key part of assessment is to ensure realistic objectives: Can these objectives be accomplished within the parameters of the course or program? Are these objectives specifically addressed in the program or curriculum? Outcomes assessment efforts of individual students can later be aggregated to department and even institutional levels to determine overall quality of education and achievement of institutional mission.

The American Council on Education (2007) provides a list of common intercultural learning outcomes found at the intersection of international and multicultural education. Those outcomes include ones found in Figure 10.4, and even these statements can be tailored more specifically to a particular course or discipline. Another resource to use for outcomes statements is the intercultural rubric developed by faculty through the American Association of Colleges and Universities (Rhodes, 2010). This rubric has been adapted for use at numerous U.S. higher education institutions to assess actual student work, especially in student portfolios.

Knowledge/Content Oriented

- Understand the interconnectedness and interdependence of global systems
- Understand the historical, cultural, economic, and political forces that shape society and explain own situation in this context
- Develop a nuanced/complex understanding of culture as a concept and the deep/complex/dynamic nature of culture.
- Understand various cultures and how culture is created
- Understand the relationship of power and language and how language interacts with culture
- Understand the connections between power, knowledge, privilege, gender, and class (locally and globally)
- Understand conflict and power relationships
- Understand how language frames thinking and perspective
- Recognize how stereotypes develop and where they come from

Attitudinal

- Develop a sense of perspective and social responsibility
- Overcome provincial/parochial thinking
- Reduce own prejudice
- Appreciate difference; value and acknowledge other cultures as legitimate
- Improve cultural self-awareness and understanding of one's self in the global context
- Demonstrate greater appreciation of or an interest in learning about different cultures
- Develop empathy and perspective consciousness
- Demonstrate open-mindedness and an understanding of complexity

Skills

- Think, work, and move across boundaries and in diverse environments
- Develop and use skills in conflict resolution

- Develop and use intercultural communication skills
- Demonstrate language proficiency
- Take informed responsibility for actions in a globally connected world
- Link theory and practice through own experience both as citizens and professionals
- Internalize and apply cultural understandings and knowledge
- Seek out multiple perspectives

Figure 10.4   Shared Learning Outcomes of International Education and Multicultural Education

Source: Adapted from Olson, Evans, & Schoenberg, 2007.

Given the complexity of intercultural competence, an assessment plan involving a multimethod, multiperspective approach is desired. Advocating the use of multiple measures in assessing competence, Pottinger (1979) stresses that "how one defines the domain of competence will greatly affect one's choice of measurement procedures" (p. 30) and notes that pen and paper assessment tests have been widely criticized, due in part to the effect of the test format and also due to the limits a paper test places on the complex phenomena being measured (pp. 33–34). Since competence varies by setting, context, and individual, using a variety of assessments, both *direct* and *indirect*, ensures a stronger measurement. Direct measures are actual evidence of student learning (such as course assignments, performance, and capstone projects). Indirect measures are perceptions of student learning (as collected through surveys, interviews, and focus groups). The key question to ask is "what is the evidence of student learning" regarding the stated outcomes.

Furthermore, using the definition of "effective and appropriate behavior and communication in intercultural settings" (Deardorff, 2006), measures need to be multiperspective, beyond the learner perspective. Learners can indicate to what degree they have been *effective* in an intercultural setting, but only the other person in the interaction can determine the *appropriateness* of behavior/communication.

What does this all mean in assessing intercultural competence? Given the complexity of this concept, it would be challenging—if not impossible—for one tool to measure an individual's intercultural competence. There are numerous questions to answer: Intercultural competence from whose perspective and according to whom? Intercultural competence to what degree? Intercultural competence to what end—that is, for what purpose? Furthermore, specific priorities of intercultural competence aspects for a course, department, or institution will vary as determined by mission statement and goals. Thus, the tool being used in one course or program may not be appropriate for another course or program if the goals for those are different. This last point is also valid for the impact of internationalization in general on the quality of education.

FUTURE TRENDS IN OUTCOMES ASSESSMENT OF INTERNATIONALIZATION

In the previous sections, we discussed the current state of learning outcomes assessment in the context of internationalization. Future developments in this area will partly depend on factors that lie outside the scope of internationalization or even higher education in general. Several developments or trends are relevant in this respect, such as the increased call for accountability and transparency, a trend to mainstream internationalization and developments in instrumentation.

Accountability within higher education is crucial, particularly in determining overall quality of educational efforts. The trend in measuring (learning) outcomes seems to be here to stay and, in fact, in the United States, it is spreading beyond undergraduate education to include graduation education. This is spurred in part by the increasing emphasis accrediting bodies put on learning outcomes and accountability. In the

United States, not only regional accrediting bodies but also disciplinary accrediting bodies such as ABET (for engineering) and NCATE (for education) are incorporating standards on global competence development for students.

In Europe, there is a clear trend toward assessing all aspects of education, each through a specifically designed tool. Apart from the obvious accountability issue toward accreditation organizations and the public, knowing whether an institution meets its own set expectations can help allocate resources more efficiently and effectively. The European Commission finances the development of many evaluation and assessment tools, for example, Maunimo and EMQT (Erasmus Mobility Quality Tools, http://www .emqt.org/home.html) tools, as well as the Tuning project. There is significant overlap in these tools, and at the same time, there is a consistent shortcoming: measurement of impact rather than output or outcomes continues to receive less emphasis.

A development that is much related to accountability is transparency. Publishing results of assessments can boost the institution's reputation among students, their parents, future employers, and other stakeholders. This information can be a valuable source for advocacy toward political and financial stakeholders. Communicating the results to the various stakeholders, especially students, is the key to transparency and would be part of any assessment plan.

The trend of mainstreaming internationalization has complicated the efforts for transparency somewhat. Internationalization has become mainstream in some educational programs, yet it is still a marginal concept in others. As Hudzik and Stohl (2009) point out, mainstreaming of internationalization causes a broadened perspective on impact assessment. Assessment efforts within internationalization are also becoming more mainstream, as noted by the increased hiring of staff tasked specifically with assessment in their job portfolios. Growth in both resources and strategic implementation can help increase achievement of outcomes and, ultimately, the level of impact.

Finally, individuals and companies are rushing to design instruments and software to assist institutions in collecting assessment data on intercultural learning. Some of these tools are more reliable and valid than others—many have inherent cultural biases—and they measure various aspects of intercultural learning. In moving forward, it will be important that assessment efforts remain true to quality assessment principles, which include alignment of assessment tools/methods with overall mission, goals and outcomes statements, use of collected data, and review of the assessment process itself.

Conclusion

A familiar adage within the assessment field states that "it is important to measure what we value instead of valuing what we measure." What is valued within international higher education? Within higher education in general? Assessing outcomes within international higher education is a critical area in which to focus efforts and attention, given that outcomes provide data on the quality of education and the overall preparation of students. This chapter has provided some frameworks in which to situate outcomes assessment. It has highlighted numerous efforts related to outcomes assessment and offered some concrete strategies available to higher education institutions for outcomes assessment of internationalization efforts. Specifically, quality of education and intercultural competence were explored, given that intercultural competence is often mentioned as a desirable student learning outcome of international education. Noting the complexity of assessing intercultural competence and related learning outcomes of international education, other questions can be raised: How do educators avoid oversimplification of key learning outcomes and yet develop reliable methods with which to measure outcomes of internationalization? How can educators avoid the inherent limits of assessment methods (such as those associated with tests, inventories, and self-report instruments)? How can outcomes assessment be integrated throughout a student's university experience, so as to create a more holistic picture of students' learning and thus provide a clearer picture of educational quality? These questions point to the need for additional research on outcomes assessment in internationalization.

In sum: Current work suggests that assessment of internationalization begins with a clear mission and well-defined goals derived from the literature that translate into concrete, measurable outcomes.

These specific, prioritized outcomes are then assessed through both direct and indirect measures. Despite the desire for easy ways to measure outcomes, such assessment, when done well to yield meaningful results, remains a complex undertaking within internationalization. The higher education contexts vary so much (i.e., type of institution, institutional missions, national policies, etc.) that the assessment approach must be tailored to each context, and thus, one size does *not* fit all, nor does one assessment tool fit all circumstances. Nonetheless, assessment remains a vital component in determining the success of internationalization efforts and in increasing the quality of education in general.

Ultimately, assessment and learning are integral to student development, and thus, assessment goes beyond simply documenting students' overseas experiences or international courses completed. Rather, outcomes assessment of internationalization provides evidence that students are learning interculturally and globally. Educators need to use assessment data to improve the quality of their programs and to guide students in their development. Assessment is hard work but well worth the investment in determining the impact of institutions on student learning and in preparing students for the global world in which they live and work.

REFERENCES

American Council on Education (2007). *Web guide: Assessing international learning outcomes.* Retrieved from http://www.acenet.edu/Content/NavigationMenu/ProgramsServices/cii/res/assess/index.htm

American Council on Education. (2008). *Web guide: Preparing for assessment.* Retrieved from http://www.acenet.edu/Content/NavigationMenu/ProgramsServices/International/Campus/GoodPractice/fipse/preparing/index.htm

Association of Universities and Colleges of Canada (AUCC). (2009). *Internationalization of the curriculum: A practical guide to support Canadian universities' efforts.* Ottawa: Author.

Banta, T. (2007, January 26). A warning on measuring learning outcomes. *Inside Higher Education.* Retrieved from http://www.Insidehighered.com

Beerkens, E., Brandenburg, U., Evers N., Van Gaalen A., Leichsenring, H., &

Zimmermann, V. (2010). *Indicator projects on internationalization: Approaches, methods and findings.* A report in the context of the European project "Indicators for Mapping & Profiling Internationalization" (IMPI). www.impi-project.eu

Birtwistle, T., & McKiernan, H. H. (2011, May). Trans-atlantic "ping-pong" & the Bologna Process. *Internationalization of European Higher Education*, pp. 1–21.

Cutberth, D., Smith, W., & Boey, J. (2008). What do we really know about outcomes of Australian international Education? A critical review and prospectus for future research. *Journal of Studies in International Education, 10,* 1–21.

Deardorff, D. K. (2005, May/June). A matter of logic? *International Educator,* 26–31.

Deardorff, D. K. (2006). Identification and assessment of intercultural competence as a student outcome of internationlisation. *Journal of Studies in International Education, 10,* 241–266.

Deardorff, D.K. (2007, Spring). *Principles of international education assessment. IIENetworker.* Retrieved from http://www.nxtbook.com/nxtbooks/naylor/IIEB0107/index.php?startid=51#/50

Deardorff, D. K. (Ed.). (2009). *The SAGE handbook of intercultural competence.* Thousand Oaks, CA: Sage.

De Decker, F. (2003). An evaluation of the impact of internationalisation on the higher education curricula (in Flanders). Background Paper for the Session, *"What are we doing it for?"* at the European Association for International Education conference, Vienna. Retrieved August 4, 2011, from http://www.eaie.org/pdf/conf2003/817.pdf

de Wit, H. (Ed.). (2009). *Measuring success in the internationalisation of higher education.* Amsterdam: European Association for International Education.

Driscoll. A., & Wood, S. (2007). *Developing outcomes-based assessment for learner-centered education.* Sterling, VA: Stylus.

Dwyer, M., & Peters, C. (2004, March/April). Benefits of study abroad. *Transitions Abroad Magazine, 37*(5). Retrieved July 29, 2011, from http://www.transitionsabroad.com/publications/magazine/0403/benefits_study_abroad.shtml

Earl, S., Carden, F., & Smutylo, T. (2001). *Outcome mapping: Building learning and reflection into development programs.* Ottawa, Canada: International Development Research Centre (IDRC).

Hudzik, J., & Stohl, M. (2009). Modelling assessment of the outcomes and impacts of internationalization. In H. de Wit (Ed.), *Measuring success in the internationalisation of higher education* (pp. 9–21). Amsterdam: European Association for International Education.

Huisman, J. (2007). Research on the internationalisation of higher education: The state of the art. Paper prepared for the *Seminar on the Internationalisation of Higher Education*, University of Bath.

Jang, J. (2009). *Analysis of the relationship between internationalization and the quality of higher education.* Doctoral dissertation, University of Minnesota.

Knight, J. (2004). Internationalization remodelled: Definition, approaches, and rationales. *Journal of Studies in International Education, 1,* 5–31. doi: 10.1177/1028315303260832

Knowles, M. S. (1975). *Self-directed learning: a guide for learners and teachers.* New York: Associated Press.

Leask, B. (2004). International outcomes for all students using information and communication technologies (ICTs). *Journal of Studies in International Education, 4,* 336–351.

Leeuw, F., & Vaessen, J. (2009). *Impact evaluations and development: NONIE guidance on impact evaluation.* Washington, DC: The Network of Networks on Impact Evaluation.

Martin, M., & Sauvageot, C. (2011). *Constructing an indicator system or scorecard for higher education A practical guide.* Paris: UNESCO.

McGowan, S., & Potter, L. (2008). The implications of the Chinese learner for the internationalization of the curriculum: An Australian perspective. *Critical Perspectives on Accounting, 19,* 81–198. doi:10.1016/j.cpa.2005.12.006

Molas-Gallart, J., Salter, A., Patel, P., Scott, A., and Duran, X. (2002). *Measuring third stream activities: Final report to the Russell Group of Universities.* United Kingdom: University of Sussex, Science and Techonology Policy Research (SPRU).

Morgan, B., & Lydon, J. (2009). Bologna: Some thoughts on its effect on the internationalization of higher education. *Journal of Applied Research in Higher Education, 1,* 63–72.

NVAO. (2011). *Frameworks for the assessment of internationalisation.* The Hague: Author. Retrieved from http://nvao.com/page/downloads/Kaders_BKK_Internationalisering_Frameworks_for_the_Assessment_of_Internationalisation_14-11-2011.pdf

Olson, C., Evans, R., & Schoenberg, R. F. (2007). *At home in the world: Bridging the gap between internationalization and multicultural education.* Washington, DC: American Council on Education.

Organization for Economic Cooperation and Development (OECD). (2002). *Glossary of key terms in evaluation and results based management.* Paris: Author.

Organization for Economic Cooperation and Development (OECD). (2010). *Assessment of higher education learning outcomes (AHELO).* Paris: Author. Retrieved from *http://www.oecd.org/dataoecd/37/49/45755875.pdf*

Paige, R., Fry, G., Stallman, E., Josić, J., & Jon, J. (2009). Study abroad for global engagement: The long-term impact of mobility experiences. *Intercultural Education, 20,* 29–44. DOI:10.1080/14675980903370847

Palomba, C. A., & Banta, T. W. (2001). *Assessing student competence in accredited disciplines: Pioneering approaches to assessment in higher education.* Sterling, VA: Stylus.

Parey, M., & Waldinger, F. (2011). Studying abroad and the effect on international labour market mobility: Evidence from the introduction of Erasmus. *Economic Journal, Royal Economic Society, 121*(551), 194–222. doi:http://hdl.handle.net/10.1111/j.1468-0297.2010.02369.x

Parsons, R. (2010). The effects of an internationalized university experience on domestic students in the United States and Australia. *Journal of Studies in International Education, 14*(4), 313–334. doi: 10.1177/1028315309331390

Pottinger, P. S. (1979). Competence assessment: Comments on current practices. *Defining and measuring competence.* San Francisco: Jossey-Bass.

Rauhvargers, A. (2011). *Global university rankings and their impact.* Belgium, Brussels: European University Association.

Rhodes, T. (Ed.). (2010). *Assessing outcomes and improving achievement: Tips and tools for using rubrics.* Washington, DC: Association of American Colleges and Universities.

Rogers, P. J. (2000). Program theory: Not whether programs work but how they work. In D. L. Stufflebeam, G. F. Madaus, & T. Kellaghan (Eds.), *Evaluation models: Viewpoints on educational and human services evaluation* (2nd ed., pp. 209–232). Boston: Kluwer Academic.

Sakurai, T., McCall-Wolf, F.. & Kashima, E. (2010). Building intercultural links: The impact of a multicultural intervention program on social ties of international students in Australia. *International Journal of Intercultural Relations, 2,* 176–185. doi:10.1016/j.ijintrel.2009.11.002

Sindt, P. (2007). *Internationalization and higher education: Understanding the impact of short-term study abroad.* Doctoral dissertation, Arizona State University.

Sutton, R., & Rubin, D. (2010). *The GLOSSARI Project: Initial findings from a system-wide research initiative on study abroad learning outcomes.* Retrieved from www.frontiersjournal.com

Teekens, H. (2011, Spring). Rethinking mobility. *Forum*, pp. 39–41.

Thomson, G., & Douglas, D. (2009). *Decoding learning gains: Outcomes and the pivotal role of the major and student backgrounds* (Research and Occasional Paper Series: Center for Studies in Higher Education). Berkeley: University of California. Retrieved from http://cshe.berkeley.edu

Vickers, P., & Bekhradnia, B. (2007). *The economic costs and benefits of international students.UK.* Oxford, UK: Higher Education Policy Institute.

Van Gaalen, A. (2009). Developing a tool for measuring internationalisation: A case study. *Measuring success in the internationalisation of higher education* (pp. 77–91). Amsterdam: European Association for International Education.

Van Gaalen, A. (Ed.). (2010). *Internationalisation and quality assurance.* Amsterdam: European Association for International Education.

Ward, C. (2006). *International students: Interpersonal, institutional and community impacts.* Wellington, New Zealand: Ministry of Education.

Westerheijden, D. (2010). *Internationalisation and its quality assurance: Modern European platform higher education modernisation.* Brussels, Belgium: European Centre for Strategic Management of Universities.

Wildavsky, B. (2010). *The great brain race: How global universities are reshaping the world.* Princeton, NJ: Princeton University Press.

Williams, S. (2008). *Internationalization of the curriculum: A remedy for international students' academic adjustment difficulties?* A final paper for the degree of Master of Education. Memorial University of Newfoundland, St. John's, Canada.

NOTES

1   Molas-Gallart, Salter, Patel, Scott, and Duran (2002) define third mission of higher education institutions as: "all activities concerned with the generation, use, application and exploitation of knowledge and other university capabilities outside academic environments."

2   NONIE has published a manual to develop impact evaluations in the area of development cooperation. Though developed for a different sector, this manual is applicable for the most part to internationalisation in the higher education sector. NONIE is comprised of the Development Assistance Committee of the Organization for Economic Co-operation and Development (OECD/DAC) Evaluation Network, the United Nations Evaluation Group (UNEG), the Evaluation Cooperation Group (ECG) and the International Organization for Cooperation in Evaluation (IOCE).

3   http://www.eua.be/maunimo

4   Both direct and indirect impacts can be identified. This chapter focuses primarily on the most direct effects on learning outcomes and the quality of education. Impact of internationalisation on students and staff will eventually also effect the program or institution in which these individuals are involved. Therefore the theoretical division between the different levels is somewhat arbitrary

5   http://www.cehd.umn.edu/projects/sage/

6   As always in education the challenge lies in the fact that the 'client' is part of the input. And therefore, as pointed out by Leask (2004), the achievement of internationalization outcomes requires student support and involvement, such as intentional development of students' intercultural communication skills, transition programs for international endeavors and so on. Some scholars (Knowles, 1975) even go so far as to advocate for students' direct involvement in articulating their own learning outcomes.

11

EMPLOYER PERSPECTIVES ON INTERNATIONAL EDUCATION

MARTIN TILLMAN

Because innovation requires continual collaboration, workers in the 21st century can no longer rely on the expertise they learned early in life to keep them in front of the skills queue . . . it is unlikely that universities and other educational institutions will be able to keep abreast of the fast-changing dynamic nature of work . . . as we step deeper into the 21st century, aspiring knowledge workers will need cross-disciplinary programs and degrees in order to compete. Historically, universities have found it difficult to provide such programs. There are many reasons for that. But to overcome it, we recommend a much tighter collaboration between academia and industry. And as required skills become more and more dynamic, business enterprises will need to assume an increasingly important role as educators. *(Donofrio, 2005, emphasis added)*

This chapter will discuss the emergence of an expanded rationale for international education in light of the convergence of mutual interests between academic institutions and employers to better prepare students to enter the global workforce, using primarily U.S. cases and sources, but at the end making reference to other cases as well. The discussion in no way implies that the central purpose of institutional efforts to provide students with international educational experiences—both on and off campus—is merely to serve the needs of businesses to identify talent with skills and intercultural competencies.

However, it is important to recognize that globalization of the workplace, coupled with the rise of a more mobile international workforce,

has resulted in a new transnational academic narrative supporting the realignment of international programs to achieve gains in competencies that add value to student career decision-making and postgraduate job searches.

According to Laurette Bennhold-Samaan, managing director, global assignment services, at Aperian Global, an intercultural consulting, training, and Web tools company, corporations need global talent more than ever:

In today's global economy, where complexity and change are the norm, attracting and retaining culturally competent talent will continue to be a challenge for companies globally. International experience has become a critical asset for all global organizations and will continue to create a competitive advantage—both for the individuals and for the companies that hire them. (Personal correspondence with author, June 14, 2011)

Unquestionably, the forces unleashed by globalization in the past decade have changed the expectations of professionals entering the workplace. They have also altered the landscape of how higher education institutions prepare students to develop global competencies through expanded opportunities to study, work, intern, and serve abroad as well as through more global opportunities created by internationalization of the curriculum and in their local community (Matherly & Nolting, 2007; Matherly & Robinson, 2001).

Furthermore, economic globalization and the expansion of institutional policies and practices that impact internationalization give rise to important questions. How should campuses prepare students to succeed in the global economy? How should universities align campus internationalization priorities and strategies with expectations of the global marketplace? Should preparing global-ready graduates be solely the domain and responsibility of colleges and universities? What is the role of business and industry in contributing to the applied knowledge and skill development of students?

In many instances, business leaders are new actors, who have been increasingly vocal about the direction of international education as they seek to recruit talent to meet the needs of their global workforce. They are more engaged because there is uncertainty about whether academic institutions, acting alone, can adequately prepare students for dynamic changes taking place in the global workforce. This is borne out by research conducted on behalf of the Association of American Colleges and Universities. Peter D. Hart Research Associates (2006, 2010) found that "only one in four employers [of 302 in their survey] thinks that two- and four-year colleges are doing a good job in preparing students for the challenges of the global economy." However, this concern goes beyond American business leaders and educators.

A global report prepared by the German engineering company, Continental AG (2006), surveyed eight universities in Asia, Europe, and South America and found there was

"insufficient evidence" (p. 1) as to whether their sponsored international programs (commonly including cooperative education, internships, research experience, service-learning, and study abroad) actually prepare students to practice on a global scale. The survey did not dispute the importance of such experiential learning; rather, the findings suggest there was "a significant lack of knowledge about proven theories and effective practices for instilling global competence" (p. 41).

In writing this global engineering report, team members conducted a review and analyses of what they refer to as the

> globalization programs and practices [with regard to their engineering programs] at each of the participating eight universities in Europe, Asia, North and South America. They acknowledged that campuses surveyed had both formulated policies for an overall institutional or organizational framework for globalization and . . . devised specific activities as part of their efforts to internationalize their campuses. However, the team found four conditions which they characterized as impeding "the worldwide capacity to better prepare global engineers. (p. 41)

These were:

• Preparation for global practice is generally not viewed as central to the education of an engineer; often, it is an isolated element or add-on to the engineering curriculum.

• Sustaining international mobility is a challenge in terms of sustaining successful international collaborations, despite the fact that living, working, or studying in a foreign culture is critical to the development of global engineers.

• Although globalization and collaboration may complement each other, many partnerships that have been attempted are more form than substance.

• There is a lack of knowledge about proven theories and effective practices for instilling global competence; such programs are seldom rigorously and scientifically evaluated for their educational impact.

The findings of the report, although focused solely on engineering education, have implications for the broader discussion about aligning international educational experience and workforce needs. The report sought answers to key questions that have implications across all disciplines, as well as specialized professional schools on campuses. What new skills are required, now and in the future, in the training of global engineers? How do we instill those skills? Will globalization increasingly lead to an employability and status gap between engineers who comfortably maneuver in an international environment and engineers who do not?

These questions raise challenges facing academic policymakers and program administrators regardless of whether they are responsible for developing undergraduate international programs or for training professionals (and not only engineers) at graduate schools in all fields.

The need for cooperation and collaboration was emphasized in the 2011 symposium held by the National Association of Colleges and Employers, which supported efforts toward building deep relationships between universities and employers (Wheeler, 2011).

Manny Contomanolis, associate vice president at the Rochester Institute of Technology, noted that corporations are looking for fewer but deeper partnerships with universities. At this meeting, the association held its first ever Global Campus Recruitment Symposium, which was a concrete expression of growing interest by universities and employers in making the conversation between university career service professionals and industry more international.

Williamson (2011) explains why "strategic collaboration" between universities and employers and between campuses and community-based partners is essential. She says, "The beauty of strategic collaboration is that it helps colleges and universities with little or no additional resources. This is critical given all the financial difficulties that universities are facing with state budget cuts and other forms of revenue losses." She also points out that despite the efforts of university presidents to globalize campuses in recent years, and despite the relatively large increase in the number of students studying abroad, the actual percentage of all students who study abroad is only 1.5% (as of the 2008–2009 academic year). In her view, collaboration offers a way to attract greater numbers of students to enroll in education-abroad programs while at the same time building important bridges to prospective employers.

Global workforce development has increasingly become a focus within higher education in the past decade and, in particular, an integral component of the global agenda of professional development organizations such as NAFSA: Association of International Educators. For example, in 2003, global workforce development was added to the mission of the association: "NAFSA serves its members, their institutions and organizations, and others engaged in international education and exchange and global workforce development ("Bazaar del Mundo," 2003)."

Despite the global economic downturn that began in 2008, and the difficulty that academic institutions and governments face to sustain support for international educational initiatives, there remains a high degree of support for the "inter-connectedness of higher education systems." New interuniversity linkages increased and broadened to include a more diverse group of nations. Turmoil in the Middle East and North Africa has opened up prospects for both student and faculty mobility and economic development with implications for the future of global workforce development in the region (McMurtrie, 2011).

The new grant program launched in 2011 by the Coca-Cola Foundation, the global philanthropic arm of the Coca-Cola Company, is a good example of how university collaboration with the private sector can impact and support international higher education. Grants totaling $1 million were awarded to six U.S. colleges and universities to send about 160 students to study in China over the next 4 years in support of the U.S. State Department's "100,000 Strong Initiative." The initiative is designed to enhance and strengthen ties between the United States and China in the areas of education, culture, sports, science and technology, and women's issues. It has received strong support from the Chinese government and a number of U.S. multinational companies, including Citigroup and Caterpillar, as well as Coca-Cola.

The issues facing the education and training of engineering students cited in the Continental AG report are challenging academic leaders in business education. A report issued by the Association to Advance Collegiate Schools of Business, the result of a 3-year study by a task force of deans and scholars from top business schools worldwide, examined case studies from nine institutions on several continents. It found that a "frustratingly wide curriculum gap remains alongside large risks of misdirected and incoherent strategies." The report concluded that most business schools placed more emphasis on studying abroad than on "developing and integrating global content within the curriculum" (Mangan, 2011).

On many levels, business schools throughout the world are trying to catch up to the needs of their students to gain international experience so they can compete more effectively—and become more marketable—for jobs in a global environment (Schumpeter, 2011). Some signs of this trend are new interuniversity linkages (Wharton at the University of Pennsylvania and the Harvard Business School with the China Europe International Business School in Shanghai), new requirements for MBAs to gain work-abroad experience (University of Michigan Ross School of Business requires all first-year students to spend seven weeks working abroad), and an increased demand to recruit international students to bring the world home (34% of students attending 55 of the leading MBA programs in the United States were foreign (as ranked by the *Financial Times*), as were 85% of those at Europe's top 55 courses).

The dean of the Harvard Business School, Nitin Nohria, believes that business schools need to adjust to the new realities in the global marketplace. Speaking about several changes he has instituted in the Harvard curriculum, he states

> A second theme is globalization, and the need to educate the next generation of business leaders to be far more savvy about what is going on around the world ... All of our students will go abroad, too, to some emerging market and think about a new product or service that a company can introduce in that emerging market. ("Looking Ahead," 2011)

However, despite the effort by campuses to advance international educational experiences, there may be a disconnect between schools' globalization efforts and specific skills employers want and need in candidates they screen for jobs. "Many business schools offer opportunities for students to go abroad, but I don't know if

that's sufficient in its own right," according to Russ Hagey, senior partner and worldwide chief talent officer at Bain (Middleton, 2011).

Clearly, companies want to provide students with skills and competencies that reflect their best practices, provide domain knowledge, and also introduce students to those cognitive, social, and personal skills that are a good fit with the company's human resource needs. However, according to Deardorff (2009), the evidence is clear that from the perspective of employers, international experience by itself is not enough.

> Intercultural competence doesn't just happen; if it did, there would be far fewer cross-cultural misunderstandings. Rather, we must be intentional about developing learners' intercultural competence. Such development can occur through adequate preparation, substantive intercultural interactions, and relationship building. (p. xiii)

To better understand the perceptions of international experiences among students and employers alike, Malerich (2009) surveyed the literature on the value of international internships in global workforce development. She found that

> while increasingly utilized by students in an effort to increase marketability in the global economy, the real value of the international internship is limited by both lack of understanding on the part of the American employers regarding internships as skill and quality building platforms, as well as by a lack of understanding and skill on the part of [recent graduates] in effectively communicating their gained competencies. (p. 2)

In her view, the stakeholders—academic institutions, employers, and students—need to "create new levels of partnerships to develop international internship experiences through which all stakeholders gain" (p. 2).

The cases in this chapter citing the partnerships of KPMG, Continental AG, Infosys, and Sodexo illustrate the benefits of carefully designed partnerships between campuses and corporations to bridge gaps in the education and training of students. These partnerships emphasize structured internship experiences and the training of students (KPMG and Sodexo's programs train only U.S. students) for careers in selected fields; nevertheless, they are useful examples of a new paradigm for realigning the structure of domestic and international educational experiences to develop and nurture competencies and skills that add value to industry global workforce requirements. At the same time, they offer students invaluable experiential learning experiences in diverse international workforces providing intensive interaction between students and experienced professionals.

Infosys developed InStep, its global internship program, in 1999. The program's goal was to build the Infosys brand and establish mind-share in its future clients, partners, and employees. The company sought to provide interns with a clear understanding of how the company's business model operates and, in particular, to bridge those "theoretical frameworks taught in classrooms with real-world applications."

BOX 11.1 InStep: INFOSYS Global Internship Program

Soraya Mohideen
Program Manager, Global Academic Relations (India)

Infosys Ltd. is a consulting and information technology (IT) services company established in 1981. The founders quickly realized that the biggest market consuming IT services in the 1980s was the United States and pioneered the Global Delivery Model. Today, Infosys manages over 7,000 projects at any time, with highly integrated teams working across countries, cultures, and time zones to deliver best-in-class software tools and transformational insights into clients' business.

Infosys continuously searches for bright professionals who understand the importance of working as a global team. Now, a global team requires that even junior staff interact with their team members around the world, which is very different from yesterday, when only senior management interacted with country heads in Japan or Germany.

To answer some of these needs, Infosys created the InStep Global Internship Program aimed at introducing tomorrow's leaders to the company's model of doing business; with teammates of many nationalities, leveraging the Global Delivery Model with an emerging markets perspective. Best-in-class students from many of the top technology, business, and liberal arts colleges pursuing bachelor, master, and PhD degrees are hand-selected to pursue company-relevant projects. During their 6-week to 6-month internship, interns are exposed to working with a large multinational corporation born in an emerging market with clients across the globe. The majority of interns come to one of the Infosys offices in India, where the company is headquartered, learning about the growth and opportunities in an emerging market.

Interns learn a variety of skills during their internship. Each has a specific project in broad areas such as research, software development, internal consulting, marketing, employee relations, and brand-building.

One liberal arts intern shares:

I worked on the sustainability theme for my internship project. The aim of the project was to interview Infoscions, ranging from the Infosys board of directors to active members in volunteer groups, and analyze the current sustainability initiatives at work to identify areas of improvement. This project was strategically important as it helped the company identify focus areas and move ahead. Being part of this project also helped me to understand how to work on sustainability within a large organization.

(Continued)

(Continued)

One of the MBA interns shares:

My InStep project was designed to look at innovation in management practices of some of the world's most innovative companies. Aside from distilling best practices, I also traced patterns across different industries and geographies and tried to determine the impact of innovation on financial performance indicators. It was a challenging project that required me to draw from my experience in finance, accounting, marketing and general management. I also took part in the InStep Business Plan Competition and got the chance to develop and pitch my ideas to the top management at Infosys. This was an invaluable experience."

Students who have interned with Infosys develop four critical skills and insights applicable across industries and roles:

1. Ability to work across cultural boundaries, requiring respect and flexibility

2. Leveraging technology to address business and real world situations

3. Understanding of the importance of emerging economies economically, politically, and culturally

4. Bridging theoretical frameworks taught in classrooms with real-world applications

Students who have finished the InStep Global Internship Program are respected professionals across business, the public sector, nonprofits, and academia. They are quickly identified as having gained valuable international experience critical to leading a global workforce.

KPMG took a similar route in creating its Global Internship Program in 2007. Because more U.S. students have international study and work experiences than ever before, the company found a rise in the number of multilingual students joining the firm. They determined that students with previous overseas experience will be able to quickly leverage this knowledge for the benefit of their teams and clients.

BOX 11.2 KPMG Global Internship Program

Simon Kho
Former director, KPMG National Student Programs & Global Initiatives (USA)

KPMG, one of the world's leading professional organizations, provides audit, advisory, and tax services to 85% of the companies listed on the Fortune Global 500. To be able to respond to its clients' evolving international needs, KPMG's people agenda must include attracting and developing a mobile workforce with global views and perspectives. "Our firm needs to become a much more global enterprise with strong global recruiting, global career paths for our people, globally consistent client service, and a global culture," says John Veihmeyer, who serves as chairman and CEO of KPMG's U.S. member firm and as chairman of KPMG's Americas Region.

The U.S. member firm of KPMG alone recruits about 3,000 university graduates and more than 2,000 interns each year. To support the firm's global business requirements, the U.S. firm has developed multiple student programs that promote the importance of cross-border awareness and exposure. "As part of our continuing efforts to advance KPMG's global connectivity, we have a number of global development opportunities for professionals at every level of their career from interns to partners. The objective is to provide exposure to the global business environment, deliver a consistent training experience, and help us attract and develop global professionals, which is essential for our success as an organization," cites Brian Ambrose, global chief operation officer, KPMG International.

KPMG's award-winning Global Internship Program was first introduced in 2007. Through the program, students complete a 4-week overseas assignment as part of their internship experience. Over the past 5 years, there has been a dramatic increase in the skills and experiences of the students choosing to join KPMG. More students have international study and work experiences than ever before. In addition, KPMG actively partners with faculty in promoting international study opportunities. Universities who sponsor business courses that include an overseas travel component or study tour can also visit one of KPMG's international offices. During the 2010–2011 academic year, the U.S. firm coordinated more than 20 global office visits to locations ranging from Sydney to Sao Paulo to Shanghai. "We are very impressed with KPMG's programs and opportunities. I have noticed more of our students looking to study abroad in either their sophomore and/or junior year so the student interest is definitely there. The business world is no longer local and we have to change the way we do business to address the global community. Offering international exposure as part of our academic curriculum will only help our students as they enter the workforce," shares Dr. Barbara Porco, accounting faculty, Fordham University.

KPMG expects to recruit more talented people than ever—up to 250,000 over the next 5 years. KPMG's teams will be working across borders in increasing numbers to support the ever-changing global marketplace. "Global experiences, especially those gained early in a career, allow our people to grow as individuals and as professionals. They develop additional skills that make them even more valuable when working with clients and teams, wherever they are in the world," says Stacy Sturgeon, KPMG's national managing partner, university relations and recruiting.

Creating opportunities to attract students with international experience who also have been exposed to the organizational culture of a particular business or organization is critical to the long-term workforce development strategies of global companies. It is especially important for multilateral institutions and international organizations like the United Nations. The case of the International Organization for Migration highlights the importance of identifying candidates whose good intentions match up with the unique skills and competencies required by multilateral institutions.

Sodexo has more than 380,000 employees providing on-site services to clients in educational institutions, hospitals, senior living facilities, government organizations, and private businesses in 80 countries worldwide. It is the 21st largest employer in the world. Given the global marketplace in which it works, the company places a high value on hiring and developing employees who offer a diverse array of international experience, education, global perspectives, and language skills.

BOX 11.3 Hiring Practices in International Organizations

Michael Emery
Director of Human Resources Management, International Organization for Migration

Many actors are competing for what was once the traditional core business of a handful of international organizations, and more than ever, employers have the luxury of choosing from huge numbers of exceptionally well educated graduates from all corners of the globe. How do you *actually* get a job in international organizations? That is a difficult question to answer, as all organizations are different, and all individuals bring something different to each organization.

When considering applications to vacancies with an initial assessment, two aspects of the application are relevant: the minimum requirements (the objective criteria such as academic requirements) and then the competency and value proposition of candidates. While the first aspect is important to be in the mix, what will get candidates onto a short-list is the competency and value proposition that is evident in the overall application.

I was involved in the short-listing for a training position in Afghanistan, and one of the long-listed candidates had excellent pedagogical academic credentials from reputable universities in Western Europe but little other relevant experience. Another candidate, while meeting the minimum requirement of a master's degree, had been posted to Mawson Station in Antarctica, where staffs are isolated for 11 months straight. Between the two candidates, the one favored was the candidate with the exposure to an isolated, confined work environment as a track record of success in stressful conditions was more relevant to the Afghanistan context.

A further trend in selection in the multilateral sector is the increasing use of psychometric testing to assess external candidates and internal staff for career advancement. In a recent talent management initiative introduced by a United Nations agency, candidates interviewed with an organizational psychologist who provided feedback on multirater and psychometric assessments. These were expected to measure a variety of aptitudes, skills, and IQ (related to the capacity for reasoning) on several levels (tendencies, inclinations, and capacity for learning) that related to the work, operational tasks, administrative, verbal, numerical, and practical abilities. In the design of these assessments, it was stressed that the resulting test scores did not indicate a systematic discrimination of specific persons because of their membership to ethnic, socio-cultural or gender-specific groups. Thus, introduction of psychometric tests as a tool in a basket of assessment methodologies as part of a holistic assessment of candidates is adding to a more objective view of selection and recruitment.

As important as contextual experience are the "soft competencies" or "emotional competencies" of candidates. During one round of the selection process for UNDP's young professional program, the selection panel wanted to explore cultural awareness and cross-cultural navigation, and asked the following two questions: "I see you have had opportunity to work in cross cultural teams. What have you learned about yourself in the way you interact with people from other cultures?" The follow-up question was, "Tell me about a time when you have made a cultural mistake. What was the context and what did you learn from the experience?"

In my view, getting a job in an international organization requires aspirants to address a range of career variables in a holistic manner. Apart from minimum relevant experience and qualifications (and today's master's degree is the bachelor's of yesteryear), constant attention must be paid to effective networking, often described as building and nurturing long-term, reciprocal professional relationships where there is a constant exchange of knowledge, resources, and information. A second variable to consider is how one builds a professional reputation. Reputation management is probably the most underestimated aspect of career self-management, recognizing that everyone has a reputation (likely multiple reputations), and it is not what an individual *thinks* other people think about them; it's what other people think about them. Protecting one's reputation is as important as effective networking in building a career.

These are just two of many essential variables to address in career self-management.

BOX 11.4 Sodexo Future Leaders Internship Program

Sherie Valderrama
Senior Director, Talent Acquisition Group, Sodexo (USA)

At Sodexo, Corporate Human Resources' aim is to attract, hire, and develop "citizens of the world"—highly talented professionals who have a key interest in global trends and an understanding of how these trends impact our business. We value those who know how to anticipate, innovate, act differently, understand cultural differences, and have the potential to become global executives within our company.

In the United States, Sodexo has formal relationships with about 28 institutions selected to conduct academic programs in our industry because their highly diverse student enrollment supports our company's diversity goals. The hires we make from these schools are entry-level graduates. Each institution is assigned a recruiter who prepares a formal annual strategy that involves a combination of supporting student activities, speaking on campus about the industry, providing guidance on career/job search strategies, attending career events, and so on. All schools have designated operational relationship managers, who work with the recruiters to represent Sodexo on campus, and ultimately, drive college hires. For six of the schools, six members of our Sodexo North American CEO's executive team have taken ownership and attend an annual event and provide input into overall strategy.

As part of college recruiting, we have a Future Leaders Internship program that is focused on students from these schools. Each intern is assigned a formal mentor in our company in addition to a direct supervisor for the internship, and all interns attend several professional development events throughout the duration of the internship. Following completion of their internships, our top interns return to campus as student ambassadors, and we provide a stipend for their representation on campus.

The company also sponsors a STAR faculty program, which targets a group of top faculty from key schools who advise us on our college relations program.

Several efforts have been made to better define and categorize global competencies over the years. In a pioneering study for the RAND Institute on Education and Training, Bikson and Law (1994) sought to identify the perceived human resource implications of what the authors referred to as *globalism.* The study also examined the "characteristics needed by professionals to perform in the new world economy." Interviews were conducted at 16 corporate sites and 16 academic institutions.

The findings, while anecdotal, track closely with subsequent research examining the hard and soft attributes and skills needed by businesses to succeed in building their global workforce, as well as the issues facing campuses trying to prepare their graduates to enter the workforce after building a portfolio of both academic knowledge and practical [international] experience. Numerous frameworks and definitions of global or intercultural competence can be found in Spitzberg and Changnon's work (2009), including two research-based frameworks, those of Deardorff (2006) and Hunter, White, and Godbey (2006).

Employers cited four categories as key human resource needs:

- *Domain knowledge:* This involves knowledge gained in specific subject areas.

- *Cognitive, social, and personal skills:* These include problem-solving ability, decision-making, working effectively in groups with colleagues of different backgrounds, flexibility and adaptability, and other similar skills.

- *Prior work experience and on-the-job training:* In this particular area, campuses have realized large gains in the past 15 years through expansion of all forms of off-campus domestic and international experiential educational programs as well as traditional study abroad programs.

- *Cross-cultural competence:* Authors called this a "critical new human resource requirement created by globalism"; here, too, there have been enormous advances in preparing students to adapt and adjust in different cross-cultural settings as the field of international education has moved away from its early predominantly Eurocentric model to one that embraces a wider range of countries in the developing world.

Regardless of the structure of the experience, or whether it takes place in a domestic or international setting, there needs to be a purposeful focus on assisting students to fully integrate the learning that takes place and to interpret, evaluate, and articulate the skills and competencies that resulted from their experience.

PURPOSEFUL INTERNATIONAL EDUCATIONAL EXPERIENCE STRENGTHENS INTERCULTURAL COMPETENCIES AND EMPLOYABILITY

While efforts to internationalize campuses have risen dramatically in recent years, there remains a need for more purposeful and structured intercultural experience to provide students with the skills and competencies employers are looking for to build their global workforces, whether those experiences are in local communities or in other countries.

Research supports the conclusion that "the design of international education programs, with regard to student intercultural learning and development, should be intentional rather than by 'trial-and-error'" (Deardorff, 2009, p. 340). Furthermore, it is important to note that building intercultural skills can occur without international experiences—and not all students who have those experiences will be employed outside the United States. As Deardorff states: "One doesn't have to go overseas to work with people from different cultures. Exposure to intercultural communication even at home is becoming more important as our population becomes more diverse" (Bremer, 2006, p. 42). There is certainly much recent evidence that such exposure is important in many parts of the world where communities are struggling to assimilate and acculturate increasingly diverse emigrant communities.

These are some of the key issues that must be considered by senior international officers (SIOs) and their campus colleagues:

- The competencies employers believe are necessary to build their global workforces are disconnected from the learning outcomes that students value during their college experience/career.

- Job opportunities are growing with companies doing increasing business in the developing world/emerging markets, but most students do not study, work or intern in these countries.

- Institutions need to place greater emphasis on the impact of education abroad—and work, internships or service learning—on student career development. The value-added of international education experience is diminished if students cannot clearly articulate the way that such experience has strengthened specific intercultural competencies of interest to prospective employers (Tillman, 2005).

- Institutions must adequately prepare students before, during, and after international experiences to maximize the intercultural learning experience (Deardorff, 2008; Tillman, 2011).

- Institutions must maximize their resources to enhance students' intercultural competence at the home campus (especially for the majority of students who do not have the opportunity to go abroad), through the curriculum, co-curriculum, and community service.

In the Institute of International Education (2009) briefing paper, "The Value of International Education to U.S. Business and Industry Leaders: Key Findings from a Survey of CEOs," 60% of all respondents (a group of more than 200 senior-level U.S. and international business leaders) reported that their company's hiring and promotion strategy acknowledged the importance of a study abroad experience. Of those surveyed, 90% of senior managers who reported that they studied abroad during their careers (62 respondents) also reported that their company had a "hiring or promotion strategy that actively sought out and rewarded study abroad experience."

Skills that received the overall highest rankings by survey respondents included:

- Ability to work in a cross-cultural (globalized) work environment
- Knowledge and understanding of international systems (languages, policies, practices)
- Interpersonal and communications skills
- Initiative and creative thinking

Also valued was technical knowledge, hands-on experience in a particular field (e.g., internship), adaptability, positive response to change, and enthusiasm for substance of job.

The most recent and comprehensive survey of global employers, *QS Global Employer Survey 2011* (Moloney, Sowter, & Potts, 2011), asked hiring managers and CEOs whether or not they "value" international study experience. The report is unique among recent research because it is based on responses from 10,000 respondents in 116 nations. It found that 60% of respondents said they do "value an international study experience and the attributes that the experience may confer to mobile students" (p. 6). Interestingly, support was strongest among CEOs and less so among human resources personnel. The report analyzes, by industry, what skills and competencies are valued by employers in different nations. It finds that language competency, above all other skills, is highly valued by all respondents. The immense scope of this survey supports Malerich's finding that all stakeholders gain if international experience is structured to build skills employers value in hiring talent.

Continental AG has joined forces with eight leading international universities to launch the Global Engineering Excellence Initiative (GEEI). For many years, as a leading international automotive supplier in the high-tech sector, Continental has actively promoted engineering education, reforms in academic systems, and the development of young engineers. This commitment has been integrated into the GEEI in close cooperation with eight international universities on three continents, including Georgia Tech.

Some Non-U.S. Cases

A study conducted by the Canadian Association of Universities and Colleges (Kaznowska & Usher, 2011) of how Canadian students view the value of internationalization in terms of their career advancement, showed a favorable view of the correlation between global competencies and future employment. "Overall, students were nearly uniform in indicating that the ability to work in diverse cultural settings" was important in terms of getting a job, "with 93% agreeing this was important or very important." (p. 6)

In a 2008 survey of participants in the Congress-Bundestag Youth Exchange (CBYX) for Young Professionals, administered by Cultural Vistas (a merger of the former Association for International Practical Training and the Carl Duisberg Society), nearly 95% of the respondents indicated that the program had a positive impact on their career.

BOX 11.5 Georgia Institute of Technology-Continental AG Global Engineering Internship Program

Debbie Donohue
Former Director, Work Abroad Program
Division of Professional Practice, Georgia Tech (USA)

With the Global Engineering Internship Program (GEIP), Continental has implemented a key recommendation of the Global Engineering Excellence study. Students from the eight partner universities have had the opportunity to participate in an internship abroad at one of 190 Continental locations worldwide (the partnership with Georgia Tech concluded in 2011).

Continental selected Georgia Tech as a partner due to Georgia Tech's longstanding tradition of applying technical knowledge in a practical fashion, blending theory with practice. A great part of that culture comes from the 98-year-old cooperative education program, which links industry to academia through experiential education to develop a local, national, and now international workforce. The Division of Professional Practice (DoPP) at Georgia Tech houses the co-op, internship, graduate co-op, and work-abroad programs. The co-op program is one of the stronger experiential education programs due to the strong partnerships with industry in preparing the workforce through three alternating work terms with each student. The work-abroad program started in 2005 as DoPP's fourth program and as a part of the International Plan initiative. DoPP serves as a pipeline to industry around the world in creating the workforce that they need through experiential education.

The International Plan offers a challenging four-year academic program that develops global competence within the context of each participating student's major. It requires students to engage in a minimum of 26 weeks of international experience (work, research, or study) related to their discipline, to develop a proficiency in a second language, and to take internationally oriented coursework. This experience provides students a deeper global competency than traditional international opportunities. The university viewed educating students about their major in a global context as key to enhancing their education at Georgia Tech. University leaders also saw the importance of international experiential education as part of the International Plan and formed the work-abroad program.

The work-abroad program consists of undergraduate and graduate students within any field of study. Typically, Georgia Tech students work for one semester. All of the work-abroad opportunities are full-time internships or co-op jobs outside the United States, and the majority are paid. Students can work during the fall, spring, or summer semester.

Georgia Tech's leadership believes that partnering with industry, government, and nongovernmental organizations to offer internships around the world is a key part of a student's education today.

Ian Bolin, a 1997–1998 program alumnus who now works for Audi of America, is absolutely convinced his international internship impacted his career:

Upon completion of the program in 1998, I returned to the States and utilized my contacts

gained at Bosch during my internship to land a position with Rolls Royce & Bentley Motor Cars. My background and German skills were exactly what the President & CEO was looking for in his personal assistant; the company had just been acquired by Volkswagen AG. Assisting in managing the US operations while helping my boss understand "the Germans" launched my career. Nine years later, I am still with the Volkswagen Group. Without my German language and cultural skills none of this would have been possible. (CBYX alumni survey, 2008)

Rob Fenstermacher, president and CEO of Cultural Vistas, states:

Employers consistently indicate that the global workforce of today and the future needs to have individuals who are adaptable and flexible to meet changing job requirements and work environments, possess technological skills to make use of information and communication tools, are able to work in teams (often from different cultures and nations), are able to examine issues from different perspectives to increase problem-solving abilities, and . . . possess an interest and motivation to continually learn new things. Exchange experiences help develop all of these skills and those who participate in exchanges are often risk-takers and individuals interested in expanding their horizons. It's no wonder CBYX participants believe their experience impacted their careers. They have what employers are looking for in a future employee. (Personal correspondence, May 2011)

Exploring the linkage between international experience and employability in the Canadian context, Arthur (2004) cites research suggesting that more than 50,000 Canadians are employed in multinational corporations. She states that "the value of international experience for mobility within the labor market has received little research in Canadian contexts." While employers may be seeking employees with global literacies and specific skills, she cites the problem of the "ad hoc entry" of employees into the global workforce, an issue she has been writing about throughout the past decade in terms of creating effective ways to integrate the international experience of students into their long-range career planning along with reducing barriers of employers to recognizing the value of such experience in their hiring practices.

More recent research confirms a strong correlation between international experience and employability. In the United Kingdom, for example, researchers found that "65% of international employers indicate that having overseas professional work experience makes graduates

more employable" (Archer & Davison, 2008). Likewise, an Australian study found that

all stakeholders identify clear connections between international experience and employability, given outcomes associated with the forging of networks, opportunities for experiential learning, language acquisition and the development of soft skills related to cultural understandings, personal characteristics and ways of thinking. (Crossman & Clarke, 2009)

The authors concluded, "International experience appears to support the development of cultural sensitivity and adaptability as well as enhancing graduate attractiveness in a globalized and internationalized labor market, all key factors in determining individual employability."

In a study of German students who graduated between 1989 and 2005 and studied abroad through the Erasmus (European Action Scheme for the Mobility of University Students) program, Parey and Waldinger (2011) found that "students who have studied abroad are about 15% more likely to work abroad after graduation." Their findings demonstrate that "mobility decisions during university have long-run effects on the careers and labour-market outcomes of individuals."

The necessity of creating conditions that support and foster the linkage between academic study and practical work experience poses unique challenges in the developing world. Educators and industry leaders—albeit given highly diverse and divergent educational and economic systems—are grappling with aligning institutional priorities with labor conditions and rising expectations of students to obtain workplace skills and competencies. "Skills development and unemployment is a matter of core concern not just in India but worldwide and public private partnerships are the key to realising India's vast potential in this area and achieving socially equitable and inclusive growth, said Sharda Prasad, director general employment and training, ministry of labour and employment" (Rediff India Abroad, 2008).

Similarly, building partnerships is recognized as essential with respect to the current state of higher education in Nigeria:

Putting the Nigerian graduate to gainful work also implies that its higher education institutions should partner with business to develop employability content in higher education curriculum and provide formal life skills training for students. They should use more life case analysis in teaching that brings the real work problems to life. Entrepreneurial studies should be made compulsory because many may find themselves self-employed after school. Formal career services and employability performance tracking working through a formal alumni network will also be critical along with the exchange of best practices locally and internationally. (Akanmu, 2011)

In Bangladesh, globalization and new market conditions for graduates are creating conditions for curricula change and linkages with the private sector:

In today's fluctuating market, academic institutions should be kept under pressure to armor their students to be equipped with those types of qualifications that are relevant and contain marketable skills. Because the ultimate goal of the academic is to impart skills, thus, providing the opportunity for employment within the students' chosen industry. Hence they will need to re-evaluate their traditional approach to delivering higher education qualifications. And findings of this paper suggest that to make students more work ready the teaching method of higher education establishment of this country needs to be more work based, not too distant from industry requirements and develop a better understanding of modern business. (Chisty, Uddin, & Kumar, 2007)

Citing the difficulty of multinationals in China, Dodyk, Richardson, and Wu (2012) discuss how companies like GM, Microsoft, P&G, PepsiCo and others have developed unique educational initiatives to support their local efforts to hire Chinese talent. Due to the inadequate preparation of Chinese college graduates, " ... many firms note their involvement with local universities, either through collaborative curriculum-building and/or sponsoring or participating in industry events...Companies also consistently point to their advocacy for more rigorous general management training (p. 10)."

CONCLUSION

Globalization of the workforce, increased mobility of students, rising demand from

employers for "global-ready" graduates, are but a few of the new forces of change impacting the traditional structure of international educational experiences offered to students. These forces are found to influence the focus of higher education policy and planning with respect to campus internationalization and in particular, the development of partnerships with business and industry to widen opportunities for experiential learning and practical work experience.

In a comprehensive report of original research by KPMG International (Salt, 2008), leading global managers shared their views on talent needs in the future and on policy issues associated with demographic changes in both developed and developing nations. Three of the managers expressed strikingly similar views:

- "The international mobility of talent delivers diversity of viewpoint . . . our business, all business, needs different viewpoints," Brian Ambrose, Global Mobility, KPMG.

- "There is a shortage of talent with the right skills in certain emerging markets . . . if we can't find that talent locally, we will increasingly rely on expats with global skills and mindsets," Ryan Larsen, Wal-Mart.

- "Technology and globalization [have] changed the nature of our workforce . . . we have to be flexible to ensure we attract and retain talent with a global perspective," Rodney Scaife, AOL.

Colleges and universities need to educate students to thrive and succeed in both international and domestic markets. International experience, internationalized curriculum, and intercultural learning opportunities domestically and internationally, along with a "global mindset" developed through such experiences, can have an important impact on local and regional economic development within any country around the world.

A country's economic competitiveness in the future will be dependent on the educational readiness of its workforce. Thus, it is a mistake to think of workforce development and higher education separately. Traditional higher education must have an intentional focus on, and commitment to, regional workforce development needs" (Mattes, 2008). The persistent and long-standing "employability and status gap" due to unequal access of students to both domestic and international education experiences will have a long-term impact on the readiness of a country to be competitive.

University policymakers and administrators need to take a fresh look at the design and structure of international education programs if these experiences are intended to have a maximum impact on the career direction and near- and long-term employability of students. Work-abroad programs and internships, as illustrated by the cases of KPMG, Infosys, Sodexo, and Continental AG, have succeeded due to their alignment with the needs of these companies to attract and retain talent.

The importance of building connections for students with employers and undertaking efforts to internationalize curriculum is a concern that extends beyond higher education institutions in the developed world:

> Academic administration decision-makers from non-OECD [Organization for Economic Cooperation and Development] academic institutions are concerned about advancing the students' personal and career progression. It is a reflection on that school of its global and forward-looking stance where it has actively supported growth channels like internships. Schools which partner with firms enjoy a greater reputation of interconnectedness and industry relevance. Students participate in an international internship offering high impact assignments and a global network of colleagues . . . universities can leverage these alumni relations down the line. (Personal communication, Soraya Mohideen, Program Manager, Global Academic Relations, Infosys Limited

In a highly competitive global marketplace, the best and the brightest students—selected to participate in competitive internship programs— will have an advantage and the opportunity to build outstanding career "toolkits." This begs the question of articulating the value added—in terms of intercultural skills and competencies— of classroom-based study abroad programs, for the majority of students participating in international educational programs, absent any linkage to "practical" skill-building experiences.

Higher education around the world will need to address both the availability of such programs and the student's ability to articulate how their newly gained skills and competencies are connected to their career choice if internationalization is to realize its full potential. There is clearly much work to be done in the years ahead.

REFERENCES

Akanmu, O. (2011, January 19). *Graduate employment and employability challenges in Nigeria.* Retrieved from http://olusfile.blogspot .com/2011/01/putting-nigerian-graduate-to -work.html.

Archer, W., & Davison, J. (2008). *Graduate employability: The views of employers.* London: The Council for Industry and Higher Education, retrieved from http://employability .ulster.ac.uk/ppts/Hermann%20CIHE.pdf

Arthur, N. (2004). *Show off your international experience.* The National Consultation on Career Development, Canada. Retrieved from http://www.natcon.org/archive/natcon/papers/ natcon_papers_2004_arthur.pdf.

Bazaar del Mundo revisited: NAFSA and the global workforce. (2003, Summer). *International Educator, 12*(3), 53–55. Washington, DC: NAFSA: Association of International Educators.

Bikson, T. K., & Law, S. A. (1994). *Global preparedness and human resources.* Santa Monica, CA: RAND Institute on Education and Training.

Bremer, D. (2006, May/June). Global workforce development. *International Educator,* pp. 40–45. Washington, DC, NAFSA: Association of International Educators.

Chisty, K. K. S., Uddin, G. M., & Kumar, G. S. (2007). The business graduate employability in Bangladesh: Dilemma and expected skills by corporate world. *BRAC University Journal, 4*(1), 1–8.

Congress-Bundestag Youth Exchange (CBYX) for Young Professionals. (2008). Alumni survey. New York: CDS International (now known as Cultural Vistas).

Crossman, J., & Clarke, M. (2009 August 12). *International experience and graduate employability.* Retrieved from http://www .springerlink.com/content/fqk1337344360215

Deardorff, D. K. (2006). Identification and assessment of intercultural competence as a student outcome of internationlisation. *Journal of Studies in International Education, 10,* 241–266.

Deardorff, D. K. (2008). Intercultural competence: A definition, model, and implications for education abroad. In V. Savicki (Ed.), *Intercultural competence and transformation: Theory, research, and application.* Sterling, VA: Stylus.

Deardorff, D. K. (Ed). (2009). *The SAGE handbook of intercultural competence.* Thousand Oaks, CA: Sage.

Dodyk, P., Richardson, A., & Wu, M. (2012). Talent management at multinational firms in China. In *The Lauder global business insight report 2012: Transformative times: New opportunities for business in an era of upheaval* (pp. 7–10). Philadelphia: University of Pennsylvania, The Lauder Institute. Retrieved from http:// knowledge.wharton.upenn.edu/papers/ download/012012_Lauder-Report -Transformative-Times.pdf.

Donofrio, N. (2005, June 16–17). *The evolving global talent pool: issues, challenges and strategic implications.* Albany: State University of New York, The Levin Institute.

Continental AG. (2006). Final report of the global engineering excellence initiative. Hanover, Germany: Author.

Hunter, W. D. White, G. P., & Godbey, G. C. (2006). What does it mean to be globally competent? *Journal of Studies in International Education, 10*(No. 3), 267–285.

Institute of International Education. (2009, October). *The value of international education to U.S. business and industry leaders: Key findings from a survey of CEOs.* Retrieved from www.iie .org/research/evaluation

Kaznowska, E., & Usher, A. (2011, January 6). *Internationalization at Canadian universities: Are students seeing the value?* Toronto, Canada: Higher Education Strategy Associates.

Looking ahead behind the ivy (Interview with Nitin Nohria). (2011, July 24). *The New York Times Education Life*, p. 14.

Malerich, J. (2009). *The value of international internships in global workforce development.* Tempe: Arizona State University.

Mangan, K. (2011, February 10). Business schools worldwide fall short on globalization, report says. *Chronicle of Higher Education*, Washington, DC.

Matherly, C., & Nolting, W. (2007, March). Educational experience abroad: Preparation for a globalized workplace. *National Association of Colleges and Employers (NACE) Journal*, 14–44.

Matherly, C., & Robinson, D. (2001, September 9). *Get ready for the global workplace.* Retrieved from http://public.wsj.com/careers/resources/ documents/20000125-matherly.htm

Mattes, B. (August 7, 2008). *Higher education should link workforce development to economic needs.* Retrieved from http://archives. huntingtonnews.net/columns/080807-mattes -columnshighereducation.html

McMurtrie, B. (2011, August 21). Cross-border connections multiply, despite tight budgets. *Chronicle of Higher Education Almanac of Higher Education.*

Middleton, D. (2011, April 12). Schools set global track, for students and programs. *Wall Street Journal Online.* Retrieved from http://online .wsj.com/article/SB1000142405274870380630457 6244980620638072.html

Moloney, J., Sowter, B., & Potts, D. (2011). *QS global employer survey report 2011: How employers value an international study experience.* Retrieved from http://content.qs.com/qs/ qs-global-employer-survey-2011.pdf

Parey, M., & Waldinger, F. (2011, March 27). *Studying abroad and international labour market mobility.* Retrieved from http://www.voxeu.org/ index.php?q=node/6287

Peter D. Hart Research Associates, Inc. (2006, December 28). *How should colleges prepare students to succeed in today's global economy?* Washington, DC: Author.

Peter D. Hart Research Associates, Inc. (2010, January 20). *Raising the bar: Employers' views on college learning in the wake of the economic downturn.* Washington, DC: Author.

Rediff India Abroad. (2008, May 16). *Only 39.5% Indian graduates employable.* Retrieved from http://www.rediff.com/money/2008/may/16job .htm

Salt, B. (2008, September). *The global skills convergence: Issues and ideas for the management of an international workforce.* Geneva: KPMG International.

Schumpeter (blog). (2011, June 11). Tutors to the world: Business schools are globalizing at a furious pace—which is largely a good thing. *The Economist.* Retrieved March 21, 2012, from http://www.economist.com/node/18802722

Spitzberg, B., & Changnon, G. (2009). Conceptualizing intercultural competence. In D. Deardorff (Ed.), *The SAGE handbook of intercultural competence* (pp. 2–52). Thousand Oaks, CA: Sage.

Tillman, M. (2005, August). The right tool for the job. *International Education.* Washington, DC: NAFSA: Association of International Educators, Retrieved from http://www.nafsa.org/_/File/_/ therighttool.pdf.

Tillman, M. (2011, June). *AIFS student guide to study abroad and career development.* Stamford, CT: American Institute for Foreign Study. Retrieved from http://clscholarship.org/files/Tillman _AIFS_Student_Guide_Career.pdf.

Wheeler, D. (2011, July 8). Global companies want universities to help scoop up student talent. *Chronicle of Higher Education.* Retrieved from http://chronicle.com/blogs/worldwise/global -companies-want-universities-to-help-scoop -up-student-talent/28448

Williamson, W. (2011, June 23). The quest for collaboration in study abroad. *Chronicle of Higher Education.* Retrieved from http:// chronicle.com/article/The-Quest-for -Collaboration-in/12798.

12

INTERNATIONAL STUDENT SECURITY

SIMON MARGINSON

I nternational students have different lives than the students who are citizens of the nations where they are educated. The international student experience is mediated by noncitizen outsider status, the often-related fact of cultural difference, and often-associated problems of information asymmetry and communication difficulty.

International students face many issues as students and as human beings, inside and outside the classroom. These issues can be defined as matters of *international student security,* the topic of this chapter. They range from novel requirements in relation to academic and administrative systems, to dealings with unfamiliar government authorities, problems of language proficiency and intercultural relations, loneliness, economic survival, health, and personal safety. Unlike issues in teaching and learning (see Chapters 14 and 15, this volume), matters of international student security are mostly discussed through the lens of student counselling or welfare. This approach, however, typically positions international students as supplicant, dependent, and in cultural and social deficit. This fits easy but retrograde assumptions that international students are outsiders, assumptions that undermine potential for

cultural interaction. Notions of dependence and deficit carry a grain of truth, especially early in the sojourn, but they are unduly limiting, given that international tertiary students are mostly adults in the legal sense. Notions of dependence and deficit also seem anomalous given that pedagogical and welfare programs aim to facilitate the self-adjustment of autonomous learning international students to local requirements. Self-adjustment requires personal agency, which is weakened by notions of deficit.

This chapter presents an alternative approach to international students, which is to define them as rights-bearing individuals who enjoy the same scope for self-determination as local citizens. This raises the problem of how to provide rights to noncitizens, an issue explored in this chapter. The chapter proceeds as follows: First, it discusses international students as rights-bearing subjects and provides an agency-centered theorization of international student security. Second, it briefly discusses the main domains of international student security, illustrating this with examples from research on international education in Australia, New Zealand, and the United States. Finally, this chapter considers how to more effectively provide for the rights of globally mobile noncitizen students, subject to national jurisdictions.

INTERNATIONAL STUDENT SECURITY

Human Agency and Security

What is meant by *security*? The term is variously discussed in sociology, cultural studies, and international relations. It often carries a connotation of protection and preservation; yet, for mobile students, it also involves the capacity to cope with new requirements. Religious traditions have differing understandings of security. Islam balances individual motivation with cooperation and mutual responsibility, social justice, and equity. Liberal Christianity calls on the charity of individuals, especially leaders, to provide what is needed for security. State security practices take different meanings according to traditions and attitudes. In English-speaking countries influenced by neoliberal values, personal effort makes security. Europeans are more inclined to see the community as a primary source of security. The United States might be seen as spending less than Europeans on the security needs of citizens but more than Europeans on the security of the state. Chinese people maintain a strong belief in the need for the state to provide social protection. All these traditions are at play in international education.

Contemporary notions of human security are also partly shaped by the global agencies with responsibility for peace, refugees, and poverty relief. At the United Nations, *human security* suggests an individual "made secure from two basic kinds of threats: freedom from fear and freedom from want" (Nesadurai, 2005, p. 9). The *1994 Human Development Report* formalizes human security as "protection from sudden and hurtful disruptions in the patterns of daily life; whether in homes, jobs or in communities" and "safety from chronic threats such as hunger, disease and repression" (UN Development Program, 1994, p. 23). This notion encompasses security relating to food, health, safety of the person, and the economic and political order. It is defensive in relation to risk but proactive in economics. Yet, there is more to security than this.

In *Development as Freedom* (2000), Amartya Sen discusses the intersection of human agency, security, and social and economic development.

For Sen, free self-responsible human agents, in charge of their own identity and values, are the prior condition of economic and social evolution (Sen, 2000, pp. 287–288). "Any affirmation of social responsibility that *replaces* individual responsibility cannot but be, to varying extents, counterproductive" (p. 283), he says. Nevertheless, the capacity to exercise individual responsibility cannot be taken for granted. It depends on social conditions, including policies, education, democratic political participation, and human rights (pp. 284, 288). Collective policies, in turn, are shaped by norms of individual freedom. For Sen (1985, 1992), free agency embodies three elements. The first is an active human will and conscious identity, the seat of self-directed activity, which Sen calls *agency freedom*. The second is freedom from external threat or constraint, which Sen calls *control freedom* and others call *negative freedom*. The third, freedom as the capacity to act, Sen calls *effective freedom* or *freedom as power*, and others call it *positive freedom*. Control freedom and effective freedom are the defensive and proactive moments of agency.

Sen's approach fosters a broad understanding of human security as shaped both by individual freedoms and social relations and arrangements. Once we admit human agency as constructive of social practices *and* vice versa, we circumvent the barren either/or argument of individual versus social responsibility, although the individual-society balance can be fixed in differing ways. Human agency is both product and producer of human security. International students make their own security, in circumstances that they do not entirely control, including the scope for agency itself. This includes the rights regime in which agency is nested. State policy and regulation, institutional management, the civil and private sphere—all influence the practices of security and the potentials of students as agents. International students may affect the wider setting in which their rights and responsibilities are defined, even as temporary residents. The more they can do so, the more their security is advanced. "Basic civil rights and political freedoms are indispensable for the emergence of social values," as Sen (2000, p. 287) explains. "The freedom to participate in critical evaluation and the process of value formation is among the most crucial freedoms of social existence."

In sum, international student security lies in the maintenance of a stable capacity for self-determining human agency. *Maintenance* and *stable capacity* capture the defensive and protective element that is part of security. Here protection is not an end in itself but one of the conditions essential to active human agency. The term *self-determining human agency* offers scope for variation in identity and values and for the subjective element of self-defined needs that must be part of any humanist construct of human security. At the same time, a capacity for stable agency is only guaranteed within a human rights regime that encompasses all people. International student security and student rights are interdependent.

International Students as Bearers of Human Rights

It is widely understood that all people are normed as bearers of comprehensive human rights and entitlements to human security. Most national governments have signed the 1948 United Nations (UN) *Universal Declaration of Human Rights* (UN, 2010). It provides for the rights of self-determining people in a broad set of domains including personal safety and privacy; access to justice and equal recognition before the law; freedom of movement and expression; and "economic, social and cultural rights" including access to social security, to work in "just and favourable" conditions, and to education and health care. Article 28 states: "Everyone is entitled to a social and international order in which the rights and freedoms set forth in this Declaration can be fully realized." All people, wherever located, are entitled to live under a regime enabling them to exercise self-determination, in which they are not just nominal but effective rights-bearers.

If effective and stable human agency rests on both control freedom and effective freedom, to be the self-determining people envisioned by the UN Declaration, international students require security from want and coercion while sustaining the capability (Sen, 2000) to act on their own behalf. These are the ultimate measuring sticks of international student rights and security. By definition, on the soil of any nation that signs the UN Declaration, universal human rights must apply to noncitizens as well as citizens. The principle is shattered if confined to selected people or groups. Taylor (1988) notes it is "utterly wrong and unfounded to draw the boundaries of respect and concern for others "any narrower than the whole human race" (pp. 6–7). But for mobile students, self-determining agency and rights are closely affected by the conditions provided by host governments and institutions.

Specific Conditions

For international students, there are four corollaries. First, student rights and security are affected by the degree of tolerance and scope for expression of cultural difference. Second, many international students speak languages other than the official language(s) of the host nation. Language proficiency is key to effective agency. Third, most international students experience information asymmetry in their relationship with host-country education institutions. Access to knowledge, information, and communicative resources are crucial to self-determining agency. Among the tests of the host country in its provision of international student security are the extent of intercultural tolerance, access to language learning, and access to the necessary information. Finally, the exercise of security and rights is not solely dependent on formal law and regulation, policy, and institutional programs. It is also affected by what happens in the private and informal sphere.

National jurisdictions differ markedly in the manner in which they define and position international students, the extent to which they provide formal rights, and the extent to which they differentiate the conditions of international and local students.

Those nations that regulate international education as a commercial industry, led by the United Kingdom, Australia, and New Zealand, position international students as consumers of a business service and provide for consumer rights (see Box 12.1). Students are entitled to certain kinds of information prior to signing a contract, and they are protected from fraud and default, but they are not provided with civil, political, or industrial rights. Consumer power is far-reaching in one respect, in that it is freely extended to noncitizens, but limited in that it imagines the person in terms of only one kind of right. For example, in its detailed national legislation on international education, Australia says little about mandated rights to student services.

Most international students experience asymmetry of treatment, in that their defined entitlements are different from (and mostly inferior to) those applying to local students. In 2008, a study was conducted that compared the rights and entitlements of international and local students in Australia (Marginson, Nyland, Sawir, & Forbes-Mewett, 2010, pp. 17–20). The position of international students was inferior in 28 domains. Nearly all forms of public financial support, including public welfare and finance for housing, were inaccessible to them. In the two largest Australian states, they paid full fares on public transport while local students paid concession rates. Public schooling was free for locals, but most internationals paid full-cost fees for student children. International students received less financial support from universities but paid higher tuition. Not all postgraduate research scholarships were available to them. Bank services were attenuated. Both groups had access to health coverage, but internationals were excluded from the public Medicare scheme and had to take out private insurance, which was more costly than the Medicare levy paid by locals via taxation. During semester, international students could work for only 20 hours per week, while local students had unrestricted rights to work. International students from certain countries faced implied restrictions on political activity. Their visas included Condition 8303: "You must not become involved in any activities that are disruptive to, or in violence threaten harm to, the Australian community or a group within the Australian community." Only some international students were restricted in this way, and their selection appeared arbitrary. Boxes 12.1 and 12.2 provide information on the frameworks for consumer protection developed in Australia and in New Zealand.

BOX 12.1 Consumer protection jurisdictions in Australia

In 2008, Australia enrolled 230,635 onshore international tertiary students; New Zealand had 59,636 (Organization for Economic Cooperation and Development [OECD], 2010). Both nations pursue commercial international education designed to generate export revenues. Between 2008 and 2010, education was the third-largest export in Australia (Australian Bureau of Statistics, 2011) and fifth largest in New Zealand (Education New Zealand, 2011). Both nations defined international students as economic consumers with consumer rights.

International education in Australia was governed by the Education Services for Overseas Students (ESOS) Act and its *National Code of Practice* (Department of Education, Employment, and Workplace Relations [DEEWR], 2007). Government devolved responsibility for student security to providers. There was no contract between students and government and no reference to political representation. The act and code emphasized the obligations of educational providers in immigration law compliance and consumer protection (DEEWR, 2007). The notion of student as consumer was used only for international students, not local students. The provider entered into a written agreement with the student, specifying program of study, monies payable, and "information in relation to refunds of course money." Marketing had to provide information "of a high standard, clear and unambiguous, so that intending students and their parents can make informed decisions about their preferred provider and course." Consumers received "information about the course, fees, facilities, services and resources offered by the registered provider prior to enrolment," as well as data on the cost of living and housing options. Providers could not offer "false or misleading information or advice" in areas like "the employment outcomes associated with a course, automatic acceptance into another course," or "possible migration outcomes." Students had a mechanism for complaints and appeals, but an independent external body was not required.

The code was less detailed about service delivery and student support. Academic staffing had to be adequate with "the capabilities as required by the quality assurance framework applying to the course," enabling variable standards. Statements about learning resources and facilities were similar (DEEWR, 2007). Providers had to ensure "access to support services and support staff to meet the needs of the students enrolled in their courses" and "assist students to adjust to study and life in Australia," but *assist* and *needs* were undefined. Providers had to offer information on "support services available to students in the transition to life and study in a new environment, legal services, emergency and health services, facilities and resources," and "complaints and appeals processes"—information, but not services—although providers were required to offer free "welfare-related support services" to assist students "with issues that may arise during their study, including . . . accommodation issues" (Standard 6, Section 6.2). This is the only reference to housing. There was no mandatory obligation to provide counselling.

The legal framework only feinted toward comprehensive student care. By framing rights in terms of consumer protection, Australia limited potential claims. It was assumed that international students as consumers would regulate standards by making market choices—although, as the code noted, "overseas students usually cannot evaluate the quality of a course before purchase" (DEEWR, 2007). The consumer had leverage only when the provider breaches its contractual undertaking to provide the specified program. This was rare. Beyond the jurisdiction of the ESOS Act there was no legal basis for international student security in the general community, where most of the problems occurred, such as personal safety, and access to accommodation, transport, health, and other services. International students could take issues of discrimination to the Australian Human Rights Commission, but the avenue was little known and proceedings lengthy. There were just a handful of claims.

BOX 12.2 The New Zealand Framework

The framework in New Zealand was similar but not identical to the one in Australia. Student security was regulated by the Code of Practice for the Pastoral Care of International Students. The government delegated to providers responsibility for certain services and protections and supervised them to ensure these functions were carried out. The code set standards for ethical and responsible recruitment, contractual dealings, and requirements for staff training. Information supplied to prospective international students had to be comprehensive, accurate, and up-to-date and had to be received prior to signing. The code provided for rights and processes in educational and linguistic preparation; cultural adaptation; supervised temporary accommodation and advice on later accommodation, travel, health, and welfare; advice on harassment and discrimination; and grievance procedures. The provisions concerning housing, language, and cultural adaptation moved beyond consumer protection to pastoral care. However, the main difference with Australia was an International Education Appeal Authority (IEAA), fully independent of the providers, to deal with complaints from students and their agents. But research on the operation of the code and the IEAA indicated the IEAA was little used. Few international students even knew it existed (Sawir, Marginson, Nyland, Ramia, & Rawlings-Sanaei, 2009).

No national jurisdiction provides for the comprehensive regulation of international students. In all jurisdictions, including those treating international students as consumers, there are large areas of silence in regulation, which make explicit regulation more significant. Informal, extragovernmental aspects of student security probably vary even more. These have been investigated in one jurisdiction, Australia (Marginson et al., 2010), but as yet there is a lack of comparative studies. The discussion that follows is largely about formal aspects of security.

ASPECTS OF INTERNATIONAL STUDENT SECURITY

The social and economic security of cross-border students includes financial means and safe conditions of work; adequate housing; health and ancillary welfare services; help with communication where host language proficiency is entailed; the maintenance of adequate personal and social networks including family, community, and affinity groups; personal safety, including freedom from abuse and discrimination inside and outside education; and noncoercive relationships with government and university authorities. All of these aspects of international student security are essential to the exercise of agency and rights. All are accessible to research and monitoring, and most can be furthered through formal governmental regulation or educational policy and provision.

Language Proficiency and Communications

In research on international students, the difficulties most frequently reported relate to host-language proficiency and communication in both academic and nonacademic settings. Effective communication is fundamental to the exercise of effective agency and the maintenance of successful cross-cultural relations (for a discussion of the literature, see Marginson et al., 2010). For example, in a study of international students at one United Kingdom (UK) university, Li and Kaye (1998) found that communication difficulties and problems of cross-cultural separation or segregation are circularly linked.

> Students who have English language problems tend to have difficulties in mixing with UK students; on the other hand, the students who do not mix with UK students have less [sic] opportunities to communicate in English and are likely to continue to have English language problems. (p. 48)

Such problems affect many students from Asian and African countries who enter education systems in the English-speaking world, Western Europe, Japan, and China. Tests of language proficiency at the point of entry are insufficient to guarantee communicative competence, particularly in everyday speech (e.g., Carroll, 2005; Coley, 1999; Pantelides, 1999). The host nation can contribute to student security by providing diagnostic services at the point of entry, foundation and bridging programs in academic language and day-to-day communication requirements, and academic support services. Evidence from the systems that provide international education on a mass scale suggests that such ongoing support is often inadequate (e.g., Cownie & Addison, 1996; Marginson et al., 2010).

Finances and Work

As with local students, a significant proportion of international students experience financial difficulties, for example, in the United Kingdom (UNITE, 2006), New Zealand (Ward & Masgoret, 2004), and Australia (Krause, Hartley, James, & McInnis, 2005). Some governments attempt to ensure financial support by requiring students to demonstrate access to a specified level of finance as a condition of the student visa. For example, in 2010, Australia required students to demonstrate that they had held $18,000 per year of study for a minimum of 6 months. This constituted $72,000 for a 4-year program. However, this amount was well short of the actual cost of tuition and living expenses, together estimated at $55,205 per student per year in higher education in 2009 (Deloitte Access Economics, 2011, p. 4).

Studies in a number of countries indicate that most international students work at some stage during their studies, and many are crucially dependent on this. Whereas the UN Declaration (2010) provides for access to work in "just and favorable" conditions, most education exporting nations restrict the right of international students to work. Restrictions include requiring specific work visas or amendments to the student visa and limiting the number of hours of work, especially during study weeks. There is tension between students' needs for income and the restriction of their work rights, and as a result, some international students experience special vulnerability. Like local students, some are exploited at work. What makes the international student experience distinct, aside from a lesser knowledge of local labor markets, is their immigration status. For example, in Australia, international students are limited to 20 hours of paid work a week during the academic semester. Some work for longer periods to make ends meet, but students working outside their visa conditions are scarcely in a position to complain to the public authorities about low rates of pay, demands for excessive hours, or sexual harassment in the workplace.

Accommodation

The human security of international students is also affected by the adequacy and stability of accommodation. Practices vary significantly among countries. In much of Asia and also parts of the United States, subsidized on-campus or near-campus student housing is the norm, and many international students make use of it. Culturally mixed housing offers the most favorable conditions for the evolution of deep cross-cultural friendships, an objective common to international students but one that for most students remains largely unfulfilled (e.g., Marginson et al., 2010).

The situation in most of the English-speaking world is less favorable. On-campus housing is scarce—and where it exists it is often unsubsidized and out of reach of most students—and most students find themselves in the private rental market. Studies in the United Kingdom, United States, and Australia suggest students are especially vulnerable to exploitation early in the stay, and some are crowded in same-culture households in conditions often unsanitary and unsafe (e.g., Bozick, 2007; Christie, Munro, & Rettig, 2002; Marginson et al., 2010; Patiniotis & Holdsworth, 2005). The only export nation that guarantees housing is New Zealand, but this extends only to transitional housing at the time of arrival. After that, education providers are obliged to provide accommodation-related advice to students but not accommodation itself.

Health, Welfare, and Counseling Services

In part of Western Europe and the United Kingdom, international students and their families use free health services through the National Health Service; in the United States and Australia, they may be required to enter into private insurance arrangements. In the insurance regimes and in some other nations, there are issues of cost or coverage, for example, in relation to dental services, emergency and ambulance costs, high-technology care, and pharmaceutics. In all nations, there are issues of access to preferred forms of medicine and health treatment—for example, many Chinese students prefer herbal and diet-based forms of care—and the cost of nonmainstream forms of care. On-campus medical services vary in access and quality, within nations as well as between them.

Student counseling services are normally provided in universities offering doctoral degrees but are not always available in other institutions, such as private training colleges. Counselors can have a broad role, from academic development to mental health treatments and referrals. Most international students experience loneliness or isolation at some point during their stay. For most, these problems occur largely in the early months, but for some students, loneliness becomes a chronic condition (Sawir, Marginson, Deumert, Nyland, & Ramia, 2008). Research also suggests that the incidence of ongoing mental health problems is greater than generally realized (e.g., Bradley, 2000, in the United Kingdom). There are no clear guidelines and cross-border protocols concerning financial responsibility for long-term mental health conditions. Sometimes the education institutions carry this cost, sometimes public authorities, often the students' family, or a mix of the different agencies. The literature on counseling indicates lack of cultural congruence between students and some counselors is a serious problem (e.g., Mori, 2000; Zhang & Dixon, 2003). Cultural tensions are also associated with tendencies to both individual unhappiness and physical health problems (Rosenthal, Russell, & Thomson, 2006).

Personal Safety

Personal safety is an emotive issue that draws more media publicity than any other issue affecting international students. At any given time, only a small minority of students report problems. Precisely because safety is an emotive issue, however, education provider nations are reluctant to acknowledge safety problems or take steps to remedy them when they arise, a pattern that showed itself successively in the United Kingdom, New Zealand, Russia, and Australia in the first decade of the twenty-first century.

BOX 12.3 The United States: Information and Security

On April 5, 1986, in the United States, 19-year-old Lehigh University student Jeanne Ann Clery was raped and murdered while asleep in her residence hall room. Jeanne's parents, Connie and Howard Clery, discovered that students had not been told about 38 violent crimes on the Lehigh campus in the three years prior to her murder. A public audit of 25 education providers later found 23 understated the level of crime associated with their institutions. Joining with other campus crime victims, the Clerys persuaded Congress to enact a law in 1990, later known as the Jeanne Clery Disclosure of Campus Security Policy and Campus Crime Statistics Act. This requires institutions to compile and publicly report statistics of crime occurring on and near campus. It also mandates implementation of law enforcement procedures and "safety from crime" policies. Public data generated by the act shows the crimes most frequently reported on U.S. campuses are theft of personal belongings, burglary, violence, racial or hate crime, and sexual abuse and rape. Most on-campus crime is committed by students. The Clery Act is enforced by the federal Department of Education. Institutions can be fined for noncompliance (Brinkley, 2005; Janosik & Gregory, 2002).

The Clery Act is premised on the power of open information to contribute to student security (McNeal, 2007). Information diffusion promotes awareness of risks to safety and programs of student self-protection (Brinkley, 2005; Janosik & Gregory, 2002). Janosik and Plummer (2005) note the act has led to more consistent gathering and reporting of crime statistics. Notably, international student families tend to select campuses with low crime rates (Volkwein, Szelest, & Lizotte, 1995; Larsen, 2008).

Policy on international education after the September 11, 2001, attacks on the New York World Trade Center and the Pentagon highlighted another and different relationship between information and security. Some suicide attackers had entered the United States as international students and trained in aviation in American institutions. There was a spate of hostile media on international students and an observable increase in both hate crime and discriminatory racial profiling of certain students by police and other authorities. In the booklet, *Know your Rights on Campus: A guide to racial profiling and hate crime for international students in the United States,* The Civil Rights Project at Harvard University (2003) noted that Middle Eastern, Arab, and South Asian students were "viewed suspiciously" because of "their appearance or religious and cultural affiliations." This affected not just the individuals, triggering problems from academic difficulties to physical trauma, but "everyone in the targeted group" (p. 2). However, the government did not protect the security of international students from American hostility. It acted to protect the security of the United States from international students.

One month after 9/11, the Bush government implemented the SEVIS surveillance system, already developed before 9/11. This positioned all international students as potentially dangerous, infringed their liberties, and imposed a regulatory burden on universities and their staff (Rosser,

Hermsen, Mamiseishvili, & Wood, 2007). By August 2003, all international students were required to have a record in the SEVIS system. According to Rosser and colleagues, "campus-based student and scholar advisors are required to maintain the SEVIS data base by reporting events in intervals ranging from daily to monthly." A survey of international student advisers found that 86 per cent said that SEVIS required them to focus more on regulatory compliance than student assistance (p. 532). SEVIS was modified only in the last months of the Bush administration in 2008.

More recently, the United Kingdom has been candid in acknowledging safety problems and in providing not just research (e.g., Home Office, 2004) and advisory services but extra policing in trouble spots. Relatively few issues of personal safety arise on campus, although assaults and robberies occur. Most issues arise in the general community well away from campus. International students are most vulnerable when using public transport or walking home at night. Problems of physical student safety intersect with cross-cultural problems of discrimination and abuse. In English-language and European environments, nonwhite students are much more likely than white students to experience both kinds of problem (e.g., Lee & Rice, 2007).

Cross-Cultural Relations

For many international students, cross-cultural issues begin with their encounters with the immigration department in the host country. These experiences are rarely easy and often unpleasant. But cross-cultural problems fall largely on those students whose appearance or difficulty in communicating more readily open them to informal segregation, stereotyping, marginalization, and abuse (e.g., Hanassah, 2006; Robertson, Line, Jones, & Thomas, 2000; Spencer-Rodgers, 2001; UK Council for International Education, 2004. For example, wearing a head scarf renders Muslim women more vulnerable to abuse in English-speaking countries, particularly at times of international military conflict (Marginson et al., 2010).

Many international students face barriers in achieving social integration with local people. This is a recurring theme in the literature. A primary difficulty is that local students often lack motivation to engage (e.g., Li & Gasser,

2005; Rosenthal et al., 2006). However, there are strong positive associations between communicative proficiency, personal agency, and cross-cultural efficacy. This provides international students and their educators with strategic avenues for advancing cross-cultural relations (Marginson & Sawir, 2011).

FUTURE EVOLUTION OF STUDENT SECURITY

There is growing awareness of global interdependence in education as in other domains. However, there is no global state or any other form of comprehensive global governance. A sketchy system of international law rests on multilateral consent; global agencies operate partly inside and partly outside national governments; and a thickening global civil society is outside formal rules. Dual citizenship is provided by some countries but rarely accessed by students and other temporary migrants like tourists, workers, and business executives. Thus, the universal principles enshrined in the UN Declaration are implemented within a multilateral framework in which national government is sovereign and national law, regulation, and convention are the engine of human protections and entitlements. Where national regulation reaches its limit, the application of the universal principle also falters. Thus mobile students are relatively undersupported by the human rights regime. While in practice the application of the UN Declaration is often incomplete for citizens, it is more incomplete for noncitizens. How might this limitation be overcome, at least as far as international students are concerned?

No international protocols specify for governments whether, how much, and how they should differentiate noncitizen students from citizens. Which rights of the person, if any, should be extended to these students? Which services universally accessed by citizens? And to what extent should government provide specific services in areas of international student need and vulnerability?

Mobile noncitizen students have ambiguous meanings for the host country. International students are managed within two conflicting normative policy frameworks. On one hand, international education is a global exchange where the student is nominally valued and welcomed. International students are variously seen to offer revenues, research labor, international goodwill, and future human capital as citizens. On the other hand, international education triggers border anxiety, bureaucratic categorization, and coercion. Officials from immigration or homeland security, perhaps reflecting antimigration sensitivities in the host-country population, focus on the potential expenditure burdens in relation to scarce national resources in education,

health, welfare, and housing; and the dangers to property, life, and national character. It is variously feared that international students will overstay their student visas and attempt backdoor migration, engage in crime, or commit acts of terrorism. In threat mode, the nation-state focuses on its own welfare and security, asserts its own interests as a right, and models the students as outsiders without intrinsic rights. In this mode, it is difficult for nation-states to conceive of international students as (temporary) insiders with legitimate issues of *their* human security and rights.

Double Regulation, Partial Security

International students are affected by two national regimes and the political and legal relationship between them. The host nation has greater practical regulatory power, but the home country is not irrelevant. From time to time, home governments, for example, China, take up student-related issues with the host nation.

BOX 12.4 New Zealand Ignores Student Security and Pays the Price

In 2003, Chinese Embassy officials advised the New Zealand government that they were dissatisfied with the level of attention given to the safety of Chinese students (Li, 2007). China was concerned about the paucity of provision for student safety, the license allowed fraudulent suppliers, hostile media coverage and the racial vilification of Asians, and the number of Chinese students who were victims or perpetrators of crime. The New Zealand government failed to appreciate the warning. It merely referred to the nation's Code of Practice for the Pastoral Care of International Students and stepped up its marketing claim that New Zealand was a safe venue. China's Ministry of Education responded by branding New Zealand as unable to protect Chinese students. It posted this advisory on its website:

In recent years, the number of Chinese full fee-paying students studying in New Zealand is increasing rapidly. The number reached over 30,000 by the end of 2002. New Zealand's limited number of tertiary institutions, its inadequate transport and infrastructure do not have capacity to accommodate such a large number of international students. Most Chinese students are very young and study low-level subjects and courses. They do not have a sense of self-control and self-protection. Therefore, there are many problems with these Chinese students, such as tension with home-stay families, traffic offences, violence, prostitution, gambling, crimes, fraudulence, drugs, kidnapping, and murdering. (Chinese Ministry of Education, cited by Li, 2007)

China was much the largest importer of New Zealand education. After the warning, total international students fell from 126,919 in 2002 to 92,246 in 2005 (Education New Zealand,

2011). The decline triggered research on the nature of the risks affecting international students and how to restore New Zealand's reputation as a provider of safe conditions (Butcher & McGrath, 2004; Collins, 2006; Jackson, 2005; Lewis, 2005; Tan & Simpson, 2008; Ward & Masgoret, 2004; Xi & Ning, 2006). The government moved to strengthen the Code of Practice for Pastoral Care, imposing on education institutions a stronger strategy for reputation management. It even discussed measures to enhance student safety (McGrath, Beaven, Chong, & Eriquez, 2008). But international enrolments never fully recovered (Figure 12.1):

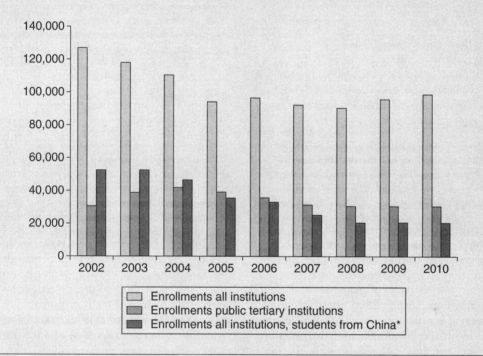

Figure 12.1   Enrollments of international students in New Zealand after Chinese government issued warning in 2002

* From 2006 onward, enrollments from China include Hong Kong SAR. Student enrollments from Hong Kong constituted about 2% of total enrollments from mainland China and Hong Kong in 2005.

Source: New Zealand Ministry of Education; "Levy Statistics" 2007, 2011. For more current information visit: http://www.educationnz.org/nz/strategyresearchstats.

Nevertheless, international students experience an incomplete framework of security and rights. They cannot exercise the full entitlements of citizens in either the home country or country of temporary residence. They cannot fully access home legal, welfare, and political systems. The main point of formal contact is the embassy or consulate, itself a guest and unable to replicate all home-government functions. As aliens in the foreign country, international students have a different and inferior status to local citizens. The exact meaning of this varies by nation. International students are affected by laws concerning aliens, and some nations with large numbers of international students have specific laws, regulations, or programs for them. Status can vary according to nation of origin. European Union (EU) countries grant other EU citizens favored treatment; they pay lower tuition than non-EU foreigners. Australia offers quasi-citizen status to students from New Zealand. Most nations discriminate against particular categories of foreigners in the regulation of temporary migration, for example, in relation to the ease of access to visas.

International education is simultaneously local and institutional, national and global. Globalization invokes the challenge of regulating activities such as education, which cross more than one national space. The rights and protection of mobile persons are a matter of global public good. However, global governance and regulation are underdeveloped. This suggests a new approach is needed to ensure international student security.

What Can National Governments Do?

Individual nations can advance international student security by formally providing for international student rights and by their stance on international education—by positioning international students as self-determining people managing their own identities and life trajectories, defining their own needs and values, and holding the full range of acknowledged rights including legal, civil, political, social, economic, industrial, and educational rights. This can be done most simply and effectively by extending to noncitizen international students the same rights and entitlements as citizen students enjoy. For their part, postsecondary education institutions can advocate such an approach by their nation-state. In nations that hitherto have had little or no policy on international education, the advocacy of postsecondary institutions is likely to have significant impact.

The norm of equivalence with citizens would minimize the outsider element in the international student experience. Nevertheless, many are likely to balk at the suggestion. In most political cultures, the foreign identity of international students is deeply ingrained. It is likely that, in the first instance, the proposal will be taken up by those nations (and institutions) that are commercial exporters of education services, for whom a more inclusive policy has the potential to expand market share.

Note that the idea of equivalence between international and local students does not mean the need for particularized services and supports disappears. To exercise fuller human rights, such services are essential for many students, especially during the early months of their stay.

Global Approaches

Action by single governments is not enough to address this problem. A more global approach could evolve in two possibly interdependent ways: through the accumulation of bilateral negotiations and via the work of global agencies.

The regulatory role of home-country governments can be exercised only in collaboration with the host-country government. This suggests that the student-sending (education-importing) countries might negotiate with receiving (exporting) governments a set of protocols concerning the rights and entitlements of mobile students. These protocols could be developed with reference to the UN's Universal Declaration (UN, 2010), with provisions in student-specific domains such as education, housing, and intercultural relations. If enough such agreements are reached on a bilateral basis, this would create momentum for the emergence of an informal global standard subject to widespread policy imitation. With each nation turning its education system into a more globally responsible space, a regime of international student security and rights could be constructed by an incremental process of voluntary agreement.

In turn, this would create favorable conditions for development of a universal global standard for multilateral consideration, which would be monitored and regulated by a global organization, existing or purpose-built. (Here international education could also lead the development of global approaches to other, more difficult areas of cross-border people movement: not just labor and business migration, but political refugees, and people displaced by global climate change). Up to the time of writing, global organizations have been largely indifferent to international student rights and security. For example, the International Labor Organization (ILO) discusses migrant workers but does not include international students in that category (ILO, 2011), although many nations define them as temporary migrants. Global organizations are more active in relation to stateless people and refugees. No government has jurisdiction over such people, so that nations more readily accept the need for a supranational intervention (UN Development Program, 1994). For both groups, the core problem is similar: the absence, whether full or partial, of nation-state coverage, which has been the customary source of rights.

CONCLUSION

What does this all mean for leaders in international higher education? What can these leaders do at the individual level to help ensure international student security locally? A safe campus environment, mixed cultural accommodation, and appropriate services are obvious steps. On the larger issues, practice can move ahead of regulation by providing for an inclusive environment in which genuine parity of esteem for international students frames the management of their experience and their relations with local people. "Light touch" monitoring of individual students is also needed to anticipate problems of continuing loneliness and isolation, which place some students at risk. Furthermore, much is to be gained by working closely with civic authorities, the police and local government services, given that larger security problems arise off campus, and student movement between the education institution and the general community needs more attention.

Institutions that send their own students face the same set of issues but with the equations of cultural identity reversed. They can negotiate with host-country governments and institutions a set of protocols that provide for the rights and security of those students when offshore and develop information packages that are nuanced to the conditions of each study abroad site. These measures would also set useful precedents for the handling of student flows in the opposite direction.

Global mobility is increasing. The number of international students is expanding (Organization for Economic Cooperation and Development, 2010) and in future, there will be a marked increase in other mobile people also. Ultimately, cross-border people movement will have to be managed via a multilateral or global approach. No one nation can solve this problem. No one educational institution through its own practices alone is sufficient to solve it. But all can contribute to the change in values and in practices that is needed.

Ultimately, it will be necessary to denationalize, globalize, and humanize international student rights. The bedrock of a global student rights regime is not national interest, but a global humanism in which every person is understood as a self-determining subject and worthy of equal respect.

REFERENCES

Australian Bureau of Statistics. (2011). *International trade in services by country, by state and by detailed services category, financial year 2009–10.* Canberra: Author.

Bozick, R. (2007). Making it through the first year of college: The role of students' economic resources, employment, and living arrangements. *Sociology of Education, 80,* 261–285.

Bradley, G. (2000). Responding effectively to the mental health needs of international students. *Higher Education, 39,* 417–433.

Brinkley, W. (2005). *The Clery Act: An examination of the Clery Act and the influence of the Clery Act on crime statistics reported by four year colleges and universities.* Doctoral dissertation, Central Missouri State University.

Butcher, A., & McGrath, T. (2004). International students in New Zealand: Needs and responses. *International Education Journal, 5,* 540–551.

Carroll, J. (2005). Lightening the load: Teaching in English, learning in English. In J. Carroll & J. Ryan (Eds), *Teaching international students* (pp. 35–42). London: Routledge.

Christie, H., Munro, M., & Rettig, H. (2002). Accommodating students. *Journal of Youth Studies, 5,* 209–235.

The Civil Rights Project at Harvard University. (2003). *Know your rights on campus: A guide on racial profiling, and hate crime for international students in the United States.* Cambridge, MA: Author.

Coley, M. (1999). The English language entry requirements of Australian universities for students of non-English speaking background. *Higher Education Research and Development, 18,* 7–17.

Collins, F. (2006). Making Asian students, making students Asian: The racialisation of export education in Auckland, New Zealand. *Asia Pacific Viewpoint, 47,* 217–234.

Cownie, F., & Addison, W. (1996). International students and language support: A new survey. *Studies in Higher Education 21,* 221–231.

Deloitte Access Economics. (2011). *Broader implications from a downturn in international students*. Canberra: Universities Australia.

Department of Education, Employment, and Workplace Relations (DEEWR). (2007). *National code of practice for registration authorities and providers of education and training to overseas students, Australian Government*. Canberra, Australia: Author.

Education New Zealand (ENZ). (2011). Statistics. Retrieved from http://www.educationnz.org.nz/policy-research-stats/statistics

Hanassah, S. (2006). Diversity, international students, and perceived discrimination: Implications for educators and counsellors. *Journal of Studies in International Education, 10*(2), 157–172.

Home Office, UK. (2004). *Crimes against students: Emerging lessons for reducing student victimization*. London: Author.

International Labor Organization. (2011). *International Migration Branch*. Retrieved August 22, 2011, from http://www.ilo.org/public/english/protection/migrant/ Accessed 22 August 2011.

Jackson, J. (2005). Regulation of international education: Australia and New Zealand. *Australia & New Zealand Journal of Law and Education, 10/11*(1), 67–82.

Janosik, S., & Gregory, D. (2002). *The Clery Act and the views of campus law enforcement officers* (EPI Policy Paper Number 12). Blacksburg: Virginia Tech.

Janosik, S., & Plummer, E. (2005). The Clery Act, campus safety, and the views of assault victim advocates. *College Student Affairs Journal, 25*, 116–131.

Krause, K-L., Hartley, R., James, R., & McInnis, C. (2005). *The first-year experience in Australian universities: Findings from a decade of national studies, Final Report*. Canberra, Australia: Department of Education, Science and Training.

Larsen, M. (2008). North American insecurities, fears and anxieties: Educational implications. *Comparative Education, 44*, 265–278.

Lee, J., & Rice, C. (2007). Welcome to America? International student perceptions of discrimination. *Higher Education, 53*, 381–409.

Lewis, N. (2005). Code of practice for the pastoral care of international students: Making a globalising industry in New Zealand. *Globalisation, Societies, and Education, 3*, 5–47.

Li, A., & Gasser, M. (2005). Predicting Asian international students' sociocultural adjustment: A test of two mediation models. *International Journal of Intercultural Relations, 29*, 561–576.

Li, M. (2007, September 22–24). *The impact of the media on the New Zealand export education industry*. Paper presented at the University of International Business and Economics, Beijing, China.

Li, R., & Kaye, M. (1998). Understanding overseas students' concerns and problems. *Journal of Higher Education Policy and Management, 20*, 41–50.

Marginson, S., Nyland, C., Sawir, E., & Forbes-Mewett, H. (2010). *International student security*. Cambridge, UK: Cambridge University Press.

Marginson, S., & Sawir, E. (2011). *Ideas for intercultural education*. New York: Palgrave Macmillan.

McGrath, T., Beaven, S., Chong, J., & Eriquez, R. (2008, December 2–5). *Connecting international students, domestic students and community people in campus, classroom and community situations*. Paper presented to The 19th ISANA International Education Conference, Auckland.

McNeal, L. (2007). Clery Act: Road to compliance. *Journal of Personal Evaluation in Education, 19*, 105–113.

Ministry of Education, New Zealand. (2011). *International student enrolments in New Zealand, 2000–2006* and *2004–2010*. Retrieved from http://www.educationcounts.govt.nz/publications/series/15260

Mori, S. (2000). Addressing the mental health concerns of international students. *Journal of Counseling and Development, 78*, 137–144.

Nesadurai, H. (2005). *Conceptualizing economic security in an era of globalization: What does the East Asian experience reveal?* Coventry, UK: University of Warwick, Centre for the Study of Globalization and Regionalization.

Organization for Economic Cooperation and Development (OECD). (2010). *Education at a glance, 2010*. Paris: Author.

Pantelides, U. (1999). Meeting the language needs of tertiary NESB students. *The Australian Journal of Language and Literacy, 22*, 60–76.

Patiniotis, J., & Holdsworth, C. (2005). Seize that chance! Leaving home and transitions to higher education. *Journal of Youth Studies, 8*, 81–95.

Robertson, M., Line, M., Jones, S., & Thomas, S. (2000). International students, learning environments and perceptions: A case study using the Delphi technique. *Higher Education Research and Development, 19*, 89–102.

Rosenthal, D., Russell, V., & Thomson, G. (2006). *A growing experience: The health and the wealth-being of international students at the University of Melbourne*. Melbourne, Australia: University of Melbourne.

Rosser, V., Hermsen, J., Mamiseishvili, K., & Wood, M. (2007). A national study examining the impact of SEVIS on international student and scholar advisers. *Higher Education, 54,* 525–542.

Sawir, E., Marginson, S., Deumert, A., Nyland, C., & Ramia, G. (2008). Loneliness and international students: An Australian study. *Journal of Studies in International Education, 12,* 148–180.

Sawir, E., Marginson, S., Nyland, C., Ramia, G., & Rawlings-Sanaei, F. (2009). The Pastoral care of international students in New Zealand: Is it more than a consumer protection regime? *Journal of Asia-Pacific Education, 29,* 45–59.

Sen, A. (1985). Well-being, agency and freedom: The Dewey Lectures 1984. *The Journal of Philosophy 82,* 169–221.

Sen, A. (1992). *Inequality reexamined.* Cambridge: Harvard University Press.

Sen, A. (2000). *Development as freedom.* New York: Anchor Books.

Spencer-Rodgers, J. (2001). Consensual and individual stereotypic beliefs about international students among American host nationals. *International Journal of Intercultural Relations, 25,* 639–657.

Tan, W., & Simpson, K. (2008). Overseas educational experience of Chinese students. *Journal of Research in International Education, 7,* 93–112.

Taylor, C. (1988). *Sources of the self: The making of modern identity.* Cambridge: Harvard University Press.

UK Council for International Education (UKCISA). (2004). *International students in UK universities and colleges.* London: Author.

UNITE. (2006). *The international student experience report 2006.* London: UNITE/UKCISA.

United Nations. (2010). *The universal declaration of human rights.* Retrieved October 20, 2010, from http://www.un.org/en/documents/udhr/index.shtml

United Nations Development Program, UNDP (1994). *Human development report.* New York: United Nations Development Program.

Volkwein, J., Szelest, B., & Lizotte, A. (1995). The relationship of campus crime to campus and student characteristics. *Research in Higher Education, 36*(6), 647–669.

Ward, C., & Masgoret, A.-M. (2004). *The experiences of international students in New Zealand: Report on the results of the national survey.* Wellington: Ministry of Education, New Zealand.

Xi, M., & Ning, G. (2006). *Christmas in summer: Chinese students in New Zealand.* Shenzhen, Guangdong: Haitian Publisher.

Zhang, N., & Dixon, D. (2003). Acculturation and attitudes of Asian international students toward seeking psychological help. *Multicultural Counselling and Development, 31,* 205–222.

13

LEGAL, HEALTH, AND SAFETY ISSUES

Crisis Management and Student Services in International Higher Education

GARY RHODES AND ROGER LUDEMAN

This chapter focuses on important emerging responsibilities in international education administration. A key to success in administering internationalization initiatives is to implement effective programs for providing specialized support on campus and around the world while limiting institutional liability.

While some senior international officers (SIOs) at higher education institutions have experience in the areas of risk management, health and safety support, and aspects of student affairs and international program administration, many come from a faculty/academic background that does not include training in practical program administration on campus or internationally (see also Chapter 7, this volume, on SIO leadership).

Institutional infrastructures also vary. While some SIOs have large programs with comprehensive staff and directors from many areas reporting to them, many higher education institutions have limited infrastructure for internationalization activities. In fact, some institutions do not have an SIO, while others have the SIO managing an office with little or no administrative support. In such cases, the SIO must turn to other administrative offices for assistance in dealing with issues ranging from contract development to accidents and injuries, any of which may have serious consequences for faculty, staff, students, and the institution itself.

Operating programs globally offers the potential to confront significant risks and liabilities. Entering into contracts, operating under local laws and traditions, engaging in risk and crisis management, and offering quality student services all require careful planning. This includes implementing effective policies and procedures, collaborating with international partners on their support capabilities, and dedicating resources to enable faculty, staff, and students to respond, both to minor incidents and to major crises that may occur abroad. In addition, special issues arise on the SIO's home campus when accepting international students for degree programs and when collaborating to provide support for visiting international students, faculty, and staff.

This chapter provides an overview of some of the issues an SIO may need to address to effectively implement cross-border programs. This area is still in development. In some countries, SIOs and support services for international initiatives are not expected to deal directly with health, safety, risk management, and legal issues. In other countries, implementing student support programs is viewed as too much "hand-holding," and as a result there is hesitancy to focus on this area. However, other places and institutions have experienced significant growth in the SIO role devoted to student affairs and services, risk management, legal issues, and health and safety. With the environmental, political, and general health and safety issues continuing to impact international programs, this area will grow. Although the documents referenced in this chapter will

need to be continually updated, it is important for the SIO to consider how to respond to these issues and challenges. Because laws, cultural traditions, and availability of resources vary by country, region, institution, and program, this chapter will provide a general overview of the problems that may arise and how to organize the necessary support to deal with them effectively. This asymmetry in the resources of SIOs within countries and across regions, as discussed in Box 13.1, results in challenges for operating programs that meet an appropriate set of standards.

In addition to the wide range in resources available to develop expertise in such areas as risk management, there is also a wide range of cultural and legal traditions that are relevant to this and other related issues. Just as institutional rules may differ from institution to institution,

BOX 13.1 Managing Risk Globally: The Challenge of Uneven Resources

Francisco Marmolejo

Consortium for North American Higher Education Cooperation (USA)

The level of sophistication of the international enterprise varies in different countries around the world. As the executive director of an organization that provides support for university partnerships in Mexico, Canada, and the United States, I see these differences on a regular basis. It is important to pay attention to health, safety, risk management, and legal issues in the internationalization enterprise. It is evident that institutions in some countries have gone far in being careful about issues related to security. While focusing on these issues is important, going too far sometimes hinders international academic cooperation.

In universities all across the world, there has been an increasing pressure for global linkages, programs, and partnerships. Typically, this process begins by designating an administrator to take the lead. The challenge for institutions in developing countries is that many times they need to implement these programs and initiatives with limited infrastructure at their home university and even less support for international initiatives. Without training, information, and support resources, new SIOs may implement programs that are destined to fail. In my work with the Organization for Economic Cooperation and Development (OECD), the challenge of uneven resources was always present.

Regional, national, and international organizations can play an important role in providing guidance to the SIO at a less-resourced institution on differences in laws, administrative practices, and expectations of partner institutions. It is important that national and regional organizations engage in a review of standards for international linkages to provide guidance and potentially to develop reasonable standards for universities in their country or region to help SIOs develop appropriate practice.

United States of America	United Kingdom	The Netherlands
Risk averse		Manage the crisis

Figure 13.1   Risk Management Approaches: Different Cultures React Differently

Source: Birtwistle, 2009.

approaches to risk and risk tolerance differ from country to country. As Birtwistle (2009) notes, "different cultures react differently." To make this point, he presents a spectrum of risk management approaches in three developed countries (see Figure 13.1).

One of the challenges for SIOs is the variation in the ways that universities are regulated in countries around the world. The roles of the federal and regional governments vary, laws for operating programs vary, and the level of the "duty of care" for faculty, staff, and students vary as well. As already noted, the focus on this set of issues varies significantly from country to country and from region to region. In Box 13.2, a South African SIO highlights the differences in perspective in South Africa as compared with the United States.

It needs to be recognized that functioning in environments where the focus is on the main event, the comprehensive internationalization of the university, the SIO's focus would primarily be on the activities that enhance internationalization and not on issues of health and safety

BOX 13.2 Legal Issues From an African Perspective

Nico Jooste

Director, Office of International Education, Nelson Mandela Metropolitan University (South Africa)

On our campus, issues of health and safety for our students and for visiting international students and faculty are important as we internationalize our university. However, in South Africa and many other countries outside of the United States, most risk management and legal efforts cover general on-campus university practices, from fire safety to personnel issues to housing safety, transportation safety, limits on student high-risk activities, insurance practices, and immigration issues. Although our campuses experience issues that provide safety challenges, these risk management issues, as most international campuses are not as litigious as the United States, have not engaged SIOs' time, energy, and focus at the same level as in the United States. We share the challenge that most international offices do: limited resources and the many responsibilities of the international office. At U.S. colleges and universities, there are publications focusing on health and safety issues, which have supported a need for the training of internationalization office staff on ways to respond to the issues raised in these publications. The number of staff dealing with health and safety issues for internationalization offices has increased. Abroad, however, the number of publications focused on responding to health and safety issues is still limited, and hiring a special staff member to focus on this role has not been embraced by universities in South Africa and most universities outside the United States.

from a pure compliance point of view. It needs to be recognized that the legal environment is totally different and allows for a more laissez-faire approach.

This chapter is written from the risk-averse U.S. perspective. Not surprisingly, the interest and expertise in this area has been developed most extensively in the relatively litigious U.S. context. Wherever possible, however, other country perspectives are brought to bear in the discussion. It is the authors' contention that the dramatic growth of transnational programs and the expansion of academic mobility will make this topic of increasing interest globally in the years ahead.

First, it is useful to review the responsibilities and competencies for implementing international initiatives in terms of the support required at the SIO's home institution as well as the support needed to implement programs in the various parts of the world where students will study, where faculty may conduct research, and where joint- or dual-degree programs or other international initiatives may take place. Since international initiatives at home and abroad may require various types of support services, to successfully implement programs, it is important for SIOs to include experts both at home and abroad. As the range of administrative support services varies, in some cases, the SIO's home institution may have more or less expertise and support services than the partner institution or international program abroad.

The challenge for the SIO is that the realities of laws, level of risk, and responsibilities for program administration on campus and abroad may vary substantially by program and institution. A faculty member taking part in a small research project abroad may need little support, whereas implementing a full research project, dual-degree program, or branch campus may require a significant amount of planning, consultation with experts on the legal system in another country, and significant start-up and support costs.

KEY LIABILITY ISSUES IN POLICY AND PROGRAM DEVELOPMENT SUPPORT IN INTERNATIONAL HIGHER EDUCATION

Legal Issues

Higher education institutions are obligated to maintain a safe environment where academic learning can take place. In some countries, such as the United States, legal issues affect important day-to-day activities of campus administrators, and most faculty and staff are aware of their impact. For them, everyday interaction brings the potential for criminal or civil penalties. In other countries, there may be lesser potential for legal action stemming from an institutional environment. In these settings, liability is less of a concern.

Managing international activities where these divergent worlds collide is a challenge for an SIO. An SIO from a country with greater legal liability has a responsibility to remain well-informed of program risks to make sure their institution's legal concerns are addressed. The SIO must also provide information to international partners to help prevent legal challenges resulting from program operation. Similarly, an SIO from a country with lesser legal liability must be aware of the potential for legal issues in countries with higher or varied levels of legal liability related to such things as contracts, appropriate minimum standards, housing, fire safety, sexual harassment, and assault. However, while SIOs should evaluate the readiness of their own institution as well as partner institutions to address the emergencies of students abroad, it is unreasonable to expect partner institutions to apply the rules of the SIO's home institution (Lindsay & van Liempd, 2010).

It is a common feature of SIO responsibility to assure that individual programs, level of support, and risk tolerance are appropriate for the leadership of the SIO's home institution. At the same time, when operating in countries abroad, it is important to take into account interpretations of the "duty of care" required at the international location. At the very least, an SIO should be aware that courts in an increasing number of countries take seriously claims against academic institutions and sponsoring organizations that breach their "duty of care" (D'Ancona & Walloga, 2010). In fact, legal experts often remind institutions of their duty to provide students participating in study abroad programs with a reasonable standard of care (Brown et al., 2001a, 2001b).

At one time, only faculty and students from wealthy backgrounds and with a significant amount of travel experience and language skills were academically mobile. However, in most parts of the world, there has been a drive to make the international experience available for far greater numbers of faculty, staff, and students. As a result, more academic travelers have limited travel experience and limited expertise in the language and culture of the countries where programs take place. There is also a growing commitment to send abroad faculty, staff, and students who may have physical and mental health needs that may require special assistance. In these cases, successful mobility requires that institutions offer a broader level of support than in the past.

One of the critical issues in looking at liability in student activity abroad is addressed by the UK Council for International Student Affairs (see Box 13.3).

BOX 13.3 Risk Assessment: A UK Perspective on Liability and Student Activity Abroad

UK Council for International Student Affairs

Question: What liability do institutions have generally with respect to student activity abroad?

Answer: There is the contract with the student to deliver in accordance with the terms of the agreement (prospectus, website, promotional materials, charter, etc.). In addition there is a sufficiently close relationship between the university and the student (proximity) for a duty of care to be owed.

This means that the normal law of negligence applies—a duty of care (acting as a reasonable person acting in that capacity would) is owed; if there is a breach of duty of care (lack of reasonableness) and damage results, then there is liability. This also relates to vicarious liability (employer liable for the acts of employees "acting in the normal course of employment"). There is liability for negligent statements.

The extent of the duty of care an institution has for student activity abroad will vary according to the extent to which it undertakes actively to provide placements, as opposed to sanctioning those arranged by students. The greater the degree of institutional involvement in the placement, the greater its duty of care.

The decision in *McLean v. The University of St Andrews,* heard in the Scottish Court of Session (February 25, 2004) to a large extent confirmed the orthodox view regarding university liability. It is generally acknowledged that a university does owe a duty of care to those it is reasonably foreseeable may be affected by its acts or omissions. The difficult analysis is to determine where the boundaries of that liability lie.

In the McLean case, it does appear to reinforce the notion of boundaries. The university will be liable for that which it is responsible for if the duty of care is not met and damage results. The university will not be liable for those things "outwith University control" (para 10). If a person "removes themselves" from the duty of care, then this is beyond the scope of the duty of care.

Universities will no doubt look at this case, place it in the overall context of negligence, and arrive at the conclusion that care must be taken, responsible and robust procedures must be in place, and a responsible attitude maintained *but* given all of this, activities, placements, field trips, study exchanges, joint programs, and so on can be continued. Normal risk assessment procedures plus a realistic mapping of the boundaries should result in the duty of care being fulfilled.

Source: UK Council for International Student Affairs, *Student Activity Abroad: Risk Assessment,* Tim Birtwistle of Leeds Metropolitan University and Dennis Farrington, following up a survey of institutions about their policies and practices with regard to student activity abroad (http://www.ukcisa.org.uk/about/liability.php).

In the United States, many colleges and universities have full-time attorneys whose sole responsibility is responding to legal issues that could impact the campus. The National Association of College and University Attorneys (NACUA) provides continuing education and research to these attorneys and their institutions through conferences and workshops focusing on legal issues commonly related to international programs. From an international viewpoint, an institution's legal counsel can assist in authorizing partner institutions to run a study abroad program and to ensure that appropriate written agreements are in place with program faculty, staff, and service providers (Hoye, 2008). However, in most countries outside the United States, a university would hire outside attorneys for legal cases and not see legal issues as a primary issue in operating the university. Yet, as universities increase the number of programs operated outside of their home country and realize the importance of adhering to local country law as a part of their international initiatives, the role of the attorney as a permanent staff member of the university or as outside counsel will continue to grow.

It is critical that SIOs work with legal counsel to ensure programs account for potential legal issues. Addressing areas such as entering into international contracts, securing health and safety, and providing legal counsel to represent the campus abroad will better guarantee that the laws of countries where programs take place are taken into account. According to Alexander Koff (n.d.), as universities operate abroad, they should be aware of legal implications of the business practices of doing so (see Box 13.4).

BOX 13.4 Global Issues With Legal Implications for Universities

Alexander Koff

Whiteford, Taylor & Preston LLC (USA)

Universities around the world are increasingly becoming engaged globally. This means that they need to respond to both home-country and international laws. Although they are not businesses, universities engage in work around the world in ways similar to what a global company faces. To operate effectively in the global arena, the senior international officer (SIO) at a university should be aware of international law and engage attorneys at home and abroad in discussions about how to implement international programs and draft agreements. It is less time consuming and safer to seek the advice of competent counsel before producing and rolling out a program than to spend time and energy unraveling a problem created unknowingly by signing an international agreement without proper guidance. Without effective policies and procedures in place, the SIO's actions could result in financial loss to the university and civil, or even criminal, liability under the laws of the home country or the countries where the university operates abroad.

Colleges and universities have led the way for domestic nonprofits to venture abroad. Many such ventures began simply, with a handshake and a signed agreement to collaborate between two university presidents, but the implementation of these international collaborations has become more complicated as the vision has grown far beyond just sending a few students between the universities in different countries. Along with agreements and collaborations between institutions, there has been a growth in branch campuses, joint degrees, international research, development projects, and so on. Responding to the following issues is critical for the development of effective international business practice for universities around the world:

1. Strategic business services
   - compliance and ethics
   - crisis management and public affairs

- international business advice, transactions and investment
- technology and intellectual property
- trade policy and government relations

2. Dispute Resolution
   - alternative dispute resolution
   - domestic litigation
   - intellectual property disputes
   - international disputes
   - unfair trade litigation

3. Regulatory guidance
   - customs
   - export controls, other sanctions, and foreign corrupt practices
   - immigration
   - transportation
   - specialty areas

4. Development assistance
   - fair trade
   - intellectual asset protection
   - legal reform
   - microfinance
   - nongovernmental organizations

Source: Alexander Koff (July 2011), partner and chair of global practice at Whiteford, Taylor & Preston LLC. Personal communication and website: http://www.wtplaw.com/public_document.cfm?id=369

RISK MANAGEMENT

According to Hoye (2008), some of the leading causes of court cases and claims against colleges and universities sponsoring international programs include sexual harassment/assault, personal injury and accidental death, unlawful discrimination, motor vehicle and pedestrian accidents, oversight or lack of medical treatment, and lack of due process or unfair dismissal claims. Hoye suggests that it is imperative for faculty and staff to work closely with student affairs personnel and legal counsel when investigating and responding to complaints of sexual harassment, assault, discrimination, and harassment; they should also be familiar with their institution's policies and procedures for responding to such allegations. Legal counsel should be well-versed in the actions required for the institution to comply with the law, which will also contribute to protecting the rights and welfare of all involved parties. Furthermore, it is suggested that legal counsel review policies and procedures to ensure their realistic application and suggest possible amendment to better fit an institution's international programs. As far as managing the risk exposure of an institution in cases of personal injury or death, Hoye urges that program materials clearly delineate activities that are program-sponsored. In addition, vehicle usage policies should explicitly state restrictions of motor vehicle operation. To further reduce the likelihood of legal claims against an institution, it is advised that programs make use of public transportation or private transportation companies rather than relying on vehicles owned or rented by the institution.

There is only limited information about the financial implications of problems that occur abroad. As a result, at this time, there is not enough data to help SIOs obtain a clear picture about which incidents have resulted in legal claims against institutions as a result of international programs and projects abroad. Figure 13.2 shows one liability insurance

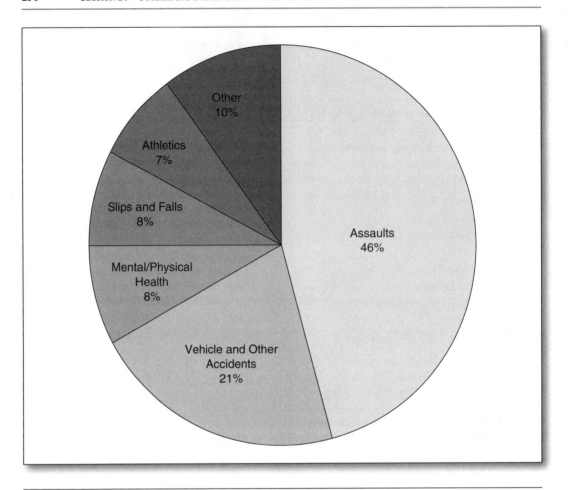

Figure 13.2   Reported International Insurance Claims to United Educators (UE), 2006–2010

company's claims experience for international operations at the colleges and universities they insure.

Between 2006 and November 2011, United Educators (UE), the insurer, processed 61 claims. Four of those claims resulted in a loss to UE (although there may have been other claims by UE members not reported to UE, and they may have been paid through other sources, for example, the home campus). The total loss from those four claims was nearly $200,000. The largest loss, about $130,000, was from a sexual assault claim. This dollar amount includes the money paid by both UE and the home campus (personal communication, United Educators, October 2011).

It has been argued that the main responsibility of an institution is to inform students that they are responsible for their own actions (Lindsay & van Liempd, 2010). In this regard, as institutions implement specialized programs both on campus and abroad, developing standards and plans for safety, program implementation, and crisis or risk management is critical. Protocols must be developed to limit risk in crisis situations abroad. At the same time, plans must be prepared for responding when problems arise. It is important that institutions consider various contingencies when setting up crisis plans (Hack & Bergman, 2010). Overall, effective risk management requires identifying consequences potentially arising from exposure to hazards, determining an institution's willingness to accept potential loss, and deciding how to manage the risk (Lindeman, Mello, Brockington, Johnson, & McCabe, 2005).

At the same time, universities operate programs abroad, sometimes in war-torn and developing countries with special health and safety risks in supporting mobility by university students, a population prone to look for adventure and challenges that may include high-risk behaviors. The SIO needs to be able to accept the uncertainty that comes with operating programs abroad while managing the risks involved. The different legal jurisdictions add complexity, whether in operating joint-degree programs, distance learning programs, development programs, or staff and student exchanges.

Higher education institutions staff their risk management departments in various ways. While most colleges and universities have risk management efforts in place for students in study abroad programs, such efforts may not be coordinated, adding cost while minimizing the benefits of these efforts (D'Ancona & Walloga, 2010). Some colleges and universities have an office with one or more staff in the role of risk manager. The University Risk Management and Insurance Association (URMIA; https://www .urmia.org/urmia.cfm), in collaboration with the National Association of College and University Business Officers (NACUBO), has developed an International Resource Center (http://irc .nacubo.org/Pages/default.aspx) to help institutions develop protocols and insurance support for programs on the home campus and abroad. They also hold conferences and workshops focusing on internationalization activities.

OTHER ROLES TO BE CONSIDERED IN EFFECTIVE SUPPORT

Although legal and risk management personnel are the primary units for addressing legal issues and crisis management, other campus staff serve important roles in developing effective policies and procedures. At minimum, planning and managing crises require working with institutional personnel who are the primary stakeholders in such situations (Hoffa, Burak, & Smithee, 2001). On the other hand, the involvement of other campus staff is necessary since the risks of international travel potentially touch on almost every aspect of campus life (Gallagher Higher Education Practice Group, 2007).

Many universities have a group of staff who review services across campus. A smaller group of administrators across campus may have been brought together to ensure that general policies and procedures support faculty, staff, student, and visitor safety. One of their areas of focus will likely be responding to potential crises that arise, from fire to sexual harassment and assault. One of the focus areas of the group should be the response to issues facing faculty, staff, and students abroad, including faculty or staff involved in research, development projects, branch campuses, and other international initiatives. This group should develop an emergency action planning team for international initiatives. At a U.S. institution, the team's typical membership could include:

- Senior international officer
- Key program administrators
- On-site health provider
- On-site counseling provider
- Insurance representative
- 24-hour assistance
- University international program support team:
  o Student affairs administrators
  o Study-abroad administrators
  o Campus security officer
  o Risk manager
  o Legal counsel
  o Health center
  o Counseling center
  o Public relations
  o President or chancellor's office
- Government/embassy representative
- Student representative

Student Support Programs

Enhancing students' international learning is one of the most important and challenging roles of an SIO. Working to effectively integrate curricular and co-curricular elements into student development is critical to international learning. Although each year thousands of students, faculty, and staff members travel internationally with few negative experiences reported, distance, foreign laws, and language barriers complicate matters in emergency situations (Gallagher Higher Education Practice Group, 2007). Developing prevention and response protocols to limit risk and enhance the safety and health of students is important. The bottom line remains that properly prepared students are well-informed about what is acceptable, legal, and safe. Furthermore, preparation efforts are a shared responsibility between the home and host institutions and the students themselves (Lindsay & van Liempd, 2010).

Students in many areas of the world are more mobile than at any other time in the history of higher education. For example, the development of the European Union's Erasmus (European Action Scheme for the Mobility of University Students) program has accelerated the expansion of such preparation, the message being that student mobility is now for all students (Rhodes, 2011). The more recent growth in the use of technology in higher education, the domestic and global competition for student talent, and the pressure to compete with peer institutions have all led to an increasing number of higher education institutions offering academic study across borders. This flurry of global activity comes at a time when the higher education community has identified the need for higher education institutions and organizations around the world to work together to resolve issues confronting students.

In light of the limited resources available on some campuses, meeting this challenge requires collaboration, cooperation, and increased communication. It may also involve integrating the efforts of international educators who carry out student mobility programs with student affairs practitioners who work with students domestically. In fact, although study abroad professionals face numerous elements unique to overseas environments, many of the emergency response protocols are similar to those used by domestic student affairs professionals (Lindeman et al., 2005). While risk cannot be entirely eliminated, well-thought-out planning, risk management, and crisis management can help make travel abroad a positive experience for all concerned (Gallagher Higher Education Practice Group, 2007).

Centrality of Student
Services to Student Learning

The premise that student learning is central to the mission of higher education—serving students in every capacity, including teaching them in multiple settings—is imperative to the collaborative hypothesis. Regardless of institutional structures that divide the roles of institutional departments and staff, every effort must be made to ensure students are given

opportunities to acquire the knowledge and skills they will need when seeking employment or pursuing advanced study. Some believe that the risks of study abroad are an unavoidable part of the learning process (Gore & Green, 2005). Therefore, discussion about health and safety often centers on what injury or loss the institution is willing to assume to provide opportunities that lead to desired outcomes for students (Lindeman et al., 2005).

Setting High Expectations for Students

While students are independent adults able to fend for themselves, they are also traveling to unfamiliar countries and have limited language skills and travel experience. Both aspects need to be taken into account when selecting student participants and determining the level of support they will require. But ultimately, while programs should feel responsible for their students, students must also be made aware of their own personal responsibilities (Hack & Bergman, 2010). Students are a key in planning, carrying out, and evaluating student programs and services. Likewise, they must also be encouraged to use those programs and services to enhance their learning outcomes and subsequent chances for success during and after their university education. These two principles are cornerstones of student affairs and student services.

INTERNATIONAL STUDENT SUPPORT

International students can significantly enhance and support an international learning environment at a higher education institution. These students bring diversity to the institutional environment and provide for cross-cultural opportunities (Owen, 2008). In addition, the tuition paid by these students may be a source of institutional financial support (Rhodes & Ebner, 2009). In turn, these institutions have a reciprocal responsibility to provide assistance to international students, offering specialized support for issues including visas and immigration, student orientation, cross-cultural training, language skills, housing, lawful conduct, academic policies, and appropriate relationships with faculty, staff, and other students. Some of these students bring with them or develop serious personal problems, making it a primary responsibility of an international educator to ensure that existing programs also serve international students (Hoffa, et al., 2001). In some cases, international students may find these specialized services, in addition to the academic curriculum itself, the decisive factor for enrolling in a particular institution (Rhodes & Ebner, 2009).

For international students, the level of campus resources available to them may differ from those available in their home country. Understanding that these differences may exist should encourage institutions to provide an appropriate level of specialized services for these students to succeed. In the United States, NAFSA: Association of International Educators provides specialized professional support for advisers of international students. In addition, the Council of International Schools (COIS) has published a Code of Ethics for Higher Education focusing on recruiting and admitting international students. The code deals with a range of issues including marketing, non-discrimination, and complaint resolution. NAFSA also maintains a Code of Ethics for International Student Recruitment. (See also Chapters 12 and 22, this volume.)

The UK Council for International Student Affairs, Universities Australia, and a joint initiative of the Dutch government in association with independent higher education institutions in the Netherlands (internationalstudy.nl) have published similar codes of ethics for international students. If an institution is receiving students from a country with its own code of ethics, it is prudent to review whether or not the institution's level of support meets student expectations. In some cases, independent organizations are responsible for the creation of codes of ethics or other standards. In other cases, government agencies may be involved in the development of regulations and ensuring adherence to them.

It is especially critical that health and safety issues are considered before international students enroll at an institution. In Australia, a resource called "Think Before: A Student Safety Initiative" has been developed providing international students safety information before studying in Australia.

STUDY-ABROAD PROGRAM SUPPORT

By 2025, almost 8 million students will be educated transnationally, according to some estimates.

Students sometimes study in other countries as international students with limited or no connection to their home institution. In some cases, study abroad results from institutional agreements. In others, there are country-based (the German Academic Exchange Service [DAAD], the British Council, etc.) or regional/state-based institutions supporting student mobility within a country. In still others, regional organizations like the European Union promote student mobility across the region. In the United States, the number of programs lasting a semester or less is increasing, many operated by nonprofit or for-profit organizations other than universities. In addition, a number of programs are administered by universities outside of the country where the program takes place. When developing and implementing these programs, a critical role of the SIO is to support the academic, student affairs, and health and safety aspects of these programs. In addition to addressing academic issues, program approval processes should also include the opinions of an institution's risk management department and legal counsel to identify health, safety, risk, and legal compliance issues associated with the institution's academic goals, policies, and interests (Hoye, 2008).

In the United States, an increasing number of universities have a staff member whose role is to focus solely on the student affairs, health and safety, and crisis management aspects of study abroad programs. Julie Friend, the international analyst for travel health, safety, and security at Michigan State University, is an example of someone operating in this role. According to Friend,

> In 2006, there were two institutions in the United States with education-abroad professionals whose sole function was to manage health, safety and security risks for international programs. Today [2011], there are 16, including . . . five positions that were recently posted . . . Pressure to "internationalize" the campus, demand for more "exotic" study abroad experiences, growth in programming in areas of the world with heightened risk, the rise in study abroad related litigation and increased scrutiny of international activities by campus insurance underwriters support the development of such positions. Other factors, such as the need for consistency in the management of crises, the increasing

complexity of insurance options, and the necessity to identify trends that may predict political instability support such job creation. Current experts in the field come from diverse backgrounds with prior employment in the following sectors: government, medicine, counseling, risk management, law enforcement, diplomacy, law, and public administration. (personal communication, July 2011)

Study-abroad programs may provide SIOs with some of the most significant challenges in the area of health, safety, and liability. Complicating matters is the fact that no international entity exists to evaluate and accredit these programs, increasing the legal liability of colleges or universities and their partners (Rhodes & Ebner, 2010). Thus, it is beneficial for education-abroad administrators to collect as much information as possible on the health and safety risks of the countries where programs are being managed by outside institutions (Gore & Green, 2005). The role of the SIO is critical in developing effective policies and procedures for an institution, such as setting up a study abroad office; deciding what programs to offer; developing forms and other materials to manage risk exposure for students, faculty, and staff; and preparing for situations abroad that could lead to health, safety, and other legal challenges for the institution. In many instances, these are short-term programs with no permanent office or staff in the country where they take place. Furthermore, more students are traveling to less developed areas of the world with higher risk that demand greater emergency response benefits (D'Ancona & Walloga, 2010).

As a result, it is paramount that the SIO provide support to implement a legal, risk management, and health and safety audit on their campus to evaluate the level of support for programs abroad. After all, the greatest risk lies in approaching an overseas program as though it were taking place on the home campus (Lindeman et al., 2005). What does a comprehensive study-abroad safety policy and process look like? Queen's University (2010) in Ontario, Canada, has implemented such a policy, which states:

> The fundamental premise of this Off-Campus Activity Safety Policy is that from the initial stages of planning, off-campus activities must be

evaluated from a safety perspective . . . When hazards lying outside local expertise are identified, the Policy requires that planners/organizers consult appropriate experts for advice. (See also Figure 13.3.)

THE INTERORGANIZATIONAL TASK FORCE: RESPONSIBLE STUDY ABROAD: GOOD PRACTICES FOR HEALTH AND SAFETY

The next section discusses U.S.-based documents that offer models for enhancing practice in diverse settings. These are important reading for sending campuses and international partners. In the case of a problem occurring on a program sponsored by a U.S. university, for example, the plaintiff's attorney will likely propose that the U.S. campus staff and international partner(s) should have been aware of these standards and have implemented effective policies and procedures in response to them.

Interorganizational Task Force on Safety and Responsibility in Study Abroad

In 1996, several highly publicized health and safety incidents took place. In response, representatives in the study abroad field developed a set of best practices for health and safety and requested that colleges, universities, and study abroad providers send letters to affirm support for these *Guidelines*, initially published in 1998 and later published as *Responsible Study Abroad: Good Practices for Health and Safety* in 2002 (http://www.nafsa.org/uploadedFiles/responsible_study_abroad.pdf). The document begins with the following Statement of Purpose:

> Because the health and safety of study abroad participants are primary concerns, these statements of good practice have been developed to provide guidance to institutions, participants (including faculty and staff), and parents/guardians/families. These statements are intended to be aspirational in nature. They address issues that merit attention and thoughtful consideration by everyone involved with study abroad. They are intentionally general; they are not intended to account for all the many variations in study abroad programs and actual health, safety, and

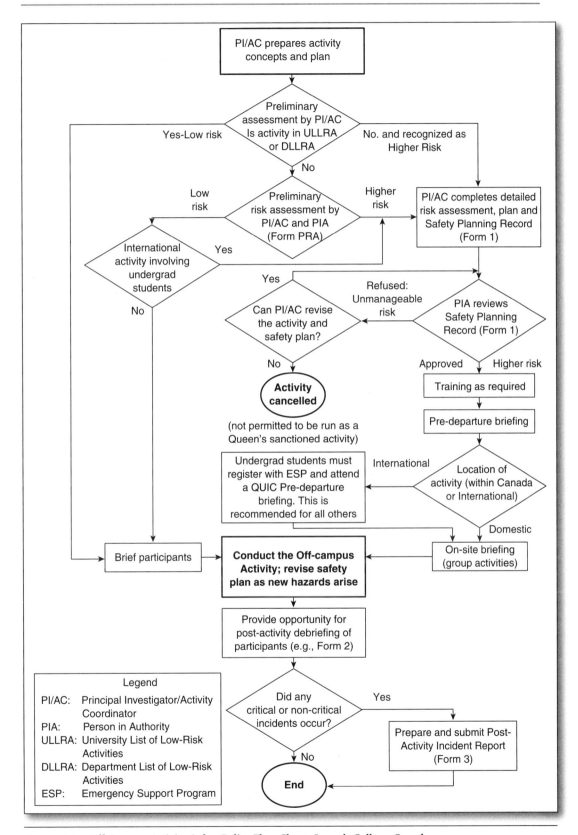

Figure 13.3   Off-Campus Activity Safety Policy Flow Chart, Queen's College, Canada

Source: Queen's University, Off-Campus Activity Safety Policy (https://www.queensu.ca/safety/ocasp/Guide/OCASP_The_Policy.pdf)

security cases that will inevitably occur. In dealing with any specific situation, those responsible must also rely upon their collective experience and judgment while considering their specific circumstances.

Although the language describing the *Good Practices* seems to provide only general ideas, the language in the document itself includes the modifier *should*. As a result, the content in the document does not mandate what an institution has to do, nor is there an organization verifying how institutions respond to the good practices. However, the use of the term *should* allows a plaintiff's attorney to argue that the field has suggested that institutions go beyond thinking about these concepts and *should* implement them. This language thus provides a strong argument for a plaintiff's attorney if they were to review and evaluate institutional policies and procedures since 1998, when the first document was published. The document is presented with a focus on the responsibilities of the institution, responsibilities of participants, and recommendations to parents, families, and guardians.

Forum on Education Abroad: Standards, Short-Term Standards, and Code of Ethics

The Forum on Education Abroad was created in 2001 to respond to the study abroad field's desire to increase the resources and information supporting the study abroad field. In January 2005, the U.S. Department of Justice's Anti-Trust Division and the Federal Trade Commission designated the forum as the standards development organization (SDO) for the field of education abroad. The standards were developed by and relate to many different types of study abroad providers.

The Forum has developed Standards of Good Practice for Education Abroad, Standards of Good Practice for Short-Term Education Abroad, and a Code of Ethics for Education Abroad (http://www.forumea.org/standards-standards.cfm).

Institutions that have undergone a successful quality improvement program (QUIP) peer review of their program or evaluation scheme are recognized by the forum as "meeting its standards (http://forumea.org/quip-aboutquip .cfm). Thus, if a college or university is a member of the forum or accepts students from universities

that are members of the forum, these standards and code of ethics documents could be used to determine the quality of program support put in place by an institution. Parts of each document have health and safety implications connected to effective development of programs and support of students.

The Council for the Advancement of Standards in Higher Education (CAS)

This group has provided standards in student affairs, student services, and student development programs since its inception in 1979. The council has published a set of standards and guidelines specifically for education-abroad programs and services. Individuals and institutions from the 41 member organizations comprise a professional constituency of more than 100,000 professionals. Although many in the U.S. study abroad field are not aware of the CAS standards, these provide good guidance, and health and safety support services could be viewed with these as one set of minimum standards.

Rhodes' Legal Audit of Study Abroad

First published in 1994 and updated since then, the Legal Audit Checklist for Study Abroad was created to provide a framework for reviewing institutional policies and procedures that have direct legal implications. Institutions can use this as a checklist for evaluating study abroad policies and procedures. This document can be used with staff as well as other campus experts to provide a framework for review of program policies and procedures (http://www .globaled.us/safeti/legalaudit.pdf).

SAFETI Clearinghouse Program Audit Checklist

The SAFETI Program Audit Checklist, developed by the Center for Global Education at UCLA, was created to help institutions evaluate their health and safety policies and procedures. The checklist is linked to the Internet Resource Links, which provide background information about each item and samples of policies and procedures from other study abroad programs as well as useful World Wide Web links (http:// www.globaled.us/safeti/auditchklst.html).

NAFSA: Association of International Education Resources for Education Abroad Professionals

This website includes resources for supporting effective program development and administration of study abroad. It includes a wide variety of resources that support health and safety issues (http://www.nafsa.org/resourcelibrary/default.aspx?catId=429104).

The resources here provide information with a clear message to college and university SIOs: Study-abroad program development and administration includes clear legal, risk management, and health and safety challenges for an institution. By working with study abroad administrators and bringing together a campus team to take part in a legal, risk management, and health and safety audit, an institution can better protect itself as well as its faculty, staff, and students. These resources can assist institutions in finding examples of good policies and procedures to improve institutional study abroad practices.

Some administrative decisions are made through local control by an individual university. However, some issues are outlined by government regulations in various countries. In Australia, there are regulations in place for dealing with health care and insurance for international students. According to Marginson, Nyland, Sawir, and Forbes-Mewett (2010), the purposes of the Deed of Agreement between the Australian government and insurance providers are quite comprehensive, including:

> To ensure that the cost of health insurance does not serve as a disincentive to prospective overseas students coming to Australia to study
>
> To ensure that overseas students and their accompanying dependents have access to affordable medical and hospital treatment while studying in Australia
>
> To minimize the risk of personal financial crisis for overseas students requiring medical treatment
>
> To minimize the risk of bad debt to hospitals, doctors, and other health professionals
>
> To ensure the costs of providing health services to government-sponsored students are clearly attributable
>
> To ensure that there is no, or minimal, cost to the Australian taxpayer for the provision of health services to overseas students

> To ensure that a level of service is available enabling overseas students accessibility and a clear understanding of their benefit

The challenge for an SIO is to collaborate with colleagues on their home campus and with representatives of government agencies; regional, national, and international organizations; and colleagues at partner institutions around the world. SIOs must understand that highly prescriptive rules apply in some areas, while in others, a balance must be sought between the rules in the home country and the realities in many countries around the world where programs and collaboration take place.

CONNECTIONS TO STUDENT AFFAIRS/ STUDENT SERVICES PROFESSIONALS

The development of student affairs/student services as a profession within university administration has a long history in the United States and in other Anglo-American contexts. This is largely the legacy of the Oxford/Cambridge "college" tradition in the United Kingdom. *In loco parentis*, an important element behind expanding student services, has been a much stronger feature of higher education in Anglo-American countries than elsewhere (Bateson, 2009, p. 4). Continental Europe has only recently begun discussions of the role student services might play in institutional support. Bateson (2009) writes:

> In contrast [to the Anglo-American context], the traditions of continental Europe are more diverse. European higher education has been influenced in turn by classical Greek and Italian academic cultures, the German university tradition of the 19th century, or the French system of practically-oriented *grande écoles*, none of which placed special emphasis on a "service" culture. (p. 5)

The European mix of traditions tended to emphasize the heightened role of the state in directing the purposes of higher education and the primacy of the professor-student relationship in teaching and learning. All of this worked against integrated institutional support for students' nonacademic needs or even the development of the concept of the "co-curriculum."

Interestingly, the European Union (EU) Bologna Process played an important role in encouraging European universities to expand student services in the 1990s as the flood of international students—that is, European students visiting other institutions in other EU countries—posed special needs for orientation, language training, counseling, housing, and related support services. Although this development remained marginalized with the international component of the institution, recent policies tend to extend this kind of thinking to domestic students as well.

Whether in well-established administrative structures as in the United States and United Kingdom or in new private institutions in central Europe, no other division of an institution has a better knowledge of the changing needs and profiles of students than student affairs. In addition to knowledge gained from working directly with students, many student affairs divisions now include research units that are continually conducting studies and surveying students about their needs and development (Ludeman, 2002; Upcraft & Schuh, 1997). For years, international conferences and workshops have been organized to do comparative analyses of the similarities and differences among student services delivery systems around the world. Early on, the World Conference on Higher Education, held in Paris in 1998, laid the foundation for institutions and countries around the world to ensure that all their efforts should be centered on students and to place more emphasis on exchanges of both students and academic staff through study and research (UNESCO, 1998). More recently, "Putting Students at the Center: A Transatlantic Dialogue on Student Affairs and Services," a 2008 international conference sponsored by the Université du Luxembourg, is an example of an event with this focus. Lipka (2010) has discussed the emergence of the first global organization for student services practitioners and their work to collaborate within tertiary education circles across cultures and countries.

How are institutions dealing with the shifting sentiment regarding *in loco parentis* and parent involvement in their children's lives? What are the social issues facing students—for example, alcohol, drugs, sexual behavior, STDs, sexual assault/harassment, psychological histories, racism, homophobia—and how might these issues impact cross-border education? What are the unique health concerns that are related to studying abroad: prevention strategies, knowledge of health care systems, health insurance, prescription medications, as well as other issues? Student affairs practitioners often have the tools to help international educators deal with these persistent and complex issues (McClellen, Stringer, & Barr, 2008).

Student affairs staff are faced daily with a variety of situations that have potential legal ramifications. In the United States, the Americans with Disabilities Act (ADA), Campus Crime Reporting, Parental Notification and other aspects of Higher Education Amendments of 1998, rights to privacy (FERPA), and the Clery Act (U.S. federal requirement to disclose information about crime on and near campus) all require in-depth knowledge not only about related issues, but also about the requirements to report such matters to government officials, no matter where their students might be studying.

Delivering basic services for students studying abroad includes such areas as admissions/selection, academic advising, financial aid, accommodations, food/nutrition, career and personal counseling, cross culture training, experiential/service learning, orientation/pre-departure information, child care, services for nontraditional students, and disability services. Student affairs staff members are experts at designing such services and adapting them to meet the needs of students in international settings, and doing so based on research (Schuh & West, 2009).

One of the more valuable assets that student affairs brings to international education is experience in assessing risk management and dealing with crisis situations (Sokolow, 2001). Because of the increasing number of crisis situations occurring on campus, these staff members have learned to develop standard prevention strategies and response protocols that could be adapted for use in cross-border education programs. Developing a critical incident stress debriefing (CISD) approach to dealing with victims and survivors (friends, classmates, parents and families, spouse/partner, etc.) is an example of these skills as practiced by student affairs.

Another area that the student affairs staff faces regularly is developing a student conduct code and system that meets an institution's standards while adapting to local laws and traditions found in the countries of program sites (Ludeman, 2009). In addition, student affairs staff can assist in screening students for entry into such programs based on student conduct history.

Cross-border education carries the obvious issue of studying in a new culture and then returning to the home culture. Helping students with cross-culture communication, culture shock, isolation, and reentry are areas in which student affairs could be called on to provide expertise and support (Sue, Ivey, & Pederson, 1996; Sue & Sue, 2003). Helping students reflect on their experiences and learn to better understand the impact study abroad has on their lives is an important responsibility of international educators. Student affairs staff can be very helpful here as well.

Finally, cross-border education must be assessed and evaluated on a regular basis. Through the use of participant evaluations, overseas partner evaluations, program assessment, student learning outcomes assessment (see Chapter 10, this volume, for further discussion on outcomes assessment), and regular strategic planning, student affairs can be an important partner in seeing that these programs meet student needs and institutional objectives (Schuh & West, 2009; Upcraft & Schuh, 1997).

How can international educators get student affairs and other institutional offices involved in risk management? The simplest way to get others' assistance is to make the case for a need to improve the quality of international experiences of students. This could be achieved in part by creating an advisory group that includes student affairs' staff to advise international education staff on a wide range of issues. For program providers not based on campus, it may require creating a staff position to deal with issues related to students and student affairs and to relate to student affairs staff at the institutional level. Whatever the situation, institutions and program providers must have access to the skills and expertise that student affairs and services practitioners are able to provide. Student mobility programs will only be as strong as the expertise to carry them out and the ability of international educators to seek out the expertise of student affairs staff and other experts.

Conclusion

The role of an SIO can be as broad as managing a wide array of university initiatives with a variety of partners in locations around the world. Many universities involved in international initiatives do not have an SIO on their campus to provide central direction to internationalization efforts. The purpose of this chapter is to identify key issues to be considered as well as resources to be used to further explore legal issues, risk management, and health and safety from the perspective of the SIO.

Since potential worst-case scenarios are so wide-ranging, the question of how to respond to potential crises is not a simple one. Between countries—and within countries—different institutional philosophies and legal traditions abound. Currently, no international entity evaluates and approves administrative practices in international higher education. Moreover, national governments have been cautious in developing a regulatory role in this field. As a result, responsibility (and liability) falls to each university, program provider, international partner, and the students, faculty, and staff who participate in international activities. This may include a visiting lecturer, an insurance provider, a housing supervisor, or even the bus driver on a program-related excursion. The SIO's unique role, either directly or indirectly, includes purview over these diverse functions. For this reason, it is critical that the SIO brings together staff, faculty, and students at their own institution, as well as communicate with their international partners, to develop and implement programs supporting internationalization while limiting institutional liability.

The SIO can also impact the field itself. Developing global standards for effective crisis management practice can be facilitated through the collaboration between SIOs and national, regional, and international organizations. The standards, guidelines, codes of ethics, or best practices outlined in this chapter can be used to help develop robust institutional policies and procedures; they can also be used by a plaintiff's attorney to bring an institution into a court of law to enforce compliance and penalties. The latter is true whether or not the SIO or institution took part in their development or agreed with their directives. For the sake of broader, higher quality and sustainable internationalization inititiaves, it is prudent for SIOs to be in the forefront of the kind of collaboration that supports the growth of those initiatives while at the same time protecting participants from unwelcome legal and financial outcomes.

Authors' Note: The authors would like to thank Albert J. Biscarra, MA, doctoral student at the UCLA Graduate School of Education and Information Studies for his support for the research and editing of the article. We would also like to thank the people who provided assistance with the special citations, charts and resources. Finally, we are grateful to Hans-Georg van Liempd, Tilburg University, for his helpful suggestions on an advanced draft of the chapter.

REFERENCES

Bateson, R. (2009). "The Role of Student Services in Promoting Internationalisation." *EUA/ACA Handbook on the Internationalisation of European Higher Education.* Berlin: Raabe.

Brown, D., Buschman, J., Lindeman, B., Martin, M., McCabe, L., Rascoe, B., Rhodes, D., Robinson, B., Stephenson, S., & Wallace, J. D. (2001a). Crises prevention. In P. A. Burak & W. W. Hoffa (Eds.), *Crisis management in a cross-cultural setting* (Rev. ed., pp. 161–174). Washington, DC: NAFSA: Association of International Educators.

Brown, D., Buschman, J., Lindeman, B., Martin, M., McCabe, L., Rascoe, B., Rhodes, D., Robinson, B., Stephenson, S., & Wallace, J. D. (2001b). Introduction to crises involving U.S. students studying abroad. In P. A. Burak & W. W. Hoffa (Eds.), *Crisis management in a cross-cultural setting* (Rev. ed., pp. 157–160). Washington, DC: NAFSA: Association of International Educators.

D'Ancona, F., & Walloga, J. (2010). Foreign travel: Risk and response. *URMIA Journal,* 39–44.

Gallagher Higher Education Practice Group. (2007). *College and university international education programs: Managing the risks.* Itasca, IL: Gallagher.

Gore, J. E., & Green, J. (2005). Health issues and advising responsibilities. In J. L. Brockington, W. W. Hoffa, & P. C. Martin (Eds.), *NAFSA's guide to education abroad for advisers and administrators* (3rd ed., pp. 261–278). Washington, DC: NAFSA: Association of International Educators.

Hack, E., & Bergman, M. (2010, Summer). Better safe than sorry. *The Forum on Education abroad,* pp. 36–37.

Hoffa, W. W., Burak, P. A., & Smithee, M. B. (2001). Setting up an inclusive crisis management plan. In P. A. Burak & W. W. Hoffa (Eds.), *Crisis management in a cross-cultural setting* (Rev. ed., pp. 3–20). Washington, DC: NAFSA: Association of International Educators.

Hoye, W. (2008). *Understanding and managing the risks of short-term international programs.* Chevy Chase, MD: United Educators.

Koff, A. W. (n.d.). *Critical business issues.* Baltimore: White, Taylor & Preston, LLP. Retrieved from http://www.wtplaw.com/public_document. cfm?id=369

Lindeman, B., Mello, N., Brockington, J. L., Johnson, M., & McCabe, L. (2005). Maximizing safety and security and minimizing risk in education abroad programs. In J. L. Brockington, W. W. Hoffa, & P. C. Martin (Eds.), *NAFSA's guide to education abroad for advisers and administrators* (3rd ed., pp. 479–510). Washington, DC: NAFSA: Association of International Educators.

Lindsay, R., & van Liempd, H.-G. (2010). Differences in responsibility. *EAIE Winter Forum, 35.* Retrieved from http://issuu.com/eaie/docs/wint erforum2010?mode=embed&layout=http%3A %2F%2Fskin.issuu.com%2Fv%2Flight% 2Flayout.xml&showFlipBtn=true&page Number=30

Lipka, S. (2010, August 2). Student affairs gains a global hub. *The Chronicle of Higher Education.* Retrieved April 11, 2012, from http://chronicle .com/article/Student-Affairs-Gains-a-Global/123732/

Ludeman, R. B. (2002). Quality assurance, evaluation, accountability, assessment, continuous quality improvement: What do they mean for student affairs professionals? *Thuso– Journal of the South African Association of Senior Student Affairs Professionals, 28*(1).

Ludeman, R. B. (2009). Discipline/conduct standards. In R. B. Ludeman, K. J. Osfield, E. I. Hidalgo, D. Oste, & H. W. Wang (Eds.), *Student affairs and services in higher education: Global foundations, issues and best practices* (pp. 110– 112). Paris: UNESCO.

Marginson, M., Nyland, C., Sawir, E., & Forbes-Mewett, H. (2010). *International student security.* New York: Cambridge University Press.

McClellen, G. S., Stringer, J., & Barr, M. J. (2008). *The handbook of student affairs administration* (3rd ed.). San Francisco: Jossey-Bass.

Owen, L. A. (2008). Serving international students. In K. J. Osfield (Ed.), *Internationalization of student affairs and services* (pp. 49–56). Washington, DC: NASPA.

Queen's University. (2010). *Queen's University off-campus activity safety policy.* Retrieved from https://www.queensu.ca/safety/ocasp/Guide/ OCASP_The_Policy.pdf

Rhodes, G. (2011). Health, safety, and crisis management for student mobility programs. In M. Magnan, M. Soderqvist, H.-G van Liempd, & F. Wittmann, F. (Eds.), *Internationalisation of European higher education.* Berlin: Raabe.

Rhodes, G., & Ebner, J. (2009). International programmes/student mobility services management. In R. B. Ludeman, K. J. Osfield, E. I. Hidalgo, D. Oste, & H. W. Wang (Eds.), *Student affairs and services in higher education: Global foundations, issues, and best practices* (pp. 127–137). Paris: UNESCO.

Rhodes, G., & Ebner, J. (2010). A question of responsibility. *EAIE Spring Forum*, pp. 32–33.

Schuh, J. H., & West, A. (2009). Research, evaluation, assessment, and strategic planning in higher education student affairs and services. In R. B. Ludeman, K. J. Osfield, E. I. Hidalgo, D. Oste, & H. W. Wang (Eds.), *Student affairs and services in higher education: Global foundations, issues and best practices* (pp. 21–37). Paris: UNESCO.

Sokolow. B. A. (2001). Risk assessment in student affairs. In B. A. Sokolow (Ed.), *Instilling principles of risk management into the daily practice of student affairs* (pp. 102–122). Malvern, PA: National Center for Higher Education Risk Management, & Bloomington, IN: University Risk Management and Insurance Association.

Sue, D., Ivey, A., & Pedersen, P. (1996). *A theory of multicultural counseling and therapy.* Pacific Grove, CA: Brooks Cole.

Sue, D. W., & Sue, D. (2003). *Counseling the culturally diverse: Theory and practice* (4th. ed.). New York: John Wiley.

UNESCO. (1998). *World declaration on higher education for the twenty-first century: Vision and action and framework for priority action for change and development in higher education.* Paris: UNESCO.

Upcraft, M. L., & Schuh, J. H. (1997). *Assessment in student affairs.* San Francisco: Jossey-Bass.

SECTION C

INTERNATIONALIZATION AT HOME

14

INTERNATIONALIZATION OF THE CURRICULUM

ELIZABETH BREWER AND BETTY LEASK

The drive to internationalize the higher education curriculum has a long history (see Chapter 3, this volume). Students in medieval Europe crossed political and geographical borders to learn from scholars elsewhere. Then, students internationalized their studies themselves, while more recently, globalization has made it imperative that colleges and universities internationalize both themselves and their curricula. A process increasing the interconnections between nations and peoples of the world, globalization has transformed higher education throughout the world, engaging local institutions, their staff, students, and their graduates with the wider world (Marginson, 2003, p. 2). As those who were once far away are now our neighbors (Featherstone, 1990, p. 11), the need to build "bridges of tolerance and respect for other cultures" (Kramsch, 2002, p. 272) is more evident than ever before. Furthermore, "making higher education [more] responsive to the requirements and challenges related to the globalization of societies, economy and labour markets" has become urgent (Van der Wende, 1997, p. 19). This chapter provides a discussion of the key issues inherent in an internationalized curriculum, which is key in this process of increasing global interconnections and deepening engagement in the wider world.

THE CONTEXT FOR INTERNATIONALIZATION OF THE CURRICULUM WITHIN HIGHER EDUCATION

Internationalizing the curriculum is a response to the historical as well as contemporary contexts of universities and their local and global situatedness. Driven by both institutional and national agendas, motivations to internationalize the curriculum have included promoting national political and economic competitiveness, preserving linguistic and cultural heritage, and facilitating critical and comparative thinking for life in multicultural environments (Yershova, De Jaegbere, & Mestenhauser, 2000, p. 67) as well as intercultural competency for "personal, professional, and citizenship development" (Knight, 2004, p. 22; see also Green & Shoenberg, 2006). Key foci of an internationalized curriculum are encouraging deep learning and new ways of thinking. Indeed, given the small percentage of students who study abroad, an internationalized curriculum is the primary means by which *all* undergraduate students can be encouraged to expand their horizons beyond traditional, nationally focused boundaries and concerns.

While there is no single agreed definition of an internationalized curriculum, the one offered by the Organization for Economic Cooperation and Development (1994) has been widely used:

> A curriculum with an international orientation in content and/or form, aimed at preparing students for performing (professionally/socially) in an international and multicultural context and designed for domestic and/or foreign students. (p. 9)

Curriculum internationalization is associated with a process of constant transformation (Foucault, 1981) and is represented in ways that are both similar and different in different parts of the world:

• The development of "a sophisticated degree of global awareness as an integral part of [students'] liberal arts education" that prepares them "for the highly interdependent and multicultural world in which they live and have to function in the future" (Harari, 1992, p. 52 & p. 53) (United States)

• "A means for Canadian students to develop global perspectives and skills at home . . . (that) . . . makes the teaching/learning process more relevant for international students on campus" and develops the "breadth and depth of knowledge, skills and attitudes that graduates need to work effectively in a more global environment" (Association of Universities and Colleges of Canada, 2009, p. 5) (Canada)

• "Content (that) does not arise out of a single cultural base but engages with global plurality in terms of sources of knowledge . . . encourages students to explore how knowledge is produced, distributed and utilized globally . . . helps students to develop an understanding of the global nature of scientific, economic, political, and cultural exchange" (Webb 2005, p. 111) and "develop[s] graduates who can call on a range of international perspectives in their lives as professionals and as citizens" (Leask, 2005, p. 119) (Australia)

• "It is actually the combination of international content, the international classroom setting and a strong emphasis on interactive and collaborative learning processes, which optimally enables the acquisitions of a wide range of skills, which are essential for work and life in an international and multicultural context" (Van der Wende 2000, p. 36) (Europe)

These examples speak to the connections between internationalization and globalization; the importance of integration (as opposed to adding on); and the need to focus on teaching and learning in addition to content. However, interpretations of internationalization have depended largely on local settings, so that "what may at first appear to be similar policies may end up being quite different practices" (Lee, 2000, p. 329). Indeed, in the last 20 years in the United States, internationalization of the curriculum largely has focused on the development of intercultural skills through the outbound mobility of students (study abroad). Many European countries have focused on outbound mobility within Europe (see, e.g., Teichler 2004, p. 7), while in Australia, Japan, and the United Kingdom, international student recruitment has been both a driver and a resource for internationalization of the curriculum. Much can be learned about the internationalization of the curriculum, therefore, by studying examples from across the world, with the caveat that first-world representations of the subject in journal articles and conference papers tell only part of the story.

In 1997, Knight observed that "internationalisation means different things to different people, and as a result there is a great diversity of interpretations attributed to the concept" (p. 5). The same can be said for internationalization of the curriculum. The discussion in this chapter takes place within this context. Internationalizing the curriculum is both a concept and a process and will continue to be dynamic and challenging.

CRITIQUES

Internationalization of the curriculum has not been without its critics. One area of critique has focused on the hegemony of Western perspectives and the export/import of Western conceptions of higher education and internationalization. Goodman (1984) argued that the dominance of Western educational models defines "what is knowledge and who is qualified to understand and apply that knowledge" (p. 13), who is expert in what, and who can claim privilege, prestige, and elite status. Ashwill (2011) has written that using international exchange to remake "other societies in the United States' image is not only cynical and misguided; it is also delusional," while feminist scholars in the United States have warned against reproducing colonial relationships when incorporating non-U.S. materials into comparative Women's Studies courses, arguing that "the use of truly international perspectives in women's studies courses should fundamentally reframe the classroom" (McDermott, 1998, p. 90). Mok (2007), writing on the internationalization of universities in Asia, cautioned against simply copying Western policies and practices, lest Asian states "fall into traps of recolonialization" (p. 438).

African scholars have voiced similar concerns: Having been disconnected from their earlier African identities by colonialization and structural adjustment policies, universities in Africa need to respond to globalization and internationalization by changing internally so that they can both meet African needs and contribute to world knowledge (Mthembu, 2004; Rouhani & Kishun, 2004). Soudien (2005) suggests that this requires that Africans make critical decisions about

> how much or how little of that which we imagine to be distinctly ours, whatever that might be, we wish to have at the core of the education our children ought to receive; or, alternately, how strongly we wish them to be assimilated into that which has become the dominant culture. (p. 502)

These comments highlight the tensions between the local and the global, and the less developed South and the more developed North, in today's world. These tensions are frequently overlooked but extremely important, in the process of internationalizing the curriculum. There is also an underlying ethical question for developed countries: how to ensure that, while pursuing their own internationalization agendas, others are given the opportunity to make critical decisions about what internationalization means for them, both in the short and long term. For example, countries in Latin America and the Caribbean will need to seek a balance between exchanges with higher education institutions in the developed world and "ties to Latin American and Caribbean neighbors" (Gazzola & Didriksson, 2008, p. 182) in their internationalization efforts.

Other criticisms of internationalization of the curriculum have focused on reach and impact. Mestenhauser (1998) argued that internationalization of the curriculum in the United States had been narrowly focused on projects and programs designed to train a few students as future international affairs specialists, completely ignoring the need to prepare all graduates to work in an interconnected world no matter their profession. He also argued that those involved in internationalization of the curriculum had not sufficiently challenged the nature of the curriculum or the paradigms on which it is based (p. 21). Harari (1992) pointed out that where international studies programs did exist, their impact was "often limited to a rather small number of students with limited repercussion on the much larger pool of students attending the institution involved" (p. 57). Furthermore, despite some successful efforts to internationalize curricula in the United States, "at a national level [the U.S. remains] somewhat parochial, and monolingual, if not monocultural" (p. 56). Mestenhauser (1998) also criticized student mobility as a vehicle for internationalizing the curriculum, arguing that this does not impact faculty practice and, therefore, fails to impact teaching and learning. Indeed, in 1991, Goodwin and Nacht reported that internationalizing the curriculum was less a priority in internationalization efforts than different kinds of mobility (see also Van der Wende, 1997, p. 54). These arguments, as discussed later in this chapter, have led to calls for a more comprehensive approach to internationalization (see Chapter 4, this volume, for further discussion of this approach).

It has also been argued that the use of English as the main language of instruction in international education today contributes to the continued dominance of Western knowledge, has resulted in a decline in the status of national languages, and works against internationalization of the curriculum (Pennycook, 1994). Critics of approaches in the United Kingdom and Australia have focused on an overemphasis on the recruitment of fee-paying international students as a strategy for internationalization of the curriculum, while comparatively small numbers of UK and Australian students develop international perspectives by learning foreign languages and studying abroad. The uneven flow of students between the South and the North is also criticized as a major contributor to brain drain from the very countries that can least afford it, especially if students remain in the receiving country as migrants. Thus, poorer sending countries lose, while wealthier receiving countries benefit from both the home-country government or aid agency funding that has supported the students and the subsequent intellectual and economic contributions the students make as graduates.

INTERNATIONALIZATION AND CURRICULUM CHANGE

A variety of approaches and strategies to creating less parochial and more international curricula have emerged both across and within nations and regions. The drivers for change have varied, as have the responses. Both practical and ethical issues have been raised.

In the United States after World War II, an urgency to add elements to the curriculum that would assure greater knowledge of the world was felt at national and institutional levels (Larsen & Dutschke, 2010). The specter of Soviet domination in science and technology led to the National Defense Education Act of 1958, which in addition to providing funding for improvements in these areas in higher education, also led to the establishment of area studies centers at universities and to graduate student fellowships for language and area studies. Subsequently, in 1972, an undergraduate international studies program provided support for area studies and language study at this level. The area studies approach to curriculum internationalization has been critiqued. Area studies have been associated with cold war ideologies and the use of knowledge to gain advantage and domination over other countries. Many area studies programs lack the theoretical underpinnings associated with the social sciences, and cultural differences are looked at objectively and scientifically (Kulacki, 2000), thematic studies are given preference over interdisciplinary approaches to problems and issues, and, with

globalization, the increasing emergence of transnational issues call into question conventional conceptions of "areas." In addition, U.S. graduates of area studies programs have more often joined the professoriate than business and government. As Szanton (2004) points out, however, "the context of area studies has changed dramatically since the 1940s and 1950s" (p. 30). In dialogue with scholars in the regions of study, area studies have become more critical and much less prone to serving national interests and in at least some cases, allow for a "deeper comparative understandings of U.S. society and culture" (Szanton, 2004, p. 30).

In other nations and regions, World War II also resulted in a broadening of the curriculum to develop open mindsets, international and cross-cultural skills, and understanding in the next generation of leaders and citizens of the world. By the 1990s, however, it was clear that the strategies were reaching only a small portion of students. Organizations such as the American Council on Education (ACE) called for the extension of internationalization to subject areas not traditionally associated with internationalization (ACE, 1995). However, a 2002 ACE report showed that only 8% of American undergraduates had studied a foreign language, and only 14% had taken four or more credit hours of instruction with significant international content (Engberg & Green, 2002). Furthermore, although in 2008 more U.S. college and university mission statements referred to international or global education and faculty enjoyed more opportunities to gain international experience, curricular evidence for internationalization appeared to decline (ACE, 2008).

Since the turn of the 21st century, there has been a growing recognition across global higher education that significant changes in the way the curriculum is conceived and delivered are required if all students are to develop international and intercultural perspectives. Leask (2008) argues that internationalization of the curriculum requires innovation based on

> an understanding of the way in which discipline knowledge and professional practice are culturally constructed . . . active engagement with the diversity of cultures existing within classrooms, countries, communities and institutions . . . the development of intercultural understanding in all students and all staff, the

ability to see professional issues from a variety of national and cultural perspectives and . . . new curriculum content and teaching and learning processes. (p. 23)

Increasing the volume of student mobility, inbound or outbound, will not significantly influence learning outcomes for the majority of students. In response, some have argued that "internationalised curricula are the only way to equip all students for their roles in this world" (Beelen, 2007, p. 4). However, faculty members are not equally equipped to help with this work, nor equally willing.

Internationalization at home (IaH) emerged as a concept in a 2001 position paper published by the European Association of International Educators (Crowther et al., 2001) in recognition of the limitations of student mobility as a vehicle for internationalization. This led to formation of a special interest group and a 2003 edition of the *Journal of Studies in International Education* devoted to the topic. IaH asks that all students develop international competency through internationalized curricula and opportunities for learning beyond the campus, including through student mobility (Wächter, 2003; see also Knight, 2004). In the same period, the importance of the curriculum to Australian higher education internationalization efforts was recognized, resulting in 2005 in the formation of a special interest group on *internationalization of the curriculum* (IoC) within the newly formed International Education Association of Australia. In the United States, educational associations such as the ACE began a push toward comprehensive internationalization; more recently, NAFSA: Association of International Educators also championed the movement.

A key objective in IaH, IoC, and comprehensive internationalization is to increase the engagement of faculty members in its conceptualization and implementation, as faculty members are key to internationalizing the curriculum and student learning (Leask & Beelen, 2009). The need to focus on faculty development, rewards, and recognition to internationalize the curriculum is a recurring theme (Brewer & Cunningham, 2010, pp. 209–221; Peterson, 2000; Stohl, 2007).

The most cited definitions of internationalization link the development of intercultural

skills and attitudes to internationalization of the curriculum (see, for example, Knight, 2004). A recent literature review on educators' preparation to internationalize the curriculum looks at educators' ability to prepare students "for life in plural societies" by teaching for intercultural competence and world-mindedness (Schuerholz-Lehr, 2007, p. 181). Drawing on studies undertaken in a number of countries, the review concludes that there is little evidence that educators' own intercultural competence and world-mindedness translates into classroom practice; it suggests that targeted interventions to help educators do so may be productive. This resonates with the ACE's *At Home in the World Initiative: Educating for Global Connections and Local Commitments* (2007), which asks higher education in the United States to consider issues and commonalities around domestic diversity and internationalization. (See also Chapter 17, this volume.) The Shared Futures project of the American Association of College and Universities (AAC&U) similarly focuses on building a network of educators to facilitate "curricular change and faculty development" so that graduates will be able to both thrive in an "interdependent but unequal world" and "remedy its inequities" (AAC&U, n.d.).

The 1990s also saw institutions across the world focusing on the concept of "graduate attributes or qualities" (learning outcomes in the United States). Hough (1991) proposed that a concern for the common good be one of the criteria for educational excellence. To this end, he argued that universities needed to become more outward looking and community-focused and to foster interdisciplinary discourse that might transcend "individualism, nationalism, and anthropocentrism" as the "the larger issues of the common good are transnational" (p. 117). Such views resonate with approaches to internationalization focused on the development of intercultural and international perspectives as elements of graduate attributes. Those listed on university websites in Australia, Hong Kong, and the United States include the knowledge, skills, and attitudes needed for the exercise of citizenship in a globalized world. Considerations around political and economic integration on both a regional and a global scale have often motivated efforts to internationalize the curriculum.

STRATEGIES FOR INTERNATIONALIZING THE CURRICULUM

Efforts by higher educational institutions to internationalize the curriculum take place at system-wide, institutional, departmental, and individual course levels. Governments, educational associations, the private sector, and nongovernmental organizations (NGOs) also seek to help internationalize higher education. The varied approaches are highly context-dependent and involve challenges such as building faculty capacity to design and deliver an internationalized curriculum, providing access to an internationalized curriculum to all students, ensuring that students' international experiences (study abroad, internships, service learning) result in internationalized learning outcomes and are integrated back into the classroom, and linking institutional mission and policy to the curriculum. This section discusses specific strategies, related issues, and challenges.

International Faculty

The recruitment of faculty from diverse national, cultural, and linguistic backgrounds is one strategy to internationalize the curriculum. However, recruitment on its own is unlikely to be sufficient. Whitsed and Volet (2011) and Whitsed and Wright (2011) examined the role and place of adjunct foreign English-language teachers in the Japanese higher education sector in the context of internationalization or *kokusaika*. They found that while such teachers may seem ideally placed to encourage the development of domestic Japanese students' intercultural and global competencies, at the institutional level, the teachers are marginalized and face a "culture of indifference." Moreover, receiving no professional development and guidance, the teachers' understanding of the internationalization to which they are meant to contribute is limited and highly subjective. Their impact on the university and its curriculum is thus limited at best. These studies make clear that importing faculty will help internationalize the curriculum only if expectations for the faculty are clear, they are integrated into the work of the larger institution, and they have professional development opportunities. The strategy must also be monitored and evaluated.

Faculty Development

Faculty are central to internationalizing the curriculum, yet engaging faculty in this work can be challenging (Childress, 2010; Clifford, 2009; Leask, 2003, 2008; Leask & Beelen, 2009; Sanderson, 2008; Webb, 2005). The range of skills, knowledge, and attitudes required to internationalize the curriculum are many and varied (Deardorff, 2011; Farkas-Teekens, 1997; Sanderson, 2008). Furthermore, the educational reform involved in internationalizing the curriculum requires thinking differently about the universality of knowledge (Mestenhauser, 1998, p. 21) as well as recognizing—and, ideally, critically analyzing—the connections between culture, knowledge, and professional practice. The beliefs and perceptions of faculty are culturally influenced, and the process of change can, therefore, be personally and professional challenging.

Faculty development is critical to enabling faculty members to do this work. To start, they need the opportunity to engage in activities that will stimulate reflection on their own cultural identity, provide them with examples of curricular internationalization, and encourage them to experiment in their teaching. Eventually, they will need to undertake a meta-analysis of the curriculum and to view it from an interdisciplinary and integrative stance. Ultimately, to be effective, faculty development must be based on "faculty ownership, choice, and support," integrated with "other internationalization strategies," and it must reach an ever-expanding "circle of engaged faculty" (Green & Olson, 2003, p. 78). (See Chapter 15, this volume, for further discussion on the internationalization of teaching.)

One approach to faculty development around curriculum internationalization is to assume that faculty will learn from the experiences of international and returned study abroad students (Pickert & Turlington, 1992). Another is to allow faculty to study abroad themselves by traveling abroad individually or in groups (Peterson, 2000, pp. 3–4). Faculty development may also take place in seminars or workshops aimed at enabling faculty to "re-vision" what they know (Winston, 2001, p. 69), gain new content knowledge, and "test new pedagogical approaches encouraging experiential and intercultural learning" (Brewer & Cunningham, 2010, p. 215). International teaching collaborations;

residencies at a university or other institution abroad for the purposes of teaching, research, or collaboration; and travel abroad with students as part of a course or study abroad program are also commonly cited development activities. Ultimately, however, the success of faculty development in support of curriculum internationalization rests on its being an assessed part of a broader strategy, rather than a series of isolated and ad hoc activities with unmeasured outcomes. Box 14.1 discusses a conceptual framework for faculty development for internationalization of the business curriculum in Australia.

BOX 14.1 A Conceptual Framework to Help Faculty Internationalize the Business Curriculum.

Mark Freeman, Lesley Treleaven, and Chris Sykes

Project Team, Faculty of Business and Economics, University of Sydney (Australia)

Lyn Simpson and Simon Ridings

Project Team, Faculty of Business, Queensland University of Technology (Australia)

Betty Leask

University of South Australia (Australia)

Prem Ramburuth

Project Team, Australian School of Business, University of New South Wales (Australia)

There are three core components of this framework: communities of practice; curriculum, policies, and procedures; and resources and tools. The identification of relevant communities of practice and work within and by them is central to the framework and provides a useful alternative to customary approaches to supporting curriculum internationalization. The latter tend to provide tips and tricks and workshops for managing cultural diversity or internationalizing one aspect of a program in isolation. Such approaches encourage a view of internationalization of the curriculum as a disconnected set of activities.

Communities of practice (see Lave & Wenger, 1991) are groups of faculty and other staff who have a shared commitment to and understanding of internationalization. They are the champions who collectively are motivated, committed, and ready to take action to encourage and enact change. Sharing reflective practice and generating new knowledge open up and support possibilities for change. The communities may include individuals responsible for academic content across degree programs, course teams, student reference groups, and peer mentoring facilitators.

Policies, procedures, and curriculum can initiate or further systematic change. For example, a university or faculty policy may require the development of a graduate attribute such as intercultural competence. If embedded in procedures for approving new courses or programs, intercultural competence will be given attention in intended learning outcomes, teaching and learning activities, assessment, and assessment criteria. Alignment of these components is as important as the policy that drives it and the curriculum content that surrounds and supports it. This alignment includes the development of specific assessment criteria for self-assessment and tutor marking of each assessment task. Curriculum-mapping graduate attributes across a program facilitates the

(Continued)

(Continued)

embedding of these attributes throughout the degree. The informal curriculum is also integral to supporting the development of intercultural competence as a part of the student experience, for example, in training to be a cultural peer mentor or mentee.

Resources and tools provide new materials for embedding into learning and teaching new ways of using materials, both in a system-wide approach and in particular curricula. These might include resources faculty can use to assist students to work in multicultural teams or to design, manage, and assess multicultural group work. Tools might include mapping the integration of internationalized learning outcomes across a program using a taxonomy of intercultural competence.

This framework connects faculty with the core activity of curriculum internationalization and focuses that activity on embedding internationalized learning outcomes for all students within the context of the complete program of study.

The Australian Learning and Teaching Council funded the study. More details on the outcomes of the project are available from the Australian Government's Office of Learning and Teaching website. http://www.olt.gov.au/project-embedding-development-intercultural-sydney-2006

International Student Enrollments

Recruiting degree-seeking or exchange students to increase the cultural diversity of the campus student body has been a strategy to international-ize the curriculum in a number of European countries as well as in Japan, Australia, and the United States. However, there is little evidence to suggest that cultural diversity on campus results in, or even contributes positively toward, the development of intercultural or international perspectives in either faculty or home-campus students (Kalantzis & Cope, 2000; Leask, 2005; Wächter, 2003). Two examples illustrate the challenges.

Huang (2006) reports that Japanese higher education internationalization reforms focused mainly on the importation of "Western ideas and practices" (p. 104) until the 1980s, when policies shifted to the importation of students from other countries in response to globalization and the declining number of university-age Japanese. In addition, in the 1990s, Japanese students were given a greater push to learn foreign languages and study abroad. By 2003, Japan had surpassed its 2002 goal of enrolling 100,000 international students. University curricula included Japanese language programs as well as courses in English specifically designed for international students, but these were eventually opened to Japanese students. The curriculum for Japanese students included more international perspectives (p. 113), with private universities particularly creative in

their approach (p. 114). Nonetheless, Japan has had difficulty creating educational programs attractive to both domestic and foreign students (p. 116), and the impact of international students on the international education of Japanese students has been weaker than desired.

In Australia, for many years, the recruitment of fee-paying international students was seen as a strategy to increase contact and positive intercultural experiences for domestic students and their international peers. This was rarely the case (Leask & Carroll, 2011), however, and institutions then tried to improve the international learning outcomes of domestic students. Leask (2001, 2009) describes strategies within both the formal and the informal curriculum, which have improved the international learning outcomes of all students at one Australian university. By internationalizing the informal or co-curriculum, universities can ensure that international students and domestic students, including those from diverse cultural and linguistic backgrounds, learn from each other as part of the experience outside the classroom. International and domestic students beyond the first year of study work in pairs as mentors to mixed culture groups of first-year students. Longitudinal program evaluation has demonstrated increased levels of intercultural engagement on campus, and those involved report greater willingness to be involved in intercultural activities in class (Leask, 2010, p. 13).

Even slight, but strategic modifications made to an existing scheme resulted in significant benefits.

Ultimately, international students can help internationalize the curriculum. This requires, however, an intentional approach to incorporating their perspectives and experiences into the classroom as well as in the life of students outside the classroom. Box 14.2 contains such an example.

BOX 14.2 An International Experience "At Home" for Education Students in Amsterdam

Jos Beelen

Consultant, Center for Applied Research on Economics and Management, University of Applied Sciences (The Netherlands)

The School of Education at Hogeschool van Amsterdam, University of Applied Sciences, hosts an annual student conference as part of its Internationalisation at Home strategy.

"Teacher in Europe is a 3-day conference for students in teacher education. The event is attended by about 50 Dutch and international students, all of whom are studying to be teachers at home or in the Netherlands. The participating students, all of whom are studying in the Netherlands, typically come from more than 10 European countries. One third to one half are Dutch. The language of communication is English.

All come to the conference with the same background information. Students and coaches participate in preparatory online training, including orientation to internationalization and globalization, European educational programs (such as Comenius), and project management. The training also introduces educational and project terminology in (international) English, necessary because most participants have English as a second (or third) language.

The conference starts with a keynote talk, followed by an ice-breaker activity. Students then work in multicountry groups to develop a proposal for an international project for a secondary school. They explore different European educational systems as part of this process while being coached by former participants as well as Dutch and other European educators, who find the activity contributes to the development of their international perspectives. The dinner for coaches and speakers has become a popular tradition.

Short plenary instruction lectures focus on handling project management, budgeting, and making a convincing PowerPoint presentation. Halfway through the conference, the groups present their preliminary proposal to the coaches. At the end, they give PowerPoint presentations and receive feedback from coaches, other specialists, and the students.

The conference is a pressure cooker. The students meet for the first time at the conference and start working together almost immediately. Many students are unfamiliar with project-based work or the task of distinguishing aims, goals, and objectives. In addition, they have to use a second language to communicate with students from quite diverse educational traditions.

Financing by the European Platform for Dutch Education supports good quality catering, facilities, and hotel rooms. Students appreciate this professional atmosphere and feel challenged to perform well.

After the conference, they upload a personal evaluation report to a Moodle-based platform, which they can also use to stay in touch. Teacher in Europe is an intensive international experience for both students and coaches.

Study Abroad

The term *study abroad* is generally understood as credit-bearing undergraduate study in another country incorporated into degree studies at the home university. The form of study abroad varies and includes enrollment in universities abroad as fee-paying or exchange students, courses taught by a faculty member from the home institution who accompanies the students abroad, courses designed for study abroad students by educational organizations, and combinations of these. Exchanges are the dominant form of study abroad in many parts of the world, although in the United States, study abroad has increasingly taken the form of programs designed specifically for study abroad students. These programs may not have any connection to universities in the countries in which they take place. With long historical antecedents, formal study abroad is generally said to have emerged in the United States in the early 20th century, when eight students from Delaware College spent their junior year in France.

Engle and Engle (2003) distinguish between "culture-based" study abroad and "knowledge-transfer" (p. 4) study abroad, the latter often involving science and information exchange. Knowledge transfer may have been a goal from the beginning of modern study abroad (Gore, 2005). However, into the 1990s, students could find it difficult to earn credit toward the major in disciplines outside those traditionally associated with study abroad such as language, literature, history, and area studies (see Carlson, Burn, Useem, & Yachimowicz, 1990; Pickert & Turlington, 1992). Nevertheless, the potential of study abroad to internationalize the curriculum was being acknowledged. In the 1990s, President Peter McPherson of Michigan State University made a bold move to massively increase study abroad to reshape the university's curriculum.

Within the European Higher Education Area, the Bologna Process has aimed to "ensure more comparable, compatible, and coherent systems of higher education in Europe" (The Official Bologna Process website, http://www.ehea .info/). Forty-seven countries are participating in the process, and the model has been made available to other countries and world regions. The European Credit Transfer and Accumulation System has greatly increased study abroad on the part of European students by easing recognition of credit earned at other European universities. Offering curricula in a major European language has also been a strategy to overcome barriers to mobility when the host-country language is less commonly known. Credit transfer has also been vital to increasing study abroad enrollments in the United States, as well as providing access across the disciplines, although the decentralization of U.S. education makes this an institutional and organizational effort rather than governmental. In the 1990s, the University of Minnesota embarked on an initiative to assure that study abroad would be possible across the institution. Academic departments were asked to identify study abroad courses that could earn credit toward their majors (see Paige, 2003; University of Minnesota, 2011). Other U.S. institutions have since adapted the Minnesota model to their needs, resources, and institutional cultures (Van Deusen, 2007). ACE and NAFSA have also promoted study abroad integration. Articulation agreements allowing students to earn dual degrees at two different institutions are increasing; the partner universities identify courses of study that will integrate well with each other. (See Chapter 10, this volume, for more on this topic.)

Earning credit for study abroad is one way for students to integrate study abroad into their education. However, knowledge transfer is no longer the only goal of study abroad; another goal is cultural learning as preparation for living and working in today's globalized world. Yet simply studying in another country may not advance intercultural learning. Furthermore, knowledge transfer rests on the ability of students to successfully negotiate the host institutions' educational systems. Two different, but not incompatible approaches to yielding more robust learning outcomes are to provide interventions before, during, and after the study abroad experience for participating students (see, e.g., Deardorff, 2008; Engle & Engle, 2002; Savicki, 2008; Vande Berg, 2007), and to modify the home-campus curriculum to better equip students for study abroad as well as integrate it into their ongoing studies upon return (see Brewer & Cunningham, 2010). Research on intercultural development suggests that gains are greater during study abroad when interventions (experiential learning, structured reflection, opportunities to engage with host nationals) are provided (Paige & Goode, 2009; Vande Berg, 2007).

Study-abroad students frequently report that most of their learning takes place outside the classroom; scholarship supports this view. Increasingly, therefore, higher education is aiming to teach students how to learn both in and outside the classroom. The Bologna Process, to take one example, is now focusing on "the teaching mission of higher education institutions and the necessity for ongoing curricular reform geared toward the development of learning outcomes" and asking "higher education institutions to pay particular attention to improving the teaching quality of their study programmes at all levels" (European Higher Education Area, n.d.; Labi, 2011). Hong Kong has recently moved from a 3-year university education model to a 4-year model, in part to make study abroad possible for more students but also to introduce general education and encourage more service learning; these can lead to lifelong learning and contributions to society. This supports the notion that for study abroad to help internationalize the curriculum, students must be prepared and assisted to take advantage of the learning opportunities both in and outside the classroom.

Other efforts to use study abroad to internationalize the curriculum focus on the role of faculty. Faculty members who accompany students abroad to teach them on-site claim that this helps them incorporate content from other places into their teaching while also giving them insight into the cultural dimensions involved in locating teaching and learning abroad. Professional schools are creating opportunities for students to spend a portion of their studies abroad; nursing and medical students, for example, are undertaking rotations in other countries. Yet another possibility is for the faculty to remain at home but supervise students' work abroad (see, e.g., Brown University, 2010; Youd, 2010). Technology can bring study abroad students into the classroom on the home campus; Skype and blogging enable study abroad students to report from their host sites on topics under discussion on the home campus (Ellett, 2010). Electronic course management systems and video conferencing enable faculty members in different countries to collaborate in their teaching by connecting their classrooms (Ellett, Kiwuwa, & Roberts, 2009). However, these activities can be difficult to undertake if institutions are unable or unwilling to invest in the technology to support them, or if they do not value this kind activity as part of faculty members' responsibilities. Another challenge is that faculty may not feel comfortable taking on the role of integrating study abroad into their teaching, or that study abroad may be seen as falling under the responsibility of an administrative unit, not the faculty (Brewer & Cunningham, 2010, p. xv). Nevertheless, examples of faculty engagement with study abroad are emerging and have been fostered by engagement with such initiatives as the ACE's Internationalization Collaborative (see Brewer & Cunningham, 2010). Foundations such as the Andrew W. Mellon Foundation as well as disciplinary organizations are seeking to support such efforts.

What is the evidence that study abroad impacts the curriculum? Credit transfer is one measure used to analyze the impact on a variety of levels, ranging from an individual student's studies to departmental, institutional, system, and national levels. However, credit transfer does not get at the larger questions of learning outcomes, and therefore, increasingly there are attempts to set learning goals for study abroad and to measure their outcomes (see Chapters 10 and 16, this volume, for further discussion). More than 100 different assessment tools have been developed to assess aspects of intercultural and global learning (Deardorff, 2009). Beyond pre-post measures, assessment efforts include gathering information about students' activities post-study abroad, such as changes in grade point average, senior theses related to the study abroad experience, presentations, civic engagement, and postundergraduate study and careers. Another method is to embed assessment into course assignments as well as post-study abroad reflection essays. The outcomes of study abroad are also being made visible to wider audiences: Student writing about study abroad is sometimes attached to college and university websites, as are digital films about the study abroad experience. Other forms of visible assessment include public presentations, exhibits, and symposia devoted to learning that takes place abroad (Berzon, n.d.).

Ultimately, study abroad can serve as a vehicle for internationalizing the curriculum, but only if study abroad is approached intentionally and faculty are prepared to facilitate the integration of the study abroad experience into the curriculum. Furthermore, action is necessary not only at the individual student and faculty member level, but also at departmental and institutional levels, and, where educational systems permit, governmental levels.

Disciplinary and Interdisciplinary Approaches

Examples of curriculum internationalization could be drawn from most if not all disciplinary and interdisciplinary fields of study. This section focuses on examples of initiatives in mathematics, political science, science, and nursing rather than the fields traditionally associated with internationalization (modern languages, area studies, and international studies/relations). However, all fields of study will benefit from continuing innovation as internationalization evolves.

Applebaum, Friedler, Ortiz, and Wolff (2009) argue that as mathematics is shaped by culture, the mathematics curriculum should be internationalized, especially cultural aspects of mathematics, mathematical modeling, and math history. Furthermore, mathematics students should study abroad to gain the cultural knowledge they will need to collaborate successfully and internationally, and capstones should incorporate cultural issues. At Arcadia University, the authors are internationalizing mathematics course by course, with the goal of ultimately internationalizing them all.

Carter (2008) argues that it is critical to develop a new science curriculum that includes content focused on the way in which globalization has resulted in the uneven distribution of science while privileging Western scientists, science, and technology. In addition, the curriculum should acknowledge that commercial interests and the privatization of knowledge have virtually eliminated purely curiosity-driven science. One of the unintended consequences of globalization has been "fewer nations, and fewer individuals, working on more narrowly defined problems of Western science, controlled by a limited number of economically related interests" (p. 625), and this has had a negative impact on many peoples of the world and the environment. Thus, an internationalized curriculum in science would be suited to the needs of socially, culturally, and ethnically diverse learners and would employ problem-based methodologies that prepare students to be flexible, adaptive,

and reflexive problem solvers who can conduct community-based as well as industry-based investigations and who "respect the great diversity, both natural and cultural of our planet" (p. 629).

Science Education for New Civic Engagements and Responsibilities (SENCER), initiated by the National Science Foundation in the United States in 2001, seeks to "improve STEM (science, technology, engineering and mathematics) education by connecting learning to critical civic questions" (http://www.sencer.net/). SENCER is now the signature program of the National Center for Science and Civic Education at Harrisburg University of Science and Technology, Pennsylvania, and focuses on faculty development and education reform in science, technology, engineering, and mathematics. SENCER model courses focus on civic issues important to students' futures and draw on research about how people learn. A number of the model courses posted on the SENCER website (http://www.sencer.net/) have explicit global themes or address social justice issues relevant to both local and international contexts. Another approach to internationalizing science curricula comes from the University of Saskatchewan in Canada, where transformative pedagogies were used in the internationalization of two global health courses with the aim of increasing the "potential for social transformation" (Hanson, 2010).

Sandstrom (1998) looks at the internationalization of the nursing curriculum in Sweden. She argues that education can and should create the conditions necessary for health, peace and harmony, and human rights in every society and that nurses and midwives can make a valuable contribution to the promotion, preservation, and maintenance of these conditions (Sandstrom 1998, p. 146). Thus, the learning outcomes of an internationalized curriculum in nursing should include:

- The ability to cooperate and collaborate in joint efforts across national and cultural boundaries

- Intercultural communicative competence required for provision of professional health care to patients from diverse cultural backgrounds

- The ability to obtain and utilize ideas and experiences from different parts of the world

- The ability to function within the health-care organizations of the future

The achievement of such outcomes requires systematic, sustained efforts across the entire curriculum, rather than isolated, uncoordinated, and ad hoc efforts.

These discipline-specific examples highlight the diversity of approaches to internationalization of the curriculum. Common features include a focus on ethics to secure the future of the world and its peoples, with the approach varying by discipline. However, instrumental approaches also exist, where the intention may be to develop international perspectives and intercultural competencies to achieve benefit for the individual rather than the larger society.

CHALLENGES: ENACTING INSTITUTIONAL POLICY OR MISSION THROUGH THE CURRICULUM

College and university mission statements around the world include internationalization, international learning outcomes, and preparation of graduates for work and citizenship. However, mission does not always result in curriculum planning and enactment, even though "internationalization is ideally completely integrated in the regular curriculum" (van Gaalen, 2010, p. 36). The European Association of International Education provides seven questions to ensure that mission translates into curriculum internationalization, for example: To what extent do curricular goals explicitly mention international knowledge and skills? How much does the curriculum improve the international competencies of all students? How is the curriculum aligned with workplaces outside of the home country? and What supports are available for faculty to internationalize their teaching (van Gaalen, 2010, p. 37)?

Internationalization of the curriculum can also be "front-loaded" by requiring faculty to indicate in course planning and approval documents how course objectives, teaching, and learning will be internationalized and assessed. This approach is often linked with the development of a set of graduate attributes related to internationalization and "soft" skills such as cross-cultural communication and the ability to work in multicultural teams (see Leask, 2001).

Despite these examples, powerful deterrents to internationalizing the curriculum also exist (see e.g., Childress, 2010; Clifford, 2009). Childress (2010) provides detailed case studies of how two very different U.S. universities, Duke University and the University of Richmond, have worked to address the blockers they faced by working strategically to engage faculty with curricular change (see Box 14.3). Box 14.4 gives an example from Australia.

BOX 14.3 The Faculty Role in Internationalizing the Curriculum: Findings from a Cross-Case Study

Lisa Childress

LKC Consulting (USA)

To develop global competencies for students, internationalization of the curriculum has become a priority for many higher education institutions. This is increasingly important as the majority of college students do not study abroad (Siaya & Hayward, 2003), although study abroad is a common vehicle for developing global competencies. A strategy to ensure that the majority of students are exposed to cross-cultural vantage points is therefore to provide faculty with the time and financial resources to internationalize their pedagogies and syllabi. At Duke University and the University of Richmond (Childress, 2010), supports such as faculty seminars, differential investments, strategic use of electronic communication channels, and the customization of internationalization

(Continued)

(Continued)

goals to unique disciplines have encouraged faculty to internationalize their curricula and thus expose students to international vantage points.

Faculty Seminars

Seminars enhance the international expertise and experiences of faculty so that students can develop global competencies. At Duke, interdisciplinary, semester-long, on-campus seminars have provided teaching release time for faculty to discuss particular international topics with colleagues. Richmond's nationally recognized faculty seminar-abroad program allows faculty to gain interdisciplinary knowledge about a country for 3 weeks during the summer. In both cases, faculty have developed critical knowledge, networks, and motivation to internationalize their pedagogies and syllabi.

Differential Investment

Differential investment is the process of allocating special funds at various institutional levels for initiatives that promote strategic priorities. At Duke and Richmond, curriculum internationalization grants have encouraged faculty to develop new courses with international content and to infuse international perspectives into existing courses. For example, at Richmond, such grants allowed a law school professor to create an international intellectual property course and a psychology professor a cross-cultural psychopathology course. The proposal writing proved a productive way for applicants to engage with curriculum internationalization, even for those who did not receive funding.

Strategic Use of Electronic Communication Channels

Both Duke and Richmond have central international offices that take advantage of faculty members' frequent use of electronic media to (a) share international teaching resources with faculty and (b) collect information about faculty members' areas of international expertise and interests. At Duke, these include an international faculty database and international faculty blogs, while at Richmond, they include examples of internationalized syllabi and a faculty internationalization survey.

Customizing Internationalization Goals to the Disciplines

Customization emphasizes the importance of adapting an institution's internationalization goals to unique disciplinary priorities. With internationalization a priority in Duke's university-wide strategic plan, internationalization was also prioritized in schoolwide strategic plans. Customizing the plans to each school made connections between disciplinary priorities and internationalization explicit, thereby prompting faculty involvement.

Recommendations

Higher education leaders seeking to internationalize their curricula must ensure infrastructural supports enable the faculty to do the work. In addition to the points discussed above, the following may be useful:

1. Incorporation of global perspectives into tenure and promotion policies' definition of "excellence in teaching" can promote faculty engagement in curriculum internationalization.

2. Incorporation of deliverables, that is, internationalized syllabi, as requirements of participation in international faculty seminars and programs, builds in a structural mechanism to ensure that participation results in internationalized teaching.

Universities and colleges can strategically engage faculty to internationalize the curriculum using intentionality, investments, infrastructure, institutional networks, and individual support (Childress, 2010). That is, to internationalize the curriculum, higher education institutions should (a) intentionally articulate their goals for faculty involvement, (b) make long-term investments to provide resources to support faculty in these endeavors, (c) develop infrastructure to create foundational programmatic support, (d) streamline institutional networks so faculty are aware of international teaching opportunities and resources, and (e) provide support for individual faculty to connect international issues with their unique scholarly agendas.

BOX 14.4 Identifying Gaps and Synergies to Achieve Institutional Vision in Relation to Internationalization at an Australian University

Kay Salehi

Academic development adviser, Swinburne University (Australia)

The Swinburne University 2015 Vision Statement states that university staff and students will be international in their outlook. This is connected to internationalization of the curriculum across the university and the preparation of all students for "performing professionally/socially in an international and multicultural context" (OECD, 1996). Achievement of the vision is thus related to the application of teaching and learning and support strategies that assist staff and students to develop these skills and attitudes. Many universities' vision statements claim similar intentions. Deceptively simple, the vision statements mask a range of complex interactions between individuals and departments, their conceptualization of the rationale behind the vision, and their responsibilities and accountabilities in relation to the vision's achievement.

A literature review undertaken in conjunction with a project to evaluate progress toward achievement of the Swinburne vision suggested that within the institution, there might be different rationales for internationalization as well as differing perspectives on how to approach the task and achieve the vision. As well, despite the possibility that synergies, groups and individuals might work separately, unaware of each other's efforts. For example, some staff might focus on the international marketing of programs and the university's international standing and reputation; others on locating alliances and new partnerships to increase study abroad, exchanges, and research linkages; and others on the quality of teaching and student learning outcomes. A challenge for institutional leaders, therefore, is to ensure that the efforts of various groups and individuals contribute efficiently to the achievement of institutional vision.

To identify the gaps and synergies between the international vision of the university and the perspectives of relevant staff, the project used Knight's 2004 five institutional rationales for internationalization (profile and reputation, student and staff development, income generation, strategic alliances, and knowledge generation) and combined these with Leask's 2003 five layers of internationalization (policy, program, course, teacher/academic, and student). A conceptual matrix was developed and provided a valuable prompt and framework for discussion with institutional leaders.

(Continued)

(Continued)

Institutional leaders shared their thoughts and perspectives in relation to each of Leask's layers and Knight's rationales. This provided them with new ways to both conceptualize their role within the university's internationalization agenda and to think about how their work might relate to and impact the work done by colleagues working in other areas. Informal discussions provided opportunities for leaders in different areas of the university to both confirm and reconceptualize their own and others' roles and identify synergies and possible areas of contradiction. Potential gaps and opportunities were also identified.

For example, the research and knowledge area was expected to promote international research linkages, while the marketing/reputation area was concerned with promoting the university's reputation to attract high-caliber scholars and staff. However, the staff and student development area was expected to help staff and students take advantage of international research opportunities. While such overlaps can be useful, they can also be wasteful and counterproductive. Knowing that they exist is the first step in being able to use the opportunities and reduce duplication of effort. Ultimately, research linkages can benefit (a) faculty seeking to internationalize the curriculum, (b) students hoping to add an international dimension to their studies and prepare for future employment, and (c) institutional leaders charged with supporting the institution in achieving its international mission and goals.

This process and the matrix that guided it may help other institutions determine how best to employ resources to internationalize the curriculum.

Future Issues and Concluding Questions

A number of practical, philosophical, and ethical considerations emerge from the discussion in this chapter:

• How can the experiential and intercultural learning outcomes considered crucial to the development of all students' ability to live and work in a globalized world be developed and assessed within the context of a program of study?

• How can faculty members be engaged to internationalize the curriculum in their disciplines and in institutions and contexts where academic teaching and learning continue to be conceived of as separate from the development of students' intercultural and international perspectives?

• How can universities ensure that the intersection of the international and intercultural in the curriculum will lead to "increased understanding and appreciation of cultural diversity

and fusion" rather than "cultural homogenization?" (Knight, 2004, p. 28).

• How can teaching within higher education become flexible so as to include different cultural perspectives on, and constructions of, knowledge to reflect the diversity within and beyond the educational institution? Also, how can knowledge from outside the academy help to internationalize the curriculum?

• How can strategic, planned transformative encounters maximize the benefits of international education as well as ensure that we "become something more than we presently are" at the individual and institutional level (Sanderson, 2004, p. 9)?

• Transformative encounters will result from internationalization only if difference is valued, if there is a genuine desire and willingness to engage with cultural others, and if support for faculty, staff, and students is adequate and appropriate (Thom, 2010). How can we best support faculty, staff, and students to acquire this value so that they adjust the way they think and act?

- *Productive diversity* treats diversity as a resource rather than an annoying problem to be overcome, thereby creating "new and diverse paths of learning" (Kalantzis & Cope, 2000, p.42). How will faculty engage with and learn from other cultures so that they can become intercultural educators and avoid the colonization of the mind and the non-negotiable domination of Western ways of doing and knowing described by Goodman (1984)?

- New technologies have made it far easier than in the past to access information from around the world as well as facilitate communication, and educators have been experimenting with ways to take advantage of these to internationalize the curriculum. Yet, access to new technologies is uneven, as is the ability of educators and students to use them effectively for teaching and learning. How will the use of technology to internationalize the curriculum evolve, both on the traditional campus and in distance learning? Will its use act as a mechanism to create greater equality between nations, or will it exacerbate disadvantage?

These and other questions highlight the complexity and rich potential of internationalization of the curriculum as both an established and an evolving concept and set of processes. Thus, this chapter concludes with lessons for those seeking to internationalize the curriculum in their institutions.

CONCLUSION: EIGHT LESSONS

Internationalization of college and university curricula is challenging but also imperative as a response to globalization; it must involve many actors. This chapter, therefore, concludes with eight lessons that have emerged from experience.

First, it is critical that institutions work to develop an internal understanding of what it means to internationalize the curriculum. The literature can help institutions develop definitions that respond to their missions in processes that will likely be iterative and should involve students, faculty, administrators, and institutional leaders. This is not the work of an individual or a single office or group.

Second, inventories of courses with international content can be a starting point for measuring the internationalization of the curriculum, but the lists need to be supplemented by information on degree requirements for specific courses of study (foreign language study, courses with international content, as well as data on study abroad participation). In addition, other kinds of courses may also be developing the knowledge and skills students need to succeed in an internationalized and globalized world. Thus, it is important to develop learning goals around internationalization, assessment tasks, and graduate attributes.

Third, collaborative effort within and beyond the institution is needed to advance internationalization of the curriculum. Within institutions, partnerships can be between and among individuals, academic departments, administrative offices, and student groups. Beyond the institution, productive partnerships can be built with local organizations, other institutions of higher education (within or beyond the country in which the institution is located), organizations working to help internationalize the curriculum, government agencies, and professional associations.

Fourth, faculty members are central, and their role must be recognized and valued, as they control the curriculum and must, therefore, take the lead in its internationalization. Thus, they must be given opportunities for reflection on what internationalization of the curriculum means for them personally as well as for their disciplines, their departments, their own teaching and scholarship, their students' learning, and the institution. Financial resources can be helpful, but even in the absence of dedicated funding, much can be accomplished if faculty members are given the space in which to think about internationalization of the curriculum and take action. Curriculum internationalization must also be embedded in the institutional mission, curricular structure, and faculty responsibilities and compensation.

Fifth, the learning outcomes of an internationalized curriculum must be assessable and assessed. This provides evidence that the internationalization is taking place and that the institution is producing graduates able to succeed personally and professionally in an internationalized and globalized world. Faculty and institutional researchers can assist with this work; external organizations and researchers can also provide models.

Sixth, students have an important role to play in shaping as well as receiving an internationalized education. They need to both understand their institutions' goals in internationalizing the curriculum and identify their own goals within these. Developing meta-cognition will allow them to understand what they are learning and how, as well as identify and address the gaps in their knowledge and skills.

Seventh, while institutions and their leaders may want to justify internationalizing the curriculum as a means to compete nationally and internationally, they may want to balance that with recognition that internationalization can also lead to greater cooperation.

Finally, eighth, none of this will happen without adequate resourcing. What is clear from the past is that without adequate funding, employed strategically, we can claim much but achieve little.

Internationalization of the curriculum is a complex, multidimensional and iterative process. With learning and teaching at its heart, it requires collaboration and reflective practice. The past can provide valuable lessons, as can the experience of others working in other places toward similar goals.

References

American Council on Education (ACE). (1995). *Educating Americans for a world in flux: Ten ground rules for internationalizing American higher education.* Washington, DC: Author.

American Council on Education (ACE). (2008). *Mapping internationalization on U.S. campuses.* Washington, DC: Author.

Applebaum, P., Friedler, L. M., Ortiz, C. E. & Wolff, E. F. (2009). Internationalizing the university mathematics curriculum. *Journal of Studies in International Education, 13*(3), 365–381.

Ashwill, M. A. (2011). *Higher ed as a weapon.* Retrieved April 28, 2011, from http://www .insidehighered.com/views/2011/04/12/ashwill _international_higher_education_used_for _political_purposes

Association of American Colleges and Universities (n.d.). *Shared futures.* Retrieved June 26, 2010 from http://www.aacu.org/SharedFutures/index .cfm

Association of Universities and Colleges of Canada (AUCC). (2009). *Internationalization of the curriculum: A practical guide to support Canadian universities' efforts.* Canada: Author.

Beelen, J. (Ed.). (2007). EAIE professional development series for international educators: Vol. 2. Implementing internationalisation at home. Amsterdam: European Association for International Education.

Berzon, R. (n.d.). Making the world a smaller place: The international symposium at Beloit College. *Abroad View.* Retrieved November 30, 2011, from http://www.abroadview.org/academics/ beloitsymposium.html

Brewer, E., & Cunningham, K. (Eds.). (2010). *Integrating study abroad into the curriculum: Theory and practice across the disciplines.* Sterling, VA: Stylus.

Brown University (2010). *The global independent study initiative.* Retrieved from http://www .brown.edu/Administration/OIP/programs/gis/

Carlson, J. S., Burn, B. B., Useem, J., & Yachimowicz, D. (1990). *Study abroad: The experience of American undergraduates.* Westport, CT: Greenwood.

Carter, L. (2008). Globalization and science education: The implications of science in the new economy. *Journal of Research in Science Teaching, 45*(5), 617–633.

Childress, L. K. (2010). *The twenty-first century university: Developing faculty engagement in internationalization.* New York: Peter Lang.

Clifford, V. (2009). Engaging the disciplines in internationalising the curriculum. *International Journal for Academic Development, 14*(2), 133–143.

Crowther, P., Joris, M., Otten, M., Nilsson, B., Teekens, H., & Wächter, B. (2001). *Internationalisation at home: A position paper.* Amsterdam: European Association for International Education.

Deardorff, D. K. (2008). Intercultural competence: A definition, model and implications for education abroad. In V. Savicki (Ed.), *Intercultural competence and transformation: Theory, research, and application.* Sterling, VA: Stylus.

Deardorff, D. K. (2009). *The SAGE handbook of intercultural competence.* Thousand Oaks, CA: Sage.

Deardorff, D. K. (2011). Exploring a framework for interculturally competent teaching in diverse classrooms. In M. Magnan, M. Soderqvist, H.-G.van Liempd, & F. Wittmann, F. (Eds.), *Internationalisation of European higher education.* Berlin: Raabe Academic Publishers.

Ellett, R. (2010, September/October). Bringing study abroad into the political science classroom. *EDUCAUSE Review, 45*(5), 102–103. Retrieved May 8, 2011 from http://www .educause.edu/EDUCAUSE+Review/ EDUCAUSEReviewMagazineVolume45/ BringingStudyAbroadintotheColl/213958

Ellett, R., Kiwuwa, D., & Roberts, J. W. (2009). *Track six: Internationalizing the curriculum, 2009 teaching and learning conference,* American Political Science Association. Retrieved May 8, 2011, from http://www.apsanet.org/content_65116.cfm

Engberg, D., & Green, M. F. (2002). *Promising practices: Spotlighting excellence in comprehensive internationalization.* Washington, D.C.: American Council on Education.

Engle, J., & Engle, L. (2002). Neither international nor educative: Study abroad in the time of globalization. In W. Grünzweig & N. Rinehard (Eds.), *Rockin' in Red Square: Critical approaches to international education in the age of cyberculture* (pp. 25–39). Münster: Lit Verlag.

Engle, L., & Engle, J. (2003, Fall). Study abroad levels: Toward a classification of program types. *Frontiers: Interdisciplinary Journal of Study Abroad, 9.*

European Higher Education Area. (n.d.). *Student centered learning.* Retrieved May 7, 2011 from http://www.ehea.info/article-details.aspx?ArticleId=147

Farkas-Teekens, H. (1997). A profile of the "ideal lecturer" for the international classroom: Teaching in the international classroom. In H. Farkas-Teekens & M. van der Wende (Eds.), *Nuffic Papers 8.* Amsterdam: Nuffic.

Featherstone, M. (1990). Global culture: An introduction. In M. Featherstone (Ed.), *Global culture: Nationalism, globalization, and modernity* (pp. 1–13). London: Sage.

Foucault, M. (1981). *The history of sexuality:* Vol. 1. *An introduction* (R. Hurley, Trans.). Harmondsworth, Middlesex, UK: Penguin.

Gazzola, A. L., & Didriksson, A. (Eds.). (2008). *Trends in higher education in Latin America and the Caribbean.* Caracas: IESALC-UNESCO.

Goodman, N. (1984). The institutionalization of overseas education. In E. Barber, P. Altbach, & R. G. Myers (Eds.), *Bridges to knowledge: Foreign students in comparative perspective* (pp. 7–18). Chicago: The University of Chicago Press.

Goodwin, C. D., & Nacht, M. (1991). *Missing the boat: The failure to internationalize American higher education.* Cambridge, UK: Cambridge University Press.

Gore, J. E. (2005). *Dominant beliefs and alternative voices: Discourse, belief, and gender in American study abroad.* New York: Routledge.

Green, M., & Olson, C. (2003). *Internationalizing the campus: A user's guide.* Washington, DC: American Council on Education.

Green, M., & Shoenberg, R. (2006). *Where faculty live: Internationalizing the disciplines.* Washington, DC: American Council on Education.

Hanson, L. (2010). Global citizenship, global health, and the internationalization of curriculum: A study of transformative potential. *Journal of Studies in International Education, 14*(1), 70–88.

Harari, M. (1992). The internationalization of the curriculum. In C. B. Klasek (Ed.), *Bridges to the future: Strategies for internationalizing higher education* (pp. 52–79). Carbondale, IL: Association of International Education Administrators.

Hough, J. C., Jr. (1991). The university and the common good. In Dr. Griffin & J. C. Hough, Jr. (Eds.), *Theology and the university* (pp. 97–124). New York: State University of New York Press.

Huang, F. (2006). Internationalization of university curricula in Japan: Major policies and practice since the 1980s. *Journal of Studies in International Education, 10*(2), 102–118.

Kalantzis, M., & Cope, B. (2000). Towards an inclusive and international higher education. In R. King, D. Hill, & B. Hemmings (Eds.), *University and diversity: Changing perspectives, policies, and practices in Australia* (pp. 30–53). Wagga Wagga: Keon Publications.

Knight, J. (1997). Internationalisation of higher education: A conceptual framework. In J. Knight & H. de Wit (Eds.), *Internationalisation of higher education in Asia Pacific countries* (pp. 5–19). Amsterdam: European Association for International Education.

Knight, J. (2004). Internationalisation remodelled: Definition, approaches, and rationales, *Journal of Studies in International Education, 8*(1), 5–31.

Kramsch, C. (2002). In search of the intercultural. *Journal of Sociolinguistics, 6*(2), 275–285.

Kulacki, G. (2000, Winter). Area studies and study abroad: The Chinese experience. *Frontiers: The Interdisciplinary Journal of Study Abroad, 15,* 23–46.

Labi, A. (2011). New international ranking system has a DIY twist. *The Chronicle of Higher Education.* Retrieved November 17, 2011, from: http://chronicle.com/article/New-International-Ranking/127871/

Larsen, D., and Dutschke, D. (2010). Campus internationalization and study abroad. In W. Hoffa & S. DePaul, S. (Eds.), *A history of U.S. study abroad: Vol. 2. 1965 to present* (pp. 325–367). Lancaster, PA: Whitmore.

Lave, J., & Wenger, E. (1991). *Situated learning: Legitimate peripheral participation.* Cambridge, UK: University of Cambridge Press.

Leask, B. (2001). Bridging the gap: Internationalising university curricula. *Journal of Studies in International Education, 5*(2), 100-115.

Leask, B. (2003, October). *Beyond the numbers: Levels and layers of internationalisation to utilise and support growth and diversity.* Paper presented at the 17th IDP Australian International Education Conference, Melbourne, Australia.

Leask, B. (2005). Internationalisation of the curriculum: Teaching and learning. In J. Carroll & J. Ryan (Eds.), *Teaching international students: Enhancing learning for all students* (pp. 119–129). London: Routledge Falmer.

Leask, B. (2008). Internationalisation, globalization, and curriculum innovation. In A. Reed & M. Hellsten (Eds.), *Researching international pedagogies: Sustainable practice for teaching and learning in higher education* (pp. 9–26). The Netherlands: Springer.

Leask, B. (2009). Using formal and informal curricula to improve interactions between home and international students. *Journal of Studies in International Education, 13*(2), 205–221.

Leask, B. (2010). Beside me is an empty chair: The student experience of internationalization. In E. Jones (Ed.), *Internationalisation and the student voice: Higher education perspectives* (pp. 3–17). New York: Routledge.

Leask, B., & Beelen, J. (2009). Enhancing the engagement of academic staff in international education. In *Advancing Europe-Australia cooperation in international education: proceedings of a Joint Symposium* (pp. 28–42). Melbourne: IEAA & EAIE.

Leask, B., & Carroll, J. (2011). Moving beyond "wishing and hoping": Internationalisation and student experiences of inclusion and engagement. *Higher Education Research and Development, 30*(5), 647–659.

Lee, M. (2000). The impacts of globalization on education in Malaysia. In N. P. Stromquist & K. Monkman (Eds.), *Globalization and education: Integration and contestation across cultures* (pp. 315–332). Lanham: Rowman & Littlefield.

Marginson, S. (2003, November 29–December 3). *AARE Radford Lecture (revised) Markets in Higher Education: National and global competition.* Paper presented at the ANZARE/ AARE Joint Conference, Auckland, New Zealand.

McDermott, P. (1998). Internationalizing the core curriculum. *Women's Studies Quarterly, 26*(3/4), 88–98.

Mestenhauser, J. (1998). Portaits of an internationalized curriculum. In J. Mestenhauser & B. Ellingboe (Eds.), *Reforming the higher education curriculum* (pp. 3–35). Phoenix AZ: The Oryx Press.

Mok, K. H. (2007). Questing for internationalization of universities in Asia: Critical reflections. *Journal of Studies in International Education, 11*(3/4), 433–454.

Mthembu, T. (2004). Creating a niche in internationalization for (South) African higher education institutions. *Journal of Studies in International Education, 8*(3), 282–296.

Olson, C., Evans, R., & Schoenberg, R. E. (2007). *At home in the world: Bridging the gap between internationalization and multicultural education.* Washington, DC: American Council on Education.

Organization for Economic Cooperation and Development (OECD). (1996). *Internationalising the curriculum in higher education. Paris: Author.*

Paige, R. M. (2003). The American case: The University of Minnesota model. *Journal of Studies in International Education, 7*(1), 52-63.

Paige, R. M., & Goode, M. L. (2009.). Cultural mentoring: International education professionals and the development of intercultural competence. In D. Deardorff (Ed.), *The SAGE handbook of intercultural competence* (pp. 333–349). Thousand Oaks, CA: Sage.

Pennycook, A. (1994). The cultural politics of English as an international language. Harlow, Essex, UK: Longman Group.

Peterson, P. (2000). The worthy goal of a world faculty. *Peer Review, 3*(1), 3–7.

Pickert, S., & Turlington, B. (1992). *Internationalizing the undergraduate curriculum: A handbook for campus leaders.* Washington, DC: American Council on Education.

Rouhani, S., & Kishun, R. (2004). Introduction: Internationalization of higher education in (South) Africa. *Journal of Studies in International Education, 8*(3), 235–243.

Sanderson, G. (2004). Existentialism, globalisation, and the cultural other. *International Education Journal, 4*(4), 1–20.

Sanderson, G. (2008). A foundation for the internationalization of the academic self. *Journal of Studies in International Education, 12*(3), 276–307.

Sandstrom, S. (1998). *Internationalisation in Swedish undergraduate nursing education: Its interpretation and implementation in the context of nursing with tender loving care* (Research Bulletin 96). Helsinki: University of Helsinki, Faculty of Education.

Savicki, V. (Ed.). (2008). *Developing intercultural competence and transformation: Theory, research and application in international education.* Sterling, VA: Stylus.

Schuerholz-Lehr, S. (2007). Teaching for global literacy in higher education: How prepared are the educators? *Journal of Studies in International Education, 11*(2), 180–204.

Siaya, L., & Hayward, F. (2003). *Mapping internationalization on U.S. campuses: Final report*. Washington, DC: American Council on Education.

Soudien, C. (2005). Inside out but below: The puzzle of education in the global order. In J. I Zajda (Ed.), *International handbook on globalisation, education, and policy research* (pp. 501–516). Dordrecht, the Netherlands: Springer.

Stohl, M. (2007, Fall/Winter). We have met the enemy and he is us: The role of the faculty in the internationalization of higher education in the coming decade. *Journal of Studies in International Education, 11*(3/4), 359–372.

Szanton, D. (Ed.). (2004). *The politics of knowledge: Area studies and the disciplines*. Berkeley: University of California Press.

Teichler, U. (2004). The changing debate on internationalisation of higher education. *Higher Education, 48*(1), 5–26.

Thom, V. (2010). Mutual cultures: Engaging with interculturalism in higher education. In E. Jones (Ed.), *Internationalisation and the student voice* (pp. 155–168). New York: Routledge.

Vande Berg, M. (2007). Intervening in the learning of U.S. students abroad. *Journal of Studies in International Education, 11*(3/4), 392–399.

Van der Wende, M. (1997). Internationalising the curriculum in Dutch higher education: An international comparative perspective. *Journal of Studies in International Education, 1,* 53–72.

Van der Wende, M. (2000). Internationalising the curriculum: New perspectives and challenges. In B. Hudson & M. Todd (Eds.), *Internationalising the curriculum in higher education: Reflecting on practice* (pp. 25–38). Sheffield, UK: Sheffield Hallam University Press.

Van Deusen, B. G. (2007). *Moving beyond marketing study abroad: Comparative case studies of the implementation of the Minnesota model of curriculum integration, A five college report*

(2006-07). Master's Paper. Retrieved June 26, 2010, from http://umabroad.umn.edu/ci/documents/B.VanDeusenCIcasestudiespaper.pdf

Van Gaalen, A. (Ed.). (2010). *Internationalisation and quality assurance* (Professional Development Series for International Educators). Amsterdam: European Association of International Education.

Wächter, B. (2003). An introduction: Internationalisation at home in context. *Journal of Studies in International Education, 7*(1), 35–11.

Webb, G. (2005). Internationalisation of curriculum: An institutional approach. In J. Carroll & J. Ryan (Eds.), *Teaching international students improving learning for all* (pp. 109–118). Abingdon: Routledge.

Whitsed, C., & Volet, S. (2011). Fostering the intercultural dimensions of internationalisation in higher education: Metaphors and challenges in the Japanese context. *Journal of Studies in International Education, 15*(2), 146–170.

Whitsed, C., & Wright, P. (2011). Perspectives from within: Adjunct foreign English-language teachers in the internationalization of Japanese universities. *Journal of Research in International Education, 10*(1), 28–45.

Winston, R. P. (2001, Fall). Discipline and interdiscipline: Approaches to study abroad. *Frontiers: The Interdisciplinary Journal of Study Abroad, 6,* 61–93.

Yershova, Y., De Jaegbere, J., & Mestenhauser, J. (2000). Thinking not as usual: Adding the intercultural perspective. *Journal of Studies in International Education, 4* (spring), 39–78.

Youd, D. (2010). Chinese cities in transition. In E. Brewer & K. Cunningham (Eds.), *Integrating study abroad into the curriculum* (pp. 137–153). Sterling, VA: Stylus.

15

Leveraging Technology and the International Classroom for Cross-Cultural Learning

Jane Edwards and Hanneke Teekens

This chapter attempts to address some of the issues surrounding the processes of leveraging technology and the international classroom to support student learning in the globalized educational environment of the 21st century teaching and learning. Innovation in teaching toward global awareness and intercultural competence (see Chapter 16, this volume, and Deardorff, 2009, for further discussion of these concepts) tracks to a large extent with innovation in other areas of the curriculum. Incorporation of directed experience outside the classroom, implementation of strategies that foster active and group learning, and the use of new technologies to provide learning platforms, access resources, and make connections that were impossible a few years ago have been the principal elements in innovation in pedagogy in the 21st century. Additional significant variables to be considered are the growth of cultural diversity in the classroom as a result of student mobility and the implications of the spread of English as the principal classroom language in countries where English is not the dominant language.

As higher education struggles to meet the challenges of globalization, institutions are experiencing pressure to structure the educational experience, particularly at the undergraduate level, to incorporate an international and intercultural dimension in the teaching and learning processes. Institutional strategies to prepare students for success in a globalized world are for the most part implemented by administrators and involve the movement of people—students, faculty, researchers—the development of partnerships, and the sponsoring of special extracurricular activities abroad (Bhandari, Belyavina, & Gutierrez, 2011). The dilemma for international educators is that, within the U.S. system and in many others, what happens within the classroom at the home institution is essentially owned by the faculty, whose primary goal must be to teach in their area of expertise. Bringing an international dimension into the curriculum (see Chapter 14, this volume) and infusing such a dimension into classrooms where the subject of the coursework is not explicitly intercultural education places an additional burden on the instructor. This can become difficult to mandate, reward, or even monitor. Because this is truly the domain of the faculty, successful strategies often start from the premise that faculty will need encouragement, incentives, and support in identifying strategies and useful technologies if they are to focus energy and class time on this aspect of their teaching (Lundy Dobbert 1998, p. 53).

These pathways exist within a broader matrix, however. Globally, the main academic challenges in internationalizing teaching and learning processes vary regionally and nationally. Despite this diversity, these challenges broadly include the following: the management of classroom dynamics related to student mobility across borders, including cultural and language issues faced by faculty and students; expectations that come with the growth of transborder and international partnership initiatives; the utilization of communications technologies to enhance learning; and the pressure to develop global awareness throughout the student body. In English-speaking countries like Canada and Australia, there are developments comparable to these U.S. initiatives. In European countries, teaching and learning remains more closely linked to national languages, cultures, and traditions, even in international education, but the introduction of teaching in English (in non-English speaking countries) has greatly influenced the international classroom (Maiworm & Wächter, 2002). This applies particularly in northern Europe and has resulted in attracting students worldwide. In other parts of Europe, students continue to come from countries with the same language, as from francophone Africa to France or to Spain from Latin America. But increasingly, all European countries offer courses in English, and internationalization has promoted collaborative initiatives across the whole region. While the pedagogic rhetoric surrounding international education in the United States has remained rather stable underneath new rationales invoked after 2001 about national security and global competiveness, in Europe, rationales for internationalization have become a more complex mix of national, economic, political, and cultural objectives.

Perhaps the single most important trend in classroom dynamics worldwide relates to the rapidly growing awareness of the significance of globalization for what is studied and how it is studied. This has contributed, with other factors, to the escalating debate on the validity of academic disciplines (see for example Jacobs, 2009). Thematic study—interdisciplinary by necessity—of climate change, human rights, global health, and political economy is now recognized as an essential mode of inquiry and course design. This results in new imperatives to think beyond national and cultural boundaries as well as those of the disciplines. Students who take these courses develop a new awareness of their place on the planet, and the international experience of faculty and students has new salience in immediate and pragmatic ways. This dynamic is mirrored in curriculum planning across many educational systems. A new recognition of urgency is fostered by communications technologies that allow classroom discussion of, for example, a nuclear accident in Japan in real time elsewhere in the world, sourced from the Internet, possibly in direct video contact with students in Japan. Such work is facilitated by the accelerated dissemination of information, which results in data sets, the most current theoretical papers, and multimedia presentations of all kinds being rapidly and readily available. This new reality permits faculty and students to work together to understand what is happening elsewhere on the planet and to examine its implications for their own country or region.

This change in the modalities of coursework and the concomitant growth of online education, together with the growing acceptance of experiential learning as an essential component of education in the 21st century, are the primary drivers for teaching innovation in international education as in so many other areas.

Literature Review

Research and discussion on the pedagogies of international education are often found embedded in larger discussions of the curriculum and the learning process. Thus, important contributions are found in such collections as Mestenhauser and Ellingboe's (1998) *Reforming the Higher Education Curriculum: Internationalizing the Campus*, which examines the multidisciplinary nature of the pedagogies of international education within the context of institutional internationalization strategies. *European Studies in Education* has published various studies in pedagogy with a focus on the international and intercultural component of education reform and teacher education. Central are questions on which forms of learning and experience further the formation of an intercultural consciousness with corresponding attitudes and reactions (Wulf, 1995). Developing new rationales for learning and teaching has constituted the single most important dimension in creating the European Higher Education Area (EHEA), as is illustrated in the first thick handbook on the *Internationalisation of European Higher Education,* published under the aegis of the European University Association (Gaebel, Purser, Wächter, & Wilson, 2008). One could claim that this is perhaps more Europeanization than internationalization, but experience suggests that recognizable dilemmas surface across nations. In countries where international education and incoming student mobility are relatively new phenomena, as in China, we see that the same pedagogical issues soon emerge, as became clear in an international workshop on this specific issue (Chan & Luk, 2006).

Specific fields of study offer distinct possibilities. Music is a field that offers students the possibility of understanding both universals and nonuniversals (Fung, 1998). Fung describes possibilities for a course in world music built around cultural-geographical, musical, and topical approaches (p. 122) and discusses the ways in which such a course can open students' minds to cultural difference. Graham (1998) clarifies, using examples from Latin America, the ways in which the internationalization of courses in soil science and agronomy—which he regards as important for effective practice in agriculture globally—can be achieved both through the designation of a course as international (p. 129) and through the inclusion of international examples in courses not so-designated. Mestenhauser exposes the complexity of the debate surrounding the internationalization of courses and curriculum and provides a comprehensive introduction to the most significant issues in a discourse that, albeit not new, remains most relevant (Mestenhauser & Ellingboe, 1998). Those complexities derive from the fact that international education is a system in which discrete disciplines, although they may overlap, have different expectations and assumptions:

"Our problem is how to develop new pedagogical and curricular practices that introduce multivaried modes of thinking and learning without openly challenging the system, and how to educate the system itself to embrace change in the direction of the maximalist approach proposed here" (Mestenhauser & Ellingboe, 1998, p. 27). Grunzweig and Rinehart (2002) take a similar approach in gathering a collection of thought-provoking studies that together reinforce the need to examine pedagogy within a larger context. The significance of the use of personal experience as part of pedagogy is examined in Holzmüller, Stöttinger, and Wittkop's (2002) chapter on business education, which proposes "new training programs that combine information technology tools with face-to-face cultural exposure and provide a more comprehensive learning experience synthesizing cognitive and affective skills development" (p. 143). Klahr (2002) writes about a paradigm shift in engineering education, which now includes the expectation that engineers will have "the ability to work in a group, adaptability and creativity, and the ability to manage and motivate" (p. 125). Experience abroad becomes itself the pedagogy under discussion, since these "are aspects of personal growth students generally gain as a result of having studied or interned in another culture" (Klahr, 2002, p. 125).

Hellstén and Reid (2008), in *Researching International Pedagogies,* go further in developing resources entirely focused on teaching and learning for international education in a broad range of fields. The need to develop new pedagogies for the classroom where participants, or faculty and students, come from more than one cultural background is explored in several essays. Within a discussion of the rising numbers of Asian students in Australian university classrooms, Singh and Shrestha (2008) raise the possibility of a pedagogical strategy of "double-knowing," which "favours critical, collaborative, reciprocal interactions around multiple sources of knowledge" (p. 77), as a way of changing the classroom experience for all participants. Hellstén and Reid (2008) advocate the use of the "reflective teaching framework" (p. 96) to recalibrate the cultural basis of teaching, which can "open communication channels, by signaling active listening, straight talk, and questioning taken-for-granted cognitions between teacher and learner" (p. 97). Bell's (2008) case study of an Australian field program serving students from Singapore examines the potential of the fieldwork environment to go "beyond disciplinary understanding and encompass broader skills such as problem posing and solving, independent and critical thinking/reflection" (p. 134).

The significance of information technologies for pedagogy is examined in six essays in Hellstén and Reid's volume (2008). Notably, Sorensen (2008) probes e-learning as a process that to develop students' capacity as responsible global citizens, must be designed to include interhuman dialogue and intercultural processes of democratic negotiation. Sorensen proposes critical examination of the pedagogical methodology inherent in e-learning, illustrating the outcomes through an examination of a collaborative endeavor among Danish universities. Bretag and Hannon (2008) present case studies of e-mail communication and online discussion as elements in diverse Australian classrooms, demonstrating the value of the development of a community of inquiry that allows self-disclosure and collaboration among students of different backgrounds; they see computer-mediated communication as an essential tool for developing such a community. Eurydice, the information network on education in Europe, reports regularly on initiatives to internationalize education developments and objectives. Improving language learning and opening up to the wider world are important aims and, specified in key competencies and subject matter, are vital for the information society (European Commission [EC], 2002). These studies form part of a growing literature on the dimensions and management of the intercultural classroom. In Europe, this is largely contextualized within the framework known as "internationalization at home," to which a special issue of the *Journal of Studies in International Education* (Otten & Nilsson, 2003) provides an excellent introduction. Teekens's *Internationalization at Home: A Global Perspective* (2006) brings together studies at the level of the institution (e.g., Joris, 2006) and the classroom (e.g., Paige & Kippa, 2006). It is characterized by a consistent focus on individual student learning outcomes and the need to reach all students, and not the minority who will travel abroad as part of their education. A central feature of this approach is the re-visioning of the classroom at home as an environment in which cross-cultural engagement can occur. Students can, with

guidance, discuss their own reactions and those of their classmates as culturally situated responses to materials presented. Chang (2006) and Leask (2009) discuss strategies for engaging students' experience and interest, such as group work in which students from different backgrounds must share cultural perspectives to succeed (Leask, p. 21) and the use of datasets from other countries for learning about analytical methodologies (Chang, p. 373). Kingston and Forland (2008) discuss a related theme that has been a subject of research for many years in the Australian context: how to assist teaching faculty in working with the different expectations and learning styles of international students. Bringing a comparison of the Confucian and Socratic traditions to bear on the classroom experience of East Asian students in the United Kingdom, they propose that faculty review with students expectations about lecturers and assessment, issues of plagiarism, and knowledge of available support systems (pp. 214–215). The very different classroom behaviors and expectations of Asian students enrolled in Australian universities, for example, are addressed in detail in the work of Ballard and Clanchy (1991), with suggestions for specific strategies and exercises to help faculty modify their teaching. Nisbett (2003) argues that "the geography of thought" that represents the great differences in teaching and learning between the East Asian and Western schools of thought might be bridged by a shift in characteristic social practices (p. 229). The international classroom is a setting where a shift can be expected to produce a change in patterns of perception and thought (Bodelier, 2008).

Facing constantly rising expectations to publish research in their own fields, faculty can be expected to make a relatively small investment in writing about pedagogy, but for those in the field of education, there are greater incentives. Cushner and Brennan (2007) offer an introduction to a collection of explorations of teaching placement abroad as a tool that allows student teachers to develop skills in international collaboration, including perspective consciousness, an ethno-relative orientation, cross-cultural communications, interpersonal skills, and an understanding of the adjustment process that accompanies international transitions (p. 2). There are many such programs in the United States and in Europe; perhaps the best known and most acclaimed is Indiana University's

Cultural Immersion Projects, which place students in eight-week teaching assignments in one of 15 countries, following at least 10 weeks of student teaching at home (http://education .indiana.edu/Default.aspx?alias=education.indi ana.edu/cultural). Tang and Choi (2004) document the development of professional competence as well as personal growth for Hong Kong participants teaching in Australia and Canada, for whom the teaching experience was part of a language immersion program. This in-depth qualitative study of four students' experiences emphasizes the importance of linking experience abroad to students' other professional experiences to maximize impact.

STRATEGIES AND PRACTICE

Developments in Pedagogy in U.S. Education Abroad

Pedagogy in U.S. study abroad programs has made great strides in the early 21st century. Some of the lessons learned in study abroad about student learning for intercultural competence have entered the U.S. classroom, often in conjunction with initiatives connected to the concept of global citizenship and the methodologies of service learning. Teaching toward global competence implies attitudinal and skill as well as cognitive dimensions (Deardorff, 2009). The difficulty of grappling with this within the conventional expectations of the classroom drives the similar pedagogical strategies advocated by so much of the literature: interaction, reflection, and experience are proposed to supplement knowledge building. The experience abroad is, to some extent, the pedagogy.

While the tension between the goal of preparing students for success in a competitive global environment and the goal of preparing them to be good citizens of that environment remains a reality, there has been convergence in recent years around an approach similar to the mission articulated by SIT Study Abroad (a program of World Learning), which aims "to prepare students to be interculturally effective leaders, professionals, and citizens through programs that incorporate field-based practice, reflection, and application" (see http://www.sit .edu/studyabroad/studyabroad.htm).

Strategies for preparation of this kind include the increased use of experiential, outside-the-classroom, field-based activity. Existing syllabi can be revised to include case work or thematic study, usually interdisciplinary, which is global in nature. The model of international service learning, in which service to a community is supported by credit-bearing classroom activity, has been redefined as itself a transformative pedagogy. Students "engage in regular, structured reflection activities that integrate academic content with real-world practice and ask students to explore their own values, their sense of social responsibility, and their ability to work collaboratively with individuals and groups from diverse backgrounds" (Plater, Jones, Bringle, & Clayton, 2009, p. 486). The creation of the Building Bridges Coalition through the Brookings Institution is providing new structures for institutional programs such as DukeEngage (http://dukeengage.duke.edu/about-dukeengage) to collaborate in developing a research agenda and shared practices and pedagogies regarding international service learning. Iverson and Espenschied-Reilly (2010) suggest that while service learning calls for a student-centered pedagogy, teaching practices continue in many systems to be predominantly instructor-centered. Writing about Ireland, they found that students preferred to be given clear instructions rather than to generate their own goals and project ideas (p. 8). Writing about South Africa, Erasmus (2011) notes that the connections between students and partner organizations in service learning are complicated by political and power relations. Thus, the pedagogies of service learning, developed primarily within the U.S. educational system, must be calibrated to local contexts.

All these initiatives depend on the knowledge and sensitivity of the faculty, and developing those qualities has become a significant concern for many institutions (see Chapter 14, this volume, for further discussion). Faculty development seminars, conferences, and workshops, structured expectations for faculty direct involvement with study abroad, and support from centers for teaching and learning have become part of the repertoire of strategies for changing the way in which faculty think about their role in this aspect of student learning. Childress (2010) presents case materials from faculty internationalization initiatives at Duke University and Richmond University and offers a detailed typology for intentional development of a program involving teaching, research, and service both on-campus and abroad (p. 145). As evidence of the recognition of the importance of pedagogical discussion across borders, a group of scholars from around the world founded in 2004 the International Society for the Scholarship of Teaching and Learning (http://www.issotl.org/). In addition, the online *International Journal for the Scholarship of Teaching and Learning* was established in 2007.

BOX 15.1 Liberal Learning Abroad: Globalization in Comparative Perspective

Michael D. Monahan

President of BCA Study Abroad

Former Director of the International Center, Macalester College (USA)

"The imagination thrives . . . on oblique attention; it never stirs so magically as when the intellect is austerely absorbed in worthy inquiries."

Eva Brann

The Macalester College Globalization in Comparative Perspective program involves a full academic year in which each participant pursues studies individually during the fall semester in one country (usually in the global South or, for international students, in the United States). The group then convenes in the Netherlands for an intensive January seminar, coordinated and taught by Macalester faculty and staff and focused on the interdisciplinary and comparative study of globalization. Students then spend the spring semester enrolled in vetted courses at Maastricht University.

The educational linchpin of this year-long venture is the January seminar. This is theme-driven, intellectually challenging, and experientially rich. Students are required to become intellectually familiar and civically engaged with the concept and practical consequences of globalization through carefully selected texts, lectures, and educational excursions. Both classroom and field learning focus on three selected subthemes of globalization: human rights (with special attention to war crimes); urban diversity (including the challenges of immigration and integration of ethnic minorities); and global governance (with the European Union as a case study). For the three educational excursions, students undertake serious preparatory readings, participate in classroom lectures and discussions, and engage with practitioners and community members. These excursions include visits with lawyers and observations of trials at the International Criminal Tribunal of the former Yugoslavia (ICTY) in The Hague; direct engagement with immigrants (e.g., Somali, Moroccan) and public intellectuals in Amsterdam; and discussions with academics and practitioners connected with the European Commission in Brussels. The combination of classroom and experience-based learning is a critical pedagogical goal of this program and represents a dynamic interplay between ideas and practices in teaching and learning in study abroad.

The culmination of student learning is a full-year independent study project dedicated to a topic within the program theme and a final paper that must draw on student learning across two cultures. Research topics have included: immigrant integration, the politics of language and identity, the political ecology of water, and human trafficking. Final papers are published in the journal *Macalester International.*

Macalester's dedication in this program is to the life of the mind for a purpose: teaching and learning in an international and intercultural context that leads to a deeper understanding of globalization. And in this process—this movement from the world of ideas to the world of action and back again—there is also an underlying ethical dimension: our alertness to better learning helps us lead better lives.

Some institutions have long been engaged in the development of pedagogies across disciplines, and among liberal arts colleges, there are many models of success, from Kalamazoo and St. Olaf to Elon and Whitman, all of which have developed differing strategic plans for incorporating education for global competence into the education of all undergraduates, both through study abroad and through engagement of the faculty with internationalization of coursework. Examples of successful strategies at a wide variety of U.S. institutions can be found in NAFSA's series, *Internationalizing the Campus: Profiles of Success at Colleges and Universities* (http://www.nafsa.org/resourcelibrary/default.aspx?id=8502). The University of Minnesota's curriculum integration project, much analyzed and reported (http://www.umabroad.umn.edu/ci/), models a strategy to engage the faculty across schools in a large research institution in a comprehensive effort to integrate experience abroad into major fields of study on the home campus, and information about this and other similar initiatives can be found on the NAFSA website in its resource section (http://www.nafsa.org/resourcelibrary/default.aspx?id=17487).

In the United States, a strong cultural bias toward the value of American pedagogical methodologies has led faculty to expect international students to adapt and conform to their American peers and to the process-oriented, interactive, clearly delineated style of the typical U.S. classroom. The shift toward interdisciplinary study of global issues may result in a recognition that other educational systems have developed pedagogies as a result of cultural difference, and that examining the merits of outcome-based learning, for example, building on the work of others rather than striving for originality, could change the dynamic of a classroom including students from different societies in significant ways, requiring students to question their own assumptions about the learning process. Perhaps most significant, and in part in recognition of the expectations students now have concerning active learning and the engagement of their own experience, faculty draw on the diversity of background and experience among students to increase the cross-cultural dimension of classroom learning, regardless of the content of the course. In a transborder initiative drawing on this model, courses offered as part of the Global Summer Program of the International Alliance of Research Universities, a collaborative organization of universities in eight countries (http://www.iaruni.org/gsp), are structured around the expectations of a classroom in which students from seven or eight countries are learning together about a theme of global interest by sharing the different perspectives they bring, with the guidance of a faculty member who has structured the course to include exercises and discussion of this kind. Students evaluate these courses as highly conducive to learning how to bring understanding and empathy to the values and opinions of people from other societies.

Where it is not possible to bring students together physically, some innovative programs have been developed to build on this dimension to help students develop a global perspective through working with peers from other countries. The Center for European Studies at Harvard University leveraged a strong faculty connection with their French partner institution, Sciences Po in Paris, to develop a course using a model that is increasingly popular where time differences and technology permit: regular video-conferencing shared classes for a course taught on two or more campuses. In these sessions, students can talk with their counterparts abroad and benefit from the dialogue between faculty members teaching in different institutional environments. East Carolina University's

Global Academic Initiatives program has been recognized for innovative strategies in its freshman course "Global Understanding" (http://www.ecu.edu/cs-acad/globalinitiatives/course.cfm) in which chat technology and videoconferencing bring students together with their overseas counterparts in pairings among 23 partner universities abroad throughout the semester. The same university has been recognized for its International Lecture Exchange Program, in which faculty present a lecture through video in a course at a partner institution. Strong institutional partnerships, resource commitment on the home campus, and engaged faculty are the primary determinants of success in such arrangements.

BOX 15.2 The Global Honors College

Michael Mooney

Special Adviser to the President, Waseda University (Japan)

Nine universities in the United States and Asia—Columbia, Harvard, Korea, MIT, National University of Singapore, Peking, Waseda, University of Washington, and Yale—are combining traditional strengths with emerging technologies to form what they are calling a Global Honors College. Once built out, the college will embrace 20 to 30 similar institutions from every region of the world, forming international cohorts of faculty and students to investigate jointly, both online and on-site, some of the world's most intractable problems.

This initiative attempts to escape the innate limits of space and time in the typical classroom. Through dedicated Web platforms, faculty and students are together building courses that begin before they begin and end after they end—if ever they do. Students may be loath to abandon their rich campus lives during term time, but online they are relentlessly creative, tapping into open courses at other institutions, uploading, downloading, exchanging all manner of information, blogging, and joining discussions that cross all spatial and temporal boundaries.

The Global Honors College attempts to harness this energy by pooling the talent of its member schools and structuring sustained inquiries, online and on-site, into issues that, by definition, demand the attention of multiple disciplines and multiple cultures. It proceeds this way:

• Canvassing their joint interests and unique strengths, members decide a theme for year-long inquiry and select a campus to host the "on site" summer seminar. Sustainability was the theme of the inaugural seminar; one on cities is now being formed, and others on migration, water, and liberty are being discussed.

• Faculty from four universities and as many disciplines are chosen to lead the seminar, and students are nominated by their home institutions—four or five from each—to take part in it. Students are drawn in equal number from natural science and social science or humanities majors.

• Technical staff create for the seminar a dedicated website with multiple interactive capacities, including blogs, forums, Voice Threads (collaborative multimedia slide presentations that allow comment and annotation by multiple users), and spaces for public and private communications. A simultaneous translation tool is added.

• Faculty prepare and mount distinct online course modules with readings, lectures, videos, and links to scientific literature. Each runs for about 2 weeks during June and July, during which time students discuss the modules, add materials from their own research, compile and annotate a common bibliography, and complete written assignments online. Forums run continuously.

- After the modules are completed, students are paired (from different countries and disciplines) to prepare joint presentations on aspects of the seminar theme.

- In August, faculty and students gather at the host university for 3 weeks of intense research. During the first 2 days, each student pair presents the results of its work to the seminar. Thereafter, students are reconstituted into four research groups, each a mix of countries and disciplines and each headed by a member of the seminar faculty. Common field trips and seminar meetings complement the work of the groups.

- The research groups make periodic oral reports to the seminar at large, and final written reports are prepared. Together with the various threads and forums, they are kept online as the permanent archive of the seminar.

- Students return to their home universities (or visit one another's) and continue their inquiries with disciplinary courses on aspects of the seminar theme. Academic credit for the program or any course that makes it up is determined by the students' home universities according to their normal standards and procedures. A certificate of completion is issued to students by the Global Honors College.

The ultimate success of the college will be measured, over time, by the number of students who sustain their interest in global issues, build the network of talented peers who share them, cultivate the intercultural and interdisciplinary strategies needed to engage them, and enter the careers in public service and private enterprise that might mitigate, if not solve, them.

CLASSROOM DYNAMICS IN EUROPEAN INSTITUTIONS

Europe after World War II experienced its first significant influx of international students and scholars, mainly from developing countries, often from former colonies. Those students were usually fluent in the language of the receiving country (English, French, German, Dutch, etc.) and were supposed to simply fit in. At the same time, they created an image of the exotic in international education. Sometimes specialized courses were provided catering to the demands of countries in development. This was a first attempt to adapt teaching and learning to a targeted international group of students, but with a marginal impact on national systems as a whole.

The launch of the Erasmus (European Action Scheme for the Mobility of University Students) program in 1987 attempted to change the nature of academic exchange and teaching. Inter-European student mobility became an end in itself, and cooperation through projects and agreements demanded the involvement of groups of academics rather than individuals. The number of mobile European students continued to rise over the following two decades, and the international classroom that resulted required new pedagogical skills to cater to the needs of students with widely different backgrounds. The rise of student mobility in Europe, outside the English-speaking countries, confronted the continent with the issue of language. Unlike students from the former colonies, European students did not have the same command of the various European languages, and for shorter exchanges, they were not willing to learn them. With more exchanges and joint programs, it was no longer feasible to require command of local languages as a precondition for participation in international programs. In most cases, English has become the language of communication for speakers of languages not mainstream in the host country, but few staff were adequately prepared for this situation (Woolf, 2005).

BOX 15.3 Preparing Staff for the International University

Els van der Werf

Senior Policy Advisor on International Relations,

Hanze University of Applied Sciences (The Netherlands)

For Hanzehogeschool Groningen, a university of applied sciences in the north of the Netherlands, the process of internationalization began in the 1980s, inspired by the launch of the Erasmus program. In the early years, the internationalization process was largely limited to degree programs that had a clear international focus, and consequently, the number of faculty members involved was also limited to a "happy few." This changed when the university adopted an internationalization policy requiring that all study programs were to prepare their students to be able to function well—socially, emotionally, and professionally—in an international working environment. All programs were:

- To embed a clearly defined international dimension in the curriculum, aimed at improving both cognitive and attitude-related skills in relation to the international professional practice

- To teach at least one semester (30 ECTS credits) of the program in English in order to be able to receive foreign (exchange) students and create an international classroom

- To create mobility opportunities for students, either in the form of a study abroad period or a work placement abroad.

This new policy meant that internationalization became mainstream and that all faculty members would need to become involved. There were questions: Did they have the competences for the new tasks that they would be required to carry out? Were they sufficiently aware of the international dimension of the professions for which they trained students? Would they be able to deal with an international classroom? Were they sufficiently proficient in English to use it as a working language? These were issues that had so far not received the attention they merited and that heads of department had been loath to address, not only in relation to the recruitment of new staff, but particularly in relation to current staff.

A large-scale survey of the university's faculty 2006 examining their personal experience in living and working in an international environment, their language skills, and their intercultural competences, uncovered a lot of enthusiasm for the university's new international policy, but an overall strategy was needed to improve related competences. This led to two important initiatives.

Via the so-called Corporate Academy, a range of personal and professional development options have been made available to faculty members. Besides a choice of language courses, they can also take courses that focus on the development of intercultural competences, especially in relation to the international classroom. Through best-practice seminars and workshops, staff are invited to learn from their colleagues about topics such as "Internationalisation@Home" and "Developing an international semester."

In addition, an International Competences Matrix was developed in 2007 (and up-dated in 2011), a tool that helps to assess whether a faculty member has the competences required to carry out various tasks related to the internationalization process. For each task, the matrix indicates which competences a lecturer should have and, if possible, the level of competence. The tool is based on the assumption that not all faculty members have the same tasks and that they therefore may also need different sets of competences. Some may be required to teach in English but have few research tasks. Others may teach only in the national language but be involved in the supervision of foreign students. Heads of department are advised to use the matrix during job interviews with potential new members of staff but also in relation to current staff, for example, in job appraisal talks. Faculty members are advised to use the tool in reflecting on their own needs for professional development. The matrix is meant to alert both parties to the fact that working in an international environment requires new and additional competences and that training in "weak" areas may be necessary to make a university's internationalization policy a success.

In 1999, the policymakers behind the Bologna Process wanted to encourage more coherence across the European higher education space, with a focus on compatibility, comparability, and access. This was predominantly a structural reform to enhance transparency and mobility. In practice, it challenged academics to adjust their ways of teaching to the new context. The two-tier degree structure (with a bachelor's and master's program instead of 5- to 6-year programs for the first degree) meant that academics had to reformulate their program profiles and had to commit to innovative teaching methods (Witte, 2006). Linking student mobility with the recognition of credits implies that courses can no longer solely be described by content only but also must contain a list of competences and learning outcomes. This meant a shift from a focus on input to a focus on output and from what a student has been taught to what a student has learned and is able to do (Lokhoff, 2010, p. 11). The emergence of the international classroom as a result of student mobility has challenged the notion of "good international education." Rhoads and Szeleny (2011) argue that in an interdependent world, the same question is equally relevant for *all* students. The role of the university in promoting global citizenship involves the whole academic community. In reality, however, this is not easily accomplished, as "home" and international students do not easily mix.

BOX 15.4 WIRE—Worldnet of Intercultural Relations in Education: Making Initial Intercultural Contacts More Relevant

Matthias Otten

Professor, Cologne University of Applied Sciences (Germany)

While enrollment of international students continues to rise at most European universities, many experts in international education are still worried about the lack of intercultural contacts on campus and in the classroom. Empirical and practical observations show the immense importance of positive intercultural interaction during the first weeks of student experience at a university as a crucial factor for their further educational development. This holds true for international and

(Continued)

(Continued)

domestic students alike. But "making people meet" (and encouraging them to remain in contact) is not as easy as most people believe.

The WIRE Internet project (http://www.wire-karlsruhe.de/) was initiated at the University of Karlsruhe (now called KIT or Karlsruhe Institute of Technology) in 2004 to foster informal intercultural contacts among all students. The acronym was chosen for two reasons. On the one hand, the technical metaphor describes nicely the basic idea of virtual communication by means of online communication and a website. On the other hand, the acronym indicates clearly that social relation building is a fundamental precondition of education.

WIRE addresses several target-groups and tries to bring them together:

- International students who intend to study at KIT but who have not yet arrived

- International and domestic students in their first months at KIT, who seek typical freshman information and support

- Students who like to meet people from all over the world, for example, for language tandems

- Students who intend to study abroad at one of KIT's partner institutions and who want to find people from these universities.

WIRE combines online and offline approaches: The website hosts a *basar* of initial basic information (housing, financial aspects, job opportunities, academic life at KIT, student life in Karlsruhe) and several interactive community functions (forum, chat, newsletter). Many students never show up at the international office or other service units. They prefer to consult with other students online. WIRE takes this communication preference seriously and tries to build an online bridge to enter the campus community. All international students get a WIRE leaflet with their enrollment documents.

The well-known phenomenon of online lurking (observing other peoples' conversation without speaking up oneself) is absolutely accepted. In fact, we found that some students prefer to observe the community in safe anonymity before beginning to attend offline meetings, excursions, or student parties offered by the WIRE team. Everyone can choose his or her preferred mode.

THE CHALLENGE OF LANGUAGE

The increased internationalizing of the curriculum posed an important additional question in the non-English speaking world. How to deal with language? For most countries in continental Europe, increased mobility of international students, and thus catering to them with an internationalized curriculum, has meant developing curricula in English (Woolf, 2005). Even in countries like Germany and France, more and more programs are now offered in English and not in the local language. For a country like the Netherlands, this has meant that within one decade the majority of graduate programs are now offered in English, catering to both home and international students. For conveners, difficult questions came up. It became clear that a simple translation of national curricula would not work and that therefore translation meant in fact creating completely new programs with distinct international and intercultural dimensions (Maiworm &Wächter, 2002). In the first stages of this process, which could be called a trajectory, the focus was on the international students and their additional needs (as compared to home students), needs that more often than not were labeled *deficiencies*. In the meantime, we see a shift toward more inclusive approaches whereby teachers and home students, as part of the international classroom, realize that all grabble for solutions in dealing with diversity. And this is not restricted to non-English speaking countries. It means a radical pedagogy involving a transformative process aimed at developing global citizens (Clifford, Henderson, & Montgomery, 2011).

In the United States and other Anglophone countries, the issue is in some ways the reverse of that in non-Anglophone countries: The pedagogical need is to break out of a unified monolingual classroom environment by finding ways for students to work in other languages as a structured part of the learning experience. An internationalized curriculum taught in English must coexist with the need for students to master foreign languages to a level useful for communication within and beyond the academic environment. The academic structures of U.S. universities, in which languages are indissolubly wedded to literature research in the hierarchies of faculty promotion and tenure, do not favor the pragmatic acquisition of language for use in other contexts. As early as 1980, the National Endowment for the Humanities was supporting programs at such institutions as Earlham College, which came to be known as FLAC (foreign language across the curriculum), characterized by the addition of foreign language readings and discussion sections added to English-language courses. FLAC programs depend on collaboration between language faculty and those in other disciplines, and the role they play in language acquisition is somewhat ambiguous (Sudermann & Cisar, 1992). Nonetheless, such curricular strategies can be very useful for some students, particularly those returning from study abroad who wish to maintain disciplinary knowledge acquired abroad.

For faculty who are proficient in another language, FLAC courses can allow all sorts of interesting things to happen, and of course active collaboration between a language teacher and a faculty member in another discipline can result in real language gains for students. The motivation of some students may be significantly higher than it would be for literary studies. Faculty who rely on teaching assistants to manage the foreign language sections will still feel the impact of students who are thinking in

more than one language—and thus, from more than a single perspective—about the content of the course. Students will experience the important opportunity to participate in focused, content-based discussion through the medium of a foreign language. The cost of managing FLAC programs has perhaps been key in limiting the growth of this pedagogical strategy, but recognition of its worth endures, and many campuses—for example, Yale University—have small but thriving FLAC programs. The new directions proposed in the Modern Language Association's (2007) report, *Foreign Languages and Higher Education: New Structures for a Changed World*, is premised on the same recognition of the complex relationship between student engagement with foreign languages and the university's curricular organization that gave rise to the FLAC movement over 30 years ago.

The broader cultural impact of global education has become increasingly important, making new pedagogical approaches essential in dealing with an increasingly diverse classroom. The new social and cultural context of the multicultural classroom poses different questions than the national one, with its hidden curriculum that is understood by local students without explicit explanation (Jones, 2010). The heterogeneity of students in terms of academic ability, ethnicity, social class, religion, and gender magnifies in situations where language and culture set a completely different agenda. Dealing with these issues has consequences for all levels of the institution, but initially for the persons directly involved, the teacher and the student. Teachers in particular need to possess certain knowledge, skills, and attitudes to deal with the complexity of the classroom setting in international education (Sanderson, 2006). Dialogue between human beings—not merely the interaction of individuals as members of one specific culture—can be enriching and instructive, provided reflection on one's own values is part of professional practice. It does not mean that cultural differences become obsolete, rather they become rewarding, often leaving academics confused about their own role.

CONCLUSION

While the convergence of higher education practices on the Western model is widespread, it is by no means uncontested. Response to globalization in higher education systems and institutions involves complex assessments of competition and collaboration, resource allocation, political reality, and the expectations of the many stakeholder constituencies. In Europe and in the United States, the international dimension of higher education has become an amalgamation of aims and objectives, realities and ambitions. University boards, professors, students, and even parents are stakeholders in a complex process of often-conflicting ideas and priorities. Economic, political, and educational rationales pose different questions and set different goals. Individual staff and institutions seek their own way in dealing with the new demands. As a result, many creative initiatives develop, making the process of internationalization an important agent of change and quality improvement. Student mobility from all parts of the world has linked the discourse on educational innovation and exchanges with the discussion of commercial tuition markets and competition. The challenge remains to educate all students to think and act beyond the confines of national borders and to give them the tools to build an understanding of the contemporary dynamic of global interconnectivity and interdependence.

This challenge also informs innovation in pedagogy in the development of curricula and course design in institutions across the globe. Increasingly, students are making decisions about higher education that are dominated by their understanding of themselves as global actors as well as members of local communities. As use of communications technologies grows and supplements the interpersonal exchanges that have traditionally enhanced cross-cultural learning in study abroad and for faculty teaching abroad, opportunities grow for new dialogues within the classroom, among instructors across the globe, and among administrators seeking to encourage pedagogical innovation on their own campus. The research and practice occasioned by the need to integrate numbers of Asian students in Australian universities, for example, illustrates the way in which local imperatives determine the direction of innovative practices. Recognition that all students need preparation to live in a globalized world, and not only those with the means and possibility to travel, is driving the development of new pedagogical models. Thus, the use of the constantly changing toolbox

of communication technologies will increasingly supplement experiential education as a primary approach for the intercultural learning and international engagement of students as well as faculty in the 21st century.

References

Ballard, B., & Clanchy, J. (1991). *Teaching students from overseas: A brief guide for lecturers and supervisors.* Melbourne: Longman.

Bell, M. (2008). Exploring fieldwork for study abroad sojourners. In M. Hellstén & A. Reid (Eds.), *Researching international pedagogies* (pp. 129–143). Dordrecht, the Netherlands: Springer.

Bhandari, R., Belyavina, R., & Gutierrez, R. (2011). *Student mobility and the internationalization of higher education: National policies and strategies from six world regions* (A Project Atlas Report). New York: Institute of International Education.

Bodelier, R. (2008). *Cosmopolitans: How international students change global society.* Tilburg, the Netherlands: Wereldpodium.

Bretag, T., & Hannon, J. (2008). Online close and personal. In M. Hellstén & A. Reid (Eds.), *Researching international pedagogies* (pp. 241–258). Dordrecht, the Netherlands: Springer.

Chan K. B., & Luk,V. (2006). *Internationalising the curriculum and learning environment: An East-West focus.* Hong Kong: David C. Lam Institute for East-West Studies.

Chang, J. (2006). A transcultural wisdom bank in the classroom: Making cultural diversity a key resource in teaching and learning. *Journal of Studies in International Education, 10(4),* 369–377.

Childress, L. (2010). *The twenty-first century university: Developing faculty engagement in internationalization.* New York: Peter Lang.

Clifford, V., Henderson, J., & Montgomery, C. (2011). Internationalizing the curriculum for all students: The role of staff dialogue. Presentation at *Internationalisation of Pedagogy and Curriculum Conference, The higher education academy,* Oxford Brookes University.

Cushner, K., & Brennan, S. (2007). The value of learning to teach in another culture. In K. Cushner & S. Brennan (Eds.), *Intercultural student teaching: A bridge to global competence* (pp. 215–225). Lanham MD: Rowman & Littlefield.

Deardorff, D. K. (Ed.). (2009). *The SAGE handbook of intercultural competence.* Thousand Oaks, CA: Sage.

Erasmus, M. (2011). A South African perspective on North American international service learning. In R. Bringle, J. A. Hatcher, & S. G. Jones (Eds.), *International service learning: Conceptual frameworks and research.* Sterling VA: Stylus.

European Commission (EC), Directorate-General for Education and Culture. (2002). *Key competencies.* Brussels: Eurydice.

Fung, C. V. (1998). Mind opening through music: An internationalized music curriculum. In J. A. Mestenhauser & B. J. Ellingboe (Eds.), *Reforming the higher education curriculum: Internationalizing the campus* (pp. 118–124). Phoenix AZ: Oryx.

Gaebel, M., Purser, L.,Wächter, B., & Wilson, L. (2008). *Internationalisation of European higher education.* Berlin: Raabe Verlag.

Graham, P. (1998). Internationalization of coursework in soil science and agronomy. In J. A. Mestenhauser & B. J. Ellingboe (Eds.), *Reforming the higher education curriculum: Internationalizing the campus* (pp. 125–134). Phoenix AZ: Oryx.

Grunzweig, W., & Rinehart, N. (Eds.). (2002). *Rockin' in Red Square: Critical approaches to international education in the age of cyberculture.* Munster: Lit Verlag.

Hellstén, M., & Reid, A. (2008). *Researching international pedagogies.* Dordrecht, the Netherlands: Springer.

Holzmüller, H. H., Stöttinger, B., & Wittkop, T. (2002). Information and communication technologies in internationalized business education: Technical opportunities and interpersonal threats. In W. Grunzweig & N. Rinehart (Eds.), *Rockin' in Red Square: Critical approaches to international education in the age of cyberculture* (pp. 127–146). Munster: Lit Verlag.

Iverson, S., & Espenschied-Reilly, A. (2010). Made in America? Assumptions about service learning pedagogy as transnational: A comparison between Ireland and the United States. *International Journal for the Scholarship of Teaching and Learning, 4*(2). Retrieved from http://www.georgiasouthern.edu/ijostl

Jacobs, J. A. (2009, November 22). Interdisciplinary hype. Chronicle of Higher Education, Retrieved from http://chronicle.com/article/Interdisciplinary-Hype/49191/

Jones, E. (Ed.). (2010). *Internationalisation and the student voice.* London: Routledge.

Joris, M. (2006). IaH: A quality tool for institutional change and management. In H. Teekens (Ed.), *Internationalisation at home: A global perspective* (pp. 91–104). The Hague: Nuffic.

Kingston, E., & Forland, H. (2008). Bridging the gap in expectations between international students and acadamic staff. *Journal of Studies in International Education, 12*(2), 204–221.

Klahr, S. (2002). Every engineer a nomad? International education as a challenge to the professions. In W. Grunzweig & N. Rinehart (Eds.), *Rockin' in Red Square: Critical approaches to international education in the age of cyberculture* (pp. 119–126). Munster: Lit Verlag.

Leask, B. (2009). Using formal and informal curricula to improve interactions between home and international students, *Journal of Studies in International Education, 13*(2), 205–221.

Lokhoff, J. E. O. (Eds.). (2010). *Tuning: A guide to formulating degree programme profiles.* Bilbao, Spain: Universidad de Deusto.

Lundy Dobbert, M. (1998). The impossibility of internationalizing students by adding materials to courses. In J. A. Mestenhauser & B. J. Ellingboe (Eds.), *Reforming the higher education curriculum: Internationalizing the campus* (pp. 53–68). Phoenix AZ: Oryx.

Maiworm, F., & Wächter, B. (2002). *English-language-taught programmes in European higher education: Trends and success factors.* Bonn: Lemmes.

Mestenhauser, J. A. (1998). Portraits on an international curriculum: An uncommon multidimensional perspective. In J. A. Mestenhauser & B. J. Ellingboe (Eds.), *Reforming the higher education curriculum: Internationalizing the campus* (pp. 3–39). Phoenix AZ: Oryx.

Mestenhauser, J. A., & Ellingboe, B. J. (Eds.). (1998). *Reforming the higher education curriculum: Internationalizing the campus.* Phoenix AZ: Oryx.

Modern Language Association. (2007, August 20). *Foreign languages and higher education: New structures for a changed world.* Retrieved from http://www.mla.org/flreport.

Nisbett, R.E. (2003). *The geography of thought: How Asians and Westerners think differently—and why.* London: Nicholas Brealey.

Otten, M., & Nilsson, B. (Eds.). (2003). Internationalisation at home [Special issue]. *Journal of Studies in International Education, 7*(1).

Paige, R. M., & Kippa, S. (2006). Curriculum transformation in study abroad: Maximizing study abroad guides. In H. Teekens (Ed.), *Internationalization at home: A global perspective* (pp. 79–91). The Hague: Nuffic.

Plater, W. M., Jones, S. G., Bringle, R. G., & Clayton, P. H. (2009). Educating globally competent citizens through international service learning. In R. Lewin (Ed.), *The handbook of practice and research in study abroad* (pp. 485–505). New York: Routledge.

Rhoads, R., & Szeleny, K. (2011). Global citizenship and the university: *Advancing social life and relations in an interdependent world.* Stanford, CA: Stanford University Press.

Sanderson, G. (2006). *Examination of a profile of the ideal lecturer for teaching international students.* Doctoral dissertation, Flinders University, Adelaide, Australia.

Singh, M. & Shrestha, M. (2008). International pedagogical structures. In M. Hellstén & A. Reid (Eds.), *Researching international pedagogies* (pp. 65–82). Dordrecht, the Netherlands: Springer.

Sorenson, E. K. (2008). Design of dialogic quality in e-learning. In M. Hellstén & A. Reid (Eds.), *Researching international pedagogies* (pp. 277–294). Dordrecht, the Netherlands: Springer.

Sudermann, D. P., & Cisar, M. (1992). Foreign language across the curriculum: A critical appraisal. *The Modern Language Journal, 76*(3), 295–308.

Tang, S., & Choi, P. (2004). The development of personal, intercultural and professional competence in international field experience in initial teacher education. *Asia Pacific Education Review, 5*(1), 50–63.

Teekens, H. (Ed.). (2006). *Internationalisation at home: Ideas and ideals (EAIE Occasional Paper 20).* Amsterdam: European Association for International Education.

Witte, J. (2006). *Change of degrees and degrees of change.* Enschede: CHEPS.

Woolf, M. (Ed.). (2005). *I gotta use words when I talk to you: English and international education* (EAIE Occasional Paper 17). Amsterdam: *European Association for International Education.*

Wulf, C. (Ed) (1995). *Education in Europe: An intercultural task.* Munster: Waxmann.

16

INTERCULTURAL COMPETENCE

An Emerging Focus in International Higher Education

DARLA K. DEARDORFF AND ELSPETH JONES

W hy do postsecondary institutions engage in international education? Why is international education considered to be "essential to our future?" (Association of International Education Administrators, 2010). Numerous chapters (Chapters 1, 2, 8, 9, 11, 23) in this volume respond to these questions, with responses range from furthering research, to strengthening the institution's reputation, to launching new revenue streams. Another response to these questions is that at the core of postsecondary institutions' missions, institutions are preparing "global-ready" graduates in the 21st century who will be able to address global challenges and live in an increasingly interconnected society (Deardorff & Hunter, 2006; Caruana, 2010). Yet, in *Our Underachieving Colleges*, Bok (2006) laments the poor job postsecondary institutions are doing in this regard. Several studies have indicated that universities are failing to maximize the opportunities presented by international and intercultural diversity on campus (Harrison & Peacock, 2010a, 2010b;

Leask, 2009; Montgomery, 2010; Summers & Volet, 2008; Thom, 2010; Volet & Ang, 1998).

Other scholars have likewise noted that the central responsibility of today's institutions of higher education is to educate students to function more effectively in an integrated world system (Cole, Barber & Graubard, 1994). This brings intercultural competence and diversity to the fore as one of the key reasons for engaging in internationalization at all. One study concluded that "the intensity of globalization in recent years has brought intercultural competence acquisition studies back to the center stage" (Kuada, 2004, p. 10). With the rising interest in the development of global perspectives through internationalization (Clifford & Montgomery, 2011) and in intercultural education for the multicultural society (Caruana & Ploner, 2010), intercultural competence development is emerging as a central focus—and outcome—of many internationalization efforts. This chapter explores definitions and frameworks of intercultural competence, highlights some practices and lessons learned in the development of intercultural competence at higher education institutions, and concludes with strategies that can be implemented in higher education institutions related to this central paradigm.

Summary of Key Literature/ Studies/Theoretical Frameworks

In any work on intercultural competence and cross-cultural communication and conflict, there are obvious variations within cultures,[1] and any generalized statements about cultures should be understood as descriptions of patterns found within and among various cultures. Such general descriptions are not meant to obscure or simplify the complexities of cultural diversity but, rather, to serve as a starting point for further discussion. It is also important to explore underlying assumptions and existing biases about culture and about the way(s) in which one approaches the concept of intercultural competence.

Definitions, Terminology, and Approaches

So what is meant by the term *intercultural competence,* and what terms are used in different professional and cultural contexts, and indeed in different countries around the world, to refer to this concept? Much scholarly effort has been invested, particularly in western cultures, in defining intercultural competence; what follows is a brief discussion of some of that work. (For a more comprehensive discussion, see Spitzberg & Changnon, 2009, and Spencer-Oatey & Franklin, 2009). In fact, the concept of *intercultural* was discussed by Comenius in the 1600s when he suggested "pedagogical universalism," or a multiplicity of perspectives, as a foundation on which to build an education and to encourage mutual understanding (Piaget, 1957; Sadler 1969). More recently, and perhaps more simply, Spencer-Oatey and Franklin (2009), adapting Žegarac's cognitive perspective, describe an intercultural situation as "one in which the cultural distance between the participants is significant enough to have an effect on interaction/communication that is noticeable to at least one of the parties" (p. 3). Meanwhile, various anthropological frameworks such as Hall's (1976) three dimensions of cultural difference have sought to explain some of the difficulties involved in cross-cultural interaction.

Scholars in the United States have been working on this concept for 50 years, and yet there is little consensus on terminology either in the United States or elsewhere. Varying by discipline and approach, terminology includes *intercultural competence, intercultural communicative competence, global competence, global citizenship, multicultural competence, cultural fluency, communicative competence, cultural competence, intercultural sensitivity, cross-cultural awareness, cultural intelligence, cultural literacy, cross-cultural capability,* and so on (see Fantini, 2009, for a longer list of terms). Much of the competence literature suggests that *competence* is comprised of knowledge, skills, and attitudes. Others, such as Killick (1997), have argued that the term *competence* is in itself flawed in that it suggests completion of the learning process and relatively low-level skills (p. 284); terms such as *development, awareness, understanding, maturity,* or *capability* would be considered more representative of the processes involved. Nevertheless, for the purpose of this chapter, *intercultural competence* is used for ease of reference, in part because that term is used frequently in the literature and is viewed as being applicable in any intercultural situation, not just ones that occur abroad.

Initially, intercultural competence research and literature in the United States were focused primarily on the identification of predictor variables for success as people were selected and trained to serve in foreign settings. Thus, a discussion of intercultural competence has usually involved a list of dimensions or components. Depending on the background of the researcher (i.e., communication, education, psychology, anthropology, business, languages), different approaches were taken in developing lists of components/predictors. For example, Lustig and Koester (1993) identified at least four different approaches to researching intercultural competence: trait approach (i.e., personality), perceptual approach (i.e., attitudes, perceptions), behavioral approach, and culture-specific approach. Collier (1989) also identified different approaches to intercultural competence including cross-cultural attitude approaches, behavioral skills approaches, ethnographic approach, and cultural identity approach, concluding that research can benefit from the "clarification of conceptualizations" (p. 298). Chen and Starosta (1996) note the confusion and ambiguity that exist in the literature regarding the distinctions between the various components of intercultural competence. Wiseman (2001) cites numerous scholars who stress different behaviors related to intercultural competence, including interaction behaviors and management, identity maintenance, relationship skills, and uncertainty reduction strategies. Spencer-Oatey and Franklin (2009) discuss a range of *etic* and *emic* approaches to cultural difference in a variety of disciplines, from sociology through linguistics to business, and in several social, professional, and religious contexts.

Scholars prioritize various components as being central to intercultural competence. Kim (2002), in utilizing a systems-theory approach to examine intercultural communication competence, sees adaptability at the heart of intercultural communication competence and defines adaptability as

> the individual's capacity to suspend or modify some of the old cultural ways, and learn and accommodate some of the new cultural ways, and creatively find ways to manage the dynamics of cultural difference/unfamiliarity, intergroup posture, and the accompanying stress. (p. 377)

Further, Kim (2002) advocates separating intercultural communication competence from cultural communication competence since the content of cultural communication competence is culture-specific and varies from culture to culture, whereas the content of intercultural communication competence "should remain constant across all intercultural situations regardless of specific cultures involved" (p. 373).

Spitzberg and Cupach (1984) concur with Kim on the role of adaptability as a critical competence that is context-independent. They note that adaptability "implies that different behaviors and skills are applied in different contexts and situations" (p. 90). Hofstede (1997) focuses on the need to understand cultural difference through underlying cultural values, while Bennett (1993) presents an intercultural sensitivity model in which one's response to cultural difference, developmental in nature, underscores one's degree of intercultural competence. Magala (2005), on the other hand, stresses identity as central to intercultural competence. This point is reinforced throughout the literature emphasizing the importance of greater understanding

of one's own identity as a crucial element of the development of intercultural competence. Alred, Byram, and Fleming (2003) talk of "the discovery of self through the discovery of otherness" (p. 109). Indeed, this can be seen as a growth spiral in that the process of learning to understand cultural otherness leads to enhanced self-understanding, which supports greater understanding of cultural others.

Different fields and professions also use a variety of terminology and definitions when exploring this concept. For example, the engineering field in the United States uses the term *global competence* (Grandin & Hedderich, 2009), while the field of social work often uses *cultural competence* (Fong, 2009). The health care field, where this can become a life or death matter, uses both *interculturally competent care* and *cultural humility* (Anand & Lahiri, 2009, Tervalon & Murray-García, 1998). Spitzberg and Changnon (2009) cite a wide range of work on intercultural competence in different fields, while also listing work on intercultural competence designed for specific contexts (p. 3). Many other fields have addressed the concept of intercultural competence, including linguistics, cultural anthropology, psychology, sociology, business, tourism and hospitality, military, international development, public administration, police/security, and even religious organizations (Yancey, 2009). As Moosmueller and Schoenhuth (2009) note, "the discourse on intercultural competence is multifaceted and often considered confusing" (p. 209). And as Spitzberg and Changnon (2009) point out, while "there is obviously no shortage of feasible approaches or models guiding conceptualizations . . . of intercultural competence," there are some common categories, including motivation, knowledge, higher order skills, macro-level skills, interpersonal skills (categorized under subcategories of attentiveness, composure, coordination, expressiveness), contextual competencies (including identity), and outcomes. Spitzberg and Changnon (2009) found that adaptability was part of nearly all models of intercultural competence in the scholarly literature in the United States, and given that there has been little concrete research to date focused specifically on adaptability, these scholars call for further research on this concept. Unresolved issues in current conceptualizations of intercultural competence include the absence of emotional aspects, the ethnocentricity found in these conceptualizations (i.e., the Western emphasis on the individual and the focus at the individual level), and research on the various definitions and models themselves, including criteria for identifying quality model(s) (and who set them).

One particular discipline in which intercultural competence development has become a significant feature is languages. As illustrated by Byram (1997) and Killick and Parry (1999), Parker (2002) argues that the discipline "has to some extent reinvented itself, focusing not on language skills, but on intercultural communication," and several studies note the incorporation of ethnographic methods into study abroad for language learning (Weber-Bosley 2010). Byram, Alred, and others (Alred et al., 2003, 2006; Byram, 1997, 2006; Deardorff, 2009b), contend that intercultural competence must be taught in addition to the language and that speaking another language does not automatically give rise to intercultural competence.

Byram and Zaraté (1994), posited four, and Byram (1997) later extended this to five *savoirs* for teaching and assessing what they term *intercultural communicative competence*. Although initially emerging from the discipline of languages, these concepts are applicable beyond that field:

Knowing (*Savoir*)— knowledge of aspects of culture, beliefs, and reference points that are familiar to cultural natives

Being or empathizing (*Savoir être*)— understanding and dealing with cultural difference with curiosity and openness and without ethnocentrism

Learning (*Savoir apprendre*)—interpreting how others live, think, feel, and communicate

Understanding (*Savoir comprendre*)—gaining insight into cultural meanings, beliefs, and practices in comparison with one's own culture

Engaging (*Savoir s'engager*)—making informed critical evaluations of aspects of one's own and other cultures

In adding the fifth *savoir*, Byram (1997) asserts that "the inclusion in Intercultural Communicative Competence of savoir s'engager/ critical cultural awareness as an educational aim for foreign language teaching is crucial" (p 113). However, Scarino (2007) argues that "the model

of *savoirs* does not elaborate on the important ways in which language affects culture and culture affects language, and what this means to the learner as an interactant or performer in communication" (p. 3).

Kraeva (n.d.) asserts that language is "an essential component of inter-cultural education in order to encourage understanding between different population groups and ensure respect for fundamental rights" and outlines a curriculum at Moscow State Linguistic University that is designed to promote intercultural awareness and competence as a general educational goal. Kraeva argues that the cultural component of language teaching and learning should be strengthened to facilitate deeper understanding of other cultures. "Languages should not be simple exercises but opportunities to reflect on other ways of life, other literatures, other customs" (p. 3).

Yet, it is important to be mindful that while understanding or speaking another language does not automatically result in the development of intercultural competence, language fluency can provide unique access to deep cultural knowledge that cannot be achieved in any other way. A measure of intercultural competence can be achieved without higher order language fluency, but higher order intercultural competence assumes both deep cultural knowledge and the ability for interlocutors to communicate with one another in ways that incorporate the nuances of the culture. This would necessarily mean that the interculturally competent party would have fluency in the language of the other party. The optimal situation would clearly be combining language fluency with the array of other skills, knowledge, attitudes, and outcomes that are most frequently associated with competence as further discussed in this chapter.

Research-Based Model of Intercultural Competence

The first research study to document consensus among leading intercultural scholars from a variety of disciplines and primarily based in the United States was conducted by Deardorff (2006, 2009b). From this national study conducted in the United States, the consensus definition on which these leading intercultural scholars agreed was broadly defined as "effective and appropriate behavior and communication in intercultural situations" (Deardorff, 2009b, p. 33). The researcher categorized these specific agreed-upon elements into attitudes, knowledge, skills, and internal/external outcomes and placed these in a visual framework. This study serves as one way to view a more foundational framework on intercultural competence, one that is based on a grounded research approach. This framework, which has found resonance in different cultural contexts, is meant to serve as a basis of further discussion for purposes of this chapter.

Attitudes

Based on the Deardorff (2009b) study, key attitudes emerged: respect, openness, curiosity, and discovery. Openness and curiosity imply a willingness to risk and to move outside one's comfort zone. Furthermore, curiosity sets a foundation for more creative ways to turn differences into opportunities while openness allows the possibility of seeing from more than one perspective, which is invaluable when negotiating and mediating cultural difference (LeBaron & Pillay, 2006). As LeBaron and Pillay (2006) note, "dialogue with genuine curiosity is a precondition for . . . addressing cultural conflicts" (p. 94).

Knowledge

In the United States, there is some debate as to what *global knowledge* is needed for intercultural competence. In that regard, intercultural scholars concurred on the following: (1) cultural self-awareness (meaning the ways in which one's culture has influenced one's identity and worldview), (2) culture-specific knowledge,[2] deep cultural knowledge including understanding other worldviews, and (3) sociolinguistic awareness. The one element all the intercultural scholars in the study agreed on was the importance of understanding the world from others' perspectives.

Skills

The skills that emerged from this study were ones that addressed the acquisition and processing of knowledge: observation, listening, evaluating, analyzing, interpreting, and relating. This concurs with an observation by Bok (2006) of the importance of "thinking interculturally."

Knowledge is not static, and given the exponential change occurring in the 21st century, it becomes critical that individuals develop the skills necessary not only to acquire knowledge but, more important, to make meaning of the knowledge and then apply that knowledge in specific ways to concrete problems.

Internal outcomes

The attitudes, knowledge, and skills outlined in this framework ideally lead to an internal outcome that consists of flexibility (LeBaron & Pillay, 2006), adaptability, an ethnorelative perspective and empathy. These are aspects that occur *within* the individual as a result of the acquired attitudes, knowledge, and skills necessary for intercultural competence. At this point, individuals are ideally able to see from others' perspectives and to respond to others according to the way in which the other person desires to be treated, thus demonstrating empathy (Calloway-Thomas, 2010). Individuals may reach these internal outcomes with varying degrees of success, depending on the attitudes, skills, and knowledge acquired within this framework.

External outcomes

The summation of the attitudes, knowledge, and skills, as well as the internal outcomes, is demonstrated through the behavior and communication of the individual. How effective and appropriate is this person in intercultural interactions? Behavior and communication become the visible external outcomes of intercultural competence. This then becomes the agreed upon definition of the intercultural scholars in this study, that intercultural competence is the effective and appropriate behavior and communication in intercultural situations. However, it is important to understand that this definition is predicated on particular requisite elements of intercultural competence. It is also important to understand the implications of *effective* and *appropriate* behavior and communication. *Effectiveness* can be determined by the interlocutor, but the *appropriateness* can be determined only by the other person—with appropriateness being directly related to language fluency, cultural sensitivity, and the adherence to cultural norms of that person.

These five overall elements of attitudes, knowledge, skills, and internal and external outcomes comprise this research-based intercultural competence model (see Figure 16.1), thereby providing a framework to further guide efforts in developing—and assessing—individuals' intercultural competence. These elements are placed within the context of intercultural interactions, with an emphasis on the process involved in the development of one's intercultural competence. It is important to note that the development of intercultural competence is a lifelong process and that there is no point at which one becomes fully interculturally competent. Furthermore, the *process* of development becomes crucial through self-reflection and mindfulness. Knowledge alone, such as learning a language, is not sufficient for intercultural competence but must be combined with other elements such as the requisite attitudes of openness, curiosity, and respect.

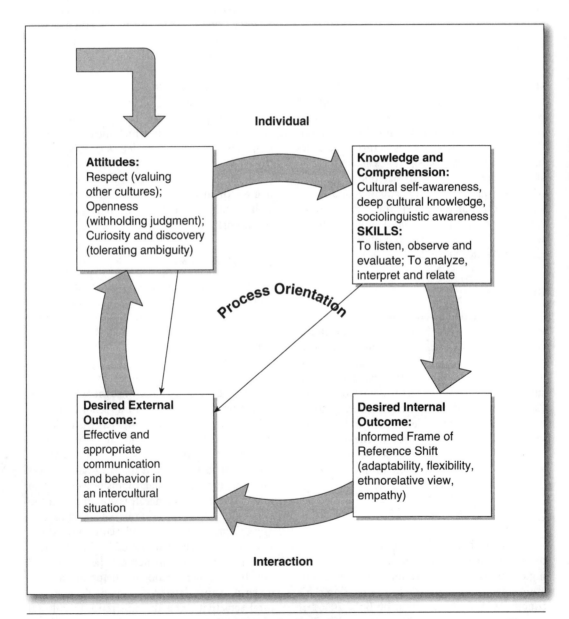

Figure 16.1   Intercultural Competence Model (Deardorff, 2006)

In the ever-evolving literature on intercultural competence, the term *cultural humility* is entering the discussion; it focuses more on respect combined with cultural self-awareness, with cultural self-awareness, with less emphasis placed on knowledge and more on fostering cultural self-awareness, interpersonal sensitivity, and an attitude of respect and learning (Tervalon, & Murray-García, 1998). This particular model lends itself well to the focus on cultural humility when interacting with others. It is also important to recognize this or other frameworks of intercultural competence occur within a much larger global context and that intercultural competence becomes a requisite component to successful engagement and relationship building.

There are practical implications of this framework within areas of the international education field, including curriculum development, faculty development (see Chapters 14 & 15, this volume, for further elaboration), assessment, and program improvement; those will be discussed in subsequent chapter sections (for further discussion on assessment, please see Chapter 10, this volume). For example, this model, while culture-general in nature, can be tailored to specific contextual situations, whether domestic or cross-border in nature, by using the elements to develop context-specific outcomes. One final note: This model is not meant to be used alone but rather in juxtaposition and combination with other frames, including ones that address more specifically the developmental, psychological, ethical, interpersonal, and engagement dimensions of human interactions.

Limitations of this research-based model are somewhat obvious, including that this is a U.S.- centric model of intercultural competence, albeit one that has resonated in other cultures. Given that understanding other worldviews was the one aspect agreed upon by all the intercultural scholars in the study, one can ask: What are other cultural perspectives on this concept of intercultural competence? For example, from an Indian perspective, intercultural competence manifests itself as "unity within diversity" (Manian & Naidu, 2009). From a Chinese perspective, there is a strong focus on harmony and relational aspects (Chen & An, 2009). See Box 16.1 for a brief history of Chinese scholarship on intercultural communicative competence.

BOX 16.1 Reviewing Developments in Teaching and Research in China on Intercultural Communication

Steve J. Kulich

Executive director, Intercultural Institute (SII), Shanghai International Studies University (China)

Ada Yanni Meng

Graduate research assistant, SII (China)

SII team

Shanghai International Studies University (China)

As China opened up in the 1980s, the revival of foreign language teaching led to the beginnings of intercultural communication (IC), first introduced in 1983 through Daokuan He (Shenzhen University). A number of other English instructors sent abroad started by first including culture in foreign language teaching; as time went on, they emphasized communicative competence, cultural awareness, and then intercultural competence. Wenzhong Hu (Beijing Foreign Studies University, BFSU) coedited some of the first IC guidebooks in the early 1990s. Other returnees wrote the early Chinese IC textbooks and launched the first IC courses in the mid-1990s, notably Shijie Guan (Peking University), Gao Yihong (Peking University), Yuxin Jia (Harbin Institute of Technology, HIT),

(Continued)

(Continued)

Hongying Wang (Nankai University), Dajin Lin (Fuzhou Normal University), and Lisheng Xu (Zhejiang University).

Doctoral dissertations with an IC focus started appearing in the late 1990s, and some of the earliest were directed by Zhaoxiong He, Shuzhong Hu, and Weidong Dai at Shanghai International Studies University (SISU), where Steve Kulich and Hongling Zhang were pioneering IC coursework. Courses, research papers, and books also appeared from scholars like Jiazu Gu and Linnell Davis (Nanjing Normal University), Ruiqing Du and Benxian Li (Xi'an Foreign Language University), and Degen Tang (Xiangtan University). Most of the institutions mentioned here have now become established as some of the leading IC programs in the country, and the presses of BFSU and SISU have provided a wide range of textbooks for the field.

The first truly international IC conference was held in Harbin at HIT in 1995; the Chinese Association for Intercultural Communication (CAFIC) was established on this occasion (cf. Guan, 2007; Kulich & Chi, 2009) with continuing support from the International Association for Intercultural Communication Studies and the Center for Intercultural Dialogue. With an official name for the field, an association that meets every 2 years, and a growing palette of texts, the field grew rapidly. IC research or educational articles exceeded 1,000 by 1997 (Hu, 1999) then 2,000 in the next 5 years (Hu, 2006). In 1999, the Chinese Ministry of Education revised the FLT curriculum and syllabus to include IC awareness and competence in the teaching of foreign languages.

Concurrently, the need to move the IC field "beyond language" was emphasized (Kulich, 2003) and the scope expanded, with intercultural communication competence (ICC) becoming a key focus (cf. Xu, 2006a). Scholars like Hongling Zhang (2001, 2007), Yihong Gao (2002), Lisheng Xu (2006b, 2011), and Li Song (2004) have been key proponents for developing the conceptualization and implementation of ICC. Competence is increasingly integrated as a core component in IC courses and research projects, like those of Wei Weifan and Hua Zhong (Huazhong University of Science and Technology, HUST) and Yi'an Wang (Hangzhou Electrical Technology University). As an example, ICC was a primary goal of the undergraduate and graduate courses started in 1999 at SISU (initially called "IC Theory and Practice"). These continue to use experiential exercises from Linell Davis's *Doing Culture* (1999) and have added Myron Lustig and Jolene Koester's IC textbook (2007). In 2010, the course was renamed "Intercultural Communication Competence."

Conceptually, scholars have been grappling with appropriate ways to adapt ICC to Chinese contexts (e.g., Gao's "going across" and "going beyond" article, 2002). Wen (2004) addresses the inadequacies in China's models of foreign language teaching and argues that languages should be taught with a focus on intercultural competence. Wen proposes a two-component ICC model to measure students' second-language proficiency and puts forward suggestions for teaching English as a second language. Her two components are (1) communicative competence, which involves linguistic, pragmatic, and strategic competence; and (2) intercultural competence, which involves sensitivity to, tolerance of, and flexibility in dealing with cultural differences. She further suggests that (a) all language-teaching programs offer a course on IC that combines the daily teaching of cultural knowledge with promoting the students' ICC, and beyond language courses, (b) ICC should be part of general education to help students develop a competitive edge in a world where "globalization has become a reality."

Some of these concerns have been addressed. Jiang (2011) notes that college English teachers now affirm the promotion of communicative competence, but methods for integrating ICC are the primary issue, some of the best being discussion/debate, role-plays, presentations, intercultural scenarios, and critical incidents. There are also larger conceptual concerns, as Xu (2011) notes. In revisiting the construction of ICC in China, he critiques the Western traditions that have long dominated communication studies; highlights the prevailing tendencies in this research toward reductionism, fragmentation, pragmatism (a preoccupation with the effectiveness), and non-cross-cultural orientations; and makes suggestions to develop true cross-cultural paradigms to further the field.

In the last decade, about 20 universities (nearly every institution listed here) have developed IC centers to advance IC teaching, comparative research, and ICC training. Among these, the centers at SISU, HIT, BFSU, and HUST in Wuhan are multistaffed and particularly influential. Li Song of HIT has national research funding to focus on the teacher's cognition of ICC in the Chinese context in foreign language teaching (primarily English). The HUST team have projects including the use of film as an interactive component in ICC teaching and assessment of the effects of ICC training. In the last 5 to 10 years, colleges of business and organizational training firms are also increasingly focusing on ICC training in international work and management contexts (e.g., Kulich et al., 2006). With such a rapidly growing market and acknowledged need, ICC research and applications in China have bright prospects.

Within some African cultures, the theme of identity emerges within intercultural competence through the concept of *Ubuntu*: "I am, therefore we are; we are, therefore, I am" (Nwosu, 2009). This relational aspect finds resonance in other cultural perspectives on intercultural competence, including some Arab perspectives (Zaharna, 2009) and the Latin American context (Medina-Lopez-Portillo & Sinnigen, 2009). Imahori and Lanigan (1989) developed a model of intercultural communication competence where the focus is on both people in the intercultural action, not just the individual, which is unique to many other definitions and models. The outcome thus becomes a relational outcome between the two participants in the intercultural interaction, which aligns with numerous non-Western conceptualizations of intercultural competence.

Some common themes emerge in this more global review that can be incorporated into practice. The first theme is the role and impact of colonialism on intercultural contact within and between societies, especially those in African, Asian, and Latin American contexts. The importance of understanding these historical, political, and social contexts of societies is crucial in the development of greater individual and societal intercultural competence. In fact, numerous scholars emphasize the importance of context in intercultural competence and while Western definitions and models of this concept tend to view this construct in a vacuum—devoid of context—work from Latin American, Arab, and Asian perspectives of intercultural competence note how crucial it is to consider the specific contexts of intercultural competence practice. For example, Medina-Lopez-Portillo and Sinnigen (2009), in writing about Latin American perspectives on intercultural competence, raise key questions about the role of equality and power in intercultural interaction, as well as the impact of such historical contexts as colonialism and its subsequent influence on indigenous cultures. This focus on context points to the importance of knowledge and awareness in intercultural competence development.

Another key theme that emerges from the literature is that of the importance of relationship within competence. Such a priority on relationship building has significant implications for trust building, interpersonal communication skills, conflict resolution, and other issues. The discussions on relationship also lead to the focus on interconnectedness and on global citizenship. To that end, Ashwill and Duong (2009), in discussing the U.S. American and Vietnamese conceptualizations of intercultural competence within global citizenship, point out the interconnectedness of multidimensional global citizens: "Global citizens think and feel themselves as part of something much grander and all-inclusive than one culture or nationality" (p. 155).

This leads to another theme, that of identity. Given the human tendency to identify oneself through in-group or out-group categorizations, what role does identity play in intercultural communication? Is it possible to transcend one's cultural identity to embrace the larger identity of global citizen? Moreover, what role does national identity play? For example, Ashwill and Duong (2009) discuss intercultural competence within the larger national identity, including the impact of Vietnamese insecurity around identity. In this age of globalization, which often leads to politicized cultural identities, transcending one's identity implies moving beyond the traditional dichotomous in/out group mentality to one that embraces and respects others' differences and focuses on the relational goals of engagement. Education abroad, service learning, and experiential learning opportunities, when combined with critical self-reflection assignments, help students to explore identity as a first step in transcending identities. From various perspectives and models of intercultural competence, this chapter now turns to the broader context in which higher education institutions around the world attempt to incorporate intercultural competence (with varied terminology) into their missions and practice.

UNIVERSITY IMPLEMENTATION OF INTERCULTURAL COMPETENCE

Working with theoretical models and operating in concrete contexts, how do institutions of higher education incorporate intercultural competence development into their internationalization projects? In the United Kingdom, the United States, and Australia, the concept of intercultural competence is increasingly linked to notions of global citizenship and multiculturalism discussed here. In Australia, for example, many universities are explicit about their expectations that graduates will have acquired certain "graduate attributes." It is common for these lists to include notions of global citizenship, multicultural perspectives, and other dimensions of intercultural competence.

The University of South Australia (UniSA), for example, lists a range of indicators in its expectation that "a graduate . . . demonstrates international perspectives as a professional and as a citizen" (University of South Australia, n.d.). These include:

Display an ability to think globally and consider issues from a variety of perspectives

Demonstrate an awareness of their own culture and its perspectives and other cultures and their perspectives

Recognize intercultural issues relevant to their professional practice

Appreciate the importance of multicultural diversity to professional practice and citizenship

Appreciate the complex and interacting factors that contribute to notions of culture and cultural relationships

Value diversity of language and culture

Demonstrate awareness of the implications of local decisions and actions for international communities and of international decisions and actions for local communities.

For another example from an Australian university, see Box 16.2.

BOX 16.2 Intercultural Competence at Macquarie University

Sabine Krajewski

Lecturer, Intercultural Communication, Macquarie University (Australia)

Macquarie University is the fourth-largest university in Sydney, Australia. Its diverse community comprises about 37,000 students and 2,500 academic and professional staff. Around 30% of its students are international students from more than 70 countries. Macquarie was one of the first universities to develop a research-based definition of intercultural competence tailored specifically to the university, grounded in literature (e.g., Deardorff, Schroeder), and using a Delphi-methodology to arrive at the definition (Krajewski, 2011). The following examples are cornerstones of Macquarie University's activities around building intercultural competence, which is a vital part of all policies, procedures, and guidelines of Macquarie University.

At Macquarie, the term *cultural diversity* is defined broadly to include language use, cultural background, race, ethnicity, national origin, gender, sexuality, Indigenous Australian identity, age, attendance pattern, family and carer responsibility, geographical location, socioeconomic status, religion, and disability. The Cultural Diversity & Inclusive Language Resource (http://www.mq.edu.au/socialinclusion/cultural_diversity/cultural_diversity.html) is designed to assist academic staff, general staff, and students in creating welcoming, supportive, and culturally competent environments in which cultural diversity is acknowledged, affirmed, and celebrated.

A research team led by scholars from Macquarie University and including scholars from the University of Newcastle and the University of Queensland focused on postgraduate research supervision in a cross-cultural context and what institutions can do to support candidates and supervisors. The team developed online resources to enhance skills in higher degree research supervision in an intercultural context that are freely available for use by both candidates and supervisors:

Ten short video clips with supporting transcripts; 17 written scenarios with key ideas and suggested discussion questions; three documents outlining strategies; a checklist to determine departmental and faculty readiness; and an annotated bibliography with over 100 entries. (http://www.mq.edu.au/ltc/altc/cross_cultural_supervision_project/)

There are numerous MQ Equity & Diversity Groups working together with faculties and offices to embed principles of inclusion, equity, and diversity in university practices. They develop equity frameworks such as the Multicultural Services and Programs Plan, and case-manage equity-related grievances (discrimination/harassment on the basis of gender, race, sexuality, disability, age, family/carer's responsibilities, political affiliation).

In 2010, the Equity & Diversity Unit (Social Inclusion) instigated a series of "Courageous Conversations about Race" workshops for staff and students, which will be followed by more themed workshops to strengthen cultural competency in the university community.

LEAP (Learning Education Aspiration Participation)

In 2010, Macquarie University introduced an innovative new undergraduate curriculum, which includes *people, planet* and *participation* units. These units encourage cross-cultural understanding by providing global perspectives and directly impacting students' local and international connectedness.

The Macquarie Global Leadership Program provides a structured 30-hour program for students to develop cross-cultural understanding through a range of elective workshops and seminars, think tanks, lectures by distinguished speakers, and internationally focused activities and internship opportunities.

The Building Inclusive Communities Awards are a joint initiative of the Ethnic Communities' Council of New South Wales and Macquarie University (Social Inclusion). The Awards recognize and showcase individuals and groups in New South Wales whose work promotes harmony and

(Continued)

(Continued)

understanding of others, and makes a significant contribution in helping to build a diverse and tolerant Australia. Macquarie's first Multicultural Policies & Services Program Plan is currently being developed by Social Inclusion staff. It will provide a framework for developing and expanding cultural competence in planning and policy, learning, teaching and research, access and equity (students and staff), and community engagement.

PACE (Participation and Community Engagement) has been developed over the last 3 years to further the capabilities of Macquarie students and staff to actively contribute to the well-being of people and the planet. This is an exciting experiential learning experience program offering a range of opportunities to apply academic learning to real world situations. PACE sets out to transform the learning, teaching, and research experience at Macquarie to enable enhanced contributions to a socially inclusive and sustainable society.

Similar examples are to be found in the United Kingdom. At the University of Sheffield (n.d.), "We want all of our students to be engaged with the communities they are living in and to have opportunities to appreciate cultures that are new to them." The British experience in this regard may be contrasted with more assimilationist approaches to multiculturalism in, for example, the United States and France. For an example from a Mexican university, see Box 16.3.

BOX 16.3 Universidad de Monterrey (UDEM)'s Journey in Intercultural Competence

Brenda Garcia Portillo

Coordinator of Internationalization Projects, Universidad de Monterrey (Mexico)

Universidad de Monterrey (UDEM) is a private institution that stands out in the context of Mexican higher education for its model of liberal arts education. Founded in 1969, UDEM believes that education should go beyond fostering the acquisition of knowledge to promoting the comprehensive and holistic development of the human being. As part of its international accreditation with the Southern Association of Colleges and Schools, UDEM chose Internationalization as its Quality Enhancement Plan. Also, in 2007, UDEM developed the Internationalization Strategic Plan, which was awarded the Andrew Heiskell Award for Innovation in International Education in 2009.

As part of UDEM's Strategic Plan, UDEM is addressing the development of intercultural competence (ICC). UDEM is well aware of the importance accomplishing this and is committed to providing its students with the following direct and indirect activities.

Compared international contexts course. This course is part of the general curriculum and is mandatory for all students. It focuses on developing specific cultural knowledge and activities and also encourages the students to discuss global issues and dilemmas.

Co-curricular courses. The formative model of UDEM requires that all students take co-curricular courses in different fields, such as sports, cultural affairs, service learning, pastoral, and leadership. In this area, UDEM enriched the model by developing a set of courses, Intercultural Competences I, II, and III, that address ICC in a more systematic and direct way. These courses are based on the theories of Kolb, Mezirow, Bennett, Paige, Hunter, and Deardorff, among others.

In the fall term 2011, UDEM ran its first pilot course called Intercultural Competences I. This course is offered, in its first phase, to all students who want to study abroad. In its second phase, it engages the entire student body, including international students. This course became mandatory for all students in Fall 2012. Within its curricula, the course includes modules in cultural knowledge, intercultural communication, intercultural sensitivity, and intercultural adaptation among others.

Intercultural Competence II is an online course for students who are abroad. The purpose of this course is to provide students with a space for reflection on their experience while they are overseas. The students apply the knowledge acquired in the first course to their current experience.

Intercultural Competence III is a seminar in which students will reflect on how to keep developing ICC in the future, since it is an ongoing process.

Global classroom. This is an online project, and UDEM is participating with different universities around the world. Students from UDEM join a virtual class with students from different parts of the world and work together on activities that prompt them to develop intercultural communication skills.

The I-Fair and the I-Link program. These are two specific activities aimed to promote the interaction with other cultures. They create an international platform in which Mexican and international students relate and collaborate together. During the I-Fair, international students have the opportunity to share their culture with all the university community: students, professors, and collaborators. The I-Link program allows a Mexican student to accompany an international student through his or her journey in the country, the city, and UDEM. These activities encourage respect, empathy, curiosity and communication with individuals of other cultures.

Foreign language proficiency requirement. To graduate, all UDEM students must obtain a 550 score in their TOEFL.

The Challenges

Faculty and staff. UDEM'S next challenge is to develop ICC in faculty and staff since most of the initial efforts have been intended only for students through activities and courses. Training faculty is a main challenge, but having identified the importance of this, the university has revised its hiring process to hire staff with ICC.

Assessment is also a challenge that needs to be addressed and one that the university continues to tackle.

This notion of global citizenship has become part of the internationalization discourse in higher education around the world (Bourn, 2010; Bourn, McKenzie, & Shiel, 2006; Fielden, 2007; Fielden, Middlehurst, & Woodfield, 2007; Lewin, 2009; McKenzie et al. 2003; Otter, 2007; Shiel, 2006) and is increasingly the focus of doctoral research and scholarly work (such as Killick 2010). On the one hand, this has emerged through disciplines such as politics, international relations, and development studies and, on the other, through languages, particularly in Byram's work on intercultural citizenship (Byram, 1997; Byram, 2006; see also Alred et al., 2003, 2006) and by Phipps (2006) on "languaging" to strengthen intercultural dialogue.

Fielden et al. (2007) argue that employers are looking for graduates with firsthand experience of living and working in other cultures and that this requirement matches the increasing desire of universities to develop global citizens. Alred et al. (2003) argue for the notion of intercultural citizenship, proposing that a fundamental purpose of education is to promote "a sense of interculturality, an intercultural competence, which is fundamental to education, perhaps always has been so, but is all the more significant in the contemporary world" (p. 6). Viewing this from the student perspective, Bourn (2010) goes so far as to suggest that "there is clear evidence from around the world that more and more students wish to have a greater sense of global connectedness" (p. 27). Fielden (2007) notes that those skills that are necessary "to operate effectively as a global citizen ... also help achieve social cohesion in a multi-cultural society" (p. 23). This reinforcement of the link between internationalization and multiculturalism is finding increasing resonance within UK higher education: the intercultural competence required to operate globally is recognized as equally significant for living within a diverse population (Caruana & Ploner, 2010). This is true within the U.S. context, as well, particularly through the American Council on Education's work in the "At Home in the World" project (Olson, Evans, & Schoenberg, 2007), in which institutions have come together to explore the intersections of international education and multiculturalism, one of which is shared learning outcomes

In this sense, the development of intercultural competence, while not necessarily articulated in this way outside the United States, has become established within the internationalization agenda. It is encompassed, for example, within the Internationalization at Home movement (Crowther et al. 2000). This movement recognized that the vast majority of students do not go abroad for study or placements, and it seeks to create a learning environment so they can acquire intercultural competence both through the formal and nonformal curricula (Beelen, 2007). Leask, Sanderson, Ridings, and Caruana (2006) consider the extent to which having cultural diversity in the student and staff population can help to develop such intercultural competence at home. And Deardorff (2009a) points out the ways in which international students, scholars, and faculty are often an underutilized resource within institutions.

The wide-ranging initiatives to internationalize university curricula (see, e.g., Jones & Killick, 2007; Leask, 2009, 2010) also incorporate notions of intercultural competence, albeit not always explicitly. More U.S. institutions, however, are explicitly setting intercultural competence development as a key goal, and national organizations are addressing this through global learning projects. For example, the American Council on Education worked with several institutions around the United States to develop specific outcomes related to global learning. This "Global Learning for All" project (see also Chapter 17, this volume) was grounded in the belief that global learning is for all students, not just those who have the opportunity to study abroad, and that global learning should be integrated throughout all degree programs. A starting point was engaging key campus stakeholders in dialogues that led to the clear articulation of these global learning outcomes for the institution.

Another national organization that has done extensive work on global learning is the American Association of Colleges and Universities, which developed a rubric on intercultural competence in 2010–2011 through working with faculty from across the United States over an 18-month period (www.aacu.org/value/rubrics/). This rubric was based on the intercultural frameworks of Bennett (1993) and Deardorff (2006) and has been used to assess students' work in various disciplines. (For further discussion, see Chapter 14, this volume, on internationalizing the curriculum, as well as Chapter 15 on internationalizing teaching and learning and Chapter 10 on outcomes assessment.)

The importance of study abroad in developing intercultural competence has long been recognized. Indeed, De Jong and Teekens (2003) go so far as to suggest that the internationalization agenda is really one of interculturalization:

> The cultural impact of a period spent abroad comes mainly from the way it increases people's understanding of their own culture or subculture and their ability to deal with cultural differences in a nonjudgmental way within their own direct environment as well as in international contexts. (p. 48)

The literature includes examples of study abroad being less beneficial (e.g., Caruana & Hanstock 2008; Coleman, 1999) and shows the danger that it can reinforce "a stronger sense of the rightness of one's own nationality and cultural identity" (Alred et al., 2003, p. 118). However, this serves to reinforce the importance of appropriate support for the development of intercultural competence in preparation for the study abroad experience. Coleman's (1997) study indicated negative results for poorly prepared language undergraduates studying abroad, leading to increased stereotyping, ethnocentrism, and prejudice. This led to a number of projects that supported UK universities in introducing elements such as ethnography and intercultural communication into university teaching as preparation for the study abroad experience (FDTL, 1997–2000a, 1997–2000b, 1997–2000c).

Authors in other countries also report on ethnographic approaches that prepare students for study abroad (Jackson, 2005, 2008, Weber-Bosley 2010), but similar techniques are also being used for faculty-led study tours and other kinds of international experiences (e.g., Russell & Vallade, 2010). Jackson's (2005) work with students in Hong Kong shows how their ethnographic writing skills can be developed to encourage reflection. Her research demonstrates "the importance of carefully planned preparation for the cognitive, affective, and behavioral dimensions of intercultural adjustment," through self-analysis and reflection (Jackson, 2008, pp. 222, 232).

Another aspect of significant intercultural competence research relates to the experience of international students at institutions around the world. Leask (2009) and Deardorff (2009a) argue the need for better integration of international and domestic students, whereas Killick (2010) suggests rather that "universities need to be devoting energies to integrating the *home* student to the *university as an international/multicultural community*, rather than focusing so exclusively upon integrating the *international* student into an Anglo-centric community" (p. 256, his italics). Montgomery (2010) suggests that domestic students may miss out on the development of intercultural competence by failing to take advantage of the social and cultural diversity being created by internationalization in higher education (p. 18). Other scholars, such as Harrison and Peacock (2010b), focus on the difficulties associated with intercultural groupwork, a context that should be beneficial to the development of intercultural competence. They find that many domestic students perceive a high level of risk associated with intercultural communication, combined with a significant amount of effort required to understand, be understood, and not offend. Leask (2009) concludes that the development of intercultural competencies in students is a key outcome of an internationalized curriculum and requires a campus culture that motivates and rewards interaction between domestic and international students, both in and out of the classroom. While arguing that interventions to enhance

intercultural engagement between domestic and international students contributes to the breaking down of stereotypes, Thom (2010) notes the increasing rarity in universities of safe opportunities for genuine engagement with other academic cultures, styles, and forms of knowledge.

While the preponderance of international education research studies in the U.S. focus on the intercultural learning of American students abroad, United Kingdom and Australian studies emphasize research that considers intercultural competence and the international student experience. Both countries have aggressively marketed themselves to students wishing to study in another country, resulting in large numbers of international students enrolled in university programs. The experience of those students is recognized as crucial, to ensure that quality and thus reputation remains high; both countries also understand that word-of-mouth marketing is the most effective way to attract more students. As an increasing number of countries promote themselves as student destinations, resulting research is giving rise to interesting reports from elsewhere. In a case study from the Philippines, Abayao (n.d.), for example, outlines an intercultural program offering a "culture sensitive" educational experience envisioned as a part of the university's extension program to enhance the relationship of the university to the surrounding communities.

Practice in Western countries can also represent non-Western approaches in the home context. Haigh (2009) invites domestic learners to take part in an exercise assessing the emotional impacts of their habitat using Smkhya's three modes of nature: self-awareness, self-realization, and self-improvement. Haigh finds that students become uncomfortable with the emphasis on personal introspection this approach requires and argues that students find it easier to deal with the international or intercultural elements of their curriculum if this is delivered by pedagogical approaches with which they are familiar. Adjusting to a curriculum constructed on different cultural foundations and pedagogy, while also being challenged in terms of cultural content, made students uneasy. However, this kind of experiment, which questions worldviews and presuppositions underpinning Western educational structures, can be a benefit both to learners and teachers through critical self-analysis.

Discussion on Implications: Strategies

In the discussion on ways in which intercultural competence is viewed and addressed in various postsecondary institutions around the world, several themes emerge that have practical implications. Intercultural competence development is often a crucial part of broader institutional goals such as global citizenship and engagement. This development occurs on campus through the curriculum, through intersections of international and domestic student interaction in meaningful ways, through faculty development (Deardorff, 2011; Cushner & Mahon, 2009), and through intercultural opportunities in the local community. This development also occurs through intercultural experiences abroad, albeit with the recognition that simply sending students abroad does not result in interculturally competent students. In fact, as noted earlier in this chapter, some research has shown that students may return more ethnocentric and close-minded, depending on a number of factors, including how the experience was constructed, what support mechanisms were in place, and the degree of intercultural learning interventions to further students' development.

Implementation Strategies

What are the first practical steps for an institution in addressing intercultural competence as a student learning outcome? Given the discussion in this chapter, it is important first for institutions to define intercultural competence, based on the literature and their institutional mission, before developing plans to address and assess intercultural competence (Deardorff, 2009b). Too often institutions fail to recognize the wealth of scholarly work on this concept when defining intercultural competence within a particular institutional context. Once intercultural competence is defined and related learning outcomes have been explicitly stated, strategies can be targeted based on the institutional context. Some of these strategies have been highlighted below, and others are discussed in Chapters 14, 15, and 17 of this volume.

Strategies for developing intercultural competence at postsecondary institutions include:

- Explicitly state intercultural competence-related learning outcomes as part of the curriculum, particularly in less obvious courses

such as those in math, science, or even music—developed through dialogue with key institutional stakeholders.

- Utilize course materials from multiple cultural perspectives (including innovative use of technology to incorporate different perspectives) and ensure that courses go beyond knowledge transmission related to intercultural materials (i.e., a few "international readings" added in) to address actual skill development

- Articulate an institutional list of graduate attributes and indicators related to intercultural competence and global citizenship

- Introduce elements such as ethnography, intercultural communication, self-analysis, experiential learning, service learning, intercultural groupwork, and critical reflection into university teaching, especially as preparation for experiences abroad and intercultural interactions in the local community. Provide feedback to students on their intercultural development.

- Intentionally create meaningful, safe ways for international and domestic students to interact substantively together outside the classroom (i.e., living arrangements, community service projects, intramural sports programs, pairing programs, etc.), which means also finding ways to motivate and reward students for these efforts

- Develop programs that intentionally connect students with the local community (i.e., service learning opportunities, volunteer projects, internships), especially immigrant populations within the community

- Provide opportunities (such as symposia, workshops, and dialogues) for faculty to explore intercultural competence frameworks and ways in which those frameworks translate into specific intercultural learning outcomes within curricula and courses (see Deardorff, 2012, for more on this)

- Implement intercultural skills training programs to help prepare staff to model and guide students' intercultural competence development

- Provide experiential learning and professional development opportunities for alumni to continue their own intercultural competence development and engagement, given that this is a lifelong process

• Develop language-across-the-curriculum initiatives that connect language skills and intercultural learning in a variety of disciplines

• Bring in a variety of guest speakers from other cultures to the institution to provide multiple viewpoints for students, staff, and faculty

• Intentionally integrate returning students' experiences abroad into courses and programs at the institution

As institutions implement strategies, both in and out of the classroom, to help develop students' intercultural competence, international educators should recognize that this is a lifelong process. (For discussion on developing intercultural competence, see Bennett, 2009). Furthermore, there are developmental aspects related to this process, and it is important to align strategies with students' own developmental level (see Bennett, 1993). Thus, it is often helpful for institutional leaders to consult with intercultural experts at their institutions to ensure appropriate alignment of strategies and learning interventions.

CONCLUSION

This chapter has highlighted various definitions and conceptions around intercultural competence, discussed some current institutional practices around the development of intercultural competence, and highlighted some strategies that can be considered by institutions. The discourse on intercultural competence has intensified in recent years, although further research and work is needed in this area. In terms of emerging issues within intercultural competence research, there remains much to discuss and explore. For example, what specifically is meant by adaptation? Who adapts to whom and to what degree? Or is it more a question of gleaning the best from various cultures and developing a new global culture to which all adapt? Moreover, what is the impact of globalization on culture and on identity? Are the frames and theories used to analyze cultures still relevant in the increasingly globalized societies of the 21st century? What does it mean to situate intercultural competence within various contexts to more fully understand the true complexity of intercultural competence?

Within higher education, there is movement toward incorporating intercultural competence within broader institutional goals of engagement, 21st-century skills, and global citizenship. In looking to the future, the preparation of "global-ready" graduates appears to be key in the design and development of future curricula and programs. (See Chapter 25, this volume, for further discussion.) As higher education institutions increasingly highlight intercultural competence development as core to achieving their mission and goals, students will not only be more prepared for the globalized workplace of the 21st century but be better equipped to take on the global challenges that confront humanity today.

REFERENCES

Abayao, L. E. (n.d.). Mainstreaming intercultural education. *Case study on intercultural learning and dialogue for the International Association of Universities.* Retrieved from http://www.iau-aiu.net/id/id_case_studies.html

Alred, G., Byram, M., & Fleming, M. (Eds.). (2003). *Intercultural experience and education.* Clevedon, UK: Multilingual Matters.

Alred, G., Byram, M., & Fleming, M. (Eds.). (2006). *Education for intercultural citizenship: Concepts and comparisons.* Clevedon, UK: Multilingual Matters.

Anand, R., & Lahiri, I. (2009). Developing skills for interculturally competence care. In D. K. Deardorff (Ed.), *The SAGE handbook of intercultural competence* (pp. 387–402). Thousand Oaks, CA: Sage.

Ashwill, M., & Duong, T. (2009). Developing globally competent citizens: The contrasting cases of the United States and Vietnam. In D. K. Deardorff (Ed.), *The SAGE handbook of intercultural competence* (pp. 141–157). Thousand Oaks, CA: Sage.

Association of International Education Administrators (AIEA). (2010). *International education: Essential to our future* (2010 AIEA Conference theme). http://www.aieaworld.org

Beelen, J. (Ed.). (2007). *Implementing internationalization at home.* Amsterdam: EAIE.

Bennett, J. M. (2009). Cultivating intercultural competence: A process perspective. In D. K. Deardorff (Ed.), *The Sage handbook of intercultural competence* (pp. 121–140). Thousand Oaks, CA: Sage.

Bennett, M. J. (1993). Towards ethnorelativism: A developmental model of intercultural sensitivity. In R. M. Paige (Ed.), *Education for the intercultural experience* (2nd ed., pp. 21–71). Yarmouth, ME: Intercultural Press.

Bok, D. (2006). *Our underachieving colleges: A candid look at how much students learn and why they should be learning more.* Princeton, NJ: Princeton University Press.

Bourn, D. (2010) Students as global citizens. In E. Jones (Ed.), *Internationalisation and the student voice* (pp. 18–29). London: Routledge.

Bourn, D., McKenzie, A., & Shiel, C. (Eds.). (2006). *The global university: The role of the curriculum.* London: Development Education Agency.

Byram, M. (1997). *Teaching and assessing intercultural communicative competence.* Clevedon, UK: Multilingual Matters.

Byram, M. (2006) Developing a concept of intercultural citizenship. In G. Alred, M. Byram, & M. Fleming (Eds.), *Education for intercultural citizenship: Concepts and comparisons* (pp. 109–129). Clevedon, UK: Multilingual Matters.

Byram, M., & Zaraté, C. (1994). *Definitions, objectifs et évaluation de la competence socio-culturelle.* Strasbourg, France: Council of Europe.

Calloway-Thomas, C. (2010). *Empathy in the global world: An intercultural perspective.* Thousand Oaks, CA: Sage.

Caruana, V. (2010). Global citizenship for all: Putting the "higher" back into UK higher education. In F. Maringe & N. Foskett (Eds.), *Globalization and internationalization in higher education.* London: Continuum.

Caruana, V., & Hanstock, J. (2008). Internationalizing the curriculum at the University of Salford: From rhetoric to reality. In C. Shiel & A. McKenzie (Eds.), *The global university: The role of senior managers* (pp. 30–35). London: DEA.

Caruana, V., & Ploner, J. (2010). *Internationalisation and equality and diversity in HE: Merging identities.* London: Equality Challenge Unit. Retrieved from http://www .ecu.ac.uk/publications/internationalisation -and-equality-and-diversity-in-he- merging -identities

Chen, G. M., & An, R. (2009). A Chinese model of intercultural leadership competence. In D. K. Deardorff (Ed.), *The SAGE handbook of intercultural competence* (pp. 196–208). Thousand Oaks, CA: Sage.

Chen, G. M., & Starosta, W. J. (1996). Intercultural communication competence: A synthesis. *Communication Yearbook, 19,* 353–383.

Clifford, V., & Montgomery, C. (Eds.). (2011). *Moving towards internationalisation of the curriculum for global citizenship in Higher Education.* Oxford, UK: Centre for Staff and Learning Development.

Cole, J., Barber, E., & Graubard. S. (1994). *The research university in a time of discontent.* Baltimore: Johns Hopkins University Press.

Coleman, J. A. (1997). State of the art article: Residence abroad within language study. *Language Teaching, 30*(1)*,* 1–20.

Coleman, J. A. (1999). Language learner attitudes and student residence abroad: New qualitative and qualitative insights. In D. Killick, M. Parry, & A. Phipps (Eds.), *Poetics and praxis of language and intercultural communication* (pp. 75–95) Leeds Metropolitan University: Glasgow University Press/Leeds Metropolitan University.

Collier, M. J. (1989). Cultural and intercultural communication competence: Current approaches and directions for future research. *International Journal of Intercultural Relations, 13,* 287–302.

Crowther, P., Joris, M., Otten, M., Nilsson, B., Teekens, H., & Wächter, B. (2000). *Internationalisation at home* (European Association for International Education position paper). Retrieved from http://www .eaie.org/IaH/IaHPositionPaper.pdf

Cushner, K., & Mahon, J. (2009). Developing the intercultural competence of educators and their students: Creating blueprints. In DK Deardorff (ed*) The SAGE handbook of intercultural competence* (pp. 304-320), Thousand Oaks, CA: Sage.

Davis, L. (1999). *Doing culture: Cross-cultural communications in action.* Beijing: Foreign Language Teaching and Research Press.

Deardorff, D. K. (2006) The identification and assessment of intercultural competence as a student outcome of internationalization at institutions of higher education in the United States. *Journal of Studies in International Education, 10*(3), 241–266.

Deardorff, D. K. (2009a). Connecting international and domestic students. In M. Andrade & N. Evans (Eds.), *International students: Strengthening a critical resource.* New York: Rowman & Littlefield Education.

Deardorff, D. K. (Ed.). (2009b). *The SAGE handbook of intercultural competence.* Thousand Oaks, CA: Sage.

Deardorff, D. K. (2011). Exploring a framework for interculturally competent teaching in diverse classrooms: An American perspective. *Internationalization of European Higher Education: An EUA/ACA Handbook.* Berlin: Raabe.

Deardorff, D. K. (2012, Spring). Building an interculturally competent faculty. *IIE Networker,* p. 39.

Deardorff, D. K., & Hunter, W. (2006). Educating global-ready graduates, *International Educator, 15*(3), 72–83.

Fantini, A. (2009). Assessing intercultural competence: Issues and Tools. In D. K. Deardorff (Ed.), *The SAGE handbook of intercultural competence* (pp. 456–476), Thousand Oaks, CA: Sage.

FDTL (1997–2000a). *The Interculture project.* Retrieved from http://www.lancs.ac.uk/users/interculture/

FDTL (1997–2000b). *Learning and residence abroad project.* Retrieved from http://www.llas.ac.uk/sites/lara/

FDTL (1997–2000c). *Residence abroad project.* Retrieved from http://www.llas.ac.uk/resources/mb/626

Fielden, J. (2007) *Global horizons for UK universities.* London: Council for Industry and Higher Education.

Fielden, J., Middlehurst, R., & Woodfield, S. (2007) *Global horizons for UK students: A guide for universities.* London: Council for Industry and Higher Education.

Fong, R. (2009). Culturally competent practice in social work. In D. K. Deardorff (Ed.), *The SAGE handbook of intercultural competence.* Thousand Oaks, CA: Sage.

Gao, Y. H. (2002). Developing intercultural communicative competence: "Going across" and "going beyond." *Foreign Languages and Their Teaching,* (10), 27–31.

Grandin, J. M. & Hedderich, N. (2009). Global competence for engineers. In D. K. Deardorff (Ed.), *The SAGE handbook of intercultural competence* (pp. 362–373). Thousand Oaks, CA: Sage.

Guan, S. J. (2007). Foreword. In S. J. Kulich & M. H. Prosser (Eds.), *Intercultural perspectives on studying the Chinese: Intercultural research* (Vol. 1, pp. i–xiii in Chinese; ix–xvi in English). Shanghai: Shanghai Foreign Language Education Press.

Haigh, M. (2009). Fostering cross-cultural empathy with non-western curricular structures. *Journal of Studies in International Education, 13*(2): 271–284.

Hall, E. T. (1976). *Beyond culture.* New York: Doubleday.

Harrison, N., & Peacock, N. (2010a). Cultural distance, mindfulness and passive xenophobia: Using Integrated Threat Theory to explore home higher education students' perspectives on "internationalisation at home." *British Educational Research Journal, 36*(6), 877–902. Retrieved from http://www.informaworld.com/smpp/content~db=all~content=a914207566

Harrison, N., & Peacock, N. (2010b). Interactions in the international classroom: The UK perspective. In E. Jones (Ed.), *Internationalisation and the student voice: Higher education perspectives.* London: Routledge.

Hofstede, G. (1997). *Cultures and organizations: Software of the mind.* New York: McGraw-Hill.

Hu, W. Z. (1999). *Intercultural communication studies: An overview.* Beijing: Foreign Language Teaching and Research Press. (In Chinese)

Hu, W. Z. (2006, May 20–22). *On empirical research in intercultural communication.* Keynote presented at the 6th Chinese Symposium for Intercultural Communications sponsored by the CAFIC, Nanjing Normal University. (In Chinese)

Imahori, T. T., & Lanigan, M. (1989). Relational model of intercultural communication competence. *International Journal of Intercultural Relations, 13,* 269–286.

Jackson, J. (2005, August). Assessing intercultural learning through introspective accounts. *Frontiers: The Interdisciplinary Journal of Study Abroad, 11,* 165–186.

Jackson, J. (2008). *Language, identity, and study abroad.* London: Equinox.

Jiang, B. (2011). The teaching of intercultural communicative competence. *Journal of Heilongjiang College of Education, 30*(3), 164–166.

Jones, E., & Killick, D. (2007). Internationalisation of the curriculum. In E. Jones & S. Brown (Eds.), *Internationalising higher education.* London: Routledge.

Killick, D. (1997, December 15–16). Conference summary. In D. Killick & M. Parry (Eds.), *Cross-cultural capability: The why, the ways, and the means* (Proceedings of the conference at Leeds Metropolitan University). Leeds, UK: Leeds Metropolitan University Press.

Killick, D. (2010). *Students as global citizens: being and becoming through the lived-experience of international mobility.* Unpublished doctoral thesis, Leeds Metropolitan University.

Killick, D., & Parry, M. (Eds.). (1999). *Languages for cross-cultural capability: Making boundaries and crossing borders.* Leeds, UK: Leeds Metropolitan University Press.

Kim, M.-S. (2002). *Non-Western perspectives on human communication: Implications for theory and practice.* Thousand Oaks, CA: Sage.

Kraeva, I. (n.d.). Curricular options for teaching language through culture. *Case study on intercultural learning and dialogue for the International Association of Universities.* Retrieved from http://www.iau-aiu.net/id/id_case_studies.html

Krajewski, S. (2011). *The next Buddha may be a community: Practising intercultural competence at Macquarie University.* Sydney: Cambridge Scholars Publishing.

Kuada, J. (2004). *Intercultural competence development of Danish managers.* Retrieved from www.business.aau.dk/ivo/publications/working/wp33

Kulich, S. J. (2003). Beyond language to culture's interdisciplinary dimensions: Toward a broader focus in intercultural communications (Introducing the "Advancing Intercultural Studies" project). In Y. F. Wu (Ed.). *Foreign language and culture studies* (Vol. 3, pp. 848–869). Shanghai: Shanghai Foreign Language Education Press.

Kulich, S. J., & Chi, R. B. (2009). Coming of age: Developing intercultural communication as a discipline in China. *Intercultural Communication Research, 1*(1).

Kulich, S. J., Zhang S. T., & Zhu, M. (2006). Global impacts on Chinese education, identity, and values: Implications for intercultural training. *International Management Review, 2*(1), 41–59.

Leask, B. (2009). Using formal and informal curricula to improve interactions between home and international students. *Journal of Studies in International Education, 13*(2), 205–221.

Leask, B. (2010) "Beside me is an empty chair": The student experience of internationalisation. In E. Jones (Ed.), *Internationalisation and the student voice: Higher education perspectives* (pp. 3–17). London: Routledge.

Leask, B., Sanderson, G., Ridings, S., & Caruana, V. (2006, September). *Developing intercultural competence at home.* Presentation to the EAIE 20th annual conference, Antwerp, Belgium. Retrieved from http://alt-resource.teams.leedsmet.ac.uk/alt-topics

LeBaron, M., & Pillay, V. (2006). *Conflict across cultures: A unique experience of bridging differences.* Yarmouth, ME: Intercultural Press.

Lewin, R. (2009). The quest for global citizenship through study abroad. In R. Lewin (Ed.), *The handbook of practice and research in study abroad* (pp. xiii–xxii). Abingdon, UK: Routledge.

Lustig, M. W., & Koester, J. (1993). *Intercultural competence: Interpersonal communication across cultures.* New York: Harper Collins.

Magala, S. (2005). *Cross-cultural competence.* Oxford, UK: Routledge.

Manian, R., & Naidu, S. (2009). India: A cross-cultural overview of intercultural competence. In D. K. Deardorff (Ed.), *The SAGE handbook of intercultural competence* (pp. 233–247). Thousand Oaks, CA: Sage.

McKenzie, A., Bourn, D., Evans, S., Brown, M., Shiel, C., Bunney, A., Collins, G., Wade, R., Parker, J., & Annette, J. (2003) *Global perspectives in higher education.* London: Development Education Association.

Medina-Lopez-Portillo, A., & Sinnigen, J. (2009). Interculturality versus intercultural competencies in Latin America. In D. K. Deardorff (Ed.), *The SAGE handbook of intercultural competence (pp. 249–263),* Thousand Oaks, CA: Sage.

Montgomery, C. (2010). *Understanding the international student experience.* Basingstoke, UK: Palgrave Macmillan.

Moosmueller, A., & Schoenhuth, M. (2009). Intercultural competence in German discourse. In D. K. Deardorff (Ed.), *The SAGE handbook of intercultural competence* (pp. 209–232). Thousand Oaks, CA: Sage.

Nwosu, P. (2009). Understanding Africans' conceptualizations of intercultural competence. In D. K. Deardorff (Ed.), *The SAGE handbook of intercultural competence* (pp. 158–178). Thousand Oaks, CA: Sage.

Olson, C. Evans, R., & Schoenberg, R. (2007). *At home in the world: Bridging the gap between internationalization and multicultural education.* Washington DC: American Council on Education.

Otter, D. (2007) Globalisation and sustainability: Global perspectives and education for sustainable development. In E. Jones & S. Brown (Eds.), *Internationalising higher education.* London: Routledge.

Parker, J. (2002). A new disciplinarity: Communities of knowledge, learning, and practice. *Teaching in Higher Education, 7*(4).

Phipps, A. (2006) *Learning the arts of linguistic survival: Languaging, tourism, life (tourism and cultural change).* London: Channel View.

Piaget, J. (1957). Jan Amos Comenius. *Prospects, 23* (1–2), 173–196. Retrieved from www.ibe.unesco.org/publications/ThinkersPdf/comeniuse.PDF on March 19, 2010.

Russell, M., & Vallade, L. (2010). Guided reflective journaling: Assessing the international study and volunteering experience. In E. Jones (Ed.), *Internationalisation and the student voice: Higher education perspectives* (pp. 98–109). London: Routledge.

Sadler, J. E. (1969). *Comenius.* London: Collier-MacMillian.

Scarino, A. (2007). *Assessing intercultural language learning* (Intercultural language teaching and learning in practice discussion paper 6). Canberra: Australian Government, Quality teacher program.

Shiel, C. (2006, April). Cultural diversity: Are we doing enough? BMAF Annual conference 2006: *Managing diversity in teaching and learning,* Oxford, UK.

Song, L. (2004). *Gateways to intercultural communication.* Harbin, China: HIT Press. (In Chinese)

Spencer-Oatey, H., & Franklin, P. (2009). *Intercultural interaction: A multidisciplinary*

approach to intercultural communication.
Basingstoke, UK: Palgrave Macmillan.

Spitzberg, B., & Changnon, G. (2009).
Conceptualizing intercultural competence. In
D. K. Deardorff (Ed.), *The SAGE handbook of
intercultural competence* (pp. 2–52). Thousand
Oaks, CA: Sage.

Spitzberg, B., & Cupach, W. R. (1984). *Interpersonal
communication competence.* Beverly Hills,
CA: Sage.

Summers, M., & Volet, S. (2008). Students' attitudes
towards culturally mixed groups on
international campuses: Impact of participation
in diverse and non-diverse groups. *Studies in
Higher Education, 33*(4), 357–370.

Tervalon, M., & Murray-García, J. (1998, May).
Cultural humility versus cultural competence: a
critical distinction in defining physician
training outcomes in multicultural education.
Journal of Health Care for the Poor and
Underserved, 9(2), 117–125.

Thom, V. (2010). Mutual cultures: Engaging with
interculturalism in higher education. In E. Jones
(Ed.), *Internationalisation and the student voice:
Higher education perspectives.* London:
Routledge.

University of Sheffield. (n.d.). Online statement of
the Sheffield graduate. Retrieved from http://
thesheffieldgraduate.group.shef.ac.uk/staff_10
.html

University of South Australia. (n.d.). Online
statement of graduate attributes for UniSA
xWen, Q. F. (2004). Globalization and
intercultural competence. In K.-K. Tam &
T. Weiss (Eds.), *English and globalization:
Perspectives from Hong Kong and Mainland
China* (pp. 169–180). Hong Kong: The Chinese
University Press.

Volet, S., & Ang, G. (1998). Culturally mixed groups
on international campuses: An opportunity for
inter-cultural learning. *Higher Education
Research & Development, 17*(1), 5–23. Retrieved
from http://www.informaworld.com/smpp/cont
ent~db=all~content=a758496236

Xu, L. S. (2006a, May 20–22). *Intercultural
communication competence.* Paper presented at
the 6th Chinese Symposium for Intercultural
Communications sponsored by the CAFIC,
Nanjing Normal University.

Xu, L. S. (2006b). *Studying language and its use: An
intercultural approach.* Shanghai: Shanghai
Foreign Language Education Press. (In Chinese)

Xu, L. S. (2011). Intercultural competence revisited.
*Journal of Zhejiang University (Humanities and
Social Science Edition).* (3), 132–139.

Weber-Bosley, G. (2010). Beyond immersion: Global
engagement and transformation through
intervention via student reflection in long term
study abroad. In E. Jones (Ed.),
*Internationalisation and the student voice: Higher
education perspectives.* London: Routledge.

Wen, Q. F. (2004). Globalization and intercultural
competence. In K.-K. Tam & T. Weiss (Eds.),
*English and globalization: Perspectives from Hong
Kong and Mainland China.* Hong Kong: Chinese
University Press.

Wiseman, R. (2001) Intercultural communication
competence. In W. Gudykunst & B. Mody
(Eds.) *Handbook of international and
intercultural communication.* Thousand Oaks,
CA: Sage.

Xu, L. S. (2006a, May 20–22). *Intercultural
communication competence.* Paper presented at
the 6th Chinese Symposium for Intercultural
Communications sponsored by the CAFIC,
Nanjing Normal University.

Xu, L. S. (2011). Intercultural competence revisited.
*Journal of Zhejiang University (Humanities and
Social Science Edition).*

Yancey, G. (2009). Neither Jew nor Gentile:
Lessons about intercultural competence in
religious organizations. In D. K. Deardorff
(Ed.), *The SAGE handbook of intercultural
competence* (pp. 374–386*).* Thousand Oaks,
CA: Sage.

Zaharna, R. (2009). An associative approach to
intercultural communication competence in
the Arab world. In D. K. Deardorff (Ed.), *The
SAGE handbook of intercultural competence* (pp.
179–195). Thousand Oaks, CA: Sage.

Zhang H. L. (2001). Reforming China's FLT from an
intercultural perspective: An investigation of
culture teaching in China's FLT. In Y. F. Wu &
Q. H. Feng (Eds.), *Foreign language and culture
studies* (Vol. 1, pp. 332–346). Shanghai:
Shanghai Foreign Language and Education
Press. (In Chinese)

Zhang, H. L. (2007). *An intercultural communication
approach to foreign language teaching.* Shanghai:
Shanghai Foreign Language and Education
Press. (In Chinese).

Notes

1 There are many definitions that have been used for
the word "culture." For purposes of this discussion,
"culture" is defined as values, beliefs and norms
shared by a group of people and is not limited to
national culture

17

GLOBALISM AND INTERCULTURALISM

Where Global and Local Meet

CHRISTA OLSON AND JAMES PEACOCK

Globalism is a key concern in contemporary higher education; the global university is a pervasive ideal and one that university administrators often seek to address. Key to addressing the global university is the understanding that global is grounded in local. Institutionally, universities depend on states, provinces, cities, regions, and international bureaucracies, which themselves are localized in headquarters and outposts or other locales. Individually, students are immigrants, migrating to universities from diverse locales—foreign or nearby, rural or urban, rich or poor, with minority or majority ethnicities and cultures. Such localized particularities encounter efforts at engendering global understandings, creating global citizens. How can higher education best synergize such global and local resources? What hinders such synergies? What designs are workable? This chapter examines these questions further by looking at the global university through the synergies of where global meets local.

Initially challenged to describe and fully capture the forces of globalization and its consequences in recent years, U.S. higher education leaders heard scholars at their institutions voice concerns and were cautious to embrace globalization as an organizing principle. Debates about terminology over the past two decades reflect concerns about the philosophical, economical, political, and sociological consequences of globalization. In the mid-1990s, the concept of internationalization was offered up by researchers from Canada and Europe – notably Knight and de Wit (1999) connected with their work on the Internationalization Quality Review Protocol. Presented as the process for integrating international/intercultural learning into the teaching, research, and service functions of an institution, internationalization was embraced by many higher education organizations and institutions as a useful, neutral frame for addressing the forces of globalization (see Green & Olson, 2003). Furthermore, global studies programs have emerged at several higher education institutions as a means of understanding these phenomena and as a counter to the nation-state focus of international relations, the regional focus of area studies, or the local focus of cultural studies. Many institutions now seek to enhance their global footprint and become players in reshaping the global landscape (see Altbach & Peterson, 2007; Marginson, 2011;

Marginson & van der Wende, 2007; Salmi, 2009; van der Wende, 2008; Wildavsky, 2010). Yet others are striving to strike a balance between student learning and institutional impact (Stearns, 2008).

An obvious point of intersection between the global and local within U.S. higher education is that of internationalization and diversity/multicultural education, which is quite new as an interdisciplinary field onto itself. Diversity/multicultural education can be traced through the emergence of the black, ethnic, and multiethnic studies movements of the early 20th century, the intergroup education movement in the mid-20th century, and the civil rights movement of the 1960s and 1970s. Since the 1960s, ethnic studies emphasizing ethnic pride, empowerment, social change, and a voice in the curriculum for historically marginalized groups has evolved through multiethnic education to strive for educational equality through systemic and structural reforms. Following on this, efforts to encompass more than race and ethnicity and to draw comparisons, connections, and interrelationships among race, ethnicity, gender, and class have emerged (Banks & Banks, 2004, Chapter 1).

Alongside these initiatives to diversify U.S. higher education curriculum and institutions, a stream of research has highlighted how diversity enhances the quality of higher education for all (Hovland, 2006; Hurtado, 2007; Jayakumar, 2008). Furthermore, Jayakumar's study demonstrates that the benefits of structural diversity depend on fostering a positive racial climate on campus. How diversity affects higher education institutions and how higher education institutions around the world engage with diversity is yet another stream of this research (Allen, Bonous-Hamouth, & Teranishi, 2006).

Akin to this development is the reemergence of global diversity and global citizenship as framing constructs for higher education leaders, scholars, and practitioners. Noting how citizenship education has been historically rooted in a zero-sum concept, Banks (2007) promotes transformative citizenship education as a means for creating cosmopolitans who are well equipped to be citizens of the global community and address pressing global issues. The Association of American Colleges and Universities (AAC&U) work on global learning and global citizenship also raises important questions about social justice and global connectedness (Hovland & McTighe Musil, 2003).

To what extent, then, are the higher education responses to these themes and forces interconnected? While some encouraging framing constructs have been presented, these responses are often unconnected in practice. As explained further here, diversity issues such as affirmative action are often treated separately—philosophically, legally, and administratively— from global issues. In U.S. institutions, one office is frequently devoted to diversity and minority affairs, others to study abroad, international students and scholars, and international affairs. Furthermore, the division is reflected in funding, administration, and populations of students and teachers. Likewise, in U.S. public institutions, concerns of locale (e.g., counties and communities) are separated from global foci of an institution's college or university curriculum, research, or outreach programs.

Should interconnections increase? If so, how? What are prospects for synergies that energize the educational process? What cautions and criticisms argue against such synergies? For example, if specialization is efficient in spheres ranging from business to science, why not in education?

This chapter addresses these questions from two points of view, using two concepts: interculturalism and grounded globalism. Interculturalism emerges in the overlap between global and local work offering frameworks, competencies, and concrete communication tools for individuals to connect across cultures. Grounded globalism addresses a similar overlap, but its frame is more spatial or geographical; global is a large space grounded in small localized spaces, and dimensions linking these spaces include cultural, economic, political, and psychological. Each perspective will be presented, after which comparisons, synthesis, and recommendations will be explored.

Interculturalism as a Bridging Construct

With the support of several foundations, the American Council on Education (ACE) has conducted multi-institutional demonstration projects seeking to advance internationalization of U.S. institutions. These projects have highlighted that campuses are host to multiple terms for naming and perspectives about educating for global and local spaces. At some institutions, differences in philosophy about how terms should be defined and initiatives advanced resulted in tensions that stymied efforts to promote any of the initiatives. Although some saw the possibilities for synergy and mutual reinforcement between internationalization and multicultural education (for example), others perceived that these educational concerns differed on a conceptual level and competed for attention and resources on a practical level.

ACE's *At Home in the World* initiative, launched in 2005, is grappling directly with these issues. The initiative has included roundtables of leaders (2006, 2007), a publication of the same title (2007), institutes for institutional teams (2008, 2009), a study (2010), and a Luce-funded project (2011). One of the drivers of this initiative is the need for collaborative strategies that transcend the divide between internationalization and multicultural education to ensure that students are empowered to live ethical, meaningful, productive lives in our increasingly diverse and complex world. Other goals include: to better understand our changing world order; to equip a more diverse group of students with skills and knowledge to thrive in a global environment; to improve instruction and advance student learning; and to address difficult social issues within the institutional or broader community context.

Through this initiative, ACE identified areas of common ground such as shared values (the appreciation of difference), shared nature of the work (interdisciplinarity and experiential pedagogy), and shared student learning outcomes (see Olson, Evans, & Schoenberg, 2007). Each of these areas of common ground presents opportunities for champions in diverse intellectual "camps" to construct potential bridges with their counterparts. Working together in identifying shared student learning outcomes, for example, has been a fruitful strategy for getting conversations started for many institutions.

Early on in the *At Home in the World* initiative, interculturalism emerged as a bridging construct between these areas. There was a precedent. The AAC&U had kindled explorations of internationalization, diversity, and intercultural education with their publication, *Globalizing Knowledge: Connecting International & Intercultural Studies* (see Cornwell & Stoddard, 1999), and their ongoing national *Shared Futures* project. Both feature intercultural skills in their reflections about the preparation of students for local and global citizenship. Several small private institutions, including Baldwin Wallace College and Arcadia University, plunged in to experiment with these and other models developed by AAC&U and brought two diverging experiences with interculturalism to the *At Home in the World* initiative. As illustrated in the adjoining boxes, Baldwin-Wallace drew on intercultural competency as the foundation for curricular work in this area, whereas Arcadia felt they had to move beyond this frame to one featuring global connections. (See Boxes 17.1 and 17.2)

BOX 17.1 Intercultural Competency: Preparing Students to be 21st-Century Global Citizens, the Baldwin-Wallace Experience

Judy B. Krutky

Professor of Political Science and International Studies

Director for Intercultural Education, Baldwin–Wallace College (USA)

Baldwin-Wallace's commitment to internationalization and multicultural education is rooted in priorities established when the college was founded in 1845. Baldwin-Wallace is one of the first colleges in Ohio to admit students without regard to race or gender. Its forward-thinking founder,

(Continued)

(Continued)

John Baldwin, also embodied concern for internationalization and started two high schools in Bangalore, India in the 1880s. Today Baldwin-Wallace is a comprehensive master's college with a regional focus, and many students enter the college with limited multicultural or international perspectives. Baldwin-Wallace's current Mission Statement, adopted in 2000, aims to prepare students to become "contributing, compassionate citizens of an increasingly global society."

This mission fit well with the college's heritage. Helping students develop appropriate knowledge, skills, and attitudes supportive of global citizenship was made easier by earlier efforts already in place focused on multicultural affairs and internationalization. Synergy between these efforts began to develop in the curriculum in 2004 with the establishment of the Office of Intercultural Education, representing an attempt to promote students' understanding of alternative cultural perspectives. Most recently, Baldwin-Wallace has reaffirmed its commitment to diversity with the addition of a director of campus diversity affairs in 2008 to promote student, faculty, and staff diversity.

Faculty incorporated elements of intercultural education into the curriculum based on AAC&U's and ACE's learning outcomes into the design of the Liberal Arts and Sciences 200 course, entitled *Enduring Questions for an Intercultural World*. This course began in 2005 as a common experience, required for all students to develop skills and attitudes needed in the 21st century. Students read foundational authors who address enduring questions faced by all cultures and analyze how cultural orientations shape alternative responses. Intercultural education is also supported through the Language Across the Curriculum program, which began in 2003 as an innovative way to allow students to use foreign language to enhance understanding of different cultures.

Baldwin-Wallace's affiliation with ACE and AAC&U has shaped campus thinking on liberal education generally and on these two issues in particular. Theoretical grounding comes from Deardorff (2006, 2009), who presents intercultural competency development as a process of internal change that moves students from individual attributes and knowledge to interactive skills and outcomes. Her conceptualization of intercultural competence pictures a developmental continuum of increasing knowledge and skill and provides a basis for assessment over time. This is reflected in the curriculum, which begins with all students taking the *Enduring Question* course, then selecting additional core courses with an international or diversity focus. The next step will be to reinforce these outcomes in the majors.

Baldwin-Wallace has received funding to develop 17 new language courses in 15 majors to promote language use appropriate to disciplinary learning outcomes. Courses will be taught by nine bilingual faculty and eight nonnative faculty with near-native fluency, who will use grant funding to improve their own language proficiency.

Baldwin-Wallace's aim is to prepare citizens who are interculturally competent and able to interact successfully across different cultures locally, nationally, and globally. While most faculty and students tend to be more oriented to one of these levels than others, depending on interests or majors, the intention is that students will develop a knowledge base that covers all levels on which they will be able to draw both personally and professionally after graduation.

BOX 17.2 Exploring Global Connections at Arcadia University

Jeffrey Shultz

Professor of Education, Assistant Provost for Special Projects,

Arcadia University (USA)

Several years ago, Arcadia University tried to use the concept of interculturalism to bridge the gap between international and domestic matters. It never quite worked right. As a result of our involvement in AAC&U's Shared Futures project, we were exposed to and greatly influenced by Hovland and McTighe Musil's (2003) notions of global learning. As we developed our new undergraduate curriculum three to four years ago, we came up with the concept of global connections, and so far, it has served us well.

In our new curriculum, we call global connections an *intellectual practice,* a course that addresses issues of interdependence, interconnections, and resulting inequities, regardless of the course's subject matter. Domestic issues such as homelessness can be looked at in this way as well as issues of migration across nations. Thus, this concept allows us to look at domestic issues in an international context and vice versa.

The curriculum has been in place for only a couple of years, so it's a bit early to tell what students are getting from their global connections courses. The new concept has, however, energized the faculty to create interesting courses. For example, I teach a course on race and ethnicity in baseball that looks both at issues of domestic (U.S.) diversity and connections between the United States and countries such as the Dominican Republic, which provide such a large number of major league players. In this way, social justice issues in the United States get connected to similar issues both in other countries and in the relationship between the United States and those countries.

Other institutions involved with the *At Home in the World* initiative, notably larger comprehensive and research institutions, found it prudent to take their time. They had found the areas of divergence between multicultural and international education to be very present at their institutions and were concerned about the potential for exacerbating sometimes latent and other times open tensions. These areas of divergence—as noted in the *At Home in the World* publication—included different histories; parallel support structures; differing motivations and objectives of scholars, professors, and students; and distinct philosophical undercurrents (social justice, Eurocentrism versus postcolonialism; globalization; American exceptionalism). Table 17.1 charts these divergences. Due largely to these differences, many people working in these areas had limited interaction with each other, limited knowledge of each other's work, and strong

perceptions (frequently erroneous) of each others motivations.

Portland State University was among those larger institutions that elected to become engaged in the *At Home in the World* initiative but to take an incremental approach to this work. Internationalization and diversity were both presidential priorities and had developed on parallel paths, each with their own institution-wide committees, structures, and programs (curricular and co-curricular). Those champions who understood the potential for collaboration between these initiatives carefully cultivated this collaboration at multiple levels of the institution. At the level of the institution, two distinct councils—which initially coveted each other's resources and were concerned about the dilution of each other's work—have over time evolved to share members, set collaboration with each other as a priority, and plan joint programs together. As the

	Diversity/Multicultural Education	International Education
Histories	Inspired by the civil rights movement as a social activist movement	International education movement post-World War II
	Reflected in ethnic studies, multiethnic education	Area studies, international relations, global studies
	Multicultural education, comparative approach	Internationalization as transformational change
	Global diversity	Globalization of higher education
Support Structures	Student affairs: Extracurricular student ethnic clubs	Academic affairs: Curricular programs (languages, area studies)
	Affirmative action officer	Service offices (study abroad)
	Chief diversity officer	
Motivations and Objectives	Redress social inequality	Create elites with focused knowledge base (area studies)
	Strengthen identity	Compete internationally (international relations, business)
	Provide diversity training	Increase quality of education
	Increase quality of education	

Table 17.1   Areas of Divergences

institution works to set campus-wide learning outcomes and university studies goals, those working both on the diversity and the internationalization learning outcomes are coming to conceptualize how intercultural awareness is an area of overlap. As professors work to imbed diversity and internationalization goals into their academic programs, they are observing how intercultural awareness can serve either as the point of entry to both global awareness and diversity awareness (in the case of a course on intercultural communication for public administrators) or as a passageway from one to the other (study abroad course, global management course, diversity in the workforce course). As the Portland State champions for collaboration chart their path forward (see Box 17.3) they anticipate identifying more cases of joint curricular initiatives.

BOX 17.3 Institutionalizing Diversity and Internationalization Initiative at Portland State University

Masami Nishishiba

Associate Director of the Center for Public Service,
Portland State University (USA)

Gil Latz

Associate Vice Chancellor for International Affairs, Purdue University (USA)

At Portland State University, the efforts to promote diversity/multiculturalism and internationalization were both initiated as presidential initiatives.

In 1999, shortly after his appointment as president, Dan Bernstine appointed a group of faculty, staff, and students to evaluate campus climate and life. The group, formerly named a Commission on Campus Climate, conducted personal interviews, focus groups, and survey of faculty, staff, and students. Based on the information they gathered, they recommended that the university adopt and implement a policy for diversity, which would be reflected in the daily personal interactions on campus, in personnel and student recruitment and support, in the physical environment, and in the development and delivery of the curriculum.

In 2000, diversity was formally declared a presidential initiative, and the Diversity Action Council (DAC) was formed to develop policy and plans to promote diversity. With the support of the Presidents' Office and the Center for Academic Excellence, DAC developed a diversity action plan for the purpose of promoting diversity. In 2007, the outgoing interim president, Michael Riordan, in consultation with DAC, established an Office of Diversity and Equity (ODE) and declared that diversity was no longer a presidential initiative, but an institutionalized effort.

The history of Portland State's institutional commitment to internationalization followed a similar path. Recognizing that faculty, staff, and students have a responsibility to exercise leadership in the global community in the 21st century, in 2002, President Bernstine inaugurated an internationalization initiative and established an Internationalization Action Council (IAC). In 2007, as a step forward in the institutionalization of the internationalization initiative, the IAC became a standing administrative committee, appointed by and reporting to the provost, and renamed as an Internationalization Council (IC).

With two parallel support structures, namely the DAC for diversity efforts and the IC for internationalization, there was some potential danger that the two efforts would diverge and potentially hinder each other's work. Those who were strongly affiliated with traditional diversity-related work voiced some concern that the university's focus on internationalization would take the attention away from the importance of being more inclusive of historically oppressed groups. There was also a perception among both the DAC and IC members that they were competing for scarce resources.

Fortunately, at Portland State, where engagement and collaboration are highly valued, faculty and staff who worked in both the diversity and the international arenas recognized the potential for conflict and consciously sought to build a bridge between groups. Also with a long history of engagement related to ACE's work, Portland State had a critically important leadership group that understood the importance of adopting an approach to institutional change that created synergy between diversity and internationalization.

At the university-wide, institutional level, the initiative to bridge diversity and internationalization was first taken up by the DAC and IC. In appointing the members, both councils made a conscious effort to pursue cross-membership appointments of those who have been active in both councils. DAC also identified collaboration with the IC as one of the priority action areas for the 2009–2010 academic year. As a result, a DAC/IC joint meeting was held twice during the 2009–2010 academic year, and DAC/IC joint task force was formed.

Another impetus for diversity/internationalization collaboration emerged from another university-wide initiative, the work of the institutional assessment initiative. In 2007, an institutional assessment initiative to develop campus-wide learning outcomes was inaugurated. After 2 years of work, the faculty senate in 2009 approved the campus-wide learning outcomes with eight areas of focus, two of which focused on diversity and internationalization. In academic year 2009–2010, members of Institutional Assessment Council were charged with operationalization of the learning outcomes, including the need to have a clear definition and expectations of what constitutes a

(Continued)

(Continued)

diversity and an internationalization outcome and where each overlaps, respectively. Members of DAC/IC together with the members of Institutional Assessment Council continued into the following academic year to work together to finalize the rubric and metrics for both diversity and international learning outcome.

Finally, a significant further step that PSU has taken, directly stemming from the work of the Diversity Action Council, and the leadership of President Wim Wiewel, is creation of a chief diversity officer. By design, this position works closely with Portland State's vice provost for international affairs and the president in identifying points of collaborative opportunity for student learning.

DISCUSSION

For each of these three cases, those working on bridging efforts have confronted the issue of how to nurture the mindset required for this work. Efforts to internationalize or to diversify, and by extension to engage in bridging work between diversity and internationalization, as well as between the local and the global, may require individuals to develop a different set of skills from those emphasized in their families of origin, their graduate training, and their disciplinary associations. The literature is full of mechanisms for promoting the mindset conducive to advancing internationalization or diversity/multicultural education, with faculty professional development repeatedly cited as critical to successful internationalization or diversification of the campus and its curriculum and co-curriculum. When reviewing these two bodies of literature, a variation of interculturalism—that is, the development of skills for communicating between and across cultures—emerges in both bodies. It makes sense that institutional leaders would reach for this framework and the tools it offers for nurturing mindsets to build bridges between these areas.

As leaders embrace interculturalism, another question frequently follows: Can interculturalism serve as the overarching construct for both internationalization and diversity/multicultural education? Some have explored collapsing internationalization and diversity or multicultural education and consolidating all of the structures, people, and so on that these initiatives involve. Yet, this strategy raises other questions about whether interculturalism (or any one framework) is sufficient as an overarching

construct for institutions and whether intercultural skills are sufficient as a toolkit for faculty and students.

Consider the example of the Bennett theoretical model (1993) for intercultural sensitivity, which offers logical bridging points between internationalization and diversity/multicultural education. Bennett's developmental model posits a spectrum of six developmental stages. Three of these are ethnocentric (denial, defense, minimization) and three of them ethnorelative (acceptance, adaptation, integration). According to the model, as we forge more intercultural communication skills and thereby become more interculturally sensitive, we are able to move through these stages. Those who arrive at the integration stage, according to Bennett, exist first in a state of *contextual evaluation* and then *constructive marginality*. Those in contextual evaluation are able to analyze and evaluate situations from one or more chosen cultural perspectives; shift from one worldview to another, selecting those cultural aspects of each worldview that are most appropriate for a given context; and evaluate those aspects of the dominant culture that cause or contribute to oppression without rejecting the entire culture. This state opens up opportunities for those trained in the international academic traditions on the one hand and the diversity/multicultural academic traditions on the other to potentially come together to work on deconstructing and alleviating oppression.

Continuing with the Bennett model, those who progress to *constructive marginality* do not have a "natural cultural identity." They are marginal to all cultures and are constantly creating their reality. They are well-suited to carry out the cultural mediation so needed in our world precisely because they are not personally invested in a particular culture and are able to "construct each appropriate worldview as needed." Here again is another bridging point. Yet, Bennett (1993) goes on to speak about how the allegiance of a constructive marginal "is only to life itself" (p. 65). The underlying ideal of this theory—full enthorelativism—and the description of this desired state raise questions about individual identity, cultural relativism, and institutional educational purposes. It also raises questions about whether intercultural tools, and intercultural sensitivity in particular, provide a sufficient competence base for 21st-century graduates or if they need to be complemented by additional knowledge, attitudes, and skill sets.

It would be a mistake to reduce interculturalism to Bennett's model of intercultural sensitivity presented in the mid 1990s. More recent work on intercultural competence expands the scope of interculturalism. Deardorff (2006) conducted a Delphi study, which asked internationalization administrators to review various definitions of intercultural competence. What emerged as the definition most applicable to internationalization strategies includes "knowledge of others; knowledge of self; skills to interpret and relate; skills to discover and/or to interact; valuing others' values, beliefs, and behaviors; and relativizing one's self" (Deardorff, 2006, p. 247). From this initial study, Deardorff has gone on to develop the pyramid and process models of intercultural competence.

At the base of these models are

Requisite attitudes: respect (valuing other cultures, cultural diversity); openness (to intercultural learning and to people from other cultures, withholding judgment); curiosity and discovery (tolerating ambiguity and uncertainty)

On this base are built

Knowledge and comprehension outcomes: Cultural self-awareness; deep understanding and knowledge of culture (including contexts, role, and impact of culture and others' worldviews); culture-specific information; sociolinguistic awareness

Skills: To listen, observe, and interpret; to analyze, evaluate, and relate

More advanced are those *internal outcomes* that allow for

an informed frame of reference/filter shift: adaptability (to different communication styles and behaviors; adjustment to new cultural environments); flexibility (selecting and using appropriate communication styles and behaviors; cognitive flexibility); ethnorelative view; empathy

All of these outcomes are intended to be reflected in the *desired external outcome:*

behaving and communicating effectively and appropriately (based on one's intercultural knowledge, skills, and attitudes) to achieve one's goals to some degree. (Deardorff, 2006)

As noted in the Baldwin-Wallace case study cited earlier, Deardorff's expanded definition of intercultural competence has served the institution well as a bridging construct between international and diversity/multicultural education. It is, for many institutions and individuals, a comfortable and productive space of overlap. Individuals working in these areas have found intercultural principles useful in finding common ground and intercultural skills valuable in forging connections with their counterparts. However, interculturalism as an overarching construct for institutional initiatives, as suggested by the Arcadia case study, may have its limitations.

Positioning interculturalism as an overarching institutional initiative may raise questions about institutional commitments to the development of in-depth knowledge of cultures and global systems as well to addressing social injustices and the need for identity affirmation. Interculturalism may be best presented, as it has been at Portland State University, not as encompassing but rather complementing other initiatives and offering useful tools for faculty and student development. As intercultural tools offer ways to communicate more effectively across cultures, interculturalism offers bridges to more effectively link people across disciplines and initiatives.

GROUNDED GLOBALISM

The concept of *grounded globalism* explicates how global domains are grounded in local contexts. Obvious as this point is, many usages obscure it, conceptually, pedagogically, and administratively. Take the slogan "Think globally, act locally." One can ask: Don't locals think, and don't globals act? Is thinking purely global and local action simply labor without thought? What crept into the admirable slogan is a dichotomy between thought and action that became inadvertently connected to another dichotomy, that between global and local. Perhaps the slogan even expresses a bias by globalistic thinkers, planners, and policymakers that they know what is best, hence, local people should carry out their policies, or, more subtly, that only by thinking globally can anyone act wisely locally. The slogan was probably not intended to express such a dichotomy, but in fact one often does dichotomize this way in one's own thought and work.

Looking at the implications of these issues in higher education, one extreme is the example of global studies within U.S. postsecondary institutions. Specifically, the teaching of global or international studies is often accomplished by separate disciplines such as economics, political science, and policy studies, perhaps in separate schools of policy studies and international studies. At the other extreme, there are local studies, for example, folklore, community-focused social work and public health, regional and ethnic programs. Moving from studies to life itself, we experience face-to-face human relationships such as those involving contact between immigrants and natives, minorities and majorities. Such face-to-face relationships entail cultural differences, class differences, and even language differences that are quite immediate and pressing and sometimes cause conflict, difficulties of adjustment, and academic failure. Just as the global systems entail specific disciplines, schools of study, and also policies, so do such "diversities" entail specific disciplines and also specialized programs to treat problems, for example, social work or cross-cultural counseling. The separation of global and local tends to correlate with distinction between global and diversity inasmuch as diversity is frequently encountered in immediate, face-to-face contexts such as migrants or minorities entering a foreign or majority culture and institution (such as a school or university) and adapting to languages, cultures, and regulations.

What, then, is the point of *grounded globalism*? Grounded globalism presses for understanding and practice that recognize the unity of human experience, an experience that encompasses both global and local contexts, the latter including diversity. Grounded globalism addresses the experience of both global and local contexts (including diversity) holistically, seeking synergies in various contexts, including higher education (cf. Ross Lewin on global citizenship, 2009). Where did grounded globalism originate and where might it go in guiding internationalization and diversity efforts at postsecondary institutions?

GROUNDED GLOBALISM: FOUNDATIONS

Grounded globalism builds on several well-known perspectives and bodies of research: (a) cultural and multicultural perspectives; (b) international/global perspectives; (c) area studies, ethnic studies, regional studies, and folklore. This section discusses each of these in further detail.

Cultural and Multicultural Perspectives

Beginning with Sir Edward Tylor (late 1800s) in Britain and Franz Boas (early 1900s) in the United States, one can trace the development of both the concept of culture in an anthropological sense and the discipline of anthropology as a perspective and an academic discipline. Tylor (1871/1958) gave the classic definition of *culture* in 1871: "Culture . . . taken in its wide ethnographic sense is that complex whole which includes knowledge, belief, arts, morals, law, custom, and any other capabilities and habits acquired by man as a member of society" (p. 1). Boas, meanwhile, drawing on a German cultural heritage including Herder, Goethe, Toennies (1887), and Kant, featured a rather holistic *Gestalt* notion of culture as shared learning that deeply penetrated thought and action (Kluckhohn & Kroeber, 1952). Parallel to the concept of culture came the method of fieldwork, especially emphasized by Bronislaw Malinowski's (1914 to 1918) fieldwork in the Trobriand islands and later by Boas's students, such as Margaret Mead in the Pacific and British social anthropologists in Africa. A required component of this methodology is deep immersion in a single place or community or tribe.

One must learn the language and culture during a period of at least 1 or 2 years of *participant observation*. One then writes an ethnography describing that culture: the Nuer, the Trobriands, the Tikopia. Despite multiple innovations, this classic formula remains intact as the basic requirement for earning a doctorate in cultural, social, or sociocultural anthropology.

Spinoffs into other disciplines include the use of ethnographic methods in education, business, and other fields and the extension of culture concepts as well. One extension is *multiculturalism*. Where culture was seen as a unitary *Gestalt* of a single tribe or community, multiculturalism focuses on a diversity of cultures, including ethnic or minority, and emphasizes their interaction. Multiculturalism, whether in anthropology or other fields, was influenced by the civil rights era, partially driven by a quest for educational and social equality for students from diverse racial, ethnic, social class, and cultural backgrounds. While civil rights in the U.S. context and human rights internationally were involved in this development, similar quests were occurring globally, for example, by minority tribal groups in numerous nations, from China to Malaysia to Latin America.

The following is a rough typology of kinds of interdisciplinary studies within the United States that have tried to interpret both global and local processes.

Global studies place emphasis on macrosystems, governance structures, and issues that transcend borders (especially environment, health, migration), distinguished from international studies where the organizing principle is the nation-state. International relations in diplomacy, economic or market exchanges globally, and military conflict or peaceful resolution by treaties and negotiation predominate as themes in international studies. Particular cultural identities and social interactions within communities, families, or other localized units are de-emphasized, although some attention is paid to incorporating anthropological insights into particular cultures and using the concept of culture to understand the dynamics of the international relations and global systems (Appadarai, 1996; Cernea, 1995; Edelman & Hanugerud, 2005; Gudeman, 2008; Hannerz, 1996; Harvey, 1996; Massey, Jess, & Massey, 1995; Niezen, 2004; Rischard, 2002; Schafer, 2008).

Regional studies focus on a particular area of the world, such as Asia, Africa, or Latin America; or it may focus on an area of a country, such as southeastern United States or an international region such as Southeast Asia, East Asia, or South Asia (Honighaussen, Apitzsch, & Reger, 2004; Honighaussen, Frey, Peacock, Steiner, & Matthews, 2005; Honighaussen, Ortlepp, Peacock, Steiner, & Matthews, 2005). Distinct from area studies, which are globally organized while focusing on particular geographic areas, regional studies also focus on particular geographic areas but emphasize localized cultural traditions. Folklore or some equivalent exemplifies this focus.

Local studies focus on communities, states, or ethnic groups, often with an applied focus: for example, public health or safety issues of a certain unit, whether a city, state, or community (Escobar, 1995). Rather than developing new knowledge for its own sake, local studies apply knowledge to solve local problems such as access to health care.

All of the above define useful and important aspects, but each emphasizes a different context and frequently different methods, drivers, and overall rationales. Each area has developed separate literatures, leaders, organizations, and perspectives or practices. One result is the separation of global and local contexts. The concept of grounded *globalism*, then, was rooted in a range of disciplines, in fieldwork, and in scholarly work; it both derived from and shaped efforts to shape an institution. One such institutional effort is described in Box 17.4.

GLOBAL AND LOCAL BEYOND THE UNITED STATES

A brief exploration of an institution in Indonesia with which the University of North Carolina has a relationship expands the discussion beyond the U.S. higher education context and illustrates that the complex interplay between global and local in higher education is not uniquely relevant to the U.S. context.

Comparable in size of population to the United States (fourth in size, United States third) and in many other ways including even the national slogan (*Bhinekka Tunggal ika*, which means E Pluribus Unum: unity in diversity),

BOX 17.4 Global and Local at the University of North Carolina at Chapel Hill

The University of North Carolina-Chapel Hill (UNC), which is considered the first public university to open its doors in the United States (1793), passed through several phases: local/regional/state until early twentieth century, adding a national focus after World War II, and moving into a global/international focus as the 21st century began. The first international student (from Japan) arrived in 1893, and the university engaged many international people, connections, and programs, but the major focus remained on the state and secondarily on region and nation. However, the early to mid 1990s saw several developments: first, creation of the University Center for International Studies in 1993; second, creation of a regional center (Center for Southern Studies, 1990); and third, shortly after the university's bicentennial, the Sonja Hanes Stone Center, with its minority/ethnic foci. This latter evoked the most passion and conflict.

University students, upon the passing of revered teacher Sonja Hanes Stone, director of the UNC program in African American studies, wished to honor Dr. Stone by erecting a new separate structure to house the center. Administrators, led by the chancellor, favored an integrated rather than separate structure. The chancellor, whose father had been allied with Martin Luther King, Jr., took a liberal stance supporting integration and opposing a separate center, which he saw as a step back toward segregation; he called for a "forum not a fortress," meaning an integrated rather than segregated center. Reactions were violent. Thousands of students and others marched on the house of the chancellor. Led by film director Spike Lee, a nephew of Sonja Stone, thousands more gathered in the basketball stadium, where speakers condemned opponents of a separate structure. Those condemned included black faculty such as Chuck Stone, a former Tuskegee airman and distinguished journalism professor, who favored an integrated multicultural model. The "action arm" of the Black Student Movement threatened unspecified action, and death threats were issued against the chancellor and others. The cry was for a "free standing" center, representing freedom, as opposed to a center that was part of a larger entity, representing oppression, even slavery. Thus, students erected shacks advertising the campus as the chancellor's "plantation."

The author chaired the faculty senate at the time, which represented 2,500 faculty. Differing somewhat from the chancellor's position, he proposed an alternative to both the separatist and anti-separatist stance: create a center for black culture whose separate identity is moderated by reaching out to be "inclusive" of other cultures. Hundreds of hours of protest, discussion, and planning ensued, eventually resulting in a proposal about the building of the center. The Board of Trustees approved the proposal, and the Sonja Hanes Stone Center for Black Culture, bridging global and local as well as ethnic divisions, was built.

In 1993, UNC established the University Center for International Studies (UCIS, now the Center for Global Initiatives) to serve as a catalyst and coordinator for globalizing Carolina on a pan-university basis. Most if not all of Uno's 14 schools had their own international programs, but UCIS spurred university-wide development and mission. Many programs were developed (e.g., global studies, now approaching a thousand majors, and other programs now housed in an 83,000-square-foot building). An international/global priority became salient for the university, both on the Chapel Hill campus and throughout the other 16 campuses in the North Carolina public university system.

How firmly did this globalizing effort connect to local and diversity situations? A guiding concept from the start was grounded globalism (an acronym was GLOBGRO). One of the strongest connections between global programs and local contexts is Worldview. Worldview extends global resources at Carolina to K–12 and community colleges in nearly all 100 counties of North Carolina, thus "grounding" globalism. Other notable global/local connections include a continuing interest in global forces within the region. Numerous conferences, publications (e.g., forthcoming online magazine *South Writ Large*; Barcott, 2010), seminars, and workshops have featured aspects of the global South and the U.S. South (Peacock, 2007; Peacock & Tyson, 1989; Peacock, Watson, & Matthews, 2006).

Note: This text box was prepared by chapter coauthor James Peacock.

Indonesia also includes major universities and a vast K through 12 system, public and private. Like the United States, Indonesia is grappling with transitions toward the global in relation to abiding local diversities. Box 17.5 describes a case study from that country.

BOX 17.5 Universitas Muhammadiyah Surakarta: Between Local And Global Issues

Mohammad Thoyibi

Faculty, Muhammadiya University of Surakarta (Indonesia)

Universitas Muhammadiyah Surakarta (Muhammadiyah University of Surakarta), commonly referred to as UMS, is one of the 170 higher learning institutions coordinated by Muhammadiyah throughout Indonesia. As an Islamic and Muhammadiyah higher learning institution in the Javanese community, located at a site that was once an important center of the Javanese culture and surrounded by the agrarian larger community, UMS has some strategic issues to consider in playing its role in the local, national, and global contexts.

Middle Java is one of the most densely populated provinces (approximately 12,555 people per km^2) in Indonesia, and Surakarta, popularly called Sala or Solo, is the most populated town in the province. Like other main towns in Java, Surakarta has a significant Chinese community in addition to a small minority of Arabs and other ethnic groups that are more assimilated, such as Banjarese and Madurese.

Ethnic relations, particularly Javanese-Chinese, have been a problem in Surakarta throughout history. There were riots targeting the Chinese community but not all were directly related to the ethnic relationships. The most recent riot victimizing Chinese ethnic groups in a number of cities in Java, including Surakarta, was the 1998 riot. This student protest against the repressive government led to the fall of Soeharto and the New Order regime.

Although they did not lead to physical violence, some incidents could be classified as religious conflicts, particularly between Christians and Muslims. Among other incidents in which Muslims acted against Christians were the protest against the building of a new church and the sale of low-priced food for *iftar* (fasting break) at the church during the month of *ramadhan*. These religious

(Continued)

(Continued)

conflicts must be seen as part of religious phenomena within the different Muslim communities in Surakarta. Since the mid 1990s, Islamic hard-liners began to assert their scriptural and monolithic interpretations of Islamic teachings.

Like other higher learning institutions coordinated by Muhammadiyah, UMS is an autonomous organization that is free to set its own goals, manage itself, develop its own leadership, build its own structure, and characterize its own specific features. However, UMS is obliged to maintain the core values of Muhammadiyah as a reformist Islamic organization, a middle path between extremes, committing itself to the progress and welfare of the nation.

To address those different interests, Muhammadiyah defines itself as an open university that serves the needs not only of Muhammadiyah members, the Muslim community, or the Javanese population but also of the larger nation, disregarding ethnic, religious, and cultural (subcultural) backgrounds. However, unlike the Indonesian Islamic University (UII) of Yogyakarta, which has relatively more students from the Chinese and non-Muslim community, UMS has not been successful in promoting itself to the Chinese and non-Muslim community groups in the neighborhood. To counter the common misconception that non-Muslim students would be forced to convert to Islam, UMS founded an office that serves and addresses the needs of the non-Muslim students. It also established a center that promotes peace, pluralism, and multiculturalism; it has conducted some projects involving high school students of various ethnic and religious backgrounds.

Now, UMS is beginning to recruit students from other countries, particularly Thailand, Germany, and China, to study Indonesian language, Islam, Javanese culture, and performing arts. For the last 10 years, students from Thailand have studied Indonesian language and Islam at UMS, and some students from Germany have studied Indonesian language and culture. In the near future, students from China will be studying acting and performing arts. UMS has assigned an office, International Cooperation, to accommodate the specific needs of the international students.

There has been a growing awareness among leaders of the present administration that it is strategic to establish cooperation with some colleges and universities in the United States, not only for academic purposes but also for intercultural understanding. Some areas of study may become the shared interests between UMS and those U.S. universities, in ways that are beneficial for both parties and nations.

When considering the UMS alongside of U.S. university settings, the following points of comparison and questions emerge. Given that Muslims are a majority in Indonesia and minority in the United States, what are the dynamics between majority and minorities as well as the role of Islam in both contexts? UMS is a Muslim university. How does this reality contrast with U.S. institutions of religious origin? Chinese are a wealthy minority in Indonesia and are non-Muslim in this Muslim university. How does this complex interplay between income and status play out in Indonesia? Is there an equivalent in the U.S. context? A non-Muslim (Buddhist, Hindu, animistic) syncretism underlies Java and UMS and is somewhat linked to Chinese syncretism (via Buddhism). Again, what religious syncretism is at play in the U.S. context? In short, broad issues such as globalism, diversity, and localism interweave in the UMS context as in U.S. and other contexts, while the specific chemistry of the varied contexts compares suggestively, for example, a Muslim majority versus minority in relation to a non-Muslim majority versus minority (cf. Peacock 1968, 1978). This glimpse suggests the complexity of dynamics and wealth of potential insights available in taking this discussion global, while remaining grounded in local realities.

In Europe, the global-local debate is still in its initial phase. Jeanine Hermans (2005), addressing the issue of culture as part of internationalization of higher education in Europe, comes to a rather critical analysis on the way culture is included as an important dimension, both in staff and student mobility, enrollment of international students, curriculum, advising international students, internationalization of staff, internationalization of facilities and services, positioning in international networks, international accreditation, policy relating to international student affairs, and institutional intercultural policy development. She concludes,

> Awareness in higher education institutions of cultural diversity as a critical factor in successful internationalisation, although well established in international offices and with staff working internationally, is largely lacking in other parts of the institution. The awareness that exists is fragmented, and competence in dealing with diversity is more an exception at the level of an individual than common practice. (p. 112)

Her conclusion that "intercultural issues are so far still largely unresolved in the process of European higher education" and that "intercultural learning in individuals and organisations tends to occur accidentally and haphazardly" (Hermans, 2005, p. 113) according to de Wit (2009), gives a clear picture of the state of internationalization in Europe and the lack of linkage between the global and local. The one place where this is being realized more is in the classroom, as European classrooms become more international. (See Chapters 14 and 15, this volume, for further discussion on how this is manifested in the curriculum and in teaching and learning.)

Conclusions and Recommendations

This chapter has approached the key to a global university through the local/global lens and, specifically, the question of how higher education can best synergize between global and local resources. This discussion utilized a description of the American Council on Education's work on internationalization and diversity with illustrations from a range of colleges and universities; one author's experience at a single university, UNC; and a glimpse at wider contexts. The concept of interculturalism was examined as a

bridging construct and grounded globalism as a conceptual framework supportive of synergistic work.

What can be recommended for those senior international officers (SIOs) who lead efforts to build and sustain global programs at their institutions that are grounded in local contexts? A general rule is that where such a division is heavily institutionalized, in bureaucracy, in scholarship, in power structures and funding structures, some kind of innovative and entrepreneurial effort is necessary to create change. Exactly what shape that effort should take depends on context. A few specific suggestions are provided:

1. Organize at multiple levels. Levels could range from a small (three to five members) action committee within a particular college or school to a large cross-cutting interdisciplinary group of administrators and faculty.

2. Consider the engagement of stakeholders beyond the institution; advisory and advancement boards of alumni and citizens are helpful, perhaps essential, to support the effort vis-à-vis administrators, legislators, and perhaps donors.

3. Assess resources, both in the institution and beyond, including alumni, citizens, students, faculty, and administration.

4. Define global objectives, connecting them to local realities, and define local objectives, connecting them to global realities.

5. Determine a set of shared student learning goals that transcend the global, local, diversity foci.

6. Collaboratively formulate a plan, naming steps and phases, and integrate that plan into long-range overarching plans for the institution.

7. Raise funds and other resources, preferably by delegating that task to a person or part of a position in addition to the leader.

8. Take most affordable (and perhaps safest) steps first (e.g., revising existing courses to include connections between the global and the local).

9. Balance comprehensive assessment and action; think and act both globally and locally to overcome disconnects between global and local.

In 2010, ACE conducted a qualitative study of 15 institutions that had made some demonstrable progress in fostering connections (Davies & Butto, 2010). This study sought to answer the following questions: (a) From what context is collaborative work between multicultural education and internationalization begun on campuses? (b) What is the process by which an institution moves from conceptualization to implementation of collaborative work between multicultural education and internationalization? and, (c) What are key strategies employed by institutions to frame and advance collaborative work between multicultural education and internationalization? There is no one-size-fits-all model or magic formula to ensure success, however, this study did identify several common trends that are relevant for this discussion.

First, there is a need for a balance between strong, visible support from senior leadership and a culture that permits and rewards innovation and engagement of a wide variety of stakeholders, including community members, students, faculty, and staff. The primary implication of this for institutions is that leadership has to be fully committed to the development of collaborative practices while allowing campus stakeholders to go fully through the process associated with the formation of effective collaborative practices.

Second, the development of collaborative initiatives is a process that, like any other institutional change, occurs slowly and incrementally. Time is needed to identify key stakeholders, to facilitate group learning about the differences and commonalities within the fields, to adequately and sensitively address tensions and concerns, and to plan for implementation in a way that proactively addresses issues before or as they arise. This process is ever evolving and will shift with institutional demographics, social trends, and the political landscape. As a result, institutional representatives must engage in an ongoing cycle of innovation, reflection, and evaluation.

Finally, and perhaps most important, successful and meaningful collaborative work between diversity/multicultural education and internationalization requires that students, faculty, and staff develop an awareness of and appreciation for the work of their colleagues across a wide variety of disciplines. It can be challenging to critically examine the strengths and limitations of the fields to which one's life's work has been dedicated and to acknowledge the validity and value of the contributions of colleagues, who might otherwise be viewed as competitors in the struggle for finite pools of prestige and funding on campus. However, this open frame of mind is precisely what is needed to allow for the development of synergistic programming. To be successful in this work, campus stakeholders must be able to identify the areas in which diversity/multicultural education and internationalization paradigms are strongest in isolation and the areas in which more is gained through collaboration. In sum, faculty and practitioners must have support from their leaders and be empowered to act proactively and flexibly.

The example of the University of North Carolina-Chapel Hill highlighted additional dimensions. Regarding balance between leaders and stakeholders, the UNC case study showed that this balance was negotiated. Conflict, strategic planning mixed with confrontation and opportunistic collaboration, and firm goals were part of the balance. Second, the slow and incremental process was apparent; it took seven years to work through these issues. However, overnight demands and sudden crises energized that process. Third, the essential collaboration across disciplines and domains competes with careers and rewards that are largely based in departments and disciplines; goodwill and intellectual interests are usefully enhanced by incentives (e.g., course development grants that reward faculty and staff for collaborative projects). What is clear is that nurturing connections energetically but carefully can bear impressive fruit.

Do institutional supports mesh with the ramified activities and energies? Not entirely. Students are increasingly enthusiastic about global and community work but uneven in their engagement. Faculty remain primarily occupied with their disciplines, professions, and careers, although interdisciplinary synergies continue to grow. Public officials still focus on domestic needs but are increasingly aware of global dimensions and the role of immigration and international commerce. Alumni, while focused primarily on careers, are increasingly global in work, residency, and thinking, which presents some opportunities for higher education institutions to further their work beyond students. Administrators have uneven global exposure as well as local grounding since many are recruited nationally rather than globally or locally. Achievements, thus far, come from work with a wide variety of constituencies—faculty, students, government, administrators, business, alumni—and vary from policy (formulating long-range plans and priorities) to projects and events. Especially because these global/local interconnections and diversity/international initiatives cross established departmental and school lines of authority and budgeting, sustainability is both challenging and crucial. Commitment and energy must be sustained for progress to be made in joining the global and local, and that commitment and energy must pass to younger leaders as world situations develop through economic cycles, ecological crises, and conflict.

REFERENCES

Allen, W. R., Bonous-Hamouth, M., & Teranishi, R. T. (2006). *Higher education in a global society achieving diversity, equity and excellence.* Amsterdam: Elsevier.

Altbach, P. G., & Peterson, P. M. (2007). *Higher education in the new century.* Rotterdam, the Netherlands: Sense Publishers.

Appadarai, A. (1996). *Modernity at large: Cultural dimensions of globalization.* Minneapolis: University of Minnesota Press.

Banks, J. A. (Ed.). (2007). *Diversity and citizenship education: Global perspectives.* San Francisco: Jossey-Bass Education.

Banks, J. A., & McGee Banks, C. A. (Eds.). (2004). *Handbook of research on multicultural education* (2nd ed.). San Francisco: Jossey-Bass.

Barcott, R. (2010). *It happened on the way to war.* New York: Bloomsbury.

Bennett. M. (1993). Toward a developmental model of intercultural sensitivity. In R. M. Paige (Ed.), *Education for the intercultural experience.* Yarmouth, ME: Intercultural Press.

Cernea, M. (1995) The Malinowski lecture: Social organization and development in anthropology. *Human Organization, 54*(3), 340–352.

Cornwell, G., & Stoddard, E. W. (1999). *Globalizing knowledge: Connecting international and intercultural studies.* Washington, DC: Association of American Colleges and Universities.

Davies, G., & Butto, J. (2010). *At home in the world: Bridging the gap between diversity/multicultural education and internationalization.* Annual meeting of the Association for the Study of Higher Education, Indiana, Indianapolis.

Deardorff, D. K. (2006). The identification and assessment of intercultural competence as a student outcome of internationalization at institutions of higher education in the United States. *Journal of Studies in International Education, 10*(3), 241–266.

Deardorff, D. K. (Ed.). (2009). *The SAGE handbook of intercultural competence.* Thousand Oaks, CA: Sage.

de Wit, H. (2009). Global citizenship and study abroad: a European comparative perspective. In L. Ross (Ed.), *The handbook of practice and research in study abroad: Higher education and the quest for global citizenship* (pp. 212–229). New York: Routledge, AACU.

Edelman, M., & Hanugerud, A. (Eds.). (2005). *The anthropology of development and globalization.* Hoboken, NJ: Blackwell.

Escobar, A. (1995). *Encountering development.* Princeton, NJ: Princeton University Press.

Green, M. F., & Olson, C. (2003). *Internationalizing the campus: A user's guide.* Washington, DC: American Council on Education.

Gudeman, S. (2008). *Economy's tension: The dialectics of community and market.* New York and Oxford: Berghahn Books.

Hannerz, U. (1996). *Transnational connections: Culture, people, places.* London: Routledge.

Harvey, D. (1996). *Justice, nature, and the geography of difference.* Oxford, UK: Blackwell.

Hermans, J. (2005). The X factor, internationalization with a small 'c'. In B. Kehm & H. de Wit (Eds.), *European responses to the global perspective* (pp. 134–153). Amsterdam: EAIE/EAIR.

Honighaussen, L., Apitzsch, J., & Reger, W. (Eds.). (2004). *Space-place-environment.* Tubingen, Germany: Stauffenburg Verlag.

Honighaussen, L., Frey, M., Peacock, J., Steiner, N., & Matthews, C. (2005). *Regionalism in the age of globalism: Concepts of regionalism.* Madison: University of Wisconsin Press.

Honighaussen, L., Ortlepp, A., Peacock, J., Steiner, N., & Matthews, C. (2005). *Regionalism in the age of globalism: Forms of regionalism.* Madison: University of Wisconsin Press.

Hovland, K. (2006). *Shared futures: Global learning and liberal education.* Washington DC: Association of Colleges and Universities.

Hovland, K., & McTighe Musil, C. (2003). Shared futures? The interconnections of global and U.S. diversity. *Diversity Digest, 8*(3).

Hurtado, S. (2007). Linking diversity with the educational and civic missions of higher education. *Review of Higher Education, 30*(2), 185–196.

Jayakumar, U. (2008). Can higher education meet the need of an increasingly divers and global society? Campus diversity and cross-cultural work-force competency. *Harvard Education Revew, 78*(4).

Kluckhohn, C., & Kroeber, A. (1952). *Culture: A critical review of concepts and definitions.* Cambridge, MA: The Museum.

Knight, J., & de Wit, H. (Ed.). (1999). *Quality and internationalisation of higher education.* Paris: Organization for Economic Cooperation and Development.

Lewin, R. (Ed.). (2009). *The handbook of practice and research in study abroad: Higher education and the quest for global citizenship.* New York: Routledge/AACU.

Marginson, S. (2011). Imagining the global. In R. King, S. Marginson, & R. Naidoo (Eds.), *Handbook on globalization and higher education.* Cheltenham, UK: Edward Elgar.

Marginson, S., & van der Wende, M. (2007). *Globalization and higher education* (OECD Education Working Paper, No. 8). Paris: OECD.

Massey, J., Jess, P., & Massey, D. (Eds.). (1995). *A place in the world: Places, cultures, and globalization.* New York: Oxford University Press and the Open University.

Niezen, R. (2004). *A world beyond difference.* Oxford, UK: Blackwell.

Olson, C., Evans, R., & Schoenberg, R. (2007). *At home in the world: Bridging the gap between internationalization and multicultural education.* Washington DC: American Council on Education.

Peacock, J. (1968). *Rites of modernization.* Chicago: University of Chicago Press.

Peacock, J. (1978). *Muslim Puritans.* Berkeley: University of California Press.

Peacock, J. (2007). *Grounded globalism: How the U.S. South embraces the world.* Athens: University of Georgia Press.

Peacock, J., & Tyson, R. W. (1989). *Pilgrims of paradox.* Washington, DC: Smithsonian Press.

Peacock, J., Watson, H., & Matthews, C. (2006). *The American South in a global world.* Chapel Hill: University of North Carolina Press.

Rischard, J. F. (2002). *High noon: 20 global problems, 20 years to solve them.* New York: Basic Books.

Salmi, J. (2009). *The challenge of establishing world-class universities.* Washington DC: The International Bank for Reconstruction and Development/World Bank.

Schafer, P. (2008). *Revolution or renaissance: Making the transition from an economic age to a cultural age.* Ottawa: University of Ottawa Press.

Stearns, P. (2008). Goals: Where we should be heading. *Educating Global Citizens in Colleges and Universities.* New York: Routledge.

Toennies, F. (1887). *Gemeinschaft und Gesellschaft.* Leipzig: Fues's Verlag.

Tylor, E. (1958). *Primitive culture.* New York: Harper & Row. (Original work published 1871)

van der Wende, M. (2008). Rankings and classifications in higher education: A European perspective. In J. Smart (Ed.), *Higher education: Handbook of theory and research,* Dordrecht, the Netherlands: Springer.

Wildavksy, B. (2010). *The great brain race: How global universities are reshaping the world.* Princeton, NJ: Princeton University Press.

SECTION D

INTERNATIONALIZATION ABROAD

18

CROSS-BORDER DELIVERY

Projects, Programs, and Providers

PETER BURGESS AND BRETT BERQUIST

C ross-border education is not a new concept. The spread of religious education across the globe over many decades is but one example that attests to its historical significance. Knight (2006) describes cross border education as

> higher education that takes place in situations where the teacher, student, program, institution/provider or course materials cross-national jurisdictional borders. Cross-border education may include higher education by public/private and not-for-profit/for–profit providers. It encompasses a wide range of modalities in a continuum from face-to-face (taking various forms from students travelling abroad and campuses abroad) to distance learning (using a range of technologies and including e-learning). (p. 18)

One could therefore conclude that cross-border education is a catch-all phase that provides a platform for international cooperation and exchange that can lead to the delivery of degree and non-degree programs in foreign locations, staff and student mobility, cross-border accreditation, research collaboration, and many other applicable forms of the internationalization process. Research into the topic also indicates that cross-border education has evolved in different ways and forms across the globe. The Organization for Economic Cooperation and Development (2004) suggests that whereas the United States is seen as a magnet for international students, in Europe, student mobility has been largely policy driven, and in the Asia-Pacific region, it is demand driven. Transnational education (TNE), which addresses program or institution mobility, on the other hand, has evolved through initiatives that have been largely driven at the micro level by educational institutions themselves and by policies implemented by receiving countries.

In this chapter, our raison d'être is to examine and comment on cross-border delivery of projects, programs, and providers in this new century. This fits comfortably with the program/institution-oriented focus presented in the various transnational definitions often used interchangeably with cross-border education. More than a decade ago, Knight (1999, p. 14) identified the imprecision in the terminology, pointing to the complexity and evolution of the international, global/transnational/regional dimension of higher education.

UNESCO/ Council of Europe (2001) provides a broad yet descriptive TNE definition that refers to all types of higher education study programmes, or sets of courses of study, or educational services (including those of distance education) in which the learners are located in a country different from the one where the awarding institution is based. (p. 1)

The UNESCO definition addresses any form of educational arrangements that can result in the establishment of either collaborative pathway or articulation arrangements, where study programs, or parts of a particular course of study, or other educational services of the awarding institution are provided by another partner institution. This definition also refers to noncollaborative arrangements, which include branch campuses or corporate or international institutions, where degree courses, study, or other educational services are provided directly by an awarding institution.

MARKET FORCES

Background

Higher education institutions began to pursue transnational interests in the 1980s, when full-fee onshore degrees were introduced in the United Kingdom and Australia. This occurred at a time when the governments reduced expenditure in the tertiary education sector. TNE then came of age during the early 1990s when it began to be acknowledged as a legitimate higher education activity that could complement strategic internationalization objectives and provide opportunities for additional revenue generation.

Table 18.1 presents selected findings from research undertaken by the Academic Cooperation Association (ACA) between March 2007 and July 2008 as part of the European Commission's Erasmus Mundus Global Promotion Project (http://ec.europa.eu/education/erasmus-mundus/doc/studies/tnesum_en.pdf); the British Council 2007 (http://international.ac.uk/statistics/transnational_education.cfm); and Australian Education International (AEI) Research Snapshot Dec 2011: (http://www.aei.gov.au/research/Research-Snapshots/Documents/RS%20Transnational%20education%20in%20HE%20sector%202010.pdf).

Such research in broad terms has investigated the extent and modes influencing the demand and supply of transnational higher education in recent years, and Table 18.1 draws heavily on the extensive knowledge and experience of the sector held by the authors.

Nation	Activities
United States	Taken together, about 50 U.S. tertiary institutions (only 1%) are reported to offer more than 200 transnational programs that vary from franchising arrangements to full branch campuses across 40 countries, which include China, South Korea, Vietnam, the Middle East, and Turkey (Berquist & Fuller, 2006)
United Kingdom	In 2007–2008, 196,640 students were studying in more than 1,000 UK transnational programs (60% postgraduate, 40% undergraduate) (Higher Education Statistics Agency [HESA], 2010)
	About 65% of the 145 registered UK higher education institutions offer TNE programs, with 60% of the activity directed toward Asia (ACA, 2008)
	UK modes of transnational engagement vary from full multidisciplinary branch campuses to distance learning programs, with joint/dual degrees being particularly popular (ACA, 2008)
	In 2006–2007, 20 UK higher education institutions offered undergraduate and postgraduate degree courses through Indian partner institutions to about 4,100 Indian students (British Council, 2009)
	In Hong Kong, 81 UK higher education institutions offer between them 617 undergraduate and postgraduate programs (British Council, 2009)
France	Twenty-four institutions offer more than 200 programs, of which a majority (126) are at master's level. The main French transnational target countries include North Africa (58% of operations), Europe, and Asia (ACA, 2008)

Nation	Activities
Germany	About 8,000 students were enrolled in 85 transnational programs outside Europe in 2006–2007 (ACA, 2008)
Netherlands	A total of 20 transnational programs with between 1,000 and 2,000 enrollments are in its program portfolio, which seems to focus on master's-level courses that include MBAs, hospitality management, engineering, and public health (ACA, 2008)
Australia	In 2010, 104,678 transnational students were studying in Australian higher education programs outside Australia. This represented 31.2% of all international students undertaking Australian higher education programs. The top five nationalities engaging in offshore Australian higher education programs were Singapore, China, Malaysia, Hong Kong, and Vietnam—somewhat different than the top five nationalities (China, India, Malaysia, Vietnam, and Indonesia) represented in enrollments onshore in Australia. The most popular transnational programs in 2010 were bachelor's degree (68%) and master's degree by coursework (21%); discipline preferences were: management and commerce (57%), information technology (8%), engineering and related technologies (7%), society and culture (7%), and health (6%) (Australian Education International (AEI) Research Snapshot, December 2011)

Table 18.1   Examples of Recent Transnational Project and Program Activities

However, even with all the cross-border information that is available, Knight (2005) and de Wit (2008) make the point that there remains a dearth of data regarding cross-border policy and TNE development across the sector, particularly in the United States (Berquist & Fuller, 2006). The ACA in 2008 also confirmed that Europe still has no central register of TNE programs and little if any data to ascertain the number of institutions or students involved. What can safely be assumed is that supply of and the demand for higher education transnational programs has expanded over this decade. Even in a climate where Australia has reported reductions in the actual number of transnational programs offered since 2007, total transnational student enrollments are reported to be growing (Banks, Kevat, Ziguras, Ciccarelli, & Clayton, 2010). The reduction of Australian programs is believed to be the result of a number of risk reduction strategies designed to address market forces which include the increasing rigor of the Australian quality assurance process, demand shifts in maturing transnational target markets, re-engineering of course offerings and delivery, and changes in partnership arrangements.

What is generally accepted in various parts of the world is that transnational higher education is a potentially powerful tool that completes the palette for a comprehensive internationalization policy.

Provider Motives

Mutual understanding, skilled migration, revenue generation, and capacity building have previously been identified as primary motivators for cross-border education (Larsen, Momii & Vincent-Lancrin, 2004). In the United States, mutual understanding and capacity building have driven many cross-border projects. As one component of a comprehensive internationalization strategy, such projects can jump-start or enhance a larger agenda for academic research and exchange cooperation. Capacity-building projects, when undertaken in partnership, often terminate when the knowledge has been transferred. This is particularly the case where external international development funding has been accessed to support the project or where the project parameters are narrowly defined. In other cases, capacity building has provided the platform for continued institutional strengthening and sustainable partnership engagement.

In an increasingly competitive global education market, TNE can also enhance visibility and strengthen brand positioning. Furthermore, financial motives play an important role in any decision to pursue transnational higher education opportunities. In a study conducted by IDP Education Australia as far back as 2001, Rizvi (2004) found that more than 40% of the universities surveyed stated that the generation of additional sources of revenue was a primary transnational motive. Likewise, in the United States and United Kingdom continuing declines in state funding of higher education have encouraged more universities to include transnational initiatives as an important recruitment strategy for foreign national students on- or offshore. Dual-degree development has also found increasing government support, particularly in Europe, and is an important factor influencing cross-border delivery. In the United Kingdom in 2009, the Prime Minister's Initiative (British Council PM12, 2009) provided funding to support 14 transnational projects. In addition, 47 strategic alliances and partnership grants were allocated. The United States also provided funding for many years through the Fund for the Improvement of Post Secondary Education (FIPSE), which helped tertiary institutions to create cross-Atlantic programs and strengthen institutional relationships.

Recipient Motives

A growing number of governments have identified TNE cooperation as a strategy to increase domestic education capacity. Providing foreign education access to domestic markets can support an increase in the number of available student places, facilitate knowledge transfer, and encourage collaborative academic research.

India and China are prime examples of countries employing transnational collaboration as part of their strategy to increase domestic capacity. Since the beginning of the millennium, China has more than doubled its annual investment in higher education but still sees fewer than 25% of qualified students receive seats in domestic institutions. Encouraging academic collaboration, funding students to study abroad, and increasing transnational collaboration with recognized institutions have been key government higher education strategies for several years. Li (2009) points out that China has benefited significantly from access to

prestigious international institutions, which have brought with them quality education resources, highly qualified staff, and strong research linkages that have afforded significant institutional and sector-strengthening advantages. Beyond the opportunity to build institutional reputation, transnational engagement provides a platform for cross-border staff and student exchange. It also encourages research collaboration, facilitates opportunities for additional revenue generation, and reduces cost overhead by enabling access to the western curriculum.

India faces similar capacity issues and has recently and cautiously moved to invite foreign universities to enter their market (Foreign Education Institutions [Regulations of Entry and Operations]), 2010 Bill). However, according to Dhar (cited in Stella & Bhushan, 2011, p. 184), the British Council of India study identified as many as 641 transnational programs on offer in 2008, of which most were professional courses that addressed business/management, engineering, and information technology/computing. Many of these programs are conducted with private rather than public India tertiary institutions. There are already many private higher education providers in India, such as Manipal University, NIIT, Birla, the Jaypee Institute, the Vedanta University, and many wealthy business groups in India are investing in education—some with a background in education, others with business backgrounds in other sectors (Feith, 2008).

In the Gulf States, the United Arab Emirates and Qatar have employed considerable resources to encourage reputable foreign universities to build capacity in the region, and some of the world's top universities have been attracted to the Gulf. Presentations by those leading this development highlight that more than one third of the population in the region is under 15 years old and that substantial growth in demand for education and jobs is predicted. These governments have chosen to invite expertise from established foreign universities as they seek to respond to substantial growth in demand and create regional education hubs. Even in these regions, however, careful planning, due diligence, and development as part of a sustained long-term strategy are needed. The recent economic downturn has caused several institutions to withdraw or significantly scale back their operations.

Some republics of the former Soviet Union are also seeking foreign collaboration to improve their domestic capacity. The Westminster International

University in Tashkent was established in response to a call by the Uzbekistan government (British Council PM12, 2009).

In Singapore and Malaysia, which are also regional education hubs, the respective governments have implemented controlled measures designed to accelerate education development. This is reflected in the large number of foreign education providers that are active in these two countries. The University of Nottingham established its Malaysia campus in response to the government's intention to establish itself as a regional educational hub and to reduce its dependence on foreign study to meet the demand of its population (British Council PM12, 2009). Monash University (Australia) is another example of a successful Malaysian capacity-building transnational cross-border venture.

The information cited in Tables 18.2 and 18.3 is summarized and extended from work undertaken by the ACA between March 2007 and July 2008 as part of the European Commission's Erasmus Mundus Global Promotion Project: *Transnational Education in the European Context— Provision, Approaches, and Policies: Motivations and Drivers in Transnational Education,* pp. 52–62 (http://ec.europa.eu/education/erasmus-mundus/doc/studies/tnereport_en.pdf), as well as reference to data provided by Universities Australia (2009), Leask (2004), Adams et al. (2009), and Banks et al. (2010). The actual scope and content of Tables 18.2 and 18.3 rely heavily on the experience and knowledge of the authors when framing the key supply and demand motivators that are cited.

No assessment of transnational motives would be complete without consideration of what influences the student to choose to study in a transnational program. Table 18.3 summarizes the most common considerations.

Provider Motives	Recipient Motives
Diversification of the student body	Internationalization
Internationalization	Student demand exceeding available places
Institutional strengthening	Opportunity to attract prestigious partners and partner program arrangements
Ranking, reputation, and positioning	
Location	Deregulation
Distance	Student exchange and mobility
Political and economic stability	Collaborative research opportunities
Complexity of regulatory frameworks (registration, accreditation, governance, pedagogy and nomenclature, quotas, fees, taxation, repatriation of finds, profit motive, lead times)	Staff development
	Access to Western curriculum and pedagogy
	Institutional strengthening and development
	Revenue generation
Societal/cultural issues including language of instruction, pedagogy and learning styles, gender imbalance, health and safety, consumer perceptions and expectations	Recognition of English as the language of international trade and commerce
	Technology transfer
Technology and its impact on delivery modes and infrastructure	Improved regulatory quality assurance mechanisms
Cost of entry and exit	
Partnerships and positioning	
Compliance, equivalence, and quality assurance; partner collaboration and institutional linkages	
Student demand and market gaps	
Revenue generation	
Research opportunities and collaboration	
Language and culture	

(Continued)

(Continued)

Provider Motives	Recipient Motives
New student recruitment markets	
New programs resulting from innovation and entrepreneurship	
Technological change and development	
Competition: international and domestic	
Life cycles	
Timing	
Government policies: trade, visas, etc.	
Government incentives	
Academic and societal benefits	
Recipient country incentives	
Pathway opportunities to attract high-calibre students	
Changing social/cultural/economic forces affecting student demand preferences	

Table 18.2   Examples of Foreign Provider and Recipient Country Transnational Education (TNE) Motivators

Education-Related Factors	Socioeconomic Factors
Inability to secure a place at a local university (entry requirements/limited access/quota preclusions)	Career enhancement
Reputation and ranking of foreign university	Inability to afford going abroad for all of their studies
Local partner location and reputation	Cheaper to study a foreign degree at home rather than have to study in a foreign location (price competitiveness)
University entry that can involve competency in the provider university language of instruction, recognition of previous studies and provisions for credit for prior learning	Significance of the foreign language of instruction
Shorter time span to complete the foreign degree	Cultural, family, and personal considerations and connections
Attraction of attending classes taught by senior foreign academic staff	Inability to secure a place at a local university and preference to study a foreign degree within the region (third-country choice)
Opportunity to obtain foreign qualification without leaving home	No interest in studying abroad
Students interested to undertake a degree discipline not available at a local university	Competitive advantage, perhaps those interested in employment with a foreign enterprise or the opportunity to earn Western salaries
Opportunity to complete a degree on a part-time basis	Preference to continue working while studying with a foreign provider that can broaden their cultural and intellectual horizons
Campus/partner location and reputation	Opportunity to subsequently enter and remain in the host country under permanent resident status

Table 18.3   Examples of Student Motives

Managing Across Borders

Opportunity Assessment

Transnational opportunities may originate from a variety of sources, which may include proposals from existing partners, staff, agents, and competitors or perhaps requests from domestic or foreign government agencies. Such proposals are often initially assessed on the basis of suitability, viability, consistency, competitiveness (internal as well as external), and sustainability. Attention is then given to defining the program parameters, identifying appropriate partner/s as required, gauging market and recipient government acceptance, assessing competitive issues, analyzing market potential, estimating financial costs and return on investment, scoping appropriate academic pathways and credit for prior study options, and appraising academic and business risk.

Partner Selection

Assuming that the demand and supply prerequisites line up, the next step in the process may involve the selection of an appropriate host-country partner (where a partner is required or sought). The usual partner due-diligence assessments address organizational history, goals, structure, and legal/business relationships; financial standing; positioning and reputation; infrastructure, resources and student services; and courses and conduct. In addition, the choice of a partner is generally influenced by

- location and student access
- prior experience in transnational activities
- contractual considerations

- competitive offerings and complementarity
- local, regional, and national regulatory frameworks and compliance issues
- language and cross-cultural considerations
- student quotas
- timing

The weighting given to such assessment considerations is likely to vary from provider to provider, and once a choice is made, the dynamics of the partner relationship can almost always be expected to change over time. Partner commitment is essential to the success of transnational projects, and failure to engage in an effective collaborative relationship can result in reputational risk, problems with enrollments, and inappropriate operations. Once approval to proceed is obtained, a nonbinding Memorandum of Understanding (MOU) or similar agreement is generally signed between the parties. (See Chapter 9, this volume, for further discussion on strategic partnerships.)

Transnational Project Assessment, Performance, and Appraisal

The TNE assessment, performance, and appraisal process is likely to involve a comprehensive business case analysis that addresses strategic, academic, student, financial, operations, and marketing and internationalization considerations, similar to those presented in Box 18.1. Following all internal approvals, a contract is prepared for partner consideration, negotiation, and subsequent signature. At the same time, work can commence with the partner to prepare host government registration/accreditation documentation along with marketing, operations, quality assurance, and governance processes.

BOX 18.1 Transnational Education (TNE): Key Performance Considerations

The following table represents a collection of key appraisal and performance considerations that can promote successful management of transnational projects and minimize operational risk. Although not a definitive list, it does represent a comprehensive overview of the issues that should be considered when scoping out a project or appraising program performance.

(Continued)

(Continued)

Operations	*Academic*
Implementation of effective administrative procedures and processes	Compliance with regulatory requirements (registration approval and accreditation)
Instigation of business case and formal review processes	Benchmark student and academic performance
Preparation of TNE operations manual that is compliant with provider mission statement, plans, ethical practices, domestic regulatory requirements; risk adverse; equitable; of comparable quality to those delivered in the home country; and fully approved by the provider	Implementation of a quality assurance framework for teaching and learning that the partner agrees and commits to
	Pathway arrangements are understood and in place
Identify realistic duration for Partner agreement	Course duration and dates to adhere to Partner requirements and accreditation guidelines
Identify project implementation management team that are able to competently resource and manage an operation of significant complexity	Course content to comply with provider curriculum and unit descriptions
Ensure ownership/tenancy of partner facilities is clear of medium term disruption	Appointment of provider course/unit moderators in cases where units are being taught by partner academic staff
Ensure premises/facilities/learning resources are in accordance with acceptable Provider standards (classrooms, library, student facilities)	Provision for student laboratories and practicals
	Moderation and validation of student coursework complies with agreement
Manage relationships between internal and external TNE partners	Curriculum is made available to students in a timely fashion
Make sure that there is an adequate level of Partner administrative support	Delivery modes meet partner requirements
Make sure that issues relating to copyright and privacy are secure and protected	Equivalence and compliance issues are addressed and tracked
	Course advisory board/s meet regularly
Ensure that there is sufficient senior University representation and engagement in the collaborative venture.	Recruitment, enrollment and advanced standing
	Curriculum compliance and equivalence
	Service agreements formalized with teaching staff
Ensure administrative systems and reporting measures can effectively and efficiently monitor TNE performance. Allow for regular communications through effective two-way channels	Full/part time enrollment implication
	Partner academic and sessional staff are approved prior to lecturing/tutoring on TNE programs
Regularly review the appropriateness of partner campus location/s	Staff/student ratio's are preplanned and accepted
Responsibility for selection and enrollment— guarantee that entry standards are being maintained	Compulsory Induction programs addressing teaching and learning nuances and standards, policy and regulatory requirements, compliance and equivalence, student services and briefing on goals, objectives, service provisions, alumni and achievements.
Facilities and support (library provisions, access to computers, student access to library).	
Infrastructure provisions; monitoring standards	Academic rigor, pedagogy, standards and support

Resource and responsibility management—e.g., unit moderators	Examinations are arranged and supervised in accordance with Provider guidelines
Staff selection and professional development	Assessment and benchmarking to ensure comparable standards
Service provisions and pastoral support	Appropriate examination and assessment security measures are in place
Internationalization process	
Reporting, monitoring and responses/actions	Arrangements for timely moderation and assessment
Community linkages	Pathway and advanced standing is understood and communicated
Contractual arrangements	
Student support services—help desk, student feedback	Quality assurance compliance and oversight
	Fraudulent documentation for entry; plagiarism; conduct of examinations
	Accurate student record keeping—enrollments, demographics, credit precedents, academic results, records of attendance, fee payments, refunds, graduations (student records must be kept for a minimum period of two years following completion of studies)
	Teach-out Plans are in place
	Timeliness of delivery, assessment and reporting
Financial	*Marketing*
Return on investment	Clear, unambiguous and accurate marketing, communication and recruitment initiatives in line with conditions of engagement and operations
Fees associated with foreign course approval/ registration and renewal	
Partner indemnity insurance cover	Preparation and maintenance of transnational web-based information and print material
Student fees (will students pay by subject/unit, term/semester or an annual fee?)	Compliance with all course entry requirements
Fees paid to whom?	Roles for partner regarding offers and acceptance
Are there in-country caps on fees/student entry quotas?	Approval for advanced standing and credit transfers
	Clear and unambiguous commencement dates
Will there be a guarantee of minimum level of revenue?	Contingency plans in place to address situations where minimum student intakes are not achieved
Are there any taxation implications (Withholding Tax, etc.)?	Target market/s and estimated demand (who, what, where, how, when, why)
Assuming fees are made payable to the partner, are there processes in place to allow for the gap that may occur between the time of receipt of fees from the partner and the date at which the student commences studies? What are the implications for issuance of student library cards, student ID cards, etc?	Commission systems for transnational agents
	Impact on existing international student recruitment targets
	Competition (both domestic and international)
	Recruitment responsibilities
	Advertising and promotion

(Continued)

(Continued)

Compliance with Provider refund terms Budgets/cash flow projections Costing, expenditure, funding and reporting Repatriation of profit/earnings Currency hedging	
Students Planning for the student experience Equitable and ethical treatment of students (entry, access, assessment, privacy, pastoral care, etc.) Consumer protection provisions and compliance Student induction programs and preparation of student induction packs Provision of transnational scholarship scheme Maintain a student help desk Manage transnational student pastoral care initiative Support and attend transnational graduations Monitor and communicate credit for prior study Induction programs provided for all new students Arrangements for special consideration and appeals Provision of transnational scholarships Maintain a transnational student help desk Importance of transnational graduations Recommend/monitor credit precedents for advanced standing Clarify and scrutinize transnational student entry requirements Provision of timely offers	*Strategic* Relevance to internationalization policies and plans Priority given to market expansion over program development Senior management engagement and support Effective internal governance and partner project management provisions Compliance with internal program approval procedures Partner due diligence Partner registration/accredited to conduct higher education programs TNE Programs registration/approval with education authorities in host country/s (legal and ethical compliance, duration) Compatibility of partner goals, objectives and strategies Partner reputation and positioning implications Sustainability Exit/withdrawal strategies Competing strategic interests/initiatives Support for transnational alumni
Internationalization Professional recognition (i.e., CPA if accounting degree is offered) Compliance and equivalence issues Integrity and consistency Governance issues	

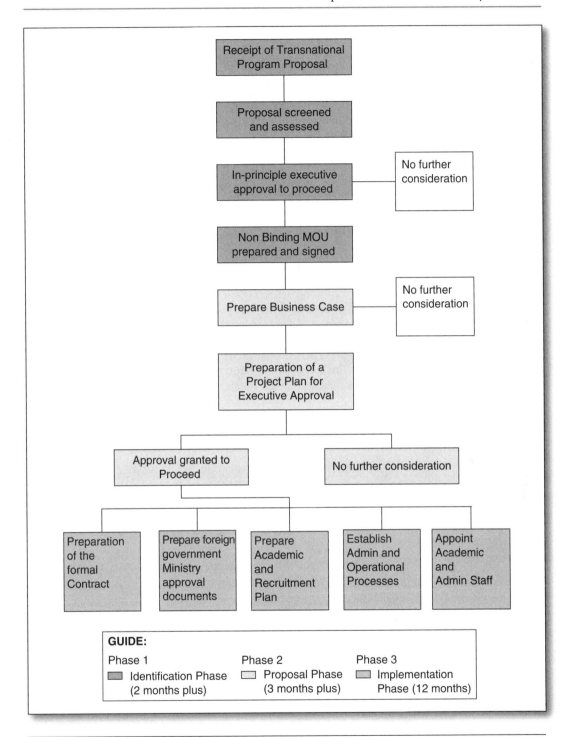

Figure 18.1 Model of the TNE Project Appraisal Process

For planning purposes, the reader should be aware that it can take well over 12 months to move from the initial project screening and appraisal stage to implementation, depending on the complexity of the project. Figure 18.1 identifies examples of the various steps that may be included in the project appraisal process.

Transnational Entry Strategies

Institutions and transnational programs can cross borders in many different ways. Knight (2005) identified six discrete TNE categories, which include virtual universities, branch campuses, independent institutions, acquisition and mergers, study centers or teaching sites, and affiliations or networks. For the practitioner, the more common definitions for the modes of transnational market entry appraisal include:

- *Twinning* arrangements provide a pathway for students to commence studies through a partner in one country and complete the agreed upon program of studies through a partner in another country. There are essentially two types of twinning programs. One involves an articulation/pathway agreement between the home institution and an education provider based in another country where the home institution approves and recognizes with appropriate credit a specific course or particular subjects taught by the foreign partner as being equivalent to those offered at the home institution. In such circumstances twinning can

also encompass cross-sectoral linkages that bridge differing qualifications to form a dual award or double or joint degree (Adams, Burgess, & Phillips, 2009). The NAFSA Resources Library provides useful reference for the establishment of U.S. dual or double degrees.

The second twinning model involves conduct and delivery of the home institution program on the foreign partner campus. This may be taught wholly or partially by home institution academic staff or wholly or partially by approved foreign-provider academic staff.

In either case, cross-crediting arrangements need to be in place to support tandem delivery of the programs. Furthermore, all conditions and rules concerning entry admission, credit recognition, awards, and testamurs (degree certificates) need to take account of the home-country provider requirements, and students must satisfy the home-country visa entry requirements as a condition of offer.

Western Michigan University, Troy University, and State University of New York are examples

BOX 18.2 Western Michigan University's Twinning Programs

The growing middle class in Malaysia surpassed the capacity of the country's six universities in the 1980s, causing the government to consider options for responding rapidly to this growing demand. In 1987, Western Michigan University (WMU) partnered with a corporation that was establishing Malaysia's first private college. The project allowed Sunway College to replicate the first 2 years of WMU's curriculum in defined degree paths so that students could transfer to WMU's campus in Kalamazoo in their third year, thereby saving about 40% of the cost of a U.S. undergraduate degree. This project helped this regional university establish a stronger international brand, with almost 700 Malaysian students studying in Kalamazoo at the highest point. For Sunway, this innovative model helped them develop educational capacity, starting from scratch in 1987. Sunway College eventually partnered with other British and Australian universities to offer several different paths to higher education in English-speaking countries. As Sunway's own capacity grew and it eventually gained university status in its own right, the partnership with WMU transformed to collaboration on a general pathway program, delivering U.S. general education curriculum that students can use to transfer to a long list of overseas universities that have recognized or articulated WMU's curriculum taught by Sunway in Kuala Lumpur.

This collaboration established WMU as a significant player in TNE, leading to subsequent projects in other parts of Asia, Latin America, and Africa. With up to eight active twinning programs and an offshore enrollment approaching 1,000 students at its high point, the university's TNE program has played a very significant role in WMU's internationalization agenda.

of U.S. institutions that operate twinning programs in foreign locations.

- *Branch campus* is generally interpreted to be a wholly foreign owned and operated or joint-venture campus facility. Some excellent branch campus facilities are operating in the Middle East, Malaysia, Australia, Vietnam, South Africa, India, China, and other parts of the globe. Most of the wholly owned campuses emanate out of the United States, Europe, and Australia and examples include the University of Richmond in London; RMIT University in Vietnam; Monash University in Malaysia and South Africa; the Universities of Liverpool and Nottingham in China; British and U.S. Universities in Dubai; University of Carnegie Melon in Australia, Greece, Japan, Qatar, and Seoul; and Webster University in Austria, Bermuda, China, Greece, Switzerland, Thailand (Academic Cooperation Association, 2008).

- *Online Learning* (distance learning or e-learning as it is commonly referred to) is today acknowledged as an important transnational teaching and learning tool. Although it has not replaced traditional transnational "chalk and talk" pedagogy, it does afford the advantage of access to a virtual learning environment that encourages, facilitates, and supports student access, engagement, and learning outcomes.

Critics of on-line learning raise concerns regarding recipient-country technology capacity, suitability to education environments where pedagogy is highly structured, and teacher-directed sensitivity to cultural norms and language of instruction (Marginson, 2004). However, given that

> 50 percent of all US higher education institutions offer distance education (34 percent award degrees via distance education) and that about 2.9 million students are enrolled in distance education programs, it is clear that this mode of delivery has great potential in transnational education. (Academic Cooperation Association, 2008, p. 84)

- *Franchising* is where the provider institution authorizes an institution in another country to teach all or some part of an accredited award program or syllabi, for a negotiated fee. Under such arrangements, the contractual agreement would normally stipulate that the provider institution maintain academic and administrative quality control over delivery.

GOVERNANCE AND QUALITY ASSURANCE

Today, in what is described as a global climate of financial constraints, risk aversion, intense competition, stringent regulatory frameworks, technological advancements, student mobility, consumer protection, and expectations of quality outcomes, TNE is undergoing rigorous scrutiny. The net result is that the international higher education sector is under continuing pressure to rethink, reassess, refine, re-engineer, and review TNE policies and practices.

At the macro level, the measures promoted through the Bologna Process (2007) have encouraged many non-European nations to seek to be more closely aligned to the Bologna structures to ensure international acceptance of higher education degrees and options for student mobility. This includes processes that address a three-cycle degree model, a national register of education providers, detailed descriptions of awards, accreditation based on national protocols and standards, credit mapping, regular audit cycles, and publication of performance data that form part of an advanced framework and quality assurance system. According to the Department of Education, Employment, and Workplace Relations (2006), the Bologna Process has significant political support within Europe and applies to about 4,000 institutions hosting 16 million students. It therefore presents implications for any nation's higher education relationships, both inside and outside Europe.

At the operational level, the World Bank (2007) makes the following point:

> There is no common definition of quality in tertiary education, and certainly no common metric with which to measure it. Yet, through the influence of the Bologna Process and the need for harmonization of learning and recognition of credentials for the purposes of mobility, quality assurance has become important as a way to develop common metrics and provide information to stakeholders. There is clearly a convergence on quality assurance methodologies and increasing agreement on the general principles of good practice. Nevertheless, each country context is unique and therefore each country has its own purposes for quality

assurance—whether to protect consumers from poor quality or encourage excellence. (p. 14)

Other particularly useful references concerning quality frameworks can be found in the UNESCO-APQN toolkit: *Regulating the Quality of Cross-border Education* (UNESCO, 2006) and the UNESCO *Guidelines for Quality Provision in Cross-border Higher Education* (UNESCO/ OECD, 2005). In the United States, quality assurance oversight is the responsibility of regional accreditation bodies, with little federal oversight or intervention systems in place to ensure consistency. U.S. institutions need to ascertain regional accreditation requirements at the early stage of transnational development. Whereas many countries have clearly embraced transnational higher education and encouraged the export and/or import of transnational projects, quality assurance of transitional education is still evolving as a management process. All too often, the provider institution is left to decide on the systems and processes necessary, and legitimate concerns remain regarding quality as it applies to equivalence, compliance, consistency, standards, and purpose. In circumstances where providers and partners are revenue driven,

there are unfortunately many examples of private institutions that have paid less attention to quality outcomes than to their short-term revenue aspirations. Furthermore, while higher education institutions may have a genuine commitment to quality, their oversight practices and processes may fall short of the expected outcomes. In a transnational setting, the recipient partner can have very different aims and objectives and may not have any legal obligation to the provider institution beyond what is specified in the contract to the provider institution or the source country.

What becomes evident is that practitioners need to give serious consideration to the internal alignment between transnational operations and their respective missions, goals, policies, and strategies as well as ensure compliance with regulatory frameworks and consumer protection and privacy laws. Successful cross-border education ultimately depends on long-term alignment of mission and internationalization strategies of both parties and excellent communication and engagement. In partnerships where the operations are transparent, there is senior staff commitment, and all the stakeholders involved benefit.

BOX 18.3 Pathways: A Case Study on Successful Cross-Border Collaboration

Higher education pathway arrangements can be described as a cross-sectoral bridge that recognizes prior study as being appropriate for higher education entry. For the prospective transnational student, many institutions now have structured credit arrangements in place that recognize prior study against foundation, partially complete, or completed diplomas and degrees or other recognized courses that have been approved and undertaken under a TNE model in collaboration with a foreign partner. Although many cross-border partnerships involve establishing a relationship with a foreign entity, a growing number of home-based non-self-accrediting provider institutions provide pathway programs in foreign locations.

IIBT—A Case Study

The International Institute of Business and Technology (IIBT) is a private fully accredited Western Australia-based higher education institution established in 1999 and accounts for a significant flow of international students from China into Australia. More than 1,500 IIBT China students have already crossed borders and successfully transited into Australian partner-university courses, with credit as advanced standing awarded for prior IIBT studies. Furthermore, IIBT currently has just over

1,400 students studying across its non-award pathway programs in China in preparation for future tertiary studies at one of IIBT's partner universities.

The IIBT China operations can be described as somewhat unusual as a TNE model. The Institute currently runs five pathway programs that form part of fully accredited Chinese higher education diplomas at 12 tertiary institutions and training colleges strategically located across the country. On successful completion of such programs, students are eligible to articulate with advanced-standing credit toward a specific degree course (i.e., business, information technology, engineering) offered in Australian public tertiary institutions that include Edith Cowan University, Curtin University, Central Queensland University, University of Wollongong, and the University of Tasmania. This approach has the approval of Chinese provincial authorities because it draws on the collective education strengths of the partners to provide a unique cross-cultural learning experience. It includes English language of instruction and the equivalent of eight Australian undergraduate first-year subjects that form part of the China qualification.

IIBT recognizes that its success in China has been attributable to a number of factors, not the least of which is the relationship it enjoys with its Chinese and Australian university partners, its networking with Chinese education authorities, its well-earned reputation, its knowledge of the market, its best-practice approach to its pedagogy, and the pastoral care and support that it provides for its cross-border pathway students in the course of transition to study at an Australian partner-university campus. IIBT also has expatriate staff based in China teaching all of its courses at Anhui Agriculture University, Anhui Economic Management Institute, Anhui Vocational College of Art, China University of Petroleum, Fujian Normal University, Zhejiang Normal University, Jinan University, Shenyang Financial Institute, South China Agriculture University, Wuhan University, Xuzhou Jiu-Zhou Professional Institute, and Xuzhou College of Industrial Technology.

The IIBT Academic Board plays a pivotal role in ensuring that quality teaching and learning outcomes are achieved within a framework that bridges language and culture, pedagogy, and learning styles, as well as relevance, compliance, and equivalence. IIBT's curriculum has achieved high levels of academic currency in terms of credit for prior learning, and its students generally receive between 1 and 1.5 years of advanced standing credit (up to 12 course units) toward partner university programs.

To ensure compliance with its higher education partners, IIBT operates within a framework that satisfies university partner policies and procedures. This involves ensuring that staff have appropriate academic credentials; appropriate infrastructure is in place and teaching/learning resources are accessible, effective, and timely; and the curriculum remains relevant. In addition, IIBT maintains an open-door policy that encourages partner engagement and participation in the quality assurance process.

IIBT is now in the process of taking its model to other Asian locations and expanding its network to provide opportunities for cross-border tertiary studies through university partners in Europe and in particular, North America.

NOTE: This box was prepared by chapter author Peter Burgess.

New Trends and Future Challenges

Mention has already been made of the many existing challenges facing the transnational educator, among them the ethics and merits of both the concept and the strategy. Stella (2005) suggests that those opposed to a commercial or transnational trade orientation might argue that it is not in the best interest of developing nations. Those that support the World Trade Organization

(WTO) General Agreement on Trade in Services (GATS) framework argue that commercialization is an unavoidable consequence of globalization. Nonetheless, some predict that "the demand for international education is forecast to increase from 1.8 million international students in 2000 to 7.2 million international students in 2025" (Knight, 2006, p 21).

In the United States, the relatively low level of engagement in this sector, compared with the United Kingdom and Australia, may reflect concerns for brand dilution, the absence of widely recognized quality control mechanisms, and an internationalization agenda that only recently has become increasingly driven by revenue considerations. Many senior international officers in the United States recall the effort in the 1980s to establish branch campuses in Japan. Very few projects were ultimately sustainable and remain today.

Given the various negative commercial, pedagogical, and cultural concerns, TNE providers remain under continued pressure to re-engineer processes that reflect changing market needs and to anticipate and respond to the multiple regulatory and quality assurance frameworks and regimes that are evolving in the global marketplace.

McBurnie and Ziguras (2011) propose four possible scenarios for the future of TNE.

Scenario 1: In this scenario the rapid growth of TNE continues apace with governments putting in place quality assurance measures that allow the scale and quality of provision to continue to grow. Importer countries see it as a rapid means of meeting student demand, and less costly than mass expansion of domestic infrastructure. Exporters are attracted to the revenue and perceived reputational benefits.

Scenario 2: That enrollment, sequentially grow, peak, and then decline on a country-by-country basis according to the phase of development and demand in the host nation. Whilst TNE would still have a strong presence in many parts of the world, its overall growth would be modest.

Scenario 3: That following the "hub" strategies of several nations, TNE develops into a limited number of international "branch campus clusters" of prestigious institutions, concentrated in major cities serving as "regional education hubs" in Asia, the Middle East, Latin America and Africa. These hubs would attract students from the region and beyond, combining institutional mobility with student mobility.

Scenario 4: Host governments apply increasingly stringent quality assurance requirements and demand greater (and more expensive) commitments from transnational providers to the highest standard, to deter over-commercialization, and to protect the integrity of the domestic system. In parallel, exporter governments, in response to negative publicity about offshore course and campus closures, place stricter regulations on provider institutions, in order to weed out low quality offerings that may damage the nation's reputation and market share. The overall effect is an enhancement of the quality of TNE, but a marked reduction in its quantity. (pp. 34, 35)

What can be safely assumed is that in the future, public accountability for financial commitments will increase, quality assurance measures will be tested in the public domain, and academic and administrative standards will be benchmarked and scrutinized. Indeed, one of the greatest challenges facing the future transnational manager will be to remain entrepreneurial in a regulatory climate that is not necessarily conducive to entrepreneurial initiatives.

Some of the more obvious TNE trends include:

- growth of double/dual degrees
- focus on long-term partner relationships
- provision of student-related information that addresses performance outcomes, access and entry conditions, student services, academic inputs, benchmarking, attrition, realistic contact hours, employment opportunities, pathways, credit precedents, and the like
- opportunities for home study
- industry and community linkages
- provision of scholarship opportunities
- inclusion of distance education in the transnational mix

TNE forums provide opportunity to share templates for good practice that give greater consideration to contractual agreements established between partners; appointment and induction of teaching staff; language of instruction issues; pedagogy considerations; student selection and assessment; benchmarking; credit for prior study; measures for institution-wide engagement; administrative systems and processes; marketing initiatives and support; opportunities for agent engagement; and examples of key performance indicators.

CONCLUSION

This chapter has attempted to demonstrate the growth of transnational programs, the motivators that support engagement, and many of the key considerations and processes involved in the management of cross-border TNE.

Today, TNE providers and programs are very often more regulated and reviewed than domestic providers and provisions. According to McBurnie and Ziguras (2011),

> Rather than flying under the radar, TNE is increasingly in the purview of both sending and receiving governments, professional bodies of both sending and receiving countries, and subject to the internal quality assurance procedures of both the foreign provider and its local partner. There are also voluntary codes and guidelines at regional and global levels and a raft of institutional studies and reports in the public domain. Beyond the debate as to whether TNE should be aid or trade oriented, what is generally accepted is the shared commitment to the development of high standard TNE through rigorous quality assurance regimes. (p. 28)

Cross-border education is not a panacea for short-term financial problems. When deployed as part of strategic and comprehensive internationalization strategy, it can produce positive internationalization outcomes in many ways. As global learning mobility is projected to continue to grow, higher education institutions should consider this opportunity within the breadth of their engagement strategies.

REFERENCES

Academic Cooperation Association (ACA). (2008). *Transnational education in the European context: Provisions, approaches and policy* (Report produced on behalf of the European Commission). Brussels: Author.

Adams A., Burgess P., & Phillips R. (2009). Pathways in international education: An analysis of global pathways in a transnational context. In M. Field & J. Fegan (Eds.), *Education across borders: Politics, policy and legislative action*. London: Springer.

Australian Education International (AEI). (2011). Research snapshot. *Transnational education in the higher education sector*. Retrieved from http://www.deewr.gov.au/HigherEducation/Publications/HEStatistics/Publications/Pages/Home.aspx

Banks M., Kevat P., Ziguras C., Ciccarelli A., & Clayton D. (2010). *The changing fortunes of Australian transnational higher education*. Retrieved from http://www.obhe.ac.uk/documents/view_details?id=835

Berquist, B., & Fuller, C. (2006). *Development of transnational education programs from a U.S. perspective*. Paper presented at the Australian International Education Conference, Perth, Australia.

Bologna Process. (2007). *European higher education in a global setting - a strategy for the external dimension of the Bologna Process*. Retrieved from http://www.ond.vlaanderen.be/hogeronderwijs/bologna/documents/wgr2007/strategy-for-ehea-in-global-setting.pdf

British Council. (2009). *The Prime Ministers Initiative PMI2*. Retrieved from www.britishcouncil.org/pmi2-connect

British Council. (2010). *Transnational education student decision-making research*. Retrieved from *www.britishcouncil.org/eumd-information-research-tne-student-decision-making.htm*

Department of Education, Employment, and Workplace Relations (2006). *The Bologna Process and Australia: Next steps* (Discussion Paper 4/2006 Australian Government). Canberra: Author. Retrieved from http://www.dest.gov.au/sectors/higher_education/publications_resources/profiles/bologna_process_and_australia.htm

de Wit, H. (2008, October). *Changing trends in the internationalization of higher education*. Paper presented at the University of Melbourne. Retrieved from http://www.cshe.unimelb.edu.au/research/seminarpapers/deWittpres061008.pdf

Feith, D. (2008, July). *India's higher education sector in the twenty first century: A growing market and the need for international engagement*. Paper presented at the 17th Biennial Conference of the Asian Studies Association of Australia Conference, Melbourne Retrieved from http://arts.monash.edu.au/mai/asaa/davidfeith.pdf

Higher Education Statistics Agency. (2010). *Transnational education*. Cheltenham, UK: Author. Retrieved from http://www.international.ac.uk/home/index.cfm

Knight, J. (1999). Internationalisation of higher education. In H. de Wit & J. Knight (Eds.), *Quality and internationalisation in higher education*. Paris: Organisation for Economic Co-operation and Development.

Knight, J. (2005). *Cross-border education: Not just students on the move*. Boston: Boston College,

Center for International Higher Education. Retrieved from http://www.bc.edu/bc_org/avp/soe/cihe/newsletter/Number41/Number41.htm

Knight, J. (2006). *Higher education crossing borders: A guide to the implications of the General Agreement on Trade in Services (GATS) for cross-border education* (Report prepared for the Commonwealth of Learning and UNESCO). Retrieved from http://unesdoc.unesco.org/images/0014/001473/147363E.pdf

Larsen K., Momii, K., & Vincent-Lancrin, S. (2004). *Cross-border higher education: An analysis of current trends, policy strategies and future scenarios.* Retrieved from http://www.obhe.ac.uk/documents/view_details?id=49

Leask, B. (2004, July). *Transnational education and intercultural learning: Reconstructing the offshore teaching team to enhance internationalisation.* Paper presented at the Proceedings of the Australian Universities Quality Forum, Adelaide.

Li, S. (2009). *Transnational education in China: Thirty years* (draft paper). http://www.unescobkk.org/fileadmin/user_upload/apeid/workshops/macao08/papers/2-b-1.pdf

Marginson, S. (2004). Don't leave me hanging on the Anglophone: The potential for online distance higher education in the Asia-Pacific Region. *Higher Education Quarterly, 58*(2/3), 74–113.

Misha A. (2010, May 9). India: Foreign universities bill tabled. *University World News.* Retrieved from *www.universityworldnews.com/article.php?story=20100507210821494*

Madison, D. (2006). *A brief history of distance education.* Retrieved from http://www.isnare.com/?aid=32195&ca=education

McBurnie, G., & Ziguras, C. (2011). Global trends in quality assurance for transnational education In A. Stella & S. Bhushan (Eds.), *Quality assurance of transnational higher education: The experiences of Australia and India.* Retrieved from http://www.nafsa.org/resourcelibrary/default.aspx?id=8810

Rizvi, F. (2004). Offshore/Australian higher rducation. *International Higher Education,* No 37. Boston: The Boston College Center for International Higher Education.

Stella, A. (2005). *The challenges of transnational education* (Abstract). http://www.informaworld.com/smpp/content~content=a727335869&db=all

Stella, A., & Bhushan, S. (Ed.). (2011). *Quality assurance of transnational higher education: The experiences of Australia and India.* Canberra: Australian Universities Quality Agency and the National University of Educational Planning and Administration.

UNESCO/Council of Europe. (2001). *Code of good practice in the provision of transnational education* (Lisbon Recognition Convention Committee, Rīga). Retrieved from http://www.coe.int/t/dg4/highereducation/recognition/Codeofgoodpractice_EN.asp

UNESCO/OECD. (2005). *Guidelines for quality provision in cross-border education.* Paris: Authors. Retrieved from http://www.oecd.org/dataoecd/27/51/35779480.pdf

UNESCO (2006). *UNESCO-APQN toolkit: Regulating the quality of cross-border education.* Bangkok: UNESCO Bangkok. Retrieved from http://www2.unescobkk.org/elib/publications/087/APQN_Toolkit.pdf

UK Higher Education International Unit. (2010). *Global opportunities for UK higher education.* Retrieved from http://www.international.ac.uk/statistics/transnational_education.cfm

Universities Australia. (2009). *The nature of international education in Australian universities and its benefits, strategy policy and research in education.* Canberra: Author.

World Bank. (2007). *Cross-border tertiary education.* Washington, DC: Author.

19

INTERNATIONAL JOINT, DOUBLE, AND CONSECUTIVE DEGREE PROGRAMS

New Developments, Issues, and Challenges

JANE KNIGHT AND JACK LEE

International joint, double, and consecutive degree (JDCD) programs have an important role in the current landscape of higher education and the potential to become more numerous and influential in the coming years. As an internationalization strategy, these programs address the heartland of academia, which is the teaching and learning process and the production of new knowledge between and among countries. These programs are built on the principle of deep academic collaboration with important benefits to individuals, institutions, and national and regional education systems. Given the increasing interest in these programs, innovative models continue to emerge and diversify the opportunities available to students.

Higher education institutions worldwide are continually seeking out opportunities or responding to requests for international collaborative programs. What are the drivers for their growing popularity? First, it is important to reflect on the unprecedented increase in the internationalization of higher education in general. The number of multilateral university networks for research, teaching, and contract project work has multiplied (Schneller, Lungu, & Wächter, 2009); new regional international education organizations have been established; countries are launching national internationalization strategies and programs (Knight, 2008a); and new policy actors such as immigration, industry, and trade are engaged and collaborating with education, foreign affairs, science, and technology (Sackmann, 2007). The increase in volume, scope, and scale of cross-border movement of education programs (franchise, twinning, branch campus, etc.) and providers (commercial companies, nongovernment organizations, traditional universities) is unprecedented (Becker, 2009; Vincent-Lancrin, 2004). The overall demand for higher education is growing, and this in turn increases the interest in international education opportunities and especially the quest for foreign education credentials. This scenario helps to context the appeal of JDCD programs.

The major drivers for stimulating this interest include the increased demand for higher education and particularly international education; greater emphasis on academic mobility for students and professors; improved information and communication technologies, which permit more virtual collaboration among higher education institutions; and finally, the rather tenuous perception by many institutions that greater international involvement can only elevate one's reputation and status.

This chapter focuses on JDCD programs that are international. While these types of programs may have existed within institutions and countries for several years, the fact that they are now crossing national borders introduces a host of different issues to consider (Knight, 2005). The purpose of this chapter is to (a) clarify the meaning of international joint, double, and consecutive degrees and discuss why they are becoming more important and popular, (b) identify the major research projects and surveys from around the world and discuss major trends, (c) analyze some of the key challenges and issues facing institutions as they establish these types of collaborative programs, and finally, (d) raise questions that require ongoing debate and analysis. The discussion will not include subdegree and degree program combinations that are prevalent in many jurisdictions (i.e., preparatory studies followed by degree enrollment). Those programs are articulation models or pathways to improve access and equity in higher education via a nontraditional route, an issue that is not the primary focus of JDCD programs.

To illustrate that these programs are a global phenomenon, examples from all regions of the world are provided through boxes. The short descriptions of the JDCD programs show that they are being developed at bachelor's, master's and doctorate levels and across all disciplines. Box 19.1 highlights joint degree programs, Box 19.2 focuses on double degree programs, and Box 19.3 gives examples of some innovative online, consortium-based, and consecutive degree programs.

TERMINOLOGY AND TYPOLOGY

A review of research articles, survey reports, and university Web pages from around the world shows a plethora of terms used to describe international collaborative programs. These terms include double, dual, multiple, tri-national, joint, integrated, collaborative, international, consecutive, concurrent, *cotutelle*, twinned, overlapping, conjoint, parallel, two-tiered, simultaneous, and common degrees. They mean different things to different people within and across countries. For example, the French model of *cotutelle* to indicate co-supervision of a doctoral student is now being used by both French and non-French institutions to indicate both joint and double degree programs.

To deal with this complexity of terms, organizations, governmental bodies, and institutions have correctly tried to provide clear definitions. While this effort has added clarity at the national or institutional level, it has resulted in a multitude of definitions and increased confusion at the global level. A typology and definitions of three major types of collaborative programs have been developed to encourage common understanding and use of the terms (Knight, 2008b). The working definitions and a brief analysis of joint, double (or multiple), and consecutive programs are discussed in the next section. Important to note is that the description following each definition highlights the importance of *program* rather than simply the *qualification* awarded.

Joint Degree Program

A joint degree program awards one joint qualification upon completion of the collaborative program requirements established by the partner institutions.

Knight, 2008b

The distinguishing feature is that only one qualification is awarded jointly by the cooperating institutions. The duration of the program is normally not extended, and thus, students have the advantage of completing a joint program in the same time period as an individual program from one of the institutions. The design and integration of the course of study varies from program to program, but it normally involves the mobility (physical or virtual) of students, professors, and course content. While student mobility provides rich learning experiences, it is not always possible. The options of having visiting professors, courses by distance, and joint virtual research projects provide valuable alternatives to student mobility.

Awarding of a joint qualification can create many legal issues. National regulations often do not allow for a university to jointly confer a qualification, especially in association with a foreign institution. In this case, if both names of the collaborating institutions appear on the degree certificate, there is a risk that the joint degree will not be recognized by either of the partner countries. Thus, a student may not have a legitimate qualification, even though all program requirements have been completed. The situation becomes more complicated when one looks for an international body that will recognize a joint degree from two bona fide institutions. At this point, the Lisbon Convention for Recognition of Credentials is the only one of six UNESCO regional conventions that does so (EC/UNESCO, 2004).

Overall, the most important features of a joint degree program are the strengths that each institution brings to the program and the opportunities it allows for students to benefit from a program that draws on the teaching, curricular, and research expertise of two or more institutions located in different countries. The major drawbacks at the current time are the issues related to the legality and recognition of a jointly conferred qualification.

Double (Multiple) Degree Program

A double degree program awards two individual qualifications at equivalent levels upon completion of the collaborative program requirements established by the two partner institutions.

Knight, 2008b

Double degree programs are the most popular type of international collaborative program and are often called dual degrees. A multiple degree program is essentially the same as a double degree

---

BOX 19.1 Joint Degrees

Norway-Finland-Portugal: joint master in Higher Education

The University of Aveiro (Portugal), the University of Oslo (Norway), and the University of Helsinki (Finland) offer a joint master's degree program in higher education as part of the European Erasmus initiative. Students are required to study at all three institutions before selecting one institution to sponsor the thesis research.

http://www.uio.no/english/studies/programmes/heem-master/index.xml

Italy-Germany-Netherlands-India: joint Ph.D. in Law and Economics

Universities of Bologna, Hamburg, and Rotterdam, with the collaboration of the Indira Gandhi Institute of Development Research of Mumbai, offer a joint doctorate in law and economics as part of the Erasmus Mundus framework. Students must study at all three European universities before receiving either a joint or double doctorate degree.

http://www.edle-phd.eu/

Singapore-India: joint PhD in Engineering

National University of Singapore and the Indian Institute of Technology (Bombay or Madras) offer a joint doctoral degree in engineering. Thesis supervision and teaching involve faculty members from both institutions.

http://www.gse.nus.edu.sg/postgradprog.html

program except for the number of qualifications offered. A multiple degree program awards three or more individual qualifications at equivalent levels upon completion of the collaborative program requirements established by the three or more partner institutions.

As the titles of bachelor's, master's, and doctoral degrees differ across countries, the term *equivalent level* is used to indicate that the double or multiple degrees conferred are of the same standing. The duration of a double or multiple degree program is normally extended beyond the length of a single degree program to meet the requirements of all partners participating in the collaborative program. The legality and recognition of the qualifications awarded by double/multiple degree programs are more straightforward than those for joint degrees. It is assumed that each partner institution is officially registered or licensed in its home county. Therefore, each degree is recognized in its country of origin, while the additional degree(s) is treated like any other foreign credential.

The major hurdles facing double or multiple degree programs involve the design of the curriculum and the establishment of completion requirements. There is no standard way to establish completion requirements due to the variety of disciplines, fields of study, and national regulations involved. Each partnership operates according to the practices and legalities of the collaborating institutions. However, the approach of double or triple counting the same student workload or learning outcomes can significantly jeopardize the academic integrity of the program. The idea of having two degrees from two different institutions in two different countries is attractive to students, but careful attention needs to be given to ensure that the value and recognition of the qualifications are valid and do not violate the premise, academic purpose, and authenticity of a collaborative degree program. This is especially true for multiple degree programs.

BOX 19.2 Double Degrees

Singapore-China: double bachelors in Medicine

Nanyang Technological University (Singapore) and Beijing University of Chinese Medicine offer a double degree, 5-year program in biomedical science and medicine, respectively.
   http://global.ntu.edu.sg/joint/Pages/BeijingUniversityofChineseMedicine.aspx

Scotland-Egypt: double bachelors in Nursing

The Queen Margaret University (Scotland) and the British University in Egypt offer a double bachelor degree in nursing that allows their graduates to work in both countries. Students must complete a 1-year internship in either country.
   http://www.qmu.ac.uk/hn/

Canada-China: double bachelors in Computing Science

Simon Fraser University (Canada) and Zhejiang University (China) offer a double degree program in Computing Science. Over a 5-year period, students take courses at both institutions with structured periods of language immersion.
   http://www.cs.sfu.ca/undergraduate/programs/dual-degree-major-with-zhejiang-university.html

U.S.-Turkey: double Ph.D. in Engineering

Carnegie Mellon (U.S.) and the Middle East Technical University (Turkey) offer a double PhD degree program in civil and environmental engineering. Students must spend a minimum of 2 years at each institution.
   http://www.ce.cmu.edu/graduate/metu.html

U.S.-South Africa: double masters plus internship in Journalism

Columbia University and the University of Witwatersrand (South Africa) offer a program in journalism, which also includes internship with news agencies in South Africa.
    http://www.journalism.columbia.edu/page/285-dual-degree-johannesburg/287

Sweden-Germany-UK-India: joint or double Ph.D. in Neuroinformatics

The Royal Institute of Technology (Sweden) coordinates a collaborative doctoral program involving institutions in three other countries: University of Edinburgh (UK), Albert-Ludwigs Universität Freiburg (Germany), and the National Centre for Biological Science (India). Students are required to visit all four sites in the network. On completion, a student receives either a joint or double degree, depending on which two universities sponsor the thesis research. English is the language of instruction.
    http://www.kth.se/studies/phd/eurospin

Consecutive Degree Program

> *A consecutive degree program awards two different qualifications at successive levels upon completion of the collaborative program requirements established by the partner institutions.*
>
>   Knight, 2008b

Consecutive degree programs are different from double degrees because two *different* levels of qualifications are awarded: usually bachelor's and master's or master's and doctorate. The major focus is on linking the two degrees and more specifically on ensuring that completion requirements for the first program align closely with the entrance prerequisites for the second degree program. This requires careful attention, as requirements in each institution or country can differ and create obstacles. For consecutive degree programs, it is common for a student to be mobile and complete the coursework and research requirements for the first degree in one country and the requirements for the second degree in the partner institution located in another country. The period of study for the program is usually longer than for a single program but shorter than if the two degrees were taken separately. At the current time, international consecutive degree programs are not as numerous as joint or double degree programs, but interest in them is growing. It is important that these programs are differentiated from the other types, and thus they constitute a third category of the typology.

BOX 19.3 Innovative Initiatives

Consecutive Degrees

Tecnológico de Monterrey (Mexico) and the Illinois Institute of Technology offer a B.Sc. and M.Sc., respectively, in environmental management and sustainability. Mexican students must spend 1 year at IIT.
    http://www.stuart.iit.edu/graduateprograms/ms/environmentalmanagement/itesm_dual_degree.shtml

(Continued)

(Continued)

La Sabana University (Colombia) and Macquarie University (Australia) offer consecutive bachelor's and master's degrees, respectively, in business, commerce, and international relations. http://www.international.mq.edu.au/studyabroad/prospectivestudents/double_degree

Online Platform

Carnegie Mellon and the Tecnológico de Monterrey (Mexico) offer a double master's degree program in information technology that is completely online. Students only meet face-to-face in Pittsburgh and Monterrey for the orientation week and closing week, respectively. http://www.ruv.itesm.mx/portal/promocion/oe/m/mti_doubledegree/homedoc.htm

International Consortium: joint PhD

The University of Nice coordinates a joint doctoral program in astrophysics that provides students with academic and research opportunities at 13 different institutions. The consortium contains mostly European universities but also includes research institutes in Europe, China, Brazil, and India. The official language of instruction is English. http://www.irap-phd.org/

Different Disciplines

The National University of Singapore and the Australian National University offer a joint bachelor degree program in Science (B.Sc. in either Chemistry, Physics or Mathematics) and Philosophy (B.A.), respectively. Students must study in both Singapore and Australia during the duration of this 4-year program. http://www.usp.nus.edu.sg/joint_deg/anu_fos/index.html

Ritsumeikan Asia Pacific University (Japan) and the Trier University of Applied Sciences (Germany) offer a program granting both a M.Sc. in International Cooperation Policy and a M.Eng. in International Material Flow Management, respectively. This program is taught completely in English. http://www.imat-master.com/

WHY COLLABORATIVE DEGREE PROGRAMS ARE IMPORTANT AND POPULAR

The rationales driving collaborative degree programs vary significantly when examined from different perspectives. This section discusses the primary reasons and anticipated benefits of JDCD programs as well as the potential disadvantages from the viewpoint of students and professors, higher education institutions, national education systems, and regional organizations.

Students and Professors

Students are attracted to these types of collaborative programs for a number of reasons. The opportunity to be part of a program that offers two degrees from two universities located in different countries is seen to enhance their employability prospects and career path. In some countries, students who complete a professional collaborative program such as engineering also receive accreditation from the professional body in each partner country, thereby enhancing job opportunities. Some students believe that a collaborative program is of higher quality, given that the expertise of two universities has shaped the academic program. This is especially true for joint degrees. Other students are less interested in enhanced quality but more enticed by the opportunity to obtain two degrees "for the price of one." Compared to pursuing two single degrees separately, students often believe that participating in consecutive degree programs provides a shorter study period, a lighter workload, and often a lower financial burden as well. These beliefs are not valid for all such programs, but there is an element of truth to these claims. Double degree programs are being presented by a leading European international education organization as "a lot easier to achieve and not necessarily less valid" and "two degrees for the price of one." Finally, students with a desire to study in another country, understand another culture, and interact with professors and students working in a different policy and problem context see many advantages of a collaborative program over an exchange or semester-abroad experience. Studying in a second or third language, often English, is seen as a huge benefit for students, as well. On a more practical note, students see the advantages of studying abroad without any loss of time or the risk of credits not being counted. Finally, the status factor cannot be ignored. There is a certain sense of elitism attached to holding academic credentials from universities in different countries, even if the student never studied abroad but instead benefited from distance education and visiting foreign professors.

On the other hand, some students may find these collaborative programs unappealing. Some collaborative programs require extra time and cost, thereby delaying graduation compared to a single degree program. The additional demand of language skills, cultural adjustment, visa issues, and other bureaucratic procedures might be daunting. Some students simply prefer traditional study abroad options to gain international and intercultural experience. Finally, the uncertainty of qualification recognition after graduating from a collaborative program might deter students from participating.

From the perspective of professors, a range of issues can influence their decision to participate in collaborative programs. Many professors are attracted to the collaborative program, given the diversity of students, as well as the opportunity to engage in an innovative teaching and learning process, to work with fellow scholars on a joint research project, to collect data or access specialized equipment, and to broaden their professional network. The appeal of exposure to another culture, new problem-solving strategies, and a different academic institution should not be underestimated for faculty members as well as students. While extra workload and new problems may be involved in collaborative programs, especially at the master's and doctoral levels, some faculty members view these programs as a win-win situation for all involved. Nevertheless, other professors may shun collaborative programs given the demands of traveling, language barriers, and increased supervision of students. The loss of complete control over the curriculum in a collaborative program is a real concern facing professors (Lee, 2009). In addition, ethical concerns about academic integrity and rigor and the general lack of recognition in the tenure and promotion process for such collaborations can ultimately dissuade professors from participating.

Higher Education Institutions

Collaborative degree programs lead to a deeper level and more sustainable type of relationship than many other internationalization strategies and can consequently bring important academic benefits. Academic benefits in terms of innovation of curriculum, exchange of professors and researchers, and access to expertise at a partner university and its research networks make joint degrees especially attractive. Consecutive degree programs allow institutions to work with overseas partners that may offer a master's or doctoral program or a speciality that is not available locally.

For other institutions, the primary rationale is to increase their reputation and ranking as an international university. This is accomplished by deliberately collaborating with partners of equal or greater status. This type of status-building applies to institutions in both developed and developing countries. For instance, institutions in developing countries seek double degree programs with developed country partners, as it indirectly verifies the quality of their program, given that courses are judged to be equivalent to count toward a double or multiple degree. Some institutions believe that a collaborative program with a partner of greater status will also help their national accreditation process.

The financial investment required to launch such programs is a subject worthy of further investigation. In some cases, the bulk of the extra costs can be borne by increasing student tuition fees, which in turn makes the program quite elitist and only accessible by financially independent or supported students. In other situations, institutions absorb the costs. At this point in time, revenue generation does not appear to be a strong driving rationale in these collaborative programs, as is the case with other cross-border activities such as franchise and twinning programs and the recruitment of foreign students. Institutions with successful joint, double, multiple degree programs have indicated that staff have mixed views on the issue. For some, it is definitely an opportunity for innovation and extension of program curriculum and research projects. For others, the upheaval and change of joint program design, development, and delivery are not welcomed.

National and Regional Levels

At the national level, profile, status, capacity-building, and competitiveness appear to be the primary rationales guiding the establishment of collaborative programs. Whereas institutions in developing countries may see the potential for capacity-building through collaborative programs, this is not often a priority for countries with a well developed higher education system. Hence, the capacity-building rationale is often motivated and shaped by self-interest status-building. This is another example where North–South international education initiatives are veering away from international development cooperation. Perhaps with time, more attention will be paid to using collaborative degree programs as a tool for building capacity in both developed and developing higher education systems and more opportunities for South-South-North cooperation will be available.

Multinational companies, especially those located in countries with a bilateral trade agreement, are interested in hiring multilingual students who have studied in both countries and understand the similarities and differences in the regulatory and cultural contexts. Collaborative programs are perceived by some countries as a way to attract talented students who may want to stay for a work experience after graduation and perhaps immigrate permanently.

Joint and double degree programs are effective tools to promote regionalization as well as inter-regional cooperation. Europe is an excellent example (European University Association, 2004). Three communiqués from Bologna ministerial meetings have emphasized the central role of these types of programs in building the European Higher Education Area (EHEA) (Schüle, 2006). In terms of inter-regional cooperation, the Atlantis Program between the Europe Union and the United States is one example of how networks of European and U.S. institutions are collaborating to offer joint or double degrees at bachelor's and master's levels (Kuder & Obst, 2009). Erasmus Mundus is a worldwide program that enables European universities to establish mobility, networks, and joint degree initiatives. This type of strategic programming and investment by the European Union is not evident in other regions of the world yet, but the potential is present. As Europe's success at using joint and double degrees to promote collaboration and increase competitiveness becomes more evident, one may see greater priority given to international collaborative degree programs as an effective instrument for both intra-regional and inter-regional cooperation.

AN OVERVIEW OF RESEARCH AND SURVEYS ON JDCD PROGRAMS

Due to the relatively short history of international JDCD programs compared to other types of academic partnerships, research on these programs remains very limited. However, several large-scale regional surveys and other reports show a distinct increase in international collaborative programs in the last few years and forecast further growth even if the definitions of joint, double, and consecutive are not consistently used among researchers, policymakers, and practitioners.

In the United States, the Council of Graduate Schools (CGS) documented the diversity and growth of collaborative degree programs between U.S. and international higher education institutions in its annual *International Graduate Admissions Survey,* both in 2007 and 2008 (CGS, 2007, 2008). These initial efforts at investigating international JDCD programs reveal significant growth in double compared to joint degree programs, an increasing number of institutions with one or more JDCD programs, and partnerships with institutions mostly in Europe, China,

India, and South Korea (Redd, 2008). In 2009, the Institute of International Education (U.S.) and Freie Universität Berlin produced a survey report on transatlantic joint and double degree programs based on responses from 180 U.S. and European higher education institutions (Kuder & Obst, 2009). The data show that U.S. institutions are more likely to offer joint and double degrees at the undergraduate level, whereas European institutions prefer the graduate level. Interestingly, U.S. institutions are more likely to use student fees to cover the cost of these programs while European institutions rely on institutional budgets and external funding (e.g., government, foundations, etc.).

In Europe, the European University Association (EUA) has highlighted the growth of JDCD programs in several survey reports as early as 2002 (Tauch & Rauhvargers, 2002). It is important to note that the term *joint degree* is commonly used in Europe to include both joint and double degrees. The *Trends V* report documents the growth of joint degree programs, particularly at the master's level (Crosier, Purser, & Smidt, 2007). However, this report also cautions that the additional financial cost required by these programs could ultimately limit their development and impact on institutional and regional goals for internationalization. The latest *Trends 2010* report also surveys institutions on the types of joint degree programs (bachelor's, master's, doctorate), new developments, and legislative changes in permitting joint degrees. *Trends 2010* indicates that many institutions are developing joint degree programs as a response to an increasingly global job market (Sursock & Smidt, 2010). EUA's 2009 *Survey of Master Degrees in Europe* confirms further growth in joint degree programs and modest progress in legislative changes to allow the awarding of joint degrees (Davies, 2009).

In Latin America, Gacel-Avila (2009) surveyed higher education institutions on international collaborative programs in a report for The Observatory on Borderless Higher Education. The survey confirms the growth of double degree programs compared to joint ones and indicates that private higher education institutions are using JDCD programs to recruit fee-paying students while public colleges and universities view these programs as capacity-building tools to strengthen graduate education. Unlike the European case, graduate employability ranks low as a rationale for developing these programs. Instead, the top rationales are the internationalization of the curriculum and the provision of innovative programs. The report concludes that Latin American colleges and universities are "some of the least internationalized in the world," and JDCD programs could overcome regional shortcomings, particularly in the internationalization of the curriculum (Gacel-Avila, 2009, p. 3).

At present, data on JDCD programs in Asia, Africa, and the Middle East are not available. However, the EU-Asia Higher Education Platform (EAHEP) met in 2009 to discuss the use of joint degree programs to promote student and staff mobility and cultural exchanges between the two regions. In a presentation from Malaysia, an international joint degree program was viewed as a strategic tool for improving the attractiveness and competitiveness of Malaysia as a regional education hub (EAHEP, 2009). This symposium also examined the benefits and challenges of international JDCD programs and recommended best practices for such collaborations.

Several other nation- or institution-based reports also address the growth of international JDCD programs. At the national level, the German Academic Exchange Service (DAAD) provides a regional survey report with mostly respondents from Germany (Maiworm, 2006); another study examines German-Dutch joint degree programs (Nickel, Zdebel, & Westerheijden, 2009); and the Finnish Ministry of Education makes several recommendations for the development of joint and double degree programs (Ministry of Education, 2004). At the institutional level, there are reports from the University of Graz, Austria (Maierhofer & Kriebernegg, 2009) and the National University of Singapore (Kong, 2008). Last, the European Consortium for Accreditation recently published a report on quality assurance and accreditation issues related to international joint degree programs (Aerden & Reczulska, 2010).

Major Trends and New Developments

Several trends are evident in the landscape of JDCD programs worldwide. Some of these trends are highlighted in the boxes while others are supported by data from the regional surveys mentioned above. First, double degree programs are far more common than joint degree programs, most likely due to legal barriers and administrative challenges in granting a joint qualification. Consecutive degree programs are the least common. Second, most joint degree programs involve two rather than multiple institutions. Joint degrees such as the one offered by Norway, Finland, and Portugal (Box 19.1) are uncommon outside Europe. It is worth noting that the European Erasmus Mundus framework currently promotes multilateral partnerships that include non-European institutions (Erasmus Mundus, 2009). Third, joint and double degree programs are mostly at the master's level, but there is increasing interest in developing collaborative doctoral degree programs that draw on expertise from different institutions (i.e., teaching, thesis supervision, research niche, etc.). Several countries are now using the French model of *cotutelle* (co-supervision, co-teaching) to label both joint and double doctoral degree programs. The short length and flexibility of many master's programs compared to bachelor's and doctorates likely facilitate international collaborative programming. Fourth, many JDCD programs are in the disciplines of business or engineering, two areas that are often considered highly mobile and international in nature. Countless international joint and double MBA degree programs already exist, therefore the boxes in this chapter specifically highlight examples from other disciplines. Last, many JDCD programs are now incorporating an overseas internship component, especially in professional fields (e.g., nursing and journalism in Box 19.2).

Although many MBA programs exhibit diverse international partners, joint degree programs in most disciplines are commonly intraregional rather than inter-regional (Box 19.1). The added complexity in developing joint degree programs may be mitigated when institutions are located in the same region with similar higher education infrastructure and policies. This geographical affinity is certainly true in Europe with a common degree structure and credit system that facilitate collaborations. On the contrary, double degree programs exhibit more interregional pairings that are remarkably international in scope (e.g., Scotland-Egypt and U.S.-Turkey in Box 19.2).

Elite higher education institutions also appear to be disproportionally represented in JDCD programs compared to other institutions. Institutions such as Columbia, Sciences Po,

London School of Economics, and the National University of Singapore all boast numerous JDCD programs. These programs generally link two elite institutions and exhibit a longer history than the collaborative programs offered by other institutions. For example, the National University of Singapore and the Australian National University offer numerous joint and double degree programs together. On the contrary, the unique example of Columbia University (U.S.) partnering with the University of Witwatersrand (Africa) in Box 19.2 could stem from a strategic move to link content expertise to a professional network in another country (i.e., access to internships) or to build capacity in a less developed institution. The boxes in this chapter purposely include both public and private institutions as well as elites to illustrate the different types of partnerships.

Innovative developments in JDCD programs include online, consortium-based, and consecutive degree programs as well as partnerships that offer degrees in two very different disciplines (Box 19.3). Advances in information and communication technologies coupled with the challenges of student mobility have led some institutions to create collaborative programs that require minimal to no traveling on the part of students. Some collaborative programs rely on faculty mobility rather than student mobility or require student mobility only for the internship component. Conceivably, students could complete an entire international JDCD program without ever leaving their home country. Although online programs may be more accessible to students with demanding schedules or limited resources, these students are deprived of the cultural immersion that epitomizes many JDCD programs. Another innovative development is the creation of large consortia to provide a wide range of learning opportunities for students. For example, in 2010, Europe launched the Erasmus Mundus joint doctorate program in astrophysics through the collaboration of 13 institutions. This international consortium includes both traditional universities in Europe and advanced research institutes worldwide. The research institutes provide cutting-edge scientific equipment and a community of highly skilled scientists to complement the academic environment of universities. Another innovative measure is the consecutive degree program that offers two degrees at separate levels from two different countries, for example B.Sc. and M.Sc. Some of these programs appear to act as new channels for graduate schools to recruit international students rather than a collaborative program designed for both local and international students. Finally, some double degree programs also offer diplomas in two very different disciplines such as science and philosophy in a timeframe that is equivalent to a standard single-discipline degree.

Issues and Challenges

Institutions face practical and substantive issues in establishing these types of initiatives. Different regulatory systems, academic calendars, credit systems, tuition and scholarship schemes, teaching approaches, and examination requirements are only a few of the more technical issues to address while quality assurance, accreditation, language, and financing present more substantive challenges.

Design and Operational Technical Issues

National and institutional regulations and customs differ and present many challenges for the design and implementation of international collaborative programs. For instance, regulations may prevent students from enrolling in more than one university at a time, or laws may require students to spend their last year or semester at the home university. Nonrecognition of or restrictions on the number of courses/credits taken outside the home institution are additional barriers. Different academic calendars can present problems for student mobility but also provide more opportunities for faculty exchange. Examination/evaluation requirements and procedures often present obstacles to double degree programs.

Professional and applied programs are popular areas for double and joint degree programs due to market demand and fewer restrictions compared to traditional academic programs (Maierhofer & Kriebernegg, 2009). The opportunity to choose an internship in one of the partner countries is appealing to students but often difficult to arrange because of visa issues, academic workload requirements, and language proficiency.

Quality Assurance and Accreditation

Quality assurance and accreditation are fundamentally important, and they pose significant challenges for JDCD programs. When institutions have their own internal quality assurance procedures in place, attaining quality in the local portion of the program is fairly straightforward. It is more difficult to assure the quality of the education or training offered by the partner university. Common entrance and exit requirements are often used as quality proxies, but it would be helpful if mutual recognition of the respective quality assurance programs (where they exist) is included in the agreement for the collaborative program.

Accreditation is even more challenging, as national systems do not exist in all countries around the world and, even if they did, accreditation agencies differ enormously: Some focus on programs and others on institutions, some focus on inputs and others on process or outputs. Furthermore, the establishment of procedures for accrediting international collaborative programs is a relatively new territory for many agencies. For the present time, the best case scenario is that accreditation is completed by each partner institution involved in the double, joint, consecutive degree program. International accreditation agencies like ABET or EQUIS may be appropriate for professional joint or double degree programs, but at present more institutions have their home program accredited rather than the collaborative degree program in its entirety.

Fees and Financing

Financial issues such as tuition fees and funding can be quite complex. It is clear that revenue generation is not usually the primary motive for these kinds of programs, as they often require extra investments by the institutions or higher tuition fees charged to students (Maierhofer & Kriebernegg, 2009). In countries that do not charge tuition fees per se or have limited autonomy to set fees, the extra costs must be borne by the institutions or external funders. However, the sustainability of a program can often be at risk when it is dependent on external funds. The development of the program becomes more complicated when multiple partners with different tuition fees are involved or when there are extra costs for the physical and virtual mobility for professors. Arrangements for joint costs regarding marketing, recruiting, assessments, and administration also need to be negotiated. In situations where revenue generation is possible, an agreement for income distribution is necessary.

Language of Instruction

The language of instruction can create serious challenges. Each partner usually offers its programs in the local language and, in some cases, English. This means that courses could be offered in at least three different languages and more if multiple partners are involved. Students need to be at least bilingual, usually their native language(s) plus English. There are two issues here. First is the dominance of English in cases where English is not the native language of any of the partners. This speaks to the Anglicization trend, or what some call linguistic imperialism. The second issue relates to the required proficiency level of students and professors in the second language of instruction or research and the training needed to help them attain sufficient proficiency. The positive side of the language issue is that students are required to be bilingual or multilingual, which helps their communication skills, employability, and understanding of another culture. The collaborative agreement must be crystal clear about each partner's responsibility in establishing language requirements and providing upgrading courses.

Certification

The granting of the legal certification for the award and the subsequent recognition of the qualifications awarded are by far the most vexing issues. As already discussed, only a few countries legally allow its universities to confer a joint qualification in partnership with an institution in another country (i.e., the official seals of all participating institutions on the same certificate). In cases where this is not possible, students often receive a formal diploma from one university and a second certificate from the partner(s), indicating that it was a collaborative degree program (Schüle, 2006). For some students, this is not a problem because the international and intercultural experience gained through the program is far more important than the resulting qualifications. However, for other students, the lack of a joint qualification remains highly problematic, given the importance placed on credentialism.

Recognition and Legitimacy of Qualifications

Employers, academic institutions, and credential evaluation agencies all need to be cognizant of what is entailed in granting and recognizing double or multiple and consecutive qualifications. A common perception is that some collaborative programs are more legitimate than others; however, this is perception and difficult to prove. The recognition process raises the legitimacy or misrepresentation issues often associated with double or multiple degree qualifications—more so than with joint or consecutive qualifications. Part of the concern rests with the double counting of course credits and workload for two or more qualifications. This has led to the "two for the cost of one" label for double degrees. Cost in this case is not measured in monetary terms alone as student workload is also involved.

Completion Requirements

The diversity of models used to determine the completion requirements for double or multiple degree programs is extremely varied. There is no one explanation or correct framework used to set program completion requirements. This raises the critical question: Is the framework based on (a) the number of completed courses/credits, (b) the student workload, or (c) required learning outcomes/competencies? These three approaches lead to different explanations and arguments in the analysis of the legitimacy of the double or multiple degrees awarded. The value of a qualification or credential is at the root of the murkiness surrounding the acceptability of double or multiple degrees emanating from a collaborative program. Many would argue that counting the same courses or workload toward two or more degrees from two or more institutions in different countries devalues the validity of a qualification (Schüle, 2006). Others believe that if students meet the stated learning outcomes and competencies required to obtain a qualification, regardless of where or how these were acquired, the credential is legitimate. This latter logic suggests that double and multiple degrees are academically sound and legitimate when based on a set of core courses or competencies and augmented by any additional requirements of the collaborating institutions—in other words, the process for recognizing these qualifications requires more attention than the completion requirements per se. Both arguments are valid, but the variety of models used prevents a clear resolution to the question of legitimacy.

Questions for Further Reflection

Interesting new questions are being raised as the volume, scope, and types of JDCD programs increase. Several of these questions are included in this section to stimulate further reflection, research, and debate about enhancing the benefits of these types of programs and minimizing risks and unintended consequences.

Is national, binational, or international accreditation the best route for recognizing international JDCD programs?

How can international JDCD programs mitigate the overuse of English and the standardization of curricula?

What sources of additional funding can sustain international JDCD programs beyond the point of program creation?

Can one thesis/dissertation fulfil the requirements of two graduate programs that are research-based?

How can national/regional qualification frameworks best recognize international JDCD programs?

What role might prior learning assessment recognition play in double or consecutive degree programs?

Could the status-building and credentialism motives eventually jeopardize the quality and academic objectives of international JDCD programs?

How can international JDCD programs broaden access by students from multiple countries rather than serve only students from a single institution or country?

The challenge facing the higher education sector is to develop a common understanding of the meanings and requirements of international JDCD programs and to address many of the academic alignment issues inherent to working in different national regulatory frameworks, cultures, and practices. Most important, a rigorous debate on the vexing questions of accreditation, recognition, and legitimacy of the qualifications needs to take place to ensure that international collaborative programs and their awards are respected and recognized by students, higher education institutions, and employers around the world.

Author's Note: Material from the following two documents has been updated and used in this chapter: Knight, J. (2008b). *Joint and double degree programmes: Vexing questions and issues.* London: The Observatory on Borderless Higher Education; Lee, J. (2009). *International joint and double degree programs: A comparative analysis of rationales and challenges.* Unpublished. University of Toronto. Text boxes in this chapter were prepared by its authors.

References

Aerden, A., & Reczulska, H. (2010). *The recognition of qualifications awarded by joint programmes: An analysis of current practices by national recognition centres.* European Consortium for Accreditation in Higher Education. Retrieved November 18, 2011, from http://www .ecaconsortium.net/admin/files/assets/ subsites/1/documenten/1270211409_eca---the -recognition-of-qualifications-awarded-by -joint-programmes---2010.pdf

Becker, R. (2009). *International branch campuses: Markets and strategies.* London: The Observatory on Borderless Higher Education.

Council of Graduate Schools (CGS). (2007). *2007 CGS international graduate admissions survey: Phase II final applications and initial offers of admission.* Retrieved November 18, 2011, from http://www.cgsnet.org/portals/0/pdf/ R_IntlAdm07_II.pdf

Council of Graduate Schools (CGS). (2008). *2008 CGS international graduate admissions survey: Phase II final applications and initial offers of admission.* Retrieved November 18, 2011, from http://www.cgsnet.org/portals/0/pdf/R_ IntlAdm08_II.pdf

Crosier, D., Purser, L., & Smidt, H. (2007). *Trends V: Universities shaping the European higher education area.* Brussels: European University Association.

Davies, H. (2009). *Survey of master degrees in Europe.* Brussels: European University Association. Retrieved on November 18, 2011, from http://www.eua.be/publications/

EU-Asia Higher Education Platform (EAHEP). (2009, February 16–17). Student mobility, joint degree programmes, and institutional development. *The Second EAHEP Workshop Outcome Report,* Kuala Lumpur, Malaysia. Retrieved on November 18, 2011, from http://www.eahep.org/web/images/Malaysia/annex%202%20second%20eahep%20workshop%20final%20outcome%20report_final.pdf

EC/UNESCO. (2004*). Recommendation on the recognition of joint degrees, adopted by the Committee of the Convention on the Recognition of Qualifications concerning Higher Education in the European Region.* Brussels: Author.

Erasmus Mundus. (2009). *Action 2: Partnerships with third country higher education institutions and scholarships for mobility.* Retrieved November 18, 2011, from http://eacea.ec.europa.eu/erasmus_mundus/programme/action2_en.php

European University Association (EUA). (2004). *Developing joint masters programmes for Europe: Results of the EUA Joint Masters Project.* Brussels: European University Association. Retrieved on November 18, 2011, from http://www.eua.be/publications/

Gacel-Avila, J. (2009). *Joint and double degree programmes in Latin America: Patterns and trends.* London: The Observatory on Borderless Higher Education.

Kong, L. (2008). Engaging globally through joint and double degree programmes: A view from Singapore. *Global Higher Education.* Retrieved November 18, 2011, from http://globalhighered.wordpress.com/2008/02/15/engaging-globally-through-joint-and-double-degree-programmes-a-view-from-singapore/

Knight, J. (2005). *Borderless, offshore, transnational and cross-border education: Definition and data dilemmas.* London: The Observatory on Borderless Higher Education.

Knight, J. (2008a). *Higher education in turmoil: The changing world of internationalization.* Rotterdam, the Netherlands: Sense Publishers.

Knight, J. (2008b). *Joint and double degree programmes: Vexing questions and issues.* London: The Observatory on Borderless Higher Education.

Kuder, M. & Obst, D. (2009). *Joint and double degree programs in the transatlantic context.* Institute of International Education & Freie Universitaet, Berlin. Retrieved November 18, 2011, from http://www.iienetwork.org/file_depot/0

-10000000/0-10000/1710/folder/80205/TDP+Report_2009_Final21.pdf

Lee, J. (2009). *International joint and double degree programs: A comparative analysis of rationales and challenges.* Toronto: University of Toronto.

Maierhofer, R., & Kriebernegg, U. (2009). Joint and dual degree programs: New ventures in academic mobility. In R. Bhandari & S. Laughlin (Eds.), *Higher education on the move: New developments in global mobility* (pp. 65–77). New York: The Institute of International Education.

Maiworm, F. (2006). *Results of the survey on study programmes awarding double, multiple or joint degrees.* Kassel, Germany: German Academic Exchange Service (DAAD) and the German Rector's Conference (HRK). Retrieved November 18, 2011, from http://www.eu.daad.de/imperia/md/content/eu/sokrates/veranstaltungen/jd_report2.pdf

Ministry of Education, Finland. (2004). *Development of international joint degrees and double degrees: Recommendation of the Ministry of Education.* Helsinki, Finland. Retrieved November 18, 2011, from http://www.minedu.fi/export/sites/default/OPM/Koulutus/koulutusjaerjestelmae/tutkintojen_tunnustaminen/opetusministerioen_suositus_kansainvaelisten_yhteistutkintojen_ja_kaksoistutkintojen_kehittaemisestae/liitteet/JointDegrees_recommendations.pdf

Nickel, S., Zdebel, T., & Westerheijden, D. (2009). *Joint degrees in European higher education: Obstacles and opportunities for transnational programme partnerships based on the example of the German-Dutch EUREGIO.* The Centre for Higher Education Development (Germany) and the Center for Higher Education Policy Studies (Holland).

Redd, K. (2008, October). Data sources: International graduate programs: 2007 & 2008. *CGS Communicator.* Retrieved November 18, 2011, from http://www.cgsnet.org/portals/0/pdf/DataSources_2008_10.pdf

Sackmann, R. (2007). Internationalization of markets for education: New actors within nationals and increasing flows between nations. In K. Martens, A. Rusconi, & K. Leuze (Eds.), *New arenas of education governance* (pp. 155–175). New York: Palgrave MacMillan.

Schneller, C., Lungu, I., & Wächter, B. (2009). *Handbook of international associations in higher education: A practical guide to 100 academic networks world-wide.* Brussels: Academic Cooperation Association.

Schüle, U. (2006). *Joint and double degrees within the European Higher Education Area: Towards further internationalization of business degrees.* Paris: Consortium of International Double Degrees. www.CIDD.org

Sursock, A., & Smidt, H. (2010). *Trends 2010: A decade of change in European higher education.* Brussels: European University Association. Retrieved on November 18, 2011, from http://www.eua.be/publications/

Tauch, C., & Rauhvargers, A. (2002). *Survey on master degrees and joint degrees in Europe.* Brussels: European University Association. Retrieved November 18, 2011, from http://www.eua.be/eua/jsp/en/upload/Survey_Master_Joint_degrees_en.1068806054837.pdf

Vincent-Lancrin, S. (2004). *Internationalisation and trade in higher education.* Paris: OECD.

20

TRANSNATIONAL RESEARCH AND DEVELOPMENT PARTNERSHIPS IN HIGHER EDUCATION

Global Perspectives

PETER H. KOEHN AND MILTON ODHIAMBO OBAMBA

When we talk about international work, we often talk about building bridges . . . in academic environments. . . . The most effective international linkages, regardless of their size, scope, goals, and context begin with people who put the common good before their own and cut across barriers to pull together whatever it takes to form that bridge.

Takoi K. H. Tartir (2007)

In our knowledge-driven and skill-led world, the leaders of Southern and Northern tertiary education institutions[1] and donor agencies increasingly recognize common interests in promoting *transnational* partnerships.[2] This chapter focuses on partnerships that involve *research and sustainable-development* objectives.[3] Establishing and enhancing sustainable research and development partnerships that connect a country's universities with transnational networks of scholars and practitioners constitutes "the intellectual project that will define the contribution of higher education in the 21st century" (Moja, 2008, p. 166).

The transformative role of transnational research and sustainable development activity in international higher education tends to be overlooked or underestimated. This chapter explores specific ways in which transnational research and development partnerships deepen three core missions of the contemporary university: preparation of competent professionals, public engagement, and campus internationalization. Illustrations are drawn from approaches specific to Asia, Finland-Tanzania, and Nigeria in boxes. The chapter also addresses problems and potential embedded within South-South and diasporic collaborations. The concluding discussion advances a preferred pathway to mutually rewarding and sustainably partnered futures for higher education through collaboration in cross-border research, development projects, and professional-curriculum enhancement.

THE PARTNERSHIP MODEL

The *partnership model* emerged during the 1990s as the dominant framework for transacting international development assistance (Organization for Economic Cooperation and Development [OECD], 1996). Through transnational development partnerships, donors seek to address societal priorities in tandem with developing-country institutions (OECD, 1996, p. 13). In recent years, major intergovernmental agencies, particularly the World Bank, have promoted the partnership approach (Obamba, forthcoming). Both the Paris Declaration on Aid Effectiveness (2005) and the Accra Agenda (2008) clearly emphasize partnership designs within the changing landscape of international development cooperation.

Under the partnership paradigm, international development is no longer conceptualized in terms of the unidirectional exchange of financial and technical assistance from the North to the South (King, 2008; Koehn, 2011). Samoff and Carrol (2004, p. 115) describe partnership as an organizational arrangement "that goes beyond technical assistance and external support" and should be based on equality and mutual benefit among partners. Partnerships of varying stripes are driven by the appeal of complementarity and synergy for the mutual benefit of all participating parties (Beerkens, 2004, p. 63).

Partnerships encompass a broad spectrum of activities and stakeholders, including higher education institutions. With specific reference to higher education, Kinser and Green (2009) define partnerships as "cooperative agreements between a higher education institution and another distinct organization to coordinate activities, share resources, and divide responsibilities related to a specific project or goal" (p. 4). Many university partnerships initially emerge from and are built around personal networks.

This chapter focuses on transnational academic partnerships of the bilateral and consortial variety. Although higher education partnerships vary in size, purpose, scope, coherence, intensity, location, and duration, those that are reciprocally fruitful and experience extensive and continuous interpersonal interactions are likely to be the most effective when addressing arising interdependence challenges. Thrift (2010) states that university portfolios of 10 to 30 partners provide "a platform upon which to build limited but vital forms of cooperation." Beyond a manageable number, research and development partnerships resemble "trophy internationalization" in that they offer "a sense of international involvement and inclusion without doing much except making dents in the travel budgets of presidents and provosts" (p. A72).

TRANSNATIONAL HIGHER EDUCATION PARTNERSHIPS

In the new millennium, transnational higher education partnerships have gained increasing traction as effective instruments both for building institutional capacity and for strengthening the contributions of higher education to economic competitiveness and development cooperation (African Union, 2008; Department of Innovation Universities and Skills [DIUS], 2008a; European University Association [EUA], 2010; Million+, 2009). The core interface between higher education and international development cooperation is clearly articulated in the 2010 *Africa-Europe Partnership Strategy White Paper* (EUA, 2010). The White Paper emphasizes "the evolving and increasingly important overlap between the internationalization agenda of universities and their role as actors [stakeholders] in development cooperation" (p. 6).

Among today's universities, external networks, alliances, and partnerships are deliberate mechanisms for campus internationalization. Partnerships can be placed at one end of a collaboration continuum with networks at the other end and alliances in between (Buse & Walt, 2002, p. 44). At the partnership end, one finds formal agreements, few parties, and collaborative projects. Alliances include temporary and long-term self-aware collaborations in pursuit or advocacy of shared objectives. Networks consist of looser and shifting interactions among numerous participants who engage irregularly without screening. While some networks are purposive, the occupants of others "may be entirely unaware of one another—for example, people who . . . visit the same website" (Tarrow, 2005, pp. 163–164). All networks are useful, however, in identifying the potential for alliance, coalition, and partnership formation (see de Wit, 2010, p. 6). In an information-driven age, it is not surprising that universities seek to position themselves at the hub of transnationally interconnected networks.

Strategic Planning

In recent decades, the dynamics of transnational academic cooperation have taken on increasing importance and complexity. For today's universities, external networks, alliances, and partnerships are pivotal mechanisms for the advancement of research, public engagement, curricular offerings, and institutional reputations as well as for the mobilization of financial and technical resources across national and organizational boundaries. The growing importance for strategic planning of transnational higher education partnerships can be attributed to a combination of factors, including rapid internationalization of learning content and pedagogy, the emergence of the global knowledge economy (Salmi, 2003), and the imperative that "local needs require local prospects in global frameworks, and global challenges need global solutions that are locally acceptable" (Escrigas & Lobera, 2009, pp. 12–13; Taylor, 2008a, p. xxiv). The quest for collaborative knowledge production also has been accelerated by recognition that no amount of research in any one country, nor any single academic discipline, can fully comprehend, let alone resolve, the interconnected problems that face humanity today—from poverty and HIV/AIDS to global warming and international terrorism (see Koehn & Rosenau, 2010). Although education is not a panacea (see McGrath, 2010, especially pp. 248–251), transnational academic partnerships and competence-building across boundaries are critical ingredients for achieving sustainable development.

Global Landscape of Higher Education Partnerships for Development

Higher education partnerships have become ubiquitous as multilateral development agencies and the governments of industrialized nations invest financial and technical resources in promoting transnational research and development linkages (Maassen, Pinheiro, & Cloete, 2007; Samoff & Carrol, 2004). Transnational higher education partnerships aimed at promoting sustainable development and capacity-building have been supported by the African Union and the European Union (African Union, 2008; Angula, 2009, pp. 21–22), by the UK Department for International Development (DfID), by the U.S. Agency for International Development (USAID), and by the Canadian International Development Agency (CIDA), among others (Maassen et al., 2007). In Britain, for instance, support for international academic and development partnerships has penetrated deep into the government's policy agenda. The prime minister's second initiative (PMI-2) constitutes an unprecedented strategic shift by the United Kingdom's government toward strengthening the country's global competitiveness in education and development through a well-structured mobilization of international academic partnerships. Launched in 2006, PMI-2 is aimed at "supporting UK institutions in the development of lasting and mutually beneficial international partnerships" (British Council, 2010, p. 4). An evaluation report prepared by DTZ Holdings plc, a technical consulting company, shows that the PMI-2 has supported nearly 500 partnerships in higher education and further education, which cover joint research, collaborative development and delivery of teaching programs, student exchanges, and policy dialogue among British universities and their foreign counterparts (DTZ, 2011, p. 4). Other recent British initiatives include DfID and British Council support for 122 partnership projects in Africa and Asia under the Development Partnerships in Higher Education programme, which focuses specifically on building the capacities of developing countries to achieve the millennium development goals through collaborative projects between United Kingdom and African institutions (British Council, 2008, pp. 3–6).

The United Kingdom has rolled out major transnational partnership initiatives since 2008: the UKIERI (UK-India Education and Research Initiative) facilitated 182 partnerships involving 600 UK and Indian institutions (http://www .ukieri.org/docs/UKIERI_Brochure.pdf); the UK-Russia BRIDGE Program supported 58 partnerships (SQW Consulting, 2010, pp. i–ii);

the INSPIRE (International Strategic Partnerships in Research and Education) program made it possible for 55 partnerships involving 100 institutions to flourish among UK universities and their counterparts in south and central Asia; 72 partnerships between British and African institutions were supported through the Education Partnerships in Africa program (http://www.britishcouncil.org/learning-epa). This evolving supportive policy landscape for transnational partnerships has captured the imagination of UK universities and precipitated an unprecedented increase in the number and complexity of international collaborative activities (DIUS, 2008a, 2008b). Leeds Metropolitan University, for example, is one of the first UK universities to develop an integrated *internationalization strategy* (Leeds Metropolitan University, 2008). LMU delivers a wide range of collaborative teaching and capacity-building programs in several African countries, including Ethiopia, Gambia, Namibia, South Africa, Uganda, Tanzania, Malawi, and Zambia. Million+, a leading think tank in UK higher education, concluded in 2009 that "many UK universities have identified . . . the task of increasing the number of overseas partnerships or further developing (by deepening and broadening) their existing institutional partnerships" (Million+, 2009, p. 5) and later found that "the international activities of UK universities have important social benefits that are closely linked with other specialist government policy agendas related to foreign policy, national security, and international development" (Million+, 2011, p. 3).

The European Commission also has recognized the importance of higher education partnerships in low-income countries (Smith, 2007). With financing from the European Seventh Framework Programme, the commission has supported 19 flagship research and capacity-building partnerships in Africa that focus on science and information/communication technology (Community Research & Development Information Service, 2008). In 2007, the European Council and the African Union signed the Joint Africa-Europe Strategic Partnership to provide a framework for biregional cooperation in multiple areas of development and capacity-building in Africa, including tertiary education (European Council, 2007). In 2006, the 15-member countries of the European Union (EU) and their 79 counterparts in the Africa Caribbean Pacific

region (ACP) launched the EDULINK Cooperation Program with funding from the EU's Ninth European Development Fund (ACP, 2006). The paramount aim of EDULINK is to strengthen linkages between higher education and the millennium development goals in low-income countries of the ACP region by promoting collaborative research, strengthening governance and quality assurance, and fostering academic networking and mobility (ACP, 2009). In a demonstration of interest in deepening partnership, the African Association of Universities and the European University Association (EUA) launched a White Paper on Africa-Europe Higher Education Cooperation for Development in September 2010. The White Paper focuses on "the need to strengthen higher education cooperation between Africa and Europe, both as a response to global challenges and to contribute to African development" (EUA, 2010, p. 8). It explicitly encourages universities in both regions to "integrate development cooperation into the overall institutional internationalization strategy" (EUA, 2010, p. 21).

Canada also is a leading player in the evolving field of academic and development collaboration with developing regions, including Africa (AUCC, 2009). A large part of Canada's official investment in support of international cooperation and development research is channeled through the International Development Research Centre and the Association of Universities and Colleges of Canada (AUCC). In 2009, for instance, the AUCC and the Association of African Universities (AAU) signed a joint partnership agreement to launch the Strengthening Higher Education Stakeholder Relations program. This 3-year partnership program involves 27 African universities and focuses on strengthening university-industry linkages in Africa and enhancing the effectiveness of the AAU's relations with its stakeholders (http://www.aau.org/?q=shesra/background; accessed 22 Nov 2011).

Furthermore, the landscape of partnership between Africa and the United States has been expanded in recent decades through a wide range of collaborative initiatives aimed at building human and institutional capacity through collaborative research that addresses development problems (Gore & Odell, 2009, p. 55; Koehn, Demment, & Hervy, 2008). The breadth and scope of U.S. university involvement in transnational research and development activity is apparent from the 1,000 project profiles at 77 member institutions posted at the Association of Public and Land Grant Universities (APLU) website (http:\\www.nasulgc.org/NetCommunity/ Page.apx?pid=776&srcid=776; accessed 9 November 2011). Nevertheless, donors have not pursued many promising opportunities to support higher education partnership initiatives in the global South. USAID, in particular, "has grown to be a less consistent partner of universities seeking sustained beneficial ties with developing countries" (Smuckler, 2003, p. 169), and the support that has been forthcoming in USAID grants awarded directly to universities tends to be short-term in duration and limited in funding (Koehn, 2012).

China is rapidly emerging as a prominent player in transnational education and development partnerships with Africa (Brautigam, 2009). The Fourth Ministerial Conference of the Forum on China-Africa Cooperation heralded China's emerging role as a donor in transnational higher education partnerships. At the 2009 conference, China and 49 African countries "agreed on a three-year action plan for establishing strategic partnerships in . . . higher education to promote knowledge-based sustainable development" (Sawahel, 2009). In addition, collaboration between Africa and India also has expanded after the signing of the Delhi Declaration (2008) and, thereafter, the Africa-India Framework for Enhanced Cooperation at the Addis Ababa Summit in May 2011. Both joint instruments focus on promoting a more structured and intensive cooperation between Africa and India in a broad array of strategic areas that are critical for capacity-building and sustainable development.

Among other North-North collaborations, British and U.S. universities are developing large-scale multidisciplinary research partnerships designed to tackle major global challenges (Labi, 2009a, p. A23). For instance, Lancaster University and the University of Kansas have partnered to "develop a test bed for the Internet of the future" and the Stanford-Scotland Photonics Innovation Collaboration involves six universities linked with businesses "on leading research in the photonics sector—fields including life sciences and renewable energy—and the commercial opportunities such research offers" (Wellings, 2010, p. A29). In March 2010, the British Council called for closer and more

numerous UK-U.S. higher education partnerships and for leveraging historic and institutional connections to build tripartite collaborations and undertake joint projects in the global South (Fischer, 2010, p. A29).

Declining and Contested Resources

The critical importance of transnational knowledge-based partnerships for revitalizing the capacity of global South universities to respond to the growing challenges of sustainable development is widely recognized (EUA, 2010; UNESCO, 2009). Concomitantly, the contemporary backdrop for our discussion of transnational partnerships is one of declining resources for higher education initiatives in the face of escalating demand for cross-border cooperation in research and transnational competence-building.

While the partnership discourse evokes images of neutrality and mutual benefit and has become ubiquitous, its boundaries and participants are fluid phenomena embedded within varying and contested configurations of power and resource-flow asymmetries (Obamba & Mwema, 2009, p. 356). For instance, Gutierrez (2008) asserts that "the main problem with the partnership and participation ideology is that it implies that it is possible to mitigate power asymmetries without *first* reducing *capital endowment asymmetries*" (p. 20, emphasis in original). Important questions also have emerged around whether North-South partnerships build and strengthen, or erode and undermine, the imaginative capacity of Southern universities to produce and utilize knowledge systems that are appropriately contextualized to national development challenges and priorities (King, 2008).

Undertaking transnational partnership activity of any form involves elaborate organizational engineering and substantial financial costs, which are not evenly distributed among and within different countries and individual higher education institutions. While stakeholders increasingly appreciate the core transformative power of universities in the global South, many higher education institutions in low-income countries confront acute financial and connectivity deficits (Bloom, 2003, pp. 140–145). Tertiary institutions are in a particularly precarious position in sub-Saharan Africa (Damtew Teferra, 2003, pp. 129–130). In the words of Mamphela Ramphele (2003), there is "a cruel irony in the inverse relationship between the size of the development challenges that nations face and the capacity of their university systems to rise to meet them" (p. 1).

Public investment in transnational research cooperation has been "the driver of change in China and Singapore and the mainstay of European research strength" (Marginson, 2007, pp. 70–71). A vast and complex initiative in this regard is the European Research Area, an EU-supported Europe-wide research consortium to promote development, research, education, and innovation. The European Research Area aims to enable researchers, research institutions, and businesses to circulate, compete, and cooperate across borders in order to exploit "transnational synergies and complementarities" (European Commission, 2008, pp. 8, 21). Nationally, with support from TEKES, the publicly resourced Finnish Funding Agency for Technology and Innovation, higher education institutions in Finland have successfully supported knowledge-based regional development and participation in the global economy (Valimaa & Hoffman, 2007, pp. 188, 190; Yusuf, Saint, & Nabeshima, 2009, p. xxvi). Flagship consortiums in the Asian-Pacific region include University Mobility in Asia Pacific and the Association of Universities of Asia and the Pacific; both aim at promoting cooperation, academic mobility, and capacity-building among universities and governments in the region (Beerkens, 2004, pp. 38–39).

Nevertheless, universities in the global North face competing institutional agendas and financial constraints that limit their involvement in cross-border research and development initiatives (Childress, 2010, pp. 30–31; Kinser & Green, 2009, p. 11; Labi, 2009b, p. A23). Today, many Northern universities find themselves challenged when seeking to engage in transnational research and development activity, particularly in the wake of the global economic recession, which has been accompanied by severe declines in public funding for universities.

THREE INTERCONNECTED MISSIONS

Universities are distinguished by three interconnected and accelerating missions: the development of human capabilities, the conduct of

basic and applied research, and commitment to public service. This triple expectation and commitment leads many 21st-century universities to participate in development cooperation and transnational competence-building. Participation by higher education institutions in transnational connectivity and capacity-building is essential for the creation of sustainable knowledge-driven economies at a time when "new sites of knowledge production are continually emerging that, in their turn, provide intellectual points of departure for further combinations or configurations of researchers" (Gibbons, 2003, p. 112).

The various forms of transnational linkages and partnerships mobilized by universities in pursuit of these three dynamic missions are organized and administered in a variety of ways and with varying degrees of intensity and consistency. In pursuing each mission, the approach to the organization and production of knowledge has followed the dynamic path of problem-based, socially contextualized, multidisciplinary, and nonhierarchical knowledge regimes, commonly described as Mode 2 knowledge rather than the rigid Mode 1 knowledge-production regime characterized by the traditional hierarchical, monodisciplinary design (Gibbons, 2003, p. 111). Strategic cross-border partnerships are primarily supported by central international offices on some campuses (Sutton, 2007). Specialized schools or colleges, especially at major universities, maintain partnerships through their own international offices. In many other cases, individual faculty members directly arrange and manage transnational research and development collaborations. The organizational scale and complexity of inter-university research and development programs range from a team of faculty members working independently without formal involvement of central university management, at one extreme, to consortia of universities operating under multisector agreements managed at the highest institution-wide levels, at the other extreme.

Preparing Transnationally Competent Professionals

From global climatic change to applications of nano-scale technologies, renewed urgency and intensity energizes the emergence of transboundary learning objectives across the planet.

From vast and rising disparities in health care, poverty, and employment to vulnerable and threatened natural resources, daunting borderless challenges await graduating professionals. As Dunn (2002) suggests, "we need a curriculum for our border-crossing, migration-prone, multiple-identity-taking planet, not one that relies on old-fashioned, essentialist, historically lifeless categories that only deter students from tackling the marvelous complexities of current affairs and the human past" (p. 13). Increasing spatial connectedness and accelerated mobility has intensified realization that the contemporary problems facing humankind are complex and boundary-spanning; their analysis and resolutions can best be achieved through an integrated human-capabilities-building, problem-focused approach characterized by multidisciplinary perspectives and transnational collaboration. Sustainability and consciousness-shifting will be common components of forward-looking domestic and transnational curricula (see Taylor, 2008b, pp. 95–96).

A new-millennium study, based on a survey of high-level officials, concluded that

> the traditional ways that universities conceived of "internationalizing" their curriculums—by developing academic area studies and language training—may no longer be the best ways of producing broad-gauged professionals. Instead, universities need to devise ways to give students a grounding in *thinking and acting across cultures.* (Bikson, Treverton, Moini, & Gustav, 2003, p. xxi; emphasis added)

The future of professional education in most fields is tied to institutional and faculty capacity to graduate practitioners, including an increasing proportion of women, who will serve in multiple sectors and mitigate complex boundary-spanning problems. New-millennium graduates need to be prepared for effective participation on and leadership of multinational and transdisciplinary teams, for creativity in the face of cascading change and uncertainty (Kellogg & Hervy, 2009, p. 3; Koehn, 2011; Williams, 2002, p. 106), for employers' demands for transnational acumen, for lifelong learning, and for humanity's need for equitable and sustainable actions and directions (Teichler, 1999, pp. 22–23).

Today, there is general agreement in scholarly and professional circles that competence across

boundaries[4] is necessary if graduates are to succeed in addressing the world's expanding list of urgent and interdependent social and technical challenges (Deardorff, 2009; National Association of State Universities and Land Grant Colleges, 2007, p. 6). Boundary-spanning competence can be created and developed through the educational process (Lambert, 1994, p. 11). The skill-focused transnational-competence curriculum offers an emerging educational platform that promises to prepare men and women in the global North and South who pursue professional careers for navigating the multiscale (Vessuri, 2008, p. 128) issues arising in the twenty-first century.[5] The transnational competence educational framework calls for the reinforcing augmentation of analytic, emotional, creative, communicative, and functional skills (see Koehn & Rosenau, 2010; also Taylor, 2008b, p. 98). Moreover, "third-stage" educational initiatives offer experienced professionals opportunities to engage in encore-career programs designed to develop new skills that are useful in addressing emerging transnational challenges to human and social development (Brown, 2008, p. 153). In short, the forward-looking, capacity-building, higher education institution will initiate a full life-cycle transnational competence curriculum.

Public Engagement and International Development

Public engagement constitutes a second vital mission of the 21st-century university. Public engagement embraces outreach and extension; it bridges with critical community contexts and issues and "connotes a more interactive relationship where the faculty and students from [higher education] institutions learn from people with whom they interact in society as well as impart knowledge and advice" (Kellogg & Hervy, 2009, p. 8). In short, public engagement provides the practical vehicle through which higher education contributes to sustainable development and cross-boundary learning.

In the global South, community service and outreach increasingly are linked to national development goals, including poverty reduction and knowledge generation initiatives, as part of the core mission of universities (Samoff & Carrol, 2004, pp. 93, 143). In the words of forward-looking political leaders such as Namibia's

Prime Minister Nahas Angula (2009), "Higher Education in the 21st century should define its relevance in terms of the contribution it makes to national economic performance and to the enhancement of the quality of life of the people" (p. 23). Goolam Mohamedbhai (2008) adds that African higher education institutions must simultaneously participate in transnational efforts that address global challenges "facing humanity, such as sustainable development and climate change" (p. 201). The Delphi poll results reported in Lobera (2008, pp. 310–315, 326) confirm that a majority of responding experts worldwide agree that contemporary higher education institutions should play an active role in sustainable social and human development and poverty reduction. Transnational research collaboration and participation in international development and capacity-building projects also ranked among the top seven internationalization priorities among the 115 higher education institutions around the world (predominantly in Europe and Asia) reporting in the International Association of Universities' (IAU) 2009 survey (http://www.unesco.org/iau/internationalization/pdf/key_results_2009_pdf).

Sustainable-development project activity recognizes the socially distributed and contextual nature of contemporary knowledge production (Gibbons, 2003, p. 111); therefore, it typically occurs away from campuses and engages additional participants—host national/subnational governments, transnational nongovernmental organizations (NGOs), indigenous NGOs, community members and associations, and private enterprises or entrepreneurs (see Box 20.1). For instance, Harvard University's Hauser Center for Nonprofit Organizations "works with university and civil society partners in developing countries to build executive education programmes for civil society leaders, which enable them to carry out research on topics critical to local development" (Brown, 2008, p. 154). The United States International University in Nairobi offers another example of transboundary engagement in knowledge production and sustainable development. International University's Centre for Excellence in Enterprise Development collaborates with the business community, donor agencies, government departments, NGOs, and other stakeholders involved in enterprise development and poverty reduction programs (Isalanoh, 2009, pp. 22–23). Participants in the 2010 Going Global Conference in London stressed the value of partnership projects among universities, research institutes, and businesses that facilitate knowledge transfer and utilization for sustainable development and solving problems and that promote innovation and entrepreneurship in both global South and North.

BOX 20.1 Transformative Transnational Higher Education and Industry Partnership: Nigeria's Institute of Petroleum Studies

Olatunde J. B. Ojo

Professor Emeritus of Political and Administrative Studies,
University of Port Harcourt (Nigeria)

Of interest because of its visible impact and potential as a model of transnational linkage for African development is the innovative program of the Institute of Petroleum Studies, which began in 2003. Dissatisfied with the quality of graduates from Nigerian universities, Elf Petroleum (EPNL), now Total, initiated a partnership with the University of Port Harcourt and the Institute Francaise du Petrole in France to develop a sustainable manpower development program of global standards to meet oil industry needs for Nigeria and the entire oil Gulf of Guinea from Senegal to Angola. The one-calendar-year M.Sc. degree in petroleum engineering and project development is limited to 20 annual intakes, sponsored initially by Elf Petroleum and now increasingly by the Nigerian National Petroleum Corporation. To ensure that its M.Sc. graduates engage in best practices, are sensitive to environmental issues, and can perform the transformative role expected of them, the Institute of Petroleum Studies trains them to combine economics and project-management skills with engineering skills and also presents them for the International Well Control Forum Certification examination as well as the National Registry for Environmental Practitioners certification examination for associate environmental professionals.

Other unique features of the institute are:

Its industry-oriented courses run in six modules that include exposure to high-tech software used in the industry, giving graduates the ability to solve complex problems while keeping them up-to-date with the industry—thereby enhancing their technical foundation, marketability, and ability to fit easily into the industry.

Faculty members are drawn from the University of Port Harcourt and other local universities, from the Institute Francaise du Petrole, and from highly placed industry captains. More significant, candidates are found by tapping intellectual migrants from their host countries for capacity-building at home (the so-called brain-circulation phenomenon that tends to dampen the effect of brain drain). Tapping intellectual migrants permits innovative changes and improvements in the curriculum. An example is the introduction (first time in Nigeria) of a reservoir geo-statistics graduate course by a Nigerian scholar based at the University of Alaska.

Faculty members have considerable exposure to and expertise drawn from the various petroleum regions of the world. Thus, they are able to impart broad long-range and comprehensive training to empower students to cope with the peculiarities of petroleum regions beyond the Niger delta.

Accomplishments: The oil and gas industry has been effusive in its praises for the Institute's highly trained, operations-ready, and internationally exposed graduates, who need minimal retraining on the job, thus saving companies considerable cost. The industry also gains from the institute's field-research data and software. In its first year, in addition to faculty presentations, five research papers by students were accepted for presentation, following normal peer review, at the Society of Petroleum Engineers conference.

Most transnational higher education research and development partnerships are project-based.[6] For instance, University College Cork (Ireland) and Mekelle University (Ethiopia) collaborate to offer a joint MSc that prepares mid- to senior-level professionals in governmental and NGO positions with multidisciplinary skills that will enhance Ethiopia's capacity to promote rural development (Johanson & Saint, 2007, p. 62). A few higher education partnerships connect consortia of universities and pursue multiple projects. An example of the latter is Universitas 21, an association of 23 higher education institutions from 13 industrialized countries with four regional nodes engaged in multidisciplinary undertakings aimed at building innovative water-system strategies (see Ervine & Usherwood, 2010, pp. A9–A10). Other research consortia include the League of European Research Universities (LERU), the International Alliance of Research Universities (IARU) (Kim, 2009, p. 400), and the Southern and Eastern Africa Policy Research Network (Maassen et al., 2007; Obamba & Mwema, 2009, pp. 368–369).

In the interest of fostering sustainable development through human capability-building, some universities in South America, Africa, and Asia explicitly strive to educate and provide field experience for "graduates who serve as agents of socioeconomic change" (Juma & Yee-Cheong, 2005, p. 96). Ghana's University for Development Studies, for instance, ensures that all students study subjects that cultivate skill in addressing poverty by, among other measures, requiring that they spend one term per year for 3 years engaged in "practice-oriented, community-based, problem-solving, gender-sensitive, and interactive learning" (Zaglul & Sherrard, 2005, pp. 39–40). The Autonomous University of Mexico's master's in rural development combines formal coursework with grassroots student research and action learning in Chiapas. The Earth University in Costa Rica focuses on experiential sustainable farming in the context of tropical agriculture (Taylor, 2008b, pp. 96–97). After 1 year of study, masters and Ph.D. students at TERI University in India participate in semester-long projects that address problems of poverty and environmental degradation (Neelakantan, 2009, p. A20).

Academic Internationalization

Individual scholars and higher education institutions participate in transnational partnerships for a variety of overlapping reasons related to campus internationalization. Respondents to a survey of higher education institutions in 150 countries ($N = 745$) conducted by the IAU in June 2009 ranked improved student preparedness, internationalized curricula, the institution's international reputation, and research and knowledge-production opportunities as their top four priorities (IAU, 2009). Other internationalization objectives that commonly inspire higher education partnership initiatives include student overseas-study opportunities and positioning at the cutting edge of knowledge breakthroughs and innovative activity (McPherson, 2008, pp. 9–10).

To help expand the base of understanding, Table 20.1 presents a survey snapshot of U.S. senior international officer (SIO) perspectives on the relationship of international research and development activity to campus internationalization.[7] Four beneficial outcomes are mentioned by at least 70% of the 37 SIOs who indicated that transnational research and development activity had enhanced campus internationalization over the past year. Three fourths of the SIOs cited "enhanced faculty competence in transnational interactions" (also Knight, 2008, p. 3) and "increased interaction with international scholars." Two thirds or more of the respondents affirmed that participation in transnational research and development activity had opened up research opportunities for faculty members, enhanced their university's overseas reputation (also Biddle, 2002, p. 7), and enriched campus course offerings (also IAU, 2009; Knight, 2008, p. 3). About half of the SIOs agreed that their campus had experienced six additional benefits: opening up of overseas study opportunities (which often provides participating students with a bridge to employment); increased capacity to compete for external funding (also Biddle, 2002, p. 7); enhanced administrative competence in transnational interactions; enhanced recruitment of recruit international students; promotion of curriculum innovations; and expanded student overseas internship/research opportunities.

Ways Campus Internationalization Has Been Strengthened	Number	%
Enhanced faculty competence in transnational interactions	28	75.7
Increased interaction with international scholars	28	75.7
Opened up research opportunities for faculty	27	73.0
Enhanced this university's reputation overseas	26	70.3
Enriched course offerings	24	64.9
Opened up overseas study opportunities	21	56.8
Increased capacity to compete for external funding	20	54.1
Enhanced administrative competence in transnational interactions	20	54.1

Ways Campus Internationalization Has Been Strengthened	Number	%
Helped recruit international students	20	54.1
Promoted curriculum innovations	18	48.6
Opened up student overseas internship/research opportunities	18	48.6
Opened up overseas teaching opportunities for faculty	17	45.9
Enhanced relations with international alumni	13	35.1

Table 20.1   U.S. Senior International Officer Reports on Ways in Which Engagement in International Research and Development Activity Strengthened Campus Internationalization (*N* = 37)

Each of these outcomes supports the mission and strategic international objectives of contemporary higher education institutions. In light of the pivotal position SIOs occupy at the nexus of institutional transnational activity, their assessments of internationalization outcomes are richly informed and especially illuminating. We can be confident, therefore, that promoting involvement in transnational research and development projects holds considerable promise for enhancing additional, parallel internationalization objectives on campuses throughout the global South and the North.

OTHER KEY LINKAGE DEVELOPMENTS

From the perspective of universities in the global South, research and sustainable development also are promoted by linkages outside the boundaries of formal North-South partnerships. Among these additional facilitators, two developments stand out. These are the expansion of South-South partnerships and the rise of diasporic linkages.

South-South Partnerships

International development initiatives are advanced by South-South partnerships (see Jowi, 2009). The IAU found, for instance, that higher education institutions in Asia and Africa "regard their home region as their main geographic priority in efforts to internationalize" (Labi, 2009b, p. A23). While transnational and regional relationships have expanded in Africa, the establishment of *national* networks and partnerships typically remains underdeveloped (see Obamba, Mwena, & Riechi, 2011). National and regional partnering can provide important stepping stones to additional resources. The World Bank reports that regional and subregional networks often provide an avenue for "national tertiary systems and institutions to 'bridge' into the sphere of experiences, best practices, and innovation that exist at the international level, and to use scarce resources more efficiently" (Johanson & Saint, 2007, p. 11; Yusuf et al., 2009, p. 99). Yusuf and colleagues (2009, p. 103) cite the Malaria Research and Training Center in Mali as a "superb example" of cooperative regional research combined with strong transnational partnerships.

Since 2000, the seven major U.S.-based foundations participating in the Partnership for Higher Education in Africa have focused on developing regional research and training networks and Internet capacity in a select group of countries (Fischer & Lindlow, 2008, p. A22; also Balan, 2009, p. 247; Maassen et al., 2007, pp. 5, 72). In addition, the African Capacity Building Foundation has provided more than $70 million in grants to support higher education capacity development in leadership and economic policy management and has supported efforts by CODESRIA (the Council for Development of Economic and Social Research in Africa) "to strengthen research in social sciences, to retain talents and scholars in African universities, and to strengthen networking in social sciences" (Shabani, 2008, pp. 470–471). McGrath and

Badroodien (2006, p. 489) caution, however, that policies and approaches that emerge in one Southern country can lead to acute problems if applied without adaptation in different Southern contexts.

Diasporic Knowledge Networks

Brain drain threatens sustainable human capability-building for national and community development among higher education institutions in low-income countries. The pull of the global knowledge economy has made it difficult to prevent or control the transnational mobility of urgently needed skilled professionals (Damtew Teferra, 2003; Rizvi, 2007). In recent decades, however, policymakers and analysts have recognized that building "diasporic-knowledge networks" provides an effective strategy for tapping into the intellectual capital that resides within diasporic scientific communities and mainstreaming it to promote capacity-building and development in low-income countries (Meyer & Brown, 1999; UNESCO, 2007; World Bank, 2007). John Sarpong, founder of the flagship African diasporic Internet portal, Africast.com, emphasizes that diasporic networks offer "a major opportunity to transform the historical brain drain . . . into the new African 'brain trust'" (cited in UNESCO, 2007, p. 6). In addition, Zeleza (2007) shows that a compelling case based on mutual enlightenment can be made for joint research projects among "African academics based on the continent, the contemporary African academic migrants or diaspora, and academics from the historic African diaspora" (p. 104).

Brain chains and the temporary transfer of transnational talent are challenging conventional brain-drain assessments (Chaparro, Hernan, & Vladimir, 2006, pp. 190–191; Kim, 2009, p. 401). In recent years, intergovernmental agencies have stepped to the frontline of promoting stronger connectivity and exchange between Africa and its growing academic and economic diaspora. Key examples include the UN Development Program's TOKTEN Program (Transfer of Knowledge through Expatriate Nationals); the World Bank's Mobilizing the African Diaspora for Development (World Bank, 2007); UNESCO's Academics Across Borders (AAB) Initiative (UNESCO, 2005); and the collaborative UNESCO-Hewlett Packard *Reverse* the Brain Drain to Brain Gain in Africa project. Diasporic network-building also enables highly skilled academics and professionals based abroad to exchange knowledge and create synergies with counterparts in countries of origin without necessarily relocating physically (Rizvi, 2007). Transnational higher education partnerships present a powerful framework for inspiring and consolidating diasporic networks among knowledge practitioners who cross the North-South epistemic divide (see Box 20.2). Concomitantly, the incorporation of diaspora academics has been "immensely useful" in arranging off-campus participation in sustainable development projects (Mohamedbhai, 2008, p. 201).

BOX 20.2 Partnerships for Knowledge-Based Development in Asia

Phyllis Bo-yuen Ngai

Department of Communication Studies, University of Montana-Missoula (USA)

Transnational higher education engagements play a key role in enhancing development in both the Asian South and the Asian North. In low-income Asia, the scale of educational advancement required for knowledge-based development is "daunting in countries of massive populations" (Richmond, 2007, p. 11). In India, to cite one case, "the number of extra doctors and nurses required to service the growing population by 2012 have been estimated to be around 450,000 and 1.2 million respectively, which cannot be met by the current higher educational system" (Emery, 2008, p. 353). In contemporary high-income Asia, investment in transnational higher education engagements addresses a different development need; it is viewed as an essential vehicle for integration into the global knowledge-based community (Wu & Yu, 2006, p. 220). Looking ahead, university presidents recognize that "the global economic crisis has accelerated the need for Asian universities . . . to engage internationally" (Hvistendahl, 2009).

Development in Asia means moving "from being passengers on the bus of globalization to becoming co-drivers" (Loveland, 2007, p. 18). Specifically, to move Asia forward, development professionals will require critical thinking skills that enable them to identify and question planning and operating assumptions that often are based on a Western model. While scientific and technological knowledge is commonly perceived in Asia as crucial for eradicating poverty, disease, and illiteracy, importing it from the West poses challenges of adaptation and use. Asian higher education leaders stress that professionals need the creativity to design responses to local problems that are sensitive to local needs and use approaches that vary from imported ones (Richmond, 2007, p. 1).

In recent years, brain circulation has been profuse in and out of Asia. The multidirectional movement of knowledge energizes collaborative research that addresses development needs. High-income Asian countries, such as Singapore, provide transnational field experience by moving students from traditional classroom learning into positions with innovative start-ups, where they work alongside and share the same struggle and excitement as the real-life entrepreneur (Mahbubani, 2010, p. A72). Singapore also helps low-income Asian countries by supporting courses offered by nonprofit organizations, such as Asian International, for students from Bangladesh, Cambodia, India, Nepal, Pakistan, the Philippines, and Thailand (Richmond, 2007, p. 13). In some cases, brain currents flow both ways simultaneously; high-income non-Asian universities, NGOs, and Asian governments collaborate on development projects involving research that benefits both global North and South. For instance, the Institute for Global Health (University College London), NGOs, and city agencies collaborate on a development project that aims to improve the health and survival of mothers and newborn infants in vulnerable urban communities in Mumbai at the same time that British researchers gain in-depth understanding of an under-researched context that parallels marginalized communities in the North (Emery, 2008, p. 356).

The development gains of multidirectional knowledge-sharing through transnational collaborative research and human capacity-building are manifold and dynamic. According to the National University of Singapore's Kishore Mahbubani, "if you want to understand why Asia is rising today, a large part of it is due to the large number of Asian students . . . who have studied in North American universities. When they returned home, they have brought back with them skills . . . [and] the positive and optimistic ethos that you find in U.S. society'" (Loveland, 2007, p. 17). While the East still learns from the West, the current generation of Asian higher education leaders have expanded their vision beyond the unidirectional flow of knowledge to include new forms of transnational partnerships, including Asian North-Asian South collaboration, that address development needs. As these initiatives expand and flourish, the West will discover additional benefits, both financially and intellectually, from engaging the East on equal footing. The gravity-defying transnational brain circulation required to fuel future knowledge-based glocal development will be multidirectional.

TOWARD A FRUITFULLY PARTNERED FUTURE

In the contexts of contemporary higher education administration and societal impact, a university's "power is determined not by its internal resources but by the set of resources it can mobilize through its contacts" (Brinkerhoff, 2002, p. 4; see also Beerkens, 2004, p. 64). While they are increasing in number and diversifying in scope and importance, transnational higher education partnerships that address shared needs for sustainable development remain the exception rather than the rule (Bloom, 2003, p. 143), an institutional appendage rather than a core faculty and student activity.

What are the decisive criteria for successful transnational higher education partnerships? Available evidence suggests that fruitful research and development partnerships are grounded in recognition that sustainable development "must be locally owned" (OECD, 1996, p. 13) and incorporate strong domestic commitment (UN Conference on Trade and Development [UNCTAD], 2008, p. 95). In curriculum development partnerships, instructional and human capacity is built up gradually based on thorough needs-assessment exercises (Holm & Malete, 2010, p. 6) and mutual trust (see Box 20.3). The learning process is multidirectional and incorporates diverse knowledge systems (Tandon, 2008, pp. 147–148; Vessuri, 2007). The curriculum is context-sensitive and engaged with challenges of development (Singh, 2007, p. 67).

BOX 20.3 Computer Science Curriculum Partnership: University of Eastern Finland and Tumaini University, Tanzania

Erkki Sutinen

Professor of Computer Science, University of Eastern Finland (Finland)

In 2000, the University of Eastern Finland (then University of Joensuu) and Tumaini University's Iringa University College (IUCO), located in southern Tanzania, initiated a partnership that is extending its original modest objective of exploring ways to integrate information and communication technology (ICT) into education. The leadership of IUCO, particularly its provost, Nicholas Bangu, had a much wider vision: to make IUCO an institution that would train self-confident experts who make a difference to the country by creating tangible tools for national development.

The commitment of both universities to seeking innovative and creative research and curriculum solutions became clear early on. Award of a competitive grant (2003–2005) by the Academy of Finland for researching the contextualization of an ICT curriculum, along with reported project results, attracted other research groups to join the collaboration. Colleagues at the University of Southern Denmark analyzed the usability of I-BLOCKS robotics set in Tanzania, and a group of Tanzanian students created a new design for African I-BLOCKS based on field studies in a rural Ilembula hospital. Other African universities, including South Africa's North-West University, joined in, forging a productive African network. Teacher and student exchanges among the two original partners and several newcomers intensified subsequent grants received from Finland's Center of International Mobility and the EU's EduLink program. These multilateral projects have focused on the theme of ICT4D, or how to promote development by appropriate uses of ICT.

In 2007, the partnership launched an undergraduate program in contextualized ICT, the first of its kind in Africa, if not globally. The innovative program is not dependent on external funding, as Tumaini is a private university. Tumaini is training graduates who will—in person—integrate understanding of ICT highlighted in international curricula with competence to design authentic ICTs for Tanzanian settings in a creative and problem-based way. The first graduates of the contextualized ICT program began to contribute to Tanzania's development in 2011.

The partnership also has resulted in unexpected spin-offs. In 2006, Tumaini opened a Science Park, the first in East Africa. The partnership has refreshed computer science education in the global North, where it previously suffered from little interest among high school students. Tumaini also has become an attractive location for researchers from all over the world.

Looking back, the partnership's success can be attributed to organic growth, mutual ownership, and trust building. Rather than follow a predefined strategic path, the program has enjoyed an organic growth process that is open to new opportunities. Partnership flexibility inspired the interest of parties beyond the two initial collaborators and attracted unexpected and rewarding inputs. Because everyone involved has benefitted from and contributed in concrete terms, including human resources and money (based on expectations and resources), the program embodies mutual ownership. Finnish and EU-funded programs that have facilitated the in-person exchange of academics have created mutual trust—the *sine qua non* of any sustainable higher education partnership.

Furthermore, meaningful transnational higher education partnerships are grounded in the ethical principles set forth in Articles 15 and 17 of the 1998 World Declaration on Higher Education for the Twenty-First Century: Vision and Action (http://www.unesco.org/education/educprog/wche/declaration_eng.htm). They encompass mutually determined project objectives pursued "through a shared understanding of the most rational division of labor based on the respective comparative advantages of each partner" (Brinkerhoff, 2002, pp. 14–18). They also involve transparency and shared accountability for results (UNCTAD, 2008, p. 96). Higher education capacity-building objectives are linked to national and subnational development strategies (Fischer, 2009, p. A14), requisite policy actions (Yusuf et al., 2009, p. xxv), institutional sustainability plans and commitments (Barcelo & Ferrer, 2008, pp. 172–173), and appropriate evaluation metrics. All partners share in the benefits of partnership projects (Moja, 2003, p. 173; Sutton, 2007). Finally, in the genuine development-cooperation partnership, local actors "progressively take the lead while external partners back their efforts to assume greater responsibility for their own development" (OECD, 1996, p. 13).

This chapter provides evidence that the ability of higher education institutions to contribute to and benefit from "connected" research undertakings, sustainable-development project activity, and institutional and human capacity-building endeavors is enhanced by transnational partnering (also see Koehn & Demment, 2010, pp. 11–12). Engagement in cross-border research and development partnerships extends and deepens faculty and staff interaction with overseas innovators, opens up faculty and student

research opportunities, enhances the transnational competence of one's own faculty and students, and facilitates brain circulation. The presence of institutional commitments and additional external support enables international education leaders around the world to undertake active roles in advancing transnationally partnered research and development activity on their respective campuses.

REFERENCES

Africa Caribbean and Pacific Secretariat (ACP). (2006). *Brussels declaration on education for sustainable development in the African, Caribbean and Pacific States*. Brussels: Africa Caribbean and Pacific Secretariat.

Africa Caribbean and Pacific Secretariat (ACP). (2009). *EDULINK in action: Empowering the people of Africa, Caribbean, and the Pacific through higher education*. Brussels: Africa Caribbean and Pacific Secretariat.

African Union (AU). (2008). *The AU/NEPAD Africa Action Plan*. Addis Ababa: Author.

Angula, N. A. (2009). The new dynamics for higher education in Africa. *UNESCO in Africa* (Special Issue), 21–25.

Association of Universities and Colleges of Canada (AUCC). (2009). *Canadian university engagement in international development cooperation*. Ottawa: Author.

Balan, J. (2009). American foundations and higher education in developing countries: Shifting rationales and strategies for support. In R. M. Bassett & A. Maldonado (Eds.), *International organizations and higher education policy: thinking globally, acting locally?* (pp. 231–250). London: Routledge.

Barcelo, M., & Ferrer, D. (2008). Institutional learning: Participatory design of the 2015 UPC sustainability plan (Technical University of Catalonia, Spain). In *Higher education in the world 3: New challenges and emerging roles for human and social development* (pp. 171–174). London: Palgrave Macmillan.

Beerkens, H.J.J.G. (2004). *Global opportunities and institutional embeddedness*. Unpublished Ph.D. dissertation, University of Twente, the Netherlands.

Biddle, S. (2002). *Internationalization: Rhetoric or reality?* New York: American Council of Learned Societies.

Bikson, T. K., Treverton, G. F., Moini, J., & Gustav, L. (2003). *New challenges for international leadership: Lessons from organizations with global missions.* Santa Monica, CA: RAND.

Bloom, D. E. (2003). Mastering globalization: From ideas to action on higher education reform. In G. Breton & M. Lambert (Eds.), *Universities and globalization: Private linkages, public trust* (pp. 140–149). Paris: UNESCO.

Brautigam, D. (2009). *The dragon's gift: The real story of China in Africa.* New York: Oxford University Press.

Brinkerhoff, J. M. (2002). *Partnerships for international development: rhetoric or results?* Boulder, CO: Lynne Reinner.

British Council. (2008). *DELPHE Annual Report 2007–2008.* London: Author.

British Council. (2010). *Making it happen: The prime minister's second initiative for international education.* London: Department for Business Innovation and Skills.

Brown, L. D. (2008). Practice-research engagement for human and social development in a globalizing world. In GUNI (Global University Network for Innovation) (Eds.), *Higher education in the world 3: New challenges and emerging roles for human and social development* (pp. 152–156). London: Palgrave Macmillan.

Brundtland Commission. (1987). *Our common future.* London: Oxford University Press.

Buse, K., & Walt, G. (2002). Globalization and multilateral public-private health partnerships: Issues for health policy. In K. Lee, K. Buse, & S. Fustukian (Eds.), *Health policy in a globalizing world* (pp. 41–62). Cambridge, UK: Cambridge University Press.

Chaparro, F., Hernan, J., & Vladimir, Q. (2006). Promise and frustration of diaspora networks: Lessons from the network of Columbian researchers abroad. In Y. Kuznetsov (Ed.). *Diaspora networks and the international migration of skills: How countries can draw on their talent abroad* (pp. 187–198). Washington, DC: World Bank.

Childress, L. K. (2010). *The twenty-first century university: Developing faculty engagement in internationalization.* New York: Peter Lang.

Community Research & Development Information Service. (2008). *EU–Africa science partnership presents flagship projects.* Retrieved from http://www.eubusiness.com/rd/eu-au-science.20/

Damtew Teferra. (2003). Scientific communication and research in African universities: challenges and opportunities in the twenty-first century. In Damtew Teferra & P. G. Altbach (Eds.), *African higher education: An international reference handbook* (pp. 128–142). Bloomington: Indiana University.

Deardorff, D. K. (Ed.). (2009). *The SAGE handbook of intercultural competence.* Thousand Oaks, CA: Sage.

Department for Innovation Universities and Skills (DIUS). (2008a). *International research collaboration in UK higher education institutions* (DIUS Research Report 08-08). London: Author.

Department for Innovation Universities and Skills (DIUS). (2008b). *Transnational education and higher education institutions: Exploring patterns of higher education institutional activity* (DIUS Research Report 08-07). London: Author.

de Wit, K. (2010). The networked university. *Tertiary Education and Management, 16,* 1–14.

DTZ. (2011). *Prime Minister's initiative for international education phase two: Final evaluation report* (Report commissioned by the UK Department for Business Innovation and Skills). London: DTZ.

Dunn, R. E. (2002). Growing good citizens with a world-centered curriculum. *Educational Leadership, 60,* 10–13.

Emery, V. C. (2008). Forging academic links with Asia. *Asian Affairs, 39*(3), 352–361.

Ervine, A., & Usherwood, J. (2010). We must create new models of international interaction. *Chronicle of Higher Education, 19,* A9–A10.

Escrigas, C., & Lobera, J. (2009). Introduction: New dynamics for social responsibility. In C. Escrigas & J. Lobera (Eds.), *Higher education at a time of transformation: New dynamics for social responsibility* (pp. 1–16). London: Palgrave Macmillan.

European Commission. (2008). *Challenging Europe's research: Rationale for the European research area.* Brussels: Author.

European Council. (2007). *The Africa-Europe strategic partnership.* Lisbon: Council of European Union.

European University Association (EUA). (2010). *The Africa-Europe higher education cooperation for development white paper: Meeting regional and global challenges.* Brussels: EUA/AAU.

Fischer, K. (2009). Universities offer international resources to help economy at home. *Chronicle of Higher Education, 27,* A14.

Fischer, K. (2010). British Council calls on colleges in Britain and America to collaborate more. *Chronicle of Higher Education, 12,* A29.

Fischer, K., & Lindow, M. (2008, July 18). Africa attracts renewed attention from American universities. *Chronicle of Higher Education,* A21–23.

Gibbons, M. (2003). Globalization and the future of higher education. In G. Breton & M. Lambert (Eds.), *Universities and globalization: Private linkages, public trust* (pp. 107–116). Paris: UNESCO.

Gore, J. S.,& Odell, M. J., Jr. (2009). *Higher education partnerships in sub-Saharan Africa: An impact assessment of 12 higher education partnerships.* Washington, DC: USAID, Bureau for Economic Growth, Agriculture and Trade (EGAT).

Gutierrez, D. (2008). Beyond disappointment: Transforming ideology and practice in north-south research partnerships. *NORRAG News,* p. 41.

Holm, J. D., & Malete, L. (2010, March 24–26). The asymmetries of university partnerships between Africa and the developed world: Our experience in Botswana. Paper delivered at *2010 Going Global 4 Conference – The British Council's International Education Conference,* London.

Hvistendahl, M. (2009). Presidents of Asian universities call for more international partnerships. *The Chronicle of Higher Education,* 55(34).

International Association of Universities (IAU). (2009). *Initial results: 2009 IAU global survey on internationalization of higher education.* Paris: Author.

Isalanoh, G. (2009, March/April). USIU strives for excellence in entrepreneurship development. *CEO Africa* (Nairobi), pp. 22–24.

Johanson, R., & Saint, W. (2007). *Cultivating knowledge and skills to grow Africa's agriculture: A synthesis of an institutional, regional, and international review.* Washington, DC: World Bank.

Jowi, J. O. (2009). Internationalization of higher education in Africa: developments, emerging trends, issues and policy implications. *Higher Education Policy, 22,* 263–281.

Juma, C., &Yee-Cheong, L. (2005). *Innovation: Applying knowledge in development.* London: EarthScan.

Kapur, D., & Crowley, M. (2008, February). *Beyond the ABCs: Higher education and developing countries* (Working Paper No. 139). Washington, DC: Center for Global Development.

Kellogg, E. D., & Hervy, A.-C. (2009). Contributions of higher education investments to development and implications for African higher education. Paper Presented at the *Conference on Reshaping Human and*

Institutional Capacity Building through Higher-Education Partnerships, Accra.

Kim, T. (2009). Transnational academic mobility, internationalization, and interculturality in higher education. *Intercultural Education, 20,* 395–405.

King, K. (2008). The promise and peril of partnership. *NORRAG News, 41,* 5–6.

Kinser, K., & Green, M. (2009). *The power of partnerships: A transatlantic dialogue.* Washington, DC: American Council on Education.

Knight, J. (2008). Internationalization in Africa: In relation to other world regions. *IIE Networker,* pp. 1–6.

Koehn, P. H. (2011, September 1). *Institutionalized chaos, access, and governance: Turbulence and bifurcation in north-south higher education partnerships for research and development.* Paper presented at the 2011 Annual Meeting of the American Political Science Association, Seattle.

Koehn, P. H. (2012). Donors and higher education partners: A critical assessment of U.S. and Canadian support for transnational research and sustainable development. *Compare: A Journal of Comparative and International Education, 42*(3).

Koehn, P. H., Deardorff, D. K., & Bolognese, K. D. (2011). Enhancing international research and development project activity on university campuses: Insights from U.S. senior international officers. *Journal of Studies in International Education, 15*(4), 332–350.

Koehn, P. H., & Demment, M. (2010, November 16). *Higher education and sustainable development in Africa: Why partner transnationally?* Background Paper for the Ministerial Conference on Higher Education in Agriculture in Africa. Kampala, Uganda.

Koehn, P. K., Demment, M., & Hervy, A.-C. (2008). Enhancing higher education's engagement in international development: Africa-U.S. partnerships. *Journal of the World Universities Forum, 1,* 127–140.

Koehn, P. H., & Rosenau, J. N. (2010). *Transnational competence: Empowering professional curricula for horizon-rising challenges.* Boulder, CO: Paradigm Press.

Labi, A. (2009a, August 7). Educators propose trust to globalize British and American universities. *Chronicle of Higher Education,* p. A23.

Labi, A. (2009b, October 2). Global survey finds shifts in universities' international priorities. *Chronicle of Higher Education,* p. A23.

Lambert, R. D. (1994). Summary and prospectus. In R. D. Lambert (Ed.), *Educational exchange and global competence* (pp. 281–293). Portland, ME: Council on International Educational Exchange.

Leeds Metropolitan University. (2008). *Internationalization strategy 2008–2012: Worldwide horizons*. Leeds, UK: Leeds Metropolitan University.

Lobera, J. (2008). Delphi Poll: Higher education for human and social development. In Global University Network for Innovation (Ed.), *Higher education in the world 3: New challenges and emerging roles for human and social development* (pp. 307–327). London: Palgrave Macmillan.

Loveland, E. (2007, May/June). Re-envisioning Asia. *International Educator*, pp. 16–20.

Maassen, P., Pinheiro, R., & Cloete, N. (2007). *Bilateral country investments and foundations partnership projects to support higher education across Africa*. Wynberg, UK: Center for Higher Education Transformation.

Mahbubani, K. (2010, March 12). 5 lessons America can learn from Asia about higher education. *The Chronicle of Higher Education*, p. A72.

Marginson, S. (2007). The new higher education landscape: Public and private goods in global-national-local settings. In *Prospects of higher education: Globalization, market competition, public goods and the future of the university* (pp. 29–77). Rotterdam: Sense Publishers.

McGrath, S. (2010). The role of education in development: An educationalist's response to some recent work in development economics. *Comparative Education, 46*, 237–253.

McGrath, S., & Badroodien, A. (2006). International influences on the evolution of skills development in South Africa. *International Journal of Educational Development, 26*, 483–494.

McPherson, P. (2008, May 6). *Higher education in Africa: Making a link between intellectual capital and regional development*. Testimony before the House Committee on Foreign Affairs, Subcommittee on Africa and Global Health. Washington, DC: NASULGC.

Meyer, J., & Brown, M. (1999). *Scientific diasporas: A new approach to the brain drain*. Paper prepared for the UNESCO World Conference on Science, Budapest, Hungary.

Million+. (2009). *Universities and international higher education partnerships: Making a difference*. London: Author.

Million +. (2011). *International higher education: Missing an opportunity?* London: Author.

Mohamedbhai, G. (2008). The role of higher education for human and social development in sub-Saharan Africa. In Global University Network for Innovation (GUNI)(Ed.), Higher education in the world *3: New challenges and emerging roles for human and social development* (pp. 191–202). London: Palgrave Macmillan.

Moja, T. (2003). Globalization apartheid: The role of higher education in development. In G. Breton & M. Lambert (Eds.), *Universities and globalization: Private linkages, public trust* (pp. 163–175). Paris: UNESCO.

Moja, T. (2008). Institutional challenges and implications for higher education institutions: Transformation, mission, and vision for the 21st century. In Global University Network for Innovation (GUNI)(Ed.), *Higher education in the world 3: New challenges and emerging roles for human and social development* (pp. 161–169). London: Palgrave Macmillan.

National Association of State Universities and Land Grant Colleges, Commission on International Programs. (2007). *A national action agenda for internationalizing higher Education*. Washington, DC: Author.

Neelakantan, S. (2009, January 9). A young university in India focuses on real-world industry and sustainability. *Chronicle of Higher Education*, p. A20.

Obamba, M. O. (Forthcoming). Uncommon knowledge: World Bank policy and the unmaking of the knowledge economy in Africa. *Higher Education Policy*.

Obamba, M. O., & Mwema, J. K. (2009). Symmetry and asymmetry: New contours, paradigms, and politics in African academic partnerships. *Higher Education Policy, 22*, 349–371.

Obamba, M. O., Mwema, J. K., & Riechi, A. A. (2011). *What works, what doesn't: New patterns and impacts of international partnerships in Kenya's higher education* (A report commissioned by the African Network for Internationalization of Education). Eldoret, Kenya: ANIE Secretariat.

Organization for Economic Cooperation and Development (OECD). (1996). *Shaping the 21st century: The contribution of development cooperation*. Paris: OECD, Development Assistance Committee.

Ramphele, M. (2003). The university as an actor in development: New perspectives and demands. In C. R. Doss, R. E. Evanson, & N. L. Ruther (Eds.). *African Higher Education: Implications for development* (pp. 1-21). New Haven, CT: Yale Center for International and Area Studies.

Richmond, J. E. D. (2007). Bridging critical thinking to the education of developing country professionals. *International Education Journal, 8*(1), 1–29.

Rizvi, F. (2007). Brain drain and the potential of diasporic professional networks. In L. Farrel & T. Fenwick (Eds.), *Educating the global workforce: Knowledge, knowledge work, and Knowledge workers* (pp. 227–238). London: Routledge.

Salmi, J. (2003). Constructing knowledge societies: New challenges for tertiary education. In G. Bretton & M. Lambert (Eds.), *Universities and globalization: Private linkages, public trust* (pp. 51–68). Paris: UNESCO.

Samoff, J., & Carrol, B. (2004). The promise of partnership and continuities of dependence: External support to higher education in Africa. *African Studies Review, 47,* 67–199.

Sawahel, W. (2009). China-Africa: Three-year partnership plan announced. *University World News.* Retrieved from http://www.universityworldnews.com/article.php?story=20091127124452958

Shabani, J. (2008). The role of key regional actors and programs. In D. Teferra & J. Knight (Eds.), *Higher education in Africa: The international dimension* (pp. 464–474). Chestnut Hill, MA: Boston College, Center for International Higher Education.

Singh, M. (2007). Universities and society: Whose terms of engagement? In S. Sorlin & H. Vessuri (Eds.), *Knowledge society vs. knowledge economy: Knowledge, power, and politics* (pp. 53–78). Hampshire, UK: Palgrave Macmillan.

Smith, A. (2007). Going international in quest of a new "foreign policy" for European higher education. *IIE Networker* (Spring).

Smuckler, R. H. (2003). *A university turns to the world: A personal history of the Michigan State University international story.* East Lansing: Michigan State University Press.

SQW Consulting. (2010). *Evaluation of UK-Russia BRIDGE program* (Report commissioned by the United Kingdom Department for Business Innovation and Skills). London: United Kingdom Department for Business Innovation and Skills.

Sutton, S. B. (2007). Making partnerships the driving force of campus internationalization. *IIE Networker* Supplement (Spring).

Tandon, R. (2008). Civil engagement in higher education and its role in human and social development. In Global University Network for Innovation (GUNI) (Ed.), *Higher education in the world 3: New challenges and emerging roles for human and social development* (pp. 142–152). London: Palgrave Macmillan.

Tarrow, S. (2005). *The new transnational activism.* Cambridge, UK: Cambridge University Press.

Tartir, T. K. H. (2007). A multidisciplinary international linkage: An engineering faculty's viewpoint." *IIE Networker* (Spring).

Taylor, P. (2008a). Bridging the past and the present. In Global University Network for Innovation (GUNI) (Ed.), *Higher education in the world 3: New challenges and emerging roles for human and social development* (pp. xxiv–xxvii). London: Palgrave Macmillan.

Taylor, P. (2008b). Higher education curricula for human and social development. In Global University Network for Innovation (GUNI) (Ed.), *Higher education in the world 3: New challenges and emerging roles for human and social development* (pp. 89–101). London: Palgrave Macmillan.

Teichler, U. (1999). *The requirements of the world of work* (World Conference on Higher Education, Vol. 4). Paris: UNESCO.

Thrift, N. (2010, February 19). The world needs global research cooperation urgently, and now. *Chronicle of Higher Education,* p. A72.

UN Conference on Trade and Development (UNCTAD). (2008). *The least developed countries report 2008: Growth, poverty and the terms of development partnership.* New York: United Nations.

UNESCO. (2005). *Launching of the academics across borders (AAB) initiative: Report of the rappoteur-general.* Paris: Author.

UNESCO. (2007). From brain drain to brain gain. *Education Today, 18,* Newsletter of UNESCO's Education Sector. Paris: Author.

UNESCO. (2009). *Communiqué of the 2009 world conference on higher education: The new dynamics of higher education and research for societal change and development.* Paris: Author.

Valimaa, J., & Hoffman, D. M. (2007). The future of Finnish higher education challenged by global competitive horizons. In S. Marginson (Ed.), *Prospects of higher education: globalization, market competition, public goods and the future of the university* (pp.185–200). Rotterdam: Sense Publishers.

Vessuri, H. (2007). The hybridization of knowledge: Science and local knowledge in support of sustainable development. In S. Sorlin & H. Vessuri (Eds.), *Knowledge society vs. knowledge economy: Knowledge, power, and politics* (pp. 158–173). Hampshire, UK: Palgrave Macmillan.

Vessuri, H. (2008). The role of research in higher education: Implications and challenges for an active contribution to human and social development. In Global University Network for Innovation (GUNI) (Ed.), *Higher education in the world 3: New challenges and emerging roles for human and social development* (pp. 119–129). London: Palgrave Macmillan.

Vincent-Lancrin, S. (2007). Building future scenarios for universities and higher education: An international approach. In S. Marginson (Ed.), *Prospects of higher education: Globalization, market competition, public goods and the future of the university* (pp. 3–27). Rotterdam: Sense Publishers.

Wellings, P. (2010, February 19). American and British universities should forge stronger partnerships. *Chronicle of Higher Education*, pp. A29–A30.

Williams, P. (2002). The competent boundary spanner. *Public Administration, 80,* 103–124.

World Bank. (2007). *Mobilizing the African diaspora for development: Concept note.* Washington DC: Author.

Wu, M., & Yu, P. (2006). Challenges and opportunities facing Australian universities caused by the internationalization of Chinese higher education. *International Education Journal, 7*(3), 211–221.

Yusuf, S., Saint, W., & Nabeshima, K. (2009). *Accelerating catch-up: Tertiary education for growth in sub-Saharan Africa.* Washington, DC: World Bank.

Zaglul, J., & Sherrard, D. (2005). Higher education in economic transformation. In C. Juma (Ed.), *Going for growth: Science, technology and innovation in Africa.* London: Smith Institute.

Zeleza, P. T. (2007). African diasporas and academics: The struggle for a global epistemic presence. In P. T. Zeleza (Ed.). *The study of Africa:* Vol. 2. *Global and transnational engagements* (pp. 86–111). Dakar: Council for the Development of Social Science Research in Africa CODESRIA.

Notes

1   Tertiary institutions encompass all postsecondary forms of education, including private and public universities and colleges, technical institutes, teaching colleges, and "other programs that lead to the award of academic diplomas or degrees" (Yusuf, Saint, & Nabeshima, 2009, p. xxxi). In this chapter, we focus on government-assisted and private (but not in-house) universities. For discussions of corporate in-house training and development activities, including McDonald's Hamburger University, the Ruschilon Facility in Switzerland, Motorola University's operations in 21 countries (including South Africa, Brazil, Mexico, China, India, and Malaysia), and Microsoft's 1,700 world-wide Certified Technical Education Centers, see Kapur and Crowley (2008, pp. 19–20); Vincent-Lancrin (2007, pp. 16–17).

2   We reserve *global* for references that include the entire world, use *international* to refer to a particular form of organization and to relations among nations, and prefer *transnational* as a descriptor for the wide range of person-to-person and higher education relations that transcend nation-state boundaries (including, but much more encompassing than degree programs delivered across borders).

3   Following the World Commission on Environment and Development's 1987 definition, sustainable development is widely considered to involve meeting the needs and aspirations of the present without compromising the ability of future generations to meet their needs (Brundtland Commission, 1987).

4   The terms used to describe boundary-spanning competence include *transnational, international, global, transdisciplinary, cultural,* and *intercultural competence.* Darla K. Deardorff's research with international education administrators revealed "no consensus on terms." Comments from the Panel on Intercultural Competence, 25th Annual Meeting of the Association of International Education Administrators, Washington, D.C., 20 February 2008.

5   An "active skills" emphasis also characterized Lambert's (1994, p. 286) earlier notion of global competence.

6   Surveyed SIOs at 40 U.S. universities show a high degree of consensus regarding the principal impetus for international research and development-project activity on their campuses. Fully 90% of the reporting SIOs rated faculty members as key drivers (Koehn, Deardorff, & Bolognese, 2011), followed by international program leaders such as themselves (75%).

7   In November of 2007, the Association of International Education Administrators and the Association of Public and Land Grant Universities co-sponsored a short, mostly structured survey designed to tap campus-wide perspectives on the role and potential of international research and development project activity. For methodological details and a list of the institutional affiliations of reporting SIOs, see Koehn, Deardorff, and Bolognese (2011).

21

GLOBAL STUDENT MOBILITY

MELISSA BANKS AND RAJIKA BHANDARI

Over the last decade, there has been a
very substantial increase in the number of internationally mobile students,
the total now approaching more than 3.7 million
globally. This growth has been driven primarily
by the gap between demand for higher education and the ability of governments and traditional higher education institutions to provide
sufficient opportunities at both the graduate
and undergraduate levels for their citizens. In
addition, increasing numbers of students have
come to realize that study abroad will enhance
their career options, as they enter a marketplace
that requires knowledge and skills beyond what
is available at home; others will use their study
abroad experience as the first in a two-step process toward skilled migration (see Chapter 23,
this volume, for more on skilled migration).
Finally, there are growing numbers of programs through which students can combine
an international study experience with study
in their home country, often leading to dual
degrees or international qualifications by foreign
providers.

In an effort to provide international education leaders with an understanding of the mobility context of the field, this chapter provides a
comprehensive overview of global student
mobility, covering definitional and measurement issues as well as key trends and the future
outlook. The chapter begins with a look at the

different forms that mobility takes today, followed by an in-depth discussion of the many
ongoing definitional and measurement challenges. We acknowledge the difficulties involved
in measuring international student mobility but
believe enough is known to identify and analyze
relevant trends in global student mobility. The
following section analyzes current data and
trends in mobility, highlighting areas of growth
and resilience. Next, various push and pull factors that affect the demand and supply of overseas education are examined, highlighting the
intense competition for international students
and the role of emerging and nontraditional
study destinations. The chapter concludes with a
summary of current trends and a prediction of
future trends in mobility.

DIMENSIONS OF GLOBAL MOBILITY

Student mobility is part of a global phenomenon of increased mobility of people for economic opportunity, political and economic
security, cross-border trade, migration, tourism,
and study and research. The global movement
of international students across borders is
commonly referred to as the most visible form
of internationalization of higher education.
Students are moving across borders in greater
numbers than ever before, and this phenomenon

can be viewed in the context of an increasingly globalized world. Globalization and internationalization of higher education are inextricably linked. de Wit (2008b) says:

> Higher education is increasingly influenced by globalisation but is also becoming a more vigorous actor in globalisation. The internationalisation of higher education is one of the ways a country or an institution responds to the impact of globalisation, but also the internationalisation of higher education is itself an agent of globalisation. Higher education is not only passively responding to globalisation but has become an active player in the global arena. (p. 3)

In 1995, education was identified as a service in the context of the General Agreement on Trade in Services of the World Trade Organization. This formalized a connection between trade and higher education and led to the development of a typology of four modes of supply of services for exports, described here in terms of education exports.

Consumption abroad: This mode involves an international student crossing national borders to undertake an education in a foreign country. This is generally referred to as student mobility.

Commercial presence: This mode involves education institutions crossing the national border and establishing a commercial presence (such as an offshore campus) in a foreign nation, generally referred to as institutional mobility.

Cross-border supply: In this mode, the education institution remains in its home country, and the students remain in their home country, receiving education by distance education and online delivery or through a local partner. This is program mobility.

Presence of natural persons: In this mode, the teacher crosses national borders to produce and/ or deliver education services to the student on behalf of the institution. This is academic mobility.

Consumption abroad is the most significant of the four modes in terms of sheer numbers. Another common measure is the economic contribution international students make to host-country economies. In Australia, international student fees contributed 17.5 % to total revenue for Australian universities in 2009 (Department of Education, Employment, and Workplace Relations, 2011). In the broader economy, this revenue is more than doubled through expenditure on accommodation, meals, entertainment, communications, and other living costs. In 2009–2010, the total contribution international students made to the Australian economy was about $18.3 billion (Australian Education International [AEI], 2011). Similarly, in 2010–2011, international students contributed more than $20 billion to the U.S. economy through living expenses for themselves and accompanying dependents, as well as expenditures on tuition, books, fees, and other education-related expenses (Institute of International Education [IIE], 2011a). The combined value of tertiary education and English-language international students in Ireland is estimated to be worth €900 million to the Irish economy.

Often, the remaining three modes are grouped together and collectively referred to as transnational education. There is no single nationally or internationally accepted definition of modes of delivery. The United Nations Education, Scientific and Cultural Organization (UNESCO, 2001) and the Council of Europe, in their *Code of Practice in the Provision of Transnational Education,* states that transnational education includes

> all types of higher education study programme, or sets of courses of study, or educational services (including those of distance education) in which the learners are located in a country different from the one where the awarding institution is based. Such programmes may belong to the educational system of a State different from the State in which it operates, or may operate independently of any national education system.

The most common delivery modes of transnational education include

Distance education or online education: This is a form of cross-border supply and is also known as program mobility. This is a common form of transnational delivery adopted by UK providers.

Supported distance education, program articulations, or franchising: In this case, an institution establishes a commercial presence to deliver its programs across borders with the assistance of a local partner (commercial or institutional partner), which provides in-country learning support via a physical presence. This delivery mode was popular in the early phases of transnational delivery in Singapore, Hong Kong, and Malaysia, but many of these programs have since been replaced by full branch-campus developments (McBurnie & Ziguras, 2009).

Offshore campus or foreign branch campus: In some cases, a full physical presence is used to deliver entire degree programs. This form of commercial presence is gaining prominence as a major form of transnational delivery in host countries seeking to establish themselves as regional education hubs (Becker, 2009; Verbik & Merkley 2006).

Several of these modes involve academic staff from the home institution crossing borders to deliver all or part of the program to students who remain in their own countries (movement of the natural person). The various modes of cross-border supply are not mutually exclusive, and students may in fact move between the various modes (model mobility and multiple mobility).

This chapter is confined to student mobility (consumption abroad) and specifically to degree or diploma mobility, where students pursue an undergraduate or graduate degree completely or mostly in the destination country, with the host institution conferring the academic award. However, student mobility is only one form of cross-border education, and increasingly, each form is impacting other forms.

DEFINING AND MEASURING MOBILITY

The foundation for measuring any phenomenon is the ability to clearly define the very concepts on which it is based. In the case of global mobility, the key challenge is how to define an international student. Definitions of international students vary, terminology and data-gathering methodologies differ, data gaps exist, and often there is a significant time lag between data collection and publication (Bhandari, Belyavina, & Gutierrez, 2011; Bhandari & Blumenthal, 2011). Multiple players are involved (students, destination and home-country governments, education institutions), and scholar, program, and institutional mobility are added complexities in the discourse about global student mobility. While the field of global student migration is vast and complex, our ability to document and understand student mobility from a global perspective has not kept pace with this growth in numbers and variety of international study experiences.

Reliable and consistent data are needed to respond effectively to global developments in higher education. Yet, few countries outside of Australia, Germany, the United Kingdom, and the United States have developed data collection systems that produce high-quality and consistent statistics. As a result, higher education officials in countries trying to develop policies in the context of global academic mobility need better information, as do campus-level officials and those in the press and public who are trying to understand critically important issues. These include, for example: How does global academic migration affect brain drain? How does it affect the current and future capacity of countries to accommodate a growing demand for higher education? What are the implications of mobility for the labor market, the economy, and the global search for academic talent?

Definitions of international students vary across countries and regions. Many countries define international students according to their citizenship or visa status in the host country. In several host countries, including the United States, China, India, and parts of Africa, students are considered to be international if they bear a passport from another country; they are consequently required to obtain a special student visa to study in the host country. Permanent residents ("green card" holders in the United States, for example) are not considered to be international students, even though they still retain a foreign passport. Although this is the most widely used approach to defining an international student, it has its limitations. A permanent resident might have arrived in the United States from another country to attend college but would not be counted as an international student because of having a green card. The citizenship or visa-based definition of an international student can also lead to a significant undercount in mobility for closely connected regions of the world such as Europe and Africa, in which many articulation and mobility schemes allow students to move easily from one country to the other without requiring a special visa or documentation.

A second approach to defining mobility is used primarily in Europe, due in large part to the borderless nature of higher education in the region. This approach combines citizenship status with degree mobility, that is, the country where students obtained their prior degree. This approach is consistent with UNESCO mobility data, which defines internationally mobile students as those who study in a foreign country of which they are not a permanent resident. Within this definition, three key criteria are used to identify international students: residency, requiring that students are not residents in the country in which they are studying; prior education, specifying that students obtained their entry qualification to the current program of study in another country; and citizenship, in that the students must not be citizens of the host country in which they pursue their studies. This definition is used to build a dataset of internationally mobile students through the contributions of data from 153 host countries (UNESCO Institute for Statistics, 2009).

The UNESCO dataset reports degree or diploma mobility where students pursue an undergraduate or graduate degree completely or mostly in the destination country, with the host institution conferring the academic award. International students who visit institutions for a short study period but who remain enrolled in their home institution are not included in this dataset. Data on short-term mobility tends to be specific to mobility programs such as Erasmus and University Mobility in Asia and the Pacific. The Organization for Economic Cooperation and Development (OECD) and UNESCO have tried to persuade all countries to adopt the degree or diploma mobility definition, but this approach is not practicable for countries that are not part of an interconnected region and that rely primarily on citizenship data to manage and study migration flows.

A major limitation of the degree mobility approach is that it counts only students enrolled for the duration of a year or more. Since internationally mobile students from the United States, Japan, and the European Union (EU) often study abroad for less than a full academic year, it can be safely assumed that the actual number of students who are globally mobile might significantly exceed the total numbers of mobile students reported by UNESCO and OECD. Moreover, the current trend shows an increasing number of students participating in short-term overseas study opportunities rather than in traditional degree-length programs. These students are currently not captured in the degree mobility approach.

The comparison of these approaches shows that there is no perfect method for defining and measuring mobility; different countries have adopted approaches that reflect the realities of their region and academic systems.

ATTEMPTS TO MEASURE MOBILITY

Although harmonization of mobility data is an ongoing challenge, several countries have established systems for collecting information on international students, using one or more of the definitions described above. In the United States, for example, the Institute of International Education (IIE) has been collecting this type of data since the 1920s, published as the *Open Doors* Report on International Educational Exchange since 1954, with support from the U.S. Department of State since 1972 (see http://www.iie.org/opendoors). An annual census of U.S. international educational exchange, *Open Doors* presents mobility statistics based on data collected from all regionally accredited U.S. higher education institutions. Similar data for Australia is gathered by Australian Education International (AEI), for the United Kingdom by the Higher Education Statistics Agency, and for Germany by the German Academic Exchange Service (DAAD). Countries such as China (through the China Scholarship Council [CSC]) and Mexico (through the Association of Universities and Higher Education Institutions [ANUIES] and the Ministry of Education) have more recently developed mechanisms to collect this type of data.

Because most current sources of information and knowledge about international students are derived from national data collection organizations such as the ones mentioned above, the resulting data vary widely from country to country in timeliness, data definitions, and scope. Country-specific data is limited in that it tells us little about the implications of each country's mobility statistics within a global context. The variation in national degree and qualifications structures across countries also makes comparative analysis difficult. What is needed is a global and consistent source of baseline data as well as a forum within which national efforts may be compared and benchmarked.

While UNESCO and OECD have instituted large-scale data collection efforts to collect mobility data for all countries, they face a number of well-recognized limitations. For one, there is typically a significant time lag between the year the data are collected and the year they are released. Second, because the data are primarily collected through ministries of education, they do not always capture enrollments at private institutions. Last, neither of these data collection efforts captures non-degree or short-term mobility, where students study overseas for less than a year. The result is an underestimate of international students, since private institutions represent the fastest-growing education sector in many developing countries and since short-term mobility is on the rise.

Project Atlas: A Shared Framework for Student Mobility Data

One effort to build on the work of UNESCO and OECD and address some of its limitations is Project Atlas, a unique initiative that brings together a community of researchers from around the world to share more harmonized and current data on student mobility. Initiated in 2001 with support from the Ford Foundation and currently supported by the U.S. Department of State and participating members in other countries, Project Atlas and its associated Web portal, the Atlas of Student Mobility (http://www.iie.org/projectatlas), provide a comprehensive global picture of international student mobility for 19 leading destination countries. These data are gathered through data-sharing agreements with researchers based at national academic mobility agencies around the world. Current project partners include ANUIES, the Association of Indian Universities (AIU), AEI, the British Council, the CSC, DAAD, the International Education Association of South Africa (IEASA), and the Netherlands Organization for International Cooperation in Higher Education (NUFFIC), among others.

Drawing on the experience of IIE's *Open Doors* project, Project Atlas provides a shared framework within which to collect, synthesize, and disseminate data on the migration trends of the millions of students who pursue education outside of their home countries each year. The aim was to address the need for global migration data that measures student flows not just to the United States but also to several other leading and emerging destinations for transnational higher education. For instance, Project Atlas tells us how China has moved from the leading sending country for international students to one of the top 10 host countries and how South Africa is growing as a regional host for students from throughout Africa and beyond. To capture more fully the increasingly important role that newer host countries are now playing in global mobility, an ongoing priority for Project Atlas is to identify and involve more partners from Asia, Latin America, the Middle East, and Africa.

Underlying the project is an unprecedented effort to engage these leading nongovernmental and governmental agencies involved in international educational exchange to examine the broader implications of their work within a global context rather than through a narrow national lens (Bhandari et al., 2011). Project Atlas also helps IIE and the other member organizations consider how international education patterns relate to other national developments such as home-country investment in human capital, population growth, and the level of technological capacity, and how they are affected by international and transnational economic, diplomatic, and political factors. An improved understanding of these dynamics might also help potential international students make a more informed choice regarding their study destinations.

The foundations for Project Atlas were laid down in May 2001 at a meeting in France that was attended by representatives from selected national bodies and nongovernmental organizations (NGOs) involved in international educational exchanges and mobility and who had expressed an interest in developing an effective approach to a common data set for global mobility. By creating a shared image of international mobility, participants hoped to highlight the truly globe-spanning aspects of higher education, make apparent the emerging world higher education economy, and establish a conversation space for those concerned with global education mobility issues.

BOX 21.1 Project Atlas®

Country partners: Association of Indian Universities, Australian Education International, British Council, CampusFrance, Canadian Bureau for International Education, Centre for International Mobility (Finland), China Scholarship Council, Danish Agency for International Education, Education Ireland, Fundación Universidad.es (Spain), German Academic Exchange Service, International Education Association of South Africa, the Institute of International Education (United States), Japan Student Services Organization, Ministry of Higher Education Malaysia, National Association of Universities and Higher Education Institutions (Mexico), Netherlands Organization for International Cooperation in Higher Education, New Zealand Ministry of Education, Swedish Institute.

  Research Affiliates: Boston College Center for International Higher Education, International Association of Universities (IAU), Organization for Economic Co-operation and Development (OECD), UNESCO Institute for Statistics.

Current Project Activities

- Data collection on full-degree and non-degree mobility.
- Collaborative meetings among international organizations involved in research on higher education migration for continuity of data collection and research on student mobility.
- Capacity-building workshops on collecting mobility data.
- Ongoing dissemination of mobility data and information via the Project Atlas website (www .iie.org/projectatlas)
- *Student Mobility and the Internationalization of Higher Education: National Policies and Strategies from Six World Regions*, a compilation of Project Atlas partner reports on student mobility trends and internationalization policies and strategies encompassing six world regions.

Project Atlas receives support from the U.S. Department of State's Bureau of Educational and Cultural Affairs (ECA), from the Institute of International Education, and from the international partners.

These collaborative meetings not only assist partners in developing joint data collection standards and practices, but also strengthen collaboration and shrink the competitive prism through which international student mobility discussions are often viewed. A more recent goal of the project has been to engage in capacity-building activities for less-experienced emerging destinations to design and implement a system to collect mobility data.

Eurodata: A Comprehensive Study of European Mobility

In 2006, the Academic Cooperation Association released the findings of its Eurodata study, which attempted to assess the quality of mobility data available for 32 European countries, of which 25 were EU members. The goals of the project were two-fold: first, to identify the types of data that were available and, second, to analyze these data and come up with a comprehensive mobility scenario for the region. One of the key findings of the study was that most countries were basing their statistics on nationality data rather than on degree mobility, which the Eurodata study considered to be the true measure of mobility. As with the concerns that led to the formation of Project Atlas, the Eurodata study also found that definitions varied widely across countries; the quality of the data was patchy; and there was limited coverage of short-term mobility and the mobility of doctoral students (Kelo, Teichler, & Wächter, 2006). The second phase of the study, Eurodata II, was completed in 2010–2011, with results disseminated later in 2011.

GROWTH, SOURCE, AND DESTINATION COUNTRIES

Recent growth in international student mobility has been spectacular. In just over 30 years numbers of mobile degree-seeking students tripled to reach well over 3 million by 2011. UNESCO reports three notable growth surges. The first surge occurred between 1975 and 1980, when student mobility increased by 30% from 800,000 to more than 1 million. The second surge occurred between 1989 and 1994, with a rise of 34%. The third surge occurred between 1999 and 2004, with a rise of 41%, from 1.75 million to 2.5 million (UNESCO Institute for Statistics, 2006). The years since early 2000 have seen the most rapid growth. Since 2004, numbers studying abroad have increased some 50% to more than 3.7 million today, and this growth has coincided with rapid growth in global tertiary education participation. Growing participation in tertiary education has driven growth in the number of students undertaking their tertiary education abroad. Much of the growth has occurred in developing or newly developed nations, as a reflection of increasing personal wealth.

Global tertiary enrollments grew fourfold between 1970 and 2009 coming from 28.6 million and growing to 164.5 million, with the greatest growth occurring since 2000 (UNESCO Institute for Statistics, 2009). Yet, despite the rapid growth in mobility, the number of people studying abroad as a proportion of all tertiary enrolments remains relatively unchanged, at 2.2% in 2009 compared to 1.9% in 1999 (meaning just over 2 in every 100 tertiary students undertook their tertiary education abroad in 2009).

Growth in tertiary education participation in regions such as Asia and the Pacific has changed the distribution of the world's tertiary students. In 1970, less than 14% of the world's tertiary students were located in Asia and the Pacific. By 2009, this had grown to 46%. In contrast, in 1970, almost half (48%) of the world's tertiary students were located in North America and

Western Europe; by 2008, this had dropped to less than 25%. Growth in demand for tertiary education is also reflected in growth in outbound mobility rates from regions including sub-Saharan Africa, central Asia, and the Arab states, which all have mobility rates well above the global average mobility rate (2.0%) at 4.9%, 5.8%, and 3.0%, respectively (UNESCO Institute for Statistics, 2011).

Population, incomes, access to education, and spending on education affect a country's demand for international education. Looking at tertiary education participation rates per country over time, participation is closely related to real income per person, with high-income countries generally having high tertiary participation rates and low-income countries having low participation rates. As personal wealth increases, so too do participation rates (Banks, Olsen, & Pearce, 2007). Global economic and political wealth has been shifting toward developing economies. Global demographic shifts occurring in rapid-growth nations, particularly those located in Asia, are inexorably changing the distribution of global economic activity (Kharas, 2010).

In 2011, just under half of the world's mobile degree-seeking students came from Asia. The share of students from Western Europe and North America had declined steadily over time from 27.9% 20 years earlier to 16% in 2008.[1] Subregion growth has been especially strong from East Asia and the Pacific, with the region contributing 29% of the world's mobile degree-seeking students in 2008, up from 24% in 1999, and with China contributing one seventh (15%) of the global total. Numbers and shares from South and West Asia have also grown, and in 2008, this region contributed 9%, up from 6% in 1999. Numbers from other regions have grown, but the share of all outbound students remains the same in 2007 compared to 1999. In 2007, Latin America and the Caribbean, central and east Europe, Arab states, and sub-Saharan Africa had shares of 6%, 11%, 7%, and 8%, respectively (UNESCO Institute for Statistics, 2009).

Rates of growth in outbound mobility vary across geographic regions and by individual country. A nation's outbound mobility rate is related to both income and tertiary participation. As income increases then outbound mobility also tends to rise. There are a number of reasons for this, but most important, increased income means that students are more able to afford international education. At the same time, however, an increase in the tertiary participation rate is associated with a decline in outbound mobility. As participation rates increase, most countries offer greater domestic educational opportunities, and so the proportion of students undertaking their tertiary education abroad falls. China, as the largest global provider of international students, is an interesting case to consider. The average annual growth in numbers studying abroad from 1999 to 2009 was 17%, while growth in domestic tertiary enrolment was 19%. With a declining population in the prime tertiary age range and continued investment in domestic tertiary education provision, it is reasonable to expect that growth in outbound mobility from China will slow in the future. Growth in tertiary education participation at home, combined with declining tertiary-aged population can reduce outbound mobility. In Western Europe and North America, short-term mobility represents the main form of student mobility, and as tertiary systems in Asia mature and personal wealth rises, it is reasonable to expect shifts in mobility trends out of and within Asia.

In 2011, the world population reached 7 billion. The United Nations has projected that the world's population will grow to 8.3 billion by 2030 and 9.3 billion by 2050. Much of the growth is expected to occur in Asia, the Middle East, Africa, and Latin America. In the case of India, 45% of the population will be under 25 years of age by 2020. India's total population will number some 1.4 billion, making it the largest populace in the world.

The global middle class, estimated to be 1.8 billion in 2009, is expected to grow by 5.3% per annum in terms of numbers of people to 3.2 billion by 2020. Kharas (2010) asserts that much of this growth will occur in Asia and that the growth in the Asian middle class will be significant enough to become one of the main drivers of the global economy. Continued improved personal wealth in developing and newly developed nations, along with growing tertiary aged populations, will continue to drive demand for tertiary education.

Growth in other forms of cross-border education means that increasingly students can opt to obtain an international education from home. Foreign branch campuses, distance education, online delivery by foreign providers, and double degree arrangements between universities at home and foreign universities all constitute examples of how students can increasingly gain an international education at home. Asia and the Middle East host the majority of the world's foreign branch campuses. (See Chapters 18 and 19, this volume, for more on these options.)

Twenty countries combine to send 47% of the world's international tertiary students, with some changes to the composition of the top 20 source countries. In 1985, the list of top 20 sending countries included Iran, the United Kingdom, Ukraine, Spain, and Algeria; today, these have been replaced by the Russian Federation, Uzbekistan, Kazakhstan, Vietnam, and Poland. China, India, and South Korea, as the top three source countries, represent a quarter of all international students. Where they are choosing to study is of more interest, as we shall see.

Ranking	Sending Countries 1995	Number	Sending Countries 2004	Number	Sending Countries 2009	Number
1	China	115,871	China	343,126	China	510,314
2	South Korea	69,736	India	123,559	India	195,107
3	Japan	62,324	South Korea	95,885	South Korea	125,165
4	Germany	45,432	Japan	60,424	Germany	91,928
5	Greece	43,941	Germany	56,410	United States	53,251
6	Malaysia	41,159	France	53,350	Malaysia	53,121
7	India	39,626	Turkey	52,048	France	51,288

Ranking	Sending Countries 1995	Number	Sending Countries 2004	Number	Sending Countries 2009	Number
8	Turkey	37,629	Morocco	51,503	Turkey	47,275
9	Italy	36,515	Greece	49,631	Russian Federation	46,964
10	Hong Kong	35,141	United States	41,181	Kazakhstan	46,142
11	Morocco	34,908	Malaysia	40,884	Canada	45,892
12	France	23,411	Canada	38,847	Japan	44,768
13	Canada	28,280	Italy	38,544	Viet Nam	44,038
14	United States	27,749	Russia	34,473	Morocco	42,009
15	Iran	26,786	Hong Kong	34,199	Italy	39,820
16	United Kingdom	24,034	Indonesia	31,687	Poland	32,991
17	Indonesia	22,235	Portugal	28,786	Hong Kong	32,944
18	Algeria	22,104	Kazakhstan	27,356	Ukraine	32,882
19	Ukraine	20,930	Spain	25,691	Indonesia	32,346
20	Spain	20,865	Ukraine	25,188	Iran	31,542

Table 21.1   Top 20 Sending Countries, 1995–2009

Source: de Wit (2008a, p 33) and UNESCO Institute for Statistics (2006, 2011).

With some 510,000 students from China pursuing degrees in other countries, China is by far the largest supplier of international students. In 2009, 51% of students from China were studying in English-speaking destination countries: the United States (111,612), the United Kingdom (42,258), Australia (63,214), Canada (30,908), and New Zealand (12,792) (OECD, 2011). A further 21% were studying in the neighboring countries of Japan (71,333) and South Korea (35,318). Other key destinations were Germany (22,233) and France (21,195). In all, well over 84% are studying in OECD destination countries (OECD, 2011).

India has a long tradition of student mobility. Students from India primarily choose to study in English-speaking destination countries. The United States hosts 104,000 students, followed by Australia and the United Kingdom with 24,256 and 31,493 students, respectively (IIE, 2011b;

OECD, 2011). These are the top three destination countries for international students from India. In the United States alone, more than 60 years of *Open Doors* data show that Indian students have often figured among the top three groups of international students, and India was the top sending country between 2001–2002 and 2008–2009 (IIE, 2009, 2010, 2011b). Other OECD countries popular with Indian students include Germany, France, Italy, and Sweden. In total, 90% of degree-seeking Indian students are studying in OECD countries (OECD 2010).

Students from South Korea have two key destinations: In 2009, the United States hosted 72,599 students or 58% of all students from South Korea, and Japan hosted 24,435 students or 19.5%. Combined the United States, the United Kingdom, Australia, New Zealand, and Canada hosted 69% of all Korean students, and OECD countries 96% (OECD, 2011).

Main English-speaking destination countries (United States, United Kingdom, Australia, Canada, and New Zealand) combined have historically hosted half of the world's international students. An English-language education is seen as desirable in a global economy that has adopted English as its international language of commerce. However, in the face of increased competition from emerging destination countries, particularly in Asia, the combined share of these countries is declining. Students are choosing to study in a greater variety of destination countries. In 2009, 42% of all international students were studying in English-speaking countries including the United States, United Kingdom, Australia, Canada, and New Zealand. Nine years earlier, the combined share of these countries was 49%.

Growth in numbers studying in nontraditional destination countries such as Singapore, Malaysia, China, and South Korea has been strong in recent years, indicating that countries that have traditionally been sources of international students for study in Australia, United States, and the United Kingdom have themselves become destination countries for international students.

By 2011, students were increasingly choosing to study within their own regions. This is a tradition long seen in Europe and the Americas, where access to quality education providers, scholarships for mobility, and regional economic and political collaborations have shaped mobility. This pattern is emerging in other regions that have previously shown a predilection for study outside their regions. In east Asia and the Pacific, for example, the proportion of international students choosing to remain in their own region increased from 36% in 1999 to 69% in 2009. The rise in regionalism coincides with growth in tertiary education provision in

the region, improved quality of education provision, growth in foreign investment in education, and investment in strategies by destination countries in the region such as China, Singapore, Malaysia, South Korea, and Japan aiming to attract international students (UNESCO Institute for Statistics, 2011).

With students from East Asia and Pacific increasingly choosing to study in their region, China, Singapore, and Malaysia are emerging as primary study destinations. China and Malaysia now occupy positions in the top 10 study destinations or host countries for international students (see de Wit, 2008a, 2008b; IIE, 2011a, 2011b; Lasanowski, 2009). According to Project Atlas, China had a 7% share of global international students with 265,090 in 2010—an increase of 11% over the prior year (http://www .iie.org/projectatlas). Malaysia, according to its Ministry of Higher Education (2011), now has 72,259 international students enrolled in tertiary education.[11] It is likely Singapore has replaced the Russian Federation in the top 10, but it is difficult to obtain accurate data on numbers of international students enrolled in tertiary education in Singapore.

One fifth of the world's international students study in United States, down from a share of nearly one third in 1995. The shares of inbound students to Germany and Russia have also declined over this period, while shares in countries that have adopted strategies aimed at attracting and recruiting international students—such as the United Kingdom, Australia, Singapore, Malaysia, and Canada—have all grown. Of the countries that were among the top 10 destination or host countries in 1995, eight remained in 2009, with Switzerland and Belgium both dropping out, replaced by China and Malaysia.

Destination Countries 1995	Number	Share 1995	Destination Countries 2009	Number	Share 2009
United States	453787	30%	United States	660581	20%
France	170574	11%	United Kingdom	368968	11%
Germany	146126	10%	Australia	257637	8%
United Kingdom	128550	9%	France	249143	7%
Russia	73172	5%	Germany	197895	6%

Destination Countries 1995	Number	Share 1995	Destination Countries 2009	Number	Share 2009
Japan	50,801	3%	Russia	136,791	4%
Australia	42,415	3%	Japan	131,599	4%
Canada	35,451	2%	Canada	92,881	3%
Belgium	35,236	2%	Italy	68,306	2%
Switzerland	25,307	2%	China	61,211	2%

Table 21.2   Top 10 Host Countries, 1995 and 2009

Sources: de Wit (2008a, p. 36). UNESCO Institute for Statistics (2011).

In 2009, the top 10 destination countries hosted 66% of all international students, down from 78% in 1995, indicating that students are increasingly choosing destination countries outside of the top 10 host countries. UNESCO uses a dispersion index to measure the extent to which international students from a particular country are either concentrated in a small number of destination countries or dispersed across a greater range of destinations. Using China as an example, 54% of students from China were studying in United States and South Korea in 1999. In 2008, this had declined to 43%, showing a higher dispersion index (UNESCO Institute for Statistics, 2009). Multiple factors are driving the choice of destination countries for international students, and these are explored in more detail below.

Although international students have greater study destination choices and are increasingly choosing destinations within their regions, the flow of students continues to be from less developed nations to more developed nations. Continuing the work of Cummings (1993) and de Wit (2008a, 2008b), Table 21.3 compares the top 10 sending and destination countries, using number of international students and mobility ratios as indicators of student flow; development indicators are gross tertiary enrollment ratios, GNI per Capita, and the Human Development Index (HDI) and finds that the flow of international students continues to be from less developed to more developed countries in general although the development gap between source countries and destination countries is reducing.

While there are variations by individual country, combined the destination countries have higher average gross tertiary enrollment, income per capita, and HDI scores than the combined top sending countries, indicating that the flows of students continue to be to more developed destination countries. Closer analysis, however, shows that the majority of the top 10 sending countries have high (4 countries) or very high (4 countries) HDI scores. Only two countries, China and India, have medium HDIs. The development gap between source and host countries appears to be closing. Comparing the average HDI of the top 10 sending countries in 2011 (0.779) to the average HDI of the top 10 sending countries in 1995 (0.792) shows that the well-being measures of the top 10 sending countries have on average increased, while the average HDI of the destination countries in 2011 (0.862) has declined against the average HDI in 1995 (0.916).

FACTORS AFFECTING THE GROWTH AND DIRECTION OF MOBILITY

The movement of students and scholars across borders is growing rapidly, driven by many factors and involving a wide range of vehicles and modalities. Many factors, real or perceived, can affect the demand for an international education and a student's choice of study destination, including the cost and quality of higher education programs; the value of the degree or professional credential for future careers; the

Top 10 sending countries

Sending Countries (2009)	Number	Gross Enrolment Ratio (2009)	GNI Per Capita PPP (2010)	Human Development Index (2011)	Outbound Mobility Rate (2009)
China	510,314	24.3	7,640	0.687	1.75
India	195,107	16.2	3,550	0.547	1.05
South Korea	125,165	103.9	29,010	0.897	3.82
Germany	91,928	...	37,950	0.905	...
United States	53,251	89.1	47,360	0.910	...
Malaysia	53,121	...	14,220	0.761	5.45
France	51,288	54.5	34,440	0.884	2.41
Turkey	47,275	45.8	15,170	0.699	1.62
Russia	46,963.5	75.9	19,190	0.755	0.51
Kazakhstan	46,142	40.0	10,770	0.745	5.63
Averages		56.2	21,930	0.779	2.78

Top 10 destinations

Destination Countries (2009)	Number	Gross Enrolment Ratio (2009)	GNI Per Capita PPP (2010)	Human Development Index (2011)	Outbound Mobility Rate (2009)
United States	660,581	89.1	47,360	0.910	...
United Kingdom	368,968	58.5	36,410	0.863	0.94
Australia	257,637	75.9	0	0.929	0.84
France	249,143	54.5	34,440	0.884	2.41
Germany	197,895	...	37,950	0.905	...
Russia	136,791	75.9	19,190	0.755	0.51
Japan	131,599	59.0	34,640	0.901	1.16
Canada	92,881	...	38,310	0.908	...
Italy	68,306	66.0	31,130	0.874	1.98
China	61,211	24.3	7,640	0.687	1.75
Averages		62.9	31,896.67	0.862	1.37

Table 21.3 Numbers, Mobility and Development Indicators Sending and Destination Countries

Source: Numbers, Gross Enrolment and Mobility data from UNESCO Institute for Statistics (2009, 2011), GNI data from World Bank (2010), Human Development Index from United Nations (2011).

availability of certain areas of specialization; access to the education system and a country (including, but not limited to, obtaining visas for entry); desire for skilled migration; and important historical, linguistic, and geographic links between the home and destination country.

On the supply side, developed countries in Europe, North America, and Oceania have dominated the global mobility picture of the late 20th and early 21st centuries. The United States, United Kingdom, France, and Germany, in particular, have long attracted large numbers of international students. And while this overall trend continues today, the situation is nonetheless changing for these key countries, with interesting variations emerging in which several unexpected players are now engaged in what might best be described as a "global competition" for international students (Wildavsky, 2010).

These changes have been propelled by a combination of factors that include aggressive recruiting by other countries to host more foreign students; the expanding capacity of countries like China not only to provide more higher education opportunities for their own students but also to host an increasing number of international students; the availability and global spread of alternative modes of educational delivery; and domestic economic, demographic, and workforce conditions that might affect students' decisions regarding an overseas education.

The following section examines in detail five interrelated developments in international education that have contributed to a significant shift in the demand and supply equation of global mobility. When examining these developments, the focus goes beyond higher education to include skilled employment because the two are inextricable and critical components of the education-to-employment pipeline in countries that attract international students and skilled migrants.

Increased Recruiting of International Students and the Emergence of Nontraditional Destinations

Government-supported efforts by key host countries, including nationally coordinated campaigns by the United Kingdom, Australia, Germany, France, New Zealand, and others, feature sophisticated marketing strategies and expedited visa policies. Several of these host countries, along with newer players in Asia and Europe, have allocated tens of millions of dollars to launch large-scale initiatives over the past few years. These efforts are proving very persuasive, especially to self-funded students from some of the large sending countries in Asia. Launched in 1998, the United Kingdom's £5 million Prime Minister's Initiative was one of the earliest and was updated in 2000 as the Education UK brand, a coordinated approach to marketing British institutions abroad that is available for use by any UK campus. Other recent UK initiatives include the Science and Engineering Graduate Scheme (2004), the UK-China Higher Education Program (2005), and the UK-India Education and Research Initiative (2006).

Countries that were primarily sending countries have now also developed their own internationalization strategies to attract foreign students and encourage international educational exchange. This new era of internationalization is most evident in Asia. Singapore has been making strides in this area with the establishment of Education Singapore, a new agency charged with promoting and marketing Singapore abroad and with attracting 150,000 foreign students by 2015. According to reports in national and international media, the following countries have set specific targets in hosting international students: Malaysia seeks to attract 200,000 international students by 2020; Jordan announced plans to increase the number of international students to 100,000 by 2020; China seeks to host 300,000 by 2020 (a goal that is likely to be achieved much sooner); and Japan has reportedly set the ambitious goal of hosting 1 million foreign students by 2025.

Home-Country Higher Education Capacity

In China, India, South Korea, and many other countries, the number of higher education seats at home has grown dramatically as national and provincial or state governments increase their investments in public education. Within some countries, especially in Asia and Latin America, the private higher education sector is also dramatically expanding to meet growing demand. But despite the rapid expansion of the public and private education sector in many countries, it is worth noting that the burgeoning college-age population in China and India continues to exceed the domestic higher education capacity of these countries, a demand-supply imbalance that probably partly explains the growing numbers of Chinese and Indian students who continue to seek an overseas education.

Growth in Other Forms of International Education

A range of new institutions and alternative approaches to international study have emerged to meet the growing need for a cost-effective education, and as a result, many students are choosing to stay home while also acquiring an international education (Blumenthal, 2002). These new modes of education include, among others, distance learning, joint degrees, branch campuses, and "sandwich" programs involving short-term study abroad. According to Gray (2006), these types of nontraditional academic arrangements have succeeded because they offer alternative modes of organization and operation in the form of new program offerings (e.g. short courses, evening classes); new pedagogical approaches; asynchronous and collaborative learning; and distributed physical infrastructure including, but not limited to, remote campuses and distance education via the Internet.

Perhaps the most significant development in alternative forms of international education has been the advent of the branch campus, often referred to as transnational education, borderless education, or cross-border education (see Chapter 18, this volume, for further discussion). Broadly speaking, this approach involves the "the movement of education across national jurisdictional or geographic borders" (Knight, 2006)—that is, "internationalization abroad" as compared with the more traditional form of "internationalization at home." As in the case of more traditional forms of global student mobility, the movement and spread of cross-border education has primarily been from the developed North to the developing South. U.S. institutions continue to dominate this type of overseas delivery and account for more than half of all overseas higher education, followed by Australia, the United Kingdom, and Ireland (Becker, 2009). Key host countries for overseas campuses include Singapore and China in Asia, and Dubai (Knowledge Village) and Qatar (Education City) in the Middle East.

Cross-border education has significant implications for domestic and international higher education. It is conceivable, for example, that as prospective international students choose branch campuses located in their own countries over the institution's home campus, traditional student mobility, as we know it, might decline (Knight, 2006). The expansion of "virtual mobility" through Internet-based learning may also undercut the need for students to cross physical borders to obtain an international credential. Conversely, it is also possible that these diverse forms of internationalization will continue to grow rapidly, serving different types of students with varying educational needs. (See the Observatory on Borderless Higher Education [OBHE]: www.obhe.ac.uk).

Skilled Migration

Many countries also hope to attract international students by formalizing the link between higher education and the skilled job market and by implementing policies that encourage international graduates to enter the workforce of the host country, especially in scientific and technical fields. Many host countries provide poststudy work opportunities for graduating international students, and this can become the first step in a two-step pathway to skilled migration (OECD, 2010). Canada, for example, allows graduating international students to remain and work in Canada for up to 3 years, and New Zealand allows students to apply for a 1-year work permit that can be extended for a further 2 years if the work is relevant to graduates' qualifications. In Australia, international students have been able to apply for permanent residency after graduation without having to leave Australia. In the United Kingdom, until recently, graduating international students from higher education programs have been able to remain for a further 2 years; and in the United States, 1 year of optional practical training (more for graduates from science, technology, engineering and medical [STEM] programs) have provided students with opportunities to find employers to sponsor continued U.S. stays. In Singapore, international students can apply for scholarships that heavily subsidize their costs of study in return for being bonded to remain in Singapore for a period of 3 or more years on completion of their studies. These types of poststudy work opportunities provide pathways to future migration.

Supplementing efforts by individual host countries in Europe, the EU has also launched initiatives to recruit science and technology researchers from around the world in an attempt to compete with well-funded U.S. research universities and labs, which reputedly attract the world's best and brightest science and technology talent. Professional associations are also becoming increasingly internationalized and are credentialing and licensing professionals trained in other nations, providing credential portability that facilitates professional mobility. As a result, international students have become a significant group in international migration flows in OECD countries.

From the perspective of employers, especially in the science and technology fields, international student and skilled migration policies have a direct bearing on the international competition for and the availability of highly skilled workers (see Chapter 11, this volume, for more on employers' perspectives). Employers in industries experiencing labor shortages can access a ready supply of skilled and qualified labor as required, and governments regulate student visas, poststudy work opportunities, and skilled migration policies to meet their nation's demand for skilled workers.

In a post-global financial crisis climate with high unemployment levels, the United Kingdom, in particular, has recently moved to restrict the post-study work rights of graduating international students. It is anticipated that for students driven by a desire for permanent residency, the United Kingdom will also become a less desirable study destination, and growth in numbers choosing to study there will decline. Lower immigration numbers is the desired outcome of this policy shift. Australia, too, in anticipation of economic stagnation in the wake of the crisis, tightened student visa policy to reduce numbers of international students, particularly in the overheated vocational education and training sector, and at the same time, it adopted a demand-driven approach to skilled migration whereby graduating international students were able to remain in Australia, provided they had qualifications in occupations that were experiencing labor shortages and were able to gain sponsorship from an employer.

Other OECD countries facing declining demographics are actively competing to attract skilled workers to their shores. Attracting and retaining talent is critical to their ongoing economic viability and global competitiveness. The United Kingdom and Australia, too, are engaged in this race and in the longer term, commitment to attracting skilled migrants will win over contemporary anti-immigration politics. (For an in-depth discussion on skilled migration, see Chapter 23, this volume.)

Nontraditional Mobility Patterns

Although there are no hard data to support this assertion, anecdotal evidence suggests that international mobility or skilled migration no longer follows a strictly linear pattern where people move between just two countries, typically from South to North. In an increasingly connected world, a student from Asia, for example, might choose to obtain an undergraduate degree in her home country, a master's degree in the United States, and a doctoral degree in the United Kingdom, returning home subsequently to work for a European multinational firm. The mobility of international scientists and researchers, too, has become increasingly complex, as the field of science and engineering itself has evolved into a borderless enterprise. Not surprisingly, this type of multicountry mobility is difficult to measure. For instance, even though Finn's (2010) research on the "stay rates" of international postdoctoral researchers and scholars in the United States sheds light on who remains there and who leaves, it is not able to tell us whether those who leave are heading to another country or back to their home country, or even whether those who stay are commuting between the United States and their home country regularly to work in joint ventures.

WHAT THE FUTURE HOLDS

Over 60 years of Open Doors data and 30 years of UNESCO data suggest that demand for international tertiary education is resilient. UNESCO reports 3.7 million internationally mobile students in 2009, with average annual growth of 4.6% per year since 1975. Open Doors reports 723,000 international students in the United States in 2010–2011, with average annual growth of about 4% since 1975. With greater numbers participating in tertiary education globally, more students than ever before are pursuing their tertiary education abroad. Growth has been most significant in the last 10 years, and this upward trend has coincided with a range of factors that are impacting where international students come from, where they go and how they gain an international education.

Population, incomes, access to education, and spending on education affect a country's demand for international education. Unmet demand is the most robust driver of global student mobility. Global demographic shifts occurring in rapid-growth nations, particularly those located in Asia, are inexorably changing the distribution of global economic activity (Kharas, 2010).

The global middle class is expected to grow by 5.3% per annum for the next 25 years from 1.8 billion to 3.2 billion by 2020 (Kharas, 2010). Much of this growth will occur in Asia. The United Nations has projected that the world's population will grow to 8.3 billion by 2030 and 9.3 billion by 2050, and most of the growth is expected to occur in Asia, Middle East, Africa, and Latin America (United Nations, 2010). Asia, with the world's largest tertiary-aged population, rising personal wealth, and increased demand for tertiary education, is likely to supply some 50% of the world's international students, and China and India will account for one quarter of the global total. Demand from China will gradually lessen as the population declines, and India will become the largest source country for international students.

Governments in the Middle East and southeast Asian countries are increasingly seeking to position themselves as destination countries for international students. These governments have introduced various policy and marketing initiatives to encourage foreign investment in education, reduce outflows of domestic students, and increase inflows of international students. Foreign branch campuses and education hubs are core components of these initiatives, and governments or sponsors offer a range of incentives including funding and infrastructure to foreign education providers to encourage the development of foreign branch campuses. Education hubs do not follow a common formula in their composition. They reflect different strategies and different players, including public and private providers as well as foreign and domestic providers; they offer different numbers, types,

and sizes of institutions; and they reflect varying policy inputs and combinations of national, state, and city government support. Foreign branch campuses are common components of regional education hubs. "The diversity of rationales, partnerships, strategies, financing, and regulatory frameworks for establishing regional education hubs demonstrates that each country adopts an approach consistent with its national/regional context and policy" (Knight, 2011, p. 212). The long-term survival of foreign branch campuses is less than assured as host government agendas, priorities, and regulatory frameworks develop and shift overtime.

A number of indicators point to growth in other forms of cross-border education. Expansion of foreign branch campuses, franchising, and the proliferation of dual and joint degree arrangements means that students have greater access to international education than ever before from within their own borders. These developments are likely to have a profound impact on mobility:

> The growing trend in offshore education enables students to stay in their home countries or regions and receive a foreign education. This option may become increasingly attractive in light of greatly reduced costs to students and the attractiveness to governments that wish to avoid brain drain. It is not at all evident that the past will predict the future. (Green & Koch, 2010, p. 10)

Language is also emerging as one of the main determinants of who goes where. Anglophone destination countries (United States, United Kingdom, Australia, Canada, and New Zealand), combined, have historically hosted half of the world's international students. An English-language education is seen as desirable in a global economy that has adopted English as its international language of commerce. However in the face of increased competition from emerging destination countries, particularly in Asia, the combined share of these countries is declining. The growth in programs taught in English in non-English-speaking destinations is likely to impact market share of international students for the main English-speaking destination countries, in what Lasanowski (2011) describes as a depreciation of the premium value of English. Other languages will gradually become increasingly valuable for employment as employers seek multilingual graduates.

Growth in other languages including Arabic, Spanish, and Mandarin is outpacing growth in English. Population growth is occurring in countries where English is not the native language, and the greatest growth in the future middle class will also occur in countries where English is not the native language. China, Japan, South Korea, Singapore, and Malaysia all offer programs taught in English, and the number of these programs is growing. Many of these programs are being offered through transnational presences of providers from English-language countries including the United States, United Kingdom, and Australia. Host countries are able to attract students from within the region to their shores for an international education conducted by a foreign provider in English. In the case of South Korea, it is a stated government priority that its universities offer more and more programs in English to secure the country's future economic viability. European nations, including Germany, the Netherlands, Sweden, Switzerland, Denmark, and Norway, are also increasing the number of programs taught in English so as to reduce barriers to inbound and outbound mobility. The benefits for domestic students are that they can now access an English-language tertiary education from home and build global competencies. The benefits for institutions are that they can attract a share of the international student market.

Students have greater choices than ever before. They are choosing to study in a greater diversity of destinations, increasingly in countries located within their regions and via a greater diversity of learning modes. The emergence and growing popularity of alternative higher education destinations, coupled with increasing return rates for a few key source countries such as China, India, and South Korea, leads to the inevitable question whether the top host nations (the United States, the United Kingdom, Australia, and Germany) can maintain their competitive edge by attracting the best and the brightest from around the world? The United States, which remains to date the top choice of international students and scholars, is affected most by current trends in global student mobility and skilled migration. U.S. reliance on foreign-born talent grew in both absolute numbers and as a share of the science and engineering

workforce and has continued to escalate during the 1990s and the first decade of the 21st century (National Science Board, 2012). Since 2006, foreign-born students have earned more than 50% of U.S. doctoral degrees in mathematics, computer sciences, physics, engineering, and economics, with most students coming from China, India, and South Korea. In engineering alone, foreign students earned 68% of all doctorates in 2007. The presence of foreign-born faculty at U.S. research institutions also continues to increase, constituting almost half of all STEM-related departments.

"At any given time doctoral students perform about half of the research conducted in a national system. Bright international PhD students are therefore a great boon to national research systems, and no nation will exploit this more than Singapore which lives off mobile and expatriate labour" (Marginson, 2011, p. 9). Already national scholarship programs in Australia, China, Singapore, Germany, the United States, and the United Kingdom are seeking to attract doctoral students to their shores in recognition of the value these students contribute to a nation's, and its institutions', research outputs. We predict that competition for doctoral students will intensify and that the international doctoral market will expand as research continues to globalize. International research collaborations are providing opportunities for researchers located in multiple geographic locations to pool their knowledge and resources to solve some of the world's great research challenges.

Finally, for the suppliers of international education—namely, host countries and institutions—there are a variety of objectives and approaches to engaging in mobility, and those that are most effective in internationalizing are characterized by flexibility and a willingness to adapt to new realities in the complex world of higher education. Common to the best of them are certain elements such as commitment to academic excellence, to fair and open access for candidates, and to a diverse range of participants. Most also face similar challenges, such as how to cope with rapidly expanding opportunities and interest in study abroad with limited or shrinking resources.

Indeed, according to some estimates, the desire for higher education—and the subsequent demand for international education—is expanding so rapidly that in 20 years there will not be enough classroom seats in the whole world to meet the needs of students who want to pursue higher education. Creative and collaborative solutions will be needed to provide higher education and training to those who seek it. Distance learning, joint degree programs, and new approaches not yet imagined will all be needed to address the educational needs of the hundreds of millions of undergraduates around the world. Governments will of course be the primary responders to this need, but the private and nonprofit sectors are also likely to play key roles. International education leaders who understand the mobility context and future trends will be well positioned to guide the development of innovative approaches to meeting global higher education needs in the future.

REFERENCES

Australian Education International. (2011). *Export income to Australia from education services in 2010, Research Snapshot.* Retrieved from www .aei.gov.au

Banks, M., Olsen, A., & Pearce, D. (2007). *Global student mobility: An Australian perspective five years on.* Melbourne, Victoria: IDP Education Pty Ltd.

Becker, R. (2009). *International branch campuses: Markets and strategies.* London: The Observatory on Borderless Higher Education.

Bhandari, R., & Blumenthal, P. (2011). *International students and global mobility in higher education: National trends and new directions.* New York: Palgrave Macmillan.

Bhandari, R., Belyavina, R., & Gutierrez, R. (2011). *Student mobility and the internationalization of higher education: National policies and strategies from six world regions.* New York: Institute of International Education.

Blumenthal, P. (2002). Virtual and physical mobility: A view from the U.S. In B. Wächter (Ed.), *The virtual challenge to international cooperation in higher education* (ACA Papers in International Cooperation). Bonn, Germany: Lemmens.

Cummings, W. (1993). Global trends in overseas study. In C. D. Goodwin (Ed.), *International investment in human capital: Overseas education for development.* New York: IIE.

Department of Education Employment and Workplace Relations. (2011). *Finance 2010: Financial reports of higher education providers.* Canberra: Commonwealth of Australia ACT.

de Wit, H. (2008a). Changing dynamics in international student circulation: Meanings, push and pull factors, trends and data. In H. de Wit, P. Agarwal, M. Said, M. T. Sehoole, & M. Sirozi (Eds.), *The dynamics of international student circulation in a global context.* Rotterdam, Netherlands: Sense Publishers.

de Wit, H. (2008b). The internationalisation of higher education in a global context. In H. de Wit, P. Agarwal, M. Said, M. T. Sehoole, & M. Sirozi (Eds.), *The dynamics of international student circulation in a global context.* Rotterdam, Netherlands: Sense Publishers.

Finn, M. G. (2010). *Stay rates of foreign doctorate recipients from U.S. universities, 2007.* Oak Ridge, TN: Oak Ridge Institute for Science and Education.

Gray, D. (2006, September 20–22). *Global engagement in a virtual world.* Paper presented at the Assuring a Globally Engaged Science and Engineering Workforce Workshop, National Science Foundation, Washington, DC.

Green, M. F., & Koch, K. (2010, Winter). The future of international post secondary enrolments. *International Higher Education,* no. 58. Chestnut Hill, MA: Boston College Centre for International Higher Education.

Institute of International Education (IIE). (2009). *Open Doors: Report on International Educational Exchange.* New York, NY: IIE.

Institute of International Education [IIE]. (2010). *Open Doors: Report on International Educational Exchange.* New York, NY: IIE.

Institute of International Education (IIE). (2011a). *Atlas of student mobility.* New York: Author. Retrieved from http://www.atlas.iienetwork.org/

Institute of International Education [IIE]. (2011b). *Open Doors: Report on International Educational Exchange.* New York: Author.

Kelo, M., Teichler, U., & Wächter, B. (2006). Towards improved data on student mobility in Europe: Findings and concepts of the Eurodata study. *Journal of Studies in International Education, 10*(3), 194–223.

Kharas, H. (2010). *The emerging middle class in developing countries* (OECD Working Paper Number 285). Paris, France: OECD. Retrieved from http://www.oecd.org/ dataoecd/12/52/44457738.pdf

Knight, J. (2006). *Internationalization of higher education: New directions, new challenges* (2005 IAU Global Survey Report). Paris: International Association of Universities.

Knight, J. (2011). Regional education hubs: Mobility for the knowledge economy. In R. Bhandari * P. Blumenthal (Eds.), *International students and global mobility in higher education: National* *trends and new directions.* New York: Palgrave Macmillan.

Lasanowski, V. (2009). *International student mobility: Status report 2009.* London: The Observatory on Borderless Higher Education.

Lasanowski, V. (2011). Can speak will travel. In R. Bhandari & P. Blumenthal (Eds.), *International students and global mobility in higher education: National trends and new directions.* New York: Palgrave Macmillan.

Marginson, S. (2011, April). *Global context of education and the role of international education in Australia.* Paper delivered at IEAA Research Symposium, Melbourne.

McBurnie, G., & Ziguras, C. (2009). Trends and future scenarios in programme and institution mobility across borders. *Higher education to 2030:* Vol. 2. *Globalisation.* Paris: OECD.

National Science Board. (2012). *Science and engineering indicators 2012.* Arlington VA: National Science Foundation (NSB 12-01).

Organization for Economic Cooperation and Development (OECD). (2010). *Education at a glance.* Paris: Author.

Organization for Economic Cooperation and Development (OECD). (2011). *Education at a glance.* Paris: Author.

UNESCO. (2001). *Code of good practice in the provision of transnational education.* Montreal, Quebec: Author.

UNESCO Institute for Statistics. (2006). *Global education digest: Comparing education statistics across the world.* Montreal, Quebec: Author.

UNESCO Institute for Statistics. (2009). *Global education digest: Comparing education statistics across the world.* Montreal, Quebec: Author.

UNESCO Institute for Statistics. (2010). *Global education digest: Comparing education statistics across the world.* Montreal, Quebec: Author.

UNESCO Institute for Statistics. (2011). *Global education digest: Comparing education statistics across the world.* Montreal, Quebec: Author.

United Nations. (2010). *World population prospects: The 2010 revision.* Retrieved from http://esa.un.org/unpd/wpp/index.htm

United Nations. (2011). *Human development report 2011: Sustainability and equity: A better future for all.* Retrieved from http://hdr.undp.org/en/reports/global/hdr2011

Verbik, L., & Merkley, C. (2006). *The international branch campus: Models and trends.* London: The Observatory on Borderless Higher Education.

Wildavsky, B. (2010). *The great brain race: How global universities are reshaping the world.* Princeton, NJ: Princeton University Press.

World Bank. (2010). *World Bank indicators.* Retrieved August 27, 2010, from http://data.worldbank.org/indicator/NY.GNP.PCAP.PP.CD

Notes

1   Share of outbound numbers taken from de Wit (2008), quoting Cummings (1993), in The Internationalisation of Higher Education In a Global Context. In H. de Wit, P. Argawal, E. Said, S. Mohsen, T. Molatlhegi, & M. Sirozi (Eds.), *The Dynamics of International Student Circulation in a Global Context* (p. 3). Rotterdam, the Netherlands: Sense Publishers.

2   For information regarding valid student passes in public and private higher education institutions by source country in Malaysia go to the Education Malaysia website at: http://www.mohe.gov.my/educationmsia/studentpass2008.php

22

International Student Recruitment in Australia and the United States

Approaches and Attitudes

Tony Adams,[1] Mitch Leventhal and Stephen Connelly

International students do not find their way to overseas institutions by accident. International student recruitment, especially in those countries where international students pay full fees, is an increasingly professional business, undertaken by experts drawing on years of experience; it incorporates practices from other industries, such as call centers and customer relationship management, and earns substantial export revenue. With the number of globally mobile students increasing at an average of 4% per annum since the 1970s (Banks, 2010), growth trends are projecting between 4.1 million to 6.7 million students studying abroad by the year 2020 (Calderon, 2010; see Chapter 21, this volume, for an in-depth discussion on student mobility). Legislation in countries such as Singapore and Australia, and emerging industry self-regulation in the United States, endeavors to provide a degree of consumer protection to international students (see Chapter 12, this volume, for more on international student security), while commentators criticize the practice

as the most obvious manifestation of the commercialization of education. At its best, international student recruitment matches students' educational and professional needs with appropriate study programs, leading to high levels of customer satisfaction and long-lasting, positive career outcomes, while simultaneously protecting and enhancing the reputation of participating institutions.

Australia is generally recognized as the leader in international student recruitment, while the United States is perceived as either a laggard or critic. This chapter aims to track the evolution of international student recruitment practice in both countries and then to draw more general conclusions relative to global practice.

Australia's Early Engagement in Student Recruitment

Although international students have been in Australia since at least 1904 (Meadows, 2011),

Australia's initial major engagement with international students began in the 1950s, when it played a key role in the implementation of the Colombo Plan for Cooperative Economic and Social Development in Asia and the Pacific, conceived at the Commonwealth Conference on Foreign Affairs held in Colombo, Ceylon (now Sri Lanka) in January 1950 and launched on July 1, 1951, as a cooperative venture for the economic and social advancement of the peoples of South and Southeast Asia (http://www.colombo-plan.org/history.php). Through the 1950s and into the 1980s, Australia became the destination of thousands of students from throughout Asia, most of whom received their schooling on generous Australian Government scholarships (Cuthbert, Smith, & Boey, 2008).

By 1985, about 20,000 students had studied at Australian universities under the Colombo Plan, which, although the largest such scholarship scheme operating in Australia, was not the only one (Meadows, 2011). The Colombo Plan alumni of Australian universities have held significant positions of power and influence in government and industry throughout Asia, as presidents and prime ministers, senior cabinet members, university presidents, and CEOs of major airlines, banks, and other trading companies.

AUSTRALIA'S FULL-FEE PROGRAM

Although self-supported students (as distinct from scholarship students) had been present in Australia since the 1960s (Meadows, 2011), higher education reforms in the mid-1980s propelled Australia from what was primarily an aid-based mission to one that was trade-based, still backed up by a range of scholarships for developing countries (Cuthbert et al., 2008). These reforms,[2] the outcome of the reports of the Committee to Review the Australian Overseas Aid Program (Jackson Committee) and the Committee of Review of Private Overseas Student Policy (Goldring Committee), were announced in 1985 and included the encouragement of the admission of full-fee-paying international students. Trade missions reported on the export potential of education services, and enabling legislation was introduced into the Australian Parliament (Meadows, 2011). In 1986, when the first full-fee-paying overseas students were admitted to Australian universities under the new regime, few expected that large numbers of international students would pay fees to study in Australia. The reforms were aimed principally at improving the efficiency and international competitiveness of Australian education. However, realizing that many of the former countries that benefited from the Colombo Plan had become Asian Tigers in the interim, the Australian government deliberately set upon a course to develop education as a fee-based export industry, following what had already occurred in the United Kingdom. In 1986, the National Liaison Committee for Overseas Students was formed, a body set up to represent international students' rights, and in 1987, the first Australian Government Ministry of Education officers were posted overseas, to Beijing, Hong Kong, and Kuala Lumpur. At the same time, the Code of Ethical Practice in the Provision of Full-Fee Courses to Overseas Students by Australian Higher Education Institutions and a Code of Conduct for the Overseas Marketing of Australian Education Services were developed by the Australian Vice Chancellors' Committee.

By the mid-1990s, export of higher education had become an explicit strategy, with the Australian government continuing the spirit of the Colombo Plan through scholarships to developing countries, accompanied by the establishment of a strong global generic marketing capacity, creation of a regulatory framework, and establishment of high-quality market intelligence (Adams, 2009).

Institutions began to see the significant demand among international students, primarily in Asia, for education in Australia and were able to use the revenue gained from international students in a discretionary manner. Although the Australian government required components of the international tuition fee to be applied to capital works and provision of certain international student services, once costs of recruitment, teaching, and support services had been expended, any surplus could be used for whatever purpose universities desired. Most commonly, this revenue was used to subsidize critical university activities such as research. Other drivers to increase international student recruitment activity included diversification of the student population to benefit the largely stay-at-home domestic population and the competition for high-quality research students to compensate for stagnant or declining growth in the pool of domestic research candidates. As a consequence, during the 1990s, international student recruitment activity by Australian universities and other institutions (e.g., English language providers) increased significantly in scope and sophistication.

RECRUITING INTERNATIONAL STUDENTS TO AUSTRALIA

Australia's onshore international student program is an important component of the country's higher education system, with fee income providing some 21% of revenue to Australian universities (Olsen, 2010). International students at Australian universities comprise about 43% of all international students in Australia, the remaining 57% being enrolled in primary and secondary schools, English language centers, vocational education, non-award programs such as Foundation Studies (see section below), and exchange or study abroad programs (Australian Education International, 2011a). Overall, international education is Australia's third-largest export and its largest services export, contributing AUD$18.3 billion to the Australian economy in 2010 (Australian Education International, 2011b). Of that, higher education generated AUD$10.4 billion or 59% of total onshore earnings. The economic value of education exports has grown rapidly, at an average annual rate of 15% over a decade to 2006–2007 (Australian Education International, 2011b). A recent report into the economic impact of international students estimated that more than 126,000 equivalent full-time jobs across the country are directly attributable to international education (Access Economics, 2009).

The history of international recruitment in Australia has been one of innovation.

> Apple's most enduring secret is not their technology, but the culture of innovation that they have nurtured for a quarter of a century. Australia has been a great innovator in international student recruitment in the past and to remain as a significant destination for international students, must remain an innovator, as well as learning from the new innovations of others (Adams, 2010).

Whether or not Australian institutions developed the innovations that follow or adapted and improved them is not important. What is important is that Australia made them their own. So what were these innovations?

The International Office

International Offices (IOs) in Australia universities were expressly established to recruit international students, and their structures reflect this requirement. This stands in stark contrast to their counterparts in the United States, which emerged to support traditional academic exchange programs. The Australian Universities International Directors Forum benchmarking study (Olsen, 2007), conducted annually since 2002, provides a snapshot of Australian university IO responsibilities, costs, reporting lines, and other measures of performance for the universities that participate in the study. In 2010, 37 of 39 Australian universities participated (Olsen, 2010).

These annual benchmarking reports demonstrate the centralization of many student recruitment-related functions, and the relative size of Australian IOs compared with their U.S. counterparts. While the reports do show the primacy of marketing and recruitment activity for IOs, they also demonstrate the comprehensive range of internationalization activities that IOs cover, including overseeing devolved admissions functions, international student advising and support, and outbound mobility.

The Use of Agents

Although their use is a controversial practice in the United States, student recruitment agents are a critical part of the marketing and recruiting strategy of Australian institutions (Olsen, 2007). Some 50% to 60% of commencing international students in higher education are recruited via agents. The following activities are carried out in relation to agents on a routine basis:

- Providing printed materials
- Including a directory of agents by country on university websites
- Visiting the agent to ensure their premises are adequate, materials provided are available to prospective students and up to date, and locally produced materials represent the university accurately

- Training the agent and staff on academic programs, student visa issues, and other national requirements, and university processes
- Working with agents to arrange interviews for prospective students
- Participating in agent-organized student recruitment fairs and road shows
- Working with agents to ensure they have sighted and verified as authentic original student academic and English-language proficiency documentation
- Developing a student recruitment plan
- Providing selected agents with a marketing budget for agreed activities

The responsibilities of agents are part of a contractual agreement between the university and the agent, the management of which is generally the responsibility of IOs. The agreement includes clauses intended to protect the university from inappropriate behavior by agents, and it references legal requirements on universities and their agents to act in the best interests of prospective students.

Agents generally operate on a commission basis, with payments representing a proportion of the tuition fees paid to education institutions. Commissions in higher education are paid based on a percentage of first year's tuition fee, normally 10% to 15%. This means that on average, measured across a student's full program duration, universities spend about 4.1% of their gross international student tuition-fee revenue on agent commissions (Olsen, 2010). Properly managed, student recruitment agents significantly enhance the reach of education institutions in Australia seeking to recruit international students, and they are perceived as a powerful means of increasing international student enrollments.

IDP Education is Australia's major agent, providing services to all Australian education providers and recruiting about 13% of commencing international students at Australian universities annually (Olsen, 2010) via its worldwide network of 65 offices. IDP was historically fully owned directly by Australia's universities as a not-for-profit company. It is now a for-profit enterprise owned 50% by universities and 50% by SEEK Limited, a publicly listed company that operates online employment classifieds and education and training. IDP recruits for several hundred Australian institutions across higher education,

vocational education, English language, and schools sectors. It has also recently started recruiting activities for institutions in other countries, including the United States (IDP, 2010), a decision that has been controversial among Australian institutions, which have been accustomed to its exclusive attention.

Study Pathways

Study pathways are a major feature of international education recruitment in Australia and are now developing in the United Kingdom, Canada, and the United States. Pathways for international students were initially developed as a bridge between students' preuniversity education and their desired university programs, in cases where a national high school certificate from certain countries did not guarantee direct entry into Australian undergraduate programs. These programs, known as Foundation Studies, quickly developed as an alternative to the final year of high school for international students primarily from Asian countries, with in-built guaranteed entry to first year of university programs, usually linked to academic performance. Foundation Studies programs were also coupled with higher education diplomas, equivalent to the first year of an Australian university degree program and providing entry points into the second year of related university degrees. These so-called pathway programs enabled universities to access cohorts of students who did not qualify for direct entry into undergraduate studies but who could be nurtured in a more supportive environment than first year at an Australian university, in smaller classes, mainly with other international students, allowing them to improve their grades and their language proficiency before entering undergraduate programs. Navitas is the best known example of innovation and success in this aspect of international education, taking its model originally developed in Australia to the world (see http://www.navitas.com/).

Australian pathway programs are either run by the universities themselves within existing academic units, or they establish a separate college to offer the programs (see Monash College and Swinburne College, both in Australia), or they are outsourced to a private provider such as Navitas, which often sets up operations on the university campus or in close proximity. The private pathway provider will teach to the university curriculum, and the student will have guaranteed entry (by performance criteria) into first or second year of the university on satisfactory completion of the program. As part of the arrangement, the university controls assessment and maintains quality assurance over teaching. The private provider often employs retired academics or university academic staff on a casual basis to teach the diploma programs.

An analysis of pathway data (Australian Education International, 2006) shows that university-operated, university-linked programs, along with a variety of private providers operating their own diplomas without direct university involvement, are responsible for 50% to 60% of all international undergraduates entering Australian universities.

Articulation Arrangements

Credit for previous studies forms an important part of undergraduate international student recruitment for Australian universities (Olsen, 2007). Traditionally, this started with universities awarding credit to graduates of the state polytechnic system in Singapore and via twinning[3] or similar arrangements in Singapore, Malaysia, and Hong Kong. In a twinning arrangement, the student undertakes perhaps the first 2 years of the university's program through a private provider, say in Malaysia. The provider will, with the agreement and under the direction of the Australian university, use that university's curriculum, and the university will provide guaranteed entry, in this case into the third (and final) year of the degree in Australia.

Australian universities often have numerous credit arrangements with providers within Australia and overseas, in some cases numbering in the hundreds. Some universities have a Credit for Previous Study Assessor as an automated recruitment tool on the international website (see, for example, http://www-public.jcu.edu.au/study/apply/JCUPRD1_061219), highlighting the importance for some universities of articulation arrangements as part of their recruitment strategy. The obvious dilemma for Australian universities is maintaining oversight of these arrangements and the performance of articulating students, once they enter their degree programs, to ensure the arrangements give students the best chance of success as they

move from the preliminary program into the degree program.

Institutional Marketing and Recruiting Good Practice

Australian universities have over time developed strong elements of good practice in international marketing and student recruitment:

- A clear and powerful marketing message, linked to the university's domestic market position and brand strength
- Web marketing and social media, attendance at overseas student recruitment fairs, agent seminars, and other activities that generate prospective student enquiries and applications
- A state of the art website with contemporary web tools to capture inquiries and channel these toward application and admission
- Prospect management tools on the Web that maximize the opportunity for enrollment
- High-quality and concise print materials to back up the Web presence
- A network of agents in target countries that are serviced with regular visits and event participation in those countries
- Clear academic and English admission levels relevant to a broad range of home countries for students traveling for undergraduate education
- Use of an Australian generic marketing infrastructure via the Australian Government internationally, including education counsellors in overseas missions
- A scholarship strategy to provide scholarships to outstanding students as a marketing tool and collaboration with overseas scholarship authorities, foundations, and private providers
- Promotion of on-arrival, orientation, and student welfare services
- Engagement with the local Australian community to welcome and support international students
- A plan that gives international marketing staff control, or at least great influence, over marketing materials, both web and print, within agreed guidelines

Prospect or Inquiry Management

The classic image of the IO unprepared for managing student inquiries at volume is the box sitting in the corner full of printed e-mail inquiries awaiting response. State of the art inquiry management is essential in these days of immediate real-time inquiry and response for all manner of services. International education is no different: Students expect prompt and accurate responses to their inquiries. Customer relationship management (CRM) or prospect management systems have the potential to provide high standards of service to prospective students, as well as significant amounts of market intelligence and other services both to the prospect and the institution. These CRM services include:

- Frequently asked question (FAQ) databases that prospects can browse
- Brochure-builder technology to deliver specified or requested information direct to an inquirer's desktop
- Access to staff to answer more difficult questions
- Inquiry statistics by country, by level of study, and by discipline, as well as comparative current trends by week, month, and year to previous inquiry periods
- Pipeline time from inquiry to enrollment by country
- Ability to survey inquiries that didn't proceed to application and enrollment as to the reasons
- Based on inquiries, the ability to predict future enrollments by country
- The addition of prospects to mailing lists for e-newspapers
- SMS and e-mail marketing campaigns, including the ability to communicate details about marketing events in a specific country to recent prospects in that country
- Follow-up on offers

Sixteen Australian universities outsource inquiry management to Hobsons Asia Pacific, which uses a system originally developed by the Good Guides Group, an Australian company (Adams, 2009). In this system, all inquiries generated via e-mail, Web forms, and telephone are diverted from the university to a central service center in Melbourne, Australia. Account managers are employed to manage the prospect from initial inquiry through to the application stage for client institutions. Inquiries are handled based on protocols agreed by client institutions

and cannot be diverted to other client institutions. A side benefit of this system has been the pooling of information from the 16 Australian universities for market intelligence purposes, from which all client institutions benefit.

International Student Admissions

Australian universities follow a number of basic normative principles in their attempt to achieve best practice in the admission of international students. Primarily, it needs to be recognized that *the admissions function is an integral part of the recruitment function.* The best marketing and recruitment practices will be undone by slow and unresponsive admissions practices. Basic principles include:

- Admission criteria need to be provided for as many countries as possible.
- The criteria should be clear and as objective as possible.
- Subject to published quota restrictions, a student who meets the criteria should have an expectation of admission.
- Any written requirements such as essays need to recognize that prospective students from non-English speaking backgrounds may not yet have reached the English-language proficiency requirements.
- Conditional offers should be made where prospective students have not yet reached the admission requirement (for example, English); when the conditions are met, the offer becomes absolute or unconditional.
- Interviews should be done only in rare circumstances, need to be at the reasonable convenience of the prospective students, and must recognize the significant cultural differences that exist as well as that English requirements may not yet have been met.
- Offers should be made on a rolling basis, with target turnaround times (e.g., maximum 5 working days to generate offers from receipt of a complete application).
- Trusted agents should be authorized to verify that documents are legitimate and correct.
- All major international English proficiency tests should be accepted (e.g., IELTS, TOEFL, Cambridge, Pearson).
- Alternate means of satisfying English language criteria must be in place, such as

recognizing students who have studied at least 2 years in the medium of English or who have passed at an appropriate level the high school English course from certain countries, without further tests required for entry.

- Admissions and recruiting staff need to work closely together, and both will normally be within the international office and often in the same organizational unit.
- Admissions and recruiting staff will most frequently be organized in regional teams to ensure they understand specific education systems and can build knowledge and expertise in a specified number of countries, develop solid working relationships with agents, and provide better service to students, their families, and internal stakeholders such as academic units.

Compliance, Standards, and Service Levels: the Education Services for Overseas Students (ESOS) Act and the National Code[4]

The ESOS Act 2000 (Australian Government, 2010a) was introduced to regulate the education and training export industry. The act and complementary legislation provide a consumer protection framework for international students studying in Australia under a student visa and a quality assurance mechanism for ensuring the standards of education provided to international students.

Violations of the ESOS Act can include criminal penalties, including prison and fines. The ESOS legislative framework includes the following.

Commonwealth Register of Institutions and Courses for Overseas Students (CRICOS). CRICOS is a database of more than 1,200 Australian education institutions (Australian Government, 2010b). All institutions that recruit, enroll, or teach international students on a student visa must be registered on CRICOS, as must each program taught to international students.

Provider Registration and International Students Management System (PRISMS). All CRICOS-approved providers and their programs are listed on PRISMS, as is each student studying in Australia on a student visa. The system interfaces with the Department of Immigration and Citizenship (DIAC) visa data (Australian Government, 2009c). Through PRISMS, providers notify DIAC of each student's acceptance into a program, prior to the student applying for a student visa. This information generates an electronic Confirmation of Enrolment as evidence of admission to a registered, full-time program (international students in Australia must study on a full-time basis). The confirmation enables a prospective student to apply for a student visa and is proof of acceptance into a CRICOS-registered institution and program. Education providers must use PRISMS to notify DIAC of students who may have breached the terms of their student visa—for example, when the student has not been attending classes or falls below minimum pass rates (see https://prisms.deewr.gov.au). The SEVIS system in the United States mirrors a number of these developments (see http://www.ice.gov/sevis/), but lacks the sophistication of PRISMS.

The ESOS Tuition Assurance Fund. The ESOS Tuition Assurance Fund (Australian Government, 2009a) was established to protect the interests of current and intending overseas students of registered providers. It does this by ensuring that students are provided with suitable alternative programs or have their program monies refunded if, for example, the provider goes into liquidation and closes. Private providers are required to make a contribution to the fund as a proportion of their international student income.

Health Insurance. Health insurance for students under a student visa, known as Overseas Student Health Cover, is mandated by the commonwealth government and operated by a small number of licensed health insurance companies. The scheme ensures that international students can gain access to general medical practitioners and the public hospital system, with the cost to be covered by the insurer (Australian Education International, 2010b). Commencing international students in Australia must take out insurance for the duration of their student visa.

The National Code that forms a part of the ESOS Act is enforceable with both operating and criminal sanctions. It includes 15 standards of practice (Australian Government, 2009a) listed in Table 22.1.

Marketing Information and Practices

Student Engagement Before Enrollment

Formalization of Enrollment

Education Agents

Younger Overseas Students

Student Support Services

Transfer Between Registered Providers

Complaints and Appeals

Completion Within Expected Duration

Monitoring Course Progress

Monitoring Attendance

Course Credit

Deferment, Suspension, or Cancellation of Study During Enrollment

Staff Capability, Educational Resources, and Premises

Changes to Registered Providers' Ownership or Management

Table 22.1   Standards of Practice

THE RESPONSE TO EDUCATION SERVICES FOR OVERSEAS STUDENTS

Education institutions in Australia take ESOS responsibilities very seriously. Because the National Code specifies compliance issues in service delivery as well as educational program delivery, institutional compliance is the responsibility of staff right across universities. Although the IO will often manage and coordinate compliance, it cannot take on the compliance responsibility for academic departments in terms of program delivery. Typical university responses to their ESOS compliance obligations will be:

- An officer within the IO with responsibility to coordinate institution-wide ESOS compliance
- A committee with broad university membership to discuss and manage ESOS compliance issues, including coordination of internal and external audits
- Requirements that all publications (print and electronic) that are developed for domestic or international recruiting are checked for ESOS compliance

- Formal procedures for the appointment and monitoring of agents
- Formal procedures for the registration of new programs under CRICOS
- Formal procedures for monitoring student performance and reporting on PRISMS
- Published fee levels and fee refund policies, as well as complaint and grievance procedures
- Written policies covering critical incidents
- Regular audits of compliance status (some universities do this as part of ISO quality assurance processes).

Benchmarking

As previously indicated, the Australian Universities International Directors Forum is a grouping of international directors of Australia's universities. It has been extremely successful since 2002 in carrying out benchmarking into various aspects of the international operations of universities, including the costs and major operational parameters of international offices and more recently student mobility. Parameters benchmarked include costs of the operation of the international office, agent costs, recruitment costs by major market, application to enrollment conversion figures, efficiency and volume of recruitment channels, and staffing ratios for recruitment, admissions, and student services staff.

Market Research

Australia is richly served by up-to-date market intelligence. Australian university and nonuniversity providers have been fortunate that a benefit of the PRISMS system is the collection and distribution of timely market data by Australian Education International. Overview data are available in the public domain (https://aei.gov.au/research/International-Student-Data/Pages/default.aspx) and are updated monthly, approximately 2 months in arrears. Complete data for planning are available in the same timeframe electronically by subscription. Other sources of data include analysis and conversion of prospective students from the Hobsons Inquiry Management Service system for its 16 client institutions, IDP benchmarking of semester-by-semester enrollment for universities,[5] and monthly surveys undertaken by English Australia, the peak English-language teaching body. In 2011, the Department of Immigration and Citizenship has introduced a regular series of three monthly reports on student visa application and grant trends, providing invaluable information about likely prospective enrollments.

Visa Processing

Australia has been a leader in establishing a transparent framework for student visa processing. This includes international student source countries ranked via five Assessment Levels (AL) representing levels of risk associated with student visa overstay (see http://www.immi.gov.au/students/student-visa-assessment-levels.htm). AL 1 represents countries whose students have the least level of risk of overstay and AL 5 the highest level of risk (Australian Government, 2010c). Linked to this has been the migration skills on demand list (MODL), which has encouraged international students with specific Australian qualifications to seek permanent residence. The MODL was a list of skills and qualifications in demand for applications for permanent residence in Australia.

In recent years, Australia's leadership in the area of student visa programs and skilled migration has been seriously eroded. Inappropriate migration settings led to exponential growth over a number of years in international student enrollments in a range of vocational education programs, causing considerable stress in the oversight of compliance by regulatory authorities and allowing unethical practices by some student recruitment agents and some private providers to go unchecked. Subsequent attacks in a number of cities on Indian students (Adams, 2010) led to a crackdown on the international student visa program; this led to the collapse of the Indian student market for Australian institutions. The student visa application process was no longer transparent, financial requirements to qualify for a student visa were increased, and the link between education and migration became confused and confusing. The parallel rise of the Australian dollar in the wake of the global financial crisis has led to a significant short-term correction in international student recruitment for Australia. Current admissions data show that higher education commencements grew by just 2.6% in 2010, but those for India collapsed by nearly 47% (Australian Education International, 2010a). The pain has continued in 2011. At the time of writing, a student visa review, conducted by former politician Michael Knight, has been completed, with the recommendations accepted by the Australian Government[6]. The framework for international student visas had been seriously compromised by a combination of poor regulation of international education in Australia by state and federal authorities, inconsistent student visa program management, and short-sighted immigration policy development, the latter two in response to unethical practices by some agents and providers, who flourished while underresourced and uncoordinated regulatory authorities were unable to fulfill their oversight responsibilities. It is hoped the outcomes of the review will restore integrity and transparency to the student visa program, reassert Australia's competitiveness with other destination countries in student visa application processing, and support an appropriate link between education and migration in Australia.

PROFESSIONALIZING INTERNATIONAL EDUCATION AND INTERNATIONAL STUDENT RECRUITMENT

Since the mid-1980s, Australian university staff involved in international student recruitment have sought to professionalize their activity. Murray (2011) refers to the four key elements of early professional development:

1. Industry briefings, conferences, and workshops

2. Industry research

3. Targeted publications on current themes and issues

4. Specialist professional groupings

The four elements have remained constants over the years as international education in Australia has matured.

In 1987, IDP conducted the first workshop, *Overseas Students: New Approaches and Practices*, in Canberra. That initial workshop has today become the Australian International Education Conference (AIEC), which celebrated its 25th anniversary in October 2011 in Adelaide. The conference attracts more than 1,300 delegates annually, the third-largest international education conference in the world, and is jointly organized by IDP and the International Education Association Australia. While international student recruitment practice is an important part of the conference, its program canvasses a broad internationalization agenda.

Australian international education practitioners and researchers have long contributed to commentary and research in the field of internationalization, via the AIEC, conferences conducted by international education associations around the world, and publications such as the *Journal of Studies in International Education*. The IDP Database on International Education is managed by the Australian Council for Educational Research and contains details of more than 8,000 publications on various aspects of international education.

In international education, professional associations and groupings have existed in Australia for many years. Peak bodies representing different industry segments, such as the International Education Association Australia (see www.ieaa. org.au), work cooperatively for the betterment of international education, servicing their memberships with professional development opportunities and jointly lobbying government on policy issues. Groups such as the Australian Universities International Directors Forum have a specific focus on international office matters, reflecting the role of that particular group.

The maturity and level of sophistication of international student recruitment activity in Australia is evident in the above examples of engagement with policy, professional development, research, and practice. This in part reflects the fact that the export paradigm has been present in Australia since the 1980s, as it has been in the United Kingdom. However, only in the very recent past has an explicit export-oriented stance started to take hold in the United States. The debate about international student recruitment in the United States reflects its unique history as a magnet for international students, quite distinct from Australia's, although there are parallels. This next section addresses attitudes toward and approaches to international student recruitment in the United States.

INTERNATIONAL STUDENT RECRUITMENT IN THE UNITED STATES

Recruitment in the United States has progressed through three distinct phases. The first phase lasted from shortly after the end of the Second World War until about the mid-1960s to early 1970s. The second phase continued until about 2008. The most recent phase has just started and will be the most closely addressed in the following pages.

Phase 1: Postwar Dominance (1948 to mid-1960s)

In the immediate aftermath of the Second World War, U.S. attention was focused on acquiring German researchers and other European scholars, who would advance America's strategic position in the world, particularly vis-á-vis the Soviet Union (see also Chapter 3, this volume). The Fulbright Program, established in 1948, was designed to promote peace and understanding through international educational exchange and to counterbalance Soviet efforts to make political inroads in the developing world. Fulbright represented the first formal U.S. commitment to increasing cross-border student mobility. It is probably not coincidental that the National Association of Foreign Student Advisers (NAFSA) was also founded in 1948, as it was obvious to many that the number of international students in the United States was poised to grow dramatically.[7]

With the Mutual Educational and Cultural Exchange Act of 1961, the Bureau of Educational and Cultural Affairs (ECA) was created. This bureau, which has variously moved between the State Department and the U.S. Information Agency, was created to foster mutual understanding between the people of the United States and those of other countries through promotion of educational and cultural exchange.

The emphasis during this period was on traditional academic exchange, generally under the sponsorship of Fulbright or a similar program. Beyond Fulbright, however, recruitment of students was not really organized. Rather, it occurred based on personal, one-on-one relationships. In the decade from 1948–1949 to 1958–1959, international student enrollment grew from 25,464 to 47,245. Recruitment practice during the first phase can best be described as passive, opportunistic, and individualistic.

Phase 2: Increasing Professionalization (mid-1960s to late-2000s)

By the mid-1960s, international student numbers began to grow dramatically. In

1966–1967, for example, the international student population grew 21.2% over the previous year and reached 100,262. During the next decade, student numbers would more than double to 203,068. Between 1966–1967 and 1978–1979, growth was in double digits for 8 of the 13 years. During the 4 years from 1975–1976 to 1978–1979, growth ranged from 12.1% to 16% each year. Much of this growth resulted from large cohorts of fully funded students coming to the United States from oil-rich countries, such as Iran, Kuwait, Nigeria, and Saudi Arabia.

This dramatic growth led to a much higher profile for NAFSA and for other organizations that emerged to serve international students and assist with their mobility. By the mid 1970s and 1980s, some universities began to focus more explicitly on international student recruitment. This probably resulted from two factors: First, large numbers of fee-paying international students had awakened an awareness on some campuses of the revenue potential of international students. Second, the Iranian Revolution, which led to a "bust" in Iranian student mobility virtually overnight, as well as other "busts" tied to the vagaries of oil economies, led campuses to realize that a more proactive approach was warranted. During this period, the federal government's EducationUSA advising centers emerged to promote U.S. higher education around the world by offering accurate, comprehensive, objective, and timely information about educational institutions in the United States and guidance to qualified individuals on how best to access those opportunities.[8]

Also during this period, recognition of the importance of education as a traded service was advanced within government. Section 135 of the Trade Act of 1974 established the private sector advisory structure to advise the Office of the U.S. Trade Representative and key Cabinet agencies on trade policy, trade negotiations, and implementation. At that time, the General Agreement on Tariffs and Trade (GATT) covered trade only in goods. However, during the Uruguay Round of Trade Negotiations, which was launched in 1986, it was agreed that services would be on the negotiating table, and thus the World Trade Organization (WTO) was created in 1995 to supersede the GATT. In that year, an Industry Technical Advisory Committee for trade in education services was formed. Of particular issue to advisors are barriers to educational trade; these barriers are understood to be increasingly important, given the acknowledgment that educational services account for billions of dollars in trade.[9]

Also emerging during this period were significant private organizations, such as Linden Educational Services (http://www.lindentours.com), which brought a more focused and professional approach to recruitment. Related services provided by such companies and associations revolved around small group visits to various cities and countries around centerpiece fairs where schools could present their programs directly to students overseas. For a large number of colleges and universities, educational tours run by private companies represented their first organized foray into the world of international recruitment. In a sense, this approach was closely patterned on typical industrial trade shows: fly into a venue, distribute information, and fly home to await orders.

While this approach resulted in some significant flows of international students to specific institutions, it was not accompanied by any substantial modification of U.S. admissions practice on the institution side and rarely was tied to any ongoing service level at the point of origin of the international student. NAFSA's work was focused primarily on the international student intake side; marketing and recruitment was confined to tours and fairs. To generalize, then, U.S. recruitment during this period can be characterized as featuring (a) a heavy reliance on road shows and recruiting fairs, (b) minimal use of local recruiting teams, (c) long distance counseling, and (d) a lack of a specialized international recruiting unit.

This rather undifferentiated approach did not matter so much, however, as real sustained growth continued unabated, and with little effort, until the early 2000s. The general view was "We built it, and they are coming." Americans looked at the aggressive marketing tactics of the Australians, and in particular their use of agents, with disdain. With the exception of a few intrepid institutions and some proprietary schools, most U.S. colleges and universities considered agencies to be unethical and an abhorrent to their professional organizations, and most even believed the practice to be illegal.[10]

And then the shock of 9/11 resulted in the first multiyear declines in international student numbers of the postwar era.

Phase 3: Moving Forward (2008 onward)

During the second phase of U.S. development, while international student numbers in the United States were growing with relatively little effort, the Australians were aggressively developing a new approach to recruiting, which was heavily dependent on the utilization of professional educational advising companies, otherwise known as education agents.

In the United States, views regarding agents began to change slightly in the years following 9/11, when it became apparent that the recovery was not keeping pace with the growth in recruitment being experienced by Australia and the United Kingdom. At a point, it became obvious that their growth was driven by something other than expedited visa processing, that there was a substantive difference in approach that was allowing them to capture U.S. market share. In Box 22.1, a personal view on the use of agents and its debate in the United States is provided.

As illustrated in Box 22.1, the use of agents for international student recruitment remains

BOX 22.1 The Use of Agents in the United States

The decisive factor that pushed institutions over the edge in the use of agents was the 2008 financial collapse, by which time financial benefit of a more aggressive recruitment strategy was undeniable. In January 2006, the University of Cincinnati became the first public research university to openly embrace the use of agents. During that time, the coauthor of this paper, who was serving as vice provost for international affairs, publicly advocated adopting a set of practices derived from Australian experience. During the subsequent 2 years, a significant number of both public and private colleges and universities in Ohio and beyond began to use agents.

By early 2008, it became evident that a system of professionalization was required, both to assure institutions of agency quality, as well as to act as a locus for the development of best practices among U.S. institutions themselves (Leventhal, 2008). This awareness resulted in a group of U.S. universities creating the American International Recruitment Council (AIRC), which is registered with the U.S. Department of Justice and the Federal Trade Commission as a standard development organization (AIRC, 2010; McMurtrie, 2008). The AIRC developed a set of standards based on standards and practices that had been developed in Australia, as well as among many agency associations around the world (AIRC, 2010). The standards were then tied to an agency certification process, closely modeled on U.S. higher education accreditation.

By mid 2011, more than 140 accredited postsecondary institutions had become members of AIRC, and more than 40 agencies had attained certification, collectively having several hundred branches in dozens of countries. AIRC's institutional membership represents only a small fraction of U.S. institutions using agents, and its members represent the mainstream of U.S. higher education, including leading state universities, private elite universities, and community colleges. Nonetheless, the use of agents, and particularly the payment of recruitment commissions, continues to be highly controversial in the United States. The most consistent and vociferous opposition comes from those opposed to the payment of success-based commissions, which are believed by some to be a corrupting influence on agent's behavior, one that can result in steering students not to the best institutional fit, but to the highest bidder. The U.S. State Department's Bureau of Educational and Cultural Affairs (ECA) has been particularly vocal in this regard. ECA manages the EducationUSA advising network and has taken an aggressive stance against agents—in stark contrast to its Australian and British counterparts, Australian Education International and the British Council, which view agents as a marketing force multiplier. The State Department's 2009 Policy Guidance for EducationUSA Centers on Commercial Recruitment Agents (U.S. Department of State, 2009) represents a generalized position against the credibility of all international recruitment agencies and the institutions that rely on them. But the U.S. higher education export industry is moving ahead of the U.S. State Department. Realizing that agency recruitment has entered the mainstream, the National Association of College Admission Counseling, the organization that largely controls access to domestic college recruiting fairs across the United States, recently stepped back from a proposed prohibition on member institutions paying commissions, opting instead for a conciliatory approach focused on further study and consultation with all constituencies.

One large university system, the State University of New York—with 64 colleges and universities and nearly one half million students—has announced an aggressive agency recruitment strategy, although the action is debated even within the system. It has pledged that a substantial percentage of incoming student revenue will be reinvested in outbound study abroad scholarships, faculty internationalization grants, and other priorities. SUNY's progress is being closely watched, and if its "virtuous circle" succeeds, the likelihood of imitators is a certainty.

The development of the AIRC's agency certification system is being closely watched by both institutions and authorities in Australia, the United Kingdom, Canada, and elsewhere. While the jury is out on its effectiveness, it represents a significant innovation, one that may finally provide a degree of agency quality assurance and enforceability, which heretofore eluded other jurisdictions.

Note: This box was prepared by chapter author Mitch Leventhal.

---

controversial in the United States. For those who are willing to adopt global recruitment models, there is still a lag in internal expertise relative to agency-based recruitment. Unlike their Australian and British counterparts, where recruitment is firmly lodged in the IO and where revenue generated provides the resources to engage in other non-revenue generating international activity, in the United States, there is no agreed locus for international recruitment. In some universities, the function rests with the admissions office, in others, with the international office; sometimes it resides under the authority of the provost, other times with the vice president for student services. Graduate programs often do not communicate with undergraduate recruiters, or even with other graduate programs or the graduate school itself. Therefore, at most U.S. universities, there is little consensus about how international recruitment fits with overall internationalization

objectives or how it should be strategically organized and managed.

Foundation Programs, Pathways, Dual Degree Programs

These various modalities, already well established in Australia, are rapidly taking hold in the United States. Dual degree (or twinning) programs seem to be the easiest for U.S. institutions to adopt, largely because they are based on institution-to-institution relations, without the involvement of intermediaries (see Chapter 19, this volume, for in-depth discussion on dual degree programs). The concepts of Foundation Programs and Pathways, however, are not yet widely understood, nor is the concept of *conditional admission* used by many institutions. Companies such as Navitas, StudyGroup and INTO—all Australian and

British concerns—have entered the U.S. market and are actively promoting the diffusion of these models into a conservative recruiting environment, with gradual success. What is striking is that so few U.S.-based companies have as of yet emerged as major players in the global recruitment services space.

A New Virtuous Circle Emerging

A few institutions are now starting to resolve the ambiguity relative to the locus of organization and control of international recruiting activities. While presidents and provosts are now touting internationalization goals, such as increasing study abroad numbers, internationalizing the curriculum, fostering more international faculty research, and so on, the rhetoric has not been backstopped by financial resources to reach those goals. Instead, budgets have been cut across the board. A new recognition is emerging, however, that international students can help internationalize the campus experience, while also providing a source of "found money" that is not dependent on state budgets, grants, or philanthropy. Some institutions are now experimenting with reserving a small percentage of incoming international student revenue specifically to underwrite the cost of the other imperatives that have gotten short shrift. Funding models vary, but even 5% from the first year's tuition of international students can provide a substantial new pool of funds that can be redistributed into the international mission. This appears to be the newest trend, and it may be a transformative benefit of the newest phase of U.S. international recruitment (Redden 2011). For an overview of the United Kingdom's recruitment evolution, see Box 22.2.

BOX 22.2 International Student Recruitment: A UK Perspective

Andy Nicol

Director of Business Development, Hobsons Asia Pacific (Malaysia)

Aggressive international student recruitment by UK universities has become a fact of life. UK universities compete against each other—and with other emerging overseas student destinations—for international student numbers that make a significant contribution both to the universities themselves and their wider economies. In 2007, the British Council estimated the value of education and training exports to the UK economy at nearly £28 billion, more than the automotive or financial services industries. Little surprise, therefore, that professional recruitment and marketing operations have emerged in UK universities to recruit, admit, support, and retain international students (Lenton, 2007).

Overseas students represent an attractive income stream to UK universities for a number of reasons; first, they pay a premium fee for degree programs, which far outweighs the funding received from government for home and European Union students; second, their numbers are unregulated by the funding councils (which fund the UK's overwhelmingly state universities); and third, universities are free to spend the incomes generated as they wish without intervention from government. It is for these reasons primarily that UK universities have come over time to depend on a strong flow of international students, whether taught in the United Kingdom or abroad, and have increased efforts to capture greater numbers of them. Moreover, successive changes in government policy have resulted in substantially lower amounts of domestic student funding. In the United Kingdom, where almost all universities are funded by the state, government policy simultaneously sought to increase participation in higher education while eroding per capita student funding. Some commentators estimated a decrease in state funding of 38% between 1989 and 2002, while student numbers during the same period increased 94% (Brown, 2003). It is no longer marginal activity for UK universities to recruit international students; rather, it is central to their strategies and mission, critical in terms of financial income. Without the additional funding streams provided by international students, it would be difficult to see how they could maintain investment in staff, facilities, and the wider student experience. This situation is compounded by recent global events, and more so in the United Kingdom, where the government recently announced funding cuts to universities for the first time in 10 years due in large part to the UK's deficit (BBC, 2010). One could speculate that UK universities will now work even harder to protect and maintain market share of international student numbers.

So although the last 15 or so years have seen increased international activity by higher education institutions in the United Kingdom, it would be wrong to view this as a recent phenomena. There were (and still remain) particularly strong links with the Commonwealth countries (former colonies), and a steady flow of international students—particularly from countries such as Hong Kong, Malaysia, and Singapore—came to the United Kingdom for their higher education. However, it is important to note that both push and pull factors were important, in no small part due to generous fee-subsidy packages provided by the UK government until the late 1970s. Relatively low fees combined with the reputation for quality and a lack of opportunity for higher education at home guaranteed significant numbers of international students on UK campuses.

Margaret Thatcher moved quickly to withdraw these funding measures when she came to power in 1979 because the government viewed the international fees subsidy as an unnecessary burden on the taxpayer. This measure had a negative impact on student numbers, which in due course began to decline significantly. As a result of this policy, and the subsequent decline in numbers, the recruitment of international students became an issue both for government and higher education institutions. In response to the decline, the government announced the 1984 Pym Package—a precursor to Tony Blair's Prime Minister's Initiative—which aimed to promote British education internationally and released funds for both scholarships and the generic promotion of UK education opportunities overseas by the British Council. In tandem with this government activity, many UK universities, attached central resources to international recruitment by way of establishing small central international offices, and this can be viewed as the beginning of a more focused approach to international marketing, recruitment, and promotion.

Australia and the Way Forward

Even in Australia, a recognized leader in international student recruitment, the practice can be controversial. It can mean that the discourse around international education focuses on the commercial aspects and as such can be a significant deterrent to faculty engagement. The fact is that in Australia, the discretionary revenue from international students onshore subsidizes infrastructure development, student support services, and research activity, benefitting staff and domestic students, but this message can be hard to convey amid the noise of the commercialization

issue. Added to this, Australia has had a clear message from a series of countries that the practice of simply recruiting fee-paying students is unsustainable in the absence of broader internationalization engagement activity. India will provide an interesting case study in coming years: a profitable market for Australian institutions, which has recently collapsed and is now facing a revised student visa and risk assessment regime that should enable universities to revive market fortunes. Yet if Australian universities do not re-engage with India in a more holistic manner, establishing research linkages, paying attention to the student experience in Australia, actively promoting mobility of Australian students to India, and seriously engaging with Indian partner institutions to establish joint programs—as is the case for Australia's engagement with other countries—then the anticipated regeneration of India as a source country for international students will not eventuate. This needs to be the new paradigm for Australia's international student recruitment effort: holistic and strategic engagement on a broad scale. Individual institutions have known this for some time, but the system needs to do more than talk the talk. This will necessitate true collaboration within universities, for example, between international and research offices, in external facing international engagement activity, and across the university system.

CONCLUSION

This chapter has highlighted the evolution of international student recruitment in Australia, as well as outlined the debate in the United States on this topic. What can international education leaders learn from Australia's experience in international student recruitment? First, understanding how policies in other countries address international education issues can provide impetus and insight into how to develop further policies, programs, and innovations. Second, a strategic issue like international student recruitment evolves over time as a process of continued refinement, one which is influenced by many outside factors that propel the field forward, as well as hinder its growth and development at times. Third, controversial issues such as international student recruitment require leaders to engage in informed debates that are based on a more nuanced and contextual understanding of the issues involved. Given the trend of increasing international student mobility in this century, leaders will need to remain engaged with all stakeholders in developing innovative approaches for staying on the cutting edge of international student recruitment and beyond.

REFERENCES

Access Economics. (2009). *The Australian education sector and the economic contribution of international students.* Melbourne: ACPET.

Adams, T. (2009, September). EAIE. Retrieved August 2, 2010, from Tony Adams and

Associates: http://tony-adams.org/files/ Marketing_for_Employability_1_final_1_.pdf

Adams, T. (2010, April 16). Inaugural Dr Martand Joshi Memorial Lecture. Retrieved August 2, 2010, from Central Queensland University: http://uninews.cqu.edu.au/UniNews/viewStory .do?story=6813

American International Recruitment Council (AIRC). (2010). http://www.airc-education.org/

Australian Education International. (2006). *Study pathways of international students in Australia, 2002 to 2005.* Canberra: Australian Government.

Australian Education International. (2010a). *Monthly summary of international student enrolment data1—Australia: YTD August 2010.* Canberra: Australian Education International.

Australian Education International. (2010b). *Overseas student health cover.* Retrieved August 2, 2010, from Study in Australia: http:// studyinaustralia.gov.au/Sia/en/StudyCosts/ OSHC.htm

Australian Education International. (2011a). Monthly *Summary of International Student Enrolment Data—Australia: YTD June 2011.* Canberra: Australian Education International.

Australian Education International. (2011b, May). *Research snapshot: Export income to Australia from education services in 2010.* Canberra: Australian Education International.

Australian Government. (2009a). *Australian Education International.* Retrieved August 2, 2010, from ESOS Assurance Fund: http://www .aei.gov.au/AEI/ESOS/FAQs/ESOS_Act. htm#ESOSAssuranceFund

Australian Government. (2009b). *National Code— Part D: Standards for registered providers.* Retrieved October 3, 2010, from http://www.aei .gov.au/AEI/ESOS/NationalCodeExplanatory Guide/PartD/default.htm

Australian Government. (2009c). *PRISMS.* Retrieved August 2, 2010, from http://www.aei.gov.au/ AEI/ESOS/FAQs/General.htm#PRISMS

Australian Government. (2010a). *Australian Education International.* Retrieved August 2, 2010, from http://aei.gov.au/AEI/ CmsTemplates/GeneralTemplates/LandingPage. aspx?NRMODE=Published&NRNODEGUID= {2F9C1196-4B2B-49A8-A64A67B003520F81}& NRORIGINALURL=%2faei%2fesos%2fdefault. htm&NRCACHEHINT=ModifyGuest

Australian Government. (2010b). *CRICOS.* Retrieved August 2, 2010, from http://cricos .deewr.gov.au/

Australian Government. (2010c). *Visas, immigration, and refugees.* Retrieved October 3, 2010, http:// www.immi.gov.au/students/

Banks, M. (2010, May), Presentation to NEAS conference, Sydney.

BBC. (2010). *Universities facing first budget cuts in years.* Retrieved August 2, 2010, from http://news.bbc.co.uk/2/hi/uk_news/education/8573432.stm

Brown, N. (2003). *What's it worth? The case for variable graduate contribution.* London: Universities UK.

Calderon, A. (2010, September). Emerging countries for student recruitment in tertiary education. Paper presented to the IMHE-OECD Conference, *Higher Education in a World Changed Utterly: Doing More with Less,* Paris, p. 6.

Cuthbert, D., Smith, W., & Boey, J. (2008). What do we really know about the outcomes of Australian international education? A critical review and prospectus for future research. *Journal of Studies in International Education,* 255–275.

IDP Education. (2010). The independent guide to Australian study opportunities. Retrieved August 2, 2010, from http://www.idp.com/

Lenton, P. (2007). *Global value: The value of UK education and training exports: An update.* Sheffield, UK: University of Sheffield.

Leventhal, M. (2008). The legality and standards of commission-based recruiting. NAFSA: Association of International Educators. Retrieved from http://www.nafsa.org/_/File/_/agents-legality_standards.pdf

McMurtrie, B. (2008, September 10). New group aims to apply standards to international-student recruitment agents. *Chronicle of Higher Education.* Retrieved from http://chronicle.com/article/New-Group-Seeks-Standards-for/1146/

Meadows, E. (2011). From aid to industry: A history of international education in Australia. In D. Davis & B. Mackintosh (Ed.). *Making a difference: Australian international education.* Kensington, NSW: University of New South Wales Press.

Murray, D. (2011), Professionalisation and research: underpinning the industry, emergence of a profession. In D. Davis & B. Mackintosh (Ed.). *Making a difference: Australian international education.* Kensington, NSW: University of New South Wales Press.

Olsen, A. (2007). *AUIDF benchmarking 2006.* Canberra: Australian Universities International Directors Forum (AUIDF).

Olsen, A. (2010). *The benchmarking of Australian university international offices.* Canberra, Australia: AUIDF.

Redden, E. (2011, July 26). SUNY bets big on agents. *Inside Higher Education.* Retrieved from http://www.insidehighered.com/news/2011/07/26/suny_plans_broad_use_of_commission_based_agents_to_boost_international_enrollment

United States Department of State. (2009). *Policy guidance for EducationUSA centers on commercial recruitment agents.* Retrieved from http://www.educationusa.info/pdf/Policy_Guidance_for_EducationUSA_Centers.pdf

NOTES

1   In May 2011, after a brief illness, Tony Adams sadly passed away. His work on this chapter has been completed by Stephen Connelly, with assistance from Dennis Murray, Executive Director, International Education Association Australia, in collaboration with Mitch Leventhal, Tony's original co-author.

2   The well-known and so-called Dawkins Reforms, after Minister for Education John Dawkins (1987-1992), followed later, and included the introduction of the Higher Education Contribution Scheme, a funding mechanism for domestic students which is still in place. The Dawkins Reforms are often popularly cited as having provided substantial additional impetus to more aggressive export of Australian higher education.

3   Arrangements whereby Australian universities offer a portion of their degree program overseas with a partner institution. The program is a 'twin' of the onshore program, equivalent in content, standards and experience.

4   Note that at the time of writing changes were being considered to aspects of the Australian regulatory and legislative framework, including the student visa program.

5   Currently suspended as of this writing.

6   The Knight Review-proposed new visa regime, with all 41 recommendations accepted, will shift from country risk assessment to provider risk assessment, at least for universities in the first instance, thereby increasing compliance costs for institutions, but easing student visa bottlenecks.

7   In 1990, the National Association of Foreign Student Advisors formerly changed its name to NAFSA: Association of International Educators.

8   This network gradually expanded to encompass more than 400 offices worldwide by the mid-2000s.

9   International trade in educational services conservatively accounted for US $15 billion in foreign exchange in 2008, making education services the fifth most valuable component of services trade. This amount includes only income from international students who come to study in the United States and does not include U.S. education services offered in other countries through distance education, branch campuses, and other joint ventures. Some estimate that, were the data kept in a more systematic way on these cross-border services,

income would possibly double, bringing education services to third in order of trade in services, surpassed only by freight and transportation/tourism.

10 Title IV of the Higher Education Act is often misinterpreted as prohibiting agency based international student recruitment. In fact, the act states: "By entering into a program participation agreement, an institution agrees that – (22)(i) It will not provide any commission, bonus, or other incentive payment based directly or indirectly upon success in securing enrollments or financial aid to any person or entity engaged in any student recruiting or admission activities or in making decisions regarding the awarding of title IV, HEA program funds, except that *this limitation does not apply to the recruitment of foreign students residing in foreign countries who are not eligible to receive title IV, HEA program funds.* [italics added]

23

DESIGNER IMMIGRANTS[1]?

International Students and Two-Step Migration

LESLEYANNE HAWTHORNE

In recent decades, international students have emerged as a prized and contested human capital resource, in a process termed *two-step migration*. This movement of international students should be seen as an integral part of transnational migration systems, which undergird skilled labor circulation in a burgeoning global knowledge economy. Governments are increasingly aware of this trend, "seen in the increasing incidence of national programmes for students' recruitment with a specific view towards longer-term or permanent settlement" (Vertovec, 2002, p. 13). What are the current issues within this trend of two-step migration? What are the policies and strategies related to this trend? This chapter outlines the discourse on this emerging trend, including student motivations, factors influencing international student migration, and ethics. In addition, the chapter provides some practical examples in skilled migration from the United States, Australia, China, Switzerland, and The Netherlands, concluding with a look to the future. Through these discussions, international education leaders will become more informed about this multifaceted trend, which is impacting international student recruitment and mobility around the world.

LITERATURE REVIEW: FACTORS CONTRIBUTING TO TWO-STEP MIGRATION

International Student Motivation

Migration is in fact a long-standing motivation for international study. As early as 1994, an Australia-wide survey found 78% of students from China, 64% from Hong Kong, 46% from Fiji, and 43% from Malaysia and Singapore planned to migrate, despite the existence at the time of a 3-year eligibility bar (Nesdale, Simkin, Sang, Burke, & Fraser, 1995). International student enrollments soared once eligibility bars were removed in 1999. Within five years, these students constituted 52% of Australia's skilled migration category, with an extraordinary 66% from India and 38% from China electing to stay.

Multiple factors influence international student migration, and so far, the literature barely explores these. The classic pattern is relocation to developed from developing countries to enhance personal and professional life choices. This has typically involved shifts from Asia and Africa to nations in the Organization for Economic Cooperation and Development (OECD), at times with devastating impact on source countries. Motivation varies markedly, however, for different cohorts of students. At independence in 1957, for example, Malaysia's constitution sought to balance Malay political and administrative pre-eminence against Chinese and Indian economic dominance. The primary objectives of the government's New Economic Policy from 1970 were to reduce poverty, restructure society, and identify ethnic groups by economic function. This *bumiputra* measure involved securing for Malays a far greater share of the nation's wealth as well as the lion's share of education and employment opportunities. It remains national policy, despite contestation. In consequence, the great majority of Malaysian international students to the United Kingdom, Australia, Canada, and New Zealand are of Chinese and Indian descent. These educational refugees are highly motivated to remain in their host country after they receive their degrees (Andressen, 1993).

A recent study of middle-class Indian students qualifying in Australia suggests permanent resident status has come to be viewed as an entitlement rather than a privilege, offsetting the fees required to fund international education. Baas (2010) defines Indian students as "global citizens in the making," seeking an Australian passport to facilitate mobility since an Indian passport is regarded as a "limiting factor" (p. 8). Such students may have uncertain long-term commitment. They inhabit a transnational world, where "more people than ever before (have been) able to imagine that they or their children would live and work in places other than where they were born" (Appadurai, 1996, p. 6). Within this context 'PR' status may simply be Stage 1 of a global migration trajectory, allowing people to explore optional lives.

Quite different motives inform the study-migration choices of North American students, whether qualifying in Asian or OECD nations. By 2010, for example, some 3,500 Canadian students were enrolled in Irish, U.S., Australian, Caribbean, and Polish medical schools. Economic or political mobility were not key drivers. In the past decade, for instance, Canada and the United States have emerged as Australia's third and fourth top source countries for international medical students, following the introduction of graduate-entry degrees. By 2009, 72% of final-year Canadian students were intending to stay, comparable to rates for Singaporean (75%) and Malaysian (74%) medical students. By 2010, Canadian student retention had risen to 90% (Hawthorne & To, 2011). Interviews conducted with several hundred Canadian students suggest there are six key drivers. The first is being a "near miss" in securing a place in a Canadian medical school, the reason 78% of Canadian students choose to study abroad (Canadian Resident Matching Service, 2011). Additional reasons concern the prospect of global adventure, a better climate, the perceived quality of Australian medical courses, and a desire to replicate their parents' migration trajectory while exploring diasporic links (in a context where disproportionately high numbers of medical students are first-generation Canadians) (Hawthorne, 2011b).

Institutional Revenue Drivers

Institutional revenue drivers are fundamental to the study-migration trajectory, a lucrative option for both governments and educational providers. As early as 2005, the United States and the United Kingdom were earning $US14.5 billion and £7.5 billion, respectively, from international students. Recruitment had become an entrenched priority for institutions obliged to compensate for reduced public revenue through collaboration with business and industry, partnerships focused on innovative product development (e.g., biotechnology), and through the marketing of educational and business services. Since 2008 the global financial crisis has exacerbated this dependence. Across the United States, caps are being lifted on international student recruitment. In 2011–2012, 29 state governments slashed their higher education budgets, a process including:

> up to $1.5 b(illion) in states such as California. The U.S. federal government's stimulus funding also begins to run out in August and it has cut $45 m(illion) or 40 per cent of the budget for international education programs under Title IV and the Fullbright-Hays Program. . . . Recruitment of international students is receiving greater attention as a revenue source . . . Although they are at different starting points, every institution contacted for this report noted that recruiting international students was important. (Green & Ferguson, 2011, p. 2)

Comparable trends are occurring in the European Union (EU)/ European Economic Area (EEA). In 2011, the European University Association's (EUA) Prague Declaration stated it was imperative to diversify income streams. Following decades of generous government subsidy, financial sustainability has become "one of the key challenges for Europe's universities," with economies facing serious contraction. The United Kingdom and Latvia are defined by the EUA as "emblematic cases," characterized by "extensive cuts in public funding (with) the situation also alarming" in other countries. A major response is to generate non-EU/EEA international student fees; the EUA report noted that in the Netherlands these students "would pay a fee at least three times higher than the fee charged to national/EU students," and that "the English universities typically received higher than average income from international students (sometimes) a third or up to almost half of the amount collected" (EUA, 2011, pp. 6–19, 32).

As early as 1999 and 2006, the United Kingdom had launched two major international student recruitment drives to reverse student decline, while contesting Australian and New Zealand encroachment on Asian markets (e.g., Singapore, Malaysia). Scope for two-step migration was expanded in tandem with this process. In 2007, the Labour government introduced a five-tier managed migration system, setting criteria by which "nationals of countries outside the European Union and the European Economic Area (could) apply to come and remain in the UK to work, train or study" (Home Office, 2006, p. 1). Their pathway to retention was clear. At Tier 4 international students could secure part-time work to cross-subsidize tuition and stipends. On graduation, they could apply to move to Tier 1 (points-based selection as "highly skilled individuals to contribute to growth and productivity" on a permanent basis) or Tier 2 (skilled workers with a job offer to fill gaps in UK labour force, accepted in the first instance on a temporary basis) (Home Office, 2006, p. 6).

International students' response was immediate and positive. In 2008, 16,171 former students were approved as Tier 1 migrants, with Indian applicants dominating (25%), followed by those from Pakistan and China. In 2009, 34,180 post-study applicants were selected. In terms of Tier 2, from June 2009 to 2010, the majority of approvals were allocated to information technology (IT) and software professionals (16,839), nurses (3,689), and doctors (2,434)— the proportion who had qualified in Britain is currently unclear (Salt et al., 2011, pp. 35–36).

Following the election of the United Kingdom's Conservative government, in the context of the global financial crisis, non-EU migration has been slashed. This is despite the fact that "one in ten academics from British universities (comes) from outside the EU" and the threat to "international collaborations that are critical to science" (Henderson, 2010, p. 1). Draconian tertiary-sector budget cuts have been imposed, including 66% to the science capital budget. By 2011, UK university administrators were reportedly in an "air of panic," dealing with domestic fees trebling in "a wholly untested market" (Nutbeam, 2011). A key institutional response is planned expansion of international student numbers, which poses challenges to faculty and administrators. Following a decade in which student migration had almost trebled, in April 2011, the prime minister said most would be obliged to go home. Despite this, pathways were preserved for the student elite: people advantaged under the 20,700 non-EU/EEA immigration cap, who could prove they had been offered "a graduate-level skilled job, with a minimum salary" (Cameron, 2011, p. 1). In line with Australian, Canadian, and New Zealand reforms, the United Kingdom is recalibrating the study-migration pathway.

Multinational employers are likely to be major beneficiaries of this trend. While this is largely left out of the literature on international students' to date, UK corporations increasingly target foreign graduates as global employees, based on "deliberate selection of particular types of international students . . . according to their nationality or disciplinary training," who are advantaged by having UK qualifications. In a recent study, Salt (2011) suggests:

> we are now entering a potentially new paradigm in the mobility of international students, characterised by their perceived value to large employers as "global human resources" . . . For companies with operations in particular countries, recruitment of international students from those locations is a matter of course. (pp. 132–149)

The Attraction of International Students Relative to Skilled Migrants

This trend to recruit international students as skilled migrants is also fuelled by striking demographic shifts under way in developed nations. According to the OECD, "Over the next couple of decades nothing will impact on (member) economies more profoundly than demographic trends and, chief among them, ageing' (Cotis, 2005, p. 1). Within a generation, select OECD nations are at risk of contracting by a third, with severe productivity implications. Countries with traditionally high birth rates are contracting, while others were approaching free-fall. Japan's population for example, which peaked at 127.8 million in 2004, is projected to drop to 89.9 million by 2055, a cataclysmic challenge to productivity, which threatens the viability of the tertiary education sector (Gross, 2009). By 2050, Japan will have one working-age adult for every elderly person, while Germany and Italy will have two (Population Reference Bureau, 2011, p. 1). This fertility revolution is being replicated across Asia, where population growth is predicted to decline from 2.1 to 1.0, a process well under way (Central Intelligence Agency, 2010; Hugo, 2007).

In many OECD countries, the policy response is enhanced migration, the challenge being to find its most palatable and efficient form. In Canada, where within 10 years 100% of net growth in the professions will depend on migration, the government has placed extraordinary emphasis on the recruitment of skills. Recent arrivals are more than twice as likely as the Canada-born to be degree-qualified (37% compared to 15%). By 2001, 51% of all IT professionals were first-generation Canadians, along with 50% of engineers, 49% of architects/builders, 35% of doctors, and 35% of accountants (many arriving in the family and humanitarian categories). Disproportionate numbers had reached Canada in the previous 5 years from diverse source countries (most notably China, India, the Philippines, Pakistan, the United States, Colombia, the United Kingdom, South Korea, Iran, and France) (Hawthorne, 2008). By 2011, the proportion of annual places allocated to skilled migrants was 60%, with an overall annual target of 240,000 to 265,000 people.

There is a problem, however. Appropriate employment for migrant professionals in Canada has diminished rather than improved in recent years, in line with growing diversity (Aydemir & Skuterad, 2005). Recent degree-qualified arrivals from the following countries have been the most likely to secure professional work: South Africa, Australia and New Zealand, United Kingdom/Ireland, North Western Europe, and the United States (migrants from English- or French-speaking countries with directly comparable development levels). Labor market integration rates are markedly lower for other birthplace groups, including migrants trained in poorly resourced tertiary systems. Large numbers qualified in the Philippines, China, India, Vietnam, and other South/Central Asian nations have secured only low-skilled work, a significant policy issue given the prominence of these groups in recent intakes. According to a recent Statistics Canada study, the economic category is now associated with entrenched disadvantage:

> By the early 2000s, skilled class entering immigrants (to Canada) were actually more likely to enter low-income and be in chronic low-income than their family class counterparts, and the small advantage that the university educated entering immigrants had over, say, the high school educated in the early 1990s had largely disappeared by 2000, as the number of highly educated rose. What did change was the face of the chronically poor immigrant; by the late 1990s one-half were in the skilled economic class, and 41% had degrees (up from 13% in the early 1990s). (Picot, Feng, & Coulombe, 2007, pp. 5–6)

Within this context, international students represent an attractive alternative resource. In 2008, an uncapped Canadian Experience Class was established to facilitate the retention of international students and temporary foreign workers. By 2009, 196,138 international students were enrolled in Canada, compared to 114,046 in 2000. A total of 107,441 were in the university sector at this time, followed by, 34,459 in secondary education or lower, and 27,118 in other post-secondary courses (Citizenship and Immigration Canada, 2010). Tertiary students thus represent a major potential resource, along with the 282,194 temporary foreign workers then resident. While conversion to skilled migration has been modest to date (just 3,900 in the Canadian Experience Class category in 2010), the strategic framework is in place, in a context where competitor countries are seeking to retain large numbers (Tachdjian, 2011).

Demand for Knowledge Economy Workers

Beyond nation-building and compensation for demographic decline, international students are increasingly sought for their competitive edge. According to a U.S. Congress report,

> Many in the scientific community maintain that in order to compete with countries that are rapidly expanding their scientific and technological capabilities, the United States needs to bring in those whose skills will benefit society and will enable us to compete in the new technology based global economy . . . Though most of the world's top universities are currently in the US, many (countries) are determined to change this balance, and they probably will. To remain competitive in the coming decades, we must continue to embrace the most capable students and scholars of other countries. Our security and quality of life will depend on it. (Matthews, 2007, p. 17)

This issue is exemplified in the 2010 U.S. Science and Engineering (S&E) Indicators report. U.S. student outcomes in science and mathematics education have been modest for years, with Black and Hispanic students notably disadvantaged. By contrast "the rise and rise" of China and other Confucian Asian countries such as Korea continues. In 2009, the OECD's Programme for International Student Assessment (PISA) demonstrated the highest-rated education systems were those of Korea, Singapore, Finland, and Hong Kong SAR, with the performance of Shanghai rated off the charts. Confucian systems already occupied "the first five places in PISA mathematics . . . Four of the top five education systems in reading . . . five of the top six in science. A recent analyst noted:

> This is momentous, with incalculable long term consequences, given the role in education and research in shaping modernization . . . (T)he UK and the US look bad in the PISA comparison . . . China has both the world's largest student enrolment and one in five world researchers. From 1995-2007 the number of science papers

rose from 9,061 to 56,806. From 1995-2007 China's annual increase in science papers averaged 16.5 per cent. (Marginson, 2011, pp. 4–7)

In the view of the National Science Board, future U.S. growth in science and mathematics depends on three factors: increased S&E production, immigration of scientists and engineers, and relatively low-scale domestic retirements. The retirement of U.S. science and engineering workers holding doctoral degrees is set to surge, however, with international students disproportionately needed to replace them. By 2003, 25% of tertiary-educated science and engineering workers in the United States—and 40% of those who held PhDs—were born overseas. More than a third of PhDs resident in the United States were from Asia, most notably China (22%) and India (14%). About 62% of foreign 2002 PhD graduates were still resident in the United States in 2007, close to the record high of 65% retained a few years earlier (National Science Foundation 2010, 3-6,7; see also Finn, 2007; Regets 2007). By 2008, the United States included an estimated 1 million resident HIB workers, with many contributing to the science, technology, and ICT industries (visa extensions and exempt categories lifted overall numbers far beyond the 65,000 annual quota). While opening the U.S. labor market to more guest workers is deemed "one of the roughest issues facing Congress," the United States allows "an easy attestation procedure for employers seeking college-educated foreigners to fill jobs that require a college degree under the H-IB program," on condition these workers are offered wage parity, supported by some labor market testing (Martin & Ruhs, 2010, p. 1).

Dependence on high-skilled migration is rising in many other OECD countries experiencing a perceived mismatch between the skills of domestic workers and the needs of the knowledge economy. In Switzerland, which had no immigration policy until 2011, there is a new willingness to admit "urgently required qualified workers" from outside the EU/EEA, with international students a favored source. By 2010–2011, about 22% of the student body was non-Swiss, including close to 50% of all doctoral student enrollments, 30% of masters students, and 18% at the bachelor level. Pressure to open the Swiss labor market to third-country nationals is mounting, with universities a stepping stone to immigration. In Germany, similarly:

> The current situation . . . is characterized by high levels of unemployment accompanied by a simultaneous shortage of experts and specialized personnel. The existing qualificational structure of the national labour force potential is not in accordance with the qualification demands of a rapidly changing globalised economy and a national economy undergoing far-reaching structural changes (qualification mismatch).
> (Helle & Sauer, 2007, p. 3)

International students represent a homegrown and generally acceptable solution to countries with conflicted histories and views on foreign migration (Isserstedt & Schnitzer, 2005).

Compensation for Out-Migration

The out-migration of domestic workers exacerbates demand for such skilled workers, and—like retirement—it is an increasingly common phenomenon. Citizens leaving OECD nations tend to be disproportionately skilled–attracted by global career rewards and unprecedented geographic choices.

Between 1955 and 2004, for example, 2.3 million migrants were selected by New Zealand. This translated to a net population gain of just 208,000 people. By 2009, 521,223 New Zealanders were resident in Australia (12% of the New Zealand population), many holding tertiary qualifications. Within this context, "Without migration New Zealand would be unable to maintain its population or fill skill shortages, even in a time of economic slowdown . . . [O]ver the 2001–2006 period, 60 percent of the growth in the working age population was from migration" (Blake, 2009, p. 1). Expatriate flows pose an urgent challenge to New Zealand in key occupational fields. In the past 5 years, for example, 5% annual growth in engineering demand has occurred, with 1,200 to 1,300 additional engineers needed per annum. While the country graduates 1,200 to 1,500 engineers per year, these numbers are inadequate when some 30% of those engineers leave within 3 years for Australia or other OECD destinations. To compensate, New Zealand imports around 200 to 350 long-term migrant engineers annually.

Between 2004–2005 and 2008–2009, 3,405 architects, engineers, and related professionals arrived as principal applicants in the skilled migrant category. The great majority were sourced onshore in New Zealand (in 2008–2009, 73% of engineer arrivals, compared with 66% in 2004–2005), many through the study-migration pathway. New Zealand is currently expanding its international student flows, focused on applicants who are university qualified and selected through the study-to-work pathway (Hawthorne, 2011a).

Workforce Undersupply and Maldistribution

International students can address workforce maldistribution as well as undersupply, experiencing few of the problems associated with overseas-trained migrants.

The United States has a long-standing dependence on international medical graduates to fill inner-city public-sector Medicaid posts. Canada recruits thousands of foreign health professionals each year to work in areas of need: regional and remote sites where visas can be tied to specific locations. Australia currently admits about 12,000 foreign health professionals annually, most on a temporary basis. Large numbers will avoid taking, or will fail to pass, the mandatory pre-registration exams. By 2006, just 53% of recent international medical migrants secured Australian medical employment in their first 5 years. Within this context, international students constitute an attractive and efficient alternative resource. By definition, they are of prime workforce age and have self-funded to meet domestic employer requirements.

The scale of international medical and allied health enrollments has grown rapidly in Australia in recent years. By 2009 8,690 international students were undertaking nursing degrees (compared to 1,307 in 1996), in particular, migration-motivated nurses from India and China. An additional 2,772 international students were enrolled in medical schools (compared to 963 in 1996). By July 2011, such medical school enrollments had risen to about 3,000, with 78% of former students transitioning to Australian medical residencies on graduation. As demonstrated by analysis of Australia's Graduate Destination Survey from 2006 to 2010, 99% had secured full-time medical employment

4 months after graduation, including many working in undersupplied regional sites. Their employment and salary outcomes are stellar compared to medical migrants trained overseas (Hawthorne, 2011b). Identical patterns apply in other fields. For example by 2009–2010, two thirds of migrant engineers were selected onshore in Australia, the great majority qualified in the local education system.

STRATEGIES AND PRACTICAL EXAMPLES

The Scale of International Students as a Skilled Migration Resource

As demonstrated, international student migration has emerged as a policy priority for developed countries in the recent decade. The institutional and policy factors driving this seem unlikely to change. Former students represent a highly acceptable form of migration. Most are immediately absorbed into host labor markets, by definition characterized by youth, advanced host-country language ability, full credential recognition, significant acculturation, and relevant training. In 2008, the United States included

623,805 international students in its tertiary education system, followed by 389,373 in Australia, 389,330 in the United Kingdom, 260,596 in France, and 246,369 in Germany, with the next five countries in rank by international enrollments located in Asia (China, Japan, Singapore, Malaysia, and the Republic of Korea). (See Table 23.1.) These figures, however, constitute an underestimate of actual flows. By 2009, for example, 242,602 foreign students were resident in Canada (including short-term study abroad students), while Australia had 630,552 international students enrolled on-site, by distance, and across all sectors (Citizenship and Immigration Canada, 2011).

The Ethics of Student Migration and Policy Strategies

The ethics of international student migration are a matter of debate, in a context where brain drain has emerged as a major concern in recent decades (Sidhu, 2006; Skeldon, 1997). The U.S. Fulbright program, set up in 1946, was intended to support third world capacity development. Australia's Colombo Plan from the 1950s was designed to offer tertiary and technical education, at a time when just 3,000 institutions existed across all Commonwealth Asia. Many

Destination Country	International Students Enrolled in Higher/ Vocational Education
1. United States	623,805 (2008)
2. Australia	389,373 (2008)
3. United Kingdom	389,330 (2008)
4. France	260,596 (2008)
5. Germany	246,369 (2007)
6. China	223,499 (2008)
7. Japan	123,829 (2008)
8. Canada	113,996 (2007)
9. Singapore	86,000 (2007)
10. Malaysia	72,000 (2008)
11. South Korea	63,952 (2008)
12. New Zealand	39,942 (2007)

Table 23.1   Top 12 Global Destinations for International Students by 2008 (Higher and Vocational Education Sectors)

Source: Compiled from data provided in *International Student Mobility: Status Report 2009,* V. Lasanowski, The Observatory on Borderless Higher Education, United Kingdom, June 2009, from data provided in Appendix B, International Student Mobility 1998-2008—Major Destination Countries, p.45.

wealthy countries committed to offering educational aid, reflecting their status and unused training capacity. As communism (and later) Islamic fundamentalism expanded, provision of education was conceptualized as political insurance in addition to aid (allowing governments to foster goodwill, while cultivating political and trade links with future regional leaders). The expectation was that international students would train abroad and go home, thus raising the living standards of recipient countries.

By the 1980s, however, growing numbers were also enrolled as private students, including young Chinese from Singapore, Malaysia, Hong Kong, and Indonesia, driven to study abroad by a desire for better quality education, the intensity of competition for tertiary places, or discrimination against ethnic minorities. By the late 1990s, several Asian countries had achieved economic development rates ahead of OECD norms, in a context where academic capitalism and the marketization of higher education were rapidly developing (Slaughter & Leslie, 1997). Parents rather than source countries have typically resourced private students' education. From an ethical perspective, their retention can seem less problematic than the migration norm: selection of mature-age professionals fully trained by their source countries.

Global surveillance of study-migration strategies has become unprecedented, supported by neutralization of perceived barriers or disincentives. The majority of OECD countries are in the process of

1. Developing migration categories designed to attract and retain skilled workers

2. Monitoring and replicating successful competitor models, including mechanisms for selection and control

3. Expanding temporary entry options, targeting international students and employer-sponsored workers

4. Facilitating student and worker transition from temporary to extended or permanent resident status, supported by priority processing and uncapped migration categories

5. Combining government-driven with employer-driven strategies

6. Creating regional settlement incentives designed to attract skilled migrants, supported by lower entry requirements and policy input from local governments and employers

7. Supporting the above strategies through sustained and increasingly innovative global promotion strategies. (Hawthorne, 2010a)

In 2005, for example, Germany promulgated a skilled migration policy, targeting international students while maintaining a policy of zero fees. In 2006, New Zealand abolished fees for international PhD students—a key strategy in cultivating and retaining doctoral student numbers. In 2007, the United States launched fresh policy initiatives to stem the post-September 11 decline in international students, based on easing visa regulations and supported by strategic initiatives favoring flows from China, Chile, and Morocco (Lowell, Bump; & Martin, 2007). Multiple providers deliver courses taught wholly in English (including in Norway, the Netherlands, Germany, China and Japan), recognizing the attraction of English as the global language. As early as 2007, the Netherlands, for example, was offering more than 1,200 courses in English, including about 900 bachelor and masters degrees—a process promoted through seven global offices (for example, in countries as diverse as Mexico, Indonesia, and Vietnam). International students have responded with alacrity to such options.

Practical Examples

Box 23.1 The United States: Maintaining the Competitive Research Edge

The political and economic dominance of the United States, aligned with the prospect of a green card (i.e., permanent residence), has long spurred international student demand for U.S. courses. In 2009–2010, 690,923 international students were enrolled (274,431 at the undergraduate level,

293,885 at the graduate level, and 54,803 in nondegrees). By 2010, business and management courses dominated (145,514 enrollments), followed by engineering (127,441), physical and life sciences, and mathematics and computer sciences (around 61,000 each). China (127,628) and India (104,628) were the dominant source countries, India showing 2% recent growth compared to 30% from China (Institute of International Education, 2010). The United States is, however, increasingly wary of global competition. A 2009 report, assessing competitor practice, included the branding strategies used by Germany, Australia, and the United Kingdom (Government Accountability Office, 2009). In 2009–2010, 5 of the top 10 U.S. source countries showed decline since the previous year despite overall growth (in rank order, Japan, Mexico, Canada, Taiwan, and South Korea).

Despite this, the rewards of the U.S. study-migration pathway remain strong. According to one study, "In the last half of the twentieth century, America was the location of choice for the best and brightest scientific minds in the world . . . with 62 per cent of the world's stars as residents"—many first arriving as international students. In the past two decades, the U.S. share of global doctoral students has risen from 13.5% to 28.3%, with such stars frequently trained by "the research universities which produce them" (Zucker & Darby, 2007, p. 1; see also Marginson & van der Wende, 2007). Science and engineering doctorate holders have the highest patent rate activity in the United States (16%), with earnings rising even late in careers. Doctoral students have slid seamlessly into postdoctoral work in the past decade, taking positions eschewed by domestic graduates in the context of poor remuneration and long tenure-track requirements (Borjas, 2009). In 2009–2010, 60,000 doctorates overall were earned, a recession-proof qualification associated with unemployment rates of just 2.5%, with international student recruitment a growing priority (Council of Graduate Schools, 2011a, 2011b).

The presence of foreign postdoctoral students is often viewed as essential, despite recent debate on this issue (Borjas, 2009; Borjas & Doran, 2012). By 2008, U.S. employer groups were lobbying Congress for automatic provision of green cards to international students with U.S. PhD degrees. Recent studies estimate long-term stay rates to include 85% to 95% of Indian and Chinese graduates, allowing for substantial scientific contributions to be made in select fields (Finn, 2007). The National Science Foundation in 2010 estimated that 22,900 U.S. citizens and permanent residents held academic positions, compared to 26,900 people on temporary visas (National Science Foundation, 2010). The National Institutes of Health (NIH) each year host more than 2,000 foreign postdoctoral students, "to receive training and conduct biomedical research." Former international students are attracted to NIH appointments by global "prestige, its clout in financing biomedical research, and its many research opportunities." Their presence is deemed vital:

> As fewer American students select biomedical careers, U.S. training institutions are forced to increasingly rely on the admission of foreign students to maintain enrolment levels (and hence, ensure the survival of graduate academic departments) and satisfy labour market demand. [The program has become] a de facto seamless and efficient recruitment mechanism whereby American academe can, at minimal cost, indirectly evaluate, select and hire biomedical scientists from a large and constantly-renewing pool of foreign candidates that includes talented and promising young biomedical scientists from around the world. (Diaz-Briquets & Cheney, 2003, pp. 433, 438, 430)

(Continued)

(Continued)

According to Testimony to the House Subcommittee on 21st Century Competitiveness and Education, future U.S. "security and quality of life" will depend on continuing to attract "the most capable students and scholars of other countries" (Matthews, 2007, p. 18). Access to permanent residence for foreign graduates is viewed as fundamental to this:

Consider a hypothetical case of a bachelor's level engineer who enters the United States with a student F visa to pursue a doctorate, who spends 6 years completing the doctorate, followed by 2 years in a postdoc position, and then is hired by an employer for a permanent job on a temporary work visa. The employer applies for a permanent work visa for their new worker, who receives it 2 years after starting work. Now, 10 years after entering the United States, a 5-year waiting period begins after receiving a permanent visa, before the engineer can apply for citizenship. The engineer applies soon after becoming eligible, and after 1 year, becomes a US citizen, 16 years after entry to the United States. (National Science Foundation, 2008, pp. 3–52)

Within an increasingly competitive global environment, there may be risks to the United States associated with uncertain or elongated study-migration pathways.

Box 23.2 Australia: Removing Perverse Study-Migration Incentives

Like Canada, Australia is a global exemplar of nation-building through government planned and administered skilled, family, and humanitarian migration programs (with 24% of the population foreign born, compared to 20% in Canada and 11% in the United States). By 2010, Australia also included the highest proportion of international tertiary students in the world (21% or 630,000 enrolments), "more than three times the OECD average of 6.7%, and six times the proportion of United States tertiary enrolments (3.4%)" (Australian Education International, 2011; OECD, 2010). In the recent decade, 35% to 52% of skilled migrants have been former international students, following the removal of a three-year eligibility bar. By 2006, students had a 99% chance of being selected, unless they failed health or character checks. Scope for migration had fueled the development of new international student markets, with migration and export education becoming inextricably linked.

Between 2005 and 2007, Australia secured impressive outcomes from its skilled migration program in global terms, including the study-migration pathway. At 6 months postmigration, 83% of primary applicants were employed or self-employed. Birthplace groups at risk of employment disadvantage were highly protected by the study-migration pathway. For example, 74% of former students from China had work compared to 53% of Chinese migrants selected offshore. Despite this, Australia's 2006 skilled migration review identified problematic issues. Former students secured salaries $20,000 a year less at 6 months than offshore migrants and were less likely to use their qualifications in work. The problem of institutional quality control was intensifying, an unanticipated consequence of Australia allocating up to 20 bonus points to skilled applicants with technical qualifications, in the context of sustained economic boom (Birrell, Hawthorne, & Richardson, 2006; Hawthorne, 2010b). Training colleges had responded rapidly to this opportunity, including private institutions described as "wily entrepreneurial players who exist solely to funnel international students into skilled migration." By 2008, Australia was experiencing 51% annual growth in technical course enrollments, compared to just 8% in the tertiary sector. Indian students had proven the most immediately responsive: 36,045 enrolled in vocational courses, compared to 1,827 six years before. Inadequate quality assurance put such students at risk of being "treated as commodities in a marketplace that charges top dollar for low-grade education and training," in what appeared to some critics as a "government-sanctioned racket" (Das, 2009, p. 15).

Responding to concerns since 2007, successive Australian governments have transformed the skilled migration program while taking steps to remove perverse study-migration incentives. A review was commissioned of the work outcomes achieved by former international students across the professions and trades, including assessment of the attributes employers sought. This demonstrated English to be the critical determinant of early employment: High-level speakers were four times more likely to be employed at 18 months than those with poor English (Hawthorne, 2010). A review of quality assurance in Australia's export education industry was undertaken, its recommendations affirming the need for enhanced quality, accountability, and governance across all education sectors (Baird Review, 2010). Skilled intakes were downsized to 108,100 in 2009–2010, in response to the global financial crisis. International student distress became pronounced, intensified by a spate of physical attacks and the collapse of a range of low-grade financially marginal private colleges.

In May 2010, a new skilled occupation list was announced, strongly reverting to the professions. A points test review was initiated, the goal being to refine selection criteria to deliver high-level outcomes. Since July 2011, Australia's skilled migration program has markedly favored the selection of older native or near-native English speakers, qualified with bachelor or higher degrees. The government's aims are clear: to "deliver the best and brightest skilled migrants by emphasising high level qualifications, better English language levels and extensive skilled work experience" (Department of Immigration and Citizenship, 2010). By August 2010, offshore visas for international students had fallen by a third, while demand for vocational sector courses had plummeted (−59%). Despite these trends, international students proved immediately responsive to Australia's revised migration requirements. Application trends for the year to July 2010 showed 10% growth in demand for university courses, compared to just 1% for vocational sector fields, a sharp reversal of recent trends. In October 2011, the government provided international student graduates with the following guarantees to stay: 2 years for those with bachelor degrees, 3 years for masters degrees, and 4 years for doctorates. These students would be eligible to seek diverse forms of employment.

Box 23.3 China: Destination and Source of Supply

China is the dominant international student source for many OECD institutions. From 1999 to 2008, Chinese student enrollments grew as follows in major countries:

Australia: From 4,633 to 82,114

United States: From 51,000 to 81,127

(Continued)

(Continued)

Japan: From 25,907 to 72,766

United Kingdom: From 4,017 to 45,355

Canada: From 6,468 to 41,082

Germany: From 5,054 in 1999 to 27,117

France: From 1,374 in 1999 to 22,452 (Lasanowski, 2009)

In 2010, 84,700 Chinese students departed for study abroad (making a 1,273,000 total), reflecting China's strategy to enhance innovation by selecting "outstanding Chinese students" to study in "elite universities and research institutes . . . through fair and open competition" (Government of China, 2010, p. 35). At the same time, China has emerged as a leading destination as well as a source of supply, ranked sixth in the world by 2008, with 223,499 international students enrolled compared to 141,000 in 2006.

In line with China's 2010-2020 National Plan, international student intakes are now set for expansion and diversification, supported by financial incentives at all levels. While the majority of international students are derived from Asia, by 2005, the United States had become the third-largest source (10,343 students enrolled). Growing numbers in China were derived at this time from other OECD countries, including Japan (18,874), France (3,105), and Germany (2,736). These students were attracted by:

(China's status as) the world's largest and fastest growing economy . . . . a place where leading industrial players want to be doing business . . . For this reason, the international students of today understand Chinese higher education as a strategic investment in future employment. As an emerging player in the global education market . . . China is in the fortunate position of being able to select from among the more successful practices of other nations . . . By channelling as much as $US4 billion into a select few of its more research-intensive institutions, China is taking great strides to transform the overall quality of higher education in the country. (Lasanowski & Verbik, 2007, pp. 23–24)

As is clear, global study-migration pathways are diversifying, breaking out of traditional South-North and East-West migration paradigms. China's target by 2020 is 500,000 international students, including 150,000 enrolled in the rapidly expanding higher education sector. The Study-in-China Plan is under way, with 6.7% planned annual growth, and strong incentives are provided through government scholarships. In 2010, 20,385 sponsored places were available, at a time when the number of U.S. scholarships was markedly contracting. A further 10,000 China-U.S. bridge scholarships will facilitate people-to-people exchange annually between 2010 and 2020. Within the next 10 years, China will also unroll its China-ASEAN initiative, provision of 10,000 government scholarships to ASEAN countries, targeting young teachers, scholars, and students (Zong, 2011). While it is premature to assess the proportion of students likely to stay, Shanghai's fertility rate has dropped to 0.9. China is also admitting growing numbers of expatriates, who confront major credential recognition and linguistic barriers. Former international students may thus become a highly attractive long-term resource (Wang, 2008; Zong, 2011).

Study location influences career destinations across Asia, as is the case in the West. In 2005, 8,050,901 foreign workers were resident in Asia, most notably 2,640,000 in Malaysia, 2,300,000 in Thailand, 900,000 in Japan, and 620,000 in Singapore. While many were low-skilled, increasing numbers were knowledge workers recruited to the expanding Shanghai, Tokyo, Singapore, and other global financial and biotechnology hubs—many first arriving as students (Appold, 2005). By 2011, Singapore's fertility rate had hit a record low (1.16). Reliance on expatriates is growing. Marketing itself as "the best of East and West . . . the Global Schoolhouse," Singapore in 2005 set a target of 150,000 international students by 2015. By 2007, enrollments stood at 86,000, compared to 90,000 in Malaysia, and about 11,000 domestic students. Significant incentives will be implemented to retain them.

Box 23.4 Switzerland: Selective Admission

Gianni D'Amato

Director, Swiss Forum for Migration and Population Studies, Professor of Migration and Citizenship Studies, University of Neuchâtel (Switzerland)

in collaboration with Marco Pecoraro and Rosita Fibbi

Throughout the 20th century, Switzerland had one of the highest immigration rates in Europe. In 2009, 25.8% of its 7.8 million residents were foreign born, and 23%, or nearly 1.8 million, were foreign nationals. The proportion of foreign nationals is twice as high as in the United States (12.5% in 2009) and considerably higher than in Canada (19.8% in 2006), two countries widely considered as prototypes of countries of immigration. By contrast, Switzerland never considered itself to be a country of immigration. This is reflected in the absence of an immigrant policy at the federal level until 2011 and the lack of facilitated access to Swiss citizenship for the second generation or *jus soli* regulations.

Two major changes in the last few years have affected regular immigration. First, June 2002 saw entry into force of the Bilateral Agreement on the Free Movement of Persons between Switzerland and the EU member states. Second came an admission policy applicable to third-country nationals that would prove more restrictive than the policy Switzerland had pursued thus far, resulting in admitting "only urgently required qualified workers" from outside the EU/EFTA area.

During the academic period 2010–2011, roughly 22% of the student population was composed of international students coming directly from abroad for study purposes (1980: 12%). A minority of foreign students had Swiss schooling and so would not strictly be defined as international students, whereas 78% of non-Swiss students fall into this category. A large proportion of these (75%) currently hold a European passport, the majority coming from neighboring Germany (31%), France (12%), or Italy (8.5%). The proportional presence of international students increases with the level of academic enrolment. Their concentration is

(Continued)

(Continued)

highest in PhD programs (close to 50% of all students), compared to 30% in master's degrees and 18% in bachelor's degree courses. The tertiary institutions in Geneva and Zurich, both University and Eidgenössische Technische Hochschule (Polytechnical University), include the highest numbers of foreign students (more than 4,000). In relative terms, the greatest proportions are to be seen in École Polytechnique Fédérale Lausanne (at 56% almost half of the student body) and two-thirds at the University Svizzera italiana.

Observing the growing importance of international students, the federal government suggested opening the Swiss labor market to third-country nationals attending higher education institutions in Switzerland to facilitate retention. In the same period, the Swiss Parliament adopted a modification of the Alien Law, allowing such students to look for employment during a six-month period after graduation from a Swiss higher education institution.

The new bill, which came into effect on January 2011, represented a major shift from the philosophy of the new Alien Law. Formerly tailored to delineate a selective admission policy for third-country nationals favoring highly qualified personnel, it continues to hamper the passage of graduated international students to the status of foreign workers by requiring newly admitted students to sign an agreement to leave the country after graduation. Ranked third behind Australia and the United Kingdom in attracting a large share of talent in higher education, for the most part of its history and because of the leading ideology to prevent too high a share of foreign population, the Swiss provided other countries with well-qualified workers after graduation. However, it is important to note that universities have become a kind of stepping stone to immigration, in an effort to retain international students for the local labor market and to tackle the issue of the mismatch between educational credentials and occupation in the labor market with reference to highly skilled personnel. Such an approach has become increasingly common among certain European countries, converging to the solution Switzerland enacted at the beginning of 2011 with a 6-month extension of the residence permit in order to allow former students to find a job.

This scheme is absolutely new to Switzerland, and there is no assessment to date of the impact of the provision. It is also difficult to predict the sustainability of the provision, since political discourse has again turned in recent months to concern that too many foreign students might enter the Swiss educational system. Universities and cantonal governments are demanding stricter quotas to control this influx. The fact that Switzerland lacks a view of itself as an immigration country raises the issue of whether it will be able to profit from imported talents. This remains an open question.

Box 23.5 The Netherlands: Constructing the Policy Framework—But Will They Stay?

Hans de Wit

Amsterdam University of Applied Sciences (The Netherlands), and Centre for Higher Education Internationalisation (Italy)

The topic of international students and skilled immigration is a key issue in Dutch politics. The debates on the positive and negative dimensions of the multicultural society, immigration, and the economic and financial crisis have a direct link to international students and skilled immigration needs.

The number of international students in Dutch higher education has increased over past years in absolute numbers, although their percentage of overall students has stabilized at 7.4%. Growth in the past five years has been mostly in research universities, 6.3% to 9.3%, and less in the universities of applied sciences, 5.8% to 6.4%. The dominant country of origin in 2009–2010 was Germany (42.5% of all international students), followed by China (10%), Belgium (5%), Spain (3.9%), and France (3.6%). In that year, 64.4% of the international students came from other EU and EFTA countries, compared to 35.6% from the rest of the world. The Netherlands is the host country with the most German students, ahead of the United Kingdom, attracting 17% of outbound German student mobility (Nuffic, 2010). Three quarters of international students are enrolled in bachelor's degree programs, although in research universities, the focus is increasingly on masters and PhD programs.

The Netherlands global market share was 1.3% in 2007, an increase of 0.6% compared to 2000. As far as outbound mobility is concerned, 2.5% (15,000) of Dutch students were studying abroad in 2006–2007, and the trend is a gradual increase each year. There are no concrete data on international PhD students and researchers in the Netherlands. A recent guess is that one third of the PhD students in the Netherlands were foreign, a rapid growth over the past 15 years, originating primarily from Western Europe and Asia. OECD data indicate that half of all foreign knowledge workers in the Netherlands come from Europe and the other half primarily from South and East Asia, followed by North America.

It is still unclear what the impact of the introduction of full cost fees for non-EU/EFTA students in 2009 will mean for the inflow of international students to the Netherlands. Two thirds of the international students in the Netherlands come from EU/EFTA countries anyway, and the first data do not show a decline in non-EU numbers. In particular, the number of students from Brazil, Russia, India, and China, the BRIC countries, is on the rise.

Since 2007, it has been possible for international students to stay in the country for a year after completion of their studies to find a job, and since 2009, highly qualified foreigners can apply for a residence permit for a maximum of one year to find a job or to start a business. There are also tax incentives for knowledge immigrants and returning expatriates in areas where there is a lack of Dutch candidates. Furthermore, migration policies have been adapted to make immigration for lower skilled immigrants more difficult and for highly skilled immigrants easier. Several measures have been initiated to increase the number of international students, such as the provision of a 5-year visa instead of a 1-year visa that must be renewed annually; easier transfer from one university to another; easier visa application procedures; reduction of bureaucratic obstacles; and a one-year postgraduate extra stay option to look for a job.

There are no data yet on how effective these combined measures have been. Also, little is known about the language factor. Although some studies see a pull factor in the fact that Dutch people often speak and understand English and that an increasing proportion of Dutch higher education is offered in English (in particular at the masters and PhD levels), others question the level of English fluency among Dutch graduates and faculty. Also, some studies indicate that the Netherlands is not attractive enough for international and returning Dutch researchers. By contrast, other studies conclude that the Netherlands is more attractive than competitor European countries because of the relatively good salaries, career prospects, and knowledge infrastructure.

There is an increasing tension in the Netherlands between short-term anti-immigrant tendencies and budget cuts for research and development, on the one hand, and the long-term need for skilled immigration to stay competitive in the global knowledge economy on the other hand. Severe budget cuts to scholarship schemes for international students and to development aid, in combination with the economic crisis, do not allow optimism in the coming years.

Future Trends

As demonstrated, international students have emerged as a skilled migration elite. They represent a highly acceptable human capital resource to governments and employers, having self-funded to meet domestic labor market demand. They confront few of the barriers experienced by foreign-trained professionals, in terms of host-country language ability, qualification recognition, or acculturation. Their productive lives will be long, given their youth at point of enrollment. They represent a palatable option for countries with ambivalent views on migration, in a context where demographic contraction is fuelling demand. In the context of the global financial crisis, cash-strapped tertiary institutions are also increasingly motivated to recruit them.

Reflecting this, in the early 2000s, many OECD countries established two-step migration frameworks, designed to attract and retain international students. These countries are at once competitors and collaborators within this process. International students have responded with alacrity to such opportunities. Study-migration pathways have emerged as a key determinant of student flows. Modes of global delivery have diversified (Knight, 2010). Increasingly diverse source countries, destinations, sectoral providers, and motivations are now involved. Abuses have emerged and are being corrected: The United Kingdom, Australia and New Zealand, for instance, are repitching student retention to elite rather than vocational qualification levels. For many students, international education has become Stage 1 of a global career trajectory. Following graduation, they will address workforce undersupply and maldistribution, including the mismatch between the skills set of domestic workers and the needs of the knowledge economy. While their scale of long-term retention is unclear, former students will also compensate for out-migration from host countries.

Within the context of the global financial crisis and revenue drivers, the two-step migration paradigm seems certain to thrive. Tertiary education leaders, administrators, and faculty will thus face new academic and governance challenges. It is important to note international students are becoming highly informed consumers, seeking the optimal global package. While the ethics of student migration remain a matter of debate, parents rather than source countries have typically resourced their education. From this perspective, international student recruitment may be less problematic than the OECD migration norm—selection of mature-age professionals fully trained by their countries of origin.

References

Andressen, C. (1993). *Educational refugees: Malaysian students in Australia* (Monash University Papers on South-East Asia, No 29). Melbourne: Monash University.

Appadurai, A. (1996). *Modernity at large.* Minneapolis: University of Minnesota Press.

Arkoudis, S., Hawthorne, L., Baik, C., Hawthorne, G., O'Loughlin, K., Bexley, E., & Leach, D. (2009). *The impact of English language proficiency and workplace readiness on the employment outcomes of tertiary international students.* Canberra, Australia: Department of Employment, Education and Workplace Relations. Retrieved from http:// aei.gov.au/AEI/PublicationsAndResearch/Publications/ELP_Full_Report_pdf.pdf

Australian Education International. (2011). *International student enrolment data - Australia YTD 2011.* Canberra, Australia: Department of Education, Employment, and Workplace Relations.

Aydemir, A., & Skuterad, M. (2005). Explaining the deteriorating entry earnings of Canada's immigrant cohorts: 1966-2000. *Canadian Journal of Economics, 38*(2).

Baas, M. (2010). *Imagined mobility: Migration and transnationalism among Indian students in Australia.* United Kingdom: Anthem Press.

Baird Review. (2010). *Review of education services for overseas students (ESOS) Act 2000: Stronger, simpler, smarter ESOS: supporting international students* (pp. 1–2, 7–9). Canberra, Australia: Department of Education, Employment and Workplace Relations.

Birrell, B., Hawthorne, L., & Richardson, S. (2006). *Evaluation of the general skilled migration categories.* Canberra: Commonwealth of Australia.

Blake, C. (2009). Foreword by Secretary of Labour. *Migration trends and outlook 2008/09: International migration, settlement and employment dynamics.* Wellington, NZ: Department of Labor. Retrieved from www.dol.govt.nz/publications/research/migration-outlook-200809/index.asp

Borjas, G. (2009). Immigration in high-skill labour markets: The impact of foreign students on the earnings of doctorates. In R. B Freeman & D. L. Goroff (Eds.), *Science and engineering careers in the United States: An analysis of markets and employment*. Chicago: University of Chicago Press.

Borjas, G., & Doran, K. (2012). *The collapse of the Soviet Union and the productivity of American mathematicians* (National Bureau of Economic Research, Working Paper 17800). Boston: Harvard University.

Cameron, D. (2011). Migration speech. *BBC News*. Retrieved September 5, 2011, from http://www .bbc.co.uk/news/uk-politics-13083781

Canadian Resident Matching Service. (2010, October). *Canadian students studying medicine abroad*. Toronto: Author.

Central Intelligence Agency. (2010). Country comparison: Fertility rates. *World Fact Book*. Retrieved from https://www.cia.gov/library/ publications/the-world-factbook/ rankorder/2127rank.html

Citizenship and Immigration Canada. (2010). *Government of Canada announces 2011 immigration plan*. Retrieved from http://www .cic.gc/english/department/ mediareleases/2010/2010-11-01a.asp.

Citizenship and Immigration Canada. (2011). *Backgrounder: Stakeholder and public consultations on immigration levels and mix*. Retrieved from http://www.cic.gc.ca/english/department/media/ backgrounders/2011/2011-07-11.asp

Cotis, J.-P. (2005, March 11–12). *Challenges of demographics*. Keynote speech, Policy network spring retreat, Warren House, Surrey.

Council of Graduate Schools. (2011a). *Data sources: Employment trends among new doctorate recipients. Results from the 2011 CGS Pressing Issues Survey*. Retrieved October 1, 2011, from http://www.cgsnet.org/portals/0/pdf/ DataSources_2010_07.pdf

Council of Graduate Schools. (2011b). *Data sources: Trends in application and financial support deadlines. Result from the 2011 CGS Pressing Issues Survey*. Retrieved October 1, 2011, from http://www.cgsnet.org/portals/0/pdf/ DataSources_2011_06.pdf

Das, S. (2009, July 29). Millions trump truth about dodgy schools. *The Age*, p. 15.

Department of Immigration and Citizenship. (2010). *Introduction of a new point test*. Retrieved December 27 from http:// www.immi.gov.au/ skilled /general-skilled-migratoin/pdf/points -fact.pdf.

Diaz-Briquets, S., & Cheney, C. (2003). Foreign scientists at the National Institutes of Health: Ramifications of US immigration and labor policies. *International Migration Review, 37*(2), 421–443.

European University Association. (2011). *Financially sustainable universities 11: European universities diversifying income streams*. Brussels: Author.

Finn, M. (2007). *Stay rates of foreign doctorate recipients from US universities: 2005*. Oak Ridge, TN: Oak Ridge Institute for Science and Education.

Government Accountability Office. (2009). *Higher education: Approaches to attract and fund international students in the United States and abroad*. Washington, DC: Author.

Government of China. (2010, July). *Outline of China's national plan for medium and long-term education reform and development (2010-2020)*. Beijing: Author.

Green, M., & Ferguson, A. (2011). *Internationalisation of U.S. higher education in a time of declining resources*. Canberra: Australian Education International.

Gross, D. (2009, July 15). Why Japan isn't rising. *Newsweek*, p. 1. Retrieved August 30, 2011, from http://www.thedailybeast.com/newsweek/2009/ 07/15/why-japan-isn-t-rising.print.html

Hawthorne, L. (2008). *The impact of economic selection policy on labour market outcomes for degree-qualified migrants in Canada and Australia*. Ottawa, Canada: Institute for Research on Public Policy.

Hawthorne, L. (2010a). Demography, migration. and demand for international students. In C. Findlay & W. Tierney (Eds.), *Globalization and tertiary education in the Asia-Pacific: The changing nature of a dynamic market* (pp. 91–120). Singapore: World Scientific Press.

Hawthorne, L. (2010b). How valuable is "Two-Step Migration"? Labour market outcomes for international student migrants to Australia (Special Edition). *Asia-Pacific Migration Journal, 19*(1), 5–36.

Hawthorne, L. (2011a). *Competing for skills: Migration policies and trends in New Zealand and Australia*. Wellington: Government of New Zealand, Department of Labour.

Hawthorne, L. (2011b). *Health workforce migration to Australia – policy trends and outcomes 2004-2010*. Canberra: Department of Health and Ageing, Health Workforce Australia.

Hawthorne, L., & To, A. (2011). *The early migration and career trajectories of international medical students qualified in Australia*. Sydney, Australia: Medical Deans of Australasia.

Helle, B., & Sauer, L. (2007). Conditions of entry and residence of third country highly qualified and highly skilled workers: The situation in Germany. In *The framework of the European migration network* (Small Scale Study 111). Nuremburg, Germany: Bunesamt fur Migration und Fluchtlinge.

Home Office. (2006). *A points-based system: Making migration work for Britain* (Cm 6741). London: Crown.

Hugo, G. (2007, May 1–2). *Demographic change in East and Southeast Asia and the implications for the future.* Presentation to the 17th General Meeting of the Pacific Economic Cooperation Council, Sydney.

Institute of International Education. (2010). International students in the United States. *Open Doors 2010 Fast Facts,* Washington, DC. Retrieved September 5, 2010, from http://www .iie.org/en/Research-and-Publications/~/media/ Files/Corporate/Open-Doors/Fast-Facts/ Fast%20Facts%202010.ashx

Isserstedt, W., & Schnitzer, K. (2005). *Internationalisation of higher education: Foreign students in Germany (and) German students abroad.* Berlin: Federal Ministry of Education and Research.

Knight, J. (2010). Cross-border higher education. In C. Findlay & W. G. Tierney (Eds.), *Globalisation and tertiary education in the Asia-Pacific: The changing nature of a dynamic market* (Chapter 4). Singapore: World Scientific.

Lasanowski, V. (2009). *International student mobility: Patterns and trends.* London: Observatory on Borderless Higher Education.

Lasanowski, V., & Verbik, L. (2007). *International student mobility: Patterns and trends.* London: Observatory on Borderless Higher Education.

Lowell, L., Bump, M., & Martin, S. (2007). *Foreign students coming to America: The impact of policy, procedures, and economic competition.* Washington, DC: Georgetown University, Institute for the Study of International Migration.

Marginson, S. (2011). *Global context of education and the role of international education in Australia.* Paper commissioned by L H Martin Institute and Australian Education International, Centre for the Study of Higher Education, University of Melbourne.

Marginson, S., & van der Wende, M. (2007). *Globalisation and higher education.* (Education working paper No. 8). Paris: OECD, Directorate for Education.

Martin, P., & Ruhs, M. (2010). *Labour shortages and US immigration reform: Promises and perils of an independent commission* (Centre on Migration, Policy and Society, Working Paper No. 81). Oxford, UK: University of Oxford.

Matthews, C. M. (2007). Foreign science and engineering presence in US institutions and the labor force (CRS report for Congress, Congressional Research Service). In J. E. Cruthers (Ed.), *Trends in higher education* (pp. 89–110). Hauppauge, NY: Nova Science.

National Science Foundation. (2008). *Science and engineering indicators 2008.* Washington, DC: Author.

National Science Foundation. (2010). *Science and engineering indicators 2010.* Washington, DC: Author.

Nesdale, D., Simkin, K., Sang, D., Burke, B., & Fraser, S. (1995). *International students and immigration.* Canberra: Australian Government Publishing Service.

Nutbeam, D. (2011, April 27). *Change in higher education in England.* Keynote presentation, Australian Ninth Higher Education Summit, Brisbane.

Organization for Economic Cooperation and Development (OECD). (2010). *International migration outlook – SOPEMI 2010* (A8, Section 3). Paris: Author.

Picot, G., Feng, H., & Coulombe, S. (2007). *Chronic low-income and low-income dynamics among recent immigrants* (Analytical studies research papers, Catalogue No. 11F0019MIE, No. 294. Ottawa: Statistics Canada.

Population Reference Bureau. (2011). *2010 World population data sheet.* Retrieved August 30, 2011, from http://www.prb.org/Publications/ Datasheets/2010/2010wpds.aspx

Salt, J. (2011). International students and the labour market. In T. Modood & J. Salt (Eds.), *Global migration, ethnicity, and Britishness* (pp. 132–149). London: Palgrave Macmillan.

Salt, J., Latham, A., Mateos, P., Dobson, J., Wood, E., Dennett, A. & Bauere, V. (2011). *UK national report: Satisfying labour demand through migration* (Home office UK, Border Agency report). Brussels: European Migration Network.

Shu, J., & Hawthorne, L. (1996). Asian student migration to Australia. *International Migration, 34*(1), 65–96.

Sidhu, R. (2006). *Universities and globalization: To market to market.* Mahwah, NJ: Lawrence Erlbaum.

Skeldon, R. (1997). *Migration and development: A global perspective.* Essex, UK: Addison Wesley Longman Limited.

Slaughter, S., & Lesley, L. (1997). *Academic capitalism: Politics, policies, and the entrepreneurial university.* Baltimore: Johns Hopkins University Press.

Tachdjian, J.-P. (2011, May 25–27). *If you let them, they will come: International students and migration policy.* Presentation by Deputy Director and Trade Commissioner, Edu-Canada, Foreign Affairs and International Trade Canada, Observatory on Borderless Higher Education Global Forum, Vancouver.

Vertovec, S. (2002). *Transnational networks and skilled labour migration* (Compass working paper). Oxford, UK: University of Oxford.

Wang, L. (2008). *Migration, quality assurance and mutual recognition of qualifications: A country paper of the People's Republic of China*. Paris: UNESCO.

Zong, W. (2011, May 25–27). *Recent policies on China's international exchange and cooperation in education*. Presentation at Observatory on Borderless Higher Education Global Forum, Vancouver.

Zucker, L., & Darby, M. (2007). *Star scientists, innovation and regional and national immigration* (Working Paper 13547). Cambridge, MA: National Bureau of Economic Research.

Notes

1   The term *designer immigrants* was coined by A. Simmons. See Simmons, A. (1999). International migration and designer immigrants: Canadian policy in the 1990s. In M. Castro (Ed.), *Free markets, open societies, closed borders? Trends in international migration and immigration policy in the Americas*. Miami: North-South Center Press.

SECTION E

THE FUTURE OF INTERNATIONAL HIGHER EDUCATION

24

The Internationalization of Higher Education

Future Prospects

Madeleine F. Green, Francisco Marmolejo,
and Eva Egron-Polak

I t is widely recognized that the future economic and social well-being of nations
rests on their ability to participate in the
global knowledge economy (Santiago,
Tremblay, Basri, & Arnal, 2008). Higher education plays a central role in preparing the workforce, fueling innovation through basic and
applied research, disseminating knowledge,
and educating for responsible citizenship. It is
both a driver of globalization and shaped by it
(Center for Higher Education Research and
Innovation, 2009). Some trends are already
quite clear as highlighted throughout this volume: The future of higher education will be a
more global one, in which both collaboration
and competition will intensify, and knowledge
and people will flow even more freely across
borders. Research will increasingly require
global teams, and technology will continue to
facilitate international cooperation both in
teaching and research. Although most institutions will continue to be rooted in their national
agendas and funding schemes, they will look
outwards to international partnerships to

accomplish their missions (as discussed in
Chapter 9, this volume).

But within these broad visible trends lies
uncertainty. Predicting the future is risky, but to
avoid the attempt is dangerous. Thus, it is only
fitting that this volume conclude with chapters
that look ahead, however imperfect their vision
may be. Such an effort must be undertaken with
caution, knowing that disruptive and unpredict-
able change could alter what may seem like
inevitable trajectories. As one observer of the
global higher education scene put it, "Anybody
who makes confident predictions about the
future of today's fast-growing global higher-
education marketplace should be reminded that
education trend lines can shift unexpectedly and
relatively quickly" (Wildavsky, 2010b, p. 17).

Introduction: Globalization for Better and for Worse

Although there is wide agreement that the globalization of higher education will continue to

439

intensify, its impact will differ by region and country. Altbach (2008) and others point to the potential for globalization to create winners and losers and to widen the divide between the developed and developing world. The race to rise in the rankings and to attain world-class status disadvantages institutions in developing countries and may push them (or their governments) to make unwise investments. The same divide can also be found within countries, between richer and more elite universities and mass institutions, and is likely to grow. The heightened role of competition for students and revenue carries the risk of putting traditional academic values in jeopardy and affecting future access for poor or marginalized students.

Opposing views on globalization abound. Friedman (2005), an early proponent of the positive effects of globalization, points to greater equality of opportunity, the benefits of technology, and the potential of globalization to level the playing field. Wildavsky (2010a) echoes this optimism, seeing "academic free trade" as a boon, intensifying the trends of mass access, meritocracy, and greater use of technology, along with an overall increase in world knowledge. The latter, he points out, is not a zero-sum game. Others even predict that globalization could help end poverty in less developed countries (Sachs, 2005).

Whatever one's view is of the benefits and perils of globalization, it will surely continue to shape the overall higher education landscape and demand both government and institutional responses. At the national level, concern with economic development will cause governments to think anew about research policies and investment, visa and immigration policies, access, and workforce needs. Security concerns can trigger policies that affect international students and scholars, cross-border education, and higher education as an instrument of public diplomacy. As the International Association of Universities (IAU) notes in its survey of institutional internationalization practices and policies, "internationalization is an issue of far more importance in overall higher education policy than in the past, both at the institutional level and in many national public policies" (Egron-Polak & Hudson, 2010, p. 17).

The IAU survey results also demonstrate that institutions are increasingly concerned with internationalization; 87% of responding institutions indicated that internationalization is part of their institutional mission statement or overall strategic plan. In addition, 78% reported that internationalization had increased in importance over the past 3 years. At the same time, the survey results underscore some notable differences in perceptions of the importance of internationalization among respondents from different regions. Only 48% of respondents from the Middle East and 51% in Latin America and the Caribbean indicated that internationalization was an area of high importance for the leadership at their institution, compared to 71% of European respondents, 68% of North American respondents, and 65% of all respondents. Regional differences in responses on the perceived risks of internationalization are also noteworthy: Respondents from North America and Europe were most likely to answer "no reply" to that question. The second most likely response was that they saw no risks. In Africa and Latin America and the Caribbean, the risk of brain drain was the leading response, whereas in the Middle East, it was loss of cultural identity. In Asia and the Pacific, commodification of higher education was cited as the leading risk.

These results highlight the variable effects of the global forces presented in the next section. Different national and regional dynamics and capacities, policies, and cultures will shape how different countries and regions experience a particular global phenomenon. The next section outlines three important global trends that will strongly influence higher education internationalization: demographics, the world economy, and technology.

THE CONTEXT: GLOBAL TRENDS

Demographics

Demand for higher education, fueled largely by population increases, shapes the movement of students and programs across borders. Virtually all the predicted population growth will occur in Africa, Asia, and Latin America. By the year 2050, with the exception of the United States (which will still be the third-largest country in 2050) and Japan (which will occupy 14th place in terms of population), the largest countries in the world will not be among the traditional wealthier nations. These will include

India (1), China (2), Pakistan (4), Indonesia (5), Nigeria (6), Bangladesh (7), Brazil (8), Ethiopia (9), Democratic Republic of Congo (10), Mexico (11), Egypt (12), Vietnam (13), Iran (15) and Uganda (16) (United Nations, 2004.) Estimates put the world population of 15 to 24 year olds in 2050 at 1.2 billion, with 90% of those youths in the developing world (Population Reference Bureau, 2009).

Likewise, the majority of the growth in higher education will happen not in today's aging developed world but in developing countries. This uneven population growth is likely to have an impact on institutional partnerships and the work of internationalization offices, research cooperation, patterns of student and faculty mobility, curriculum, and brain drain. The demand for faculty in nations expanding their higher education systems could intensify the return of faculty from the diaspora or attract Western faculty whose employment options are limited in their static systems.

Meeting the growing demand for higher education in developing countries will also drive policy discussions of several issues. Limited financial resources will underscore the need for a differentiated system of post-secondary education, where institutions assume different missions requiring differential levels of financial support. Education delivered by foreign providers through programs or campuses in the host country or online may be a more prominent alternative; student mobility will increase as long as there is insufficient domestic capacity.

Countries where population is declining, such as Japan and those in Europe, will face a different set of issues. Attracting students from abroad will be an important way to maintain both the quantity and quality of the student population and, in some cases, to keep higher education institutions or specific programs open. Europe and Japan are both seeking to increase their international student enrollments and will likely continue to do so. Closures or mergers in the future are a real possibility in nations with declines in student-age populations. Scarcity of young faculty may also lead institutions to seek to attract faculty from abroad. At the national level, policy issues concerning visas for students and faculty, work permits, and the transportability of social benefits will emerge. Some countries, such as Canada,

anticipating a student population shortage, have already adapted their visa regulations to make it easier for international students to attend their institutions and remain after graduation. This trend is likely to continue.

Migration also shapes the population and pool of potential higher education students. There are an estimated 214 million international migrants worldwide, or 3.1% of the world's population (International Organization for Migration, n.d.), 60% of whom reside in the more developed regions, representing 10% of their population. (Marmolejo, Manley-Casimir, &Vincent-Lancrin, 2008). Migrants include highly educated individuals seeking greater opportunities, refugees displaced by war, and low-skilled people in search of a living wage. Migration will also drive several important higher education policy issues, especially student and work visas (see Chapters 21 & 23, this volume). For example, should U.S. visa and immigration policies tighten in the future, it will have serious consequences for the U.S. workforce, innovation, and higher education. The United States is highly dependent on the talent pool supplied by foreign graduates in science and engineering. In 2010, 12% of the U.S. workforce were immigrants, compared to 47% of PhDs in science and engineering (Wildavsky, 2010a).

A second issue related to migration—one that is the subject of heated debate around the world—is the education of undocumented immigrants. One view is that only legal migrants should be entitled to subsidized higher education, especially since many nations are struggling to pay for access for their own citizens. Another is that there are immense social costs of creating an underclass of uneducated undocumented migrants. Future policies that exclude undocumented immigrants from higher education will have significant repercussions on the workforce and on the economy.

A final dimension of demographics is that of mortality. Advances in medicine are increasing longevity worldwide, especially in developed countries, while high infant mortality rates take a toll on developing countries. HIV/AIDS continues to have a devastating impact on Africa and will affect national economies, quality of life, the size of the student population, and the availability of teachers at all levels. Unexpected changes in mortality rates, such as wars and pandemics, underscore the reality that unexpected events could rapidly and profoundly alter the picture for higher education.

The World Economy

The vicissitudes of the world economy will always have a direct effect on higher education. Jones and Wellman (2010) point to the trend of reduced public funding of higher education and increased transfer of costs to students and their families as the "new normal" in the United States. Their prediction that public investment in higher education per student will continue to decline is applicable to many other countries, in that the decrease is driven by a combination of scarce public funds, a growing view of higher education as a private good rather than a public investment, and in some nations, burgeoning enrollments.

BOX 24.1 The Rise of China and India

The hallmark of globalization is the interdependence of nations. Because of their size, China and India have a profound influence on the rest of the world. They are by far the most populous countries, with populations of 1.338 and 1.189 billion, respectively. Projected growth in China and India puts India as the most populous country in 2050, at 1.748 billion, when China will have a population of 1.435 billion, with the United States running third at a mere 423 million.

China has undergone rapid economic expansion since the 1990s. Estimated GDP growth rates for 2007, 2008, and 2009 were 13%, 9% and 9.1%, respectively (Central Intelligence Agency, 2010). China is also moving ahead in innovation. Between 2006 and 2009, Chinese applications for patents soared, while the U.S. and European applications were stable and Japan's declined (Trading Places, 2010). If the current growth rate continues, China will soon overtake Japan in patent applications, putting it in second place after the United States.

China has undertaken an ambitious expansion of higher education aiming to increase enrollments, enhance educational quality, and improve the quality and quantity of research. Enrollments have expanded at a breathtaking rate: It now educates about 23% of the age cohort (29 million students), up from 3% 20 years ago (Liu & Wang, 2010). It aims to raise the enrollment rate to 40% within 10 years and the number of citizens with college-level education in the workforce from 9% to 20% (Sharma, 2010). China has also vigorously attacked the quality issue. "Project 211" and "Project 985" have poured funds into about 100 higher education institutions and key disciplinary areas. These programs aim to raise the standard of education and research in 300 fields deemed essential to national economic growth and to establish these 100 institutions as national standards of academic and research quality for the rest of the higher education system to emulate. China is also investing in attracting Chinese faculty in the diaspora and improving facilities, curricula, and pedagogy (Sharma, 2011). These initiatives also aim to prepare the next generation of academics and administrative leaders.

China seeks to educate an increasing proportion of its students at home and create world-class teaching and research. If China continues to increase its capacity to educate a higher proportion of its students, it will have a profound effect on the countries that have become dependent on Chinese students and could hit hard at their graduate programs in technology and science. Similarly, as China develops into a research powerhouse, it is likely to change the global landscape for research. Already, China is moving toward a balance between the number of students it sends to study abroad and those that it hosts in China. However, corruption, academic fraud, and constraints on academic freedom can easily slow progress and diminish China's credibility as an academic force.

India presents a different picture. *The Economist* (A Bumpier Road, 2010) opines that "if India keeps growing as fast as it is now, it will change the world" (p. 76). India's GDP is expected to grow by 8.5% this year, and some predict that its growth will outpace China's in 3 to 5 years. Its working age population will increase by 136 million by 2020, compared to China's increase of 23 million. Business is thriving, and an enduring democracy bodes well for future development.

But India also faces many problems and obstacles to economic and social vibrancy. The education system is poor, the bureaucracy sclerotic, and the infrastructure weak. Political instability is a problem, along with corruption, especially in government. The road to prosperity and social well-being is a long and difficult one.

India's higher education system suffers from general poor quality (with notable but relatively few exceptions) and insufficient capacity. It has not made the same investment in higher education as China. In 2007, it enrolled 11% of the age cohort and aims to increase that rate to 15% by 2012 (Mehrotra, 2009). It has a much lower adult literacy rate than China and needs to raise both the enrollment rate and quality of primary and secondary schools. India has a long way to go to catch up with the more industrialized countries in participation rates and quality. Unless India undertakes a massive effort such China's, it is likely to continue to be a major source of mobile students and a supplier of faculty to developed countries.

The economic condition of higher education institutions, in turn, influences their internationalization strategies. In countries such as Australia and the United Kingdom, and increasingly in the United States, the drive for revenue has led to a view of internationalization as an instrument of institutional competitiveness, prestige enhancement, and revenue generation. A future scenario of public disinvestment and the search for revenue will likely result in institutions seeking greater numbers of fee-paying international students and viewing study abroad as a profit center or at least as a means to remain self-supporting, rather than as an academic program requiring financial support (Heyl, 2011).

An alternative scenario is to respond to economic difficulties by increasing investment in higher education, with a goal of stimulating the local economy and enhancing research and innovation. Some nations have maintained their funding levels or made selective investments. In spite of the worldwide recession, the governments of Mexico, the Russian Federation, and Spain provided more funding for student scholarships and some academic programs. The German government is investing in infrastructure and science and technology, and the UK government in research (Varghese, 2010). Brazil, which was in the midst of an ambitious expansion and reform process when the economic crisis hit, persisted in its efforts, maintaining a $6 billion investment plan (Almeida-Filho, 2010). In addition, in 2011, Brazil launched an ambitious mobility program called Science without Borders to support up to 10,000 students to study outside the country. (See Chapter 25, Box 25.6, for a summary of Brazil's initiatives in this area.)

A crisis may be an opportunity to undertake fundamental rethinking and changes that would not be possible in normal times. Will the need for public institutions to diversify funding sources, for example, cause them to act in fundamentally different ways over time? Or will they preserve their basic structures and modes of operation with fewer resources and a different mix of funding sources, activities, and partners? Will the influx of international students in countries with high proportions of international student enrollments, such as the United Kingdom and Australia, change the culture of higher education institutions, or will they remain fundamentally British and Australian but with a sizeable international population? Certainly, some changes are inevitable. But it is unclear whether funding alone will drive deep and enduring changes that truly alter the higher education landscape and its international and global dimensions.

Technology

The use of technology to enhance teaching and learning is widely accepted (see Chapter 15, this volume, for a discussion on technology use for internationalizing the classroom), although it is increasingly clear that it is not a panacea and that a sizeable proportion of faculty members choose not to take advantage of it. The promise of technology to transform higher education—especially teaching and learning—has simply not materialized. However, the tools of technology have grown exponentially faster and more smoothly, and they have enabled institutions to be far more efficient and sophisticated than they were even 10 years ago. Gone are the days when the fastest computers had a speed of 256 kilobits per second, floppy drives were used to store information, and noisy modems served as a basis for dialup communication. Back in those days, internationalization offices developed partnerships with peer institutions or arranged study abroad programs for their students by mailing letters and documents, making campus visits and telephone calls, and later using fax machines. By the year 2030, individuals involved in internationalization will likely see the year 2012 as similarly antiquated. New technology as yet unidentified today may replace e-mail and video conferences; virtual mobility and online automatic translation may be vastly improved. There will be a new generation (or several) of the now-novel concepts of online social networking and cloud computing. Some foreseeable changes—certain to impact the work of internationalization—include the following:

Digital natives in internationalization: By 2030, most college students and the great majority of younger international education professionals will be "digital natives," comfortable with technology as a tool for communication and internationalization, perhaps using it differently than they currently do (Bennett, Maton, & Kervin, 2008). They may drive greater use of technology by faculty, including use for internationalization. In addition, institutions will increasingly serve a larger number of today's nontraditional students, both domestically and internationally, not only in the traditional face-to-face manner, but also increasingly at a distance.

Virtual classrooms: Asynchronous online technology to deliver educational programs or specific courses is increasingly available today, and its use will undoubtedly expand in the future as with the popularity of MOOCs—Massive Open Online Courses. Technology has already made it possible to establish instant communication practically anytime and anywhere in the world and to create virtual international classrooms in which students can have instant real-time interaction with students from different institutions and with individuals outside their classroom. Sharing of knowledge and interaction among students from different countries and backgrounds will become more common, as the technology gets even better and cheaper. Greater use of technology to enhance internationalization of teaching and learning will depend on human factors more than technological ones. It is important to note that the technology exists today to facilitate joint classes and projects, as well as shared materials and lectures, and to link classes in real time. There is no guarantee, however, that the continued explosion of technology will be matched by a commensurate interest in using it to enhance international connectivity.

Student recruitment: Today's recruitment of international students relies heavily on recruiting visits and fairs as well as Web-enabled information (see Chapter 22, this volume). In the future, social networking and other means not yet known could become important ways for students to gather information on prospective institutions.

Language learning: Technological capabilities in areas such as voice recognition, language databases in the cloud, and automatic translation of texts have been rapidly advancing. In a few years, it will become easier to integrate those technologies so that language interpretation devices become a regular vehicle for dealing with language differences. The use of technology for translation and interpretation will help English speakers cope with the fact that the share of English written resources on the Web continues to shrink relative to other languages, and non-English speakers will have greater access to English Web resources. While better technology may make learning a foreign language less necessary or attractive, it can also be argued that the need for high-level language speakers will always be present; technology cannot capture the nuances of languages, regionalisms, or special meaning of words.

Institutional internationalization offices: Offices of internationalization will evolve with respect to technology in parallel to other institutional units. Whatever technology is developed and applied in the university will find its way to internationalization offices. However, given the international nature of the work of these offices, technology is likely to have an even greater impact. Mailing transcripts for credential evaluation or equivalencies of credits and paper processing of visas is likely to become obsolete. Transnational quality assurance mechanisms will probably increasingly use technology to enable institutions to verify the quality of an institution abroad and its academic programs. Also, private providers of international education support services will continue to expand technological support for internationalization offices in such areas as tracking international students, providing financial information and record-keeping, and following students after graduation.

There are, of course, potential downsides to such technological change, including risks associated with security and technological disruption, more sophisticated fraudulent use of information and technological devices, and an exacerbation of the global digital divide. If current trends continue, the technology gap will persist and even widen.

The next section focuses on five key questions concerning the future of higher education, briefly outlining the current trends and factors that will shape the responses to these questions.

Critical Questions for the Future of Internationalization

1. What Lies Ahead for International Student Mobility?

In 2008, there were an estimated 3.3 million internationally mobile students, up from 1.8 million in 1999 (OECD, 2010a). (It is important to note that because of differing data collection methodologies and definitions of international students across countries, there are often discrepancies between international student enrollment data reported by different organizations. (See Koch & Green, 2009, for different definitions.) Some project 8 million mobile students

in 2025. Institutions and governments seek international students for a variety of reasons, including income generation, prestige, cultural diplomacy, promoting innovation and productivity by gaining access to talent, and promoting campus internationalization.

Although the number of students seeking education abroad, either for an entire degree or a short-term experience, will undoubtedly continue to expand, the competition for international students is fierce and is likely to intensify. In 2009, the top five receiving countries were the United States, the United Kingdom, Germany, France, and Australia. However, in light of competition for students, changing student interest and preference, and world economic conditions, most probably, the current distribution of students will change. Indeed, the loss of U.S. share from 24% to 18.7% between 2000 and 2008 (OECD, 2010a) suggests that international student flows are not static. Similarly, Australia saw steady growth of international students until fall 2010, when enrollments decreased mainly due to tightening of visa restrictions for English-language students; further drops are predicted (Kremmer, 2010). Australia also saw a decline in applications from Indian students following some widely reported racial incidents in Australia in 2009 and 2010.

A number of factors will determine international student flows. Student preferences and perceptions of educational value and quality shape their choices. Programs taught in English are growing in number and attractiveness. Perceived climate of receptiveness, recruiting practices, visa policies, scholarship opportunities, and postgraduate work opportunities are key elements in attracting international students. All of the top five host countries except the United States have national recruiting campaigns. All host central websites and have a governmental or quasi-governmental organization that provides information and varying levels of marketing activities. The ease and expense of obtaining a visa will play a key role in a country's ability to attract international students. In 2009, the United Kingdom instituted a new points-based system for visas and experienced some implementation problems. Australia allows students to work for up to 20 hours per week under their student visa but, at the same time, has restricted the possibilities for students to become permanent residents after their studies, and it has tightened its visa policies for English-language students. Similar policy changes will have significant impact on the flows of international students.

Scholarships also help attract mobile students and the willingness of governments, institutions, and the private sector to provide financial support will shape the international student body in terms of country of origin and socioeconomic status. Australia, the United Kingdom, Germany, and France are making considerable investments relative to the size of their higher education systems (Green & Koch, 2009).

Newer entrants into the international student market may change the landscape considerably. China seeks to increase its current 196,000 visiting students to 300,000 by 2020 (Bhandari & Blumenthal, 2008), and Japan hopes to rise from its current 133,000 to 300,000 by 2020 (Japan: English Courses, 2010). Malaysia has set a goal of 150,000 international students by 2015, an increase of 70,000 over 2010 enrollments (Foreign Students, 2010).

A growing trend in international mobility is regionalization, which could alter student flows. Examples of regional hubs are Singapore for Asian students and the United Arab Emirates (UAE) and Qatar for students from the Middle East. Singapore has already reached its goal of attracting 150,000 international students by 2015. By 2007, 15 foreign institutions were operating programs mainly for international students in Singapore (Gribble & McBurnie, 2007). Over the past decade, the UAE and Qatar made immense investments to attract internationally renowned universities that will serve as higher education hubs for students from the region. The trend to regionalization is further confirmed by the IAU report, which indicates that in at least three world regions—Europe, Africa, and Asia and Pacific—institutions identified their own region as the first geographic priority for their internationalization strategies.

The availability and quality of education in one's home country will also affect global student mobility. India and China currently send the largest numbers of students abroad for their studies. The extent to which they will continue to fill the classrooms and laboratories of other countries will depend on how quickly they can expand capacity and increase quality at home. The attractiveness and price of studying in other countries could result in a greater number of U.S., Canadian, or European students seeking education outside their home countries, or in the case of Europe, outside the European region. Visa policies and scholarship support of the sending countries could change, resulting in a decreased number of students going abroad. And finally, the presence of foreign campuses or the availability of online education could result in more students staying at home. Although such options may slow the increase of students seeking a full degree abroad, increases in short-term education abroad experiences could offset these declines.

Student mobility has important social, economic, and political implications for both sending and receiving countries. Brain drain is still a serious problem for developing countries, although as countries prosper, they are able to attract their graduates home (Sharma, 2011). Given their dependency on international students to fill their engineering, science, and technology programs at the graduate level, institutions in hosting nations have a great deal at stake should the numbers of mobile students decrease. Similarly, these nations benefit immensely in currently winning the global race for talent and are not likely to cede their position voluntarily. The race is on, but the winners are not assured.

2. What Is the Future of Branch Campuses?

The growing demand for education globally has resulted in institutions crossing borders to deliver programs or establish branch campuses to educate students who seek a foreign education in their home country or region. Although only a small number of institutions have established branch campuses, mostly during the past decade, they are highly visible and closely watched by the media.

Although the Observatory on Borderless Higher Education reported 162 branch campuses in 2009 (Becker, 2009), achieving a precise count is difficult due to the ambiguity of definition and variance in national record-keeping. The United States, for example, has no single registry of branch campuses; institutional accrediting agencies require institutions to report "other locations," but no national tally exists of all institutions with locations abroad serving primarily non-U.S. students.

There are many models of academic programs and branch campuses abroad, ranging from a full-fledged campus to a few rented classrooms (Verbik & Merkley, 2006). Some programs are conducted with partners in the host country, either a university or commercial entity. A few institutions, especially those operating in the Gulf States, receive subsidies from the host governments in the form of scholarships for students, operating subsidies, complete or partial support for campus construction, or favorable terms for financing. The range of disciplines offered also varies (Green & Koch, 2009).

Whatever the actual count, and despite the global interest in branch campuses, it is important to note that relatively few institutions worldwide are creating branch campuses and that they are concentrated in relatively few countries. Becker (2009) reports that of the 162 institutions with branch campuses, 111 were set up by Anglophone nations, with the United States accounting for 48%. For the vast majority of institutions worldwide, including Anglophone nations, branch campuses and programs abroad will never be a major route to internationalization.

What lies ahead? The slowdown in the establishment of branch campuses suggests that the peak period of new initiatives has passed. The countries with high demand and generous support are not likely to continue to expand their considerable array of branch campuses. The UAE, for example, hosted 40 branch campuses in 2008 or 25% of the total (Becker, 2009; Schoepp, 2009, puts this figure at 55%). Recently, Dubai Academic City turned down 25 applications from foreign universities to set up branch campuses, citing quality issues (UAE: Academic City, 2010). Qatar and Singapore, which host the next highest number of branch campuses, are also unlikely to want much more growth. The weakened global economy and a few conspicuous branch campus closings—such as the Michigan State University (U.S.) in Dubai and George Mason University (U.S.) in the UAE, or the University of New South Wales (Australia) in Singapore—are likely to make institutions more cautious about financial and reputational risk involved in venturing abroad to establish a branch campus.

As experiences and a body of literature accumulate (Becker, 2009; Fazackerley & Worthington, 2007; Fielden & Gillard, 2011; Green, Eckel, Calderon, & Luu, 2007; Green, Eckel, & Kinser, 2008; Green & Koch, 2009, Schoepp, 2009), the potential pitfalls become clearer. Issues such as complex legal regulations in the host country, the challenges of attracting and retaining high-quality staff, maintaining linkages with the home campus, and a host of other strategic considerations and tactical difficulties are likely to cause institutions to move with greater caution than they might have when these difficulties were less apparent and when funds were more plentiful. Domestically, institutions expanding abroad face challenges associated with accreditation, differential payments to faculty members locally and abroad, and issues of reputation. In addition, questions of academic freedom will give some institutions pause, and others will continue to hold to the philosophical position that partnerships— where the benefits are reciprocal—are a better way to internationalize than establishing outposts abroad.

The wisdom and sustainability of branch campuses and other forms of cross-border education are not universally accepted. Some question the idea of foreign providers as the best way to help nations expand their capacity. Branch campuses may have a very limited effect on the receiving nation's ability to improve and expand higher education on its own. Issues of cultural relevance of a foreign education also arise. In addition, their sustainability is uncertain, as was demonstrated by the closing of most of the U.S. campuses established in Japan in the 1980s. Also uncertain is the ability of institutions to replicate the quality of the home campus or continuously adapt to changing local conditions (Altbach, 2010).

Over time, branch campuses may become a niche market, focusing on the sponsoring institution's centers of excellence (e.g., the U.S. campuses in Education City in Qatar selected for their specific programmatic strengths) or offering a prestigious foreign education by internationally renowned institutions. Receiving countries will, of course, need to see branch campuses as a positive contribution to their national development if they are to continue to host them and, in some cases, support them. In brief, the stars will need to align to support new entrants into the branch campus business and sustain the existing initiatives—so that demand and receptivity by host nations complement the strategic directions and the willingness of sponsoring institutions to venture abroad, with all the attendant problems and risks.

3. How Will Private Cross-Border Providers and Partnerships With the Private Sector Affect Global Higher Education?

The application of economic models and principles, sometimes called the "marketization" of higher education, is now firmly embedded in both the conceptualization and the practice of higher education. Markets affect student choice and enrollments, staffing, research, services to industry, and private gifts (Brown, 2009). The increasing role of the market is not a neutral topic. The corporatization and commodification of higher education are the subject of much criticism, as is the "orthodoxy of neoliberalism" (Rickford, 2010) that allegedly permeates the academy. When competition consistently trumps collaboration and solidarity, developing and sustaining international cooperation becomes much more difficult. Market forces have opened the doors to a new array of private providers—both domestic and cross border—as well as partnerships with the private sector. Both these trends are likely to increase.

Cross-border providers are considered to be private entities in the host country. Building on Jane Knight's (2005) typology, one can identify several types of private providers: recognized higher education institutions, nonrecognized higher education institutions, commercial companies (e.g., Pearsons, Microsoft), corporate universities (organizations that provide training for their employees), cross-border collaborative networks and affiliations (e.g., the World University Network), and virtual higher education institutions. Private higher education (both nonprofit and for-profit) expanded rapidly in the 1980s and 1990s. It is important to note that the distinction between public, private nonprofit, and private for-profit education is difficult to make (Levy, 2009). Levy (quoted in Redden, 2008) notes the existence of "for-profits legally cloaked as nonprofits." In some countries, the legal distinctions are blurry.

Private providers now educate some 30% of students worldwide, and in some countries, the majority of enrollments are in the private sector. More than 70% of higher education students are in private institutions in Indonesia, Japan, the Philippines, and Korea. In Chile, that proportion approaches 75%, and overall in Latin America, nearly half of postsecondary students are in private institutions (Sharma, 2009). In India, private institutions educate a third of all students and 80% of students in professional studies (Agarwal, 2010).

The rise of the private sector has also spawned the growth of for-profit universities that operate globally and whose target student population is generally similar to that of the domestic private providers. For example, Laureate enrolls nearly half a million students in 43 countries. Whitney International offers moderately priced distance-learning programs, enrolling 40,000 students in Latin America in 2008. It plans to partner with for-profit institutions around the world and expand into India and other Asian nations (Wildavsky, 2010a).

Private cross-border education raises some knotty philosophical issues that will continue to be debated in the future. For some receiving countries, such as South Africa and India, relying on foreign providers to increase capacity, especially for-profit ones, is not a welcome prospect (Panikkar, 2011). Others, such as Hong Kong and Singapore, welcome such organizations and have rigorous quality assurance processes. Yet others, such as Mexico, Chile, and Egypt, and Brazil, are facing tremendous challenges in terms of access and capacity; they have quietly allowed foreign providers in one form or another, even though it is not strictly legal. As nations increase their capacity to meet the demand for higher education places and their ability to deliver high-quality education, they are likely to turn away from foreign providers. This shift, however, is not likely in the next 10 years.

Another issue lies in the cultural nature of education. The corporate cross-border education giants are largely American. On the one hand, this may portend a greater Americanization of higher education, clearly anathema to some. On the other hand, some for-profit entities are deliberate and strategic in adapting to local circumstances, sometimes by acquiring local institutions and continuing to offer the existing array of programs. What rankles in the minds of many, however, is that private education—cross-border and domestic—affords greater access to those who can pay, begging the question of how it contributes to helping nations to expand access to all socioeconomic groups. And the notion that education should be profitable to owners and shareholders is abhorrent to those who see education as a public good.

Another new development that is likely to intensify is partnerships with different kinds of actors, including domestic or global for-profit entities. A recent report by Universities U.K. (2010) describes a wide array of UK partnership models. For example, publicly funded UK universities accredit awards from other institutions. The University of Wales accredits 10 online providers, as well as overseas providers; the Open University validation service has 29 clients in the United Kingdom and eight abroad. An important new form of partnership links traditional universities with private companies to recruit or support international students. Institutions are increasingly turning to recruiting agents to identify international students, although the practice is still controversial, especially in the United States. Bridge programs to prepare international students for full matriculation are proliferating. Cambridge Education Group, INTO, Kaplan, Navitas, and Study Group have 33 U.K. institutional partners among them, as well as partners in the United States and Australia (Universities U.K., 2010). Two of the companies are Australian owned, one is American, and two are British. (See Chapter 22, this volume, for more in-depth discussion on these issues.)

A final example of such partnerships lies in the possibility for students to combine their studies in different countries with different providers (for-profit providers and traditional universities) and receive a degree from the university. Kaplan's U.S. Sino Pathways Program (USPP) enables students to study for 2 years in China at a Kaplan college, using a curriculum developed by a consortium of U.S. universities, and then transfer to one of the partner universities to complete the degree. Similarly, in India, students can study information technology at APTECH (a private firm with worldwide training centers) and complete their degrees at partner universities in England or Australia (Wildavsky, 2010a).

Cross-border private instruction could get a boost from trade bilateral or the multilateral negotiations. The General Agreement on Trade in Services (GATS) (http://www.wto.org/english/tratop_e/serv_e/gatsqa_e.htm) could also shape the development of private cross-border education. Although the GATS is currently stalled,

should it be revived, it could further open the doors to private providers as countries remove trade restrictions through these agreements. Regardless of the future of the GATS, bilateral agreements could have the same effect. Experience to date indicates, however, that trade agreements have not played a major role, and cross-border activity of all types has proceeded on its own steam. Private providers are likely to address trade barriers, either by lobbying their trade delegations or by taking the necessary steps to comply with existing regulations while still doing business.

Private cross-border providers are likely to be a permanent feature of global higher education, and new forms of public/private partnerships are bound to grow as institutions become more global and more entrepreneurial. Indeed, the influence of the market on higher education seems unstoppable. There is too much demand for higher education and too much money at stake to put this genie back in the bottle. So the question is not whether it will proceed, but what forms it will take and how it will be managed and overseen.

4. What Will Be the Effect of Escalating Competition and Rankings?

The arms race in higher education is on; de-escalation is nowhere in sight. Although competition is ubiquitous, it tends to occur in confined spaces. On the national level, institutions and programs with similar missions and standing compete with each other for students, faculty, prestige, and resources. Global competition is a phenomenon of the so-called world-class universities, which constitute a relatively small universe, concentrated in the United States and Europe. What will be new in the next 10 to 20 years, however, is that institutions outside this circle will gain entry into the elite group and join the race.

Nations are increasingly aware that achieving the goals of growth and global competitiveness depends on an educated workforce, the generation of knowledge, and innovation and that universities are key to achieving these goals (Salmi, 2009). Thus, many nations seek to have world-class universities. The definition of a world-class university is less than precise. As Altbach (2004, quoted in Salmi, 2009, p. 4) notes, "everyone wants one, no one knows what it is, and no one knows how to get one." Salmi (2009) observes that world-class universities are characterized by a high concentration of talent, abundant resources, and favorable governance. They are research intensive and prestigious. Position in high-profile rankings (national and global) is closely tied to status as a world-class university.

The push to create world-class universities has intensified in the last 15 years. Countries such as China, Germany, France, Saudi Arabia, Qatar, Spain, Malaysia, and the UAE are making enormous investments in strengthening existing higher education institutions or building new ones. The drive to attain the status of world-class university is fuelled by global rankings such as those compiled by *Times Higher Education* and Shanghai Jiao Tong University. In turn, performance in the rankings influences institutional strategy and national policy (Hazelkorn, 2008). In Malaysia, a drop in the ranking by the University of Malaya in the *Times Higher Education* from 89 to 169 caused national headlines, and the vice chancellor departed (Wildavsky, 2010a).

Ranking fever is rooted in the need for students, parents, and policymakers to have more information to understand and compare higher education institutions. This need will only increase as choices proliferate and higher education becomes even more important to individual success and national well-being. Again, the question is not whether there will be competition, comparisons, and rankings. Rather, the question is whether such comparisons can be done so that they recognize the immense diversity of more than 17,000 institutions of postsecondary education worldwide, while at the same time providing intelligible guideposts to this complex and confusing global array of institutions and programs. The weaknesses of the current rankings are well known: They favor the developed Anglophone countries; they do not recognize teaching and learning; and they count inputs rather than outcomes (Eckel, 2008).

Efforts, however, are under way to provide comparative information that attempts to avoid the pitfalls and oversimplification of rankings. One noteworthy effort is a ranking methodology begun in 1998 by the Center for Higher Education Development in Germany (http://www.che.de/). The center, founded in 1994 by the German Rectors' Conference and a foundation, is responsible for the methodology and the data, while the newspaper *Die Zeit* publishes, markets, and distributes the findings. Unlike other ranking systems, the center's methodology focuses on individual fields of study, not whole universities. Instead of producing a single score representing the combination of weighted indicators, this methodology allows users to create their own rankings by choosing and weighting indicators according to their own preference. A similar effort is the European U-Multirank initiative, supported by the European Union and under development by the Consortium for Higher Education and Research Performance Assessment (CHERPA). (See http://www.che.de/cms/?getObject=302&getNewsID=983&getCB=309&getLang=en.) Its goal is to create a multidimensional global ranking of similar institutions and programs; currently, 107 institutions from more than 40 countries have joined the study (Myklebust, 2010).

Future efforts could combine the comparative features of rankings with the detailed and more nuanced features of Germany's Center for Higher Education. For better or worse, simplicity is a virtue, and even though capturing quality should be a complex undertaking, speaking to the public requires clarity, transparency, and performance indicators that are readily understood. Higher education needs to take the business of competition and comparisons seriously. Institution leaders, researchers, and associations would be well advised to take an active role in shaping the nature of that competition and the public telling of the story through rankings and classifications. They will need to argue for and develop comparisons according to dimensions that are important to them and make certain that these choices are well understood. If equitable access for underrepresented students is an institutional goal, should institutions be penalized if they are not as selective as others or they fare less well on some of the dimensions given higher priority? A future in which higher education institutions are not involved in the selection of the criteria and systems used to present them to their many publics is not an attractive alternative, especially since it is the higher education institutions that bear the burden (and costs) of data collection and provision for all of the existing rankings and ratings.

A more positive possibility on the horizon is that of cooperating to compete. By agreeing to harmonize their systems of higher education,

European nations joining the Bologna Process hope to make Europe a more attractive destination for international students. Other kinds of networks and institutional alliances, as well as partnerships with other actors, can help institutions do together what they cannot do alone (see Chapter 9, this volume). Although networks are not a new idea, restricted resources, combined with the drive for excellence, make the prospect of cooperating to compete more appealing (Stockley & de Wit, 2011). Such cooperation, however, tempers rather than negates competition. Because institutions prefer to cooperate with peers or institutions with greater rather than lesser prestige, such cooperation could further reinforce a class system of higher education institutions.

5. How Can Higher Education Assure and Compare Quality and Define Degrees in a Globalized World?

Intensified globalization has created a need for more and better information on the quality of higher education institutions in different countries and on greater clarity on the meaning of a specific degree. Mobile students need good information to decide where to study and at which institution; faculty need to know the quality of a particular program to initiate a partnership. Employers need to evaluate the abilities of prospective hires. Rankings have to a large extent filled this need, but as noted in the previous section, they are limited in the depth of information they provide and most suffer from methodological weaknesses. Fortunately, many other initiatives are under way that attempt to address the need for better information on institutional quality and student learning outcomes.

Two types of efforts address the need for better information on the meaning of an institutional degree and the knowledge and skills of its graduates. One set of approaches—known as quality assurance or accreditation—is concerned largely with inputs and internal institutional processes and examines whether institutions have processes in place for ongoing quality review. This approach provides a measure of confidence that institutions are being externally reviewed and judgments made about quality. This cluster of approaches includes (a) the recognition of quality assurance agencies or accreditors by a superbody; (b) the accreditation of

institutions in other countries by a nationally based agency; and (c) mutual recognition of accreditation agencies.

The second set of approaches includes three initiatives that tackle the translation process through learning outcomes: (a) national or regional qualifications frameworks (or a degree profile, as it is known in the United States), which describes the learning outcomes associated with associate's, bachelor's, master's, and doctorate degrees, and in some cases short-cycle programs; (b) initiatives to describe the learning outcomes associated with different disciplines, known as the Tuning Process; and (c) a series of global tests of learning outcomes of undergraduate education, the Assessment of Higher Education Learning Outcomes (AHELO), sponsored by the Organization for Economic Cooperation and Development (OECD). (See Chapter 10, this volume, for in-depth discussion on learning outcomes and further details on AHELO.)

The latter set of approaches has emerged relatively recently; they are in their very early stages or nonexistent in some countries; this is an area of tremendous potential growth. Even those countries that have been working on learning outcomes assessment for some time—the United States for some 25 years—still faces many difficult methodological and implementation issues. Quality assurance that looks largely at input and processes is still the most frequent approach, and it will probably continue to be so in the near term. However, it is also likely that over time, assessment of learning outcomes will gain traction and sophistication and become more fully integrated into the overall methodology of quality assurance.

Recognition of quality assurance agencies: The meta-approach

One way to assure quality across borders is to have a governmental or nongovernmental superbody recognize accrediting agencies. Such a process distinguishes real accreditors from fraudulent ones and provides quality standards for accrediting bodies. Examples in the United States are the Council for Higher Education Accreditation (CHEA)—a nongovernmental membership organization—and recognition by the federal government, through the Department of Education. In Europe, the European Quality

Assurance Register for Higher Education (EQAR; http://www.eqar.eu/) provides a list or register of recognized accrediting or quality assurance agencies. Created in 2008, EQAR is currently a European initiative, although its door is open to admit agencies outside Europe. To qualify, agencies must comply with a common set of principles, the European Standards and Guidelines for Quality Assurance.

As we look ahead, it is possible to envision EQAR or a similar agency becoming a worldwide registry. EQAR may portend future trends in mutual recognition and interchangeability of quality assurance agencies. The existence of EQAR has enabled some European governments to recognize quality assurance bodies in other European countries. For example, Denmark automatically recognizes the quality assurance conducted by an EQAR-recognized agency for the purpose of Erasmus Mundus joint degree programs between Danish and foreign universities. Austria plans to allow public universities to choose freely from among EQAR-registered agencies for their periodic audits.

Mutual recognition of accrediting bodies

A more complicated and difficult model of translating quality assurance is agreement among organizations that their standards for recognition are substantially equivalent. The Washington Accord, established in 1989, is one of the oldest such efforts and recognizes "substantial equivalence" (www.washingtonaccord.org) in the accreditation of engineering degrees among 13 signatories. Similar and more recent agreements are the Sydney Accord for engineering technology education, the Dublin Accord for engineering technician education, and the Seoul Accord for computing education.

This approach is particularly well suited to science and technology, where curricula are likely to be similar; as a complement, licensure tests speak to learning outcomes. In addition, employer demand plays a role. The Engineers Mobility Forum and the Asia-Pacific Economic Cooperation engineer agreement allow individual engineers who are graduates of programs of recognized member accrediting agencies to register to have their professional qualifications recognized in other countries. Should the concept be extended to umbrella associations or meta-accreditors such as CHEA and EQAR, that could open the door for a wider application of mutual recognition among their members so that CHEA-recognized accreditors could then recognize EQAR-recognized agencies.

Accreditation and quality assurance with a global reach

Accreditation and quality assurance are no longer purely national undertakings. With the creation of the European Association for Quality Assurance in Higher Education and EQAR, Europeans are deliberately moving quality assurance to the European level, and allowing institutions to choose their quality assurance agency from among the registered bodies is a step in denationalizing quality assurance. The United States has approached denationalization rather differently, conducting both institutional and programmatic accreditation beyond the United States. According to the *CHEA Almanac of External Quality Review* (CHEA, 2010), the regional accrediting associations accredited collectively 35 institutions or programs of non-U.S. institutions in 18 countries as of December 2009. In addition, some of the programmatic accreditors are highly active in accrediting beyond U.S. borders. ABET, Inc. and AACSB International (The Association to Advance Collegiate Schools of Business) are the most heavily engaged. Since 2007, AACSB International has accredited 181 programs in 20 countries outside the United States. U.S. accreditors are not the only ones to operate across borders. A competitor to AACSB, the European Quality Improvement System (EQUIS) serves as the accrediting body of the European Foundation for Management Development (a membership association headquartered in Brussels). EQUIS has accredited 128 institutions in 36 countries, including the United States. The trend of accrediting programs globally is likely to grow, especially in certain fields where graduates are highly mobile.

The second set of approaches—focusing on defining and assessing the achievement of learning outcomes –is described below.

Qualifications frameworks

Around the world, qualifications frameworks, as they are generally called, have been developed to define the meaning of a degree at a given level (bachelor's, master's, doctorate, and short-cycle, in some cases) and the student learning outcomes required for the degree. They are likely to be more important in the future as institutions and countries seek greater clarity and transparency on the meaning of a degree. Qualifications frameworks are based on the principle of "ratcheting up" the competencies as the degree becomes more advanced. Qualifications frameworks are an established concept in countries such as Ireland, Denmark, the Netherlands, Scotland, South Africa, and many others. The United States, like other countries, has long relied on the accumulation of credits, combined with required courses for general education and the major to define a degree. That, too, could change as the United States puts more emphasis on learning outcomes and seeks a collective definition of a degree through its own version of a qualifications framework. With support from the Lumina Foundation, *A Degree Qualifications Profile* (2011) was drafted by a group of experts. As more countries take up qualifications frameworks, they may become the global coin of the realm in defining degrees.

Conclusion

In attempting to offer educated guesses about the future contours of higher education, this chapter examined current patterns, emerging trends, and visible trajectories. In the current era of rapid and volatile change, it is necessary to reiterate that there is much that cannot be foreseen or predicted. Different regions will develop differently, and even within nations, the issues will continue to be diverse. Demographic trends, including population growth, migration, and mortality, will play a decisive role in shaping the course of higher education. Less predictable are economic trends, which will to a great extent determine public investment in higher education, the ability of students and their families to pay, and patterns of student mobility. Technology, where developments are impossible to predict, will enable individuals and institutions to transcend spatial separation, connecting students, faculty, and researchers even more closely.

Yet, many important features of the future remain obscure. Whether the gaps and inequalities among institutions and nations will widen or narrow is mainly a matter of the policy choices that will be made at institutional, national, and increasingly regional levels. If the currently growing importance of the market continues in the absence of voluntary or other measures to mitigate its effects, it may become far more difficult for higher education institutions to promote the values of equity and social responsibility and to view higher education as an investment in the common good as opposed to serving as a private benefit.

Similarly, in the future, internationalization may come to emphasize competition, prestige, and income generation—higher education as an international business—rather than focusing on its mission to prepare students for global citizenship and to enhance human progress and well-being through collaborative efforts. Although the loftier aims and the business aspects will undoubtedly continue to coexist in a state of creative tension, policy choices by institutions and governments concerning the nature and purpose of internationalization could tip the balance in either direction.

The preoccupation with quality of education will not wane, and the way quality is monitored and enhanced may itself become more fully internationalized. In turn, internationalization may become an essential means toward improved quality and a measure of the same.

Globalization is a fact of life in the 21st century, and its impact on higher education will continue to be profound. While not every higher education institution will be a global one, none can exist in isolation from the world or, in other words, outside the emerging global higher education space.

References

Agarwal, P. (2010). A new direction for private higher education in India. *International Higher Education, 58,* 12–13.

Almeida-Filho, N. (2010, April). How the global crisis affected higher education in Brazil. *IAU Horizons, 16*(1), 13–15.

Altbach, P. (2004, January-February). The costs and benefits of world-class universities. *Academe, 90.* Retrieved from http://www.aaup.org/AAUP/pubsres/academe/2004/JF/Feat/altb.htm.

Altbach, P. (2008). Globalization and forces for change in higher education. *International Higher Education, 50,* 2–4.

Altbach, P. (2010). Why branch campuses may be unsustainable. *International Higher Education, 58*, 2–3.

Becker, R. F. (2009, September). *International branch campuses: Markets and strategies.* London, UK: Observatory on Borderless Higher Education. Retrieved from http://www.obhe.ac.uk

Bennett, S., Maton, K., & Kervin, L. (2008), The "digital natives" debate: A critical review of the evidence. *British Journal of Educational Technology, 39*, 775–786.

Bhandari, R., & Blumenthal, P. (2008) Global student mobility: Moving towards brain exchange. In R. Bhandari & S. Laughlin (Eds.), *Higher education on the move: New developments in global mobility.* New York: Institute of International Education/AIFS Foundation.

Brown, R. (2009). *The role of the market in higher education.* London, UK: Higher Education Policy Institute/Leadership Foundation for Higher Education. Retrieved from http://www.lfhe.ac.uk/news/hedebate09.html

A bumpier but freer road. (2010, October 2.) *The Economist*, pp. 75–77.

Center for Higher Education Research and Innovation (2009). *Higher education to 2030:* Vol. 2. *Globalisation.* Paris: Organization for Economic Cooperation and Development.

Central Intelligence Agency (CIA). (2010). *World factbook.* Retrieved from https://www.cia.gov/library/publications/the-world-factbook/geos/ch.html

Council on Higher Education Accreditation (CHEA). (2010). *CHEA almanac of external quality review, 2010.* Washington DC: Author.

Degree qualifications profile. (2011). Indianapolis, IN: Lumina Foundation.

Eckel, P. (2008). Mission diversity and the tension between prestige and effectiveness: An overview of U.S. higher education. *Higher Education Policy, 21*, 175–192.

Egron-Polak, E., & Hudson, R. (2010). *Internationalization of higher education: Global trends, regional perspectives* (IAU 3rd global survey). Paris: International Association of Universities.

Fazackerley, A., & Worthington, P. (Eds.). (2007, December). *British universities in China: The reality beyond the rhetoric* (An Agora discussion paper). Melbourne, Australia: Agora Think Tank.

Fielden, J., & Gillard, E. (2011). *A guide to offshore staffing strategies.* London: Universities U.K.

Foreign students will boost the economy. (2010, October 17). *The Star online.* Retrieved from http://thestar.com.my/education/story.asp?file=/2010/10/17/education/7218182&sec=education

Friedman, T. (2005). *The world is flat.* New York: Farrar, Strauss, & Giroux.

Green, M., Eckel P., Calderon, L., & Luu, D. (2007). *Venturing abroad: Delivering U.S. degrees thorough overseas branch campuses and programs.* Washington DC: American Council on Education.

Green, M., Eckel, P., & Kinser, K. (2008). *On the ground overseas: U.S. degree programs and branch campuses abroad.* Washington DC: American Council on Education.

Green, M., & Koch, K. (2009, September) *U.S. branch campuses abroad* (Issue brief). Washington DC: American Council on Education. Retrieved from www.acenet.edu

Gribble, C., & McBurnie, G. (2007). Problems within Singapore's global schoolhouse. *International Higher Education, 48*, 3–4.

Hazelkorn, E. (2008). Learning to live with league tables and rankings: The experience of institutional leaders. *Higher Education Policy, 21*, 193–215.

Heyl, J. (2011). *Third party program providers and education abroad: Partner or competitor?* Retrieved at http://www.aieaworld.org/publications/contemporary-issues

International Organization for Migration. (n.d.). *Facts and figures.* Retrieved from http://www.iom.int/jahia/Jahia/about-migration/facts-and-figures/lang/en

Japan: English courses to build recruitment. (2010, January 24). *University World News, 108.* Retrieved from htttp://www.universityworldnews.com

Jones, D., & Wellman, J. (2010, May–June). Breaking bad habits: Navigating the financial crisis. *Change: The Magazine of Higher Learning.* Retrieved from http://www.changemag.org/Archives/Back%20Issues/May-June%202010/breaking-bad-full.html

Knight, J. (2005). New typologies for cross-border higher education. *International Higher Education, 38*, 3–5.

Koch, K., & Green, M. (2009). *Sizing up the competition: The future of international postsecondary student enrollment in the United States.* Washington DC: American Council on Education. Retrieved from http://www.acenet.edu/Content/NavigationMenu/ProgramsServices/cii/pubs/ace/SizingUptheCompetition_September09.pdf

Kremmer, J. (2010, September 22). Australia's chancellors turn to new government as foreign enrollments drop. *Chronicle of Higher Education.* Retrieved from http://www.chronicle.com

Levy, D. (2009). For-profit versus nonprofit private higher education. *International Higher Education, 54*, 12–13.

Liu, J., & Wang, X. (2010. Expansion and differentiation in Chinese higher education. *International Higher Education, 60,* 7–8.

Marmolejo, F., Manley-Casimir, S., & Vincent-Lancrin, S. (2008). Immigration and access to tertiary education: Integration or marginalisation? In Centre for Educational Research Innovation. *Higher education to 2030:* Vol. 1. *Demography.* Paris: Organization for Economic Development and Cooperation.

Mehrotra, S. (2009). Indian higher education: Time for a serious rethink. *International Higher Education, 56,* 5–6.

Myklebust, J. (2010, October 31). Europe: U-Multirank pilot study underway. *University World News, 143.* Retrieved from http://www .universityworldnews.com

Organization for Economic Cooperation and Development (OECD). (2010a). *Education at a glance 2010.* Paris: OECD.

Organization for Economic Cooperation and Development (OECD). (2010b). *Trends shaping education* 2010. Paris: OECD.

Panikkar, K. N. (2011, April 17). India: Foreign universities bill needs to be revised. *University World News.* Retrieved from http://www .universityworldnews.com

Population Reference Bureau. (2009). World population data. Retrieved from https://www .prb.org/pdf09/09wpds_eng.pdf

Redden, E. (2008, March 19). Private colleges proliferating, worldwide. *Inside Higher Education.* Retrieved from http://www .insidehighered.com

Rickford, R. (2010, October 22). Are we commodities? *Chronicle of Higher Education.* Retrieved from http://www.chronicle.com

Sachs, J. (2005). *The end of poverty.* New York: The Penguin Press.

Salmi, J. (2009). *The challenge of establishing world-class universities.* Washington, DC: World Bank.

Santiago, P., Tremblay, K., Basri, E., & Arnal, E. (2008). *Tertiary education for the knowledge society:* Vol. 1. *Special features, governance, funding, quality.* Paris: Organization for Economic Cooperation and Development.

Schoepp, K. (2009). The United Arab Emirates and the branch campus gold rush. *International Higher Education, 56,* 22–23.

Sharma, Y. (2009, July 12). Expansion of private higher education. *University World News.* Retrieved from http://www. universityworldnews.com.

Sharma, Y. (2010, October 3). China: Ambitious "innovation society" plan. *University World News, 142.* Retrieved from http:// universityworldnews.

Sharma, Y. (2011, April 17). "Brain reclaim" as talent returns from West. *University World News.* Retrieved from http://www. universityworldnews.com

Stockley, D., & de Wit, H. (2011). The increasing relevance of institutional networks. In H. de Wit (ed.), *Trends, issues, and challenges in internationalisation of higher education.* Amsterdam: Centre for Applied Research on Economics and Management (CAREM).

Trading places. (2010, October 2). *The Economist,* pp. 70–71.

UAE: Academic city turns down 25 universities. (2010, October 24). *University World News.* Retrieved from http://www. universityworldnews.com

United Nations. (2004). *Demographics to 2300.* Retrieved from http://www.un.org/esa/popu lation/publications/.../WorldPop2300final.pdf

Universities U.K. (2010). *The growth of for-profit higher education providers in the UK.* London: Author.

Varghese, N. V. (2010, April). Higher education and the global economic crisis. *IAU Horizons, 16*(1), 12–13.

Verbik, L., & Merkley, C. (2006, October). *The international branch campus: Models and trends.* London: Observatory on Borderless Higher Education. Retrieved from http://www.obhe.ac.uk.

Wildavsky, B. (2010a). *The great brain race: How global universities are reshaping the world.* Princeton, NJ: Princeton University Press.

Wildavsky, B. (2010b, August 22). University globalization is here to stay. *Chronicle of Higher Education.* Retrieved from http://www .chronicle.com

25

BRIDGES TO THE FUTURE

The Global Landscape of
International Higher Education

DARLA K. DEARDORFF, HANS DE WIT, AND JOHN D. HEYL

This volume has explored wide-ranging issues in international higher education, from an analysis of concepts and strategies to internationalize higher education to internationalization in a broad array of contexts. In examining the emerging themes from these discussions, several are especially salient for the future. These issues include the concept of internationalization itself, the notion of global citizenship, varieties of global engagement, the impact of technology on internationalization (e.g., the notion of virtual mobility), new dimensions in study abroad, and the role of internationalization in the broader higher education field. These themes, which have been highlighted in other chapters in this volume, will provide the focus for the first part of this concluding chapter as keys—or bridges—to future developments in international higher education. This concluding chapter, together with Chapters 1 and 24 of this Handbook, intend to bring a comparative and comprehensive perspective to the rich analysis and information discussed in the other chapters.

Given that the examples in this volume, through the inclusion of specific textboxes, are predominantly from Australia, Europe, and the United States, the second part of this chapter provides a summary of internationalization efforts in various countries and regions in other parts of the world: Africa, Latin America, Asia, and the Middle East. Concluding this volume with voices from key regions/countries is a fitting way to look to the future. Through these discussions, trends, issues, and challenges emerge in the global view of international higher education.

As discussed in the first section of this Handbook, the concept of internationalization has emerged initially from North American and European perspectives. In recent years, Australia, New Zealand, and the United Kingdom have contributed a more competitive perspective on international education. The developing countries in Asia, Africa, the Middle East, and Latin America have traditionally played roles mainly as senders of students, recipients of capacity-building funds, and more recently as locations of franchise operations, branch campuses, and other forms of cross-border delivery (as discussed in the fourth section of this handbook). This is all changing. The globalization of the world's knowledge economies and societies dramatically impacts the role of higher education and its international dimensions in the regions, as highlighted in this chapter. One can speak of a global higher education environment in which these countries and their institutions of higher education become competitors, equal partners, and key actors.

The consequences of these new developments for the way internationalization as a concept and as a process will evolve are not yet clear. For the moment, internationalization is still primarily driven by rationales, strategies, approaches, and activities from the traditional regions of North America, Europe, and Australia. A future edition of this Handbook will surely see a more prominent role of other regions in international higher education. It would have been negligent, however, not to address the increasingly proactive role these regions and countries play in international higher education.

International higher education is at a turning point, and the concept of internationalization itself requires rethinking to take into account the emerging new world and higher education realignments. Other important developments in international higher education as described below relate to this pivotal juncture. Throughout these brief discussions of thematic and regional directions in higher education, relevant questions will be raised that invite further exploration as international higher education moves into the future. Indeed, continued research and exploration of these and other questions will continue to propel the field forward and possibly even transform the nature of higher education itself.

Thematic Issues and Trends

Higher Education Institutions as Global Citizens

In terms of global citizenship, institutions are increasingly stating the need for their students to become global citizens. Yet, what does it mean for an *institution* to be a global citizen? What responsibilities does an institution need to address within a larger global context? One example in guiding this discussion is the United Nations Global Compact, a strategic policy initiative in which companies, organizations, and universities embrace 10 universally accepted principles related to human rights, labor, environment, and anticorruption (http://www.unglobalcompact.org/). Another example is the attention that institutions increasingly give to tackling global issues, particularly through research that may lead to innovative solutions to complex problems, especially if institutions are able to engage in truly interdisciplinary research and collaboration. Even within this attention to global issues, however, institutions must guard against the "expert syndrome" of providing answers rather than seeking to learn. Recent developments also caution universities' intent on establishing a global brand around the world, particularly through branch campuses. Given some of the criticisms of the more colonialist tendencies of some internationalization abroad efforts—as well as some well-publicized branch campus forays and closures—institutions and programs need to more closely examine and monitor such efforts in collaboration with a wide variety of stakeholders. Sutton and Deardorff (2012) suggest that institutions engage as global citizens through partnership, collaboration, and authentic dialogue, "measuring success in terms of mutual benefit and global action," with internationalization becoming a "process of increasing synergies among scholars, deepening student and institutional engagement in the world, and creating ever larger networks of discovery," which could transform the very nature of higher education (p. 17).

Key questions emerge in this area: Will institutions remain institution-centric or move to become more global-centric? How do global efforts align with institutional mission? How can institutions work more closely together on global efforts? Which partners do institutions need to engage in their global efforts to be more global-centric? What competencies are needed for institutions to engage as global citizens in the world? What (and whose) ethical standards are to be used to guide global engagement? What might happen if institutions understood their actions as functioning within an emerging global system of higher education? These are issues that should engage not only senior international officers (SIOs) but university presidents as well. For example, Chancellor Victor

Boschini (2011) of Texas Christian University reflects the views of many of his peers when he says, "By thinking differently, planning more strategically and utilizing and integrating the many resources already available on our campuses and in our larger communities, global education can remain at the core of the institutional mission." Through integration of leadership, strategic planning, and resources, higher education institutions will emerge as global citizens as they engage more broadly in the world.

Students as Global Citizens

As institutions explore their role in the larger global context, they are simultaneously also focused on their students' development as global citizens, which is increasingly reflected in institutional mission statements (Green, 2012). Yet, even as more universities state the desire to graduate global citizens, debates arise around terminology, definitions, and assumptions inherent in this movement. These include whether one can indeed be a citizen of the world and whether being a global citizen is a right to be enjoyed only by the privileged who have access to higher education. Furthermore, whose values, morals, and ethics are to be used to guide one's global citizenship, and is it possible and desirable to reach commonly agreed upon foundational principles? Thus, many ethical dimensions are surfacing within this more traditionally academic discourse. Other discourse centers around how institutions develop global citizens, with university curricula and programs supporting this aspiration (see Chapters 14 and 15, this volume).

Other questions that institutions need to address around students as global citizens include the following: What are the assumptions made in the pursuit of developing global citizenship in students? What specific knowledge, skills, and attitudes are desired in global citizens—and according to whom? With competencies frequently emerging in literature on global citizenship, are there generic competencies that should be addressed by every program, or are there also competencies specific to each discipline that impact students as global citizens in their future professions? (See Chapter 16, this volume.) How is global citizenship to be assessed in students? Is global citizenship more about responsibility and engagement in the world and developing a lifestyle conducive to sustainability of the planet? These questions, increasingly put to international educators as well as to other key players in higher education, will be further debated in the years to come. In addition, institutions will need to more closely examine what it means for faculty and staff to be global citizens.

Redefining Study Abroad

Study abroad is a generic term with different meanings to different people and in different regions. Regardless of terminology, the landscape of study abroad is changing as a consequence of developments in international higher education in several different ways:

• First, possible destinations for study abroad have dramatically expanded in recent decades. The end of the Cold War, the commercialization of study abroad as a higher education business, the growth of the Internet, and the diversity of program providers have extended realistic study abroad opportunities far beyond traditional destinations in the developed world.

• Second, due to the surge in global migration in recent decades, there is a stronger relation between local and global, between intercultural and international (see Chapter 17, this volume). One encounters intercultural and international not only by crossing national borders but increasingly around the corner in one's own country and neighborhood. Developing intercultural and international competencies may be as possible in communities, companies, and one's own university as in other parts of the world (as discussed in Chapter 16).

• Third, technological developments such as the Worldwide Web, Internet, and social media make interactions between different cultures and regions possible without moving across borders. The notion of virtual mobility is entering international higher education. In recent years, more students and faculty from different parts of the world are interacting online in classrooms, projects, and assignments and learning from each other's different cultural, international, and didactic views directly and interactively in a way that physical mobility may not always accomplish.

• Fourth, internationalization and study abroad have moved into primary and secondary education by classroom exchanges and online interactions, as well as by individual social media contacts. In addition, "gap year" experiences between secondary and postsecondary experiences are becoming increasingly common. Students of the current and future generations entering universities and colleges are often more internationally connected than previous ones. University-level study abroad can build on these experiences.

• Fifth, study abroad is no longer solely an undergraduate experience but increasingly takes place at the master's and doctoral levels, beyond research abroad.

• Sixth, study abroad, or education abroad, no longer means only *academic* study in another location. Increasingly, students are seeking other intercultural and international experiences, such as those involving internships, research, volunteerism, and service learning abroad.

• Seventh, study abroad is no longer an isolated activity but is integrated into the curriculum and teaching and learning process (see Chapters 14 & 15). This emphasis has stimulated efforts to assess study abroad outcomes, in terms of learning, personal growth, and self-development (see Chapter 10).

• Eighth, the demographics of those who study abroad have been changing beyond the traditional white females to represent the increased diversity of backgrounds, ages, and experiences of students in higher education. These programs now need to adapt and change to accommodate these changing demographics and needs.

• Ninth, the provider landscape for study abroad has changed dramatically in recent decades. Nonprofit and for-profit providers not directly associated with universities—and sometimes developing university-level accreditation themselves—account for a significant portion of study abroad activity. This sector represents a newly competitive environment for university-based study abroad (Heyl, 2011).

• Tenth, given the accessibility of students to direct-enroll into higher education institutions in countries abroad and given increased ease of access to many other international opportunities outside of higher education, traditional study abroad programs offered through higher education institutions may no longer seem as relevant to students of the future. Frost (2009) suggests that innovative leaders of the future will have engaged in an international experience characterized by going solo, going long, and going deep—meaning they may often obtain these experiences outside of a traditional study abroad experience.

• Eleventh, given the trend to shorter lengths abroad, universities will need to explore innovative, cutting edge models beyond summer programs to accommodate and support students in their academic and intercultural learning beyond simply getting students abroad. This could include rethinking the semester system entirely and engaging students in ways thus far not explored in learning experiences in other cultures, including in their own countries.

As a consequence of all of the above, study abroad is evolving from a one-time experience of a semester or a year in undergraduate education to a palette of intercultural and international experiences in education, even beyond what the university offers. Given these numerous trends and changes within study abroad, international higher education will need to continue to innovate study abroad offerings to meet the increasingly diverse needs and experiences of students. Questions for the future include the following: How will study abroad adapt to the rapidly changing landscape? Will there continue to be a need for traditional study abroad programs offered through higher education institutions, especially given an emerging global system of higher education? How will institutions respond to and support students who no longer come through traditional study abroad programs? What other players will emerge to provide international opportunities for students to gain knowledge and skills for a global economy? It's time to rethink traditional study abroad programs and re-imagine these programs for a rapidly changing global landscape.

Changing Rules of Institutional Engagement

Another issue moving forward is that of institutional engagement. In the current higher education environment, there is no shortage of rhetoric about being "internationally engaged." Indeed, quite a number of new positions in the United States even include this term in senior administrators' titles, such as vice president for global engagement. But what does this mean? The answer, of course, is that *engagement* can mean many different things. For some institutions, it means nothing less than winning multi-million-dollar technical assistance grants for faculty to work in the developing world or to collaborate with partners in the developed world on complex research projects. For some, it means improving the institution's position in global rankings or joining regional or global consortia and associations of like-minded institutions. For others, it means linking the Language Across the Curriculum program to appropriate study/service learning/internship opportunities abroad. For still others, it will mean offering dual degrees with partner universities abroad or having numerous overseas universities as partners through various signed agreements. New rules for engagement are emerging, including new partners, some outside higher education, such as corporations, governments, advocacy groups, and civil society organizations. Regardless of how institutional engagement takes shape, one surety is that "active engagement with the rest of the world has become fundamental to a high quality education, one that prepares students and their communities for the larger world in which they will live and work" (American Council on Education [ACE], 2011, p. 6). The job of those in senior-level administration at higher education institutions is to determine—taking into account all resources available—what kind and level of engagement would strengthen the international ethos of the institution and enhance the quality of education it offers. That is, whatever the choice of particular international initiatives, partnerships, or assessment tools, the overall effort should be mission-driven. Furthermore, strategic global institutional engagement "must take place within the framework of an overarching institutional strategy that aligns closely with the institution's mission, history, and values," versus the more ad hoc approach of many institutional engagement efforts currently (ACE, 2011, p. 19). In the end, such strategic global engagement can result in an institution that provides a higher

quality education in preparing students for the future.

Declining Public Support for Higher Education

Declining public support for higher education globally, but particularly in the United States, the United Kingdom, and parts of Europe, will force many senior-level administrators to focus on resources in the coming decade. As was noted earlier in this volume,

> Presented with a world of opportunities but only limited resources. . . [international educators face] a most daunting task. Making informed and creative choices about internationalization—with a clear sense of the interplay between risks and benefits, opportunities, and imperatives, obstacles and resources—requires unique skills and talents, real vision, and sustained commitment. (Chapter 1, p. 24)

The issue of resources—not just financial resources but also those associated with the institution's faculty, student, and alumni profile and with the institution's location and history—is leading many SIOs and administrators to think in increasingly entrepreneurial ways, such as increased recruitment of students, use of agents, and franchising. Some consider this a move toward the commercialization of international education. Some may also see this commercialization as reinforcing neocolonial mind-sets. Others embrace the challenge enthusiastically. In any case, this trend toward trying to maximize resources raises important ethical issues, such as those addressed by Knight (2008, 2011a) and de Wit (2011a). Specifically, the declining public support for higher education, has forced international educators to embrace entrepreneurial approaches to increase resources from whatever source: student tuition/fees, grants, gifts from alumni and private donors, and commercial partnerships with for-profit vendors. As noted in several chapters in this volume, collaboration is becoming a prominent pathway to maximize resources (both financial and human capital) in a period of constrained resources. When the partners are private entities, however, there will be inherent challenges, including tension over proprietary ownership, that will limit transparency and openness. There may also be a clash of business and educational cultures, which creates further tensions in overall mission and operational mandates and exacerbates questions around quality of education.

Global Competition

Another recurring issue in this Handbook is that of global rankings of higher education institutions, which has raised the stakes for institutions to compete against international entities and among each other. (See Chapter 24 for more discussion on global rankings.) This process encourages institutions to attempt to link with more prestigious ones to elevate their visibility and brand. One can question the methodologies of the various ranking agencies, but what institution would not tout its placement (in relation to "peer" institutions) if doing so put it in a stronger competitive position? The rise of global rankings exacerbates the already competitive field of higher education and escalates the tensions around competition versus collaboration.

Ben Wildavsky's (2010) *The Great Brain Race: How Global Universities Are Reshaping the World* is an important case in point. Wildavsky's title itself implies a competition in international higher education that is certainly not new but one that has increased in recent years due to several developments. First, positioning higher education as a global export service (as designated by the General Agreement on Trade in Services [GATS] in 1995) implies that it is a traded, fungible activity—not quite on the level of consumer electronics, but somehow more real than financial services. To be successful, a traded good requires competitor research, packaging, and marketing. U.S. colleges and universities, even very prestigious institutions, have done this kind of branding for a very long time, mainly in search of an ever more qualified and diverse entering class of domestic students. That competition has now become global, both for the growing cohorts of internationally mobile students and faculty and for establishing branded entities abroad (see the fourth section of this Handbook). The reality that the clear majority of the highest-ranking institutions are U.S.- and European-based—all with colonizing pasts—raises the question of whether global competition (via rankings) is resulting in a new wave of cultural imperialism. Koehn and Obamba (Chapter 23, this volume) address this matter directly in their discussion of a new era

of authentic partnerships where mutual advantage is the key to success and sustainability. Yet, given the global competition generated through rankings, it is important for institutions to also recognize that "to be competitive . . . virtually all institutions will have to collaborate to leverage scarce resources, broaden possibilities, and extend impact" (ACE, 2011, p. 7). Pol (2012) concurs by stating that "cooperation in all its dimensions, between disciplines, institutions, countries, sectors, . . . represents a competitive advantage" (p. 30). Thus, competition and collaboration sometimes represent two sides of the same coin. This new reality leads to numerous questions including the following: How do global rankings address quality? What is the end result of global rankings? How do institutional collaboration, international engagement, and global responsibilities fit with global competition, given that "collaboration is this century's necessity" (ACE, 2011, p. 7)? The answers to these questions may result in a paradigm shift in the future for international higher education.

Diversification of Higher Education

Returning to the themes from Chapter 1 of this volume, it is important to place internationalization within the larger context of global education. In the future, students will gain their education not only in postsecondary institutions but also through a wide variety of providers including not-for-profit organizations, corporations, and online venues such as Khan Academy (www.khanacademy.org), Udacity (www.udacity.com), edX (www.edexonline.org), online providers of free education, or the British Open University, one of the world's largest universities with more than 250,000 students, all enrolled in distance education modules that lead to degrees. Arthur Levine (2010, n.d.), president of the Woodrow Wilson Foundation, predicts that, in the future, such diverse providers will result in colleges and universities losing their monopoly on education. As a result, he suggests that degrees will become less important; educational outcomes, in particular skills, will grow in prominence to the point of students having "educational passports" documenting their lifelong learning and outcomes achieved (http://education.gsu.edu/ctl/Programs/Future_Colleges.htm). This means traditional functions of postsecondary educations will become "unbundled," according to Levine, and students, not institutions, will drive the educational agenda as they consume an á la carte version of education from multiple providers that best meet their needs as well as the needs of a global society, given that higher education is currently preparing many students for jobs that still do not exist. In this kind of future, international education will need to innovate as more diverse providers emerge. Even now, this is occurring, with private companies providing a myriad of services including credential evaluation, recruitment, pathway programs, education abroad programs and assessment platforms. Other experts have envisioned a future where "faculty, students, research activity, teaching models, and ideas will travel freely" (ACE, 2011, p. 7). Implications of this kind of future are immense: How will postsecondary institutions change to meet the "unbundled" education pursued by students in the future? How will institutions compete with other educational providers? In other words, what will be the value-added for continued institutional internationalization? How will programs change to truly meet the needs of students? What quality assurance mechanisms can be introduced to ensure the quality of the education being provided, especially beyond traditional mechanisms that are solely within a higher education context? These developments will dramatically change international higher education.

Access to Education

With only 10% of the world's population having access to secondary education and 1% with access to higher education, access to education is a little discussed but increasingly crucial issue within the global landscape (Bhandari, 2012). How will higher education address the increasing divide between those with access to education and those with little or no access? Furthermore, given that in the United States alone, the secondary incompletion rate (i.e., high school dropout rate) is 25% annually (which nears 50%, in some urban areas), meaning one million Americans do not complete high school each year, what responsibilities do postsecondary institutions have in addressing this issue (Sanchez & Wertheimer, 2011)? How will higher education mitigate the ever-growing divide between the "haves and have-nots," especially in regard to access? How will global

migration flows impact access to higher education? And how will the disconnect between secondary and postsecondary education be addressed, even within international education? For example, Asia Society, based in the United States, has been working on global education and global competence within U.S. primary and secondary schools, developing intercultural learning outcomes similar to those in postsecondary literature. How can the various sectors work more closely together to ensure the seamless education—and access to education—of students in regard to achieving global learning outcomes?

Other Elements

Several elements of what has hitherto been understood to comprise international higher education are clearly in motion as the 21st century unfolds. One of the certain realities in coming decades is that student and faculty mobility will increase, perhaps dramatically, which leads to the notion of a more integrated mobility approach, including integration not only of individuals, but also of curricula and ideas. Another very likely reality is that faculty, students, and institutions will find ways to use technology to expand their teaching, learning, and research networks. A third likely reality, as noted above, will be the increasing role of private entities—academic, commercial, and nonprofit/charitable—in changing the resource mix and research priorities of higher education. A fourth one is the shifting regional centers of attention and leadership in higher education. Finally, and perhaps more darkly, critical global problems—environmental degradation, sustainable energy alternatives, poverty, the future of the welfare state, infectious disease and global health issues, violence arising from economic, religious and demographic tensions, and terrorism—will likely become even more urgent. And looking more broadly at the trends that will impact the world in the next 20 to 25 years, seven have been identified by the Center for Strategic and International Studies (Aughenbaugh, Falk, Moss, & Shapiro, 2010) as being the following: (1) population; (2) resource management and climate change; (3) technological innovation and diffusion; (4) the development and dissemination of information and knowledge; (5) economics; (6) the nature and mode of security; and (7) the challenge of governance. These seven trends can serve as the basis of further discussion on how higher education will respond and adapt. The internationalization of higher education, to be fully relevant to the educational mission of institutions and to the wishes of the citizenry on which those institutions rely, will have to address these larger issues and trends.

REGIONAL TRENDS

The thematic trends and issues with respect to internationalization as described in this chapter are one important element. Regional trends are also important. As mentioned at the start of this chapter, the concept of internationalization, as well as its main actors, were for a long time shaped by North American and European experience, with a gradually increasing role for Australia and New Zealand. Given that "the rise of other systems of higher education and research, especially in Asia and to a certain extent in Latin America, is associated with the spread of modernization" (ACE, 2011, p. 15), the global landscape continues to evolve in terms of players and partners. Thus, the second part of this chapter highlights challenges and trends in internationalization in various countries and regions in those other parts of the world: Africa, Asia, Latin America, and the Middle East, as viewed by experts in those regions. Given the limited space devoted here to these regional and country discussions, it is important to recognize the challenges inherent in summarizing key trends and issues.

Africa

Africa is emerging as a player in international higher education. Given the combination of capacity-building initiatives, an emerging private sector, economic development, and presence of other global players like the Middle East and China, African higher education is on the rise. One expert provides an overview of trends, challenges, and the future of internationalization within African higher education.

BOX 25.1 In Africa: Emerging Trends, Realities, and the Unknown

James Otieno Jowi

Coordinator, African Network for Internationalization of Education, Moi University (Kenya)

Internationalization is a widely discussed phenomenon that is also shaping the higher education sector across the world in unprecedented and different ways. At the same time, it is one of the main drivers of change in higher education, including in Africa (Kishun, 2006), and is increasingly gaining a central position within the education sector. From the beginning, higher education in Africa has encountered internationalization in various ways and amid myriad challenges. Over the years, it has presented several challenges, risks, and opportunities to the sector. It continues to be a major force determining reforms in higher education in the continent.

Main Rationales

The growing influence of internationalization on higher education is not in much doubt. However, it is becoming more evident that the rationales that drive the process vary between regions, countries, and even institutions. Africa, like other parts of the world, responds to internationalization in ways peculiar to its circumstances and context. According to the International Association of Universities (IAU), *3rd Global Survey on Internationalization* (IAU, 2010), institutions in Africa consider strengthening research and knowledge production and internationalizing curricula as the major rationales for internationalization. Other recent studies have documented the same conclusion (Oyewole, 2009; Teferra & Knight, 2008). The academic rationale includes strengthening research capacity and knowledge production, internationalizing curricula, enhancing academic quality, developing human resource capacity, and increasing competitiveness (Oyewole, 2009). This is mainly to enhance the weak research and institutional academic capacities of African universities.

Emerging Trends and New Realities

In recent years, there have been new occurrences in the international dimension of higher education in Africa. Intra-Africa university cooperation is an emerging phenomenon that has led to increased mobility of students and staff (Mulumba, Obaje, Kagiso, & Kishun, 2008) and more collaborations between and among African universities. This new development could contribute to the regionaliza-tion of internationalization in Africa. It is expected to contribute to reducing the scale of brain drain as it provides new mobility alternatives within Africa. It could also strengthen capacities within African institutions and bring some local relevance in academic engagements.

Development partners are also showing renewed interest in Africa's higher education, creating more opportunities for internationalization. For example, new initiatives have emerged within the African Higher Education and Research Space (AHERS) and the Arusha Convention, modelled along the lines of the Bologna Process in Europe. Several African countries are witnessing improvements in information and communication technology infrastructure. The development of regional quality assurance frameworks and ongoing harmonization of education systems could soon begin to contribute to more internationalization within Africa.

Apart from the intra-Africa initiatives, growing opportunities must be noted for collaborations and partnerships with other parts of the world. Collaborations with Asian countries have continued to grow, surpassing those with U.S. institutions (Jowi, 2009).

Challenges, Opportunities, and Risks

Internationalization presents several opportunities to the higher education sector in Africa. The renewed interest in Africa's higher education by African organizations, governments, and development partners enhances prospects for increased internationalization. It could also play an important role in enlarging Africa's research capacity and knowledge production, which is quite marginal (Teferra, 2008) and heavily dependent on external resources.

However, institutional challenges and drawbacks render most institutions unable to respond to the demands of internationalization. Quality still remains a major concern and will continue to hinder broader internationalization efforts. The coordination of the regional frameworks and the discordance that they have with respective country policies and systems are still problematic.

Internationalization also comes with attendant risks, especially for higher education systems in developing countries. The main risk for Africa is the now perennial issue of brain drain, which has had serious consequences for the capacities of African institutions (Altbach, 2002; Mohamedbhai, 2003; Salmi, 2003). It has resulted in further marginalization of Africa in global knowledge production as it depletes the already scanty capacity. The other risk is commodification and commercialization aggravated by the privatization of the sector and the influx of foreign providers. Internationalization is also still largely rooted in the historical dominance of the global North and based on junior and senior partner relations (Jowi, Kiamba, & Some, 2008).

(Continued)

(Continued)

Contemplating the Future

Internationalization presents a mixed future for higher education in Africa. The opportunities, if well utilized, could turn around Africa's higher education. At the same time, lacking a creative response, the challenges and risks could lead to serious consequences for the already weak sector. These consequences have critical implications for policy-making in African universities. The gains that have been made through national and regional frameworks need facilitation through supportive strategies and policies. Developments in key drivers of internationalization such as funding, quality assurance, and information communication technology could play a role in ameliorating the isolation of Africa from the fast-growing knowledge society. The need to strengthen institutional capacities for research and knowledge production will remain important for future internationalization.

As internationalization grows to be one of the powerful forces in Africa's higher education, questions still abound about what it portends for the future. While the benefits are many and varied, so are the risks. It is still unclear what the long-term benefits and risks will be for Africa. It is also difficult now to foresee the type of higher education institutions that Africa will develop as a result of increased internationalization. The unfolding scene is one of greater complexity, exacerbated by the many challenges and weaknesses facing the higher education sector in Africa.

Asia

Asia is increasingly emerging as a key actor in international higher education, and in particular, three countries are taking lead roles—China, India, and Japan—although one should not ignore the higher education evolution occurring in other countries such as Korea, Singapore, Vietnam, Malaysia, and Indonesia. The following three country sections are written by experts from the region and present their views.

BOX 25.2 China: Key Issues and Trends of Internationalization of Higher Education

Futao Huang

Professor, Research Institute for Higher Education, Hiroshima University (Japan)

Context and Rationales

Although the meaning of internationalization of higher education has changed significantly in China over different periods, it has played a very important role in China's higher education reforms since the latter part of the 19th century. For example, China's first modern university, Peking University, was established in 1898 based on Western models. More important, the basic structure of the current higher educational systems was also essentially influenced by the former Soviet Union's patterns, when the People's Republic of China was established in 1949. Prior to 1978, when the implementation of the open-door policy and economic reforms were implemented, the internationalization of China's higher education had been shaped by political and ideological factors, which viewed a modern national higher education system as a key instrument for economic development. Thus, from the late 1970s to the early 1990s, a key motivation was a desire for implementing the open-door policy and economic reforms. After 1992, market mechanisms and international competition emerged as driving forces in the development of China's higher education. Internationalization of higher education in China, driven by challenges from globalization and worldwide competition, has meant focused priorities on academic quality and standards and on efforts to build world-class universities.

Changes and Current Situation

In response to increasingly complicated challenges, the internationalization of China's higher education has undergone considerable and progressively striking changes in recent years. First, given an increased number of Chinese students going abroad for their advanced studies at their own expense since the 1990s, in particular, the Chinese government developed a national strategy to fund 5,000 university students every year from 2007 to 2011 to study in leading foreign universities. The vast majority of Chinese students still select institutions in the United States, the United Kingdom, France, and Germany; recently, however, there has been rapid growth in numbers of Chinese students flowing into more diverse countries, including Australia, Canada, Japan, Singapore, Hong Kong, and South Korea. In addition, the Chinese government has continued to send both young and senior researchers, faculty members, and visiting scholars, including postdoctoral researchers, to foreign universities and research institutes through various nationally funded programs. It is estimated that every year, the highly selective central government dispatches nearly 10,000 faculty members and researchers to conduct their research abroad.

Second, the integration of an international dimension into university teaching and learning, including development of both English programs and bilingual programs (Chinese and English), has been greatly encouraged. This is especially evident in leading research-oriented universities in China. Regulated and facilitated by the Ministry of Education, more and more of these universities have been able to provide from 10% to 15% of their curricula entirely in English and bilingually at both undergraduate and graduate levels.

Third, since the mid-1990s, both the Chinese government and individual institutions have made great efforts to undertake the joint operation of higher education institutions and collaborative delivery of academic programs with foreign partners. Joint efforts include two aspects: on the one side, incoming foreign programs that are jointly provided by local universities and foreign partners in Chinese universities; on the other side, outgoing programs offered by Chinese universities in other countries, in particular via the Confucius Institutes. In addition to joint educational programs on Chinese campuses, two universities have been established by local institutions and foreign universities and approved by the Ministry of Education of China. The University of Nottingham, Ningbo, China, was established in 2004 by the UK University of Nottingham in partnership with Zhejiang Wanli University, a nongovernment institution. New York University, Shanghai, is being established by the U.S. New York University in collaboration with East China Normal University, one of the leading national universities in China. The agreement was signed in 2011, and operations will start in September 2013. In both cases, a majority of programs are imported and taught by faculty members from the United States, United Kingdom, and other countries. More important, the internal governance and management arrangements in the two jointly operated universities are

(Continued)

(Continued)

modelled on UK and U.S. patterns. These institutions and programs have constituted a highly important component of the Chinese higher education system, and the government regards them as an effective means of internationalizing China's higher education and improving academic quality and standards.

Finally, since the mid-1990s, another important strategy for promoting the internationalization of higher education in China is to introduce international academic standards and to financially support several universities with the aim of becoming world-class universities.

Issues and Trends

Like many emerging countries in Asia, China faces numerous problems with the internationalization of Chinese higher education. These include the increasing brain drain; the quality assurance of incoming foreign educational services; the regulation of joint degree programs at an institutional level; the tension in conflicting policies between foreign and Chinese institutions and governments, especially with regard to unrestricted use of the Internet; and the integration of an international orientation into teaching and learning activities without affecting traditional culture and national identity. Moreover, although both the government and individual institutions have been attempting to realize mutual communication and exchange in the internationalization of higher education in China, it is still largely being undertaken as a one-way process, overwhelmingly dominated by major English-speaking countries with relation to personal mobility, provision of educational programs, utilization of academic norm and conventions, and so on. An added problem is that only a few leading universities—all belonging to the national sector—typically advocate for the policy of internationalization. This means that internationalization is restricted to a few selected key institutions with the primary goal of training elite students. In the future, individual institutions will be encouraged to play a more active role in the internationalization of China's higher education.

However, as internationalization has become one of the most effective means to improve the quality of China's higher education, it is evident that much effort will continue to be made at both national and institutional levels. China's central government will still maintain its strong leadership in stimulating the internationalization of higher education by developing relevant policies and strategies that are responsive and adaptable to new challenges.

BOX 25.3 Internationalization of Indian Higher Education: From Intentions to Actions

Rahul Choudaha

Director of development and innovation, World Education Services (USA)

Indian higher education has recently been receiving significant interest from foreign institutions. This interest gained a big boost in March 2010 with the Cabinet approval of a bill to allow entry of foreign education providers in India. Although the bill is still awaiting approval by the Parliament, it has already created a sense of excitement and confusion at the same time for many institutions in India and abroad. About the same time, an India-U.S. Higher Education Summit supported by the U.S. Department of State indicated interest of government on both sides to promote partnerships in higher education. Despite the regulatory challenges, however, foreign universities are seeking inroads into Indian higher education. For example, Leeds Metropolitan University and Lancaster University in the United Kingdom have taken the initiative to start full-fledged branch campuses in India, despite challenges they encountered.

While these positive and strategic developments are shaping the policy and practice of internationalization of Indian higher education, there are several challenges in translating intentions to actions. This discussion outlines opportunities and challenges with the internationalization of Indian higher education and concludes with a discussion of future directions.

Opportunities

With only 12% of the relevant age cohort enrolled in higher education, India offers huge potential for growth. The Indian middle class sees foreign education as valuable both for social recognition and for career advancement, resulting in an increasing demand for international programs.

Internationalization is glamorous and attracts students: Traditional outbound mobility of Indian students has been consistently increasing, however, many who aspire to study abroad do not have the resources. In addition, institutions with an international component in their programs also command a higher tuition. This has resulted in an increase in joint academic offerings and student exchange programs.

Potential of Impact and Diversity of Institutions

Although India is the third-largest postsecondary education system, internationalization is concentrated in a handful of institutions and types of programs such as business or engineering. There is enormous potential for foreign institutions to create mutually beneficial relationships with programs in social sciences and education, at one level, and vocational colleges at another level. For example, Montgomery College is leading an initiative to advance the community college model in India with the help of a grant funded by the US-India Education Foundation. Thus, internationalization opportunities exist beyond traditional models, level of programs, types of institutions, and fields of study.

Challenges

Among many challenges faced by Indian higher education, the lack of a coherent policy framework and institutional capacity to manage internationalization are two major hindrances.

1. Incoherent policy framework and lack of a national strategy:

The policy and governance framework of Indian higher education is allegedly corrupt, incoherent, and inefficient. There have been cases of corruption with leading regulatory bodies, including All India Council for Technical Education. The nexus of business, politics, and regulation also became evident with the quality issues with several universities. This policy incoherence has resulted in a paradoxical situation, where many high-quality institutions lack approval at the same time that many poor-quality institutions have approval. In addition, India also lacks a national strategy for internationalizing higher education.

(Continued)

(Continued)

2. Lack of institutional capacity and preparedness for internationalization

Only a handful of Indian institutions such as Manipal University have taken a big leap in internationalization, and some have even started foreign campuses. However, there are hardly any exemplars for comprehensive internationalization. While several institutions have the intent and interest in internationalizing, very few have a capacity, mind-set, understanding, and the resources to develop a comprehensive internationalization strategy. Many Indian institutions also misrepresent and overpromise the international component in their programs. This has resulted in misplaced priorities and ineffective collaborations with foreign institutions.

The Way Forward

To address the need and challenges of internationalization, there is a need to develop a comprehensive internationalization strategy both at the national and institutional levels. The Indian higher education system also needs to recognize that top talent, which has the potential to achieve global excellence, is the core for achieving success with international ambitions. This includes building an ecosystem of students, faculty members, and administrators and advancing the profession of higher education.

Many foreign institutions interested in India already know that it is not an easy market, and Indian higher education is even more complex. However, opportunities and potential to make an impact are very high. This means that institutions need to take a consultative and capacity-building approach. While it is important to be cautious and vigilant in finding a partner, it is also critical to take an entrepreneurial approach in starting with low-risk engagement and using it as a learning opportunity.

Charles Klasek (1992) rightfully noted, "It is not difficult to sign an agreement with universities of all types throughout the world; it is difficult to implement the agreements so that there are mutual academic benefits to the institutions involved" (p. 108). Likewise, opportunities and intentions for internationalization of Indian higher education are ample, however, the successful execution of these intentions requires an enabling environment, institutional capacity, and a coherent policy framework.

BOX 25.4 Internationalization of Universities in Japan

Hiroshi Ota

Professor and Director of the Center for Global Education

Hitotsubashi University (Japan)

The need for the internationalization of universities is a long-standing issue in Japan. It seems that universities and internationalization have been closely intertwined ever since the beginning of modernization of the country (Meiji period: 1868–1912). The internationalization of universities was essentially a national strategy for Japan, considered a less developed country in the area of higher education during the Meiji period, and, in that sense, internationalization could be considered a government-led endeavor. The Japanese government and universities typified the approach of importing knowledge and technology from overseas and modifying them to Japanese usage for the sole purpose of the country's modernization (internationalization for modernization) under the imported models of universities from the West. However, after the early stage of Japanese higher education development, universities started to localize their institutional organizations and structures to fit in traditional Japanese culture, featuring rigid hierarchy and the low mobility of students and faculty, although those universities continued to import Western knowledge and technology and translated them for Japanese application. This is a typical case of "Japanese spirits and Western knowledge" and prevented Japanese universities from internationalizing their curricula for a long time since the vast majority of course contents originally came from the West.

With the subsequent development of the country and its universities, the Japanese government has made substantial efforts to promote international exchange programs, such as the Japanese Government Scholarship (launched in 1954), the 100,000 International Students Plan (from 1983 to 2003), the JET (Japan Exchange and Teaching) Program (started in 1987), and Japanese Fulbright Programs (organized by Japan-U.S. Educational Commission). As a result of these intentional efforts to internationalize, Japan has become one of the most popular destinations for study abroad students in Asia. Nevertheless, it seems that the internationalization of universities ended up becoming dependent primarily on the personal activities of faculty members. For instance, individual researchers collaborated with researchers abroad, participating in international conferences and international research projects; those individual researchers introduce advanced studies in foreign countries to academic circles in Japan; or they teach foreign studies courses. Thus, international activities at Japanese universities have relied heavily on the initiative of individual faculty members, and there have been few concerted organizational efforts, apart from international student exchange programs, to garner true support for internationalization within universities. Representative and common problems with hosting international researchers in Japan include visa application procedures, language, a lack of adequate housing, and schools for family members of those international researchers. In most cases, individual host researchers provide solutions to those problems without the systematic support of their university. At the same time, institutional support for Japanese researchers to conduct research abroad has been limited and so, as mentioned above, the individual-level activities have inadvertently come to play a major part in the ad hoc internationalization of Japanese universities, despite a number of funding programs for Japanese and international researchers provided by the Japan Society for the Promotion of Science and the Japan International Cooperation Agency. It is likely that this happened as a result of each faculty or department, or even each professor, having a high degree of academic autonomy, especially within national universities. This autonomy meant that the institutionally organized activities of the university were relatively weak, particularly with regard to internationalization, and there was little leadership for exploring comprehensive internationalization strategies for the university as a whole. However, under recent and rapidly changing circumstances, such as university privatization, the deteriorating demographic climate within many industrialized countries, and the increasing competition to recruit international students and researchers, it seems that this ad hoc approach is no longer viable in the global landscape of higher education.

The Japanese higher education system is currently undergoing a comprehensive process of reform, in which internationalization is a major component. This includes the corporatization of public universities (the changing role of government from direct control to supervision at the macro

(Continued)

(Continued)

level and the delegation of more autonomous powers to individual institutions). Under the reform agenda and given the low percentages of international faculty (5.0%) and students (3.8%), the Ministry of Education, Culture, Sports, Science and Technology (MEXT, 2011) has supported Japanese researchers and students' engagement in increased international activities abroad as well as supporting Japanese universities' capacity to host increased numbers of international students (under the 300,000 International Students Plan started in 2008) and researchers. The ministry also has encouraged universities to increase the number of courses and programs taught in English to enhance the diversity of the student and faculty population and to meet the increasing demand for global-minded graduates (workforce) at globalizing Japanese companies.

At the same time that internationalization grows in importance in education and research evolves into a more mainstream role in Japanese higher education, Japan's public debt is reaching 200% of its GDP under the prolonged economic stagnation. Society and taxpayers increasingly expect universities to be able to clarify the added value of the international dimensions and the impact of internationalization on the institution. Under the circumstances, a growing number of successful international liberal arts institutions and schools—Ritsumeikan Asia Pacific University, Akita International University, and Waseda University's School of International Liberal Studies— offer a truly international learning experience with a high percentage of English-taught courses, highly diversified student population and faculty, and a variety of study abroad programs. They have made internationalization the first priority within their institutions' missions and efforts.

Currently, one of the crucial challenges among Japanese universities is to develop the effective evaluation process of their internationalization efforts. This challenge lies in balancing trusted quality control (which creates a bottom line in terms of accountability), transparency, resource management, and quantitative expansion. In addition, such an approach requires a creative assessment structure and related methods, such as peer review and benchmarking, which encourages overall internationalization initiatives and adds a strategic dimension to further university internationalization.

All in all, the MEXT's initiatives (e.g., Strategic Fund for Establishing International Headquarters in Universities from 2005 to 2010 and Global 30 launched in 2009) have promoted the organizational restructuring of universities to better attune them to these institution-wide internationalization tasks, and university leaders have equally made efforts to introduce an institutionally organized, proactive, and strategic approach to university internationalization. The Japanese government is expected to continue to develop strategic policies of university internationalization in order to provide a catalyst for the functional transformation of Japanese universities toward meeting the demands of the 21st century's global knowledge-based society.

Latin America

Latin America is the third region that is emerging as a key player in the global economy and society. Its higher education sector is rapidly expanding and demonstrates particularities such as a strong private sector and an emerging regional approach. The continent as a whole and specific countries such as Mexico, Argentina, Chile, Colombia, and Brazil emerge as key actors in international higher education. Here are two discussions, one on Latin America as a whole and one specifically on Brazil as a rapidly emerging country in international higher education.

BOX 25.5 Latin America: Challenges and Trends in the Internationalization of Higher Education

Jocelyne Gacel-Ávila

Professor, University of Guadalajara (Mexico)

Latin American higher education faces the challenge to respond to globalization and the emergence of a knowledge-based society, at the same time that higher education systems of the region are still dealing with unsolved problems in terms of access, equity, quality, and relevance. The potential of internationalization as a key strategy to update and improve the quality and relevance of higher education systems, as well as the student's graduate attributes, is still not fully explored.

The knowledge-based society is challenging the limited levels of research and innovation typical of Latin American institutions. Most postgraduate studies were established relatively late, mostly in the 1980s and 1990s. Enrollment in graduate studies in the region amounts to only 4.2% of the total student population (Gazzola, 2008). Despite great efforts made in the last few decades, the region has not yet achieved a sufficient number of high-quality postgraduate programs, and most of these are at the master's level (Rama, 2006, p. 53). In several areas of study, especially in scientific fields, doctoral programs are lacking, and enrollment in doctorate studies is minimal; it represents only 1% of the enrollment in countries such as Argentina, Brazil, and Mexico. Research is mainly carried out for academic purposes and therefore has little impact on the production process and national competitiveness. Knowledge transfer to society and enterprises is scarce, largely because the productive sector itself does not actively support research and development, which is a traditional characteristic of the region. Scientific and technological knowledge production in Latin America in 2008 represents only 4.9% of the world's total (UNESCO, 2010, p. 10). All these factors result in a weak national innovation system, which is just the opposite of what is needed in a knowledge-based society.

A World Bank publication declared that "the internationalization of education appears not yet to have reached a sufficient level of importance on the political agenda," concluding that the region needs a more proactive approach to education and research by establishing strategies for the medium and long term in order to shape the agenda for the future rather than reacting to changes introduced by other international stakeholders; and to strengthen capacity to generate and analyze data on the performance of the sector. This will provide a strong basis for long-term policy decisions, which in turn would improve the prospects of reaping the full benefits of internationalization (Holm-Nielsen, Thorn, Brunner, & Balán, 2005, p. 65).

Latin America is a region where governmental support is one of the lowest in the world. The main external barriers identified are limited funding (27%, a slightly higher percentage than the world average of 25%); difficulties of recognition of qualifications or study programs (16%); and language barriers (13%) (Egron-Polak & Hudson, 2010, p. 82). As a consequence, international activities are not linked to key national programs, and the lack of national leadership leaves the internationalization process to initiatives essentially stemming from institutions. The internationalization process is still marginal to national and institutional policies.

The lack of foreign language proficiency in students and faculty hinders opportunities for mobility abroad, as well as participation in cooperative projects. The lack of curricular flexibility, a

(Continued)

(Continued)

trait of the Latin American educational model, is definitely an obstacle for the internationalization of the curriculum (Gacel-Ávila, 2007, pp. 407–408), a situation that explains, in part, little curricular change and very few international joint and double degree programs.

International offices generally occupy a low position in institutional organization charts, being on the fourth or fifth tier of the hierarchy, generally reporting to academic or planning provosts who might not have the required international training and vision (Gacel-Ávila, 2005, p. 352). This means that the international office lacks the required autonomy and capacity to implement the complex strategies required by the internationalization process. Furthermore, turnover is high among the staff managing international activities and programs because of recurring changes in institutional authorities. As a consequence, staff members generally have a low level of professionalization with insufficient international expertise, leading to a lack of institutional capacity for the successful promotion and management of the internationalization process.

Latin America has one of the lowest rates of outbound student mobility in the world with 6% (UNESCO Institute for Statistics, 2010). Nevertheless, it should be underscored that outbound mobility is on the rise. However, the region hosts only 1.9% of foreign students, with the majority coming from within the region (UNESCO Institute for Statistics, 2010, pp. 174–181). Intraregional mobility has increased since 2000 as a result of the establishment of university networks, like Red de Macrouniversidades, UNIVERSIA, Grupo Montevideo, CONAHEC, among others.

The World Bank and the Organization for Economic Cooperation and Development conclude that "very little curricular change has occurred in Latin America" in the last decade (de Wit, Jaramillo, Gacel-Ávila, & Knight, 2005, p. 346). One of the major obstacles for integrating the international dimension into the curriculum is the traditional curricular model and structure of the first-cycle prevalent in most Latin American institutions of higher education; it is characterized by a lack of flexibility, disciplinary overspecialization, and professional orientation. A survey led by the Observatory on Borderless Higher Education (Gacel-Ávila, 2009) reports that since 2002, an increasingly important strategy of curricular internationalization has been the establishment of joint and double degrees with foreign universities. Nevertheless, very few of these are in Latin America, compared with other regions, such as Europe or Asia.

Regarding international cooperation, research data show high levels of participation of the major public universities of Brazil, Mexico, Argentina, Chile, and Cuba. The most important partners are European countries, among them France, Germany, Spain and the United Kingdom, and, to a lesser degree, the United States, Canada, and Japan. These projects are generally fostered and partially funded by national organizations dedicated to the advancement of science and technology, thanks to the establishment of bi- or multilateral agreements with sister organizations abroad. This type of cooperation is more inter- than intraregional, but there has been a noticeable move away from development cooperation toward collaborative research cooperation since the 1980s, thanks to the advancement of science and knowledge in countries such as Brazil, Mexico, Argentina, and Chile. Nevertheless, countries like Peru and Bolivia are still primarily recipients of development in research (Gacel-Ávila, 2005). Worth mentioning is the case of ENLACES, (*Espacio de Encuentro Latinoamericano y Caribeño de Educación Superior*), which is a regional initiative whose main objective is the creation of a system of networks for intraregional cooperation to develop a comprehensive framework for research at the regional level (Carvalho, 2009).

The level of awareness of the need for inter- and intraregional integration of higher education, following the influence of the Bologna Process in Europe, is definitely rising in the region, evidenced by the region's participation in such projects as the Latin American and Caribbean-European Union Common Area of Higher Education, which intends to create a common higher education area between Europe and Latin America, and the Ibero-American Space for Knowledge promoted by UNIVERSIA. The feasibility of such a common space and the influence of the Bologna Process in Latin America have been subject to debate and criticism (Brunner, 2009; Gacel-Ávila, 2010). A criticism of such an integration process is its limited viability for Latin America; nonetheless, it becomes a promising avenue for further research on convergence and educational models for the region.

In conclusion, one can say that in spite of modest, but undeniable progress, the region still lags behind others. The international dimension is not yet sufficiently institutionalized in Latin American tertiary education, either at the national or institutional level. Internationalization activities are not in the mainstream but rather marginal to institutional development. Therefore, the potential of internationalization is underexplored. Latin America is not able to fully reap the benefits of the world process and to trigger the much-needed transformations required by the system. Latin American governments and decision makers must put education and higher education at the top of the agenda for development, and second, they must perceive internationalization as a key strategy for the advancement of higher education.

BOX 25.6 Internationalization of Higher Education in Brazil: Now and In The Future

Sonia Pereira Laus

Researcher on the internationalization of higher
education process and international academic cooperation (Brazil)

Brazil has over 190 million inhabitants and the biggest higher education system in Latin America, composed of almost 2,400 higher education institutions (74% of them private) where about 6.4 million students are enrolled. Although its postgraduate system was created only during the 1970s, it graduated nearly 11,000 PhDs in 2008, an increase of 278% since 1996. The most significant research in the country is produced at public universities. Brazilian scientists published more than 26,000 scientific papers in international journals indexed by Thomson Reuter's Science Citation index in 2008 (UNESCO, 2010), which ranks the country as the 13th-largest producer of science in the world. More than 90% of this work is produced at public universities.

On the other side, these numbers are out step with other government data indicating that 48% of Brazilian young people in the age group 18 to 24 years enroll at higher education institutions (Brazilian Institute of Statistics and Geography, 2010, p. 49), which means that social exclusion persists in spite of the significant advancement of science and technology as the result of a state policy developed over the last 40 years leading to higher level skills training in the country and abroad.

Government policy initiatives during the 1970s led to the creation of nationally supported fellowship programs intended to support graduates with master's and doctoral degrees. During the

(Continued)

(Continued)

late 1990s, the discussions about internationalization evolved in Brazil when the government agency for the evaluation of postgraduate education (CAPES) decided to establish international patterns. The decision led to a gradual adjustment to these new standards, mainly at the public and the private-not-for-profit pontifical Catholic universities, in order to qualify its students and teachers abroad and to improve international participation in research groups (Laus & Morosini, 2005). The gap is noticeable between those institutions that rapidly adapted their structures to these new challenges, promoting internal changes and engaging in a wide range of international cooperation, and those that did not.

We can observe over the past decade a significant growth in the numbers of academic mobility abroad and an increasing number of joint projects, joint publications, and participation of Brazilian academics in international events and networks. From 2001 to 2008, many fellowships were financed by national government agencies, including CAPES (26,789) and the National Council for Scientific and Technological Development (4,398), especially for postgraduates but also including undergraduates studying abroad.

The main Brazilian partners are France, the United States, Germany, Portugal, Spain, the United Kingdom, and Canada, but we can also observe an increasing movement toward South–South cooperation, led by a national foreign policy that, in addition to traditional partners, is increasingly focused on academic and scientific dialogue to new areas such as India, China, and its traditional and new partners in Africa. Following this same movement, there is an increase in the number of intraregional mobility programs, provided mainly by the action of the *Mercado Comum do Sul* (MERCOSUL) agreement (Argentina, Brazil, Paraguay, and Uruguay) created in the early 1990s. In this regional context, some new educational polices have been implemented, such as those concerning the accreditation of university degrees, titles and graduate courses in the region. Those actions increase regional international cooperation within the framework of postgraduate teacher training and scientific research and are contributing to the implementation of the Higher Education Space ALCUE (Latin America, Caribbean and European Union) (Laus, 2009).

The impact of these activities is manifest in the number of scientific networks, like those in the frame of the Montevideo Group University Association and the MERCOSUL Higher Education Mobility Support Program, as well as multilateral academic programs like those supported by the European Commission, the Ibero-American Summit, and UNESCO, among others. These networks, programs, and projects are agents and objects of the internationalization process, acting as strong tools for internationalization nationally, regionally, and subregionally and at the same time promoting South/South integration and enlargement of academic relations in the region.

As a result of these academic activities, we can observe in many higher education institutions an evolution in the role of the international relations offices, shifting from an unimportant staff activity to an integrated part of the academic decision process, some of them having their own budgets and an institutional status of vice rectors, which was not the reality some years ago.

In recent years, international rankings are provoking a race between Brazilian universities best evaluated under CAPES patterns to strive for so-called international standards or an "equivalent performance to that of international centers of excellence in the area," even knowing that those ranking patterns are not exactly based on the model and purposes of the universities in the region.

Brazil's political and economic stability, the increase in revenues of a growing middle class, and the needs of national science, technology, and innovation to support the competitiveness of national economy are leading the country to an aggressive policy of internationalization of its higher education.

To support national growth with qualified human resources, the Brazilian government created in 2011 the Science Without borders initiative (http://www.capes.gov.br/ciencia-sem-fronteiras/ sciencewithoutborders), which is a large-scale nationwide scholarship program. Supported by R$3.1 billion (about US$1.76 billion) mainly from the federal government and with some private financing expected, the program seeks to strengthen and expand the initiatives of science, technology, innovation, and competitiveness through international mobility. Its aims are to send abroad 100,000 undergraduate and postgraduate students and researchers between 2011 and 2014 to the top-ranked universities worldwide and also to stimulate the visit of highly qualified young researchers and senior visiting professors to Brazil. Science Without Borders is focused on those areas considered strategic for national development, mainly engineering; new technology construction engineering; physical sciences (mathematics and physics); clinical, pre-clinical, and health sciences; chemistry; biology; geosciences; computing and information technology; aerospace technology; pharmaceuticals; sustainable agricultural production; oil, gas, and coal renewable energies; minerals technology, bioprospecting, and biodiversity; biotechnology, nanotechnology, and new materials; natural disasters prevention and mitigation; creative industry; marine science; and practical technologies. The first group of students went to the United States in 2011, to be followed by those who go to Germany, France, and the United Kingdom (among others) in succeeding years.

Middle East

The Middle East is another important new regional player in international higher education. In the past, several countries like Egypt, Lebanon, and Jordan were already important international players, but they lost their position at the end of the past century. Recently, countries like Dubai, Qatar, the United Arab Emirates, and Saudi Arabia are positioning themselves as regional hubs and strive for world-class status. It is still too early in the aftermath of the Arab Spring to ascertain its impact on the future of the region in general and on its higher education sector internationally. The Middle East section below provides one perspective on the current trends, issues, and challenges in the region.

BOX 25.7 A New "Spring" for Higher Education in the Middle East: Internationalization as a Positive Challenge

Georges H. Nahas

Vice President, University of Balamand (Lebanon)

Higher education in the Middle East was driven for the last decades by ideologically oriented centralized regimes. In this geographical space, Lebanon stands out as a country with a liberal education sector having different approaches to higher education and a very strong private sector open to international cooperation. All other countries in the Middle East region, because of the centralized and politicized decision-making policies, have a homogeneity characterized by the following:

1. A democratization of the educational system leads to crowded universities, even in programs such as technology and applied sciences, [13]while the recruitment policy, based on the final degree grades, does not encourage the best students joining the higher education system.

(Continued)

(Continued)

2. A lack of flexibility within the system hinders the possibility of establishing programs able to meet fast-changing market demands.

3. A lack of academic freedom within the universities due to the reigning political atmosphere has impacted the quality of teaching and of faculty.

4. A reliance on Arabic-translated resources due to political decisions leads to lower foreign language proficiency.

5. A paucity of financial resources, which primarily cover salaries and basic infrastructure, leave few resources remaining for research and professional development.

On the other hand, due to the efforts of the Arab Universities League,[1] efforts were made:

1. To reach consensus about the programs organization to enhance student mobility within the region.

2. To establish training programs in centers of excellence established within the region.

3. To establish an Arab Accreditation Agency to help search for quality and sustain the human development in all countries, mainly those who pass through wars and trouble.

4. To establish professional boards to maintain a recognized quality level within the professions, mainly the medical ones.

5. To enhance the relations between the universities (libraries, research centers, faculty exchange, etc.) to meet the requirements of a challenging new paradigm of higher education within this globalization era.

Regarding mobility, over 220,000 (7.3%) students left the Middle East and North Africa for study in 2008, compared to 134,400 international students who studied in that region. Two thirds of North African for study international students study in France, but that country is only the fifth-largest destination for students from the Middle East. One can find North African students also in Canada and Germany (80% each), while students from the Middle East are more dispersed, studying in the United States (16.5%), Jordan (14%), the United Kingdom (13%), Saudi Arabia (11%), and France (8%) (Jaramillo, 2011). About 25% of students from the Middle East study in other nations within the region. As Jaramillo (2011) states, "This creates a significant regional education market that seems to be growing in size and importance as the region's economies diversify and as countries in the region develop internationalization strategies" (p. 4).

The Middle East and North Africa (MENA) region is also a host region for international students: Egypt, Jordan, and Lebanon are among the top 30 host countries in the world. Most MENA international students' movement is intra-regional, that is, between MENA countries, attributable to cost, culture, and language competence (Jaramillo, p. 5).

As Jaramillo (2011) states, "One of the most distinctive features of higher education in the region is the large presence of foreign providers" (p. 6). In 2009, the Middle East hosted 34% of all international branch campuses (Observatory on Borderless Higher Education, 2011). The United Arab Emirates has the most branch campuses, followed by Qatar. There are also branch campuses in Kuwait, Bahrain, Yemen, Jordan, and Tunisia. Institutions operated in partnership with foreign institutions exist in some other MENA countries. For example, there are German universities in Egypt (German University of Cairo, opened in 2003 and is operated by the universities of Ulm and Stuttgart), Jordan, and Oman. The French University of Cairo operates following a similar partnership model with the University of Paris-IX Dauphine, and there is a recent partnership of Paris-IX Dauphine in Tunis. A French business school is offering MBAs in Lebanon (ESA in Beirut), and Saint Joseph University of Beirut has a branch campus, the Law School in Abu Dhabi. In Saudi Arabia, the King Abdullah University of Science and Technology has adopted another model: It has engaged world-class universities to help design the curriculum of its programs and has created a Global Research Partnership allowing its faculty and students access to top researchers and research facilities from four world-class research universities. Given that some MENA countries have adopted these new policies regarding the presence of private institutions of higher education, some for-profit organizations are creating the challenge of maintaining quality in education due to lack of academic accountability.

Having this background in mind, it is worth mentioning that the policies toward internationalization are still very problematic. Even if a large number of faculty members are trained outside the region, the choice of universities where the future faculty members are sent is driven by political issues and not by excellence priorities. As stressed in a study of the International Association of Universities, this region is reluctant to adopt an aggressive internationalization policy mainly for cultural reasons. The identity issue seems to be crucial, along with the fear of having a brain drain. Other minor problems hinder internationalization actions in the MENA region, among them the language of instruction, degree recognition, and the accredited institutions. But the paradox in this regard is the following: As state institutions, the universities could organize excellent means for internationalization through diplomatic channels, but the prevailing atmosphere does not help due to the two major factors mentioned earlier.

For example, in Lebanon, three main Lebanese universities were established as part of foreign institutions, and these relations were maintained and strengthened through the years between the Lebanese universities and European and U.S. institutions. In Lebanon, the identity issue is not considered serious, and all other factors are not hindering the open and efficient relations universities are having with the nonprofit institutions that are operating in the country. However, academic society has experienced brain drain for many years, and this remains a serious challenge factor regarding the adoption of a national policy toward internationalization.

It is likely that the political changes the Arab countries are going through at the time of this writing will have an impact on the higher education systems in the region. A change in the political approach that supports a democratic spirit and an atmosphere of freedom might boost and enhance quality in the universities by adopting a critical approach to their status quo. At the same time, internationalization is being viewed as an opportunity to make faculty better knowledge producers rather than only knowledge consumers. Jaramillo (2011) states for the Middle Eastern and North African region:

> Internationalization is one of the most important developments that globalization has brought to higher education worldwide. In the MENA region, it has turned into quite a complex undertaking. The Arab Spring has made it clear that young people in MENA are asking for more and better opportunities: to study and work; to move about the world; and to learn and to create new knowledge and enterprises. Higher education, migration, and

(Continued)

(Continued)

labor mobility are key policy areas as MENA nations address the need for a strong skills base to underpin the economic and social development of the region's disparate economies.

Foreign universities and governments are presented with the opportunity to consider institutions in MENA region as potential partners in rebuilding and restructuring the future following the Arab Spring. Internationalization has to be presented in that process as a means and not as an objective by itself.

Concluding Regional Observations

Through these brief overviews of internationalization developments in specific world regions and countries, several common themes emerge. First, the role of national governments has been a driving force in propelling international higher education forward in many of the cases. Second, underlying motivations for internationalization often involve capacity-building within the various countries, although in a decreasing scale. Third, private higher education is becoming an important factor in these regions. Fourth, internationalization itself has become a driving factor in propelling countries forward. And fifth, the traditional role of higher education and its international dimension is rapidly changing.

Within these and other themes, there are also some ongoing challenges endemic to particular regions of the world such as counteracting the persistent issue of brain drain, the risks related to increasing privatization, and a debate about ethics and values in internationalization of higher education. Indeed, these concerns are not exclusive to these regions and countries but are also highly relevant to the traditional players in North America, Europe, and the Pacific. Future trends include a growth in regional mobility through greater development of regional networks and increased intracontinental engagements, collaborations, and reforms, which are viewed as positive indicators in internationalization efforts (Jowi, 2012).

Why is it important for international education leaders to understand the emerging themes and challenges in this global landscape of higher education? To be effective in their own work, these leaders must be able to contextualize their work in understanding the rising prominence of higher education institutions in other regions, which then impacts the different themes that have been addressed in this volume, all of which are played out at the institutional level.

This rising prominence of other regions is leading to the slow but steady growth in research and scholarship on internationalization issues from non-Western perspectives. This is a welcome development, given the dominance of Western concepts and scholarship to date in the field of international education. As Jones and de Wit (2012) observe,

> those countries with longer histories of internationalization need to learn from the varied contributions to debates and practice of other developed nations, so the voices of countries who have come on the scene more recently should be heard as offering new perspectives and dimensions to the existing landscape of international education. (p. 25)

These fresher perspectives can help guide the future developments in international education; leaders would be wise to seek out such voices and research.

RETHINKING INTERNATIONALIZATION

In Chapter 2 of this Handbook, Jane Knight writes at length about the concept of internationalization. Her definition of internationalization as "the process of integrating international, intercultural, or global dimensions into the purpose, functions, or delivery of postsecondary education" has undergirded internationalization for decades and is widely referred to in other Handbook chapters and publications. Given the rapidly changing world of the 21st century, the question becomes: Does the concept of internationalization require reconceptualization? For example, is it sufficient to focus on the internationalization of one's institution? How might global issues in sustainability, economic and social justice, and human rights lead international educators to initiate broader networks and resource-sharing among institutions? How would a "layered approach" to internationalization look that involved a mix of public, private, nonprofit, and commercial entities? Some senior international educators see the new technologies, entrepreneurship, and expanding student and faculty mobility as elements of a new matrix for both institutional internationalization and enhanced student learning (see Chapters 9, 21, and 23, this volume). Others question the increased focus on competitiveness and numbers with respect to internationalization (see Chapter 10, this volume), as well as the ethics and values related to this approach.

The emerging debate on the concept of internationalization was stimulated in early 2011 by an essay with the provocative title, "The End of Internationalization" (Brandenburg & de Wit, 2011a):

> Over the last two decades, the concept of the internationalization of higher education moved from the fringe of institutional interest to the very core. . . . In the late 1980s changes occurred: Internationalization was invented and carried on, ever increasing its importance. New components were added . . . in the past two decades, moving from simple exchange of students to the big business of recruitment, and from activities impacting on an incredibly small elite group to a mass phenomenon. (pp. 15)

The authors argued that it is time for critical reflection on the changing concept of internationalization. Others are also advocating for a review of the current conceptualizations and approaches to internationalization, including Mestenhauser (2011), who writes that "the present system of mainstreaming international dimensions, whatever they are, is neither adequate or feasible and . . . a different idea is long overdue" (p. 159). He advocates for a "systems-oriented approach" (p. 159) which not only is a "multiplier of learning, but . . . also provides a

new cognitive structure for dealing with the complexity" of the modern world (p. 161).

In the fall of 2011, the International Association of Universities (IAU) took the initiative to bring together a diverse group of international educators in a discussion on reconceptualizing internationalization of higher education with the objective to stimulate the revitalization of international education. The group addresses three questions: Is the concept and the definition of internationalization keeping up with developments in higher education? Is there a shared understanding of the concept? Has internationalization lost sight of its central purposes? (www.iau-aiu.net). The result of this initiative has been the publication of an IAU document, 'Affirming Academic Values in Internationalization of Higher Education: A Call for Action,' April 2012 (www.iau-aiu.net), in which the benefits of internationalization are acknowledged, potentially adverse unintended consequences addressed, and a call is made to higher education institutions to act to ensure that its outcomes are positive and of reciprocal benefit to institutions and countries involved. Knight (2011b) also wonders about an identity crisis in internationalization and calls for a "focus on values and not only on definitions." And Mestenhauser (2011) likewise questions the traditional definitions of internationalization involving "international dimensions" by wondering "what the 'international dimension' is, how much of it is needed, where to find it, and how to add it to the existing academic programs," concluding that "a new pattern is needed to ensure the conceptual integrity of international education" (p. 135).

What those calling for a debate have in common, according to Brandenburg and de Wit (2011a), is

> the shared feeling that international education no longer can be seen as a fragmented list of activities executed by international offices and a small group of motivated internationalists among staff and students. Internationalization should on the contrary be integrated, broad and core. (p. 15)

Moreover, senior international educators could no longer be viewed as the spearhead of innovation; rather, they "are holding firm to traditional concepts and act on them while the world around [them] moves forward" (Brandenburg & de Wit, 2011a, p. 16). Thus, it becomes crucial for leaders to explore and understand this changing nature of internationalization within higher education. However, it is important to explore multiple perspectives on this debate, which can be viewed as more of a "Western" debate as noted by Murray (2012), who states that

> In many countries, there is an excited, healthy sense of only just beginning on internationalization. There is no sense of a "mid-life crisis" and at the same time there is a global recognition that "education is changing quite fundamentally and that we are entering a new era." (p. 21)

One phenomenon in the debate on the future of internationalization of higher education is the inclination to put new broad labels on the term: *mainstreaming, comprehensive, holistic, integrated,* and *deep internationalization* are some of the main ones used in recent writings and presentations (de Wit, 2011a; Hudzik, 2011). The underlying urge to broaden and deepen the notion of internationalization is understandable, but such endeavors may be counterproductive or, at a minimum, translate into continued use of familiar approaches, albeit with new labels. For example, an instrumental approach to internationalization has led to the *why* and *what* being overtaken by the *how* and *how much.* In many cases, what can be measured has become the end goal: more exchange, more degree mobility, and more recruitment (Brandenburg & de Wit, 2011a, 2011b; Deardorff, 2005; de Wit, 2011a, 2011b), although this has gradually been shifting beyond the *how much* to the more substantive goals and outcomes as discussed by Deardorff and Van Gaalen in Chapter 10, this volume.

Nonetheless, the instrumental focus has led to myths and misconceptions about what internationalization actually has meant. These myths may be grouped in various ways (de Wit, 2011b; Knight, 2011a).

- International students are effective agents of internationalization.

- An institution's international reputation is a good proxy for its quality.

- Internationalization is synonymous with: a specific programmatic or organizational strategy; teaching in the English language; study abroad; having many international students on campus; having just a few international students in the classroom; more and more international

subjects taught; or more international agreements and accreditations.

- Higher education is international by nature.

- Internationalization is an end in itself.

These various myths and misconceptions have been explored throughout this volume and are topics for critical reflection for international educators in the future. Those who advocate for internationalization must confront key issues in the future: What are internationalization's real accomplishments in terms of improving learning and students' readiness for the future? How does the changing global landscape force international educators and leaders to rethink internationalization as a "Western concept" or as the sole model for new (non-Western) players? How do leaders internationalize internationalization? (Sutton & Deardorff, 2012) What other viable approaches and models may be utilized? How are terms such as *intercultural, international,* and *global* related to core educational values? What are indeed the bridges to the future for students?

Moving Forward

Taking an even broader look at internationalization of higher education, it is helpful to examine some of the assumptions being made as to how what has been described in this volume and this chapter will all work in the future. There are larger issues at play that can greatly impact not just internationalization but higher education in general. For example, given the increasing innovations around technology, will the traditional "bricks and mortar" concept of universities remain a viable option for education, in a world of 24/7, "point, click, study," just-in-time training and asynchronous learning? Where will international education be in a world where the rate of information is expanding exponentially and shared through gaming, virtual reality, text messaging, social reading, and social networking? What formats, beyond traditional semester systems, may work best in educating the next generation? What is the value-added in maintaining centuries-old educational traditions at "brick-and-mortar" universities in the global world of the 21st century? What impact will there be with the increasing number of nonformal providers of education?

For example, in the United States, the largest provider of professional development for science teachers is National Public Broadcasting, a public television network (Levine, 2010). And with the growing popularity of online educational venues, and other online ventures that are increasing the access to education, what are the implications for international education? How will international educators collaborate with nontraditional providers of education? How will higher education be re-imagined in a global context? Considering the future of higher education is crucial as leaders in international education envision how to achieve the preparation of global-ready students. Traditional ways of "doing international education" may no longer be viable. Innovation is needed in rethinking not only internationalization but also how it translates into a rapidly changing world. To that end, there is a danger that increased calls for homogenization of international education will stifle the innovation that is so greatly needed in the 21st century.

This Handbook has provided an overview of trends, issues, and opportunities and looked at the past, present, and future of internationalization in an effort to map the global landscape of international higher education. In the discussions found in these pages are many specific strategies for moving internationalization forward into the future. The words of Maurice Harari seem as appropriate now as when they were quoted in the predecessor to this volume (*Bridges to the Future*: Klasek, 1992), when he described an institution of the future as being one that has a

> positive attitude toward understanding better other cultures and societies, learning more about the political and economic interconnectedness of humankind, a genuine desire in interacting with representatives of these other cultures and societies, a genuine desire to understand the major issues confronting the human and ecological survival of planet earth and to learn how to cooperate with others across national and cultural boundaries in seeking solutions to world problems. (Klasek, 1992, pp. 204–205)

May this handbook serve as a bridge to the future as higher education institutions seek to fulfill this vision.

REFERENCES

Altbach, P. (2002) Centres and peripheries in the academic profession: The special challenges of developing countries. In P. Altbach (Eds.), *The decline of the guru: The academic profession in developing and middle- income countries.* Boston: CIHE.

American Council on Education (ACE). (2011). *Report of the blue ribbon panel on global engagement: Strength through global leadership and engagement.* Washington DC: Center for Internationalization and Global Engagement, American Council on Education.

Aughenbaugh, S., Falk, D., Moss, S., & Shapiro, M. (2010). *Educating globally competent citizens: A tool kit for teaching seven revolutions.* Washington, DC: ISIS.

Bhandari, R. (2012, February/March). Re-envisioning internationalization: International education for what? *IAU Horizons,* pp. 18–19.

Boschini, V. J. (2011). Learning to change the world: Making international education core to the institutional mission. *AIEA: Presidential Perspectives.* Retrieved January 6, 2012, at http://www.aieaworld.org/publications/ PresidentialPerspectives.

Brandenburg, U., & de Wit, H. (2011a). The end of internationalization. In *International Higher Education,* no. 62, pp. 15–16. Boston: Boston College Center for International Higher Education.

Brandenburg, U., & de Wit, H.(2011b). Has international education lost its way? *The Chronicle of Higher Education.* 15 November 2011, blog. http://chronicle.com/blogs/ worldwise/has-international-education-lost -its-way/28891

Brazilian Institute of Statistics and Geography. (2010). *Síntese de Indicadores Sociais Uma Análise das Condições de Vida da População Brasileira.* Retrieved from http://www.ibge.gov .br/home/estatistica/populacao/condicaodevida/ indicadoresminimos/sinteseindicsociais2010/ SIS_2010.pdf

Brunner, J. J. (2009). The Bologna Process from a Latin American perspective. *Journal of Studies in International Education, 13*(4), 417–438.

Carvalho, J. (2009). *ENLACES: Propuesta para la Creación del Espacio Latinoamericano y Caribeño de Educación Superior.* Retrieved April 30, 2010, from www.iesalc.unesco.ve/.../ Jose_Renato_Carvalho_texto.pdf

Deardorff, D.K. (2005, May/June). Matter of logic? *International Educator,* pp. 26–31.

de Wit, H. (2011a, Summer). Internationalization misconceptions. *International Higher Education,* no. 64, 6–7. Boston: Boston College Center for International Higher Education.

de Wit, H. (2011b, October 23). Naming internationalisation will not revive it. *University World News*, Issue 0194.

de Wit, H., Jaramillo, I., Gacel-Ávila, J., & Knight, J. (Eds.). (2005). *Higher education in Latin America*. Washington, DC: The World Bank.

Egron-Polak, E., & Hudson, R. (Eds.). (2010). *Internationalisation of higher education: Global trends, regional perspectives: IAU 3rd global survey*. Paris: International Association of Universities.

Frost, M. (2009). The new global student: Skip the SAT, save thousands on tuition and get a truly international education. New York: Three Rivers Press.

Gacel-Ávila, J. (2005). Internationalization of higher education in Mexico. In H. de Wit (Ed.), *Higher education in Latin America* (pp. 239–279). Washington, DC: World Bank.

Gacel-Ávila, J. (2007). The process of internationalization of Latin American higher education. *Journal of Studies in International Education, 11*(3/4), pp. 400–409.

Gacel-Ávila, J. (2009). Joint and double degree programmes in Latin America: Patterns and trends. *The Observatory on Borderless Higher Education*.

Gacel-Ávila, J. (2010). Factibilidad del Proceso de Bolonia en América Latina. In F. López Segrera & D. Rivarola (Eds.), *La Universidad ante los desafíos del siglo XXI*. Asunción, Paraguay.

Gazzola, A. (2008). *Panorama de la Educación Superior en América Latina y el Caribe*. Presentación, IESALC-UNESCO, Cartagena de las Indias.

Green, M. (2012, February/March). What is global citizenship and why does it matter? *IAU Horizons*, pp. 27–28.

Heyl, J. (2011). Third-party program providers and education abroad: Partner or competitor? *AIEA Issue Brief*. Retrieved from www.aieaworld.org/publications/contemporary-issues

Holm-Nielsen, L., Thorn, K., Brunner, J. J., & Balán, J. (2005). Regional and international challenges to higher education in Latin America. In H. de Wit, I. Jaramillo, J. Gacel-Ávila, & J. Knight (Eds.), *Higher education in Latin America* (pp. 39-70). Washington, D.C.: The World Bank.

Hudzik, J.. (2011). *Comprehensive internationalization*. Retrieved from www.nafsa.org/cizn

Jaramillo, A. (2011). *Internationalization of higher education in MENA: Policy Issues associated with skills formation and mobility* (World Bank Report No: 63762-MNA). Washington, DC: World Bank.

Jones, E., & de Wit, H. (2012). Globalization of Internationalization: Thematic and regional reflections on a traditional concept. *AUDEM: International Journal of Higher Education and Democracy, 3*.

Jowi, J. O. (2009). Internationalization of higher education in Africa: Developments, emerging trends, issues, and policy implications. *Higher Education Policy, 22*(3), 263–281.

Jowi, J. O. (2012, February/March). Re-thinking internationalization and what it portends for Africa. *IAH Horizons*, p. 29.

Jowi, J.O., Kiamba, C., & Some, D. K. (2008). Kenya. In D. Teferra & J. Knight (Eds.), *Higher education in Africa: The international dimension* (pp. 238–261). Accra/Boston: AAU/CIHE.

Kishun, R. (2006). *Internationalisation of higher education in South Africa*. Durban, South Africa: IEASA.

Klasek, C. (Ed.). (1992). *Bridges to the future*. Carbondale, IL: Association of International Education Administrators.

Knight, J.. (2008). Higher education in turmoil: The changing world of internationalization. Rotterdam: Sense Publishers.

Knight, J. (2011a). Five myths about internationalization. *International Higher Education 14*(63), 14–15. Boston: Boston College Center for International Higher Education.

Knight, J. (2011b, August). Is internationalisation having an identity crisis? *IMHE Info* (p. 1). Paris: OECD/IMHE.

Laus, S. P. (2009). Calidad y Acreditación en el MERCOSUR. In *SAFIRO II. Casos Prácticos para la Gestión de la Internacionalización en Universidades* (p. 163–179). Alicante, España: Universidad de Alicante. Retrieved from http://www.safironetwork.org/public_documents/SAFIRO%20II%20-%20libro.pdf

Laus, S. P., & Morosini, M. (2005). L'internationalisation de l'enseignement supérieur au Brésil. In *L'Enseignement Supérieur en Amérique Latine. La dimension Internationale*. Washington, DC: OECD.

Levine, A. (n.d.). *The future of colleges: Nine inevitable changes*. http://education.gsu.edu/ctl/Programs/Future_Colleges.htm

Levine, A. (2010). *The future of higher education*. Unpublished talk given at 2010 Association of International Education Administrators conference, Washington DC.

Mestenhauser, J. (2011). *Reflections on the past, present, and future of internationalizing higher education: Discovering opportunities to meet the challenges*. Minneapolis: University of Minnesota.

Ministry of Education, Culture, Sports, Science, and Technology (MEXT). (2011). *University* internationalization and international student policy. Tokyo: Author.

Mohamedbhai, G. (2003). Globalization and its implications on universities in developing countries. In G. Breton & M. Lambert (Eds.), *Universities and globalization: Private linkages, public trust* (pp. 167–168). Paris: UNESCO.

Mulumba, M., Obaje, A., Kagiso, K., & Kishun, R. (2008). International students mobility in and out of Africa: Challenges and opportunity. In D. Teferra & J. Knight (Eds.). *Higher education in Africa: The international dimension* (pp. 490–514). Accra/Boston: AAU/CIHE.

Murray, D. (2012, February/March). Alexander's sword? *IAU Horizons,* p. 21.

Observatory on Borderless Higher Education. (2011). *Perspectives on the future.* Retrieved from www.obhe.org

Oyewole, O. (2009) Internationalization and its implications for the quality of higher education in Africa. *Higher Education Policy, 22*(3), 319–329.

Pol, P. (2012, February/March). Re-thinking internationalization: Towards "coopetition" or new forms of cooperation?" *IAU Horizons,* p. 30.

Rama, C. (2006). *La Tercera Reforma de la educación superior en América Latina.* Mexico City: FCE.

Salmi, J. (2003). *Constructing knowledge societies: New challenges for tertiary education.* Washington, DC: The World Bank.

Sanchez, C., & Wertheimer, L. (2011). *School dropout rates add to fiscal burden.* National Public Radio, July 24, 2011. Retrieved from http://www.npr .org/2011/07/24/138653393/school-dropout -rates-adds-to-fiscal-burden

Sutton, S., & Deardorff, D. K. (2012, February/ March). Internationalizing internationalization: The global context. *IAU Horizons,* pp. 16–17.

Teferra, D. (2008). The international dimension of higher education in Africa: Status, challenges and prospect, In D. Teferra & J. Knight (Eds.), *Higher education in Africa: The international dimension* (pp. 44–79). Accra/Boston: AAU/CIHE.

Teferra, D., & Knight, J. (2008). *Higher education in Africa: The international dimension.* Accra/ Boston: AAU/CIHE.

UNESCO (2010). *UNESCO science report 2010.* Retrieved from http://www.unesco.org/new/en/ natural-sciences/science-technology/ prospective-studies/unesco-science-report/

UNESCO Institute for Statistics. (2010). *Global education digest 2010.* Montreal: UNESCO.

Wildavsky, B. (2010). The great brain race: How global universities are reshaping the world. Princeton: Princeton University Press.

LIST OF ACRONYMS

Acronym	Title	Function
ACE	American Council on Education www.acenet.edu	ACE, the major coordinating body for all of the nation's higher education institutions, seeks to provide leadership and a unifying voice on higher education issues and to influence public policy through advocacy, research, and program initiatives.
AU	African Union www.au.int	AU, with more than 20 member states, works toward an integrated, prosperous and peaceful Africa, driven by its own citizens and representing a dynamic force in global arenas.
AHELO	Assessment of Higher Education Learning Outcomes www.oecd.org/edu/ahelo	AHELO is a landmark project involving about 15 countries with the goal of developing frameworks and instruments in the fields of engineering and economics; it is evaluating the feasibility of assessing learning outcomes in cross-culturally relevant ways.
AIEA	Association of International Education Administrators: Leaders in International Higher Education www.aieaworld.org/	AIEA is a member-based professional association comprised of leaders in international higher education around the world who are engaged in advancing the international dimensions of higher education through opportunities of networking, exchanging ideas, sharing institutional strategies and knowledge, and being an effective voice on matters of public policy.
AIRC	American International Recruitment Council www.airc-education.org	AIRC is a nonprofit membership association of accredited U.S. postsecondary institutions and student recruitment agencies that work together to establish quality standards for international student placement within the United States.
ANIE	African Network for Internationalization of Education www.anienetwork.org	ANIE is a membership-based association aiming to take the lead in enhancing the understanding and development of the international dimension of higher education in Africa by expanding knowledge and building, strengthening, and sustaining a cohort of competent professionals in this field.

ASEAN	Association of Southeast Asian Nations www.aseansec.org	ASEAN is a broadly grounded organization of southeast Asian states, which locates education at the core of its development process, creating a knowledge-based society and contributing to the enhancement of ASEAN competitiveness.
AUCC	Association of Universities and Colleges of Canada www.aucc.ca	AUCC is the national voice for Canadian universities, representing 95 public and private not-for-profit universities and university degree-level colleges; it provides university presidents with a unified voice and a forum for collective action.
CAPRI	Centre for Academic Practice and Research in Internationalization www.leedsmet.ac.uk/ world-widehorizons /index_CAPRI.htm	Based at Leeds Metropolitan University, CAPRI seeks to revolutionize thinking through the development of a community of practitioners focusing on a forward-looking research, implementation and evaluation agenda. As a global professional community, CAPRI aims to share experience and resources, collaborate in research projects and offer insights from around the world as reference points and sources of information with a view to enhancing practice in international education.
CIBER	Centers For International Business Education and Research) better known by acronym www.ciberweb.msu.edu	CIBER were created by the U.S. Congress to increase and promote the nation's capacity for international understanding and competitiveness; administered by the U.S. Department of Education, the CIBER network links the manpower and technological needs of the U.S. business community with the international education, language training, and research capacities of universities across the country.
CIHE	Center for International Higher Education www.bc.edu/research/cihe. html	The Center for International Higher Education, based at Boston College, defines its mission as advancing knowledge about the complex realities of higher education in the contemporary world through research, publications, and conferences.
CONAHEC	Consortium for North American Higher Education Collaboration www.conahec.org	CONAHEC advises and connects institutions interested in establishing or strengthening collaborative programs in the North American region.
CONAEVA	Comisión Nacional de Evaluación de la Educación Superior	Mexico's CONAEVA is dedicated to the promotion and support of the development of a national higher education evaluation system.
CONEAU	Comisión Nacional de Evaluación y Acreditación Universitaria [known by acronym] www.coneau.edu.ar	CONEAU, a decentralized organization working within the Office of the Ministry of Education in Buenos Aires, was created with the aim of contributing to the improvement of university education.

EAIE	European Association for International Education www.eaie.org	EAIE, a nonprofit, member-led organization, is the acknowledged European leadership center for expertise, networking, and resources in the internationalization of higher education, assisting members with training, conferences, and knowledge acquisition and sharing.
ECTS	European Credit Transfer and Accumulation System www.ec.europa.eu/ education/lifelong-learning-policy/ects_en.htm	ECTS facilitates the transfer of learning experiences between different European institutions, fosters greater student mobility and more flexible routes to gain degrees, and aids curriculum design and quality assurance.
EHEA	Europe Higher Education Area www.ehea.info/	EHEA was created as part of the Bologna Process to ensure more comparable, compatible, and coherent systems of higher education in Europe; its permanent website will play a key role in this process of intense internal and external communication.
ENQA	European Network for Quality Assurance in Higher Education www.enqa.eu/	ENQA disseminates information, experiences, and good practices in the field of quality assurance (QA) in higher education to European QA agencies, public authorities, and higher education institutions.
Erasmus	European Action Scheme for the Mobility of University Students http://ec.europa.eu/ education/lifelong-learning-programme/doc80_en.htm	Erasmus is the EU's flagship education and training program, enabling 200,000 students to study and work abroad each year; it funds cooperation between higher education institutions across Europe and supports students, professors, and business staff.
EUA	European University Association www.eua.be/	EUA represents and supports higher education institutions in 47 countries, providing them with a unique forum to cooperate and keep abreast of the latest trends in higher education and research policies; it plays an essential role in shaping tomorrow's European higher education and research landscape.
EURASHE	European Association of Institutions in Higher Education www.eurashe.eu	EURASHE includes 800 higher education institutions in 32 of the Bologna signatory countries; it is traditionally an association of national associations.
IAU	International Association of Universities www.iau-aiu.net	IAU is the UNESCO-based worldwide association of higher education institutions, bringing together institutions and organizations from some 120 countries for reflection and action on common concerns.
ICHEM	International Centre for Higher Education Management www.bath.ac.uk/ichem/	ICHEM is a major interdisciplinary research center based at the University of Bath, facilitating academic work in the field of higher education management and policy.

IIE	Institute of International Education iie.org	IIE, an independent not-for-profit organization founded in 1919, is among the world's largest and most experienced international education and training organizations, committed to delivering program excellence to a diverse range of participants, sponsors, and donors.
IEAA	International Education Association of Australia www.ieaa.org.au/	IEAA is Australia's leading international education professional organization, its mission to enhance the quality and standing of Australian international education by serving the professional needs and interests of its members and by promoting international education within Australia and internationally.
IMPI	Indicators for Mapping & Profiling Internalisation www.impi-project.eu	The IMPI project focuses on mapping and profiling internationalization of higher education institutions to give them insight into their performance in internationalization and measures for improvement.
NAFSA	NAFSA: Association of International Educators www.nafsa.org	NAFSA, the world's largest nonprofit professional association dedicated to international education, seeks to advance public policies that promote international education and to support a broad public dialogue about the value and importance of international education.
NONIE	Network of Networks on Impact Evaluation www.worldbank.org/ieg/nonie/	NONIE comprises various international committees to form a network drawn from the regional evaluation associations.
NUFFIC	Netherlands organization for international cooperation in higher education www.nuffic.nl/	Based in the Netherlands, NUFFIC is an organization dedicated to linking knowledge worldwide.
NVAO	Accreditation Organisation of the Netherlands and Flanders www.nvao.com	NVAO is an independent organization aiming to ensure the quality of higher education by assessing quality control at higher education institutions and accrediting their programs.
RIACES	Red Iberoamericana Acreditación de la Calidad de la Educación Superior www.riaces.net	RIACES (in English, the Latin American Network to Accreditation of Quality of Higher Education), is a nonprofit partnership of agencies and organizations for evaluation and accreditation of the quality of higher education.
SRHE	Society for Research Into Higher Education www.srhe.ac.uk	SRHE is a UK-based international learned society aimed at advancing understanding of higher education, especially through the insights, perspectives and knowledge offered by systematic research and scholarship.
WES	World Education Services www.wes.org	WES, a not-for-profit organization that evaluates credentials, is the leading source of international education intelligence; it provides an Internet portal to trusted, accurate research and intelligence about foreign academic credentials, institutions, and trends.

INDEX

Page references followed by (box), (table), and (figure) indicates display material.

ABOUT THE EDITORS

Darla K. Deardorff

Darla K. Deardorff is currently executive director of the Association of International Education Administrators, a national professional organization based at Duke University, where she is also a research scholar in education and an educator with Duke Corporate Education. In addition, she is a visiting professor at Leeds-Metropolitan University in the United Kingdom, an adjunct professor at North Carolina State University, the University of North Carolina-Chapel Hill, the Monterey Institute for International Studies, and a faculty member of the Summer Institute for Intercultural Communication in Portland, Oregon.

Deardorff is founder of ICC Global (www .iccglobal.org), a global network of researchers on issues of intercultural competence. She has received numerous invitations from around the world to speak on her research on intercultural competence and assessment and is a noted expert on these topics. With nearly 20 years of experience in the international education field, she has published widely on topics in international education and was editor of *The SAGE Handbook of Intercultural Competence*, among other books. She serves as a consultant and trainer on international education, global leadership, faculty development, intercultural competence development and assessment for universities, corporations, and nonprofit organizations around the world, including UNESCO. She is the recipient of numerous awards including an outstanding alumnus award from her undergraduate alma mater as well as a distinguished alumnus award for the department at her graduate alma mater, and several professional awards.

She has been active in numerous international education professional organizations including as a leader in NAFSA, Forum on Education Abroad, and as a Trainer in European Association of International Education (EAIE). Deardorff serves as a reviewer for numerous journals including the *Journal of Studies in International Education* (JSIE) and is a member of IAU's Ad-Hoc Expert Group on Internationalization as well as the Network of International Education Associations (NIEA).

Deardorff holds a master's degree and a doctorate from North Carolina State University where she specialized in international education. Her dissertation, on the definition and assessment of intercultural competence, has drawn national and international attention, and her intercultural competence models developed through research are being used by organizations and postsecondary institutions worldwide. A member of International Academy of Intercultural Research, she has lived and worked in Germany, Japan, and Switzerland.

Hans de Wit

Hans de Wit is professor (lector) of internationalization of higher education at the School of Economics and Management of the Hogeschool van Amsterdam, University of Applied Sciences and, as of 2012, also professor of internationalization of higher education and academic director at the International Education Research Centre (IERC) of the Università Cattolica del Sacro Cuore (UCSC) in Milan. Since 2010, he is a visiting professor at the Centre for Academic Practice and Research in Internationalization (CAPRI) of Leeds Metropolitan University, United Kingdom. In 2005–2006, he was a New Century Scholar of the Fulbright Program, Higher Education in the 21st Century. He was a visiting scholar in the United States in 1995 and 2006 and in Australia in 2002.

He is the coeditor of the *Journal of Studies in International Education* (Association for Studies in International Education/SAGE publishers). He has (co)written several other books and articles on international education and is actively involved in assessment and consultancy in international education for organizations like the European Commission, UNESCO, World Bank, IMHE/OECD, and ESMU. His latest books are *Trends, Issues and Challenges in Internationalization of Higher Education* (2011) and, as editor, *Measuring Success in Internationalization of Higher Education* (2009).

Among his other books are: *Internationalization of Higher Education in the United States of America and Europe: a Historical, Comparative and Conceptual Analysis* (2002), United States; *Higher Education in Latin America: The International Dimension*, coedited with Isabel Cristina Jaramillo, Jocelyne Gacel Avila and Jane Knight (2005), and *European Responses to the Global Perspective*, edited with Barbara Kehm (2006).

He has undertaken quality reviews of a great number of institutions of higher education in the framework of the visiting advisors program (VAP), IQRP, IQR, Eurostrat, and NVAO. He is coeditor of *Quality and Internationalization of Higher Education'* with Jane Knight (1999).

He has been director of the Office of Foreign Relations, vice president for International Affairs, and senior advisor international at the Universiteit van Amsterdam, in the period 1986 to 2005 and director of international relations at Tilburg University from 1981 to 1985. He was assistant professor in Latin American Studies at Utrecht University, 1979 to 1981. He has a bachelor's, master's and PhD from the University of Amsterdam.

Hans de Wit is founding member and past president of the European Association for International Education (EAIE). Currently, he is a member of the Board of Trustees of World Education Services (New York), member of the ESL TOEFL Board (as of 2011), and member of the Consell Assessor de l'Institut Internacional de Postgrau de la Universitat Oberta de Catalunya.

In 2008, he received the Constance Meldrum Award for Vision and Leadership of the European Association for International Education (EAIE) in Antwerp. Previously, he received awards from the University of Amsterdam (2006), AIEA (2006), CIEE (2004 and 2006), NAFSA (2002), and EAIE (1999).

John D. Heyl

John D. Heyl's career in international higher education has included teaching at the undergraduate and graduate level at three U.S. institutions, leadership in local, regional, and national professional associations and practitioner in both the public and private sector. He is currently vice president for strategic partnerships at CEA Global Education, an education abroad program provider based in Tempe, Arizona.

He has served as senior international officer (SIO) at three U.S. universities. At Illinois Wesleyan University (Bloomington, Illinois), a private, liberal arts campus, he chaired the history department and social science division and co-founded the international studies program. At the University of Missouri-Columbia, a public land grant institution, he helped develop the award-winning Global Scholars Program for faculty development. At Old Dominion University (Norfolk, Virginia), he helped expand study abroad participation at an urban, historically commuter institution and co-founded the master's program in international higher education leadership. He has won awards for both his teaching and administrative work.

Active in professional associations, Heyl served as president of the Association of International Education Administrators (AIEA) (2000–2001) and has presented papers and led workshops at NAFSA: Association of International Educators and the European Association for International Education (EAIE). He has consulted widely at U.S. universities and has advised on global education initiatives at the middle and high school levels as well. He is the author of *The Senior International Officer (SIO) as Change Agent* (2007).

Heyl has led or co-led numerous U.S. Department of Education Title VI and U.S. State Department grants for internationalizing the curriculum, enhancing faculty development, and training high school teachers worldwide. He has also reviewed applications for funding from these agencies.

Heyl earned his BA in history from Stanford University, with Phi Beta Kappa honors. He focused his doctoral work in European and

German history at Washington University in St. Louis. He has held several Fulbright grants to Germany and has written on the interplay between politics and economics in the German depression of the 1930s. He taught for 20 years on a wide range of subjects, including German history, world history, comparative revolutionary movements, and international higher education leadership.

Tony Adams (1944-2011)

On Thursday, May 12, 2011, at the age of 67, Tony Adams, co-editor of *The SAGE Handbook of International Higher Education*, passed away.

Tony commenced as a lecturer in the Department of Computer Science at RMIT in 1978. Following five years as Head of Department of Business Computing at RMIT, he acted for a year as Dean of Business in 1990-91, being appointed to the position of Dean International Programs in 1992, a position he held until 1998. Tony was appointed a member of the Foundation Professoriate at RMIT in 1992.

In 1997 he was awarded the inaugural *IDP award for excellence in International Education* and in 2006 he received the *Charles Klasek Award* for his contribution to international education from the Association of International Education Administrators (AIEA).

In 1998 he took up the position of Director International Programs at Macquarie University. In 2004, he was appointed as Pro Vice Chancellor International at Macquarie, a position he held until January 2007. During his time at Macquarie University, he developed an extensive quality network of partnerships which made this university an institution with active international mobility and exchange. In January 2007, Tony and his wife Pauline formed *Tony Adams and Associates*, international education consultants. Together, they have worked with universities in Australia, Mexico, the Netherlands and Italy as well as with U.S. British and Canadian organizations.

Tony is widely published in the areas of educational computing and international education. Among the many publications he is (co) author of are three JSIE Published Papers: Adams, T, *The Operation of Transnational Degree and Diploma Programs, The Australian Case*, 1998; Walters, D., Adams, T. , *Global Reach Through a Strategic Operations Approach: An Australian Case Study*, 2001; and Adams, T. , *The Development of International Education in Australia*, 2007. In 2008 he became co-editor of the *Journal of Studies in International Education*.

Tony has been the founding and immediate Past President of the *International Education Association of Australia* (IEAA), Vice Chairman of the Board of the *International Student Exchange Program* (ISEP), special advisor to *Università Cattolica Del Sacre Cuore* (UCSC), and special advisor to the *Mexican Association of International Education* (AMPEI). He was a regular trainer and presenter at workshops, sessions and seminars during the conferences of NAFSA, EAIE, AIEA and his own association IEAA. He was a member of a working group that created a new Network of International Education Associations (NIEA).

As described in a tribute by IDP Education Australia, *"One of the most rewarding aspects of serving the international education community is the relationships we are able to form with people truly passionate about what they do. Perhaps no one was more passionate than Tony Adams."*

ABOUT THE AUTHORS

Foreword

Josef A. Mestenhauser

Josef A. Mestenhauser is distinguished international emeritus professor at the University of Minnesota. His 60-year career included being teacher, researcher, administrator, counselor, and consultant. He published more than 150 books, monographs, articles, and book chapters on various components of international education. His most recent publication was published by the University of Minnesota (2011) under the title "Reflections on the Past, Present and Future of Internationalizing Higher Education. Discovering Opportunities to Meet the Challenges." He is three-time holder of senior Fulbright grants in the Philippines, Japan, and Czechoslovakia. Among offices he held was president of NAFSA, International Society for Educational, Cultural and Scientific Interchanges (ISECSI), and the Fulbright Association of Minnesota. He holds a doctorate from the Charles University, Faculty of Law, and from the University of Minnesota in political science and international relations. For 10 years, he was honorary consul of the Czech Republic in Minnesota, Iowa, and North and South Dakotas.

Among honors he received is the Marita Houlihan Award for Excellence in International Education; Presidential Silver Medal from President Vaclav Havel; Jan Masaryk Silver Memorial Medal; Distinguished Global Engagement Award from the University of Minnesota and, most recently, the NAFSA/TLS Award for Innovative Research and Scholarship in Internationalization. The University of Minnesota established an annual lecture series on internationalization in his name.

Chapter Authors

Clifford Adelman

Clifford Adelman taught at Roosevelt University, CCNY, and Yale, and served five years as Associate Dean and Assistant Academic Vice-President at the William Paterson College of New Jersey before coming to the U.S. Department of Education in 1979. Managed higher education issues for *A Nation at Risk* (1983) and conducted the research on which its high school curriculum recommendations were based. Designed, managed, and served as amanuensis for the higher education follow-up, the *Involvement in Learning report* (1984), which has been cited as responsible for kick-starting the assessment movement in higher education. Conducted studies of assessment in the late 1980s, then took on the task of editing and analyzing the major national longitudinal studies data bases. Wrote eight monographs in the course of this effort, including *Women at Thirtysomething: Paradoxes of Attainment* (1991); *Women and Men of the Engineering Path* (1998); *Answers in the Tool Box: Academic Intensity, Attendance Patterns, and Bachelor's Degree Attainment* (1999), and *Moving Into Town—an Moving On: the Community College in the Lives of Traditional-age Students* (2005). *The Toolbox Revisited: Paths to Degree Completion from High School Through College* (2006) is the last of Cliff's studies for the Department.

Philip Altbach

Philip G. Altbach is J. Donald Monan, S.J., University Professor and director of the Center for International Higher Education in the Lynch School of Education at Boston College. He was the 2004–2006 distinguished scholar leader for the New Century Scholars initiative of the Fulbright program, and in 2010, he was an

Erudite Scholar of the Government of Kerala in India. He has been a senior associate of the Carnegie Foundation for the Advancement of Teaching and has taught at the State University of New York at Buffalo; the University of Wisconsin, Madison; and Harvard University. He has had awards from the German Academic Exchange Service, the Japan Society for the Promotion of Science, and others.

Melissa Banks

Melissa Banks has more than 20 years' experience encompassing a variety of roles across multiple education sectors and service providers, giving her firsthand experience and skills concerning many aspects of international education in Australia. She has held senior positions in three Australian universities, including her current role as director of Swinburne International at Swinburne University of Technology. She also led major research projects in her capacity as head of research at IDP Education Pty Ltd. And has contributed papers, presentations and chapters to various national and international forums and publications throughout her working life. Topics include global student mobility, outcomes and impacts of international education in Australia, retention and transition practices in Australian universities, and Australian transnational tertiary education.

Brett Berquist

Brett Berquist is executive director of study abroad at Michigan State University, the largest study abroad program among U.S. public universities, with more than 270 programs on all seven continents. Previously, he served as executive director of international programs at Western Michigan University, where a range of transnational programs was at the heart of internationalization strategy. He has served on internationalization task forces in four universities and has more than 20 years' experience in international education in the United States, United Kingdom, France, and Korea. He chaired modern language departments and led international programming in institutions in France, which finally granted him dual citizenship, during the development of the Erasmus program and the beginning of the Bologna Process. He holds degrees in French, music, and linguistics.

Rajika Bhandari

Rajika Bhandari is deputy vice president, research and evaluation, at the Institute of International Education (IIE) in New York where she provides strategic oversight of the institute's research and evaluation activities and leads two major research projects—Open Doors and Project Atlas—that measure international higher education mobility at the domestic U.S. and international levels. She is a frequent speaker and author on the topic of mobility and is the author of four books on global student mobility. Previously, she was a senior researcher at MPR Associates, where she conducted research for state departments of education, the National Center for Education Statistics, and foundations. She also served as the assistant director for evaluation at the Mathematics and Science Education Network at the University of North Carolina, Chapel Hill. She holds a doctoral degree in psychology from North Carolina State University and a BA (Honors) in psychology from the University of Delhi, India.

Elizabeth Brewer

Elizabeth Brewer has worked in international education for most of her professional life. Currently director of international education at Beloit College, a small, liberal arts institution in Wisconsin, she has also held positions at the New School for Social Research, Boston University, and the University of Massachusetts at Amherst. With a PhD in German literature, she gained experience in rural community development as a mid-career Peace Corps volunteer in the Slovak Republic. She has brought her experience at educational institutions and in Slovakia to bear in her current position, where she has focused on helping students approach study abroad with intentionality, providing meaningful opportunities for faculty development, and using partnerships to advance campus internationalization. Coeditor of *Integrating Study Abroad into the Curriculum: Theory and Practice Across the Disciplines* (2010), she has written and edited other publications on international education as well as community development topics.

Peter Burgess

Peter Burgess is executive director, EdBiz Pty Ltd., an Australian management education consultancy. He has held senior academic and administrative positions in two Australian universities. He was honorary chair of the Australian Higher Education Transnational Education Forum and is currently an honorary auditor with the Australian Government's Tertiary Education Quality and Standards Agency.

He is chair of Academic Board with a private higher education college in Western Australia, and his research interests focus on change management and cross-border education. He has designed, implemented, and led higher education aid and trade projects in China, Thailand, Nepal, Bangladesh, and India and directed cross-border undergraduate and postgraduate programs in Singapore, Malaysia, Hong Kong, and Vietnam. He has also worked with universities and colleges in New Zealand, Canada, and Mexico on internationalization projects and taught on prestigious MBA programs in both Australia and the United Kingdom.

Stephen Connelly

Stephen Connelly was appointed deputy vice chancellor, international and development, and vice president at RMIT University in February 2010. Prior to that, he spent 5 years at Swinburne University of Technology as pro vice chancellor (international) and later deputy vice chancellor (development and engagement). He spent 7 years at La Trobe University as director of international marketing and then director of the International Programs Office. He was chair of the Victorian International Directors Committee from 2000 to 2002 and foundation chair of the Australian Universities International Directors Forum from 2002 to 2004. He is currently president of the International Education Association Australia (IEAA). A graduate of Monash and Melbourne Universities, he has lived and worked overseas in Germany and Malaysia and has more than 20 years' experience in international education.

Jane Edwards

Jane Edwards is dean of international and professional experience at Yale University, which she joined in 2006 what was then the new position of associate dean for international affairs. Previously, she served as director of international studies at Harvard University, following 10 years in a similar position at Wesleyan University. She is coauthor with Humphrey Tonkin of *The World in the Curriculum* and is a member of the editorial board of the *Journal of Studies in International Education* and of the boards of World Learning and the Fund for Education Abroad. She publishes and presents on a range of topics in international education and has taught throughout her career. She received a PhD from the University of Pennsylvania and her BA and MA from Cambridge University.

Everett Egginton

Everett Egginton is a professor in the Department of Curriculum and Instruction in the College of Education and former dean of international and border programs at New Mexico State University. Throughout his career, he has worked in Latin America in many capacities, including the Peace Corps (Venezuela), Ford Foundation Fellowship (Peru), and Fulbright Dissertation Fellowship (Colombia); he consulted with USAID (Colombia, El Salvador), ministries of education throughout Central America, and the World Bank (El Salvador); and he was a Senior Fulbright Research and Teaching Fellow (El Salvador, 2000) and Fulbright Lecturer (Colombia, 2010). He is widely published in the areas of Latin American education and bibliography and internationalization in higher education. He currently is a member of the Board of Advisors of the American Council of Education's Internationalization Collaborative and the Board of Directors of the International Student Exchange Program. Since 2009, he has been an active member of LASPAU's Board of Trustees.

Eva Egron-Polak

Eva Egron-Polak served almost 20 years in senior positions at the Association of Universities and Colleges of Canada (AUCC) prior to becoming Secretary General of the International Association of Universities in 2002. IAU, an independent global association of universities and associations of higher education institutions, based at UNESCO in Paris tackles many of the most pressing policy issues in higher education. Under her leadership, IAU launched regular global surveys on internationalization, created a grants program for professional development and North-South and South-South collaboration called LEADHER, developed an advisory service to review and assess institutional internationalistrategies (ISAS) and adopted a policy statement on equitable access and success in higher education. Most recently, she has coordinated the effort that led to the IAU document 'Affirming Academic Values in Internationalization of Higher Education: A Call for Action' and the drafting of Guidelines for institutional codes of ethics. She is a member of many committees at UNESCO, the European Commission, the OECD and others. She is the co-author of *Internationalization of Higher Education: Global Trends, Regional Perspectives*, a report published in 2010, and has written and presented many papers on various higher ed topics.

Raul Favela

Raul Favela, MD, performed his undergraduate studies at the Autonomous University of Chihuahua where he obtained a medical doctor degree. He had his post graduate degree in the National Autonomous University of Mexico as a Plastic and reconstructive Surgeon. He has held several positions at the Autonomous University of Chihuahua as Director of International Services, Director of the Confucius Institute, Co-Director in research projects in collaboration with universities in United States through the USAID Agency. He is Honorary Director of non-governmental organizations and has been honored by the University of Texas at EL Paso as "Associate Professor of the Year 2009." He is currently in the area of research and post graduate studies in the Medical School in teaching and community outreach programs in the University of Chihuahua. He is actively involved in several research projects in the educational area.

Madeleine F. Green

Madeleine F. Green is a higher education consultant and senior fellow at the International Association of Universities (IAU) and NAFSA: the Association of International Educators. Until 2010, she served as vice president, international initiatives, American Council on Education (ACE). The Association of International Education Administrators awarded her its 2010 Charles Klasek Award for outstanding service to the field of international education administration. She served as interim president of Mount Vernon College (DC) from 1990–1991 and as a member of the board of trustees of Wilson College (PA) from 1988 to 1993 and of Sweet Briar College (VA) from 1994 to 2002; she is currently a board member at Juniata College (PA). She has served on the boards of the Forum on Education Abroad and the International Association of Universities. She is the author of numerous publications on higher education, leadership, and internationalization.

Lesleyanne Hawthorne

Lesleyanne Hawthorne is associate dean international at the University of Melbourne. Her research concerns high-skilled migration, international student mobility, and foreign credential recognition. Most recently, she has completed commissioned studies for the Australian, Canadian, and New Zealand governments; UNESCO; the Global Forum of Federations; the U.S. Migration Policy Institute; and the Pacific Economic Cooperation Council (APEC). This has included a cycle of comparative studies on international student migration trends. In 2005–2006, she was appointed to an Expert Panel of Three by Australia's Federal Cabinet to complete the most extensive evaluation of Australia's skilled migration program since 1988. The panel's recommendations from 2007 to 2010 governed the selection of up to 108,000 skilled migrants in Australia per year. She was previously the research manager of Australia's Bureau of Immigration, Multicultural, and Population Research.

John Hudzik

John K. Hudzik is professor at Michigan State University. He is past president of the Association of International Education Administrators and also past president and chair of the Board of Directors of NAFSA: Association of International Educators. He is currently NAFSA senior scholar for internationalization. From 1995 to 2010, he was dean of international studies and programs at Michigan State University and then vice president for global engagement and strategic projects. He was acting university provost and vice president for academic affairs at MSU in 2005. He has served on numerous international policy and advisory boards and is a frequently invited speaker at conferences on higher education internationalization. He is recipient of several national awards for his scholarly work in judicial systems and in international education, including the AIEA Charles Klasek Award for outstanding service to international education.

Chuo-Chun Hsieh

Chuo-Chun Hsieh is a PhD candidate at the International Centre for Higher Education Management (ICHEM), School of Management at the University of Bath, United Kingdom, working on a comparative policy policy study on quality assurance in higher education. Prior to the move to England, she enrolled the Graduate Institution of Education at National Chung Chen University in Taiwan. Her work has been published in several research journals covered in the Taiwan Social Science Citation Index (TSSCI). Most of her research concerns educational policy, with an especial interest in theories of policy process in the global context.

Jeroen Huisman

Jeroen Huisman is director of the International Centre for Higher Education Management

(ICHEM). His research interests are the impacts of the change from government to governance in higher education, the dynamics of organizational change, inertia and diversity in higher education, institutional management and governance, and internationalization and Europeanization; he has published widely on these topics. He is editor of *Higher Education Policy* and editorial board member of *Tertiary Education and Management* (TEAM), *Journal of Studies in International Education, European Journal of Higher Education,* and *Educational Researcher* (U.S.).

Fiona Hunter

Fiona Hunter is International Director at the Università Carlo Cattaneo, Castellanza, Italy and Past President of the European Association for International Education (EAIE) where she is now co-chair and founding member of the Special Interest Group, Researchers in International Education (RIE). She has been involved in professional development and consultancy on internationalisation of higher education for many years for a broad range of universities, international associations and organisations. She is a member of the Editorial Board of the Journal of Studies in International Education (JSIE) and of the Scientific Committee of the Centre for Higher Education Internationalisation (CHEI) at the Università Cattolica del Sacro Cuore, Milan, Italy. She serves on the Board of Directors at Educational Credential Evaluators, Inc. (ECE) in the United States and acts as senior expert for the European Centre for Strategic Management of Universities (ESMU) in Brussels, Belgium. In the spirit of lifelong learning she completed her Doctorate of Business Administration (DBA) in Higher Education Management in 2009 at the University of Bath in the U.K.

Elspeth Jones

Elspeth Jones is emerita professor of the Internationalization of Higher Education and a consultant on global education. As International Dean at Leeds Metropolitan University she led the comprehensive internationalization strategy and was responsible for international student recruitment, curriculum internationalization, and staff development for internationalization. In 2009, she founded the Centre for Academic Practice and Research in Internationalization (CAPRI). She has published widely on comprehensive and values-driven internationalization, including the edited collections *Internationalisation and the Student Voice* (2010) and *Internationalizing Higher Education* (2007) (with Sally Brown). Her principal fields of research include transformational learning through international and intercultural experiences, the link between curriculum internationalization and multiculturalism, and the role of internationalization in enhancing student employability. With a background in applied linguistics and TEFL, she has more than 30 years' experience in international education and worked for the British Council in Japan and Singapore for 7 years.

Jane Knight

Jane Knight, University of Toronto, focuses her research and professional interests on the international dimension of higher education at the institutional, national, regional, and international levels. Her work in more than 65 countries with universities, governments, UN agencies, and foundations helps to bring a comparative, development, and international perspective to her research, teaching, and policy work. She is the author of numerous articles and publications on internationalization concepts and strategies, quality assurance, institutional management, trade, and cross-border education. Her recent research on education hubs will result in a new book in 2012. Currently, she is leading a comparative study on regionalization of higher education. She is an adjunct professor at Ontario Institute for Studies in Education, University of Toronto and sits on the advisory boards of many international organizations and journals. She was a Fulbright New Century scholar 2007–2008 and received an honorary LLD from Exeter University in 2010.

Peter H. Koehn

Peter H. Koehn is professor of political science, the University of Montana's Distinguished Scholar for 2005, a Fulbright New Century scholar, recipient of the 2011 Michael P. Malone award for international leadership, and the 2012 George M. Dennison Presidential Faculty Award for Distinguished Accomplishment. He served as the University of Montana's founding director of international programs and senior international officer from 1987 to 1996. He currently directs the University's International Development Studies program. His teaching portfolio includes courses in development administration, rural and global health (MPH program), sustainable climate policies, comparative government, politics of global migration, issues in global public health (freshman global leadership seminar), management skills, and African politics. Over the course of his career, he has taught and conducted research in Ethiopia, Nigeria, Eritrea, Namibia, China, Hong Kong, and Finland. He was coauthor with James N. Rosenau of *Transnational Competence: Empowering Professional Curricula for Horizon-Rising Challenges* (2010). A full CV and list of publications can be found at www.cas.umt.edu/polsci/faculty/koehn.htm

Betty Leask

Betty Leask is an associate professor in internationalization of the curriculum at the University of South Australia, an Australian national teaching fellow, coeditor of the *Journal of Studies in International Education,* visiting professor at the Centre for Academic Practice and Research in Internationalization (CAPRI) at Leeds Metropolitan University in the United Kingdom, a member of the International Education Association of Australia (IEAA) Board, and convener of their Internationalization of the Curriculum Special Interest Group and their Research Committee. The focus of her work is on linking policy and practice in the area of internationalization in higher education and the internationalization of teaching and learning in the formal and informal curriculum. She has undertaken various roles in schools and universities, including director of the Australian Centre for Education in Hungary, dean of teaching and learning in the Division of Business, and coordinator of international staff and student services at UniSA. Her background is in education and applied linguistics.

Jack Lee

Jack Lee worked as a program manager and instructor at the Centre for Intercultural Communication, University of British Columbia (UBC), from 2001 to 2009. During this period, he designed, managed, and facilitated intercultural training programs and workshops for both local and international educators, students, and business executives. While pursuing a master's degree in adult education at UBC, Jack spent a year at the University of Oslo, Norway, as an exchange student to study comparative education. He is currently a doctoral candidate at the Ontario Institute for Studies in Education of the University of Toronto and an active member of its Comparative,

International, and Development Education Centre. His research interests include the internationalization of higher education, regionalization, and comparative education research methodology. His dissertation examines the development of education hubs in East and Southeast Asia from the perspective of international relations.

Mitch Leventhal

Mitch Leventhal is vice chancellor for global affairs at the State University of New York, the world's largest comprehensive university system, with 64 campuses and nearly one half million students. Leventhal is a cofounder and served as the first president of the American International Recruitment Council, an officially registered standard development organization, which has adapted U.S. higher education accreditation to a certification process for international student recruitment agencies. An advocate for standards, ethical practice, and corporate social responsibility across all dimensions of the higher education enterprise, he was appointed senior adviser for academic affairs to the United Nations Global Compact in 2010. He received his doctorate in the international political economy of higher education from the University of Chicago in 1995. He resides in New York City.

Roger Ludeman

Roger Ludeman spent his career serving students at all levels of U.S. education. Following 8 years of public school teaching and counseling, he entered student affairs work as a dean in universities in Pennsylvania and the Midwest. The last years of his career saw him going global with his writing, research, and efforts focused on identifying and connecting a student affairs and services field in 50-plus countries. In 2009, he collaborated with UNESCO, publishing the book, *Student Affairs and Services in Higher Education: Global Foundations, Issues, and Best Practices.* He received three Fulbright grants (Germany, Japan, and South Africa). Throughout the decade of the 1990s and into the 21st century, he has worked to reduce the divide between international educators and student affairs professionals so that work with international students and those who study across borders can be more effective in terms of learning outcomes, health, and safety.

Simon Marginson

Simon Marginson is a professor of higher education at the University of Melbourne, Australia, where he works in the Centre for the Study of Higher Education. His research is focused on higher education, international students, and globalization. He is one of the coordinating editors of the journal, *Higher Education*. Recent books include *International Student Security* (2010) with Chris Nyland, Erlenawati Sawir, and Helen Forbes Mewett; *Ideas for Intercultural Education* (2011) with Erlenawati Sawir; and the coedited collections *Higher Education in the Asia-Pacific* (2011) and *Handbook of Higher Education and Globalization* (2011).

Francisco Marmolejo

Francisco Marmolejo is executive director of the Consortium for North American Higher Education Collaboration (CONAHEC), a network of more than 170 higher education institutions and organizations primarily from Canada, the U.S. and Mexico, headquartered at the University of Arizona, where he also serves as assistant vice president for global initiatives. Previously, he was an American Council on Education fellow at the University of Massachusetts, and vice president for academic affairs at the University of the Americas in Mexico. He is a frequent contributor to international higher educonferences, and a blogger on international education topics for the Chronicle of Higher Education. He has served on the Board of NAFSA and AMPEI, and currently he serves on the Board of the Compostela Group of Universities and World Education Services. He consults for the Organization for Economic Cooperation and Development (OECD) and the World Bank on educational policy.

Gilbert Merkx

Gilbert W. Merkx was born in Maracaibo, Venezuela. He received his BA from Harvard University and his MA and PhD from Yale University. He was a Fulbright scholar in Perú and a visiting scholar in Buenos Aires and Stockholm. He has taught on the faculties of Yale, Göteborgs Universität (Sweden), and the University of New Mexico. He currently is director of international and area studies at Duke University, director of the Duke Center for International Studies, director of the Duke Islamic Studies Center, and professor of the practice of sociology. He is a past president of the Association of International Education Administrators and a former chairman of the Group of Advisors of the National Security Education Program. He serves as co-chairman of the Council of Title VI National Resource Center Directors and sits on the boards of Venice International University and the Scholars at Risk Network.

Riall Nolan

Riall Nolan is professor of anthropology at Purdue University, where he was associate provost and dean of international programs from 2003 to 2009. He received his doctorate in social anthropology from Sussex University and lived overseas for nearly 20 years in north and west Africa, Asia, and the southwest Pacific, working in higher education and international development. Prior to coming to Purdue, he managed international programs at the University of Pittsburgh, Golden Gate University, and the University of Cincinnati. He has also held administrative and teaching positions at the School for International Training, Georgia State University, and the University of Papua New Guinea. He writes and consults frequently on issues of international development, international education, cross-cultural adaptation, and applied anthropology.

Milton Obamba

Milton Obamba is currently research associate at the John and Elnora Ferguson Centre for African Studies at the University of Bradford. He is also visiting fellow at the Centre for Higher Education Policy Research at the Leeds Metropolitan University in Britain, where he was Carnegie Centenary scholar until he received his PhD in higher education policy in 2011. Obamba studied at Moi University in Kenya before earning his MPhil in 2005 from the Norsk Laerekademiet in Bergen, Norway. He has served as visiting fellow at Nordic Africa Institute in the University of Uppsala and at the African Studies Centre at University of Leiden, Netherlands. His current research interests and publications focus on the interdisciplinary domains of higher education including comparative policy analysis, governance, internationalization, development education, and transnational academic partnerships. His most recent publications have appeared in *Higher Education Policy* and *Journal of Higher Education in Africa*.

Christa Olson

Christa Olson recently joined Drake University as the new vice provost for international programs. Prior to Drake, she served as the associate director for international initiatives at the American Council of Education (ACE). She worked with the senior vice president of programs and services on ACE's initiatives to engage member institutions in internationalization and global engagement. She directed campus networks, managed multi-institutional projects and coauthored publications capturing good practices. Her publications include *At Home in the World: Bridging the Gap Between Internationalization and Multicultural Education* and *Internationalizing the Campus: A user's guide* (with Madeleine Green). She earned a BA from Washington State University and a PhD in French from Stanford University and served as a professor of French and Intercultural Studies at New Jersey City University. A North American studies Fulbright alumnus, she conducted the trilingual research project, *Making the Link: An Exploration of the Impact of North American Educational Partnerships.*

James Peacock

James Peacock is Kenan Professor of Anthropology at the University of North Carolina at Chapel Hill (UNC-CH). He received a BA from Duke and PhD from Harvard. He is a fellow of the American Academy of Arts and Sciences. He was president of the American Anthropological Association. His field research is primarily in Indonesia and Appalachia. Publications include *The Anthropological Lens* (rev. ed., 2001, Chinese edition, 2009) and two books published in 2007: *Grounded Globalism: How the U.S. South Embraces the World* and *Identity Matters: Ethnic and Sectarian Conflict.* Current duties include director, Carolina Seminars and co-director, Duke-UNC Rotary Center on Peace and Conflict. He previously held the administrative position of director of the University Center for International Studies at UNC-CH, in which he oversaw campus internationalization.

Liz Reisberg

Liz Reisberg is a an independent consultant in higher education working with ministries of education, donor agencies, and universities on strategies for improving higher education. Previously she was a research associate at the Center for International Higher Education at Boston College, where she coordinated several grant-funded projects, engaged in research, and contributed to center publications. Her research areas include quality assurance, internationalization,

and the challenges of providing equitable access to higher education. Most of her work has focused on Latin America. She has also worked in international admissions at several Boston-area universities. She was the founder and former executive director of the MBA Tour, a company that organizes professional recruitment tours throughout the world for business schools.

Gary Rhodes

Gary Rhodes is director of the Center for Global Education at the Graduate School of Education and Information Studies at the University of California at Los Angeles (UCLA). Through his leadership, the center has served as a national resource, supporting student mobility in higher education since 1998, with print and online resources supporting faculty, staff, and students. He received his PhD and MS in Education and MA in International Relations from the University of Southern California (USC) and his BA from the University of California at Santa Barbara. He has published articles, been cited, and presents widely at conferences across the United States and around the world. He has taught courses at the graduate level at USC and UCLA on administration of international programs in higher education. He has written and presented widely on issues of university internationalization, using online resources for international learning, and safety, risk, crisis management, legal issues and study abroad. He has received Fulbright grants to India and South Africa.

Laura Rumbley

Laura E. Rumbley is associate director of the Boston College Center for International Higher Education (CIHE). She is also the website content editor for the IREG Observatory on Academic Ranking and Excellence. Laura was previously deputy director of the Academic Cooperation Association (ACA), based in Brussels. In addition to experience as a university administrator in international programming, she has authored and coauthored a number of publications on topics including academic salaries in comparative perspective, European student mobility, curricular issues in U.S. study abroad, and internationalization in Spanish higher education. Most notably, she coauthored (with Philip G. Altbach and Liz Reisberg) the foundational document for the 2009 UNESCO World Conference on Higher Education,

Trends in Global Higher Education: Tracking an Academic Revolution. A former U.S. Foreign Service officer, she currently serves on the editorial board for the *Journal of Studies in International Education* and is active in the European Association for International Education.

Farshid Shams

Farshid Shams is a PhD candidate at the International Centre for Higher Education Management (ICHEM), School of Management, University of Bath, United Kingdom. He received his MBA from Thames Valley University of London. For a number of years, he worked in the capacity of full-time lecturer and taught various business administration courses. Farshid's research interests include organizational studies of transnational enterprises, market mechanisms in non-profit sectors, organizations' reputational arms race and globalization of higher education institutions.

Michael Stohl

Michael Stohl is professor of communication at the University of California, Santa Barbara. Previously, he was dean of international programs and professor of political science at Purdue University in West Lafayette, Indiana. From 1987 to 1992, he was director of programs for study abroad at Purdue University. He has served on the boards of numerous international education associations including as chair of CIEE's Academic Consortium Board from 1995 to 2000 and as chair of the Board from 2004 to 2010. In addition to his publications on international education, he is the author or coauthor of more than 100 scholarly journal articles and book chapters and the author, editor, or coeditor of 15 books on political violence, terrorism, human rights, and corporate social responsibility. His most recent publications include *Fragile States: Violence and the Failure of Intervention* (coauthor, 2011) and *Crime and Terrorism* (coauthor, 2010).

Susan Buck Sutton

Susan Buck Sutton is senior advisor for internationalization, Bryn Mawr College, having recently retired from Indiana University–Purdue University Indianapolis (IUPUI), where she was associate vice chancellor for international affairs and chancellor's professor of anthropology. While at IUPUI, she focused campus internationalization around a philosophy of international

dialogue and collaboration that garnered the Heiskell Award from the Institute of International Education and the Senator Paul Simon Award from NAFSA. She has published five books and more than 50 articles on international partnerships, international service-learning, and the anthropology of modern Greece. She was 2011 president of the Association of International Educators and serves on boards or advisory councils for the American Council on Education, Institute for International Education, NAFSA, and the Gennadius Library in Athens.

Hanneke Teekens

Hanneke Teekens is member of the board of directors of NUFFIC (the Netherlands organization for international cooperation in higher education). Before joining Nuffic, she worked at the Hogeschool and University of Amsterdam and the University of Twente. She held positions as a teacher and researcher, manager, and consultant and worked in many parts of the world. Previously, she was director of the Socrates National Agency and director, national structure, for Erasmus Mundus in the Netherlands. She has published on various aspects of international education. Her latest contributions have focused in particular on internationalization at home. She is a frequent speaker at conferences and seminars. She studied education and history and did her graduate studies at the University of Leiden. She was an American Field Service exchange student to the United States.

Martin Tillman

Martin Tillman is president of Global Career Compass, an international consulting practice focused on global workforce trends and the impact of education abroad on student career development. He was formerly associate director, career services, at The Johns Hopkins University School of Advanced International Studies. He has managed intercultural education and development projects in the Alaskan arctic, India, Japan, Colombia, Russia, and Central Asia. He received a Fulbright International Education Administrator grant to Japan. He is a regular contributor of book reviews and essays to NAFSA's *International Educator* magazine and conference speaker on issues of global workforce development, education abroad and its impact on career development, and intercultural competence. He also is author of the *AIFS Student Guide to Study Abroad* and *Career Development,* editor of *The Impact of Education Abroad on Career Development and Study Abroad: A 21ˢᵗ Century Perspective,* and *The Right Tool for the Job.*

Joseph D. Tullbane

Joseph D. Tullbane is the associate dean for international education and outreach at St. Norbert College, supervising all international curricular and co-curricular aspects of the college. He also serves as director, Center for International Education, supervising Study Abroad, International Student Services, ESL Institute, Language Services & Outreach, and International Programming. He holds a PhD in Russian area studies (Georgetown University), as well as two degrees in architecture (Rice University) and an MA in international relations (The American University). Prior to his current position, he served as a consultant on Russian political/military affairs to the Department of the Army. He also serves as a member of the Executive Board of the Association of International Education Administrators.

David Urias

David Urias is the new executive director of educational programming for the nonprofit, *Reach For Tomorrow.* He has an extensive educational background in international education, policy studies, and program evaluation. He was the founding director of both the master's program in global and international education at Drexel University's School of Education and of the Evaluation Research Network. He earned his doctorate in international educational policy studies and program evaluation from the Curry School of Education, University of Virginia. His professional mission is to use his expertise in international education and program evaluation to make interdisciplinary collaborations to create, disseminate, and apply knowledge to improve education; education that is broadly defined. This mission provides cohesion to and increases the efficacy of his work. In addition, his research agenda and interests reflect sensitivity to the need for innovative yet pragmatic solutions to real problems, and he places emphasis on the practical implications of his work.

Adinda van Gaalen

Adinda van Gaalen holds a master's degree in Culture organization and management from the

VU University in Amsterdam. She previously studied international tourism management and consultancy at NHTV Breda and carried out her internship at the Research Department of the Ministry of Tourism in Mexico. She started her career in the field of internationalization as head of the international office of the HES School of Business in Amsterdam. She worked for several years as a policy adviser and also taught intercultural awareness at the Hogeschool van Amsterdam. She now works as a senior policy officer at Nuffic, the Netherlands organization for international cooperation in higher education. Her fields of interest include internationalization policy, strategy, and quality assurance. She is involved in carrying out studies and is project manager of the Mapping Internationalization (MINT) project. She also works as a trainer in short courses and workshops on internationalization topics.

Stephen Wilkins

Stephen Wilkins has 15 years' experience as a lecturer in further and higher education and was formerly director of professional management programmes at Dubai University College, United Arab Emirates. He has authored/co-authored many articles on international higher education and was winner of the EAIE Tony Adams Award for Excellence in Research 2011. He is currently a PhD candidate at the International Centre for Higher Education Management (ICHEM), University of Bath, United Kingdom.

BOX AUTHORS

Shingo Ashizawa is a professor in the Division of International Cooperation at Meiji University in Japan and author/research of several evaluation studies.

Jos Beelen is a researcher and consultant on internationalization, Centre for Applied Research on Economics and Management (CAREM), Amsterdam University of Applied Sciences, The Netherlands.

Tim Birtwistle is a professor emeritus of Law and Policy of Higher Education and Jean Monnet Chair at Leeds Law School in the United Kingdom.

Chrissie Boughey is professor and Dean of Teaching & Learning at Rhodes University in Grahamstown, South Africa.

Lisa Childress is an independent higher education researcher and consultant at LKC Consulting.

Rahul Choudaha is Director of Development and Innovation at World Education Services, New York.

Gianni D'Amato, PhD in Political Sciences, is Director of the Swiss Forum for Migration and Population Studies and professor of Migration and Citizenship Studies at the University of Neuchâtel, Switzerland.

Frederik de Decker is a quality expert and senior education advisor at Ghent University Association.

Debbie Donohue is the Interim Executive Director of the Division of Professional Practice at the Georgia Institute of Technology.

Michael Emery is Director of Human Resources Management at the International Organization for Migration in Geneva, Switzerland

Irina Ferencz is policy officer at the Academic Cooperation Association (ACA) in Brussels.

Mark Freeman, Project Team, Faculty of Business and Economics, University of Sydney, Australia.

Jocelyne Gacel-Avilà is professor of the internationalization process at the University of Guadalajara, Mexico.

Brenda García Portillo is Coordinator of Internationalization Projects at Universidad de Monterrey, Mexico.

Susan Gillespie is Director of the Institute for International Liberal Education and Vice President for Global Initiatives at Bard College, U.S.

Joel Glassman is Associate Provost for Academic Affairs and Director, Center for International Studies at the University of Missouri-St. Louis.

Mark O. Hatfield (deceased) served two terms as Governor of Oregon before election to the United States Senate, where he served for thirty years.

Futao Huang is professor at the Research Institute for Higher education of Hiroshima University in Japan.

James Otieno Jowi is coordinator of the African Network for Internationalization of Education (ANIE) based at Moi University in Eldoret, Kenya.

Nico Jooste is the senior international officer and director of the Office for International Education at the Nelson Mandela Metropolitan University, South Africa..

Simon Kho, KPMG (former) Director, National Student Programs & Global Initiatives, Chicago, Illinois.

Yuto Kitamura is an associate professor at Sophia University in Japan.

Alexander Koff, Esq. is a partner and Chair of the Global Practice at the law firm of Whiteford, Taylor, and Preston LLP in Baltimore, Maryland.

Sabine Krajewski is a lecturer in International Communication in the Department of Media, Music, Communication and Cultural Studies at Macquarie University, Australia.

Judy B. Krutky is professor of Political Science and International Studies and Director for Intercultural Education at Baldwin Wallace College in Ohio.

Steve J. Kulich is Executive Director of the SISU Intercultural Institute (SII) of Shanghai International Studies University (SISU), Chief Editor of the Intercultural Research series (published by Shanghai Foreign Language Education Press), and Fellow and Board Member of the International Academy of Intercultural Research.

Gil Latz is professor of Geography and Associate Vice Chancellor for International Affairs, Indiana University–Purdue University Indianapolis; and Associate Vice President for International Affairs for Indiana University Bloomington.

Sonia Pereira Laus is a researcher on the internationalization of higher education process and international academic cooperation in Brazil.

Sonny Lim serves as Director of Public Affairs for Yale-NUS College, a unique partnership between Yale University and the National University of Singapore.

Alma Maldonado-Maldonado is a researcher in the Educational Research Department of CINVESTAV - Center for Advanced Research (Mexico).

Edilio Mazzoleni is Head of Operations, International Office at the Università Cattolica del Sacro Cuore (UCSC), Italy.

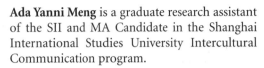

Ada Yanni Meng is a graduate research assistant of the SII and MA Candidate in the Shanghai International Studies University Intercultural Communication program.

Soraya Mohideen is Infosys Program Manager, Global Academic Relations in Bangalore, India.

Michael D. Monahan (Macalester), at the time of writing Director of the International Center at Macalester College, MN, USA; now President of BCA Study Abroad, USA.

Michael J. Mooney Special Adviser to the President, Waseda University, Japan.

Georges H. Nahas is Vice President of the University of Balamand in Lebanon.

Phyllis Bo-yuen Ngai teaches in the Department of Communication Studies at The University of Montana-Missoula.

Andy Nicol is Director of Business Development, Asia for Hobsons Asia Pacific in Kuala Lumpur, Malaysia.

Masami Nishishiba is an assistant professor in the Division of Public Administration at the Mark O. Hatfield School of Government, Portland State University and is currently serving as the Associate Director of the Center for Public Service at the Hatfield School of Government.

Olatunde J.B. Ojo is professor emeritus of political and administrative studies, past Dean of Social Sciences, and founding Director of the Emerald Energy Centre for Petroleum Economics, Policy, and Strategic Studies, University of Port Harcourt, Nigeria.

Hiroshi Ota is professor and Director of the Center for Global Education at Hitotsubashi University in Tokyo, Japan.

Matthias Otten, prof. Dr./Faculty of Applied Social Sciences, Institute for Intercultural Education and Development, Cologne University of Applied Sciences, Germany.

Prem Ramburuth, Australian School of Business, Project Team, University of New South Wales, Australia.

Simon Ridings, Project Team, Faculty of Business, Queensland University of Technology, Australia.

Kay Salehi, Academic Development Advisor, Swinburne Professional Learning, Swinburne University of Technology, Australia.

Chika Sehoole, associate professor, Faculty of Education, University of Pretoria, South Africa.

Jeffrey Shultz is an educational anthropologist who received an SB in mathematics from MIT, as well as a masters and doctorate in education from Harvard University and currently serves as Professor of Education and Assistant Provost for Special Projects at Arcadia University.

Lyn Simpson, Project Team, Faculty of Business, Queensland University of Technology, Australia

James Skelly is visiting professor of Peace Studies and Resident Director for BCA Study Abroad at the Magee campus of the University of Ulster in Derry-Londonderry, Northern Ireland.

Erkki Sutinen is professor of Computer Science and the leader of edTech$^\Delta$ research group at the University of Eastern Finland; he currently is based in Maputo, Mozambique, leading the STIFIMO program on Science, Technology, and Innovation.

Chris Sykes, Project Team, Faculty of Business and Economics, University of Sydney, Australia

Mohammad Thoyibi is on the Faculty of Muhammadiyah University at Surakarata, Indonesia.

Lesley Treleaven, Project Team, Faculty of Business and Economics, University of Sydney, Australia.

Sherie Valderrama, Sodexo Senior Director, Talent Acquisition Group, Corporate Human Resources, Gaithersburg, Maryland.

Els van der Werf is the Senior Policy Advisor on International Relations for Hanze University of Applied Sciences, Groningen, The Netherlands.

⦾SAGE research**methods**

The essential online tool for researchers from the world's leading methods publisher

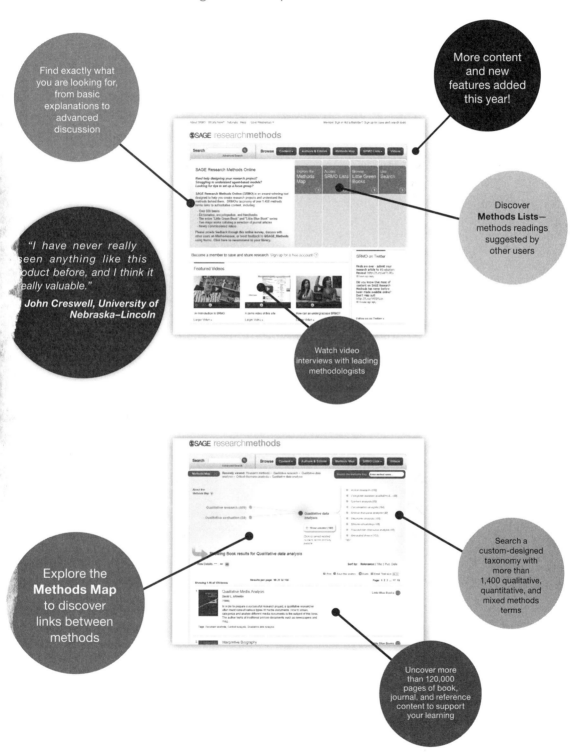

Find exactly what you are looking for, from basic explanations to advanced discussion

More content and new features added this year!

"I have never really seen anything like this product before, and I think it really valuable."
John Creswell, University of Nebraska–Lincoln

Discover **Methods Lists**— methods readings suggested by other users

Watch video interviews with leading methodologists

Explore the **Methods Map** to discover links between methods

Search a custom-designed taxonomy with more than 1,400 qualitative, quantitative, and mixed methods terms

Uncover more than 120,000 pages of book, journal, and reference content to support your learning

Find out more at
www.sageresearchmethods.com